AF725070

3ds max 6™ Animation and Visual Effects Techniques

LINN STATE TECHNICAL COLLEGE
Library Resource Center
One Technology Drive
Linn, MO 65051
WITHDRAWN

LIMITED WARRANTY AND DISCLAIMER OF LIABILITY

THE CD-ROM THAT ACCOMPANIES THIS BOOK MAY BE USED ON A SINGLE PC ONLY. THE LICENSE DOES NOT PERMIT THE USE ON A NETWORK (OF ANY KIND). YOU FURTHER AGREE THAT THIS LICENSE GRANTS PERMISSION TO USE THE PRODUCTS CONTAINED HEREIN, BUT DOES NOT GIVE YOU RIGHT OF OWNERSHIP TO ANY OF THE CONTENT OR PRODUCT CONTAINED ON THIS CD-ROM. USE OF THIRD-PARTY SOFTWARE CONTAINED ON THIS CD-ROM IS LIMITED TO AND SUBJECT TO LICENSING TERMS FOR THE RESPECTIVE PRODUCTS.

CHARLES RIVER MEDIA, INC. ("CRM") AND/OR ANYONE WHO HAS BEEN INVOLVED IN THE WRITING, CREATION, OR PRODUCTION OF THE ACCOMPANYING CODE ("THE SOFTWARE"), OR THE THIRD-PARTY PRODUCTS CONTAINED ON THIS CD-ROM, CANNOT AND DO NOT WARRANT THE PERFORMANCE OR RESULTS THAT MAY BE OBTAINED BY USING THE SOFTWARE. THE AUTHOR AND PUBLISHER HAVE USED THEIR BEST EFFORTS TO ENSURE THE ACCURACY AND FUNCTIONALITY OF THE TEXTUAL MATERIAL AND PROGRAMS CONTAINED HEREIN; WE, HOWEVER, MAKE NO WARRANTY OF THIS KIND, EXPRESS OR IMPLIED, REGARDING THE PERFORMANCE OF THESE PROGRAMS. THE SOFTWARE IS SOLD "AS IS" WITHOUT WARRANTY (EXCEPT FOR DEFECTIVE MATERIALS USED IN MANUFACTURING THE DISC OR DUE TO FAULTY WORKMANSHIP); THE SOLE REMEDY IN THE EVENT OF A DEFECT IS EXPRESSLY LIMITED TO REPLACEMENT OF THE DISC, AND ONLY AT THE DISCRETION OF CRM.

THE AUTHOR, THE PUBLISHER, DEVELOPERS OF THIRD-PARTY SOFTWARE, AND ANYONE INVOLVED IN THE PRODUCTION AND MANUFACTURING OF THIS WORK SHALL NOT BE LIABLE FOR DAMAGES OF ANY KIND ARISING OUT OF THE USE OF (OR THE INABILITY TO USE) THE PROGRAMS, SOURCE CODE, OR TEXTUAL MATERIAL CONTAINED IN THIS PUBLICATION. THIS INCLUDES, BUT IS NOT LIMITED TO, LOSS OF REVENUE OR PROFIT, OR OTHER INCIDENTAL OR CONSEQUENTIAL DAMAGES ARISING OUT OF THE USE OF THE PRODUCT.

THE SOLE REMEDY IN THE EVENT OF A CLAIM OF ANY KIND IS EXPRESSLY LIMITED TO REPLACEMENT OF THE BOOK AND/OR CD-ROM, AND ONLY AT THE DISCRETION OF CRM.

THE USE OF "IMPLIED WARRANTY" AND CERTAIN "EXCLUSIONS" VARY FROM STATE TO STATE, AND MAY NOT APPLY TO THE PURCHASER OF THIS PRODUCT.

*53276328
b16983920
i2059821x
0.11517062T
11066
TR
897.7
.K464
2003

3ds max 6™ Animation and Visual Effects Techniques

Sanford Kennedy

Charles River Media, Inc.
Hingham, Massachusetts

Copyright 2004 by CHARLES RIVER MEDIA, INC.
All rights reserved.

No part of this publication may be reproduced in any way, stored in a retrieval system of any type, or transmitted by any means or media, electronic or mechanical, including, but not limited to, photocopy, recording, or scanning, without *prior permission in writing* from the publisher.

Publisher: Jenifer Niles
Production: Paw Print Media
Cover Design: The Printed Image
Cover Image: Sanford Kennedy

CHARLES RIVER MEDIA, INC.
10 Downer Avenue
Hingham, Massachusetts 02043
781-740-0400
781-740-8816 (FAX)
info@charlesriver.com
www.charlesriver.com

This book is printed on acid-free paper.

Sanford Kennedy. *3ds max 6 Animation and Visual Effects Techniques.*
ISBN: 1-58450-334-3

All brand names and product names mentioned in this book are trademarks or service marks of their respective companies. Any omission or misuse (of any kind) of service marks or trademarks should not be regarded as intent to infringe on the property of others. The publisher recognizes and respects all marks used by companies, manufacturers, and developers as a means to distinguish their products.

Library of Congress Cataloging-in-Publication Data

Kennedy, Sanford, 1943–
3ds max 6 animation and visual effects techniques / Sanford Kennedy.
p. cm.
ISBN 1-58450-334-3 (Paperback with CD-ROM : alk. paper)
1. Computer animation. 2. 3ds max (Computer file) 3. Computer graphics. I. Title.
TR897.7.K464 2003
006.6'96—dc22

2003022999

Printed in the United States of America
03 7 6 5 4 3 2 First Edition

CHARLES RIVER MEDIA titles are available for site license or bulk purchase by institutions, user groups, corporations, etc. For additional information, please contact the Special Sales Department at 781-740-0400.

Requests for replacement of a defective CD-ROM must be accompanied by the original disc, your mailing address, telephone number, date of purchase, and purchase price. Please state the nature of the problem, and send the information to CHARLES RIVER MEDIA, INC., 10 Downer Avenue, Hingham, Massachusetts 02043. CRM's sole obligation to the purchaser is to replace the disc, based on defective materials or faulty workmanship, but not on the operation or functionality of the product.

CONTENTS

	ACKNOWLEDGMENTS	**xiii**
	PREFACE	**xv**
	What This Book Is About	xv
	What Is in This Book	xv
	How to Use This Book	xvi
	Why I Wrote This Book	xvii
CHAPTER 1	**ESSENTIALS OF 3ds max 6 FOR ANIMATION AND VISUAL EFFECTS**	**1**
	The State of the Art	2
	Animation Features	6
	Facial and Lip Sync Animation	12
	Interface Features	16
	Visual Effects Features	20
	Modeling Features	27
	The Materials Editor	30
	Rendering, Radiosity, and Global Illumination	33
	Plug-Ins	37
	MAXScript and Other Capabilities	41
	The Production Pipeline	42
	Conclusion	44
CHAPTER 2	**COMPUTER ANIMATED FILMMAKING**	**45**
	Film Design	47
	Pre-Production	48
	Storyboards	50
	Art Direction	53
	Production Design	53

Character Design 55
Environment Design 57
Visual Effects Design 59
Production 61
Post-Production 63
Conclusion 64

CHAPTER 3 MODELING ENVIRONMENTS, BUILDINGS, AND ALIENS 65

Building the Models for the Movie 66
Titan City 68
Building a Landscape Location 69
TUTORIAL 3.1: Building a Location on New Caledonia Island 70
Close-Up Environments and Interior Locations 73
TUTORIAL 3.2: Building Cell Block Zebra 74
Buildings 76
TUTORIAL 3.3: Modeling the Temple of the Horns 77
TUTORIAL 3.4: Adding Details to Buildings 80
Alien Characters 86
Modeling the Alien Vampire 86
TUTORIAL 3.5: Modeling the Alien Body 87
TUTORIAL 3.6: Creating the Alien's Leg and Buttocks 90
TUTORIAL 3.7: Finishing the Torso 93
Conclusion 96

CHAPTER 4 FINISHING THE ALIEN VAMPIRE CHARACTER 97

TUTORIAL 4.1: Creating a Character Head 99
TUTORIAL 4.2: Create the Alien's Mouth, Nose, and Eyes 100
Using NURMS 104
TUTORIAL 4.3: Increase Resolution to Create Facial Features 104
TUTORIAL 4.4: Shaping the Facial Features 108
TUTORIAL 4.5: Refining the Nose 110
TUTORIAL 4.6: Modeling the Pointed Ear 112
TUTORIAL 4.7: Attach the Ear to the Head 115
TUTORIAL 4.8: Building the Alien Hand 118
TUTORIAL 4.9: Extruding the Fingers 119
TUTORIAL 4.10: Creating a Thumb 121
TUTORIAL 4.11: Sculpt the Fingers and Add the Fingernails 123
TUTORIAL 4.12: Finish the Feet and Legs 125
Finishing Xzulixia, the Alien Vampire Character 127
TUTORIAL 4.13: Finish the Head and Body 127

TUTORIAL 4.14: Mirror Clone and Weld the Body 130
TUTORIAL 4.15: Create a Bodysuit for the Alien Using Push 132
Creating Realistic Eyes 135
TUTORIAL 4.16: Creating Realistic Human and Alien Eyes 135
TUTORIAL 4.17: Creating the Meniscus to Make the Eye Look Wet 138
Conclusion 140

CHAPTER 5 CONSTRUCTING THE GENERIC MAN CHARACTER 141

Bézier Spline Patch Modeling 142
TUTORIAL 5.1: Building the Torso 143
TUTORIAL 5.2: Add the Shoulder Spline Cage 146
TUTORIAL 5.3: Create the Arm and Attach It to the Shoulder 148
TUTORIAL 5.4: Create the Leg and Attach It to the Torso 151
TUTORIAL 5.5: Complete the Pelvis and the Neck 154
TUTORIAL 5.6: Create the Head for the Generic Man 157
TUTORIAL 5.7: Create the Facial Features 159
TUTORIAL 5.8: Refine and Sculpt the Facial Features 161
TUTORIAL 5.9: Complete the Right Half of the Face 165
TUTORIAL 5.10: Finish the Generic Man Mouth 168
TUTORIAL 5.11: Adding the Patch Ears 172
Conclusion 175

CHAPTER 6 FINISHING THE DR. QUIN/GENERIC MAN PATCH MODEL 177

TUTORIAL 6.1: Creating Patch Hands 179
TUTORIAL 6.2: Add the Fingernails to the Fingers 182
TUTORIAL 6.3: Attach the Hand to the Arm 185
TUTORIAL 6.4: Mirror Clone and Fuse the Body 188
TUTORIAL 6.5: Finishing the Feet 190
TUTORIAL 6.6: Finishing the Generic Man Head 192
TUTORIAL 6.7: Refine the Lips and Add the Inner Mouth Opening 195
TUTORIAL 6.8: Smooth the Head and Move the Neck Seam 198
TUTORIAL 6.9: Finishing the Face 201
The Final Details 204
Conclusion 204

CHAPTER 7 CHARACTER SETUP WITH BONES 205

Creating a Skeletal System 206
Constructing a Skeleton for a Specific Character 207
TUTORIAL 7.1: Build the Basic Skeleton 209

The Hands of the Doctor 213
TUTORIAL 7.2: Creating the Bones of the Hand 213
Naming the Bones 216
Applying Inverse Kinematics Solvers 218
TUTORIAL 7.3: Creating IK Chains with the HI Solver 219
Phase One, the Basic Skeleton with IK, Is Finished 221
TUTORIAL 7.4: Fit the Generic Man onto the Skeleton 223
TUTORIAL 7.5: Positioning the Hand Bones 224
What Is Rigging? 226
Rigging the Dr. Quin Skeleton for Character Animation 226
TUTORIAL 7.6: Rigging the Foot and Leg Controls 228
Body, Head, and Arm Controls 230
TUTORIAL 7.7: Rigging the Body and Head Controls 231
TUTORIAL 7.8: Rigging the Arm and Clavicle Controls 234
Conclusion 236

CHAPTER 8 PREPARING FOR CHARACTER ANIMATION 237

Using the Skin Modifier 238
TUTORIAL 8.1: Adding Bone Fins 239
Apply the Skin Modifier and Paint Weights 241
TUTORIAL 8.2: Binding the Mesh to the Skeleton with the Skin 241
TUTORIAL 8.3: Adjusting the Skin Envelope Problems 244
TUTORIAL 8.4: Adjusting the Armpits, Knee, and Elbow Skin Envelopes 246
Mirror Skin Weights 249
Sliders and Wired Parameters 251
TUTORIAL 8.5: Create a Slider and Wire It to a Finger 252
TUTORIAL 8.6: Wiring One Finger to Control All of the Fingers 255
Facial Morph Targets 258
TUTORIAL 8.7: Clone the Head for Morph Targets 260
TUTORIAL 8.8: Sculpting Facial Morph Targets 261
Creating Clothing for Dr. Quin with the Push Modifier 263
TUTORIAL 8.9: Creating Push Clothing for Dr. Quin 264
TUTORIAL 8.10: Put a Collar and Cuffs on the Coat and Pants 268
TUTORIAL 8.11: Merging the Clothing, Skin, and Skeleton 270
Schematic View Tools 272
Conclusion 274

CHAPTER 9 CHARACTER ANIMATION 275

Upper Body Movement and Gestures 277
TUTORIAL 9.1: Animate Dr. Quin Sitting at a Desk and Answering a Telephone 277
TUTORIAL 9.2: Animating the Arm and Hand 280

	TUTORIAL 9.3: Adjusting the Wrist Skin Envelopes	284
	TUTORIAL 9.4: Move the Telephone to the Ear	288
	Lip-Sync and Facial Expressions	290
	TUTORIAL 9.5: Setting Up for Lip-Sync Facial Animation	291
	Recording the Soundtrack	295
	TUTORIAL 9.6: Animating with Lip Sync	297
	Animating a Walk Cycle	301
	Body Language	301
	Character Assembly Node	302
	Breakdown of the Walk Cycle	303
	Skeletal Structure and Linking	303
	TUTORIAL 9.7: Animating a Walk Cycle	304
	Foot Movement Concepts	307
	TUTORIAL 9.8: Animate the Feet, Legs, and Arms in a Walk Cycle	309
	Acrobatic Motion of the Skeleton	311
	Putting the Xzulixia Model on the Dr. Quin Skeleton	313
	TUTORIAL 9.9: Resize the Generic Skeleton to fit Xzulixia	314
	Adding Swivel Angle Targets	315
	Animating the Iris and Eyelashes of a Realistic Eye	316
	TUTORIAL 9.10: Creating an Animated Iris for a Realistic Eye	317
	TUTORIAL 9.11: Creating Eyelashes for Morph-Animatable Eyelids	320
	Conclusion	323
CHAPTER 10	**SCENE ANIMATION**	**325**
	Making a Low-Resolution Proxy Skin for Xzulixia	328
	The Story	331
	Setting Up a Scene	334
	The First Animation	337
	TUTORIAL 10.1: Animating the Skeleton Rig in a Fast Run Cycle	340
	Multiple Scene Files	347
	TUTORIAL 10.2: Helicopter Chase	347
	Entering the Refinery	352
	Using character studio	353
	Adding Additional Characters	353
	Level of Detail and X-Refs	355
	Video Rotoscope for Scene Animation	357
	Conclusion	358
CHAPTER 11	**VISUAL EFFECTS**	**359**
	Particle Effects	360
	TUTORIAL 11.1: Setting Up a PArray Particle Rain Effect	362

	Object Fragmentation Particle Effects	365
	The Hollywood Explosion	365
	Creating an Explosion in 3ds max 6	367
	TUTORIAL 11.2: Create a Dense Explosion	368
	TUTORIAL 11.3: Set Up Atmospheric Explosions	372
	TUTORIAL 11.4: Add a Volume Light to the Explosion	376
	Instanced Geometry Particle Effects	377
	TUTORIAL 11.5: Instanced Geometry Particle Effects	378
	Facing Particle Effects	380
	Using Particle Flow for Visual Effects	381
	TUTORIAL 11.6: Creating Dusty Footsteps with Particle Flow	384
	TUTORIAL 11.7: Setting Up the Particle Flow to Generate Dust	387
	Conclusion	392
CHAPTER 12	**ADVANCED ANIMATION**	**393**
	Expressions	394
	TUTORIAL 12.1: Animate a Walk Cycle with an Expression Controller	395
	Using Reactor 2	398
	TUTORIAL 12.2: Dynamic Collisions with Characters	400
	TUTORIAL 12.3: Shooting a Rag Doll	404
	TUTORIAL 12.4: Setting Up a Reactor 2 Battle Scene	410
	Animating a Skeleton Rig with Custom Attributes	417
	Installing the Attribute Holder Modifier Script	419
	TUTORIAL 12.5: Controlling the Feet with Custom Attributes	419
	TUTORIAL 12.6: Creating a Facial Bone Network	425
	TUTORIAL 12.7: Converting Dr. Quin into Major Black	430
	Scripting	434
	TUTORIAL 12.8: Using Reactor 2 Cloth to Simulate Hair	439
	Full Body Morphing	442
	TUTORIAL 12.9: Vampire Shape Change Body Morph	443
	Conclusion	446
CHAPTER 13	**MATERIALS AND TEXTURES**	**447**
	Semi-Realism	448
	Putting a Face on Dr. Quin	451
	TUTORIAL 13.1: Applying a Texture to Dr. Quin's Face	452
	Using Unwrap UVW to Create Texture Maps	453
	TUTORIAL 13.2: Using Unwrap UVW to Make a Map for a Head	455
	TUTORIAL 13.3: Painting a Face in Adobe Photoshop	459
	Conclusion	467

CHAPTER 14	**LIGHTING AND RENDERING**	**469**
	Composition, Lighting, and Rendering	470
	Radiosity and Global Illumination	471
	Working with the Skylight and Light Tracer	473
	TUTORIAL 14.1: Using a Skylight for Global Illumination	474
	Lighting an Interior Space	477
	TUTORIAL 14.2: Adjust the Lighting of the Satellite Bridge Interior	478
	Advanced Lighting Override Material with Radiosity	482
	Using 3ds max Standard Lights for Dramatic Lighting	484
	Visual Effects Lighting	485
	Lighting the Crash of the Alien Spaceship	485
	TUTORIAL 14.3: Lighting the Alien Ship Crash	486
	Rendering a Scene	489
	TUTORIAL 14.4: Render Image Layers for Compositing and Effects	491
	Render Effects	494
	Rendering Image Elements	495
	Render to Texture	496
	Lighting and Rendering with Mental Ray	497
	Case History of a Mental Ray Image	500
	Rendering Glass and Liquids	502
	Using Backburner 2 for Network Rendering	503
	Conclusion	505
CHAPTER 15	**character studio 4**	**507**
	Sliders and Wired Parameters	511
	TUTORIAL 15.1: Animating Biped Fingers with Sliders	512
	Wired Parameters	513
	TUTORIAL 15.2: Create a Slider and Wire It to a Biped Finger	514
	TUTORIAL 15.3: Convert Biped Animation to 3ds max Bones Animation	516
	Motion Flow and Layer Animation	517
	Crowd Animation	519
	Animating a Charging Army	522
	TUTORIAL 15.4: Setting Up a Crowd Animation	522
	TUTORIAL 15.5: Setting Up a Biped Crowd Simulation	526
	TUTORIAL 15.6: Completing the Biped Crowd Simulation	528
	Conclusion	531
CHAPTER 16	**combustion 3, COMPOSITING AND 2D VISUAL EFFECTS**	**533**
	Blue- and Green-Screen Compositing	535
	TUTORIAL 16.1: Color Keying in combustion 3	538

	Adding 2D Visual Effects	543
	TUTORIAL 16.2: Create a Composite with Particle Effects	544
	Mesh Paint in 3ds max	547
	The Edit Operator	549
	Post Production	550
	Outputting Animation and Visual Effects to Film	550
	Conclusion	551
CHAPTER 17	**PLUG-INS**	**553**
	character studio 4	554
	Shag Hair	555
	The Shag Hair Plug-In	555
	TUTORIAL 17.1: Create a NURBS Scalp to Use with the Shag Hair Plug-In	556
	TUTORIAL 17.2: Create Hair Using the Shag Hair Plug-In	559
	TUTORIAL 17.3: Animating Long Hair	563
	clothfx	567
	Matching the Model Scale to Real Life	572
	TUTORIAL 17.6: Multilayer Cloth Simulation Using clothfx to Simulate Multilayer Cloth	573
	Working with Large File Sizes	575
	Digitizing a Model with the Immersion Microscribe	576
	Using Scrib-it	577
	TUTORIAL 17.7: Digitizing Clothing from a Clay Model with Scrib-it	578
	Using Surf-it	580
	Foley Studio and Sound Trax for Creating Sound Effects	581
	Phoenix—Fire that Throws Light	582
	TUTORIAL 17.11: Using Phoenix to Create Fire That Emits Light	583
	Conclusion	584
APPENDIX A	**ABOUT THE CD-ROM**	**585**
	Finding Maps	586
	System Requirements	586
APPENDIX B	**REFERENCES**	**589**
	Resources and Links	590
	Good 3ds max Sites	590
	Plug-Ins	590
	3ds max Filmography	590
	INDEX	**591**

ACKNOWLEDGMENTS

I would like to give special thanks to Jenifer Niles who has helped the creation of this book in countless ways and never wavered in her support. I would like to thank discreet, manufacturer of 3ds max 6, combustion 3, and character studio 4 for their assistance and cooperation in the preparation of this book. Special thanks go to David Marks and the 3ds max beta testing team for their insights into the intricacies of Max. Thanks to Digimation for their assistance with the plug-ins for 3ds max that were used for the tutorials. Thanks to Uncharted Territory for contributing images, and Brandon Davis for explaining how they used 3ds max for visual effects. Thanks to Imagica and Jose Parra for explaining how they create film from digital images.

PREFACE

WHAT THIS BOOK IS ABOUT

This book will provide you with insight into the tools and techniques used in 3ds max 6™ to create and animate high-quality characters, environments, and visual effects, including how to use plug-ins, and how to bring everything together into an animated rendered scene. It will explain how to use discreet combustion 3™ with 3ds max for compositing and 2D visual effects. It will also explain how make short animated films, and full-length animated motion pictures.

WHAT IS IN THIS BOOK

This book begins with an overview of the animation and visual effects features of 3ds max 6 and continues with a chapter on the animated filmmaking process. This is followed by chapters on creating environments, modeling male and female characters, skeletal rigging, character animation, lip sync, visual effects, advanced animation concepts, lighting and rendering, motion capture animation, compositing, and plug-ins. This book is organized in chapters with appendixes:

Chapter 1, *Essentials for 3ds max 6 for Animation and Visual Effects*, gives an overview of the features and functionality of 3ds max 6.

Chapter 2, *Computer Animated Filmmaking*, describes the process of creating both short animated films and animated motion pictures.

Chapter 3, *Modeling Environments, Buildings, and Aliens*, describes how to create environments and a polygonal subdivision surface female alien model.

Chapter 4, *Finishing the Alien Vampire Character,* continues the construction and finishing of the female alien model.

Chapter 5, *Constructing the Generic Man Character,* describes the spline patch modeling of a male character.

Chapter 6, *Finishing the Dr. Quin/Generic Man Patch Model,* continues the construction and finishing of the male character.

Chapter 7, *Character Setup with Bones,* describes how to build and rig a skeleton using 3ds max bones.

Chapter 8, *Preparing for Character Animation,* describes how to wire parameters and prepare a character for animation.

Chapter 9, *Character Animation,* describes hand animation techniques and lip-sync animation.

Chapter 10, *Scene Animation,* describes scene animation with a character and an environment.

Chapter 11, *Visual Effects,* describes particle and atmospheric visual effects.

Chapter 12, *Advanced Animation,* describes dynamics and other advanced animation techniques.

Chapter 13, *Materials and Textures,* describes the process of applying textures to a model.

Chapter 14, *Lighting and Rendering,* describes lighting and rendering using radiosity and Mental Ray.

Chapter 15, *character studio 4,* describes motion capture and crowd animation in character studio 4.

Chapter 16, *combustion 3, Compositing and 2D Visual Effects,* describes compositing and 2D particle visual effects in combustion 3.

Chapter 17, *Plug-Ins,* describes plug-ins for creating hair, clothing, and fire.

Appendix A, *About the CD-ROM,* describes what is on the companion CD-ROM.

Appendix B, *References,* contains a list of references and links, a list of plug-ins (both commercial and freeware) that are available for 3ds max, and a 3ds max filmography.

How to Use This Book

Each chapter in this book contains tutorials, except for Chapters 1 and 2. The tutorials cover a range of tasks from modeling to character animation, and are designed to be used with the 3ds max scene files and reference images that can be found on the companion CD-ROM. The CD-ROM is divided into sections by chapter. The folders range from Chapter 3 to Chapter 17. They contain tutorials, and most of them contain background images or sample movies of the results of the tutorials. For example, the Chapter 6 directory contains Tutorials and Images. The images are meant to be loaded into the 3ds max viewport background to use as references when modeling a character.

ON THE CD

When you start a tutorial you will be asked to load a file from the CD-ROM. After you load the scene file, you may also be asked to load a viewport background reference image, which would be located in the images folder. Since you cannot save back to the CD-ROM, you should create a directory on your computer where you can store your partially completed scene files. It is also a good idea to place the reference images in a separate directory on your hard drive, and then create a new bitmap path in 3ds max so that they are easy to locate. If you reference them only from the CD-ROM, you will need to have the disc in the computer whenever you work on a tutorial.

Why I Wrote This Book

I wrote this book because of a lack of information on applying the tools of 3ds max to real-world projects: most of the books on the market read like massively expanded help files with models thrown in that aren't particularly good. While teaching 3D animation at the college level, I watched students struggle to apply the complex tools they were learning and felt the need to supply more information about how to put an animated film project together. The purpose of this book is not to define every button in the program, but to show how to integrate all of the features of 3ds max together to create, animate, render, and finish an animation project. The book explains how I am using 3ds max in the creation of my own animated film *Homing Instinct*, which is currently in production.

My background is in aerospace and visual effects. I worked in the 1960s and 1970s in the aerospace industry as a design engineer and R & D machinist on projects like the Gemini Moon rocket, cruise missiles, and the f-16 fighter. Then I saw *Star Wars* and switched careers to visual effects in motion pictures. From 1978 until the present I have worked in visual effects designing and building computer controlled camera equipment, doing visual effects in films, building props, and doing prosthetic makeup. I have worked on 54 motion pictures to date. My most recent film work was as a modeler on *The X Men 2* and an animator on the cinematic movie for the game *Graystoke: The Temple of Ultimate Evil*. I purchased 3d studio R2 for DOS in 1992 and in 1994 began a career as a 3D animator on the film *Virtuosity*. I started teaching 3ds max in 1996 and continue to do so today at two colleges in Los Angeles. At the time I started learning 3d studio max there were no books available other than the manuals, which were technical and dry, and presented a steep learning curve. It is my wish to use this book to pass on whatever I can to make it easier for those who want to explore the exciting and creative world of 3D animation and 3ds max.

I currently own a computer animation studio in Los Angeles called Sanford Kennedy Design. Look on the *www.charlesrivermedia.com* Web site for updates on new features of 3ds max as they become available.

Sanford Kennedy
Los Angeles, California

CHAPTER

1

ESSENTIALS OF 3ds max 6 FOR ANIMATION AND VISUAL EFFECTS

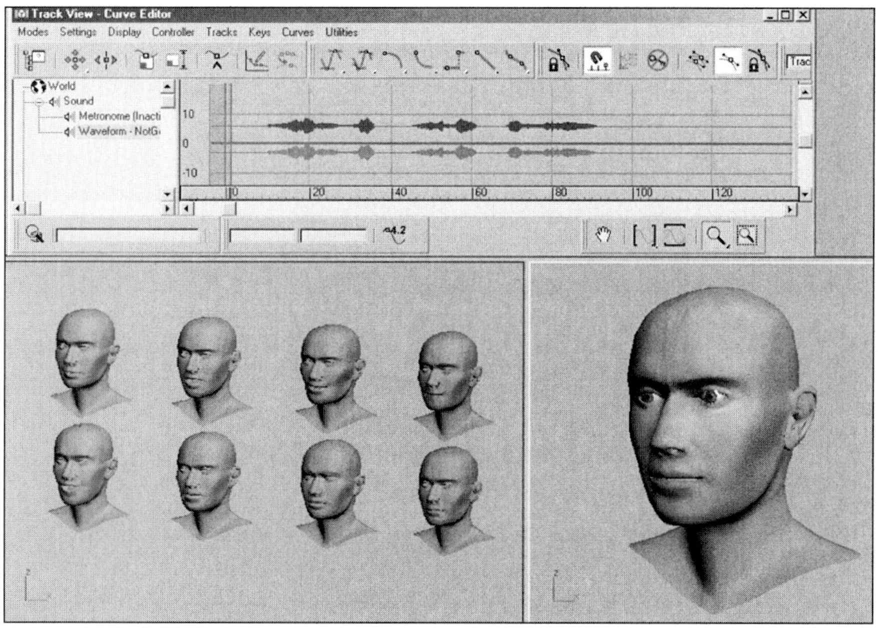

THE STATE OF THE ART

Visual effects are so important to the success of science fiction films that they often tend to overshadow the performances of the characters. In many action films, much of the screen time is spent building tension and setting up audience anticipation for the big visual effects climax. These shots are known as the "money shots" because they are usually the best and most memorable parts of a film, and are hyped in theatrical trailers and advertisements to generate interest in the movie. They commonly begin up to six months before a film is released in the hope that a great visual effects preview will create a "buzz" in the movie-going population and generate strong opening-week ticket sales.

Modern filmmaking is a mixture of old and new techniques that can be described as a "hybrid" of digital and traditional methods. Nearly all action-adventure, science fiction, and fantasy films contain digital visual effects, and almost all films of any type are composited and finished on digital editing and compositing software. Even dramatic films contain visual effects scenes in which actors are shot in front of a blue screen and then composited into background footage. In animated films like Disney's *Dinosaur*, computer animated creatures are composited into photographic backgrounds. This saves time during production and can give an air of realism to an animated film, as shown in Figure 1.1. These elements and background plates are further composited with computer-generated environments. The combination of live action footage of heroes fighting side by side with digitally animated creatures and a few pretty girls surrounded by massive rapid-fire visual effects has become a very successful formula that has spawned hit after box office hit. This type of film brings audiences into the theaters, and sells tickets.

As software becomes more complex and powerful, the level of detail and realism in computer animated films is climbing steadily. The current state of the art in pure computer animation is moving toward photorealism in the science fiction camp represented by *Final Fantasy*, and "cartoon" realism in the cartoon and family film camp, represented by *Shrek*. *Lord of the Rings* is a pure fantasy film in which real actors are mixed seamlessly with realistic computer-generated ghosts, beasts, and wraiths. Physics-based dynamic hair, as seen in *Final Fantasy*, looks real and moves with wind and inertia. Cartoon hair as seen on the hero monster in the family film *Monsters Inc.* is very dynamic and adds greatly

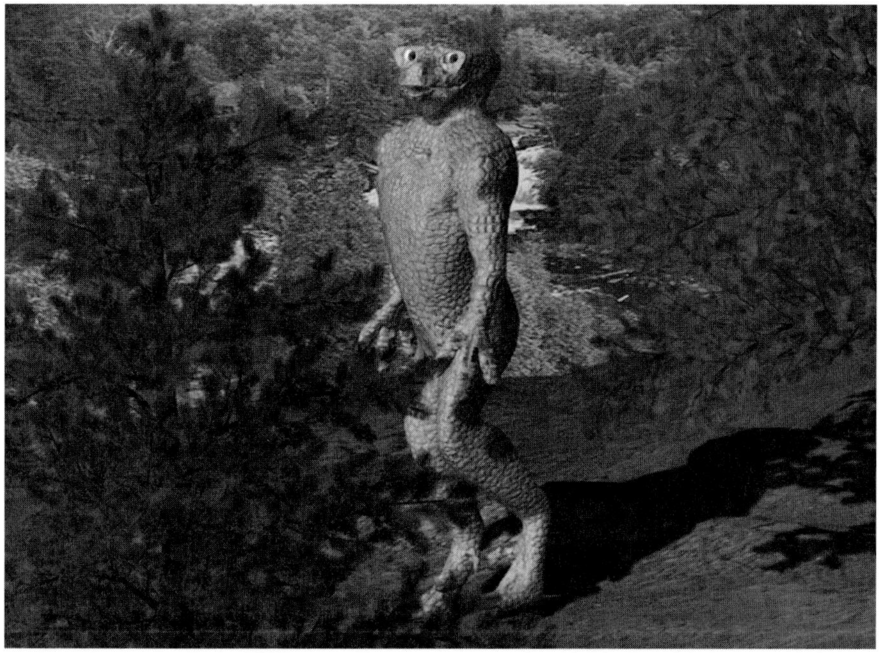

FIGURE 1.1 A Dinoman warrior composited into a photographic background image.

to the main character. Pixar, Rhythm & Hues, ILM, Sony Pictures Imageworks, and PDI are among the leading animation studios that continuously push the limits of what can be done to simulate natural phenomena in computer animation.

The new digital era has profoundly changed the movie industry. There is a controversy currently about what constitutes a virtual actor and whether the studio needs to pay union dues to the Screen Actor's Guild if it uses a digital actor. In the field of visual effects, the computer has largely done away with most miniature model-making jobs, and a big part of set building. Virtual city street sets are now being generated from Lidar laser scanned digital data, and accurate virtual buildings are being used as backgrounds in lieu of building a set.

Adobe Photoshop has made background painters and matte painting artists virtually obsolete. Traditional artists were once employed to paint all of the backgrounds on huge canvas screens or on glass for special effects films. Now, digital matte painting is done in Photoshop. Photoshop and other high-end compositing software can combine photographic images to create a castle out of an office building.

Studios can now send out a minimal crew to film background scenes or shoot background visual effects plates anywhere in the world. For example, they could send a small crew to Antarctica to film the ice flows, and then bring the footage back to the studio to be digitally combined with live actors standing in fur coats shot on a warm sound stage in downtown Los Angeles. To make it look authentic, they use visual effects software and add in falling snow, wind, and steaming breath.

In 2001, George Lucas announced that he had made the first all-digital motion picture, *Star Wars Episode II, Attack of the Clones*, which was shot completely using high-end digital cameras. The entire film is filled with computer-generated characters, combined with live actors, computer-generated environments, and miniature models. One of Lucas' main plans is to be able to distribute films directly from computers to the digital theater for public viewing. The only part of the equation that is not currently in place is the network of digital theaters to show the motion pictures.

3ds max 6 Professional Features for Animation and Visual Effects

This book is about the process of creating the animated film *Homing Instinct. Homing Instinct* is a semi-realistic animated feature film based on a science fiction vampire story written by the author. The setting is the planet-moon Titan orbiting around Saturn 400 years in the future where Alien Vampires once had a civilization. This chapter gives you an overview of the features of 3ds max 6, and how they can be used to create environments, character animation, and visual effects.

3ds max 6 is designed to be a plug-in based software that can be expanded to suit the user. There are literally hundreds of after-market, freeware plug-in programs, and MAXScripts available to expand 3ds max into a variety of different arenas. These arenas include motion picture production, visual effects, game production, television broadcast production, commercial advertising production, forensic animation, industrial product animation, cartoon animation, architectural design, and flythrough animation.

Each upgrade of 3ds max has concentrated on improving the quality of the animation tools and rendering capabilities. Both of these areas are extremely important to high-end production work. For the 3ds max 6 upgrade, some of the most significant areas of improvement are in the areas of new rendering tools, event-driven particle systems, vehicle and stunt man dynamic animation capabilities, and the Schematic View workflow. The set of character animation tools in 3ds max 6 is equal to any in the industry. For example, 3ds max bones and Inverse Kinematics (IK) system with its FK_IK capabilities and the spline IK works very much like the Maya IK skeletal system. The author teaches Max and Maya animation in two colleges and uses the same skeletal rig design and functionality to teach animation in both software packages.

Working with Character rigging and wired parameters has been improved with the new node-based Schematic View, which can display all object hierarchies, modifier connections, and parameter wiring as wires in graphic form. Reactor 2, which gives you rigid and soft body dynamics, has been more fully integrated into 3ds max 6, and gives you better dynamic impact detection, the ability to use soft selection to animate soft bodies such as cloth, and to create acrobatic and stunt action figures using the new Rag Doll constraint, as shown in Figure 1.2. Polygon modeling has been enhanced with the new Isoline display for MeshSmooth, providing a much better display of poly object edges that eliminates unnecessary edge display.

There has been extensive improvement in the area of rendering and lighting with the integration of the Mental Ray professional renderer, with its own Radiosity, Caustics, and Global Illumination. This renderer goes beyond the existing Light Tracer, Discreet Radiosity, and Max scanline rendering engines. Other improvements include a streamlined viewport layers system. Texture baking locally and across your network lets you embed lighting and shadows into a surface material on large projects. The Unwrap UVW Modifier and mapping coordinates system, which provides automatic mapping that splits the mesh and flattens it for distortion-free mapping, has been streamlined and enhanced with the Relax UV tool feature. Vertex Paint tools and Mapping Channels let you create your own layered texture maps in the Max viewport. For games, there is a new DirectX 9 shader that works with Vertex Paint Layers. Backburner, the network rendering manager, lets you render projects in both 3ds max 6 and combustion 3, with the standard renderer using up to 9,999 computers at no additional cost. All these improvements make 3ds max 6 a solid professional-level modeling and animation package—one that has been used for visual effects on numerous motion pictures, including *X-Men 2, The Core,* and *Minority Report*; it is a leader in game production on Microsoft Xbox, Sony PlayStation 2, and the Nintendo GameCube.

New tools for design visualization and architecture in 3ds max 6 include tools for creating architectural models, procedural windows, stairs,

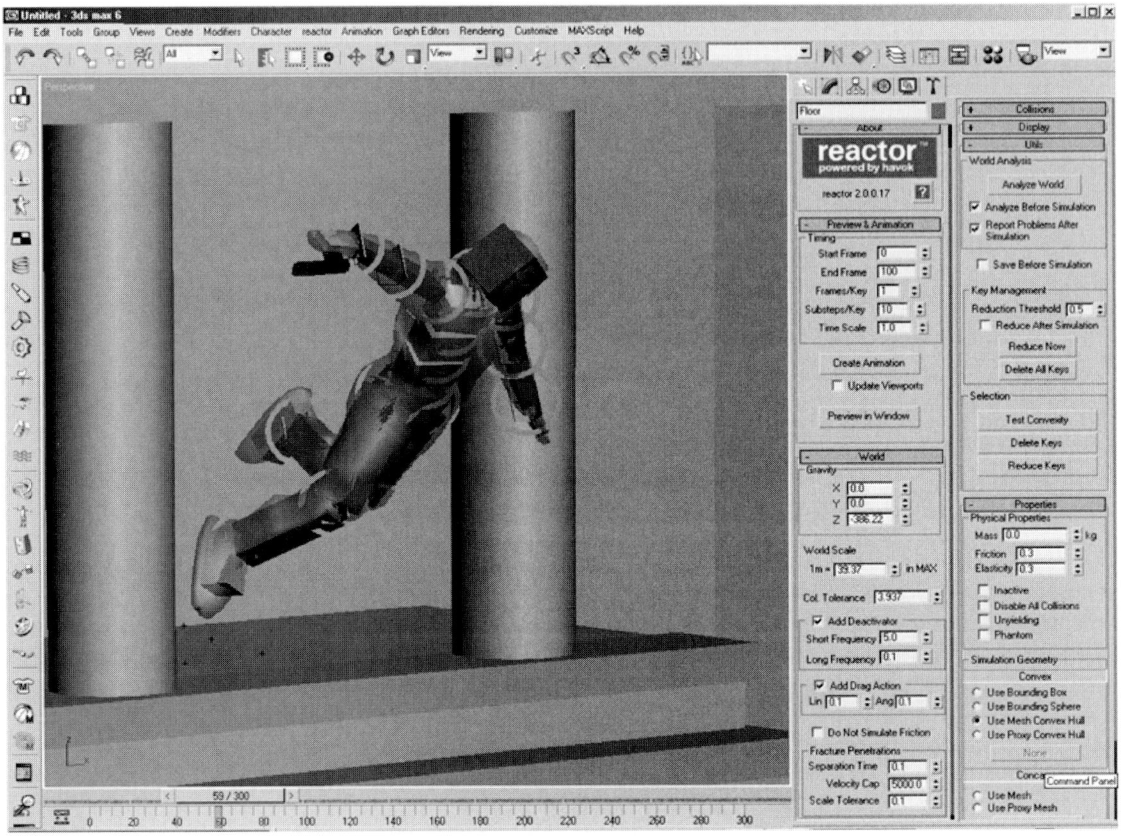

FIGURE 1.2 Reactor 2 enables you to create physical stunts with the Rag Doll.

and trees. New architectural materials make it easier to create realistic buildings. New import functions improve the import of .dxf and other CAD files. These features incorporate many of the features of 3ds max Viz, including the Panoramic Export renderer and viewer for rendering and viewing a three-dimensional panorama of an environment or a building interior.

Animation Features

We will begin the overview of 3ds max 6 features by exploring the capabilities of the skeletal deformation animation system. A typical animated character, such as those used in the film *Homing Instinct,* consists of a rigged skeleton with either sliders or custom attributes to control the hands; a polygon mesh skin model bound to the skeleton using the Skin Modifier; and facial expressions controlled by morph targets, using the Morpher Modifier, and by a facial bone network that follows the opening and closing of the jaw.

The 3ds max bones IK skeleton rig is the heart of the animated character, as shown in Figure 1.3. The process of rigging a skeleton for animation is explained in Chapter 7, "Character Setup with Bones."

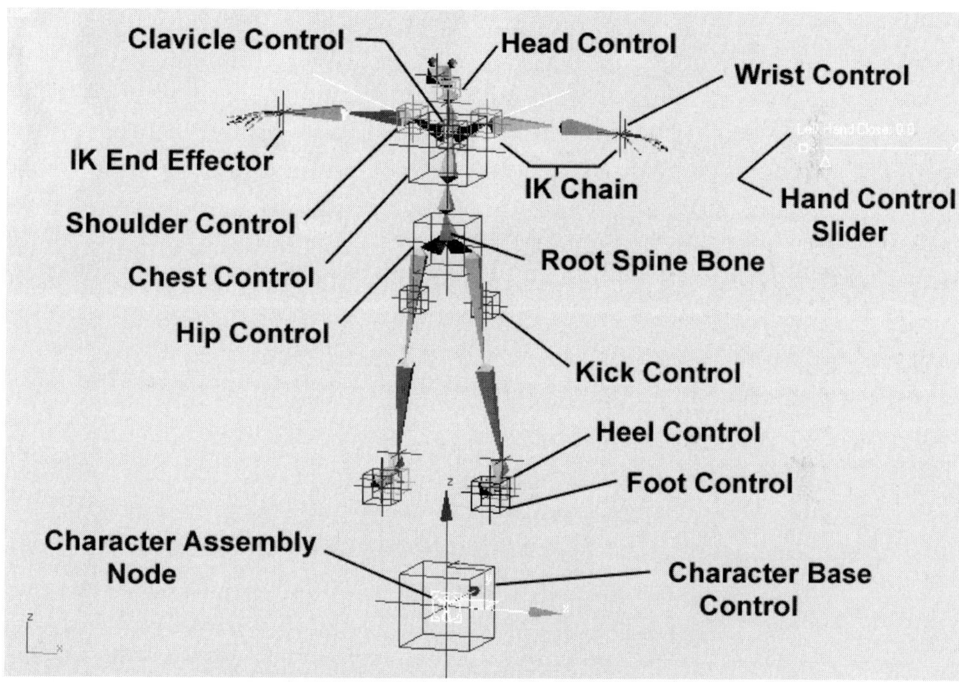

FIGURE 1.3 The parts of two different 3ds max skeleton rigs.

When the skeleton rigging is finished, the next step is to bind the skin to the skeleton. To facilitate this, bone fins are enabled, as shown in Figure 1.4, example 1. Bone fins work with the Skin Modifier to pre-set the size of the skin influence envelopes, which control how the skin deforms when the bones are animated. Fins make the fitting and adjusting of the skin much easier and quicker, as shown in Figure 1.4, example 3.

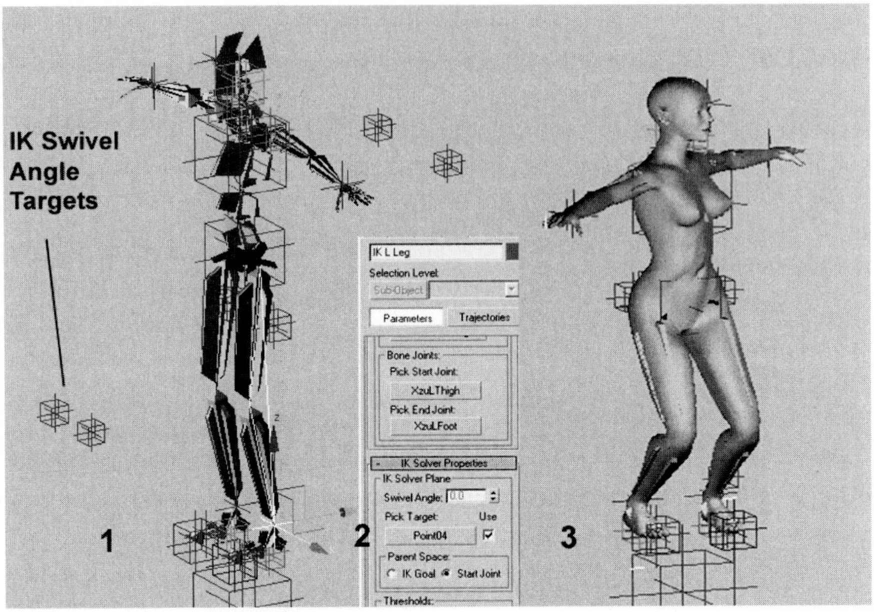

FIGURE 1.4 A polygonal skin mesh is bound to a skeleton rig with bone fins using the Skin Modifier.

The skinned character shown needed almost no adjustment after fitting because the fins took care of that. This same skinning operation done without enabling the bone fins requires manual adjustment of every influence envelope.

Detailed control of the Skin Modifier is available in 3ds max 6. The skin envelope consists of four parts: the Outer brown envelope, the Inner red envelope, the Envelope Length Control, and the Envelope Size Handles, as shown in Figure 1.5, example 1.

Bone squash or stretch can be applied to any bone to animate its length. This enables you to create a squash and stretch animation similar to "Disney style" character animation.

You can refine the behavior of the skin by painting skin weights after the initial skin envelope sizes have been adjusted, as shown in Figure 1.5, example 2. The Skin Weight Assignments Table is organized as a spreadsheet, where the weight assignment of every point on the skin is matched to its associated bone or bones. These values can be adjusted, as shown in Figure 1.6. This offers complete control over the bone-vertex assignments. The new Mirror Skin Weights commands let you assign skin

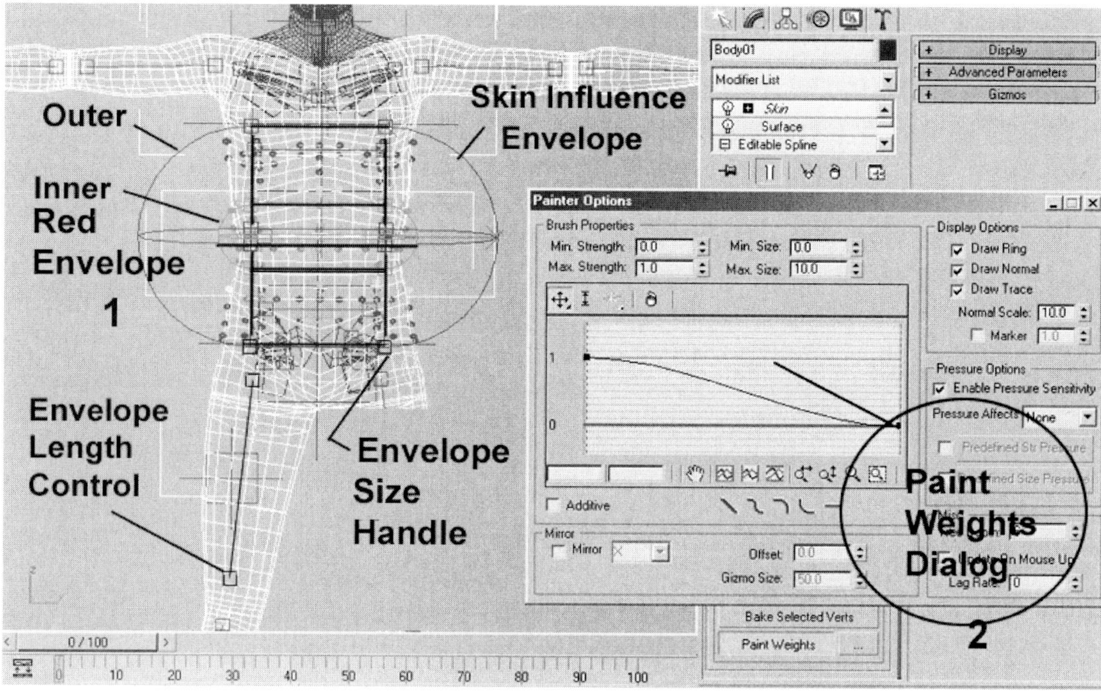

FIGURE 1.5 The skin envelope and the Paint Weights dialog.

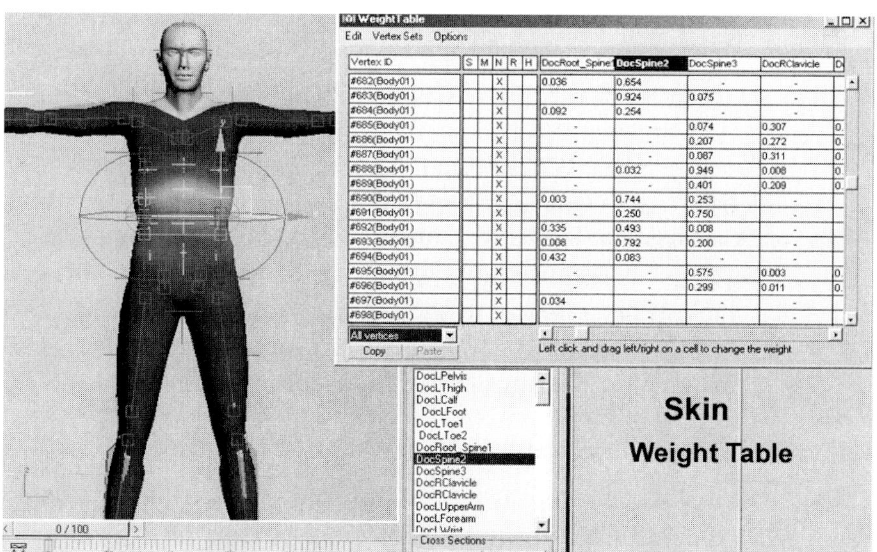

FIGURE 1.6 Skin Weight Assignments Table and Mirror Skin Weights.

weights to one side of a model and then apply the same weights automatically to the other side. This saves a tremendous amount of time during character setup.

For precise control of the skin at the joints, under the arms, or to bulge different muscle groups, the Skin Modifier has three methods: the Joint Angle Deformer, the Bulge Angle Deformer, and the Morph Angle Deformer, as shown in Figure 1.7.

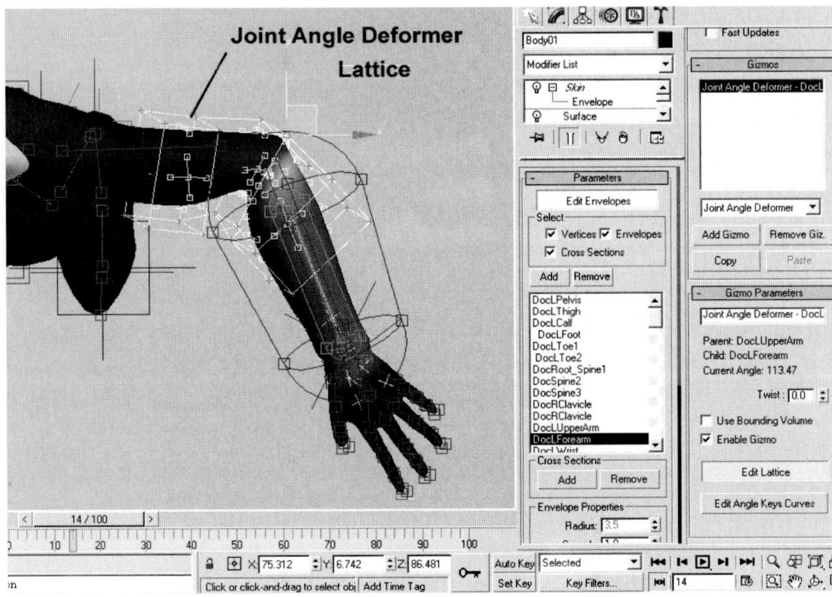

FIGURE 1.7 Using the Joint Angle Deformer to control skin behavior.

The Joint Angle Deformer is very useful for correcting minor problems such as an elbow that flattens out when the arm bends. By applying a Joint Angle Deformer Lattice to the vertices of the arm, the shape of the arm can be changed according to the bend angle of the arm. Once the skin has been bound to the skeleton and adjusted, and the skeletal rigging is done, sliders can be added to control the fingers, wrists, or any of the skeleton rig control points as shown in Figure 1.8.

A slider can be connected to an object's Z rotation parameter (or any other parameter) by using the Wired Parameters dialog or by creating Custom Attribute controls. See Chapter 8, "Preparing for Character Animation," for tutorials on using sliders. See Chapter 12, "Advanced Animation," for tutorials on setting up custom attributes.

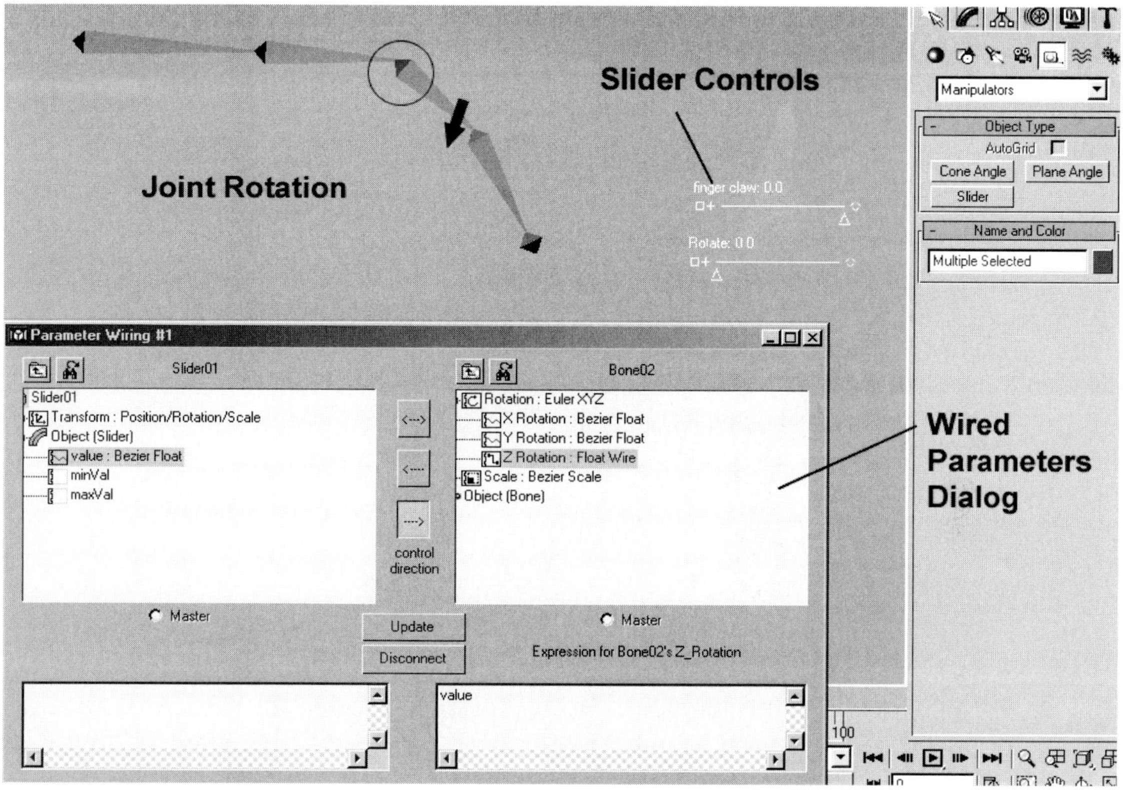

FIGURE 1.8 Wired Parameters and sliders are used to control bone rotation, which can in turn control other objects.

Secondary motion animation, such as muscle or skin jiggle, can be added with the Flex Modifier or with Reactor 2. Flex is good for adding secondary motion to a fat character, breasts, the neck skin of a massive dinosaur, or the long hanging ears of a dog. Another use of Flex is to add motion in reaction to natural forces like wind to any object in the environment such as plants, tree limbs, and flowers, as shown in Figure 1.9. For true soft-body dynamic animation, for water effects, or for wind-blown cloth or clothing, you would use Reactor 2.

A point cache can be used in all types of simulations to store vertex motion data on the hard drive, thereby speeding up playback and redraw as you work on additional animation.

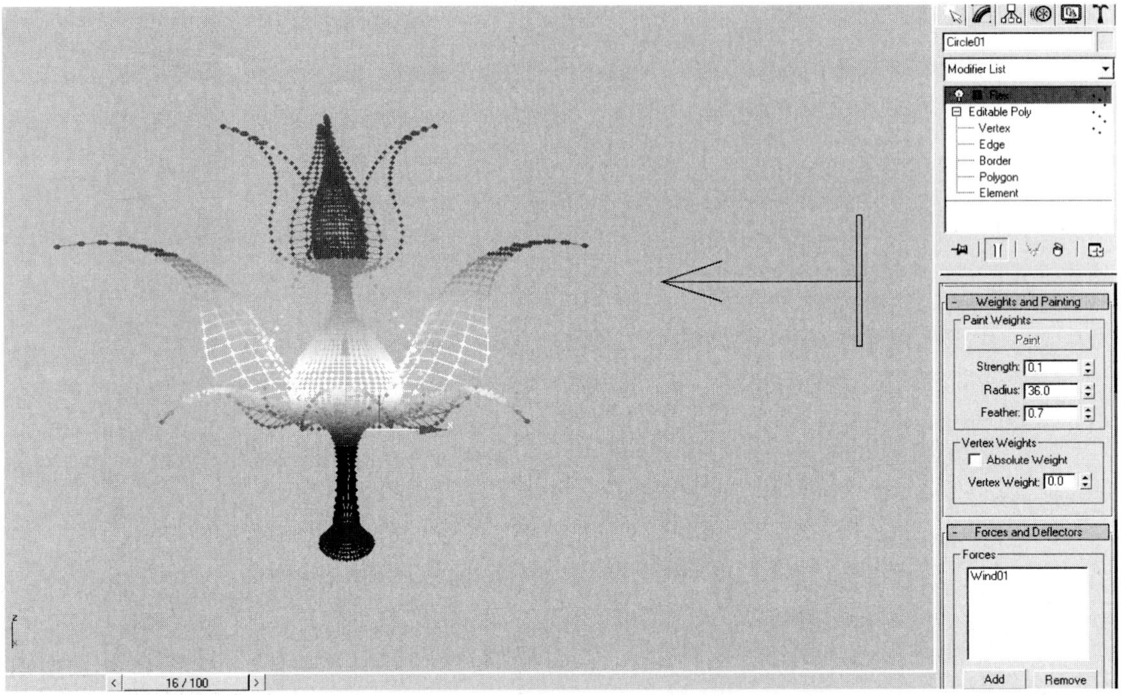

FIGURE 1.9 Secondary animation or reaction to forces like wind can be added to any object with the Flex Modifier.

FACIAL AND LIP SYNC ANIMATION

Facial animation is an important part of character animation. This goes hand in hand with lip-sync animation. The moving of the face from one mouth shape or expression to another can be done in two ways. The simplest method is to use facial morph targets and the Morpher Modifier to animate the face, as shown in Figure 1.10.

A more complicated but more sophisticated method of doing facial animation is to use a combination of morph targets with a skeletal network inside the face that is designed to open the jaw and move small lip and cheekbones with slider controls. Each emotion can then be assigned to a different slider, as shown in Figure 1.11. See Chapter 12, "Advanced Animation," for information on setting up a facial bone network.

In addition to bones, Free Form Deformation (FFD) lattices can be used to control the movement of the face, as shown in Figure 1.12. Splines can also be used as bones to animate sections of the face such as the eyebrows, or the creases in the cheeks.

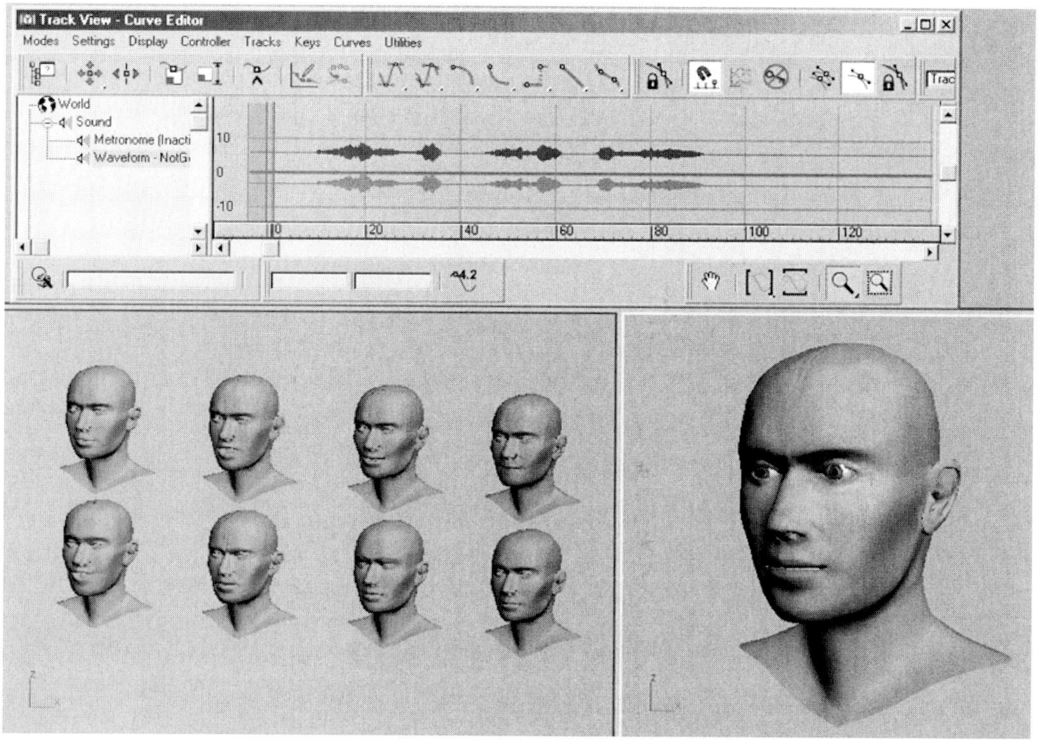

FIGURE 1.10 Facial morph targets for lip-sync animation using the Morpher Modifier.

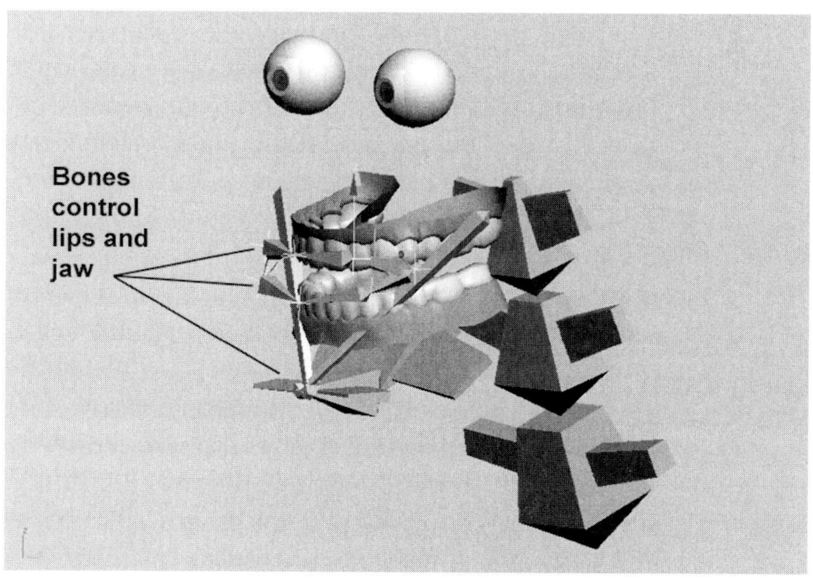

FIGURE 1.11 Animating a face with a skeletal network and sliders.

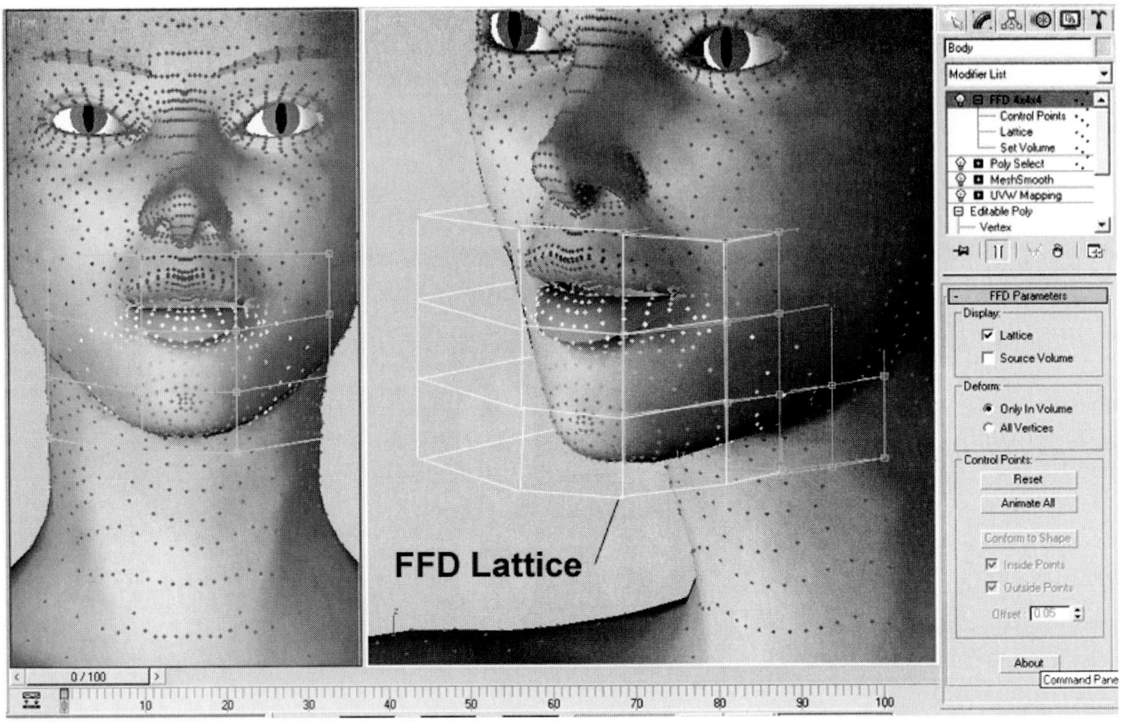

FIGURE 1.12 Facial animation using FFD modifiers and splines.

There are many different versions of the model used in an animated film production. The Level of Detail utility can be used to switch from a low-resolution to a high-resolution model dependent on the model's distance from the camera. A low-resolution version is used to work out most of the animation sequences where speed is important, as shown in Figure 1.13. A medium detail version is prepared for medium and long shots, and action shots that do not require close-ups or fine facial expressions. One or more high-resolution models are prepared for medium and close-up shots. Then, a final, more elaborate model is prepared, usually called the "Hero" model, which is lavishly textured and has a full range of facial expressions and skin detailing. On this model, special attention is paid to the lines in the face and around the eyes, the look and glossiness of the eyeballs, the realism of the eyebrows and eyelashes, and the style, density, and color of the hair. The hero model also wears the highest resolution version of the clothing, which must stand up to long close-up shots and dialog.

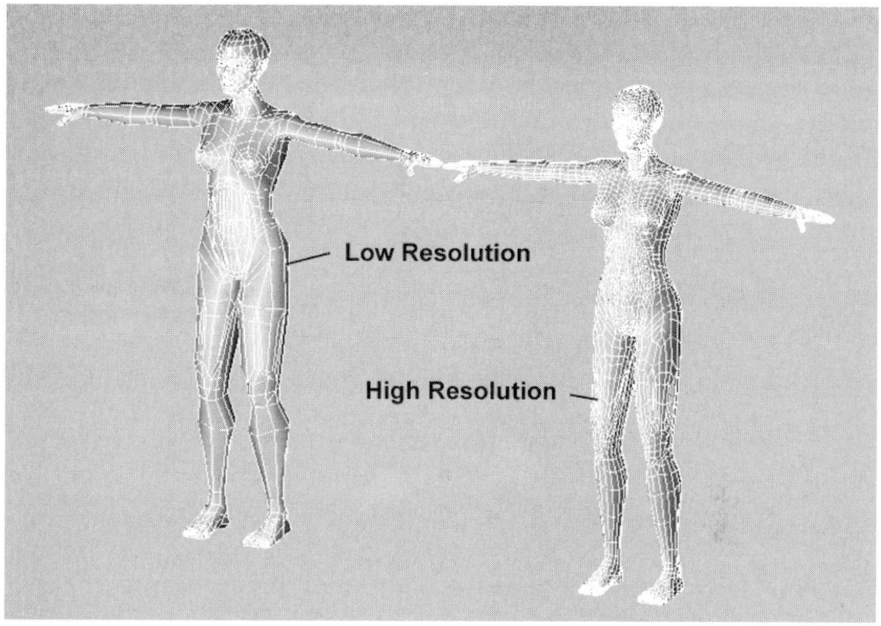

FIGURE 1.13 Low- and high-resolution versions of the Alien Vampire model.

Even if the characters are not meant to be realistic, attention to detail is just as important. Take, for example, the lead characters in the animated film *Antz*. A great deal of attention was paid to surface details, facial muscle motion, and expressions. The texture and even the teeth and lips were made nonfrightening so that the ants would look attractive in close-up shots to general audiences.

For the film *Homing Instinct,* two methods of creating clothing and costumes were used. The first method derived the clothing from the character mesh by selecting a part of the body, and then creating a clone copy of part of the mesh. That mesh was then enlarged and modeled into clothing, as shown in Figure 1.14. See Chapter 4, "Finishing the Alien Vampire Character," for information on this technique.

The second method used is a plug-in cloth garment simulation program called Stitch. See the Plug-ins section of this chapter for more information on Stitch. Reactor 2 can also be used to simulate clothing, although it does not allow you to build clothing from real clothing patterns, as Stitch does.

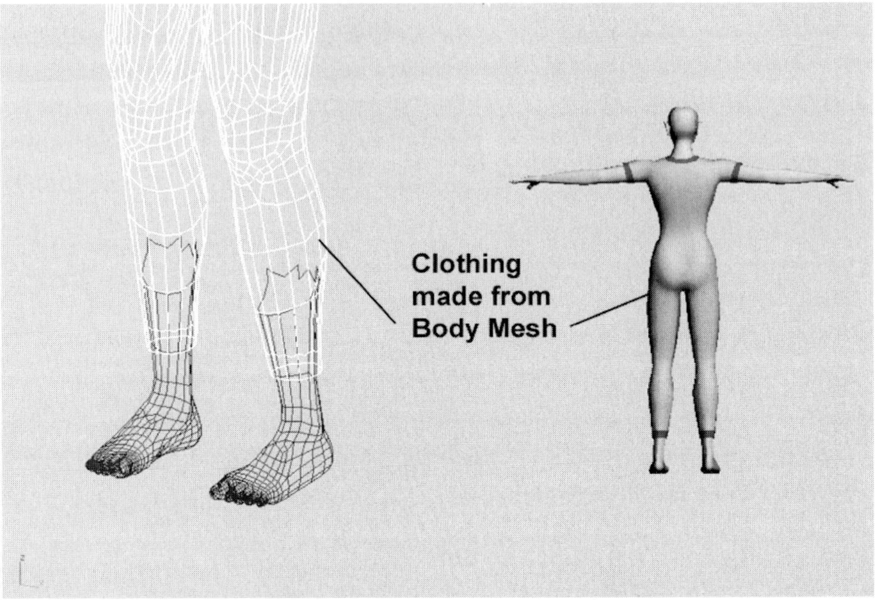

FIGURE 1.14 Clothing created by cloning the original body mesh.

Interface Features

The 3ds max 6 interface has undergone a redesign to improve workflow.

Viewport Layer manager has been improved and streamlined. Layers help you manage a complex scene in which many objects might obscure each other and make it difficult to work. Layers let you hide, freeze, or ghost different objects in a scene, which means that you can work on one layer and have another layer frozen but still visible. You no longer need to go to the properties, the modifier panel, or the track view to change visibility, selectability, or renderability because these properties can be changed in the layers. This is a real time-saver in the production environment. It can be used along with Named Selection sets to select groups of objects or sub-objects to micro-manage your scenes. The Layers toolbar does not always show in the 3ds max 6 viewport by default. To display it, right-click on the upper edge of the main toolbar, and then select Layers from the drop-down menu. This displays the Layers toolbar, as shown in Figure 1.15.

The first layer you see is named Layer 0. By default, everything in a scene is on Layer 0. If you create a new layer, make it the current layer, and then create new objects, those objects will be part of that layer. The main

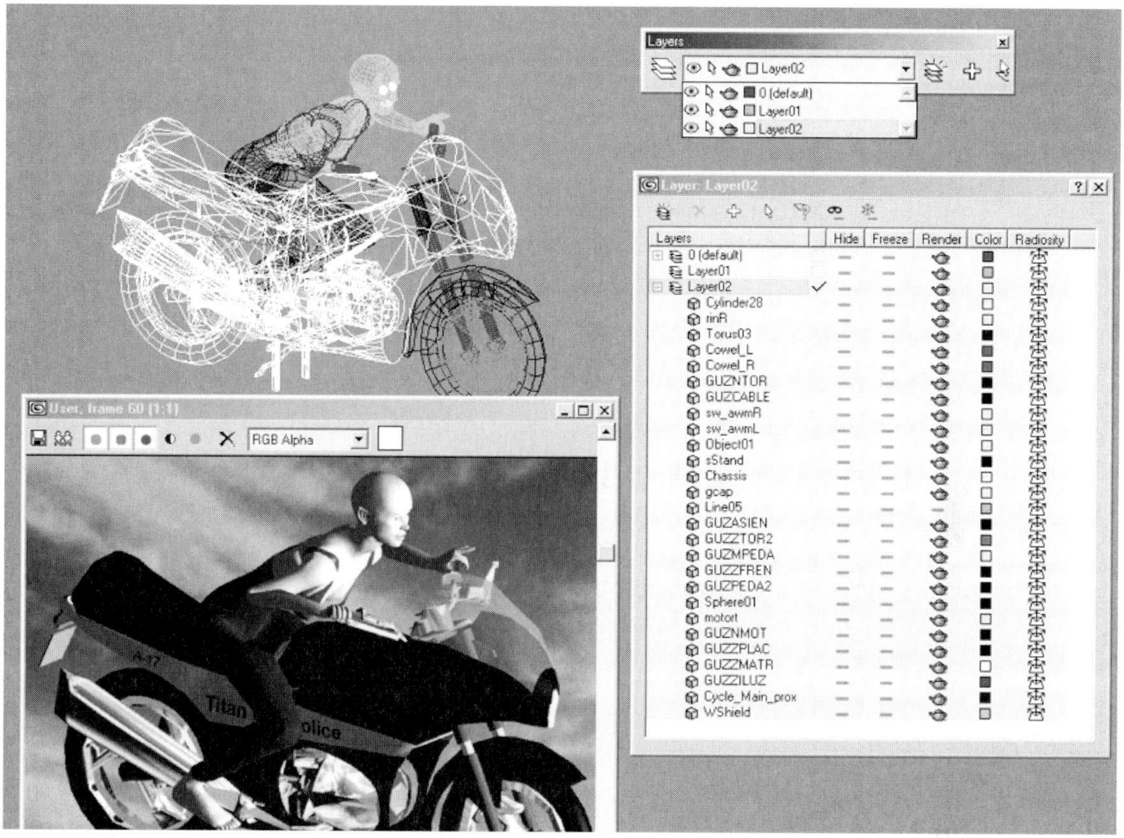

FIGURE 1.15 The Layer Properties dialog showing parts of the motorcycle model on different layers.

control for moving objects to different layers is the Add Selection to Current Layer icon. To move an object from Layer 0 to a new layer, create a new layer, and then select the object. Click on the name of the new layer in the Layers toolbar window and click the Add Selection to Current Layer icon.

The Curve Editor and the Dope Sheet

The Curve Editor and the Dope Sheet provide two different ways to view and adjust animation keyframes. The Curve Editor represents position, rotation, and scale keys using curves that can be adjusted by moving Bézier handles. The Dope Sheet represents that same information in the form of keyframe blocks, and is more suited to adjusting object controller parameters and keyframe ranges, adding keys, setting out-of-range key types, changing timing, selecting objects, or moving blocks of keys. The new Draw Curves tool lets you draw a new curve directly on the function curve graph to modify an existing animation curve.

To demonstrate how the animation curves are represented in the Curve Editor, a character skeleton was animated. In the viewport, you can see the trajectory curves of the arm movement. In the Curve Editor, those motion paths have been translated into X, Y, and Z position graph curves for each position of the arm over time. The vertical direction equals X, Y, or Z position; the horizontal direction equals time in frames or hours, minutes, and seconds. The angle of the curve expresses the velocity of the change of position over time.

The Curve Editor also displays a Time Slider (two vertical lines) that is linked to the Track Bar Time Slider for scrubbing through the motion from inside the Curve Editor window, as shown in Figure 1.16.

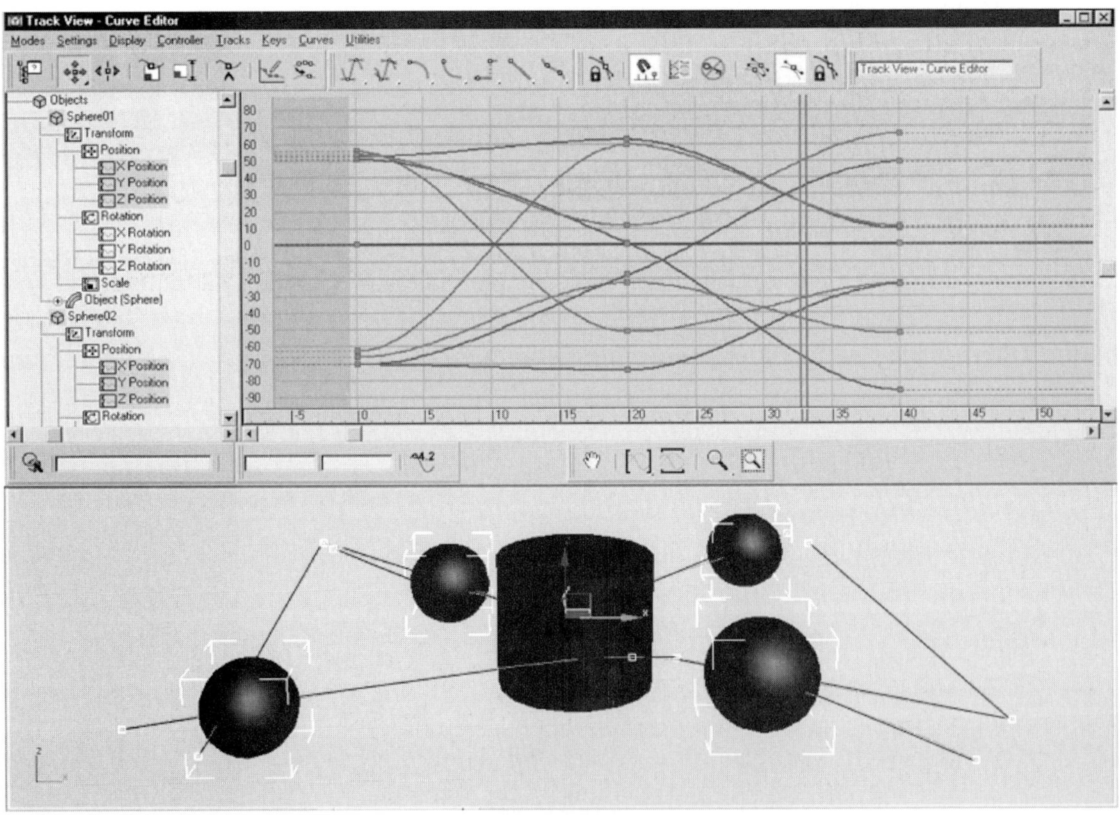

FIGURE 1.16 The Curve Editor showing the keyframe position curves for the arm animation.

These curves can be turned into Bézier curves with handles that can be pulled to change the shape of the curve. Key to Key Transition Types can also be changed quickly by clicking on a key and then clicking a Transition Type from the menu bar, which includes the new Auto Tangent, which is smoothed but does not overshoot, as well as the traditional linear, fast, slow, switch, and custom Bézier handle tangents. A powerful feature is the ability to soft select a range of keys and slide them along to stretch or compress sections of the animation, altering the way the character behaves. Two other important functions are Key Reduction, and the ability to assign controllers to tracks.

The Dope Sheet gives you the ability to adjust time ranges and to select keys and create Blocks of keys to be controlled by the Master Block Controller. This lets you copy and paste animation keys. Audio Controllers can be applied to object transformation tracks in the Dope Sheet to modify the way objects move, as shown in Figure 1.17.

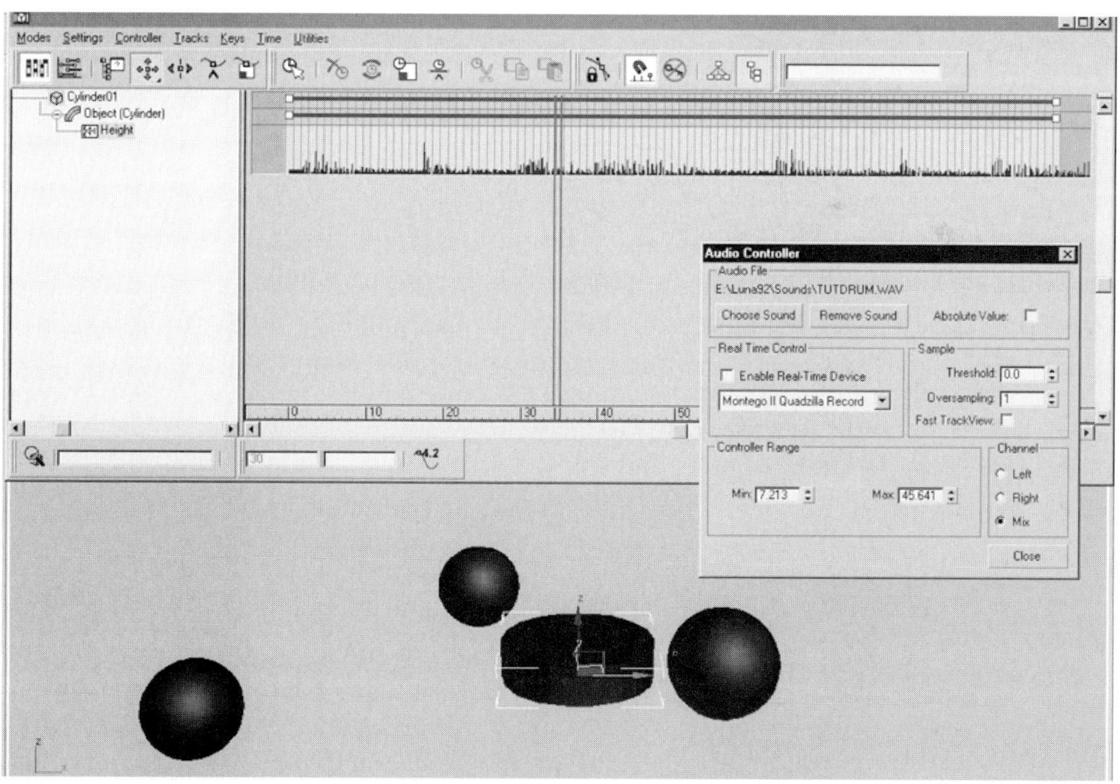

FIGURE 1.17 Applying an Audio Float Controller to an object in the Dope Sheet.

The Dope Sheet eliminates the need to open the Motion Panel for many controller functions, and lets you to manipulate the controller settings and the key positions directly to adjust the effects of the controller. The new Schematic Diagram can also be used in conjunction with the Dope Sheet to organize your animation and to apply controllers to objects, or to wire object parameters together.

The Command Panel

Many of the Command Panel menus have been expanded to include more features. When you drag the left border of the Command Panel sideways, it will expand to see all the menus of any modifier. This is especially helpful for working with particle systems or plug-in programs that contain many levels of nested menus. You can detach and float the Command Panel anywhere in the interface and dock it on the left or the right, and you can drag the submenus up or down to change the order of the menus. Switching to Expert Mode (press Ctrl > X) lets you use the entire screen as a viewport. In Master Mode, the Quad menus and hotkeys give you access to all the menus needed for most 3ds max operations while leaving the screen as free of clutter as possible.

VISUAL EFFECTS FEATURES

3ds max 6 is a powerful visual effects generation package. The visual effects used in *Homing Instinct* are of six main types: Particle, Dynamic, Atmospheric, Morphing and Transform, Compositing, and Rendering effects such as Motion Blur and Glow.

Reactor 2

Reactor 2, a powerful dynamics package from Havok, has been integrated into 3ds max 6 to give it extensive solid-body and soft-body simulation capabilities. This puts 3ds max 6 on an even footing with Maya soft-body and solid-body dynamics. The Reactor 2 toolbar can be displayed by loading the Reactor 2 User Interface (UI) in the Load Custom UI Scheme. Reactor 2 appears as a floating toolbar running up the left side of the interface. Reactor 2 can simulate a wide range of effects, including cloth, water and waves, ropes, chains, object shatter, and springs. Many different types of forces can be applied, and the keyframes that are generated in the simulation can be edited.

Objects can be made to float in water by setting the Physical Mass and Gravity of the Rag Doll stunt skeleton, the Impact Detection, and the Density and Viscosity of the water. When a Rag Doll is dropped into the water, the shoreline of a pond creates realistic waves that rebound from the edges of the pond, as shown in Figure 1.18.

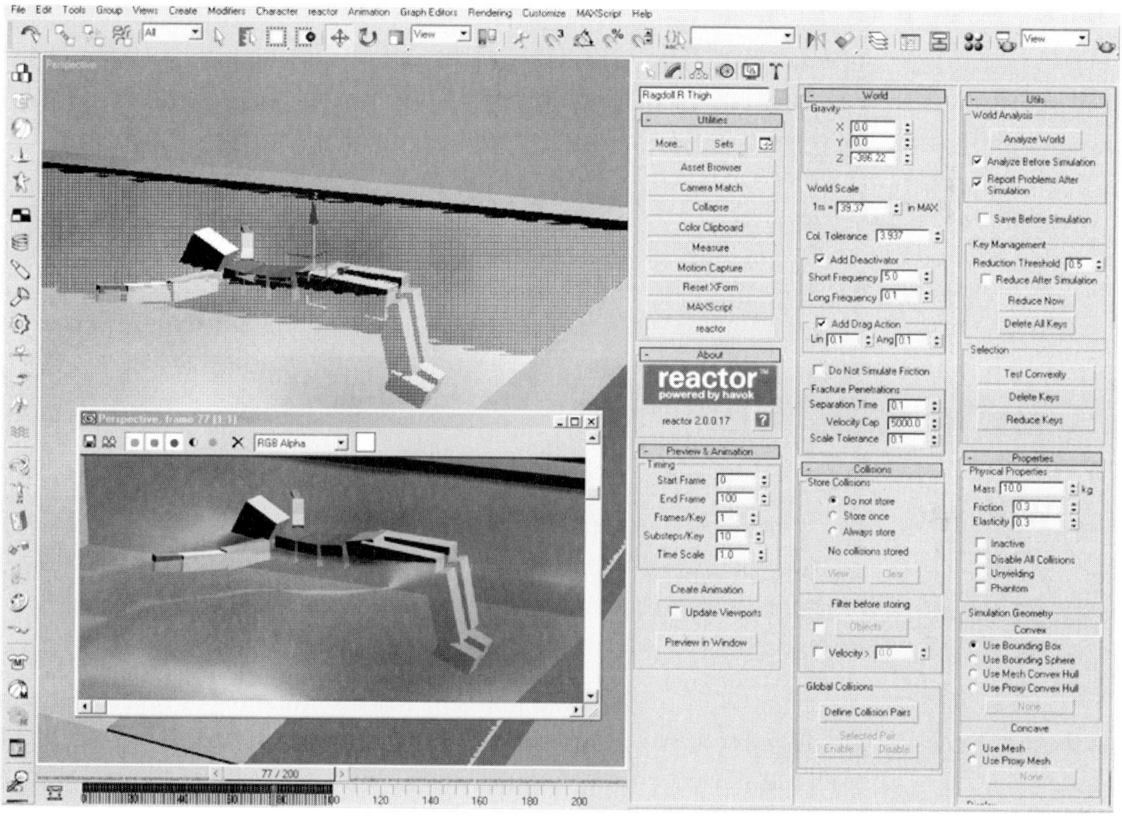

FIGURE 1.18 A Rag Doll stunt skeleton floating in the water using Reactor 2.

An important feature of Reactor 2 is the ability to pin or constrain all or part of an object to another object. This allows the top of a curtain, for example, to be pinned to a surface, and freely hang down and blow in the wind. For a tutorial on the use of Reactor 2, see Chapter 12, "Advanced Animation."

In *Homing Instinct*, particle effects are used extensively to create laser blasts, explosions, gunfire, fragmentation or disintegration, and smoke. These effects are usually augmented with light effects, as shown in Figure 1.19. When explosions go off, they are often combined with a second type of visual effect called Dynamic effects.

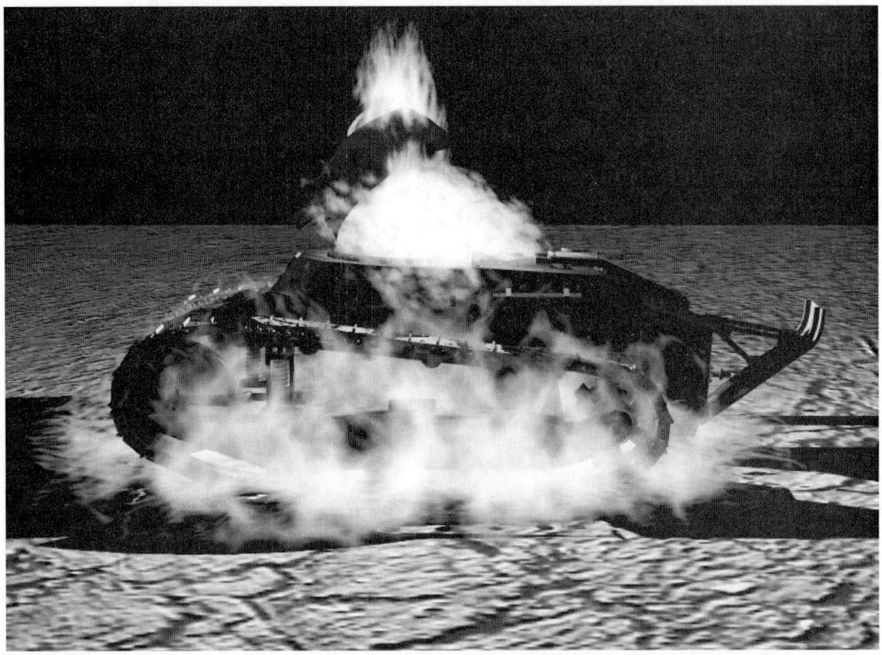

FIGURE 1.19 Particle effects are combined with Atmospheric effects to create exciting explosions.

Dynamics include solid and soft body simulation of object impacts, gravity effects, wind, turbulence, water effects, and particle effects. 3ds max 6 now has two different particle systems: the standard Max particles, and Particle Flow, which is a sophisticated, event-driven programmable particle system. Animated objects can be used as instanced geometry particles to create marching armies of soldiers, an armada of spaceships, or flocks of flying bats or birds, as shown in Figure 1.20. Facing particle types, also known as Sprites, are used for water spray, bubbles, smoke, and sparks. All of the particle effects can interact with the 3ds max Space Warps, including Deflector, Gravity, and Drag. MAXScripts can be written to control the behavior of particle systems using Particle Flow.

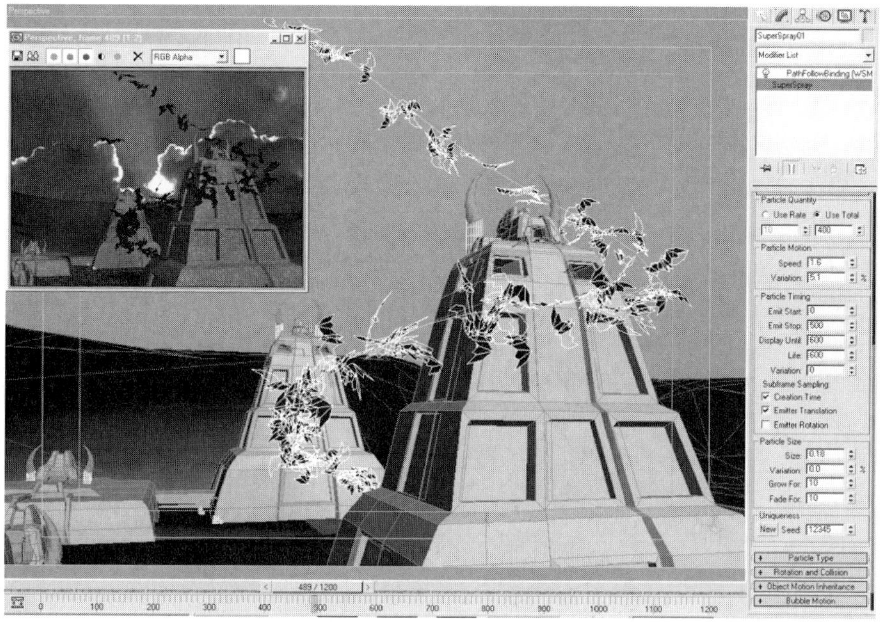

FIGURE 1.20 Instanced geometry used as particles to create a flight of bats.

Atmospheric effects include normal fog, layer fog, volume fog, rain, the Fire Effect, volume lights, and Fire Effect clouds. Fire Effect is one of the most versatile atmospheric effects in 3ds max and is not limited to making fire.

By changing the color to white or gray it become especially effective for creating low mist or wispy fog on a field or above a stream. Other uses include creating torch flames, campfires, and candle flames, as shown in Figure 1.21.

The fourth type of visual effects available in 3ds max 6 includes morphing and transform effects. Shape changing of the vampires between their human form and their demonic form was accomplished using morph animation techniques. Two of the main characters in *Homing Instinct* are vampires that undergo shape changing when they are threatened. To accomplish this type of visual effect, a series of models were built that range from the original human form to the vampire demon shape, as shown in Figure 1.22.

The fifth type of visual effect that can be created in 3ds max 6 is the Composite effect, where an object or animated character is placed as a

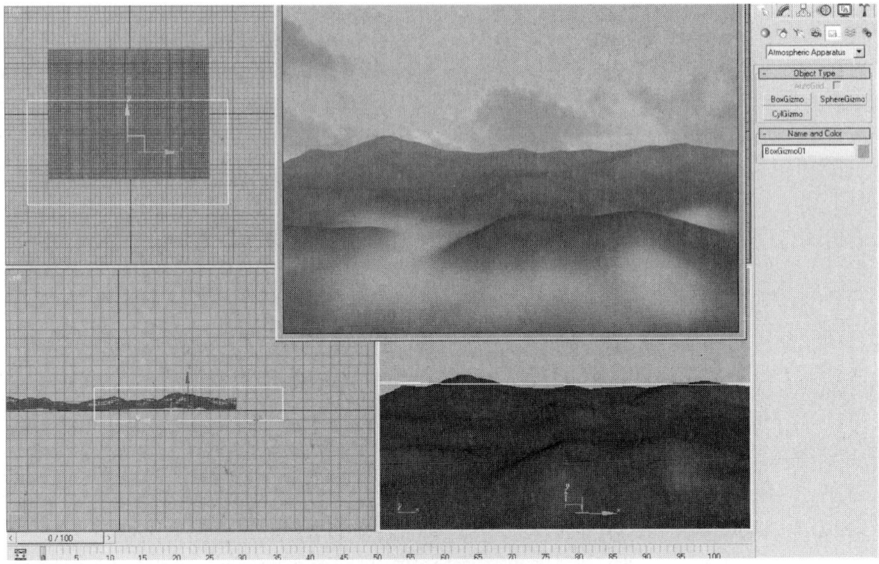

FIGURE 1.21 Wispy mist on a field made with Fire Effect.

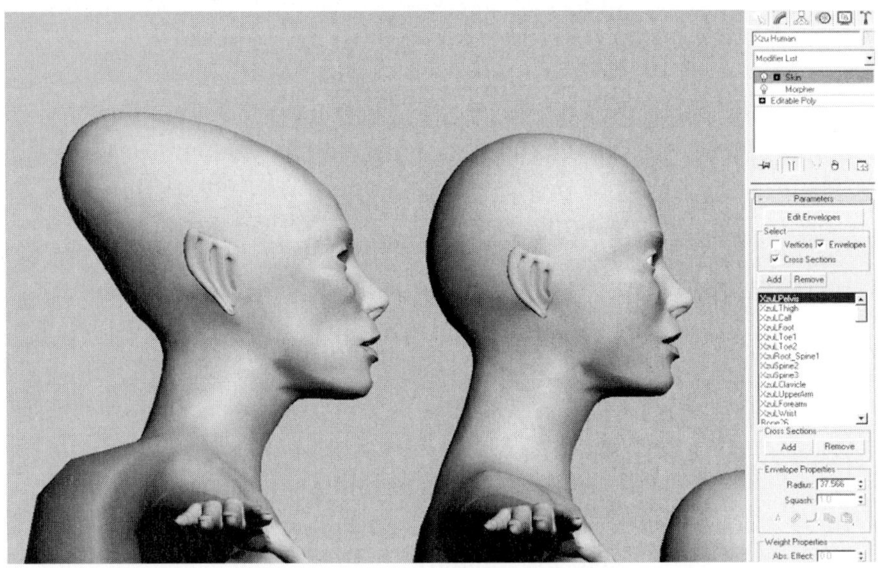

FIGURE 1.22 Shape changing effects were accomplished using morph targets.

layer into a photographic background. This includes Shadow Matte material effects where a 3D object throws a shadow on a 2D background. The Video Post module is used for rendering a series of different camera views, applying Mattes, and Image Filter effects, as shown in Figure 1.23.

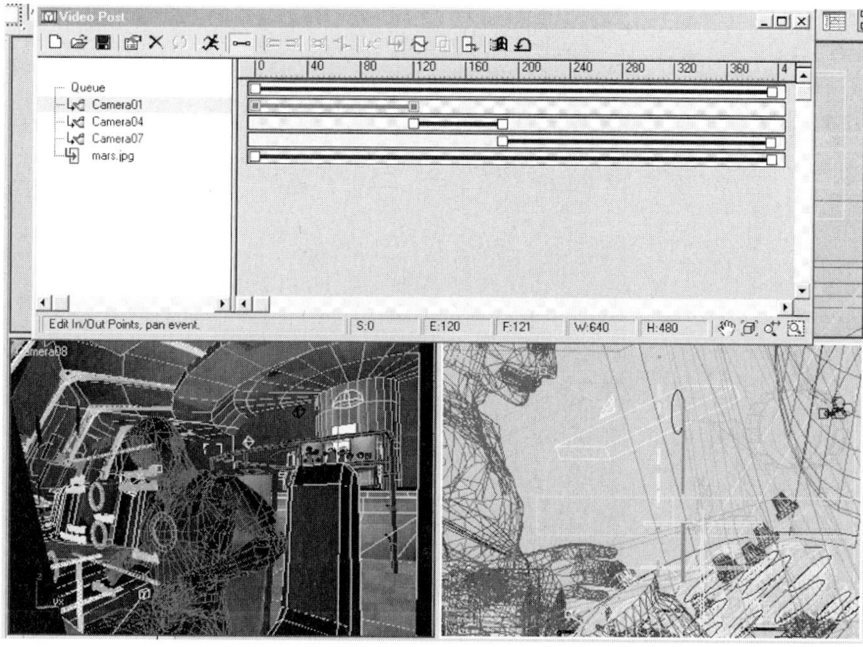

FIGURE 1.23 A scene can be rendered from different camera views in Video Post.

The sixth type of visual effects are the Render effects such as Lens Flares, Glows, Motion Blur, Radial Blur and Streaks, and Depth of Focus, as shown in Figure 1.24.

Additional useful effects include camera effects such as Camera Shake, material effects such as using a movie as a surface texture, and material morphing effects that change textures as an object changes shape. When used with animated displacement maps, the surface of an object can be animated to change radically, as shown in Figure 1.25.

Controller effects such as Audio Rotate and Audio Position use a soundtrack to drive some part of an animation or visual effect. Visibility keys can be used as a "disappearing" or materialization effect for the famous Matter Transporter of science fiction. Instancing can be used to create effects where motion is repeated in multiple copies of an object, such as creating hundreds of beetles crawling across the ground. Cracking and fracturing effects are created with a combination of particle systems, light, and atmospheric effects, as shown in Figure 1.26.

Morph Along Path or Deform Along Surface can create interesting flowing liquid effects, or slithering snake-like motion effects. Pouring

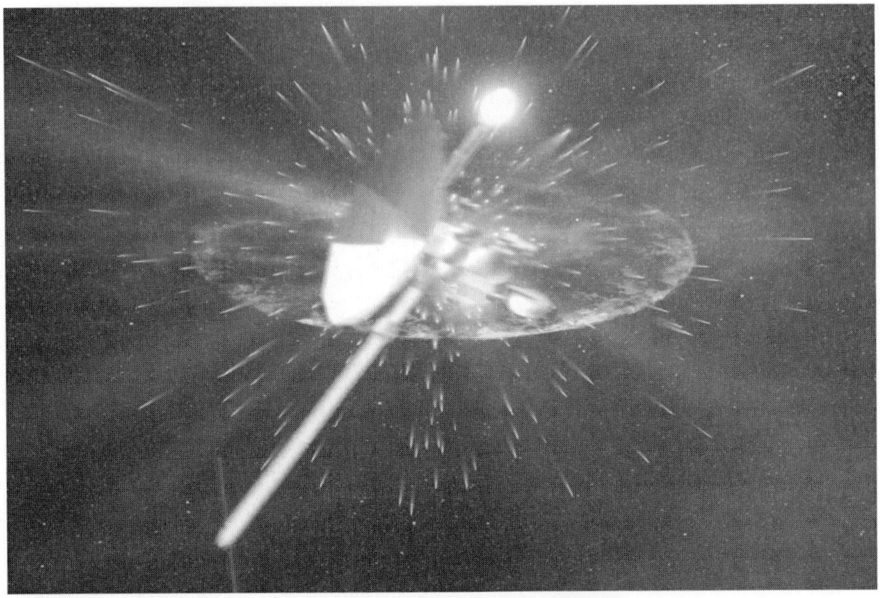

FIGURE 1.24 Rendering effects include Motion Blur and Glow.

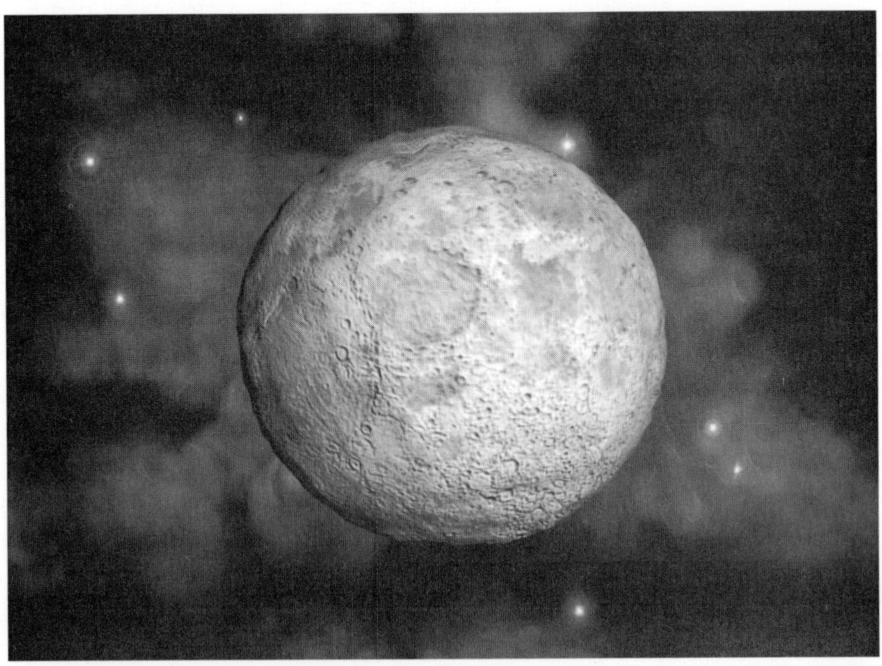

FIGURE 1.25 Displacement map effects can alter the surface of an object.

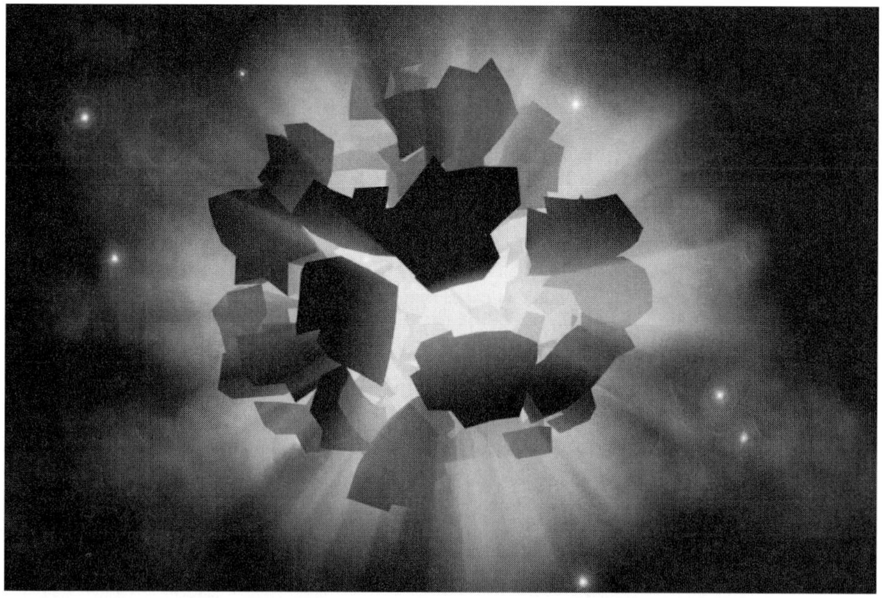

FIGURE 1.26 Cracking and fracturing effects combine particles and light effects.

liquids or liquids flowing through and out of pipes are created using the Metaparticles system and Deflector Space Warps.

The Active Shade renderer creates a floating window that updates every time you change a material parameter. Visual effects can be previewed more easily now using the Direct X 9.0, or newer video drivers, which can display animated transparency to preview particle effects such as animated flames in the viewport without rendering the scene. The Ram Player lets you view sequences of frames by loading them into RAM and splitting the screen to compare two versions of the rendering.

Modeling Features

In addition to the human character models, a large number of other models were built for *Homing Instinct*, including male and female vampires in their winged and human forms, exotic trees and plants, alien animals, insects, bat-like flying lizards, and dinosaur-like Titan aborigines. The environments included modern and ancient buildings, land and vegetation, and roads. Different flying vehicles and hovercraft were built, as well as space shuttles and helicopters. A number of interior sets were built where a scene would take place, such as Dr. Quin's laboratory, a jail, a tunnel system underground, an alien temple ruin, the interior of the alien ship, and a swamp.

For the opening battle, a Defense Satellite model was built for the exterior shots. Then, a more detailed, larger scale interior model of the Satellite bridge was built to serve as the set for the interior visual effects scene, as shown in Figure 1.27.

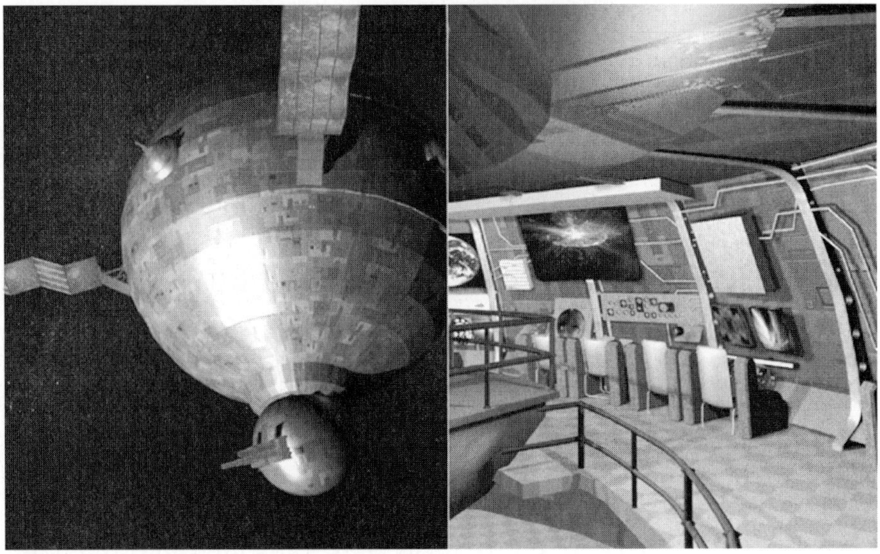

FIGURE 1.27 The Orbital Defense Satellite model and Satellite Bridge Interior model.

The satellite interior image shows the use of renderable splines to create electrical cables. Using splines speeds up the creation of pipes, wires, and tubes in detailed interiors. The Lattice Modifier was used to create railings from flat planes by turning the mesh edges of the planes into tubes. QuickTime movies were applied as animated textures to create the video screens and animated instrument readouts. During the space battle sequence the video screens were blown up using a particle system and a Fire Effect, which, when used together, can explode any object into fragments and generate a fireball with black smoke. Models can be built using four different methods: conventional mesh modeling, Bézier spline patch modeling, NURBS modeling, and polygon modeling with MeshSmooth or NURMS subdivision surfaces.

Polygon Modeling

The Polygon Selection tools have been enhanced to speed workflow. By using the Grow, Shrink, Ring, and Loop edge selection commands, you can speed up the modeling of difficult details such as eyelids, nostrils, and lips on character models, as shown in Figure 1.28.

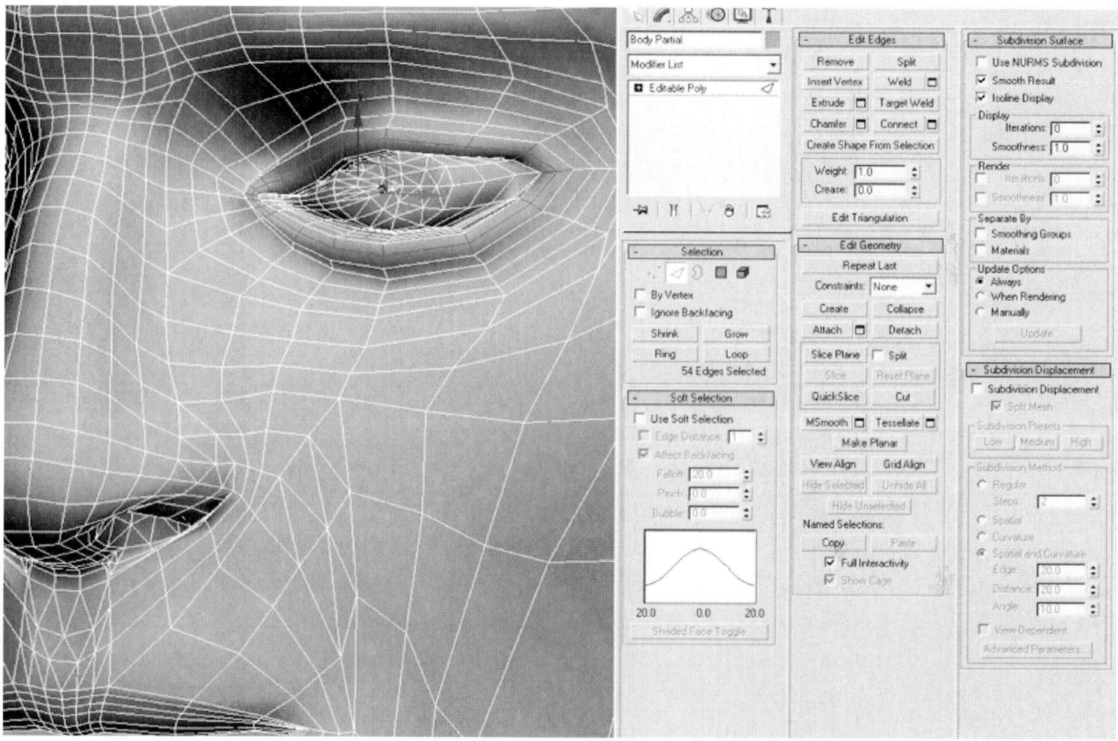

FIGURE 1.28 Polygon Modeling, Selection, and Editing tools.

Two useful Poly Modeling tools are Hinge From Edge and Extrude Along Spline, which speed up the creation of details on the surface of a polygon model. The advantage of Poly modeling over conventional triangle mesh modeling is the capability of polygons to create a polygon face with three or more vertices, allowing the filling of irregular gaps. By adding the HSDS Modifier to the polygon model, fine details can be added on top of medium resolution meshes. MeshSmooth Subdivision Surface and Subdivision Displacement can now be found in the Editable Poly menu, which eliminates the need to apply them as external modifiers. A new addition to MeshSmooth with Polys is the ability to display Isolines. These lines make it easier to see which edges you are modifying when you edit the model in the viewport. Polygon modeling tutorials can be found in Chapter 3, "Modeling Environments, Buildings, and Aliens," and Chapter 4, "Finishing the Alien Vampire Character."

THE MATERIALS EDITOR

To finish the surfaces of the models for *Homing Instinct*, and make them look realistic, a number of different types of materials and textures were designed in the Materials Editor.

The look of the environment is very important in setting the general quality of an animated motion picture. Good texture mapping with naturalistic textures enhance realism and put the finishing touches on the models. Close-up shots require high-resolution textures to prevent pixelation of the surface when the camera comes very close.

In terms of organizing the texture files, much time was spent making sure that all materials were properly named, and that all of the files associated with each model were kept together. In many cases, the same material was used for many different models, such as a basic gray metal material. A central server computer was set up with a master directory of all materials and texture maps. To manage the materials files, the 3ds max 6 Asset Browser, which can be found in the Utility panel, proved an invaluable tool. It allowed animators to look in any directory on any computer in the network to locate misplaced files, or to find where duplicate files with different names were stored.

Mapping and materials have undergone major improvements both in options and functionality. A new menu bar has been added to the Materials Editor, as shown in Figure 1.29. Combustion material is now available, which allows you to work with 3ds max and combustion 3 open at the same time, enabling you to paint on objects in the Max viewport with combustion paint tools. Materials can now be rendered with lighting baked into the material, which is valuable for game and visual effects work.

For cartoon rendering, 3ds max 6 has Ink and Paint, a new cell shader material that provides variable line widths and can render atmosphere and reflections in the line rendering. A new Translucent Shader has been added to allow light transmittance through materials. Materials

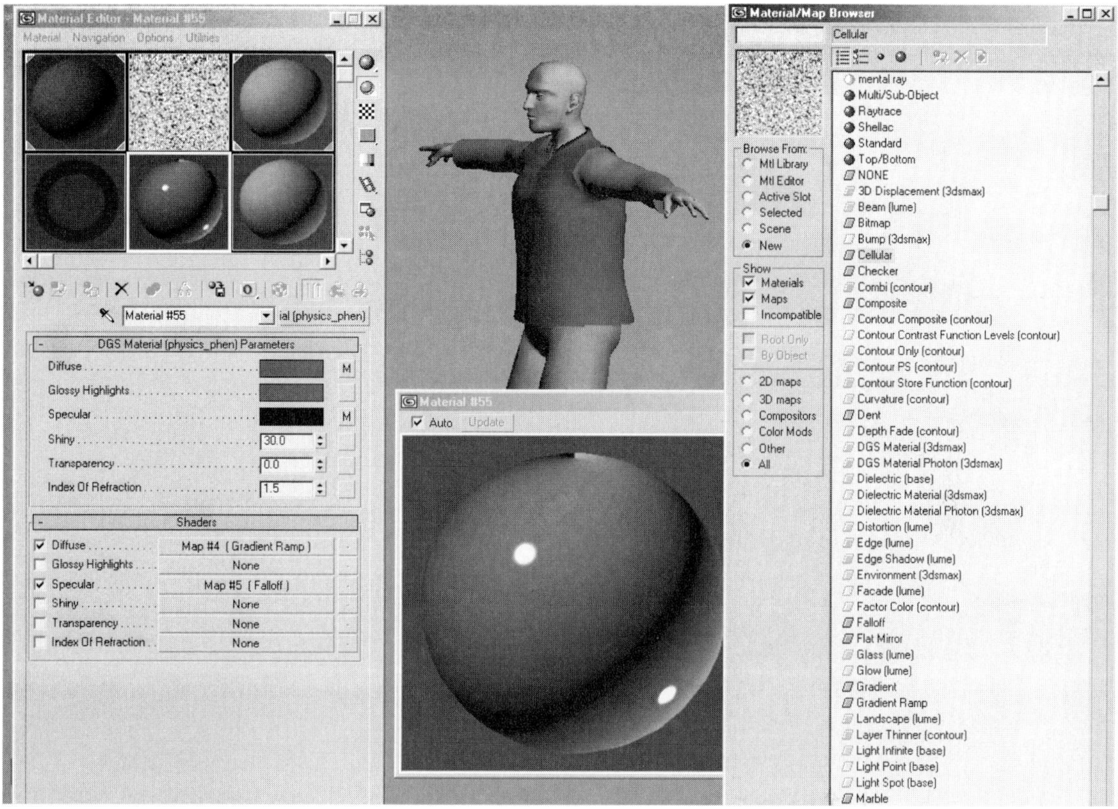

FIGURE 1.29 The Materials Editor includes Mental Ray shaders and lets you bake lighting into materials.

can now be made to emit light by setting the proper parameters in the Materials Editor and the Advanced Lighting menus.

The Unwrap UVW Modifier is a great UVW coordinate editing tool with multiple functions and flexibility. When you want to put textures on a complex model, such as a creature or a human body, many of the areas are difficult to map without distortion. Using the old planar or cylindrical coordinate projection mapping methods produced some very ugly artifacts where the textures were stretched or distorted and did not fit the model well. The Unwrap UVW Modifier has a wide array of different mapping types, and lets you edit UVs with greater control than in the previous version. A shuttle craft's texture with planar projection mapping, as shown in Figure 1.30, example 2, yields distorted and streaked textures.

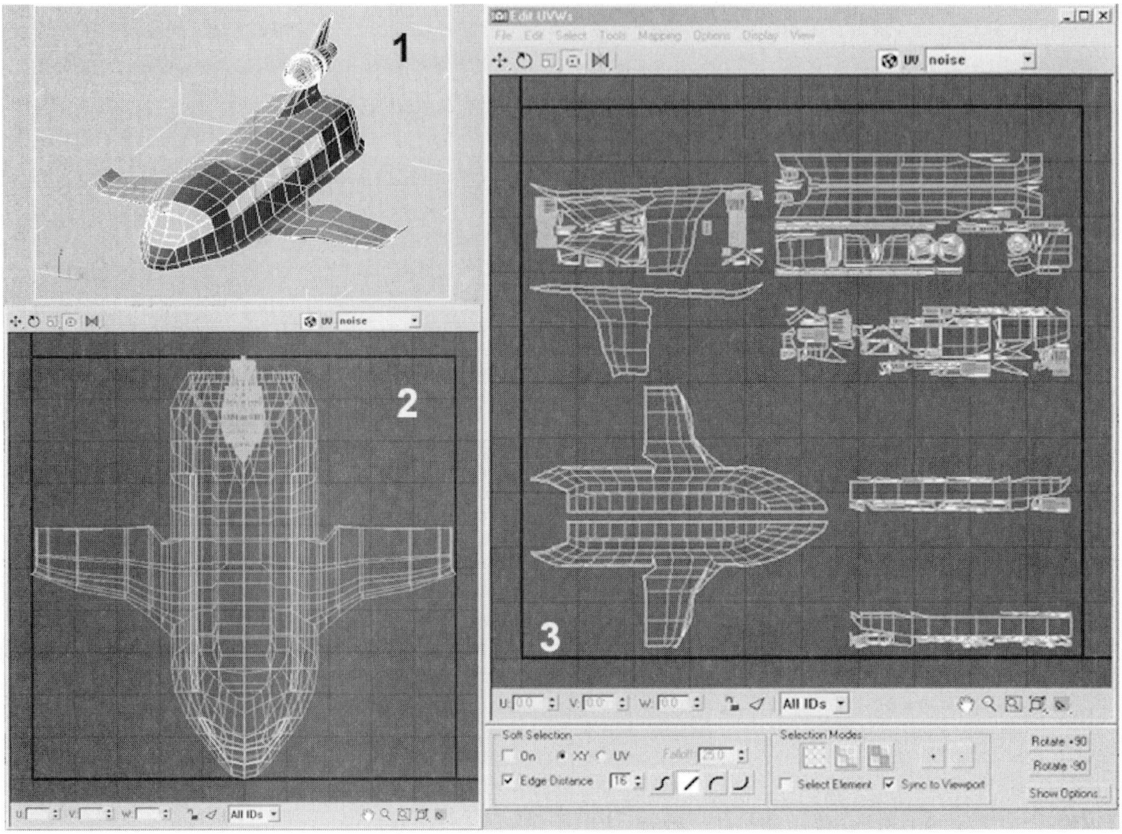

FIGURE 1.30 The new Unwrap UVW Modifier UV editing interface.

The new Flatten Mapping breaks the model into sections that let you place details on any part of the surface using only one map, and allows you to adjust the location by editing selected UVs, as shown in Figure 1.30, example 3. Flatten Mapping helps in texturing complex photo-realistic human, creature, and vehicle models, and gives 3ds max a solid tool for high-end texture mapping in production. For a tutorial on UVW Unwrap, see Chapter 13, "Materials and Textures."

Because the textures used in *Homing Instinct* are meant to be semi-realistic, photos of real surfaces became the basis for most of the materials used on the models. A favorite material type emerged after long use of the Materials Editor, the Composite material. It is made up of layers, which can themselves be made up of layers. Most of the materials are combinations of three to six different maps and masks, often mixed with noise, as shown in Figure 1.31.

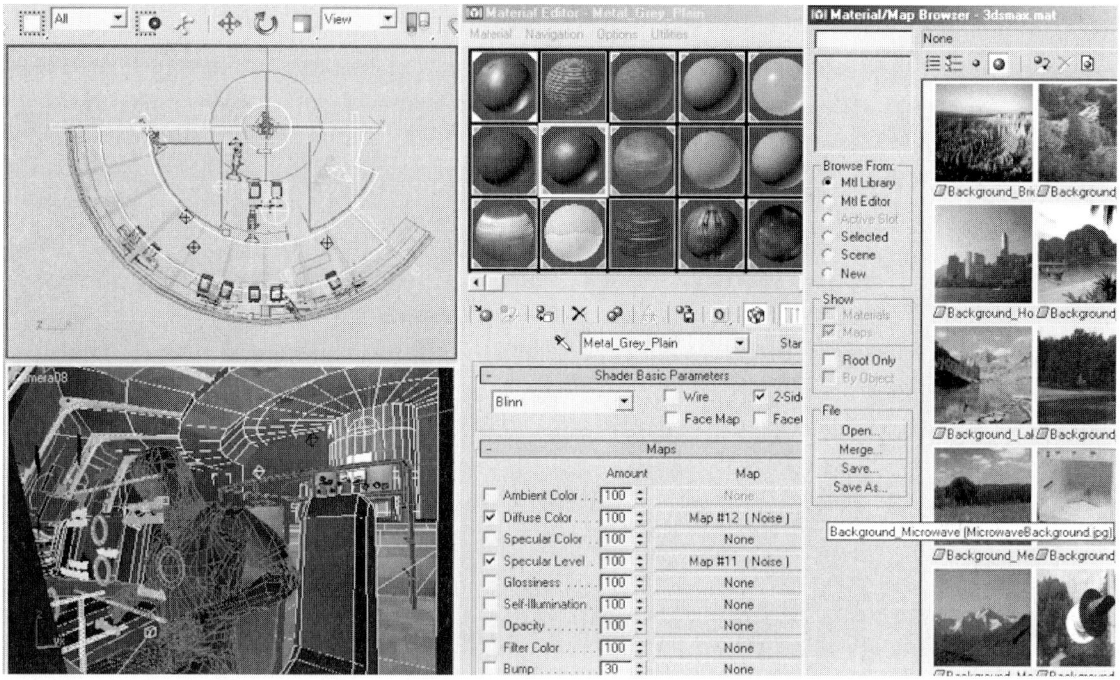

FIGURE 1.31 Use Mix and Composite materials to create multiple layer textures.

By using a mask, transparent areas in the top layer can be created that reveal the layers below, giving the textures a complex organic look.

RENDERING, RADIOSITY, AND GLOBAL ILLUMINATION

The new Mental Ray renderer has been added to the existing rendering and advanced lighting capabilities for 3ds max 6, in addition to the three existing methods of creating radiosity lighting: Skylight Global Illumination, the Light Tracer, and Radiosity. Mental Ray functions as a standalone renderer within Max and has its own menus, lights, shadow maps, shaders, and internal global illumination, called Indirect Illumination. Mental Ray has been used on a number of motion pictures and provides much more control over the rendering process than Max's standard renderer. However, the standard Radiosity is very good, and is based on light physics. Skylight and Light Tracer are designed for quicker animation rendering and do not have the exhaustive accuracy of Radiosity, which is actually discreet Lightscape ported into 3ds max. 3ds max Radiosity can be used to build and analyze the lighting solutions for architectural or virtual movie set models, and to export Lightscape lights and data to the stand-alone version of Lightscape for rendering. For more information, see Chapter 14, "Lighting and Rendering."

The Photometric Light Creation menu gives you a choice of eight different types of lights including Area, Point, and Linear lights used for Radiosity Rendering. You can control color and intensity measured in lumens or color temperature in degrees Kelvin, as well as shadow parameters and edge softness. You can also apply and control atmospheric effects such as Volume Light and Lens Effects from within the Lighting Panel, or create a rectangular Area Light to simulate fluorescent lighting, as shown in Figure 1.32.

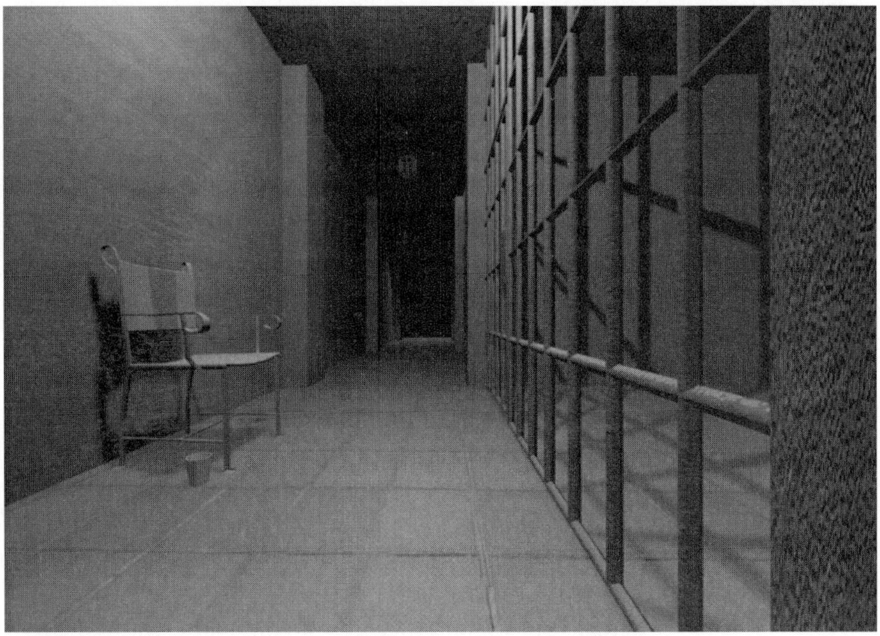

FIGURE 1.32 A prison cellblock illuminated with a rectangular Area Light.

Photometric lights are measured in lumens and foot candles, as shown in Figure 1.33. Radiosity then calculates the light falling on every surface, and the amount of light that is reflecting off those surfaces to come up with a Radiosity lighting solution that is used for the rendering. However, this is only one of four Radiosity systems in 3ds max 6. The other three are the Light Tracer, which is primarily for rendering anima-

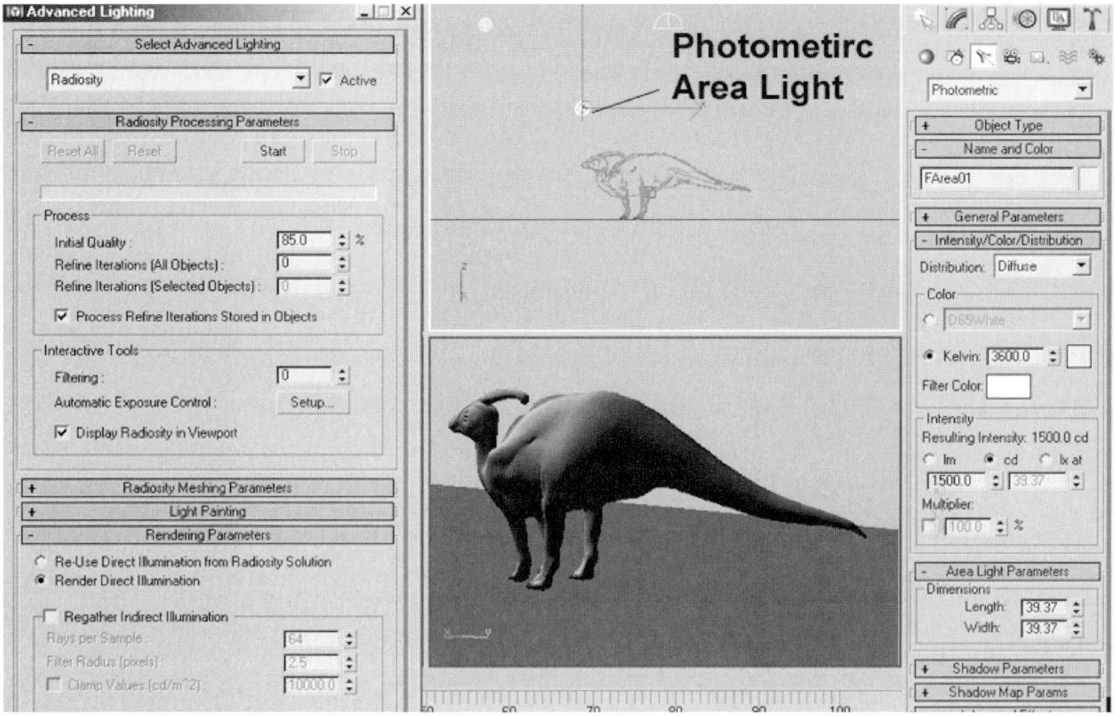

FIGURE 1.33 Radiosity rendering uses physics-based photometric lights measured in lumens and foot candles.

tions; the Skylight global illumination system, used primarily for doing exterior scenes; and Mental Ray Indirect Illumination, for doing photo-realistic rendering.

Radiosity used on a large scene can be quite demanding and can take a long time to calculate and render. For this reason, the less rigorous but very effective Light Tracer system was used to render the scenes. It was found that using the Skylight to light the scenes, and then rendering with the Light Tracer and Automatic Exposure Control gave a wonderful soft look to the character's skin, so ultimately this combination was used for all rendering throughout the film.

The Light Tracer allows you to use normal spot and omni lights with a Skylight to create a lighting solution for each scene. For more information on Radiosity rendering, see Chapter 14, "Lighting and Rendering."

3ds max 6 has three different types of Motion Blur, from a simple and quick Image Motion Blur system to an ultra-high quality Multi-Pass Motion Blur system for creating photo-realistic images. Render effects include

Film Grain, Color Balance, and Brightness and Contrast controls. Nearly all of these effects were used in *Homing Instinct* along with Global Illumination and Radiosity rendering to give the film a more cinematic quality.

The Render Elements feature lets you render different levels of the image to different channels for export to a high-end compositing program such as combustion 3 or flame, allowing you to separate background, diffuse, reflection, refraction, ink, paint, shadow, specular, alpha, and z-depth channels. By rendering in the RLA, or the more advanced RPF (.rpf) or Rich Pixel format, you are able to export Camera Path velocity and Z-depth data so that you can add visual effects such as lighting, fog, motion blur, and particles in 3D composite space using combustion 3 or flame.

Mental Ray

The Mental Ray 3.2 renderer enables the use of HDRI (High Dynamic Range Illumination) lighting maps in 3ds max 6. HDRI maps yield the most realistic lighting available for photorealistic reflections and surface materials, as shown in Figure 1.34.

Because Mental Ray is also offered as part of Maya and Softimage, Max is now capable of delivering the exact same quality renders as other high-end packages. Mental Ray is well integrated into Max, and you are able to use standard Max materials, which are automatically translated into Mental Ray shaders before rendering. The rendering types available include ray-

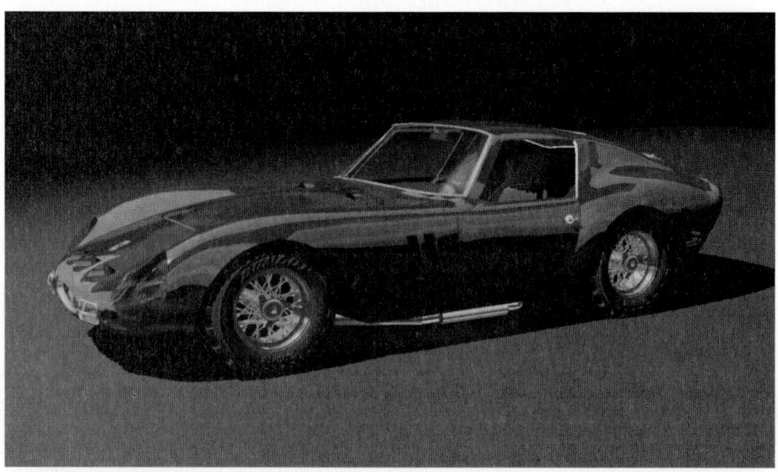

FIGURE 1.34 Using Mental Ray with a skylight and an HDRI Lighting Map to render a model car.

traced reflections and refractions, caustics for glass and water, indirect illumination, and contour shading. Mental Ray has excellent displacement map capabilities and provides physically realistic renderings that follow the laws of the physics of light. See Chapter 14, "Lighting and Rendering" for information on working with Mental Ray shaders, HDRI maps, lighting scenes with area lights, and rendering different types of objects with Mental Ray.

PLUG-INS

3ds max is designed with an open architecture that lets any developer write a plug-in that expands the capabilities of 3ds max. At the time of this writing, there are hundreds of third-party and freeware plug-ins available for 3ds max 6. All of the plug-ins for 3ds max 5 are compatible with 3ds max 6. Third-party vendors such as Digimation, Cebas, and others have extensive offerings that range from hair and fur generators to dynamic clothing made from commercial clothing patterns.

combustion 3

Combustion 3 is not a plug-in, but it can function like a plug-in to expand 3ds max's capabilities. Combustion 3 is a stand-alone program for compositing and visual effects, but it has a direct internal connection to 3ds max 6 through the Materials Editor and the combustion Paint material. To use combustion 3, you would run both programs at the same time, working on models in Max and painting the maps in combustion 3. This interactive connection gives you the capability to paint texture maps, bump maps, and specular maps directly on the surface of 3D models in the 3ds max viewport and have the 3d maps in combustion update in real time, as shown in Figure 1.35. To do this, both 3ds max and combustion 3 must be running on the same machine, and the Max combustion Paint material must be applied to the object in the viewport, and active in the 3ds max Materials Editor. For more information and a tutorial on combustion 3, see Chapter 16, "Combustion 3, Compositing and 2D Visual Effects."

character studio 4

Discreet character studio 4 is a nonlinear character animation plug-in that integrates seamlessly into 3ds max and gives you crowd animation with

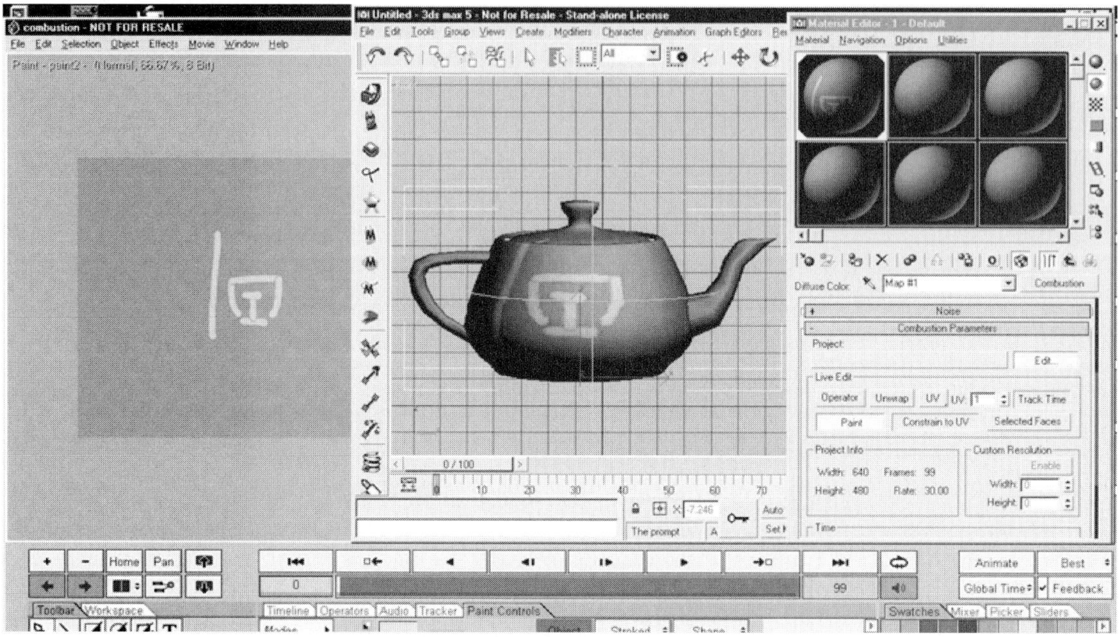

FIGURE 1.35 Using combustion 3 with 3ds max 6 for 3D mesh painting.

artificial intelligence, obstacle avoidance, flocking, and individual scriptable behaviors. Character studio was used extensively in *Homing Instinct* to animate crowds and characters such as soldiers and the satellite crew. The powerful Motion Mixer feature allows you to mix different motion files together to create new biped animations. Character studio 4 can also use MAXScript commands to control the biped animation, and export that data to different game engines. See Chapter 15, "character studio 4," for more information.

Clothfx

The clothfx cloth plug-in was used to create fitted clothing from spline shapes and patterns for the main characters. clothfx uses impact detection and dynamics to simulate cloth falling naturally on the character's body, as shown in Figure 1.36.

After creating the cloth panels from splines, the clothfx Modifier is used to pull them together by running a cloth simulation, as shown in Figure 1.37. The simulation applies real physical properties to the cloth. You can choose from a range of pre-set cloth types, including silk, cotton,

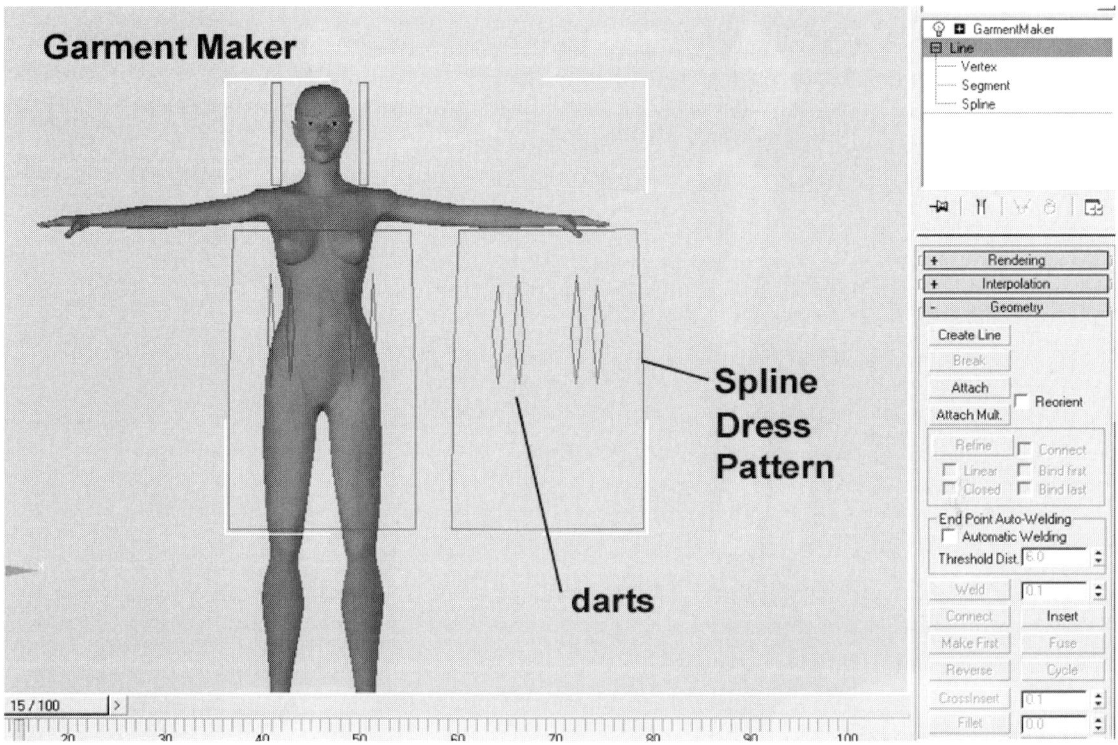

FIGURE 1.36 GarmentMaker is used to create the cloth panels from a pattern for a summer dress.

leather, wool, and rubber. Pockets and collars can be attached to the surface of the cloth to add details. See Chapter 17, "Plug-Ins," for a tutorial on using clothfx.

Shag Hair

Shag Hair, from Digimation, was used to create the hair and fur, and the grass on the ground for the characters and the environments in the film *Homing Instinct*. This plug-in program is accessed through the Environment Effects menu in 3ds max 6, as shown in Figure 1.38.

To put hair on the character models, a separate scalp mesh was created and positioned inside the head. It was then chosen as the hair emitter object. A Hair model was made from a spline that was linked to the scalp, and Shag Hair used it as a pattern to generate all of the hair on the head. An invisible Hair Cutter box was used to trim the unwanted hair by the neck, and create a hairstyle. Shag Hair is fully dynamic and reacts to gravity and

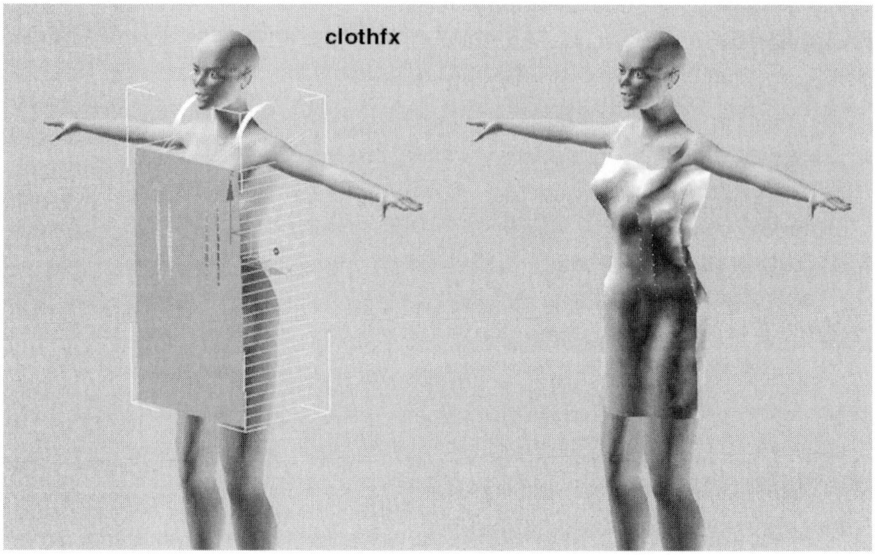

FIGURE 1.37 clothfx is used to fit the clothing and create the cloth simulation.

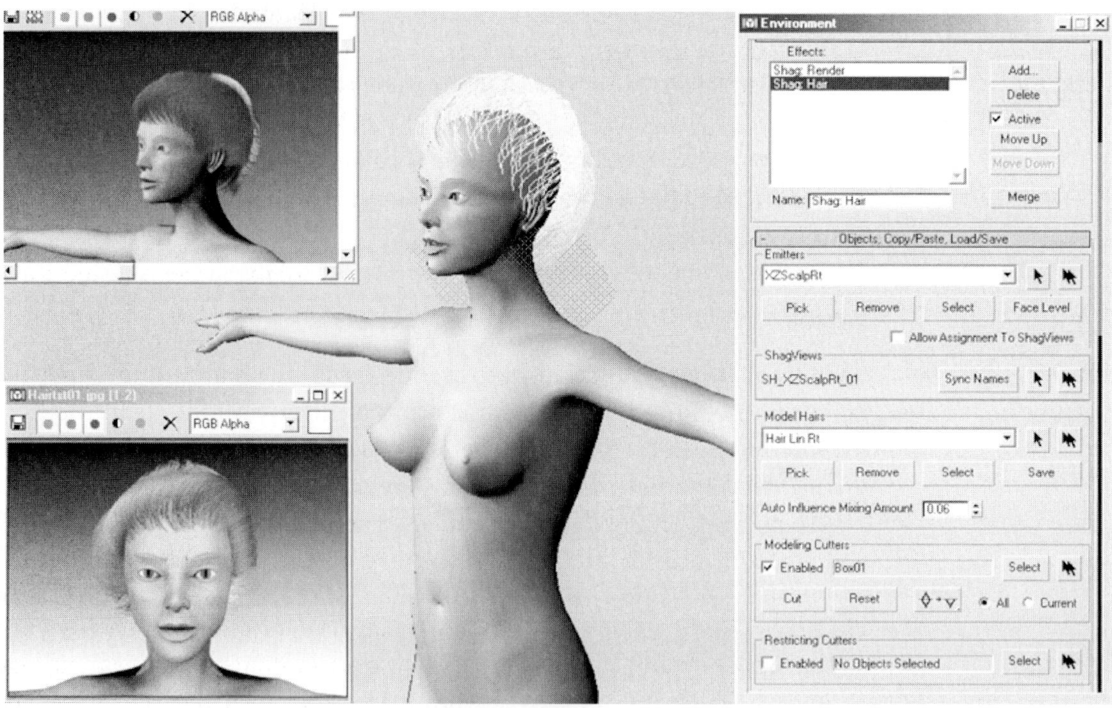

FIGURE 1.38 Shag Hair creates hair from a reference spline.

wind. It has a special Hair Shader material that can create individual highlights on each hair, and generates natural shadows for a lifelike appearance. Shag Hair uses hair vectors to control the direction of the hair. See Chapter 17, "Plug-Ins," for a tutorial and more information on Shag Hair.

Sound Trax and Foley Studio

The sound tracks and sound effects in *Homing Instinct* were created with the Sound Trax plug-in from Boomerlabs. Sound Trax adds up to 64 tracks with keyframeable volume, and sound mixing capabilities with adjustable start and end points, as well as bidirectional scrubbing of sound. Foley Studio, its more advanced sister product, is an extremely powerful sound effects production tool that lets you use objects to trigger sounds, such as a character impacting a prop, or an object hitting the floor in a scene. It also lets you slave sound to particle systems and many other events, such as the firing of a gun or an explosion. Foley Studio includes a library of sounds and has doppler and stereo panning capabilities for realistic 3D spacial sound effects.

There is a whole range of other fine third–party plug-ins, including Scene Genie for facial tracking, Vehicle Simulator for creating accurate vehicle dynamics, Brazil and Final Render for photorealistic rendering, Afterburn for volume cloud effects, and Ghost Painter, which lets you paint maps in Adobe Photoshop from within 3ds max 6.

There are many other excellent plug-ins available for 3ds max 6 that create a variety of effects, including dynamic muscles, ocean waves, and NURBS solids modeling tools. The basic 3ds max 6 package is just the starting point in a software suite that can be expanded beyond the capabilities of any other software in the 3d animation and visualization field.

MAXSCRIPT AND OTHER CAPABILITIES

MAXScript has been improved in version 6 to provide access to nearly every animatable parameter for any object. The Visual MAXScript editor allows you to build command windows of any size with various functions by dragging and dropping them into a new rollout menu. Pre-made icons include a color picker, pick button, material button, progress bar, and many others that let you build new functions and expand 3ds max's capabilities. Custom attributes can be created for any object. For an explanation of MAXScript, see Chapter 12, "Advanced Animation."

Other 3ds max 6 high-end features that help support animation and visual effects include Macro-recording and the Video Post module. The Video Post module functions as a basic compositing and sequential multicamera rendering system. It can use Photoshop and Premiere plug-ins and has built-in image-manipulation capabilities, alpha channel manipulation, wipes and dissolves, and an animated starfield generator. The Active Shade window gives you near real-time texture display to help you design materials quickly. The Ram Player provides real-time playback of rendered image sequences. The open software architecture enables studios or third-party developers to modify the program or the interface to suit their needs.

Many other features are explained in detail in the chapters that follow. These improvements are aimed at making 3ds max compatible with studio production workflow in the animation and visual effects production pipeline, which includes other software that might need to exchange files with Max. 3ds max 6 is fully integrated into the discreet products pipeline, which includes flame, flint, edit, and combustion 3. 3ds max 6 .rpf files can be read directly by flame, and 3ds max can output Cineon, or SGI RGB files for compatibility with Unix-based compositing and editing software.

THE PRODUCTION PIPELINE

Many people who work on visual effects for motion pictures are not aware that 3ds max has been able to output .RIB files to RenderMan Pro for rendering on multiple machines using the MaxMan plug-in, which has been available for the last three years from Animal Logic. File compatibility and transfer can be solved by purchasing Polytrans, a very capable file translation program that allows Maya files to be loaded into 3ds max and vice versa, or by using Rhino as an intermediary file converter. You will find that 3ds max 6 NURBS files will load directly into Maya with trims intact by using the IGES file format, one of 3ds max 6's standard file export types. The .fbx format from Kadara (Filmbox) will allow you to export 3ds max skeletons and animation keys to Maya, and to import Maya animations into 3ds max 6. Of course, some exclusive features, such as Maya NURBS Stitched surfaces, will not load into 3ds max. However, Maya Stitched NURBS surfaces won't load completely intact into Softimage, Houdini, or any other software, so it's not a 3ds max issue.

3ds max 6 has been designed to be more cross-software friendly. An example of this is the adoption of the QWERTY hotkey layout. Now, 3ds max 6 uses the Maya translation hotkey assignments by default. Another area where 3ds max is Maya-user friendly is its manipulator gizmos, for move, rotate, and scale, which look and act nearly the same as Maya. The perspective window grid looks just like the Maya perspective window grid. The 3ds max interface can be cleared completely and the Quad menus (right-click) used to work on large or complex models, as shown in Figure 1.39. Additional areas of standardization that make 3ds max 6 friendly to other software users is the replacement of the Track View with the Curve Editor, which is equivalent to Maya's Graph Editor, the Dope Sheet, which works like the Dope Sheets in Maya and Softimage XSI, and the node-based Schematic View, which functions in the same way as the Maya node-based Hypergraph.

3ds max controllers have been converted to Constraints in keeping with industry standard functionality and terminology, and they work almost the same as Maya Constraints. An additional standardization is the Character Node, which contains all of the data and animation of a character, and works the same as Maya's Character Node to allow the saving of animation clips for pose-to-pose animation.

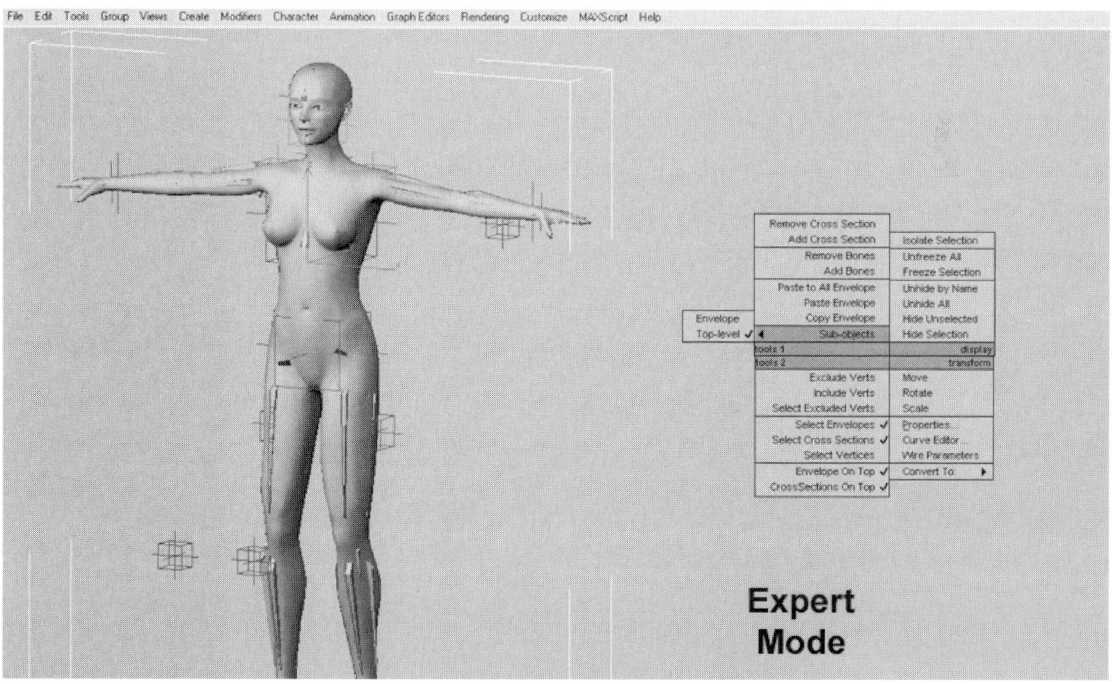

FIGURE 1.39 The full 3ds max 6 interface in Expert mode with the Quad menu.

Other capabilities include the powerful Camera Tracking utility, which has been used on a number of recent motion pictures, Camera matching, Motion Capture, XRefs (Externally Referenced Objects and scenes), and the Level of Detail controller. All of these tools and features raise 3ds max 6 to a level on an equal footing with the very best high-end production modeling and animation programs available.

3ds max 6 rendered output in the .rpf file format can be loaded directly into discreet flame™ or inferno™, or other discreet image processing and editing software, which allows it to be integrated into major studio production pipelines. Rendering output can be set to a current motion picture or broadcast aspect ratios, including 35mm Academy, 35mm Anamorphic, 70mm Panavision, 70mm IMAX, Vistavision, D-1 Video, DV Video, NTSC Video, Pal Video, and HDTV Video. 3ds max 6 is fully integrated into the discreet product pipeline, and is capable of rendering images in the Cineon (.cin), .rla, .rpf, .png, .sgi, .rgb, tga, .tif, .jpg, .avi, and .mov formats. If you add the MaxMan plug-in from Animal Logic, you can also have .rib file output to RenderMan and convert 3ds max materials to RenderMan shaders.

3ds max 6 is designed to generate content for a variety of different arenas. These arenas include motion picture production, visual effects, game production, television broadcast production, commercial advertising production, forensic animation, industrial product animation, cartoon animation, architectural design and flythrough animation, scientific process simulation, military battle and flight simulation, product design, medical illustration animation, educational multimedia, Internet content production, archeological reconstruction, book and magazine illustration, and digital fine art.

CONCLUSION

3ds max 6 is a powerful 3D animation and visual effects program that gives the game professional, the animator, and the filmmaker the powerful tools they need, and provides them with a wide array of choices in rendering, lighting, materials, modeling techniques, and character animation plus hundreds of available plug-in programs to expand its capabilities. These and many other features of 3ds max 6 help to integrate 3ds max into the studio pipeline and let animators switch from 3ds max to Maya or Softimage, and back again, with very little re-learning. In the next chapter, we will examine how animated films are designed, organized, and produced in the professional studio setting.

CHAPTER

2

COMPUTER ANIMATED FILMMAKING

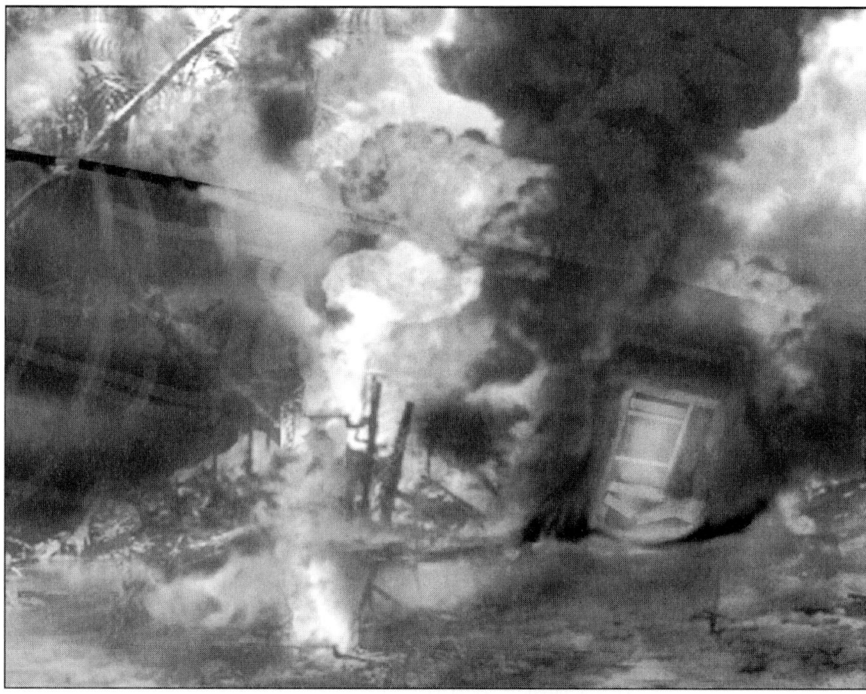

This chapter gives you an overview of the design, planning, production, and post-production phases of making an animated motion picture. We will examine the four different phases of an animated film production:

- Film design, where the script is turned into visual concepts and art work.
- Pre-production, where the storyboards are drawn, and the entire production is planned.
- Production, where the dialog is recorded, the animation and live action filmmaking is done, and the visual effects are created.
- Post-production, where all of the film and visual effects elements are brought together, composited, edited, and the sound is added.

Animated films can be created in any film or video format. They can be 2D or 3D animated shorts, or elaborate 2½-hour motion pictures that combine computer animated characters, live actors, practical special effects, miniature photography, and digital visual effects. Whatever the size or the length of your film, and whatever methods you use to create it, you will need to plan each phase of the production process.

There are differences between the structure and planning that go into an animated short film, versus a motion picture, but many of the functions that must be performed are the same. The work of the animators is also similar, regardless of the scale of the project. A short film can be created and animated by one individual. On a moderate sized small film, the animators will probably do everything themselves and have only a few nonanimators involved. On a large film, there are hundreds of people involved, and the work is divided up between departments. The creation of the imagery is shared between many animators with different specialties who work in different departments or even in different companies that have subcontracted the work on different aspects of the film.

The amount of time involved in making animated films varies wildly. Creating an animated short film could take a little as three months to complete. Some individuals have worked six or seven years creating their own animated short film. At the other end of the scale are the big studio films. Making a motion picture for theatrical release such as *Shrek* or *The Lord of the Rings: The Two Towers* requires a tremendous amount of work by hundreds of people over a period of at least one and a half to three years.

For a film to be a success, all of the work, from writing the original script to editing the final footage, must be carefully planned and executed down to the tiniest detail. The planning process begins with the analysis of the script and the creation of the concept art. Concept art consists of paintings and illustrations that present a clear picture of what the story is about. If the film project is large enough to have a staff, such as a producer, director, art director, visual effects director, and an art department, the concept art work is done by the art director in consultation with the director to create a unique vision and style for the film. If it is a small film, the design and planning is often done by one or two dedicated animator/directors who will perform every task themselves, sharing the workload.

In the making of a motion picture, the concept art, along with the script, the budget, and the projected audience demographics and revenue, are shown to the prospective investors to obtain financing for the film. The concept art also becomes the basis for a promotional campaign that might begin a year before the release of the film. On a very small animated film, there is often no budget at all, except for the savings of the animators and their credit cards. In that case, they do the concept art themselves so that they have an agreed upon artistic vision for the project.

Film Design

The design of the film begins with the close examination of the script. The verbal descriptions of each scene and the descriptions of the settings are looked at very closely and notes are taken. In a motion picture production, the director will hire an illustrator or concept artist and then they will work together to come up with a few important or pivotal scenes that would make good concept art images. In the case of an animated short film, concept art is often done by the animator/director who wrote the script. In either case, an intimate familiarity with the script should yield clear concept art images that contain all the design elements that spell out how the film is going to look. A storyboard artist will usually be hired by the director, and his or her job will be to read the script over and over until he or she has a clear mental picture of the story and its setting, and then draw out that vision in the form of storyboards. On small animated short films, the storyboards are often done by one of the animators, or by the lead animator/director.

The concept art created for *Homing Instinct* consisted of drawings and illustrations of environments, human characters, alien creatures, spaceships and satellites, buildings, and various settings on the surface of the planet-moon Titan, as shown in Figure 2.1.

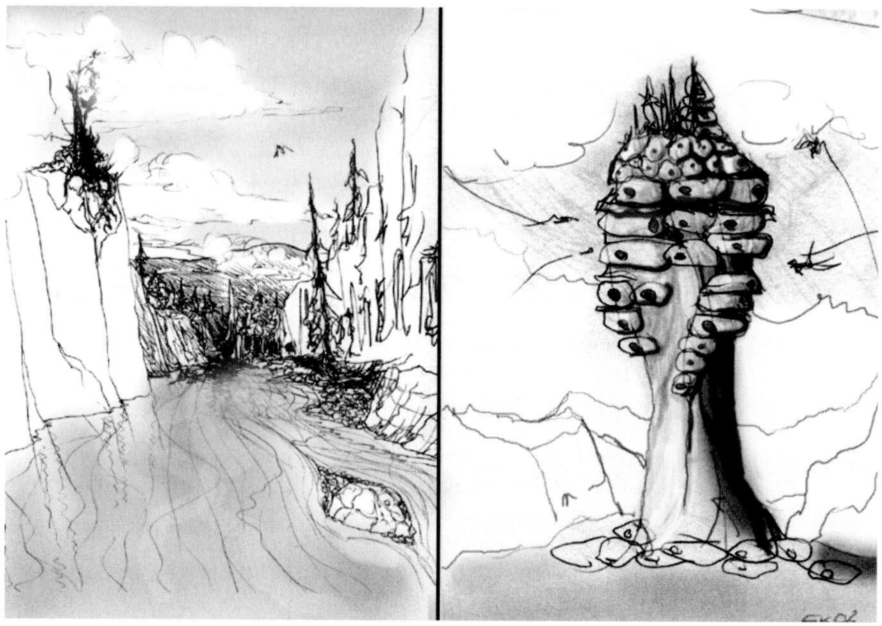

FIGURE 2.1 Concept drawings of a river gorge and a Lemur Bat city on Titan.

Concept drawings help to establish the style and look of the film, the design of the characters, and the technology used by the characters.

PRE-PRODUCTION

During the pre-production phase, the script must be analyzed before production begins, and lists made of the most important scenes and sequences. Special attention is paid to scenes that will need extensive visual effects or model construction. The visual effects required for each scene must be analyzed and broken down into a comprehensive list of requirements. Often, a shortened script containing only the pages where visual effects occur is prepared. This helps when estimating how much of the production time will be allotted to visual effects. Making a separate set of visual effects-only storyboards is a good idea for quick reference and for cost and time budgeting. Lists and breakdowns of every shot will eventually need to be made so that job assignments can be prepared, as shown in Figure 2.2.

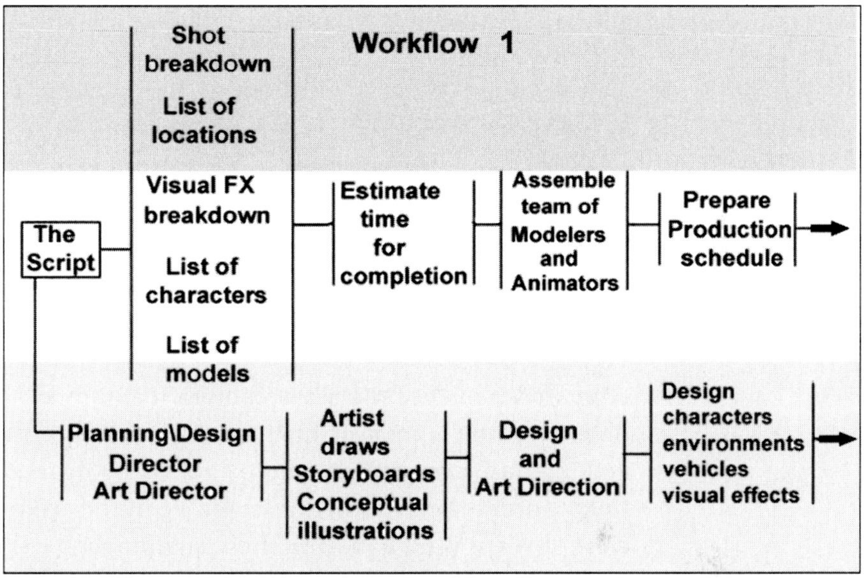

FIGURE 2.2 Pre-production phase workflow.

The breakdowns and organizational work is just as important when working with a small number of animators as it is with a big staff. A comprehensive listing of everything that will be seen on the screen should be prepared before beginning the production phase of the modeling and animation work. This will save a lot of time and avoid confusion or duplication of work. Another very useful list is the Location List, which breaks down all of the scenes that share the same environments, as shown in Figure 2.3. An additional list that should be made is a comprehensive list of all characters, their costumes, and the props they will be using in which scenes.

A shooting script is also prepared to note every shot and camera move by number in the script. To film a typical action motion picture, hundreds of shots are often required. The most successful computer

Homing Instinct - Location List				
Location	Scenes	Characters	Sets	Notes
Swamp - island	24-32, 76-80	Dr. Quin Marta Xzulixia Moxell	Burning Alien Ship ext. and interior. Hovercraft ext. and interior Edge of Water	Ship stops at island Island burns Dr. Quin enters ship Marta in Hovercraft Dr. Quin Rescues XZU.
Hospital – T. City	36-42	Doctor Nurses Patients Sick Soldiers Leut. Beckmeuler Corp. Henley	Hospital Entrance Hospital Emer. Rm. Hallway	Men brought in on Gurneys – military air ambulance.
Titan Spaceport Tow.	23-24, 27	Maj. Black Corp. Henley Reporter Videoman Shuttle crews Soldiers	Shuttle Launch Pad Govt. car Port Bldg. Entrance	Men board government shuttles. News men pushed aside

FIGURE 2.3 The Location List.

animated films use the same camera techniques as live action productions to attain a look of high-quality cinematography. Elaborate fast-action chase scenes can employ up to 20 different camera angles to fully capture the action and the dialog in the scene. Reaction shots and close-ups are used to add to the visual impact.

STORYBOARDS

Storyboards are drawn to insure that everything works and the story flows forward smoothly. Storyboards are the visual blueprint of the entire production. The storyboard artist draws each important sequence in the film to establish the images that the camera will see, based on the descriptions of the environment, setting, and action described in the script. This work is done after a long consultation with the director and the art director. In complex shots, every camera angle and move will be drawn, and indications will be made of lighting, visual effects, costumes, props, the action of vehicles, and positioning in the location environment. Good storyboards will contain every element necessary to complete a shot, and are commonly consulted many times a day during production to determine if a shot is being done correctly, or has been completed.

There are usually two sets of storyboards prepared. The first set of storyboards is used to get the production rolling and to give everyone a starting place for their work. The second set of storyboards are the production storyboards, that are constantly revised, tuned, and re-drawn as the director builds and begins to fine-tune sections of the film.

For *Homing Instinct*, a number of scenes were drawn to establish the appearance of the setting, the costumes, or the camera angles that would be used. The sample page from the *Homing Instinct* script describes a section of the battle between an alien spaceship and the orbiting planetary defense satellite in space above Titan, as shown in Figure 2.4.

12 the videoscreen flashes white and burns out. The satellite is rocked by an explosion and the bridge tilts to one side. The captain holds onto the console, presses the mic. button and yells.

Captain
Fire Control! Branson are you there?
Return fire! Return Fire! Full power!

13 Cut to: Fire control room. Smoke and sparks are in the air. Branson is coughing and frantically rubbing his eyes, but can't see anything after the flash. He lets out a guttural growl and slams down on the firing control, firing the lasers blind and screaming as he does.

Branson
Arrrrruuuh!......

Cut to: Exterior – Quick series of shots - the Satellite and Alien ship fighting

The Satellite's surface is covered with sparks and long electricity bolts crawling across the exterior like angry snakes. Some hatches have blown off and debris is blowing out into space.

14 The big plasma cannons under the Satellite open up and belch a huge blue fireball that streaks out and slams into the alien ship. The plasma outlines its shape perfectly and we see the forward cabin, the massive engines, and the stubby wings of the alien craft.

FIGURE 2.4 A page of the *Homing Instinct* script covering Scenes 12 through 14.

The storyboard for this complex action and visual effects sequence contains both interior and exterior camera shots, with close-ups and reaction shots of the characters. This sequence is rich in visual effects ranging from explosions to plasma lightening crawling across the surface of the satellite. The storyboard images shown here are from the first version of the storyboards, and only concentrate on the key turning points of the action sequence, as shown in Figure 2.5.

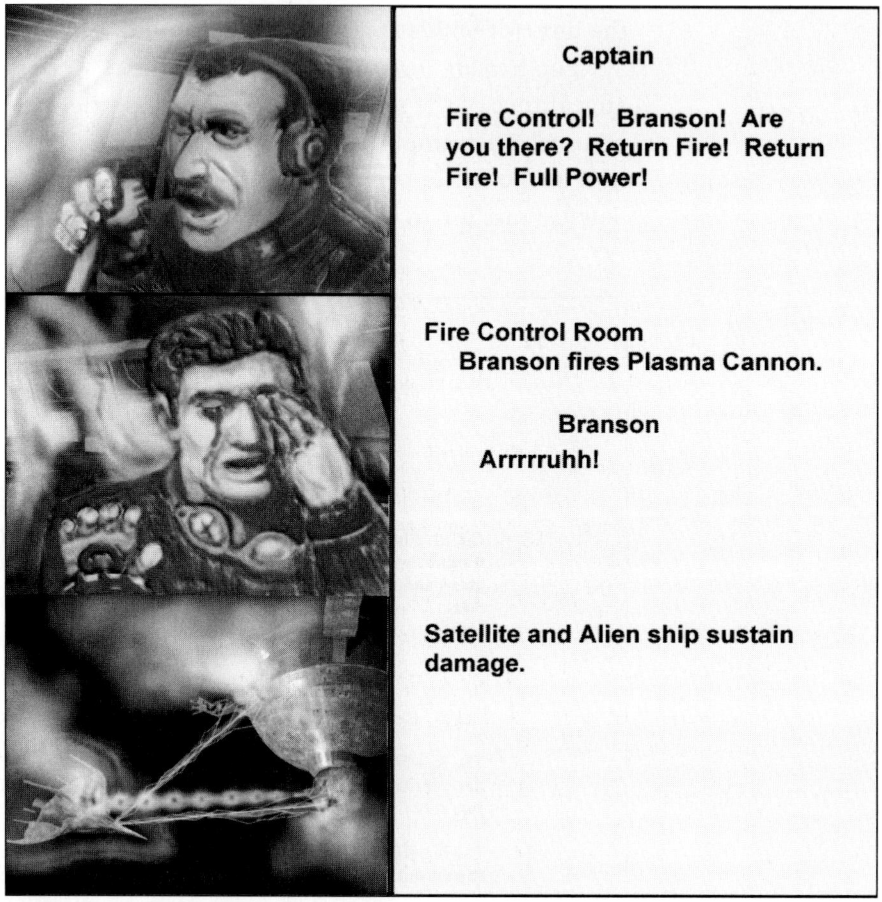

FIGURE 2.5 Storyboard drawings for Scenes 12 through 14.

A storyboard artist on a visual effects film can often be kept busy redoing and expanding the storyboards every day during the entire visual effects phase of the production. While working as an animator on the film *Starship Troopers* at Sony Pictures Imageworks, the author usually received new storyboard pages each morning at the production meeting as the director revised his vision of how the action scenes in the movie should be done.

Art Direction

The art director is one of the most important people in the production. It is his or her responsibility to examine the scene descriptions in the script and then come up with specific designs that establish the style and the era of the story. That style is then translated into the architecture, the costumes, and the technological objects that fill the environment. In the case of *Homing Instinct*, the era portrayed in the story is the future, and the location is an island-continent on Titan, the huge cloud-shrouded planet-moon orbiting Saturn. Because the era of the story was only 400 years in the future, the technology had to look advanced, but retain a feeling of familiarity where older equipment was still being used alongside new technology. An effort was made to design ordinary objects to look as they would in real life, function and move in a logical way, and have signs of use and wear on their surfaces, while having some detail that made them look futuristic.

An all-digital animated production allows a great deal of artistic freedom, but care must be taken to find a balance between stylization and realism. For *Homing Instinct*, a mix of style and realism was chosen to provide enough detail for the technology to look functional, while avoiding a slavish devotion to photo-realism. In a science fiction film, the current trend is to try for a high degree of realism, assuming that photo-realism will contribute to the process of telling the story. Unfortunately, putting too much time into attaining photo-realism can be a bad choice, as in the case of the box office failure of *Final Fantasy*, a photo-realistic animated film with a very weak storyline and little entertainment value. Clearly, a hit movie like *Monsters Inc.*, which is humorously unrealistic, shows that photo-realism has little if anything to do with box office success.

Production Design

Production design is done during pre-production, and begins with turning the ideas of the art director into preliminary models, paintings, and sculptures in the search for the right look for the sets, costumes, and models. The translation of the script into designs can take months. Attention must be paid to every detail that will be seen by the camera, including the surface detail on architecture, structure and posture of the characters, the colors of the clothing, jewelry, the hair styles, the design of the hand props, and parts of vehicles such as seats and instrument panels. Even the plants on the ground receive detailed attention, to make sure that they fit well with the other objects in the scenes.

The art director works with a small team of artists to finalize the look of everything from the clouds in the sky to the label on the bottle of soda that the hero drinks. New illustrations are prepared along with detailed construction blueprints for sets and floor plans of locations. These plans are also used to work out the sequence of camera moves. Formal 3-view plans are drawn of any special vehicles that must be constructed, as shown in Figure 2.6. Visual effects scenes are also broken down and designed in detail. The storyboard artist works with the production design team to expand the number of storyboards to include each critical camera angle and move.

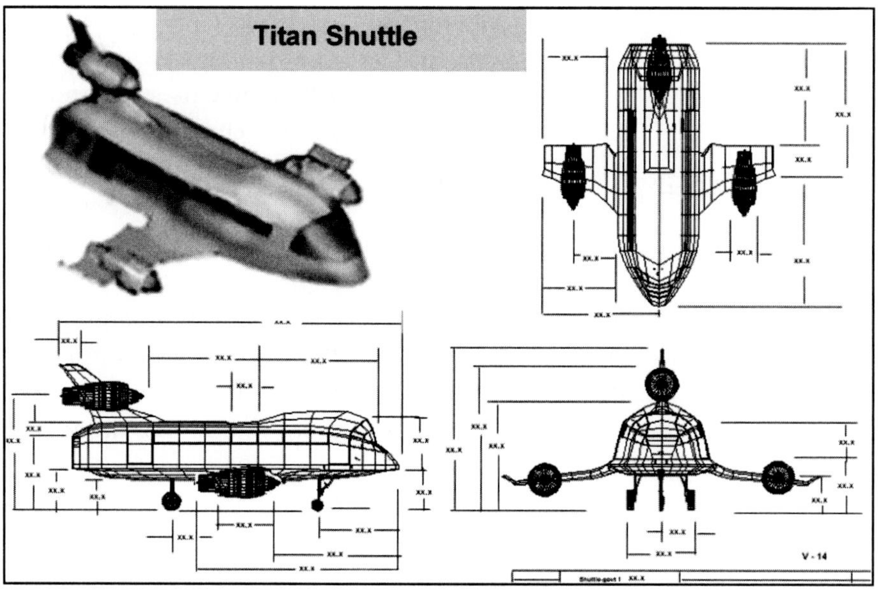

FIGURE 2.6 Plans for a civilian government shuttlecraft.

Small-scale physical models of the sets are built out of white foam-core board on a table top to better understand how a scene will play, and how the camera should move to capture it. The director can then study the layout of the set and rehearse in his mind how the shots should be done. By looking through a Director's Viewfinder (an eyepiece with a zoom camera lens), the director can determine what parts of the set are going to cause problems by blocking the camera, what changes need to be made to accomplish the shot, and what focal length lenses (wide angle, normal, or telephoto) should be used.

An animated film that will be built exclusively in the computer is not any different from a live action production in terms of the camera work that will be required. A camera in the computer has the same controls as a real camera: lens angle and a focal length, depth of field, and an aspect ratio that must be taken into account to properly compose the shot. "Shooting" an animated film is not simply a matter of choosing the right camera angle and then pushing a button. A good director will examine every shot that is animated, and maintain control over all of the camera angles used by the animators. The art director can also make a great contribution to the composition of each shot by using color and lighting wisely and placing objects in the set to emphasize the action of the scene, or to hide a distracting detail that could misdirect the attention of the audience.

CHARACTER DESIGN

Character and costume designs express of the personalities of the characters in the script. The styles chosen for each character seek to portray the lifestyle of the individual and his or her plane in society. By providing a great deal of unspoken information, costumes and hair styles tell the audience who the characters are. Information is also contained in the shapes of the furniture, the color of the interiors, and even the height of the doorways. These factors have a profound effect on the visual impact of the film. The art director strives for a clear first impression of each scene. The costuming is designed to create visual associations that indicate the economic level, job, class, rank, origin, age, and even the sexual availability of a character.

One of the main goals of character design is to make the characters seem sympathetic and accessible to the audience so that they identify with them, and respond emotionally when something disturbing happens to them. It is worth the special effort to give each character a unique appearance and persona. This helps in the difficult process of bringing an animated character to life, as shown in Figure 2.7.

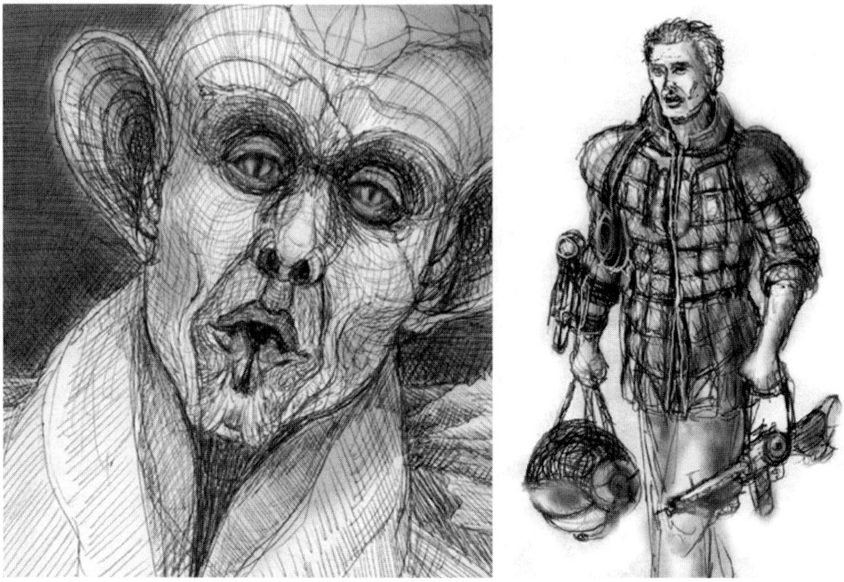

FIGURE 2.7 Sketches of Moxell the vampire and Chris, the vampire hunter.

Two characters conflict with each other in *Homing Instinct*: Moxell (Lord Moxell Raxzulantis Borranis), the immortal leader of the Alien Vampires, and Chris Christianson, the youthful bounty hunter who is hired by the Titan Corporation to assassinate Moxell. These character designs went through many revisions to arrive at an interesting contrast between the characters. Moxel is grand, elegant, powerful, and ancient, whereas Chris is informal, a bit rumpled, strong, and 26 years old. Their mannerisms, postures, and even the way they move and talk are direct opposites as they converse, threaten, and finally hunt each other.

To create an entire society and a colonial city on Titan, a large number of characters needed to be created. Some of the scenes have crowds of civilians mixed with military personnel. These characters were designed to be low-resolution models that would provide background color and movement behind the main characters who occupy the foreground. The individuals who have important scenes receive more attention, such as Kopek, the shady dealer in all things, who supplies the special rifle that will be used in hunting the vampires, as shown in Figure 2.7 on the left. Another important character is VonTaggen, the high-tech treasure hunter who discovers gold and jewels in the tomb of a vampire, as shown in Figure 2.8 on the right.

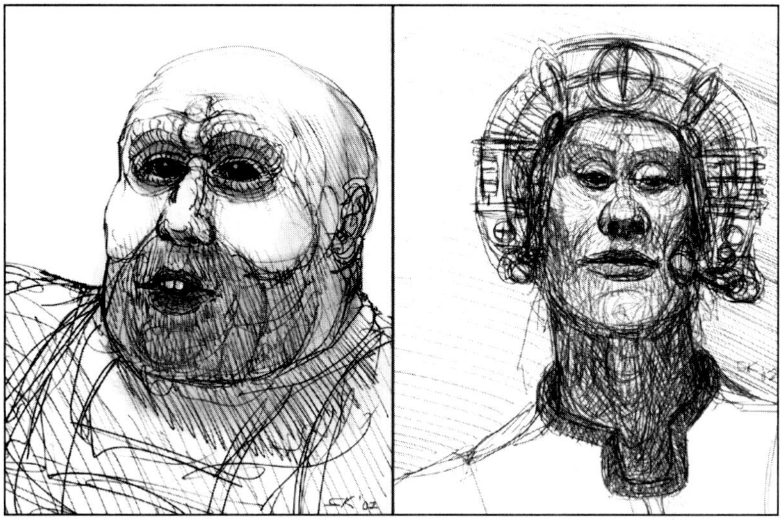

FIGURE 2.8 Kopeck the dealer, and VonTaggen, the treasure hunter.

Environment Design

The environments for the film ranged from muddy swamp to the main square of Titan City. Each location was designed to create an interesting background for the scene or scenes that would take place there. Many locations, such as the City Hall and the Hospital, were based on real places in and around Los Angeles, California. The wilder areas of Titan were based on collected images in books from all over the world that were chosen because of their unique or interesting look. The swamp environment where a number of scenes take place was based on a combination of the Mangrove swamps in Asia and the alligator infested swamps of the Louisiana bayou, as shown in Figure 2.9.

The swamp illustrations were prepared by cutting and pasting a number of different swamp photographs together to come up with a pleasing and exotic look. The swamp model that is built in the computer will be representative of what is seen here. The detail shown in the illustration will be cut down somewhat in the final environment model. The background vegetation will be created as texture maps instead of using actual geometry. Only the ground, the water, and the foreground trees and plants will be built. When the Alien Ship Crash scenes are put together by the animator, the cameras will be positioned to maximize the feeling of being in a huge muddy swamp with dense overgrowth and tangled vegetation.

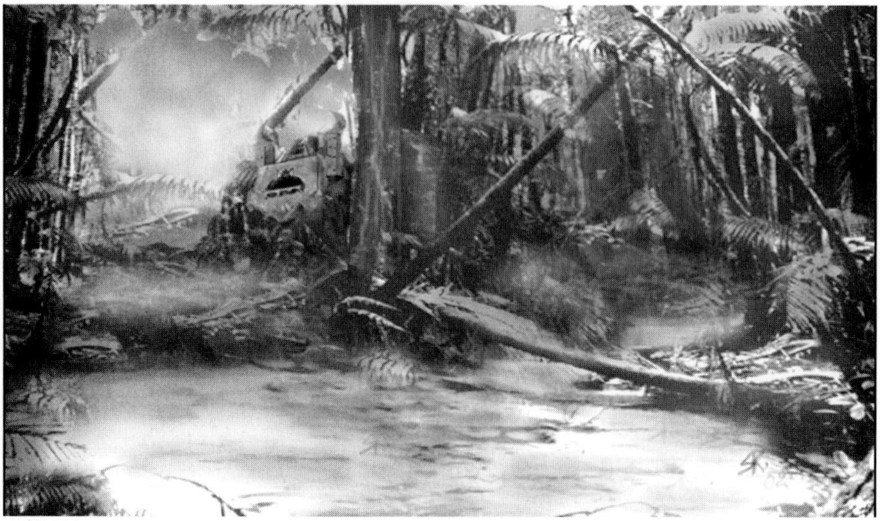

FIGURE 2.9 The northern swamps of Titan were based on photos of many swamps.

The design for the Titan Spaceport Tower was created by photographing a local high school, and then adding additional photographs of structures in Adobe Photoshop to give it a more futuristic and imposing appearance, as shown in Figure 2.10.

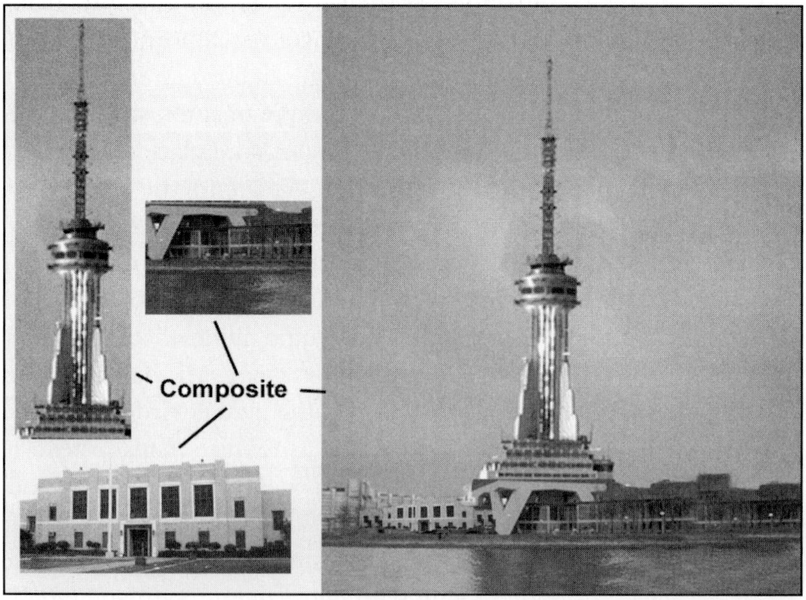

FIGURE 2.10 A high school served as the basis for the Titan Spaceport Tower.

The design for the Palace of the Vampires in the Valley of Ruins was based on a photograph of the Venice, California Public Library transformed from a pastel California modern building into a brooding castle, as shown in Figure 2.11.

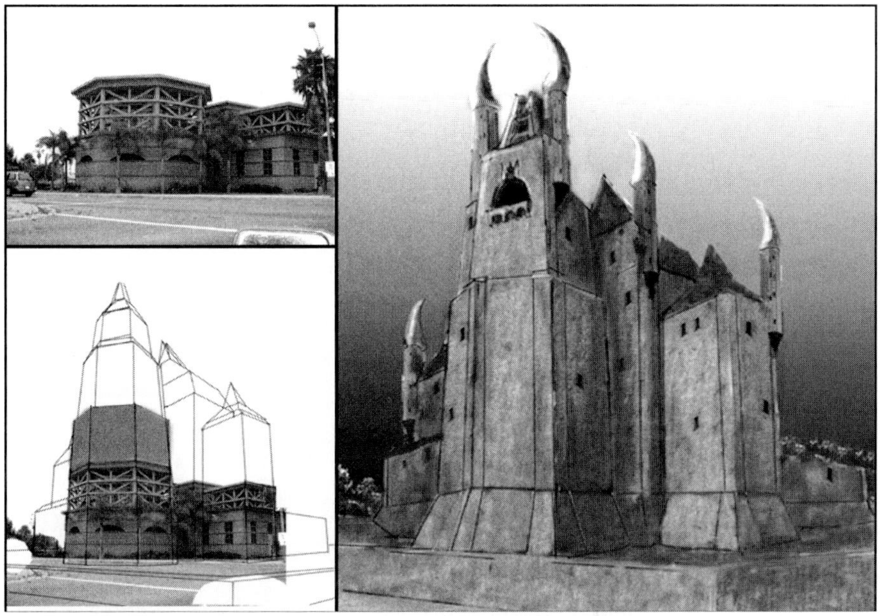

FIGURE 2.11 The transformation of a library into a Vampire Castle on a mountain.

The style of the abandoned Vampire Castle in the Valley of the Ruins is derived from early European castles designs, modified for flying vampires with the entrances at the tops of the towers.

VISUAL EFFECTS DESIGN

Visual effects are designed along with the rest of the elements in the film. The most important visual effects scenes are often drawn or painted in vibrant colors to determine the best look for the scene. Traditional visual effects in film productions consisted of practical effects such as wind, rain, fire, or explosions created by a team of technicians working on the set or on location. In the digital world, *visual effects* refers to computer effects that are produced by 2D and 3D atmospheric and particle systems, or by dynamic forces applied to particles, solid-body, and soft-body objects.

These effects are difficult to design, so their appearance is only indicated on the storyboards, and then worked out later during the production. In *Homing Instinct,* all the designs for the visual effects were created by compositing photographs in Photoshop. A big part of the visual effects in *Homing Instinct* included fire and explosions. Real explosion images, available on the companion CD-ROM from companies like Art Beats, proved very valuable when planning the explosions of buildings and vehicles in the film. In production, the real explosion images were composited into the particle system explosions to enhance their density and realism, as shown in Figure 2.12. Fog and mist were important design elements that were added to many scenes in both production and post-production to create a more mysterious and dramatic atmosphere.

ON THE CD

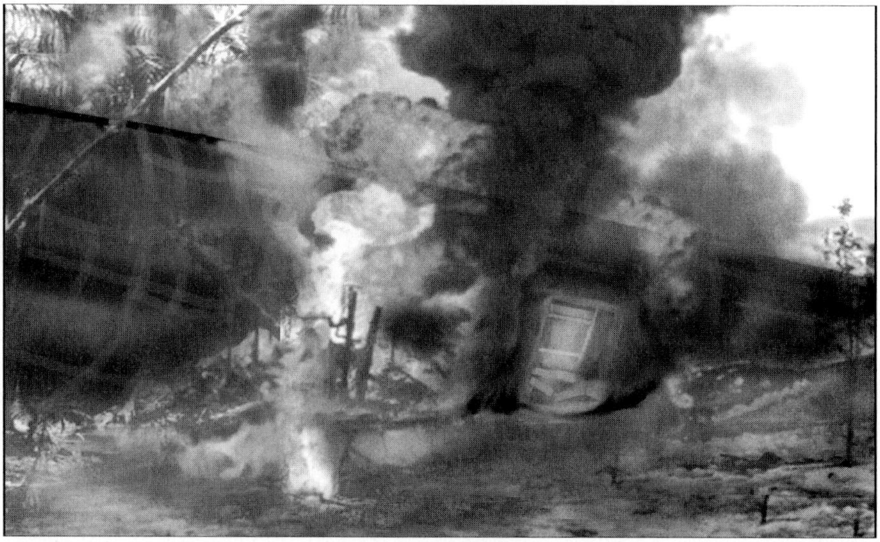

FIGURE 2.12 Visual effects design for the alien ship crash scene.

Dynamic effects were planned to add realism to many of the scenes. By simulating real physical reactions, such as impact distortions and collisions of objects, the characters are able to interact realistically with the environment in the action scenes.

Production planning is an essential part of the overall workflow of a film production. During this time, emphasis is placed on organizing the work in the animation studio, obtaining whatever supplies, tools, and computer equipment will be needed, and deciding how many animators will be needed and how many support and administration people will be required. On a big film, a production manager is hired to prepare budgets, materials lists, prop lists, and crew call sheets for each week. He or she will also be responsible for production breakdown sheets that have detailed information of all outside services and purchases that must be made during the entire production.

On an animated short film where the staff is much smaller, there might not be a formal production manager, but someone will still be needed to take care of things like buying CD-ROMs, picking up additional supplies, or arranging for a voice actor to come in to record dialog. Animators cannot work efficiently if they must also answer the telephone or go to the store two or three times a day. That is why, in many ways, a very small production is more difficult than a large production. In the small production, a myriad of small details, like forgetting to pay the power bill, or getting a virus on the rendering network and losing all your work, can constantly get in the way of doing the animation. These problems unique to very small productions cause the productions to fall behind schedule and might even cause the film never to be finished.

PRODUCTION

When the design and pre-production stages of the film are completed, the workflow moves on to the production preparations for animation, dialog recording, and live action filming, if required. By the time production is ready to begin, all the personnel should have been hired and the studio should be set up and ready to run. The Workflow 2 flow charts shown in Figure 2.13 give an overview of the sequence of tasks required to make the film.

The set of lists prepared in pre-production that must be re-checked before production begins are as follows: the shot breakdown, the list of locations, the list of characters, the visual effects breakdown, and in the case of an animated film, lists of backgrounds, environments, buildings, vehicles, and characters that must be built by computer modelers.

These lists are then analyzed by the director, the art director, the production manager, the visual effects supervisor (or director), and the animation supervisor to make sure they have covered everything they will need, and to pinpoint problem areas or complex scenes that will need

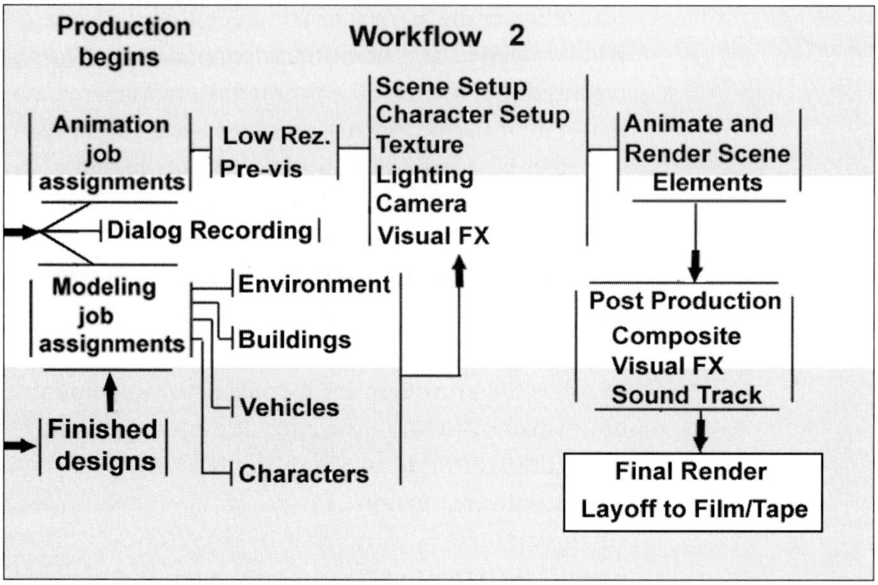

FIGURE 2.13 Production phase workflow.

special planning to complete. The production manager goes over the script, the storyboards, and the pre-production lists and prepares a final production schedule. The art director is active during this time conferring with the director, the visual effects supervisor, and the storyboard artist to perfect and tune all of the storyboards so that they are ready for production. The final production storyboards are a comprehensive guide that the production will use as the blueprint for the film. Along with the director's vision, they are the ultimate standard against which the individual animator's work will be judged.

When pre-production and planning are finished, and all the necessary preparations for animation are finished, the animators are ready to start working. As the first days of the production begin, the production manager and the animation supervisor work together to assign work to the animators and the modelers as shown in Figure 2.13. When there are extensive scenes with dialog, the recording of dialog should start early to allow finished soundtracks to be ready for lip-sync animation when the character models are ready. The coordination and completion of all the needed elements for each scene is strictly scheduled and tracked by the supervisor and the assistant director, whose job is to report to the director and relay instructions and notes back to the animation team.

During the production meetings, all the issues and problems are discussed, dailies of finished animations are shown, and the supervisor and visual effects director have input on how the scenes are coming along.

Pre-visualization is usually assigned to one or two animators. Their job is to build simple models of the more difficult visual effects scenes and animate them with simple gray colors for the purpose of judging camera angles, and moves, object scale, and most important, the timing and speed of the action. Storyboard pages are passed out to each animator. Modeling assignments for each character, building, environment, and vehicle are passed out to the modelers, and they are assigned a desired completion date based on how long the animation and production supervisors think it should take to build the models and animate the scenes. Hopefully, they have estimated wisely and the schedule will hold up without slipping too badly.

As the production moves forward and the modeling is completed, additional animators might be put on or the existing modelers might be switched to doing texture and lighting to augment the work of the animators. In many studios, there is a fairly strict division of labor, as shown in Figure 2.13. In the bigger studios, the labor force is divided into departments, such as the character animation department, the modeling department, the environment department, and the mapping and materials department, which is responsible for mapping all the sets, the environments, and the vehicles. This is to insure that the best possible people are assigned work in their specialty.

POST-PRODUCTION

Post-production is the phase of the film where all the environments, scenes, character animations, and visual effects elements are brought together and composited into a finished film. This is done scene by scene and shot by shot, with constant revision and adjustment of hundreds of separate elements and thousands of frames of rendered layers that must be assembled by the compositors. During this phase, rotoscoping and matting are done to insert visual effects into the animated scenes or to add missing elements that are necessary to complete the film. In the compositing and rendering phase, care must be taken to insure that all colors and light levels match and blend well. The final touch is to add the dialog, music, and sound effects tracks and perform what is called "sound sweetening" to insure that the dialog is clear and at the correct volume, and has no bad artifacts such as noise, pops, sibilance, or dropouts.

After post-production is finished, the movie is ready for lay-off to film for theatrical release, or to tape or digital media for presentation on television or for distribution directly to videotape or DVD for stores and the foreign markets. If it is a major studio release, this is followed by the marketing phase that consists of promotion, selling of foreign and domestic rights, making of multiple copies for theatrical release, dubbing of soundtracks for foreign release, and domestic promotion, video, and DVD sales, not to mention product marketing and tie-ins, toys, t-shirts, and books. If the film is successful, there are promotional tours and TV interviews to be done until all the potential markets for the film have been addressed and pursued. Only after all this is done will the producer start to see some return on his investment, and start thinking about making another film, or a sequel to this one, depending on box office results.

CONCLUSION

In this chapter, you explored how an animated film is designed and how the entire filmmaking process is planned out and executed from the first reading of the script to the final editing at the end of production. Rigorous design and planning work during pre-production is essential to the success of an animated film, and is equal in importance to the assembly of a top team of animators who can generate professional quality work. In the next chapter, you will begin working on tutorials that take you through building a landscape, an interior set, and the first stage of modeling Xzulixia, one of the main Alien Vampire characters in the film *Homing Instinct*.

CHAPTER

3 MODELING ENVIRONMENTS, BUILDINGS, AND ALIENS

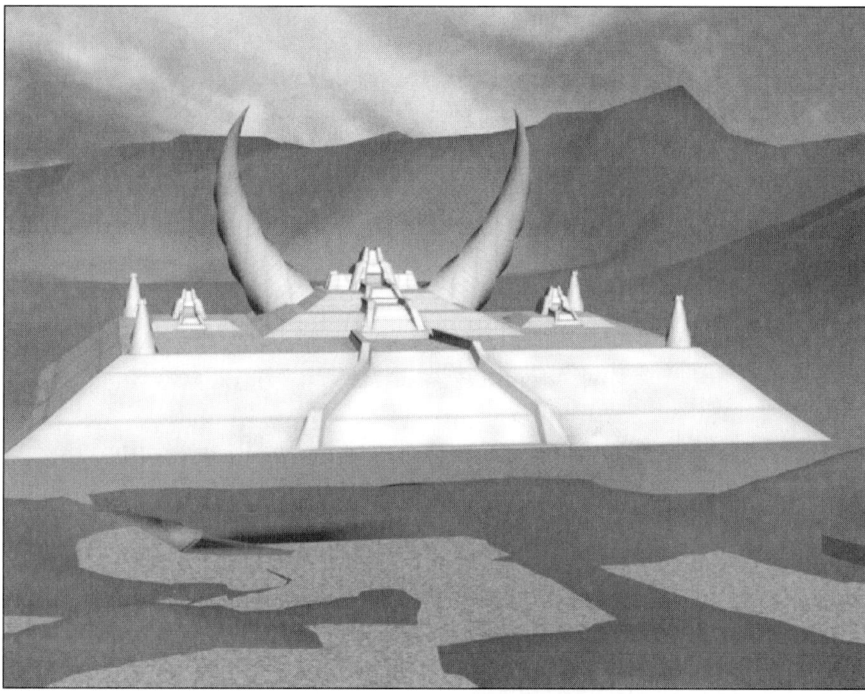

Building the Models for the Movie

3ds max 6 has a robust set of modeling tools for creating landscapes, buildings, and Alien characters. The architectural tools available in Max have been greatly expanded. Now you can take advantage of the built-in, high-end window, stair, and door generators, tree and foliage generators, and a major expansion of realistic architectural materials in the Materials Editor.

Many of the landscapes used in the *Homing Instinct* project were modeled from flat, high-resolution polygonal planes. The contours were generated by applying the Displace Modifier to a high-resolution mesh plane, and then sculpting surface details by moving vertices with the Editable Mesh Soft Selection tool. This gives you complete control over the shape of the landscape. Once built, all of the landscape meshes underwent polygon reduction using the Optimize Modifier, which is an Adaptive Subdivision tool. Optimize simplified the semi-flat areas of the mesh while maintaining a high mesh resolution in the highly curved areas.

The construction of the models for *Homing Instinct* began with the "master" landscape model of the island-continent on Titan, named New Caledonia. It includes lakes, reefs, deserts, badlands, forests, alien ruins, a human colony called Titan City, a spaceport, a waterfall, and an extinct volcano, as shown in Figure 3.1.

Every location mentioned in the script appears on the master landscape and the map derived from it. This helped tremendously in designing and placing the shots for each location. It also helped in establishing the size and shapes of all buildings, roads, natural features, and vegetation, and provided a way to experiment with the lighting and colors of each location setting described in the script.

The Master Landscape was built first, and then a Master Map was generated from it by rendering a top view. That image was labeled and printed as a reference during the production. A preliminary model of the alien temple ruins was built to provide a background to the swamp crash scene that opens the movie, as shown in Figure 3.2. This is also the location of the Xenobiology Research Center complex, which is an important location in the script. The Research Center was placed a short distance away from the largest temple ruin on the edge of the main waterway through the swamp.

Once the temple was positioned, a number of cameras were placed in the landscape to determine the best camera angles for this location. The

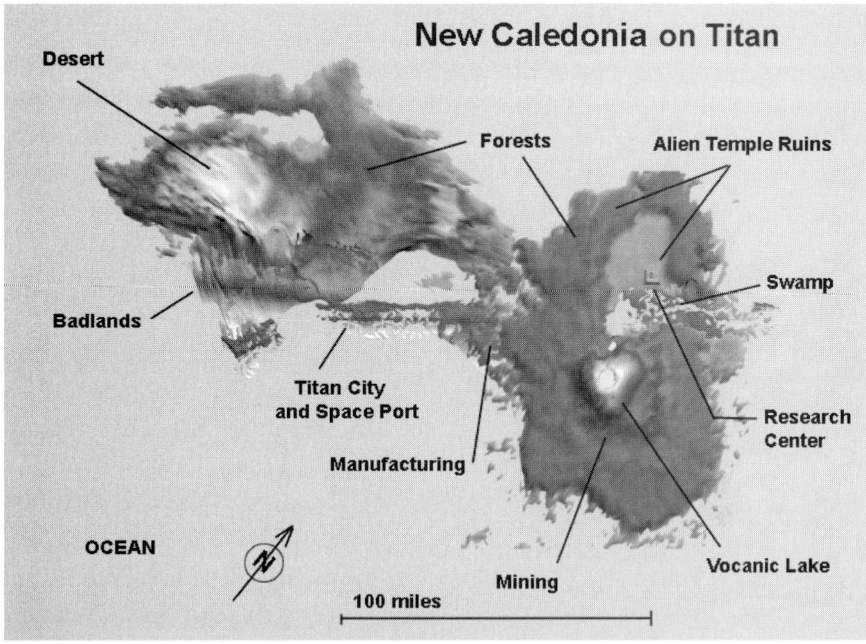

FIGURE 3.1 The Master Landscape model of New Caledonia on Titan.

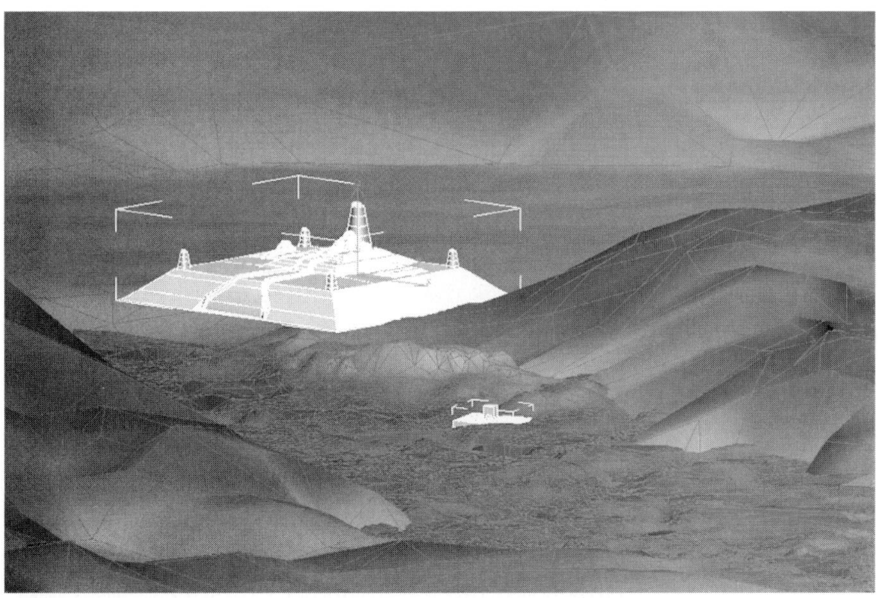

FIGURE 3.2 Placing an Alien Temple Pyramid in the Valley of the Ruins.

scene compositions and camera angles shown in the storyboards sometimes proved to be impossible to recreate with the actual models. This required constant revisions of both the location models and the storyboards during production.

Wherever close-up shots were required of a particular location, a more detailed model of that part of the landscape was made by cloning a selected section of the Master Landscape, and placing it in a separate scene file. This was necessary because the Master Landscape model was quite large, and took up 14.5MB of memory. The reason it was built so large was to keep the resolution of the land fairly high and maintain a more realistic-looking scale of the surface contours. It was a goal to be able to place a six-foot-tall man anywhere on the landscape and have him appear to be the correct scale. All doorways in the buildings were scaled to match the American Standard six-foot-eight-inch-tall door opening.

After the model of the land was finished, the next task was to create preliminary versions of all the buildings and man-made structures in their correct locations so that their design and surrounding landscape could be finalized. To set up a shot in a specific location, part of the Master model was isolated and cloned, and then saved in a separate file. Many of these locations needed increased resolution so that they looked good in an extreme close-up shot. This process included the addition of fine details and props, as well as the use of high-resolution texture maps. These techniques were necessary to preserve the appearance of realistic scale. Trees and other vegetation were added to dress up locations.

TITAN CITY

Titan City is the location of many of the scenes in the film. The first mock-up of the city was made from a stock architectural model of Houston that comes on the World Creating Tool Kit disk that shipped with 3ds max 4. This model was very handy because it already had streets laid out with city lots, and a number of different shaped buildings. It was also useful for pre-visualization because the buildings were low resolution. The stock Houston model was modified extensively as the project went on. In later versions of the city, most of the high-rise buildings were replaced with more modest structures to appear more like a small colonial city (Figure 3.3).

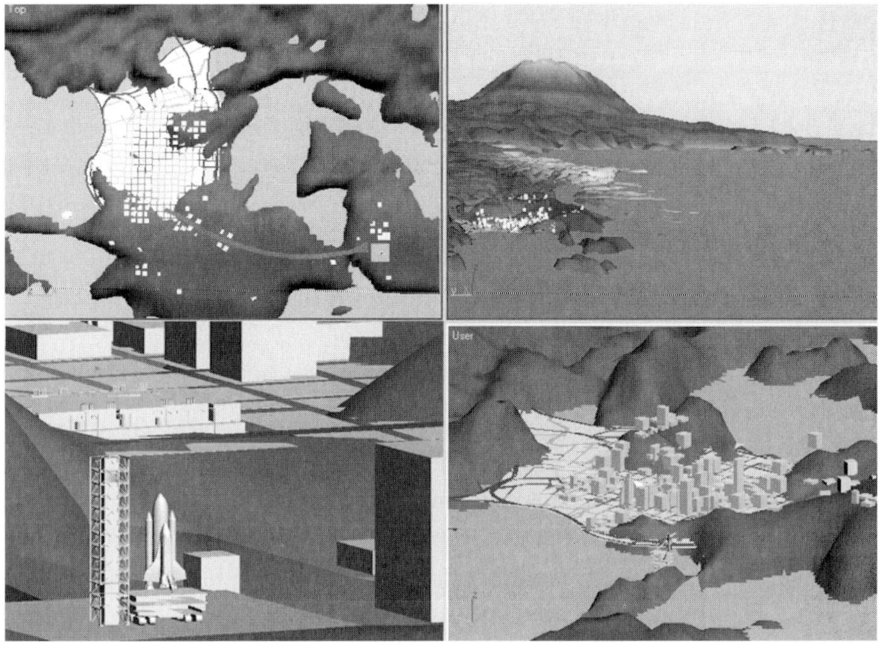

FIGURE 3.3 A low-resolution version of Titan City and the Titan Spaceport.

BUILDING A LANDSCAPE LOCATION

An area of the Master model might need to be completely rebuilt before it can be used for a scene. An example of this is the secluded section of land where a small cabin is located next to a cave that leads to underground Alien Ruins. A section of the Master model was cloned, but because of the need to build the cave entrance and the cabin, a completely new high-resolution landscape was built in place of the cloned section of the Master model.

Landscapes can be built in a number of different ways. One very good method is to use contour lines set at different heights that are skinned over with a polygonal mesh created by applying the Compound Objects > Terrain Modifier. Another is to create land from Quad Patches, pulling up patch control vertices to create the contours. The method used for all of the landscapes in this book was a little more complicated. It was built by piecing together a number of displaced planes that overlap and are pushed up through one another. A plane sculpted and textured to look like rocks protruded up through another plane that was sculpted to look like rolling hills. The combination of multiple inter-penetrating planes with different materials created a more visually exciting landscape that looked very much like the natural surface of the Earth.

In this tutorial, you will create a section of the New Caledonia landscape using the multiple displaced inter-penetrating planes.

TUTORIAL 3.1

BUILDING A LOCATION ON NEW CALEDONIA ISLAND

To build a location landscape using multiple displaced planes:

ON THE CD

1. Load the Land_Displace.max scene file from the Chap03 folder on the companion CD-ROM. The first plane has been displaced for you. Select the plane and enter the modifier to see what the settings are. Notice that the Stack has three levels: the original plane, the Displace Modifier with its bitmap, and the UVW Mapping Modifier with a different bitmap.

Colored bitmaps can be used just as well as grayscale maps to create displacements. 3ds max uses the Luminance value, not the color of the map, to determine the amount of vertical displacement.

ON THE CD

2. This plane is high resolution with both Length and Width Segments set to 160. This allows the creation of a highly detailed surface that looks good in a close-up shot. A bitmap is used by the Displace Modifier to create the bumps and hollows of the land, as shown in Figure 3.4, example 1. It is set to Strength = −33.98 and Image Blur is set to a value of 2.1, which softens the land contours. The bitmap that is applied is a color bitmap called Lake_mt.jpg and can be found in the MAX6\Maps\Backgrounds directory, or in the Chap03\Images folder on the companion CD-ROM.
3. The other two ground planes are hidden. Click Display, Unhide by Name to unhide Plane02. It is a flat plane that is correctly positioned, but has not yet had the Displace Modifier applied. Select Plane02 and click Modifier > Parametric Deformers > Displace to apply the modifier.

ON THE CD

4. In the Modify panel, in the Displace Modifier parameters, click the large map button in the Image: Bitmap menu. It is labeled "none." In the map Browser go to the Chap03\Images folder on the companion CD-ROM and load the 2Leg_Torso.tga map, and then set Displacement Strength to 9,800.0. The map is also available in the 3dsMAX6\Maps\Characters directory.

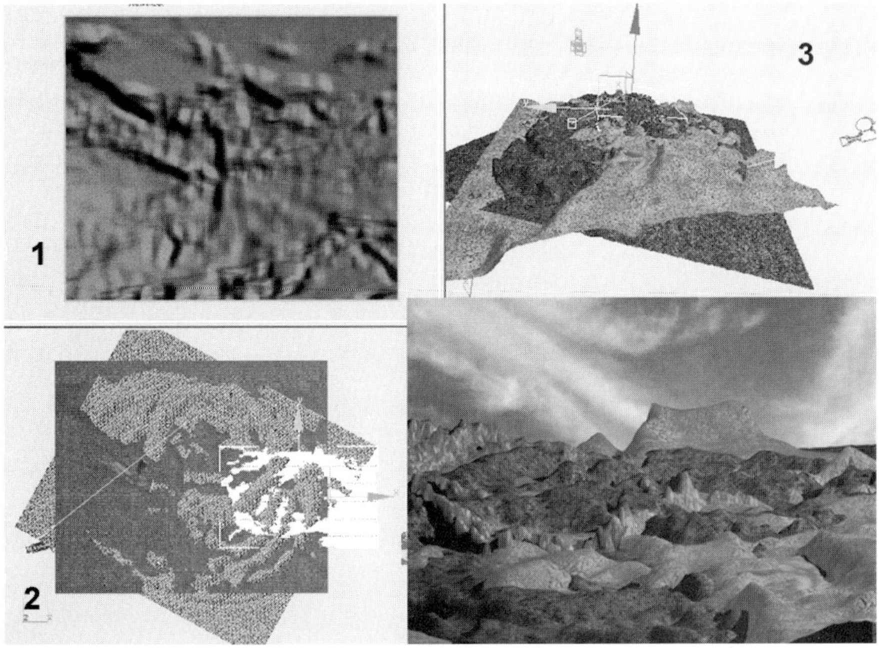

FIGURE 3.4 Multiple displaced planes simulate rocks and vegetation.

5. Notice that this map contains concentric rings, which creates a pleasing contrast between the rolling contours of the first plane and the jutting peaks of the second plane. This will become the layer that simulates the foliage.

ON THE CD

6. Unhide Plane03. It is reduced in size and has 100 x 100 segments to create smaller pointed rocks in a particular area of the landscape. Apply the Displace Modifier, and from the companion CD-ROM load the Elecswirl.jpg image from Chap03/Images, which is also in the MAX6\Maps\Misc directory. Set the Displacement Strength to 7,155.0. It should generate sharp peaks different in shape from the previous two planes, as shown in Figure 3.4, example 2.

This scene contains 122,616 faces, which will slow redraw and render speed of a computer with less than 500MB of RAM. You can use Optimize to reduce the number of faces in the planes, but the trade-off is that you will lose many of the small details, and the land will become faceted. For close-up work, it is a better idea to purchase more RAM and a faster computer rather than lowering the land resolution.

7. Do not apply the mapping in the Displace Modifier unless you are an experienced 3ds max user. Instead, apply UV map coordinates by clicking Modifiers > UV Coordinates UVW Map to each plane. Set the map tiling parameters for Plane01 to U Tile: 10.0, V Tile: 10.0. Set the map tiling parameters for Plane02 to U Tile: 8.0, V Tile: 5.0. Set the map tiling parameters for Plane03 to U Tile: 10.0, V Tile: 10.0.

ON THE CD

8. Materials already exist for these planes in the Scene file on the companion CD-ROM. Press the M key to open the Materials Editor. You should see four different materials, as shown in Figure 3.4, example 3.
9. Select Plane01 and apply the P_Ground1 material. Select Plane02 and apply the P_Foliage1 material. Select Plane03 and apply the P_Marble1 material. As a final touch, unhide the Lake object, which is a modified cylinder that simulates a mountain lake. It has the P_Water Raytrace material applied to it to simulate reflective water. In the Rendering > Environment, load the Cloud2.jpg bitmap from the 3ds max\Maps\Skys directory on your computer to create a sky background.
10. Render the scene using Camera 4 to see the image shown in Figure 3.5. Save the scene as Location301.max.

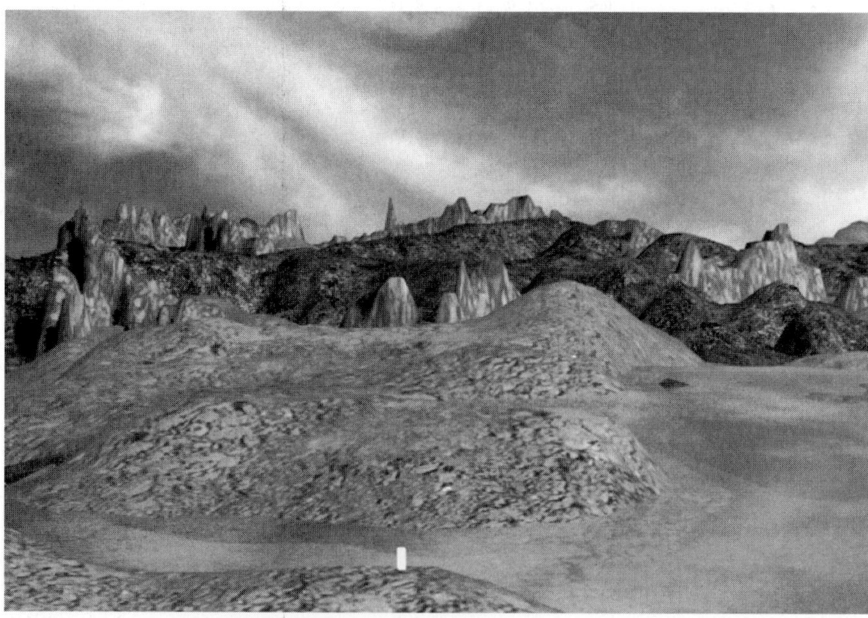

FIGURE 3.5 The white box in the foreground represents a six-foot-tall man.

Close-Up Environments and Interior Locations

The next tutorial describes what is necessary to create a detailed environment that will stand up to close-up camera shots. Interior locations are more demanding to model and texture than exterior locations are because of the need to "dress the set" with an abundance of props and details. Surface textures must be carefully applied and be of a high enough resolution so that no pixels will be noticed when a camera comes very close.

In the Spaceport Jail is a special Quarantine area where people must remain until their hospital examinations are finished and their immigration and work permit records are checked and cleared. In the script, this is known as Cell Block Zebra. The model shown in Figure 3.6 shows the cell block with default lighting.

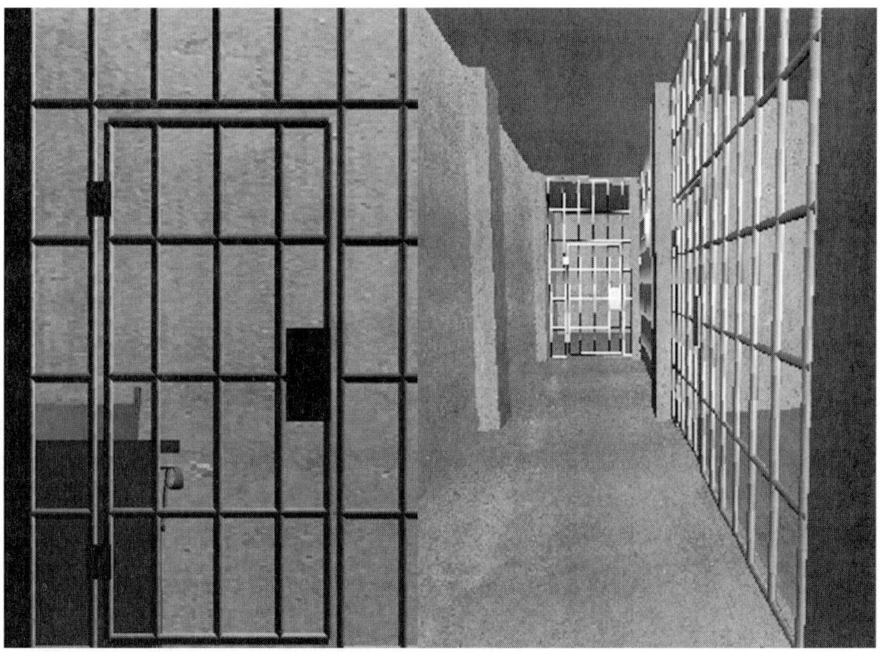

FIGURE 3.6 Interior of Cell Block Zebra.

The entire cell block is built from box, plane, and cylinder primitive objects. Construction was relatively quick because only the first cell had to be built. The other cells are all clones of the first cell.

In the next tutorial, you will construct Cell Block Zebra.

TUTORIAL 3.2

BUILDING CELL BLOCK ZEBRA

ON THE CD

To build the cell block:

1. In the background of the top view, load the Cell_Block.tif image from the Chap03\Images folder on the companion CD-ROM. Set the Aspect Ratio to Match Bitmap and turn on Lock Zoom-pan.
2. This background reference image is the floor plan of the jail. You will build your model of Cell Block Zebra on top of this image. Next, right-click the front view.
3. To build the bars and cell doors, create a plane 126 units wide by 120 high in the front view. Click the Modify tab, and in Parameters set Length Segs = 6, and Width Segs = 12. To turn the plane into prison bars, apply the Lattice Deformer by clicking Modifiers > Parametric Deformers > Lattice. The edges of the plane should turn into large rectangular boxes. To reduce them to the size of bars, change the radius in the Lattice parameters. Set Struts Radius = 1.0 and turn on Smooth to make them round. Turn off the Joint objects by setting Joints Radius = 0.0 units.
4. After the lattice is created, right-click the lattice and convert it to an Editable Mesh. Select and delete the lattice struts where the cell door area is going to be. Make a second smaller plane with 5 × 4 segments that fits into the cell door opening, apply the Lattice Deformer, and set the radius sizes as in step 3.
5. Add small boxes to the cell door to simulate the hinges and the door lock, as shown in Figure 3.7, example 1. Apply box mapping to the lattices and apply the Metal_Gray_Plain material from the Material Library in the Materials Editor. Group the cell, bars, hinges, and lock together and name them Cell_Bars.
6. The walls and pillars that form the sides and back of the cells are made from primitive boxes. Using the floor plan as a template in the top view, create a pillar that measures: Length = 19.0, Width = 17.0, and Height = 120.0 units. Apply mapping coordinates. Use Shift > Move to clone the pillar. Position the new pillars on the floor plan in the top view wherever you see a small square. You should have 22 pillars, with two scaled wider at the main entrance doors (bottom left of floor plan).
7. Next, create a box object to form the wall between one of the cells that measures: Length = 4.0, Width = 160.0, and Height = 120.0 units. Apply mapping coordinates. Position the wall to correspond with the side wall of the first cell. Clone the wall to form the back wall of the first cell. Select

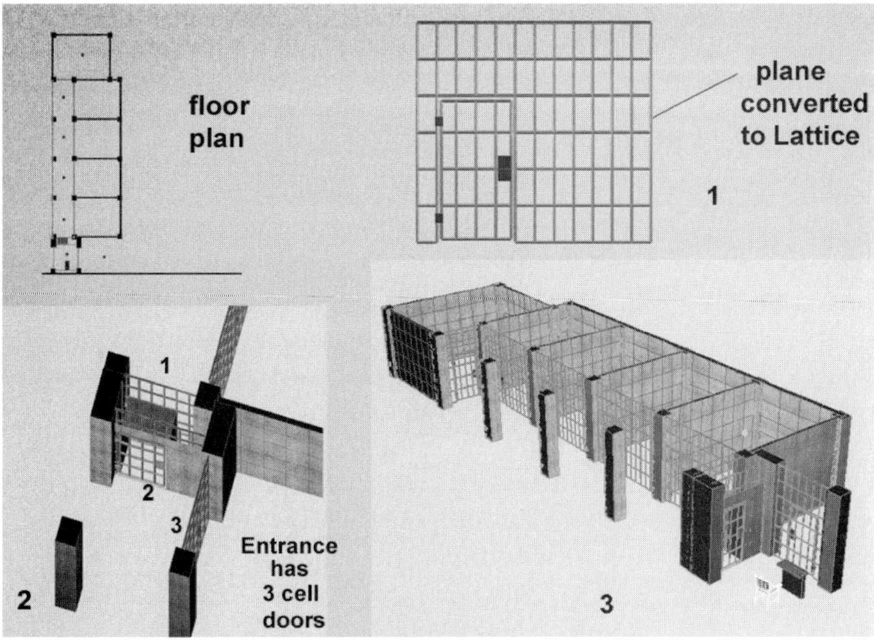

FIGURE 3.7 The construction of the Cell Block.

both walls and clone them four more times to form the side and back walls of the other cells. Clone the wall again and create the walls for the rear cell, modifying the back wall at the end of the cell block to be a bit wider.

8. Position the grouped Cell_Bars object at the front of the first cell, and then select and clone it four times to create the cell bars for the other cells. Position three of them at the front of the cells along the hallway. Put the fourth group at the end of the hall to form the rear cell door. Trim off the un-needed bars by clicking Group > Open, and then in Editable Mesh, select the parts and delete them.
9. There are three cell doors at the entrance of Cell Block Zebra. Clone another three copies of the Cell_Bars and position them at the front entrance of the Cell Block. Trim the extra bars away that extend beyond the pillars so that they fit as shown in Figure 3.7, example 2.
10. Create a long box for the hallway wall and another for the side wall of the front entrance. Last, copy the floor plane and raise it up to be the ceiling. Apply a concrete material with a slight bump map to all walls and pillars and adjust the tiling so that they look realistic. For an added touch, create the overhead lights by creating capsules and applying the Lattice Deformer.
11. Save the scene as Location302.max.

In the next tutorial, you will build one of the alien temples.

BUILDINGS

There are a variety of buildings needed for the *Homing Instinct* project. Besides the main structures of Titan City, there are various alien ruins scattered around New Caledonia with a number of temples located in and around the North Titan Swamp. One of the alien temple ruins is called the Temple of the Horns. As the name implies, it has large stone horns that thrust up toward the sky.

Temple of the Horns

The Temple of the Horns is built from primitive box objects that are modified to specific angles reminiscent of Mayan temples but without the heavy surface sculpting typical of Pre-Columbian architecture. The script describes the temple as a massive structure of "stark simplicity and huge size. The giant horns give it a familiar, yet disturbingly alien appearance."

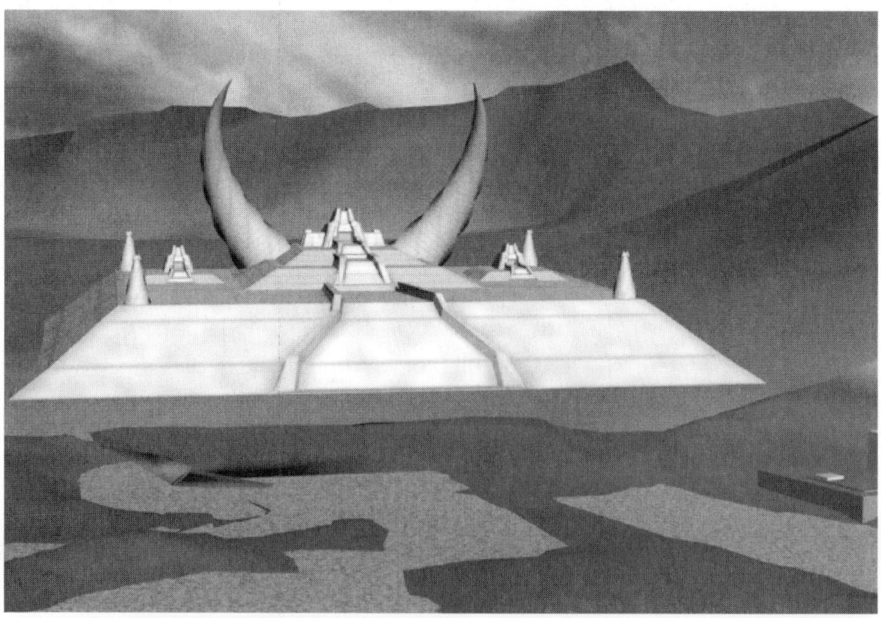

FIGURE 3.8 Temple of the Horns.

The temple shown in Figure 3.8 is a semi-final design, and at this stage, it is not finished. The model was first used for pre-visualization. Once that was done it was given its final textures and modified with cracks and age damage, including a broken tip on one of the horns. For the final scene, a number of other temple ruins were added and the location was dressed with foliage. A rendering of the finished temple ruins location can be found in the Color Plate section of this book.

TUTORIAL 3.3 MODELING THE TEMPLE OF THE HORNS

ON THE CD

1. In the front viewport background, load the Temple_Frnt.tif image from the Chap03\Images folder on the companion CD-ROM as shown in Figure 3.9, example 1. In the top viewport load Temple_Top.tif, and in the left viewport load Temple_Side.tif.
2. In the top view, create a box object the size of the outside dimensions of the temple background image. You will need to scale the model to fit into

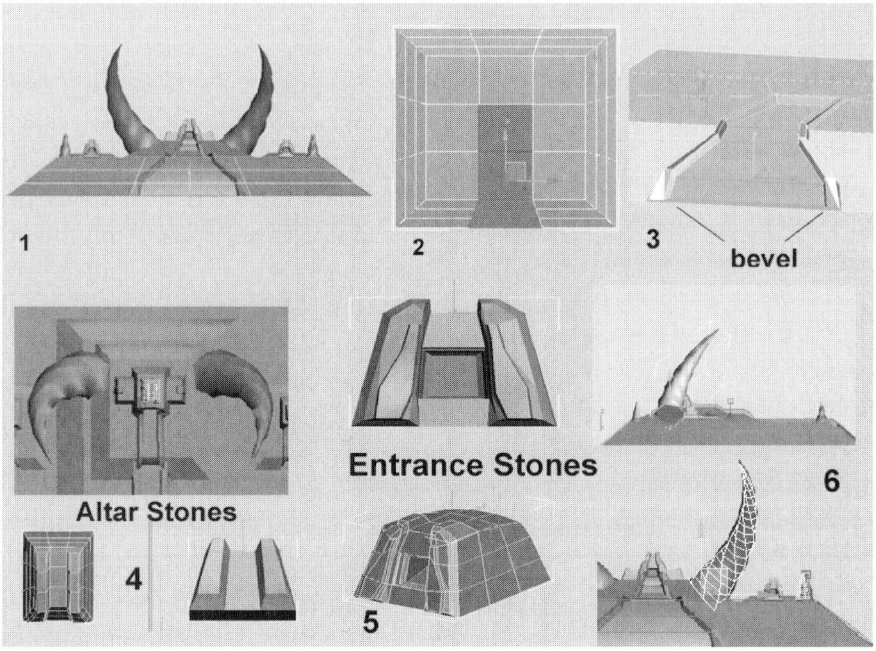

FIGURE 3.9 Creating the Alter Stones.

the Master Landscape when finished so it doesn't matter what size it is at this point. The author used the following settings in the Box parameters: Length = 330.0, Width = 360.0, Height = 40.0. Set the segments to: Length = 3, Width = 3, Height = 3.

3. Once you create this first box you will need to use the Background Lock toggle command (Ctrl > Alt > B) to unlock the foreground and zoom or pan it to match the box with the background images in all three views. When the views all match, click Ctrl > Alt > B to lock zoom-pan again. Next, convert the box to an Editable Mesh.
4. Taper the box using Modifiers > Parametric Deformers > Taper. In Modify > Parameters, set Amount to –0.28 to taper the sides to match the background image. Again, convert to an Editable Mesh. This will delete the construction history (collapse the Stack) and freeze the object in that shape.
5. Next, you will extrude the stair railings that run up the front of the pyramid. In Polygon Sub-object mode, switch to the top view and select the central polygons on top of the box, as shown in Figure 3.9, example 2. Using the Edit Geometry > Bevel tool, extrude the stair area up about 20 units, and then scale back about 10% to taper the outer edges inward. Click Bevel again and don't extrude, but instead scale this selection smaller by 20%. Now Bevel again but downward to the original level and scale smaller by 10% to create the inside face of the stair railing wall, as shown in Figure 3.9, example 3. Select vertices and move the corners of the stair railing walls to match the top view of the temple base.
6. To create the second and third levels of the pyramid, simply clone the bottom layer. Scale it smaller to match the second layer in the background image and position layer 2 on top of layer 1. Repeat for layer 3. There are also two additional smaller layer copies on the right and left sides of the large horns. There is a total of one base and four layer objects, of three different sizes. Study the background image to see where they go.
7. To make the Altar Stones that sit like thrones on the top center and sides of the pyramid, create another box over the top view of the central altar stone. Then, perform the same operations you performed on the base of the temple: select the central polygons, then Taper and Bevel/Extrude, as shown in Figure 3.9, example 4. There are seven Altar Stones of three different sizes on the pyramid.
8. The Entrance Stone is made the same way as the Altar Stone, but it has an additional set of extrusions to create a door opening in the front, as shown in Figure 3.9, example 5. There are five Entrance Stones of three different

sizes on the pyramid. Study the background image to see where they should be placed.

9. To create the spiral horns for the top of the pyramid, create a Cone with six sides in the top view. Make it 20 units high with Radius 1 = 5.0, Radius 2 = .80, Height Segments = 10, and Sides = 6. Apply the Twist Parametric Deformer and set Angle to 270 degrees. Place the small horns at the pyramid corners and place one small Alter Stone on top of each.
10. To create the large horns, create a cone with six sides in the top view. Make it 134 units in Height, with Radius 1 = 17.0, Radius 2 = 0.0, Height Segments = 10, and Sides = 6. Apply the Twist Parametric Deformer and set Angle to 360 degrees. Then apply the Bend Parametric Deformer and set Bend angle to –80.0. Rotate the bent horn to match the front and side views and move it into position on one side. Then, Mirror Clone it to create the large horn for the other side of the pyramid, as shown in Figure 3.9, example 6.
11. Apply a soft edged tile to the pyramid as a face map, and then apply noise to make it look old. Select and group all the parts of the temple and save the scene as Location303.max.

In the next tutorial, you will add details to a building.

Detailing Buildings with the New Architectural Tools

Much of the action in the film *Homing Instinct* takes place in and around the buildings of Titan City. The new 3ds max 6 architectural procedural tools enable you to quickly add details to buildings to make them look more realistic. Procedural windows give you the ability to click on a wall and drag to create details such as casement windows with built-in animatable swinging window frames. There are also tools for creating walls, spiral staircases, railings, and foliage. These tools were used in the creation of both the interior sets and the exterior locations for *Homing Instinct,* as shown in Figure 3.10.

You will use your artistic skills to add details and create a look for a group of old buildings that are set on a riverbank. There is no set position for the details such as trees and staircases. That will be up to you. The author has provided ideas for you, but the placement, size, and density of the details is up to you.

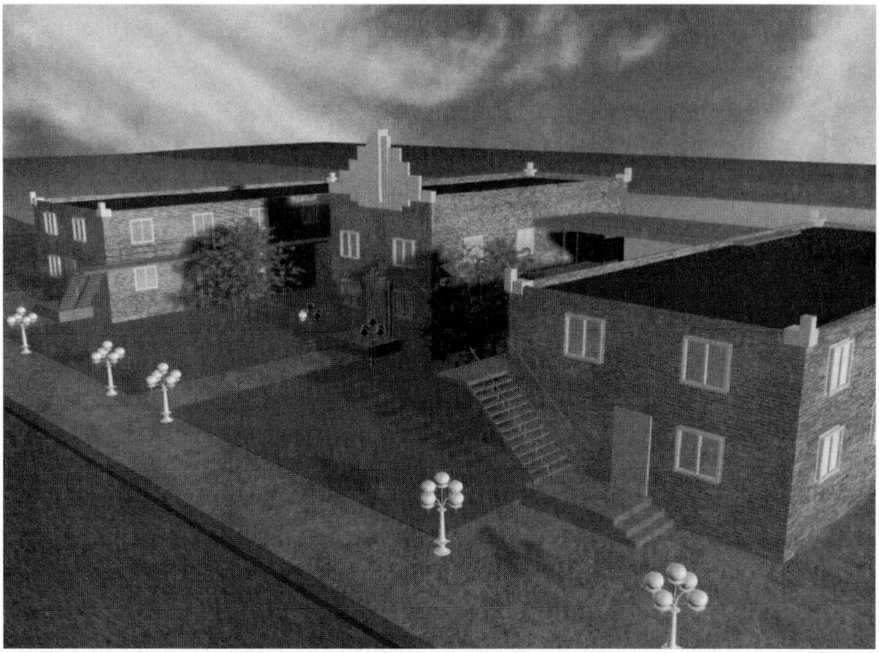

FIGURE 3.10 Old Town Buildings in the Riverside area of Titan City.

In the next tutorial, you will add details to a group of buildings to give them a more realistic appearance.

TUTORIAL 3.4

ADDING DETAILS TO BUILDINGS

To add detail to a buildings:

ON THE CD

1. Load the OldTown.max file from the Chap03 folder on the companion CD-ROM. You should see a ground plane object with a road, a group of boxy building shapes, and a dock. The dock is built on pilings and juts out into the river.
2. You will begin creating details by adding windows to the left-hand building, Building1. The two outer buildings, named Building1 and Building5, can be detailed with exactly the same windows and doors as is common practice in traditional building design. Therefore, you should place the other buildings on a different layer. Open the Layer Manager by right-

clicking the main toolbar in any gray area where there are no buttons. From the drop-down menu, select Layers. The Layer Manager will open.

3. To set up the layers, start by selecting the terrain, which is a group named Land_and_River. In the Layers toolbar, click the Create New Layer button, and name the layer Terrain. Move Selection to New layer[Layer] should be left on. Click OK. Next, select the blue dock structure, named Ground_and_Dock, and again click Create New Layer. Name that layer Dock, and then click OK. Next, create new layers for Buildings 1 through 5. You will be filling these layers with building details in the next steps. Name each of these new layers Building1, Building2, and so on. You should end up with seven layers, as shown in Figure 3.11, example 1.

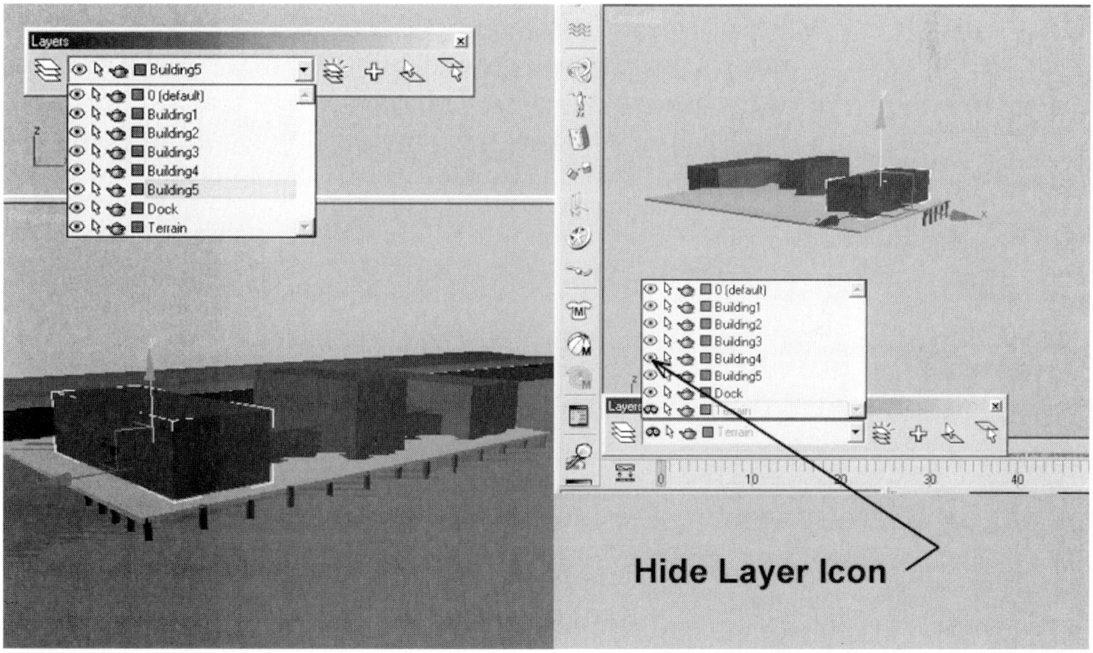

FIGURE 3.11 Setting up layers and hiding objects.

4. Drag the Layer Manager down to the lower left corner of the user interface. Next, click the arrow at the right corner of the layer list window to expand the layer list. Locate the Terrain layer and click its show/hide toggle button (the Eye icon) to hide the terrain layer, as shown in Figure 3.11, example 2. Then hide the Dock layer, and also hide buildings 2 through 5.

You should now see only Building1 in the viewports. Click Zoom Extents All. In the Command Panel > Display tab, hide cameras and lights. Next you will create procedural windows for a building.

5. You should now see only Building1. Change the Camera02 view to a Left view and click zoom extents (Ctrl+Alt+Z). Maximize the view and zoom in a little on the center area of the wall. You will begin by creating two rows of windows on the side of Building1. Be sure to check that the Layer Manager shows Building1 as the active layer. If you don't, you might not see your new window. Turn on Show Grid in the viewport, and then click the 3D Snap icon in the main toolbar. Right-click the icon and make sure it is set to Grid Points only, as shown in Figure 3.12, example 1. Next, because the building is brown, the windows should be assigned a contrasting color so you can see them as you create them. Go to the Name and Color menu in the Command Panel and click on the color swatch. In the Object Color dialog, select a light-blue color that will contrast well with the brown color of the building. Be sure to turn off the Assign Random Colors switch to prevent Max from cycling through every color as you make each window, as shown in Figure 3.12, example 2.

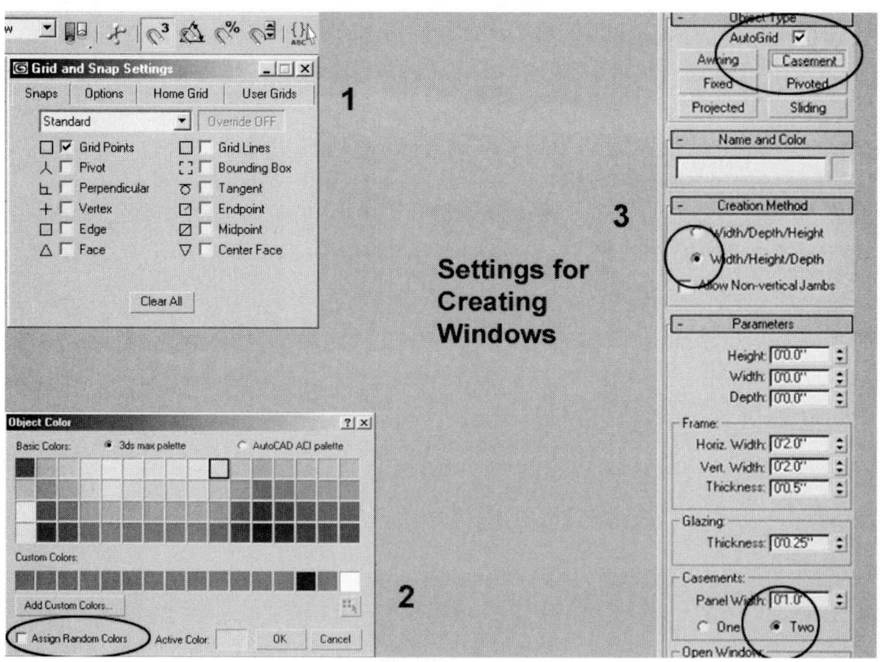

FIGURE 3.12 Setting parameters for creating a window.

6. To create a window, click Create > Geometry, and then click the word *Standard* to open the list of object creation tools. Select Windows. In the Object Type menu, select Casement and turn on the Auto Grid switch. This will ensure that the window is placed on the side of the building, and not on the Max construction plane. Before creating a window, you need to change some settings. Under Creation Method, click Width/Height/Depth. Then, in the Casements menu, click Two, as shown in Figure 3.12, example 3. Finally, after making all these settings, you are ready to create a window.
7. In the Left view, turn on Smooth and Highlight, and Edged Faces, and then click on the side of the building. The Auto Grid will activate. Hold the mouse button and drag horizontally to the right four grids. You should see the blue Snap icon jump to the next grid line as you drag. Then release the mouse button and drag the cursor upward four grid lines. Click the mouse button again and drag a very small amount to set the depth of the window casement, and finally click again to complete window creation, as shown in Figure 3.13, example 1. You should now see a light-blue window sitting on the side of the building. You can move it to just below the upper left corner of the building wall. Next, you will clone the window.

This is meant to be a two-story building, so you would create two rows of windows. Before finally positioning the window, you need to adjust its size. The building was originally measured in feet and inches. The height of the wall was about 19 feet. Each story was a little over eight feet tall, with two feet taken up by the foundation. Now the file is set to equivalent International Generic Units, so the height of the wall is 225 Units. In metric measurements, that would equal 5.72 meters high. Because this is a virtual movie set, absolute accuracy is not that important, unless you are trying to match a building from real life.

8. You need to use your artistic judgment to determine the size and spacing, and create two rows of six windows. You can use the Spacing tool to create the correct placement of the windows. The author first places the windows by eye and then does the spacing. To get accurate spacing, create a spline that goes from the center of the first window to the center of the last window. Next, create a space marker object such as a small sphere and select it. Then click Tools > Spacing. When the dialog opens, enter 6 as the Count parameter, and then click the Pick Path button and select the spline. Six spheres will appear, evenly spaced along the spline, as shown in Figure 13.13, example 2. Finally, click Align and then select and move your windows to align their centers with the marker spheres. When done,

delete the spline and marker spheres. If you are a Max "power user" or an architect, and you are very good at planning ahead, you can simply create one window, create a spline of the length you want, and then have the spacing tool clone the windows along the spline for you.

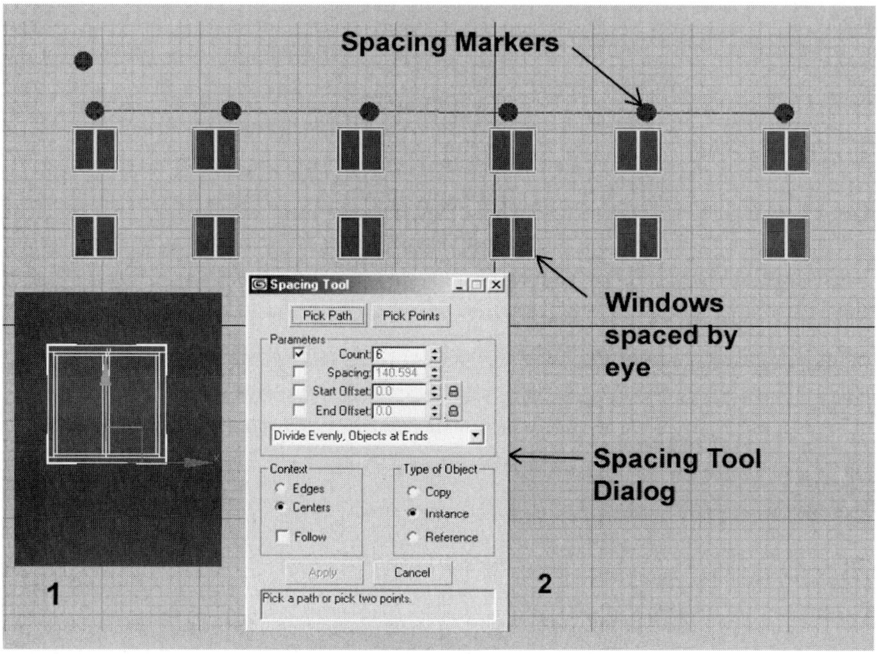

FIGURE 3.13 Creating, cloning, and spacing windows.

9. From here on, you can clone the windows and place them on all the walls on your own. The process described in the previous steps is essentially how doors are made. Stairs, steps, and trees are also created by the click-and-drag method. You can unhide buildings 2 through 5 and apply the windows and other details to those buildings as you see fit. Nearly all of the procedural architectural tools work the same way and are very intuitive. Trees are created in the AEC Extended Tools menu, and can be found in the Foliage menu. As long as you keep the proportions of the building details looking about right, so that they fit the scale of the two-story building, you will be able to create very nice buildings that will look real once they have been textured and placed in the proper lighting. Texturing these buildings is discussed in Chapter 13, "Materials and Textures."

10. Continue experimenting with each of these tools to create details and decorations for the buildings and grounds as you wish. You can also merge vehicles, streetlights, and furniture into the scene from the Standard Objects directory on the second tutorial's CD-ROM, which ships with 3ds max 6, as shown in Figure 13.14. It is a good idea to make sure that all of the details for each building are placed in the layer for that building. You will be adding a lot of details, so the layers will help you manage everything. You do not need to collapse the layers when you are done. As long as they are all visible, you can render the setting and animate a scene in the setting with all the layers intact. Save your finished file as OldTown304.max.

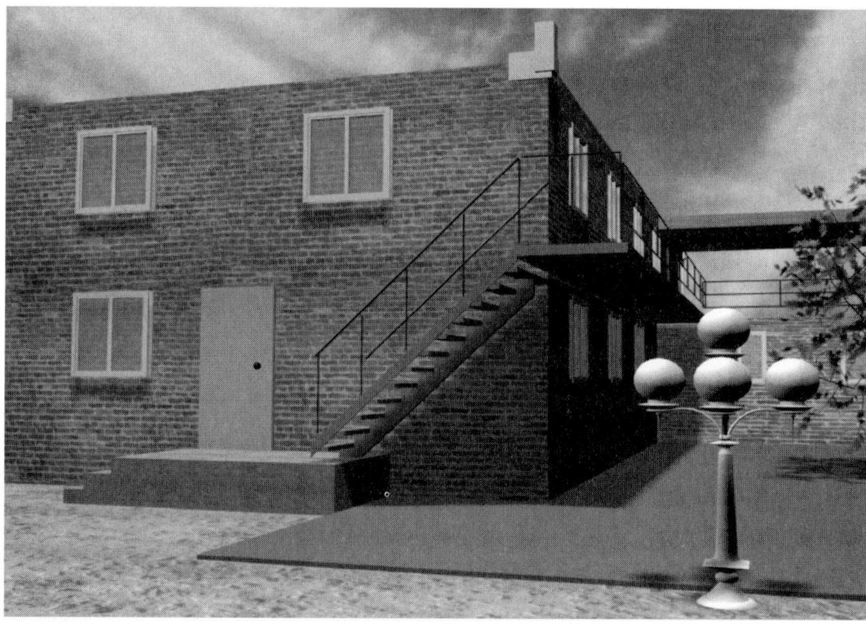

FIGURE 13.14 Building1, with additional details added to enhance realism.

ON THE CD

11. To see the author's version of the Old Town, load the OldTown304a.max file from the companion CD-ROM and examine how the details were applied to the buildings.

That concludes the Architectural Details tutorial. In the next tutorial, you will begin the creation of an alien character and work with organic modeling.

ALIEN CHARACTERS

All kinds of alien creatures live on Titan. The great thing about science fiction is that you can create a universe where exotic environments and bizarre creatures are commonplace, and human beings live next door to sentient reptiles.

Xzulixia (Xzu), the Alien Vampire character in the story (Figure 3.15), is designed to look outwardly human. However, she has alien cat eyes, fangs, and bat-like pointed ears. The model will be built using MeshSmooth, the Subdivision Surfaces Modifier, and Soft Selection, that allow you to sculpt a realistic human model from a polygonal box.

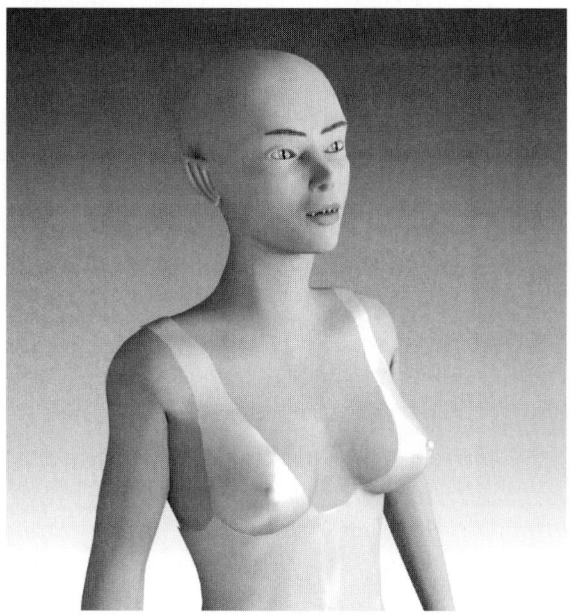

FIGURE 3.15 Xzulixia, the Alien Vampire character.

MODELING THE ALIEN VAMPIRE

During the construction of the character, the MeshSmooth Modifier will be repeatedly applied to see a preview of the result of the modifications you are making to the model. MeshSmooth can be turned on from inside the Editable Poly menu at sub-object level, or applied as a separate modifier. The method used here is to apply it as a separate modifier because that version gives you more detailed control over the mesh.

Polygon modeling in 3ds max 6 has been enhanced for improved capabilities and workflow. The polygons (which can be exported as Quads) are easier to work with than the triangle faces used in traditional mesh modeling.

The polygon modeling process typically begins by creating a box the size of the torso. You work with a symmetrical model adjusting both the right and left sides to establish good proportions. Then, when the torso's basic shape is established, the model is cut in half and one side is deleted. A reference mirror copy is created that mirrors everything done to the remaining side so you can see what the finished model will look like. After all the important features are established, the reference side is deleted and a new copy of the original half will be mirror-cloned to create the opposite side. The two sides will then be welded together and finished details added.

TUTORIAL 3.5

MODELING THE ALIEN BODY

To model an alien body:

1. Reset 3ds max 6 and change the viewport configuration to two vertical windows. Click Customize > Viewport Configuration > Layout and select layout 2 with two vertical windows. Make the window on the right the front viewport, the other one the left viewport, and then click OK. Load the background images.

ON THE CD

2. From the companion CD-ROM in the Chap03\Images folder, load the image Alien_Sid.tif, and place it in the Left view. Load Alien_Fnt.tif, and place it in the front view.
3. The body is made from a Box. In the front view, create a Standard Primitive Box. Click on the Alien's shoulder and drag the mouse to the opposite hip. In Parameters, set the box size to 50 generic units wide, 90 units high, and 30 units deep. In the Modify panel, set the Height subdivisions to 7, the width subdivisions to 4, and depth subdivisions to 2, as shown in Figure 3.16, example 1.
4. Right-click and select Convert to > Convert to Editable Poly in the Quad menu.

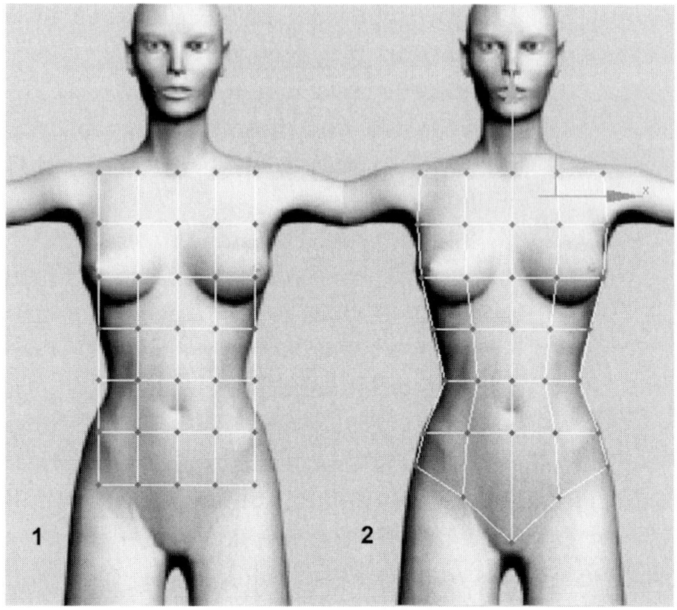

FIGURE 3.16 Fitting the wire mesh to the torso.

5. Go to Vertex mode in the Editable Poly modifier, and move the outside vertices of the box to fit the alien's profile in the front and left views. Make sure the vertical columns of vertices form smooth flowing lines that follow the body. To form the pelvic area, pull the lowest center vertices down and adjust the bottom of the box as shown in Figure 3.16, example 2.
6. Once the basic shape is made, select the corner vertices on all four corners and move them in toward the center of the torso in the X- and Y-axis. Move them only enough to "round" the edges of the model, as shown in Figure 3.17, example 1. This will help smooth the body.
7. In the front view, turn off Show Background and then use Arc Rotate to roll the viewport until you can see the top surface of the model. In Sub-object > Polygon mode, select the central four polygons, then use the Edit Polygons > Bevel tool to extrude up a short neck, and then scale it to two-thirds the original size. Then, select the four corner vertices of the new polygons and move (uniform scale) them toward the center to round them, as shown in Figure 3.17, example 2.
8. In the left view, select the vertices that form the center top of the shoulder and raise them upward a short distance to round the top of the shoulders, as shown in Figure 3.17, example 3. Next, select the four polygons that

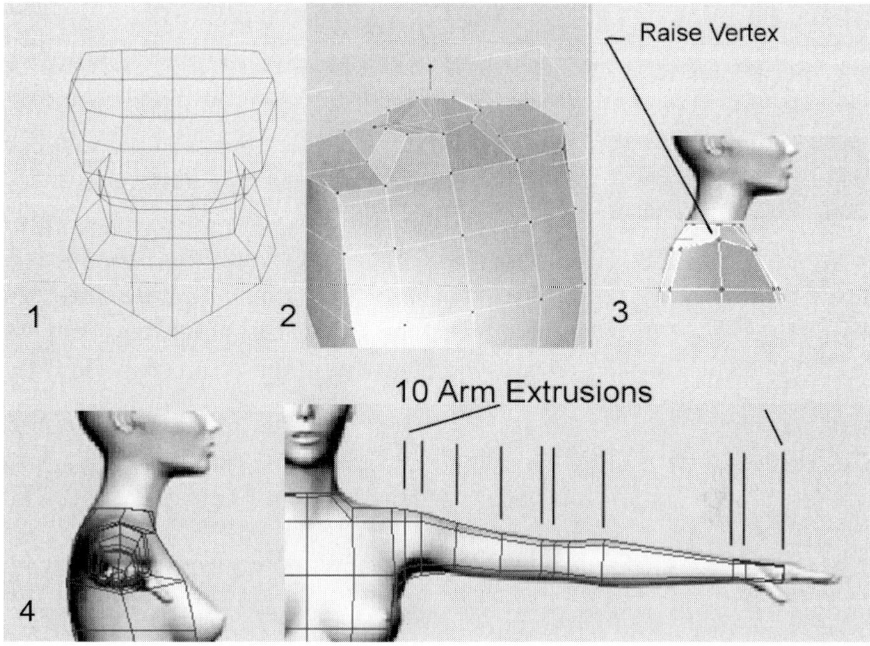

FIGURE 3.17 Extrude the neck and the arm from the torso.

correspond to the arm hole in the side of the body. Use the Edit Polygons > Bevel tool to extrude them and scale them down to two-thirds of their original size. This is the beginning of the arm.

9. Extrude the arm out in 10 steps, extruding, scaling, and positioning the selected four faces to fit the contour of the arm in the background image. You should end up with two extrusions for the shoulder, two for the upper arm, two for the elbow, two for the forearm, and two for the wrist and palm, as shown in Figure 3.17, example 4.
10. Switch the front view to the top view (press the T key). The arm will look like a straight box. Select and non-uniform scale the arm vertices to sculpt it into an arm tapering down to the wrist and forearm, and narrow the elbow. You will finish the arm when you create the hand in a subsequent tutorial. Switch the view back to the front view (press the F key).
11. Save the scene as Alien_305.max.

In the next tutorial, you will create the alien's leg and buttocks.

TUTORIAL 3.6 CREATING THE ALIEN'S LEG AND BUTTOCKS

To create the alien's leg:

1. Load your Alien_305.max scene, and then reposition the front and side views to concentrate on the hips and legs.
2. Go into Editable Poly > Polygon mode, and in the front view select the four polygon faces of the left lower side of the pelvis area as shown in Figure 3.18, example 1. Extrude a short distance. The new extruded area will be a square. Select the outside corner vertices and move them toward the center to round the shape of the leg, as shown in Figure 3.18, example 2.

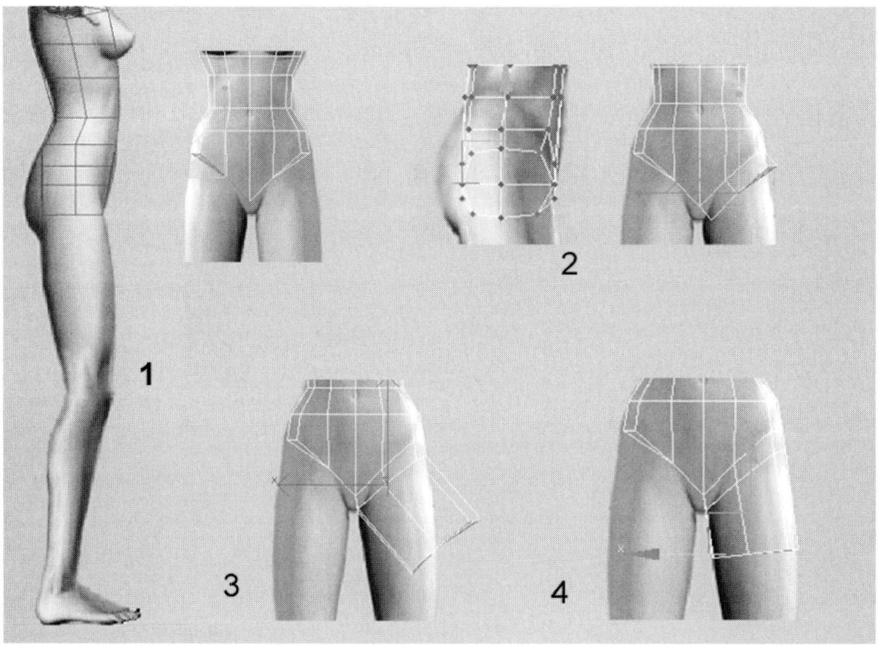

FIGURE 3.18 Extruding the leg out from the hip.

3. Control > select all four polygons on the end of the new leg extrusion and move them down and in to match the background drawing. Extrude again out to about the middle of the thigh. The extrusion will point away from the leg, as shown in Figure 3.18, example 3. In the front view, move the new polygons so that they are centered over the thigh. Then, rotate them to face down the centerline of the leg. Scale their width to fit the thigh, as shown in Figure 3.18, example 4.

4. It takes 10 extrusions to create the leg. Extrude the end polygons down to just above the knee, uniform scaling the polygons to fit the leg's width. Then, extrude down to the center of the knee, and once again to just below the knee, as shown in Figure 3.19, example 1.

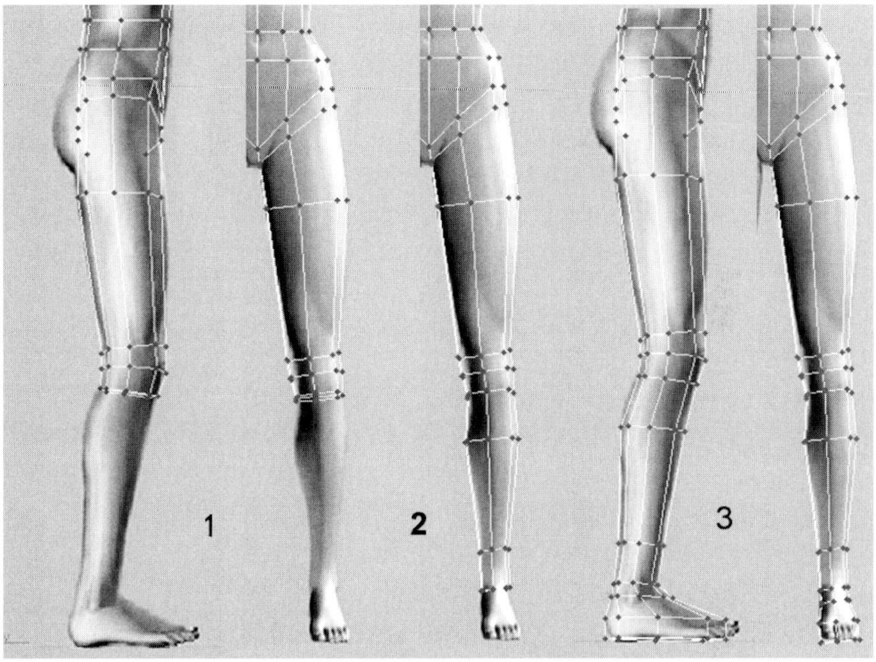

FIGURE 3.19 Extruding and scaling to create the leg and foot.

5. Next, extrude down to the calf, and then move and scale up the leg end polygons to fit the width of the calf. Extrude again to just above the ankle, then once more to below the ankle, as shown in example 2. Finally, extrude three more times to the upper foot, middle foot, and sole of the foot, as shown in Figure 3.19, example 3.
6. In both views, click Zoom Extents to center the model. You should now have a left arm and a left leg (seen on your right in the front viewport). The next step is to extrude the buttocks from the back of the hip. Change the front view to a back view by pressing the V key and selecting Back View from the pop-up menu, as shown in Figure 3.20, example 1.
7. In the Selection menu of the Editable Poly Modifier, turn on Ignore Backfacing, and then select the four polygons that make up the left buttocks

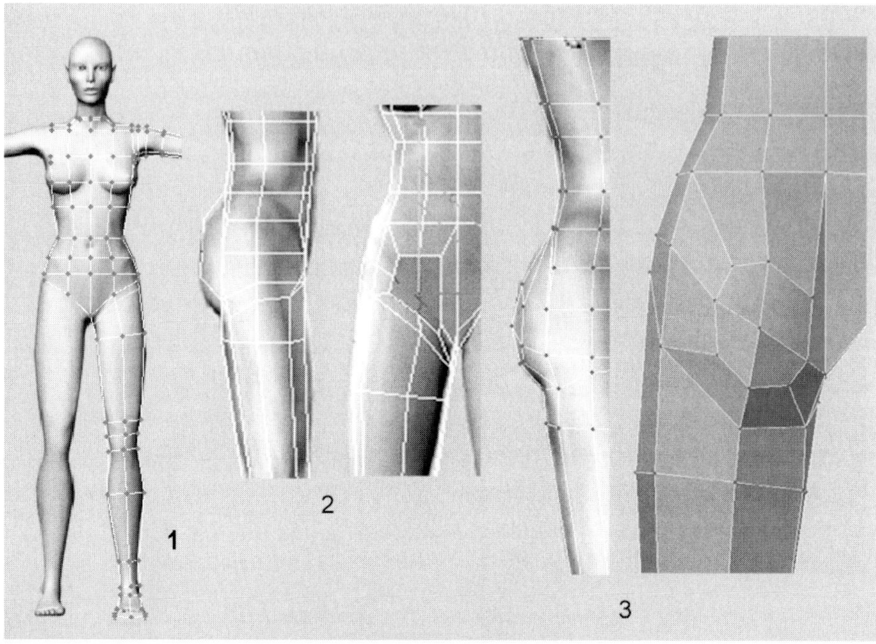

FIGURE 3.20 Extrude and scale the buttocks polygons.

area of the model. In the left view, extrude the polygons out to match the depth of the buttocks. Scale the polygons in height and width to about one-half their original size, as shown in Figure 3.20, example 2.

8. Change to Vertex Sub-object mode and move the outside corners of the buttocks polygons inward to round them, as shown in Figure 3.20, example 3. Pull the central vertex out a little.
9. To extrude the foot, turn off Ignore Backfacing, then in the Left view select the four polygons that point toward the toes of the background image and extrude them toward the toes twice, once to the middle of the foot and once to the beginnings of the toes. Do not extrude toes at this time. The toes will be added in a later tutorial.
10. Switch to vertex mode and shape the foot to match the background image.
11. Save the scene as Alien306.max.

In the next tutorial, you will finish the torso.

TUTORIAL 3.7

FINISHING THE TORSO

To finish the torso:

1. Load the Alien306.max scene. Click Z for Zoom Extents and Maximize the front view to see the arm and chest.
2. The next step is to rearrange the vertices prior to extruding the breast. Before going any farther, select the model, enter the Editable Poly Modifier, and apply MeshSmooth, with Iterations = 1. Now disable MeshSmooth until later by turning off the Lightbulb icon in the MeshSmooth Modifier window.
3. Load the Torso_Cuts.tif image from the Chap03\Images folder on the companion CD-ROM into the front viewport background. Be sure to set background Aspect Ratio to Match Bitmap to prevent distortion. Position the model over the background image as shown in Figure 3.21, example 1 using the Background Lock Toggle command (Ctrl > Alt > B) and the viewport zoom and pan tools.

   ON THE CD
4. In Editable Poly > Polygon mode, select all the polygons to the left side of the body centerline in the viewport (the model's right side). Scroll up the

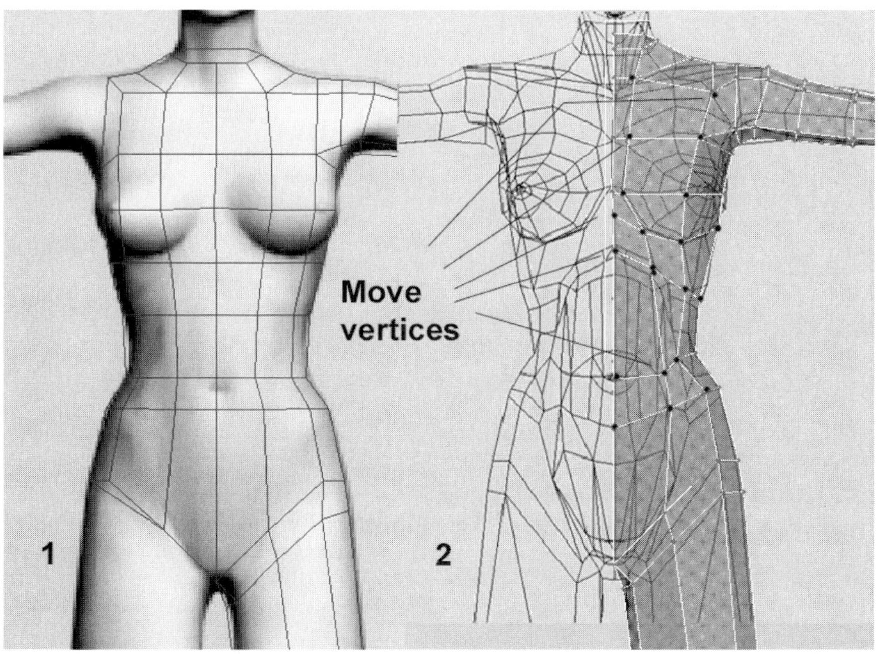

FIGURE 3.21 Torso refinement.

Edit Geometry menu and click on Hide Selected. You should now only see half of the body with the arm and leg.

5. Enter Editable Poly > Vertex mode. Then, turn on Ignore Backfacing. In the front view, select vertices and move them until they match the arrangement of vertices shown in Figure 3.21, example 2. The two horizontal lines of vertices across the middle chest should be modified to follow the curve of the rib cage and the curved line below the breast shown in the Torso_Cuts.tif background image.
6. Before the breast can be extruded, an additional line must be cut that runs from the armpit down the side of the body to the bottom of the breast line. Cut that line, and then cut another line that runs from the dip in the top of the shoulder, down the upper chest, and ends on the vertex at the nipple. This is done to add resolution to the breast and to help create the semi-circular area that will easily form the base of the breast.
7. The next step is to round out the ring of vertices around the base of the breast. These vertices enclose the group of polygons that you will extrude to form the breast, as shown in Figure 3.22, example 1. Also shown is a view of the chest area of the finished model to give you an idea of the number of polygons that are needed to form a smooth breast area when MeshSmooth is applied.

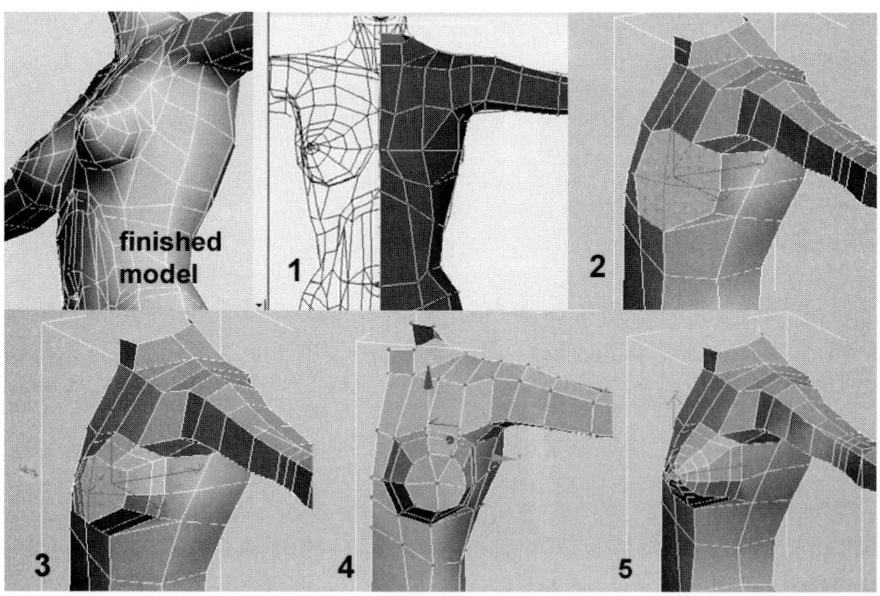

FIGURE 3.22 Extruding the breast.

8. Once the base of the breast is established, switch to Polygon mode and select the five breast base polygons. Your selection should look like Figure 3.22, example 2. Use the Editable Polygon > Edit Geometry > Bevel tool to extrude and scale down the base of the breast two times, as shown in Figure 3.22, example 3.
9. Before continuing, switch to vertex mode and form the extruded polygons of the breast into a circle, as shown in Figure 3.22, example 4. Then, resume polygon extrusion with the Bevel tool three more times, scaling the polygons smaller each time until you reach the size of the nipple. Form the nipple by extruding once more a short distance. Check the left view to make sure the breast matches the Alien_Side.tif background image.
10. The next step is to move the breast vertices to sculpt the breast into a more realistic shape. For comparison, load the image that shows the finished breast model. Using File > View Image File, load the Torso1.tif image from the Chap03\Images folder on the companion CD-ROM. Apply MeshSmooth to see if more sculpting is needed.

ON THE CD

11. Once you have sculpted the breast into a pleasing natural shape, the next step is to add the cut lines that form the stomach muscle outline and the clavicle that runs across the shoulder. Using the Torso_Cuts.tif background

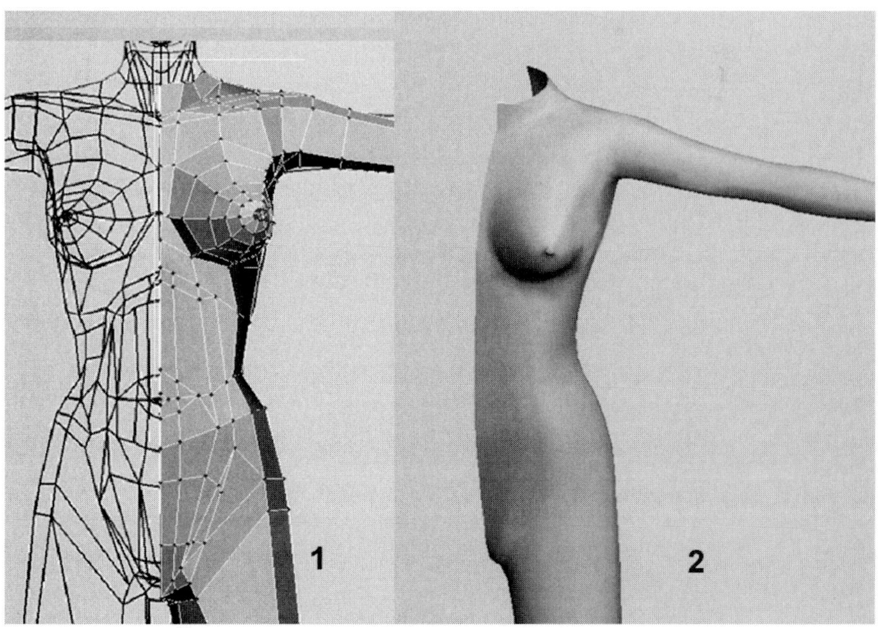

FIGURE 3.23 Cutting in the lines of the stomach muscles and clavicle.

image as a reference, cut the stomach area to form the stomach muscle outlines and the navel, as shown in Figure 3.23, example 1. Turn MeshSmooth on and off to see how the mesh looks as you cut. Final adjustment of these new cuts will be done after the entire model is assembled in a later tutorial.

12. When the stomach is finished, cut the lines across the shoulder to form the clavicle, as shown in Figure 3.23, example 2. Be sure to Unhide the right half of the body before saving the scene, which was hidden in Sub-object Polygon mode. In Sub-object Polygon mode, go to Edit Geometry and click Unhide All. Save the scene as alien 307.max.

CONCLUSION

You have completed the construction of the environments and the alien temple, and finished the first stage of the modeling of the Xzulixia character. You have been introduced to the polygonal modeling procedures that you will work with to complete the character. In the next chapter, you will finish modeling the body, hands, and face of the Xzulixia character and create a jumpsuit for her to wear.

CHAPTER

4

FINISHING THE ALIEN VAMPIRE CHARACTER

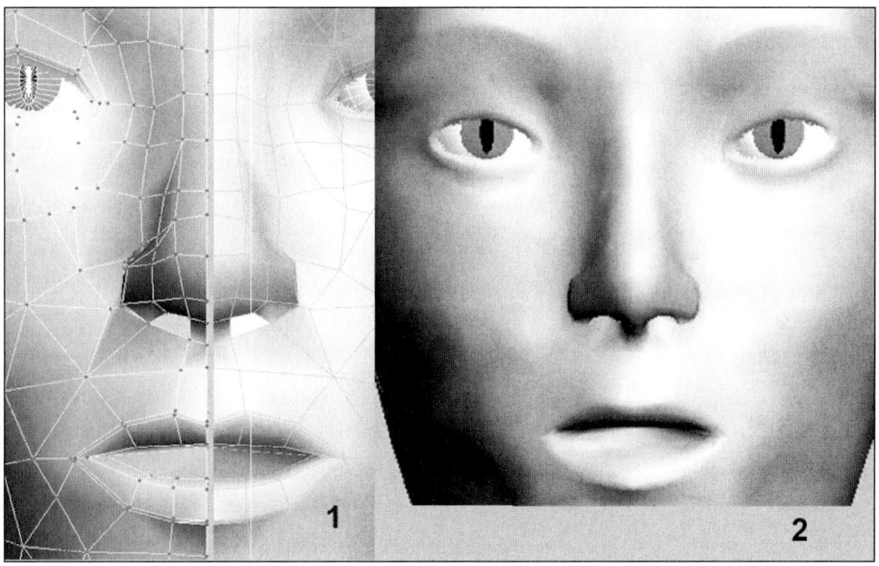

In the last chapter, you began modeling the Alien Vampire character called Xzulixia. Classical Box modeling techniques including Editable Poly Extrusion, Bevel, Cut, and MeshSmooth are used to create the model. In this chapter, those techniques are expanded on to create detailed facial features, hands with fingernails, and feet with toes. Teeth, eyes, eyelashes, and a tongue are added to enable the model to be used for lip-sync animation. Once all the modeling is done, clothing will be created for her (Figure 4.1).

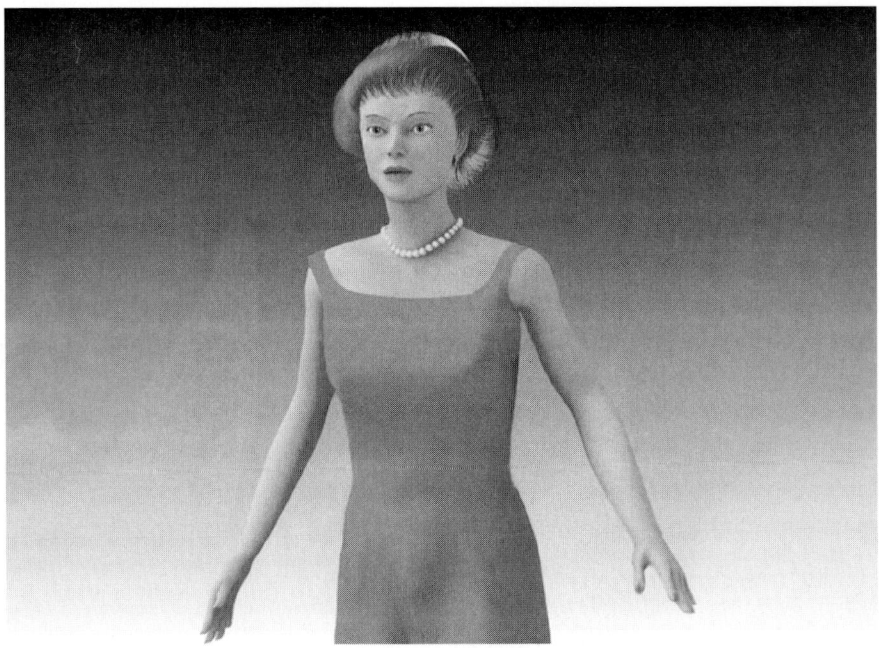

FIGURE 4.1 Xzulixia, finished and ready for animation.

Working with polygons rather than triangle mesh faces has one very important advantage: in triangle mesh models you are limited to three vertices per face. With an Editable Poly mesh, you can use three or more vertices per polygon. This gives you much greater flexibility in modeling because you can easily close irregular gaps and holes. You can also choose to output the finished model as Quads, which organizes the edges into a more uniform and smoothly flowing surface mesh.

In the next tutorial, you will continue work on the Alien Vampire model that you started in Chapter 3 by creating the Alien's head.

TUTORIAL 4.1

CREATING A CHARACTER HEAD

To create the Alien's head:

ON THE CD

1. Load the Alien306.max scene you completed in the previous chapter, or load the file from the Chap04 folder on the companion CD-ROM. When you load the file, you should see the entire model. It should have only one arm and one leg, as shown in Figure 4.2, example 1. The other half of the body has the torso but no arm or leg. It you do not see the half without the arm and leg, select the model, then go into Modify > Editable Poly > Polygon mode, and in the Edit Geometry menu click the Unhide All button. Before continuing, turn off the MeshSmooth Modifier by clicking the Lightbulb icon in the Stack.

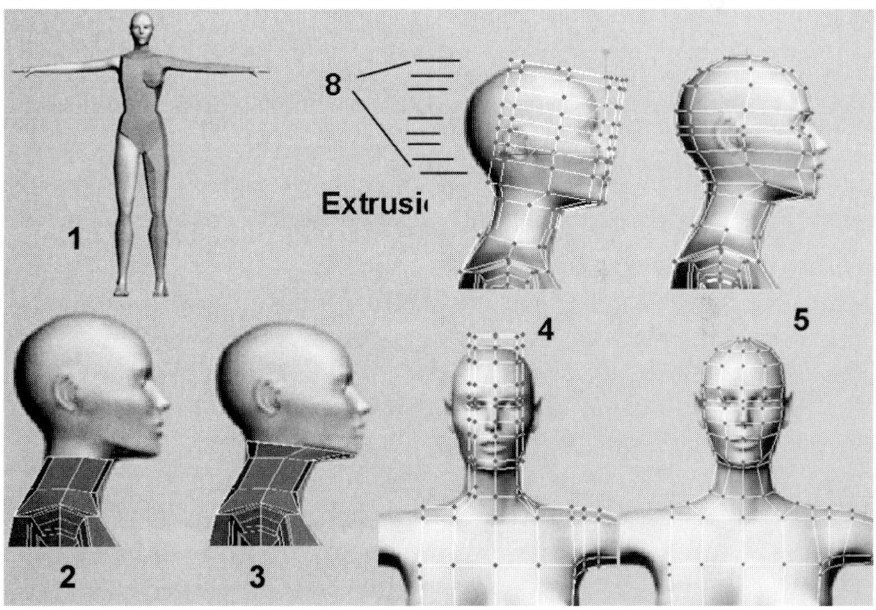

FIGURE 4.2 Extrude the neck to form the head, and then move and scale vertices.

2. The Alien_Fnt.tif and Alien_Side.tif viewport background images should load. If they do not, place them in your 3ds max\Maps directory, and use the Viewport Background menu to find and re-load them. In the Aspect Ratio dialog, turn on Match bitmap, and Lock Zoom-Pan. Re-position the model over the background images using Ctrl > Alt > B and the Zoom and Pan tools. Then, zoom in on the head and shoulder area in both views.

3. In the front view, select the polygons at the top of the neck and extrude them up once to extend the neck, stopping just below the level of the chin in the background image, as shown in Figure 4.2, Example 2. In the left view, move them forward and Non-uniform scale their width to match the outline of the neck.
4. Extrude the neck upward again to meet the chin line. In the left view, Non-uniform scale the polygons wider in the X-axis so that the top of the extrusion matches the depth of the head at the chin, as shown in Figure 4.2, example 3.
5. While still in Polygon mode, extrude the neck upward eight times all the way to the top of the head. Each extrusion should be no more than four to five units tall. (Note: All tutorials use International Generic Units.) This will create a block-like structure, as shown in Figure 4.2, example 4.
6. In vertex mode, select and scale each horizontal row of vertices in the head to match the outline drawing in both the front and left views. Be careful to match the vertical positions of the facial features with the horizontal rows of vertices, as shown in Figure 4.2, example 5.
7. The horizontal rows should pass through the major features of the face when you are finished. You should have a row at the chin, the mouth, the nose, the cheek, the eye, the brow, the middle forehead, the hairline, and the top of the head. Study Figure 4.2, example 5 and match your rows and columns of vertices to the figure.
8. Save the scene as Alien401.max.

In the next tutorial, you will subdivide the face, and create the mouth, nose, and eye openings.

TUTORIAL 4.2

CREATE THE ALIEN'S MOUTH, NOSE, AND EYES

To create the main features of the head:

1. Load the Alien401.max file. Switch background images to work close up on the features of the head. Select the front view, and then load the Alien_Fac_Fnt.tif image into the Viewport Background. Select the left view and load the Alien_Fac_Side.tif image into the Viewport Background. Turn on Match Bitmap, and Lock zoom/pan.
2. Use the background lock toggle (Ctrl > Alt > B) hotkey to unlock the foreground from the background, and then use the viewport Zoom and Pan

tools to move the head vertices to match the wire cage of the head to the Face images in both. When finished, re-lock the foreground and background so they will zoom together.

These Background Lock Toggle instructions are included for people who are new to 3ds max.

3. It is important to have the vertex rows and columns positioned correctly to build the features. Figure 4.3 shows the front and side views of the correct arrangement of vertices. In the left view, select the horizontal rows of vertices that correspond to the chin, upper neck, and lower neck, and then rotate them about 10 degrees to follow the angle of the jaw and neck in the background drawing. Move the vertices down at the cheek, as shown in Figure 4.3, examples 1 and 2. Vertical rows on both sides of the centerline should pass through the center of the eyes.

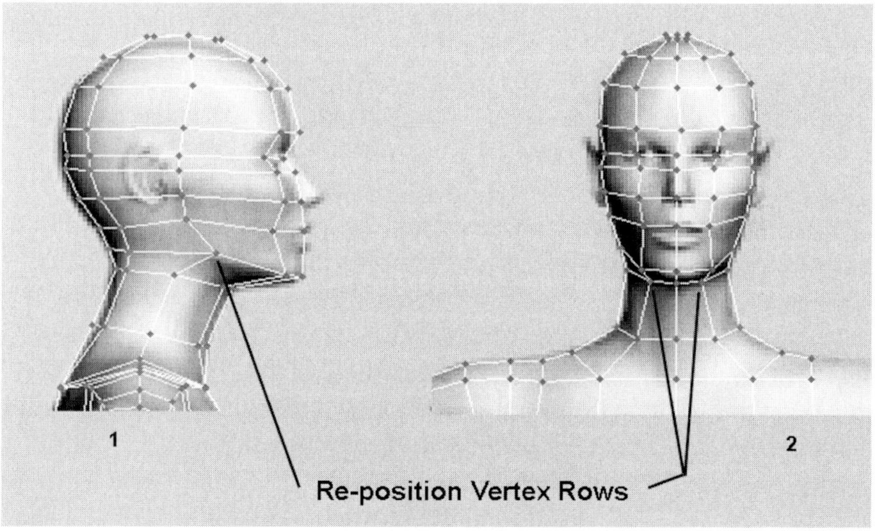

FIGURE 4.3 Positioning the rows and columns of vertices.

There are three tools to cut faces in the Editable Polygon modifier: Slice Plane, Cut, and Quick Slice. Snaps can be used with Cut to cut an edge exactly in half, or to cut from an edge to a vertex, which greatly improves accuracy. The Quick Slice tool lets you simply draw a line across the mesh with the cursor in any direction to cut a number of edges or faces.

4. To create the base shape of the nose, zoom in on the center of the face in the front view. The nose is created by subdividing the central area of the face using the Cut tool in the Edit Geometry rollout menu, as shown in Figure 4.4.

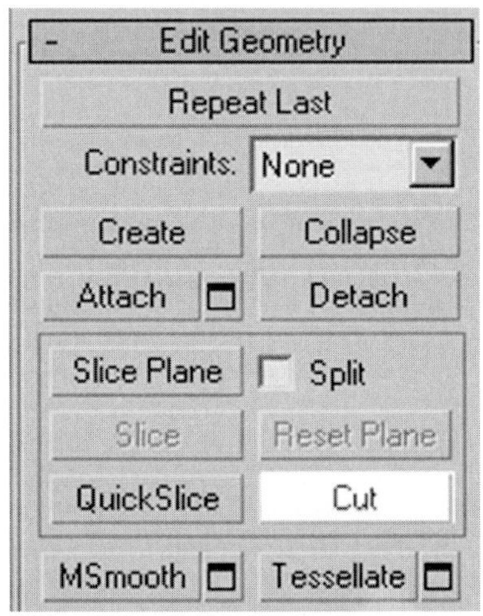

FIGURE 4.4 The Editable Polygon Edit Geometry menu showing the Cut tool.

5. Select the mesh, and then go to the Modify > Editable Poly > Edit Geometry menu and click the Cut button. Then, in the front view, place the cursor over the horizontal row of vertices that runs just below the nose, directly below the outer corner of the Alien vampire's left nostril. Move directly up toward the brow and click to cut the next horizontal edge running through the nose.
6. Repeat the Cut process until the forehead line is reached. Examine Figure 4.5, example 1 to see the path the Cut line should take as you move up the side of the nose and into the forehead. Right-click to end cutting.
7. To create the first subdivision around the eye, place the cursor over the "eye" row of vertices, which corresponds to the inner corner of the eye in the background image. Cut a diamond shape around the eye by clicking the edges around the eye clockwise, as shown in Figure 4.5, example 2.

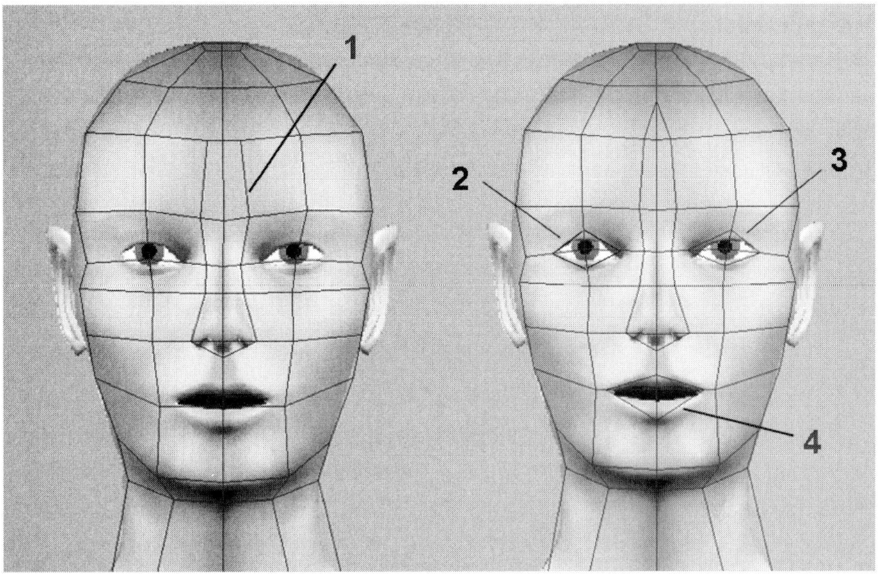

FIGURE 4.5 Cutting in the basic starting shapes of the features.

8. Cut in the opposite eye, and then cut in triangles in the Brow, vertex row No. 8, to create the eyebrows as shown in Figure 4.5, example 3.
9. To create the basic mouth diamond shape, repeat the previous process and cut a line starting at one corner of the mouth, continuing around to the other corners and back to the beginning, as shown in Figure 4.5, example 4.
10. At this point, it is time to cut the model in half. From now on, you will only work on one side of the model. Zoom out to show the head and torso. In Vertex Sub-object mode, select all the vertices on the model's right side (on your left). Do not select any of the centerline vertices. Ignore Backfacing should be turned off.
11. Delete all of the vertices on your left (the side with no arm and leg). Do not delete the centerline vertices. You should now have one half of the model with a head, arm, and leg. Save the scene as Alien402.max.

In the next tutorial, you will add resolution to the facial features to sculpt them into shapes that are more life-like.

USING NURMS

A NURMS, or Non-Uniform Rational MeshSmooth object, allows you to control the surface shape and smoothing properties by setting different weights for each control vertex. In polygon modeling, this adds greatly to the control that you have over the shape of edges. When you start dividing the polygons of the face or body to create finer details, NURMS allow you to work on the low-resolution version of the model, and then see the results of the smoothing instantly by clicking the Show End Result On/Off toggle button located at the bottom of the Modifier List window.

NURMS is one of three styles of Surface Subdivision available in the MeshSmooth tool. One of its most useful capabilities is that it lets you create a NURBS-like control Hull around an editable Poly mesh and model it smoothly like a NURBS surface model. For character modeling, this is a valuable technique for speeding up the work. It also lets you select a specific set of vertices to define a zone that will be subdivided. There is no reason to divide more of the face than is absolutely needed. That way, the model will remain as light as possible for better animation and rendering time.

The MeshSmooth tool built in as a button in the Editable Poly > Edit Geometry menu is always set to subdivide the entire model. If you want to only subdivide a local set of polygons, you must use the MeshSmooth Modifier version. As you work through these tutorials, you will see that the Mesh Smooth Modifier is nearly always present on the top of Editable Poly in the Stack, and it can be turned off and on as needed.

TUTORIAL 4.3

INCREASE RESOLUTION TO CREATE FACIAL FEATURES

To increase facial resolution:

1. Load the Alien402.max file. In the front view, select the model, and then zoom closer until the head fills the front view. The first step is to subdivide the face using the MeshSmooth Modifier.
2. To Subdivide the face using MeshSmooth, select the vertices as shown in Figure 4.6, example 1. This selection will provide adequate subdivisions to create the features without subdividing the rest of the head where it is not needed.

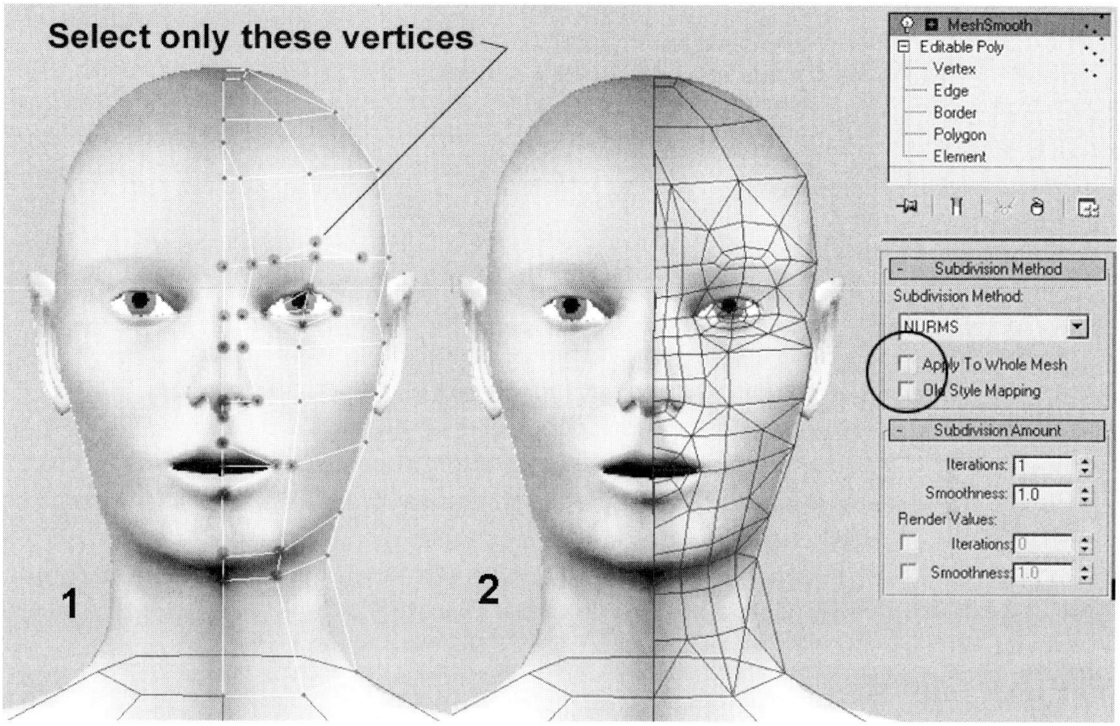

FIGURE 4.6 Selecting vertices to apply localized MeshSmooth subdivision.

3. In the Modifiers menu, select Subdivision Surfaces > MeshSmooth. Important: Under MeshSmooth > Subdivision Method, be sure to turn off Apply to Whole Mesh. Use the default NURM Subdivision Method, and set Display > Iterations to 1. This will smooth the face, as shown in Figure 4.6, example 2. Only part of the face should now be subdivided. The rest of the face and body mesh should be unchanged.
4. Next, collapse the Stack (remove the history) to lock in the subdivisions of the model at this level. To do that, right-click to open the Quad menu and then select Convert to Poly.

At this stage, the subdivided polymesh has been given all the resolution needed to establish the contours of a realistic face. Once enough vertices are available, you can rough out the shape of the character by pulling and pushing lines and areas of vertices. However, you don't want too many vertices or faces because it limits you in what you can do to change the surface. Low resolution is best to keep present at the bottom level of the Stack. That way, you can always return to the base level and correct or remodel a feature.

The new tools in Editable Poly give you many more ways of selecting complex sets of faces. This is especially useful for creating high-resolution edges around openings that will become eyelids, nostrils, ears, and lips.

5. To speed up modeling it is a good idea to hide the vertices of the back of the head so you do not inadvertently select and move it while modeling the face. Go to Editable Poly > Sub-object > Polygon mode and select all of the polygons that make up the back of the head. Hide them using Editable Poly > Edit Geometry > Hide Selected. Now you can work on the face without accidentally selecting the back of the head.
6. In order to work on one half of the head but see the results on both halves, Mirror-clone the model. In the front view, select the mesh, and then in the Main tool bar, click the Mirror Selected Objects icon. In the pop-up menu, select Reference as the Clone Selection type. A Reference Copy appears that mirrors what is done to the original half of the model, as shown in Figure 4.7.

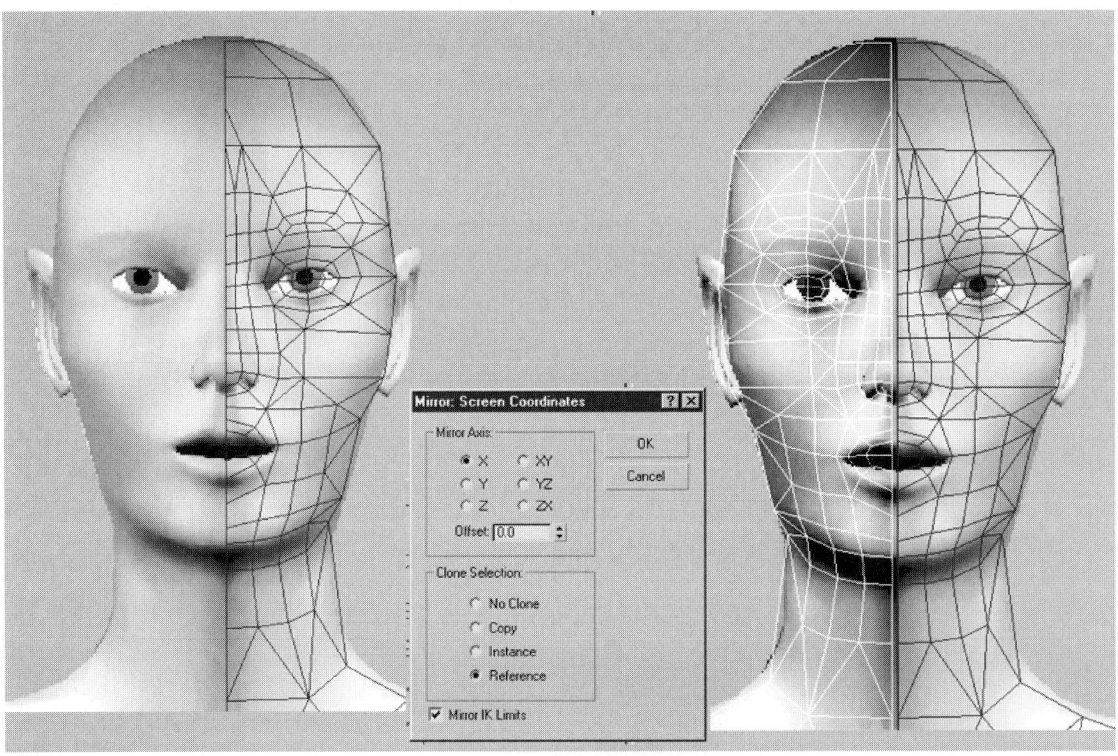

FIGURE 4.7 Mirror Clone to create a reference copy of the model.

7. Begin sculpting the face by working on the nose in the front view. Remember to only work on the model's left side (the side on your right). Selections will automatically be mirrored on the model's right side. Select the nose tip and centerline vertices, and then move them forward to match the contour of the nose of the left view background image, as shown in Figure 4.8, example 1.

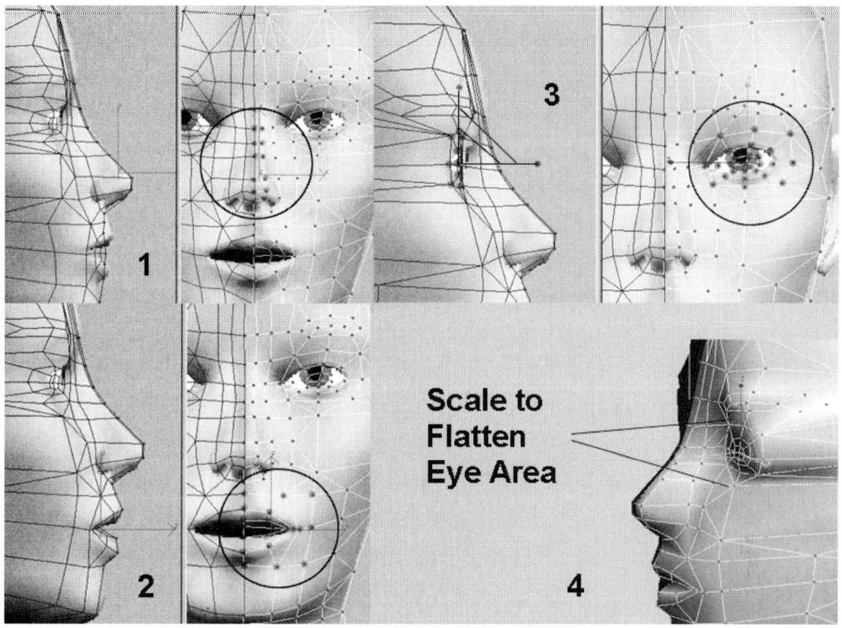

FIGURE 4.8 Sculpt the nose and lips, and then flatten the eye to make it face forward.

8. In the front view, select the three circles of vertices around the mouth and scale them down vertically in the front view to better match the shape of the mouth. Select the three vertices that will form the corner of the lips, and pull them wider and closer together to match the drawing, as shown in Figure 4.8, example 2. Then, in the left view, pull the vertices forward to match the mouth contours in the background image.
9. Select the center vertex. Then, use the new Grow button in the Editable Poly > Selection menu to grow the selection to a ring around the center of the eye. Press it two more times and it will select all three concentric rings of vertices around the eye in the front view. However, it also grabbed four additional vertices that are not part of the eye rings. Alt > Select them to deselect those vertices.

10. In the left view, pull them forward to the position of the cornea of the eye in the background image. Next, use Non-uniform Scale in the X-axis in the left view to scale them nearly flat, as shown in Figure 4.8, example 3. That should make the eye into a flat area facing forward, instead of a rounded area facing sideways as it was originally, as shown in Figure 4.8, example 4.
11. Save the scene as Alien403.max.

In the next tutorial, you will shape the facial features and contours.

TUTORIAL 4.4

SHAPING THE FACIAL FEATURES

To shape the facial features:

1. Load the Alien403.max scene file, and then zoom in on the eye area.
2. Select the inner circle of vertices of the eye, and then non-uniform scale them in the X- and Y-axis until the inner circle is almost the same size as the second ring of vertices that surrounds it. Then, select vertices from both rings and move them to position them over the eye in the background image. Work your way out to the third ring of vertices to shape the eye vertex rings as shown in Figure 4.9, example 1.
3. The eye has a central vertex. Select it and the pair of vertices above and below it (five in all), and then, in the left view, move them forward to pull out the shape of the eyelid. Then, move outward from the eye center and select the next two pairs of vertices on both sides of the centerline (eight vertices), and move them forward almost as far as the central vertices. This will round the upper and lower eyelids, as shown in Figure 4.9, example 2.
4. The eyebrow needs to be spread wider and moved down slightly. In the front view, select the inner corner of the eyebrow and move it toward the bridge of the nose. Select and move the other points of the eyebrow to make it fit the shape of the background image, as shown in Figure 4.9, example 3.
5. Select all of the eye vertices inside the circle shown in Figure 4.9, example 3. Then, in the left view, non-uniform scale the eye in the X-axis until it is almost flat, and move it forward to the position of the eye in the background image, as shown in Figure 4.9, example 4.
6. Sculpt the upper and lower eyelids to match the eye in Figure 4.9, example 5. Round the outer circle of vertices that form a ring around the eye opening.

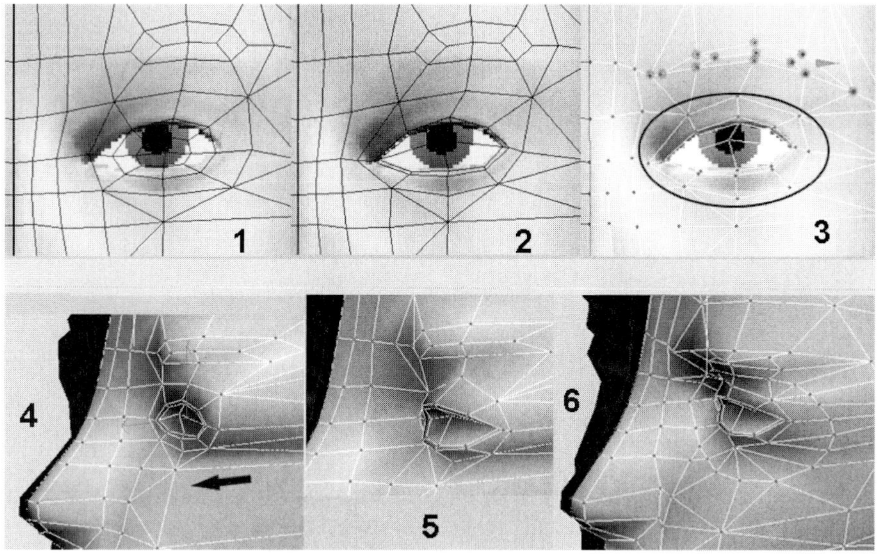

FIGURE 4.9 Shaping the eye and eyebrow.

7. To fully form the eye socket, a second ring of edges needs to be cut into the surface around the eye. Use the Cut tool to cut the polygons around the eye in the larger circle that surrounds the eye and creates the edge of the orbital eye opening in the skull, as shown in Figure 4.9, example 6.
8. Pull vertices on the cheek and above the eye to round both circles of vertices, and then move the vertices forward on the side view that form the side of the cheek and temple area. This area should be pulled outward and aligned with other rows of vertices to create smooth flowing lines in the rest of the face. This will aid in smoothing the final model.
9. Sculpt the area around the eye and eyebrow to smooth out the surface. Use soft curves for the upper eyelid area while making the lower eyelid more defined.
10. Create a white sphere with a radius of about 3.3 units. The diameter should be slightly larger than the eye opening in the background drawing. This will be the eyeball. Position it in the eye socket centered over the eye in the background image.
11. Sculpt the contours around the eye in shaded view with Shade and Highlight > Edged Faces turned on to make sure the eye does not protrude through the skin. Contour the upper and lower eyelids to follow the curvature of the eyeball, as shown in Figure 4.10.

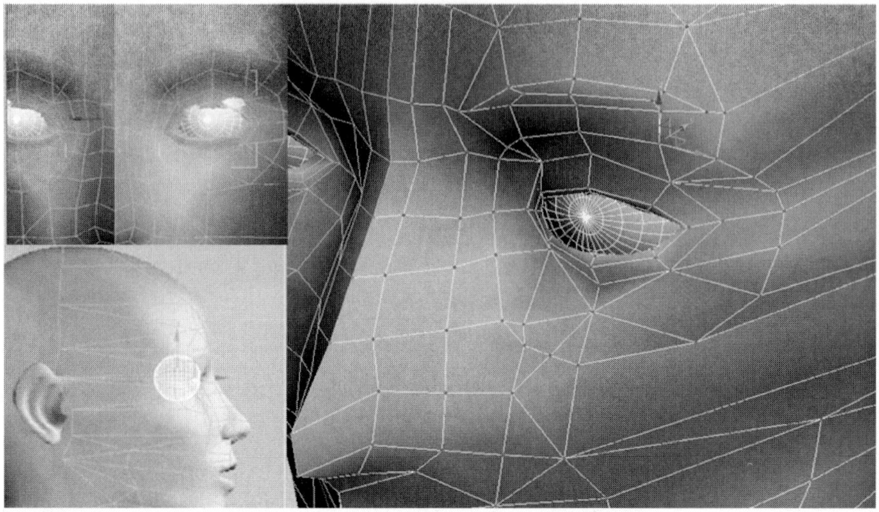

FIGURE 4.10 Adjust the eyelid contour to match the eyeball.

You will probably want to clone the eye and place the clone in the eye socket of the referenced side of the face. A tutorial on how to make a realistic eye can be found near the end of this chapter.

12. Inspect the surface of the face around the eye in the shaded view and smooth any unwanted protrusions or hollows, and then save the scene as Alien404.max.

In the next tutorial, you will refine the shape of the nose, and then sculpt the side of the nose to create the nostril protrusion.

TUTORIAL 4.5

Refining the Nose

To refine the nose:

1. Load the alien404.max scene. Be sure to load the Alien_Fac_Fnt.tif and Alien_Fac_Sid.tif background images in the front and left views, if they are not automatically loaded.
2. The first step is to cut across the nose polygons to increase the resolution of the nostril area. Zoom in on the nose in the front view.

3. Select the left half of the head (the model's left), then enter Edit Poly > Vertex mode, and then click the Edit Geometry > Cut tool button. Start in the middle of the bridge of the nose and cut down through the side of the nose.
4. To define the nostril, cut straight down from the tip of the nose to make an edge defining the inner side of the nostril. Continuing cutting down from the nostril to the upper lip to form the lip cleft, as shown in Figure 4.11, example 1.

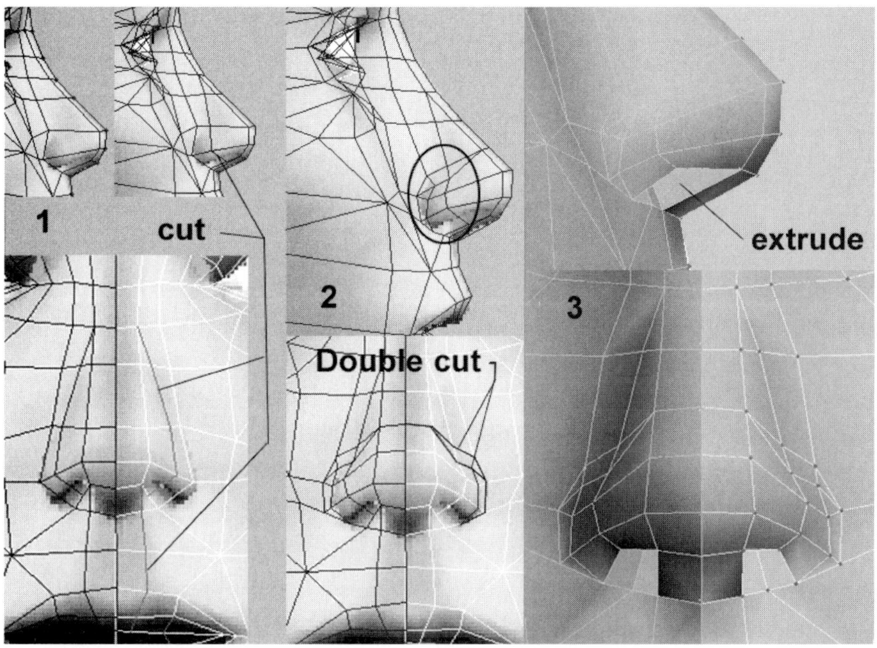

FIGURE 4.11 Refine the nostril and side of the nose.

5. Cut around the outside of the nostril protrusion on the side of the nose and bring the cuts up to the centerline at the bridge of the nose. Then, cut around the outer edge of the nose again, parallel to the first cut, to create a double line where the nose crease is, as shown in Figure 4.11, example 2.
6. Next, cut a nostril hole following the contour of the background image. Move the new vertices of the nose to insure that all lines of vertices flow smoothly and match the shape of the background image in both views.

7. To make the nostril hole, select the polygons and extrude inward, as shown in Figure 4.11, example 3.
8. Go into Polygon Sub-object mode and Unhide All polygons at the back of the head. Save the scene as Alien405.max.

In the next tutorial, you will create a pointed ear and attach it to the left side of the alien head. The design of the Alien Vampire character includes pointed ears, cat eyes, and hollow fangs. In the story, these features are hidden during the escape scene late in the film, letting her pass for human.

TUTORIAL 4.6

MODELING THE POINTED EAR

To create an ear:

1. Load the Alien 405.max file.
2. Load the Alien_Fac_Fnt.tif and Alien_Fac_Sid.tif background if they are not already loaded. Zoom in to the ear. Create a box on top of the ear with the following settings: Length = 11.0, Width = 7.0, Height = 2.0, Length Segments = 5, Width Segments = 6, and Height segments = 2.
3. In the front view, position the box beside the head so it is in front of the head mesh in the shaded left view. Turn on Shade and Highlight, then right-click the ear mesh, select Properties, and click See Through. To form it in the ear shape, click Modifiers > Parametric Deformers > Bend, then in parameters enter Bend Angle = –100, Bend Axis = Y. It should look like the box as shown in Figure 4.12, example 1.
4. Convert to editable Poly. To sculpt the shape, apply the FFD box (Lattice) Free Form Deformer. Click Modifiers > Free Form Deformers > FFD Box, and Set Number Of Points = 8x4x4. In the Modifier Stack, click the Plus and in the drop-down list select Control Points. Select the FFD control points and move them to sculpt the shape of the ear, as shown in Figure 4.12, example 3.
5. Move the box up against the head in the front view, and then sculpt the ear to roughly match the ear shown in the background views.
6. Right-click and Convert to Editable Poly again to delete the construction history and lock the ear polymesh into that shape. The ear should be next

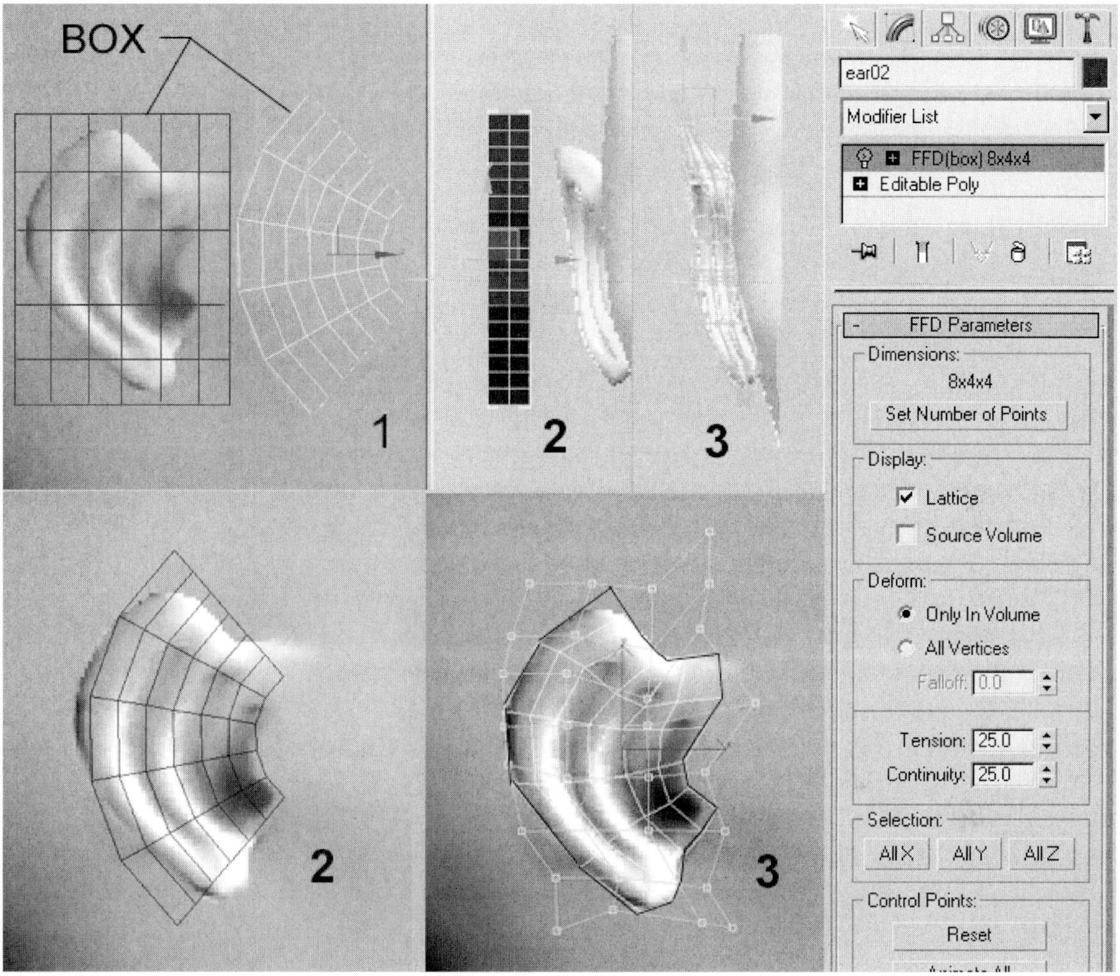

FIGURE 4.12 The Alien ear is sculpted from a box primitive using an FFD.

to the side of the head mesh. Rotate the ear in the Z-axis so that the front edge enters the head mesh, as shown in Figure 4.13, example 1.

7. In Modify > Vertex mode, select the outer edge of the ear vertices and pull them down and in toward the center of the ear a short distance to help round the edge of the ear, as shown in Figure 4.13, example 2. Round the vertices on the back edge of the ear as well.
8. In the left view, zoom in on the ear, and then move the vertices to match the outline of the darker grooves shown in the left view drawing of the ear, as shown in Figure 4.13, example 3.

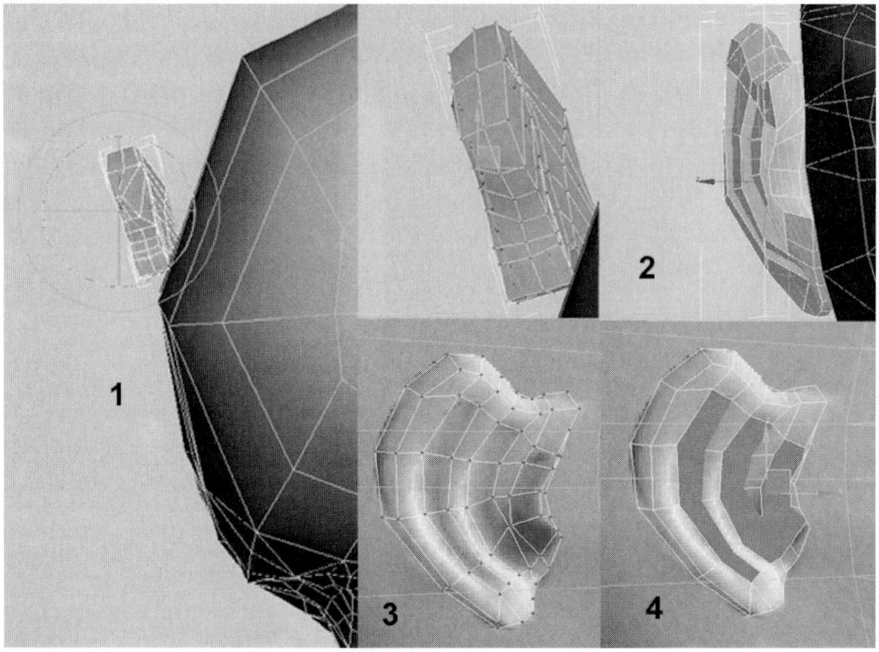

FIGURE 4.13 Round the ear edges and select polygons to extrude inward.

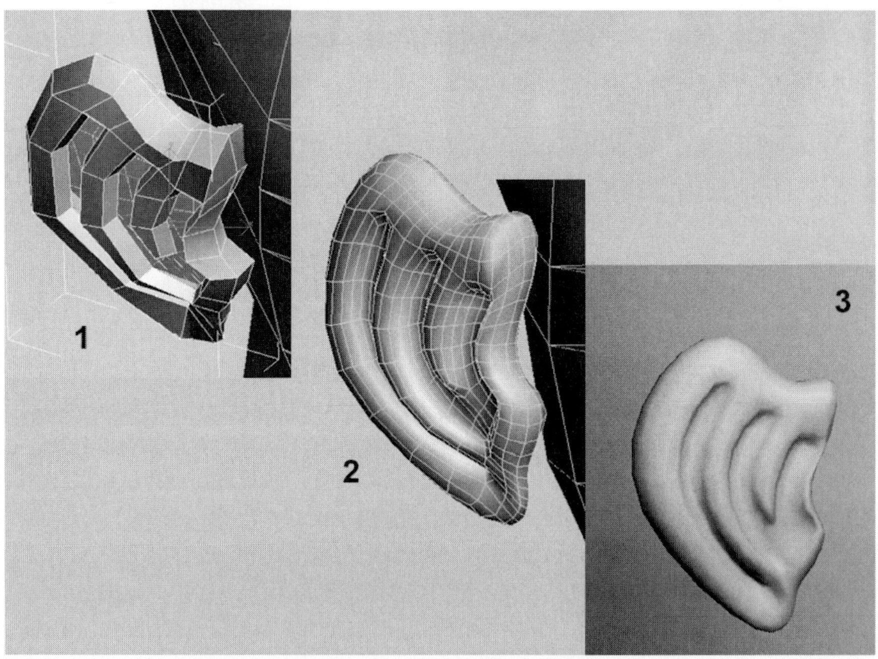

FIGURE 4.14 Bevel-extrude the ear grooves and apply MeshSmooth.

9. Go to Editable Poly > Polygon mode, select all the faces that are over the dark areas representing the grooves in the ear, and lock the selection, as shown in Figure 4.13, example 4.
10. Click the Edit Polygons > Bevel tool, and then extrude the Polys inward into the ear surface half the thickness of the ear and scale them slightly narrower to form v-shaped grooves in the ear surface as shown in Figure 4.14, examples 1 and 2. Apply MeshSmooth to see how the finished ear will look, as shown in Figure 4.14, example 3.
11. Save the scene as Alien406.max.

In the next tutorial, you will cut an ear hole in the side of the head and attach the ear.

The side of the ear that faces the head must now be opened up and polygons removed to create open edges. A corresponding hole must also be made in the head. This will allow the edges of the ear to be welded to the edges of the opening in the side of the head.

TUTORIAL 4.7 ATTACH THE EAR TO THE HEAD

To attach the ear to the head:

1. Load the Alien406.max scene file, if it isn't already loaded. Then, hide the head mesh and zoom in on the ear in the front view.
2. To prepare the ear for attachment, select the ear, and turn off MeshSmooth. Next, select and delete the polygons on the forward edge and the backside (facing the head) of the ear to make a roughly circular hole in the ear mesh while keeping all of the polygons that form the outside surface of the ear, as shown in Figure 4.15, example 1.
3. When finished you can use the Editable Poly > Border selection mode to select the open edge of the ear. Straighten and round out the border edge by moving vertices until it forms a semi-circular opening that will mate fairly nicely with the side of the head, as shown in Figure 4.15, example 2.
4. Hide the ear and then Unhide the head mesh. In the left view, select the entire centerline of the head and move it forward toward the front of the face, as shown in Figure 4.15, example 2. Use the Cut tool to create a vertical line that goes behind the ear up the side of the head. Further refine the

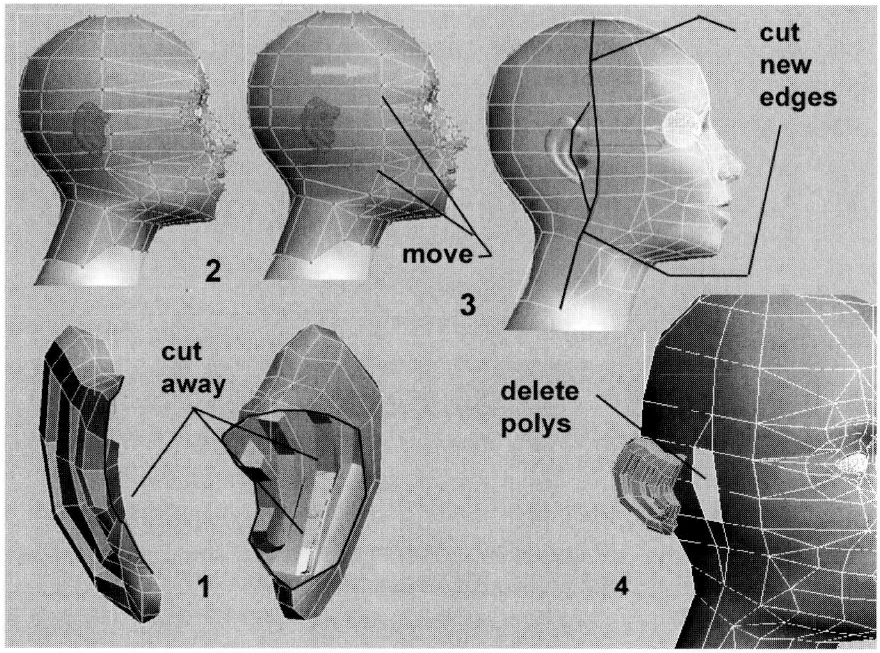

FIGURE 4.15 Prepare the ear to be welded into the head.

area with more cuts to create an ear opening, and then delete the polygons from the opening, as shown in Figure 4.15, examples 3 and 4.

5. Unhide the ear and make sure it is aligned in the left view with the background image. Move the ear in close to the head, but don't quite touch it. Use the Attach command to attach the ear to the head mesh, and then move vertices on the facing openings in the ear and the head to make a few vertices match, as shown in Figure 4.16, example 1. Use the Edit Geometry > Collapse tool to select those corresponding pairs of vertices, pull them together, and weld them.

There are about 20 vertices on the open edge of the ear that you will be trying to weld to 6 vertices on the head. There are two solutions: The first is to use the Cut tool to cut edges and thereby add vertices to the ear opening on the head. The Second solution is to use the Edit Geometry > Create Polygon tool. It will let you create a multisided polygons to bridge gaps like this.

6. To create a multisided polygon to fill the gap at the front or forward side of the ear, Click Edit Geometry > Create Polygon, and in the left view, click on

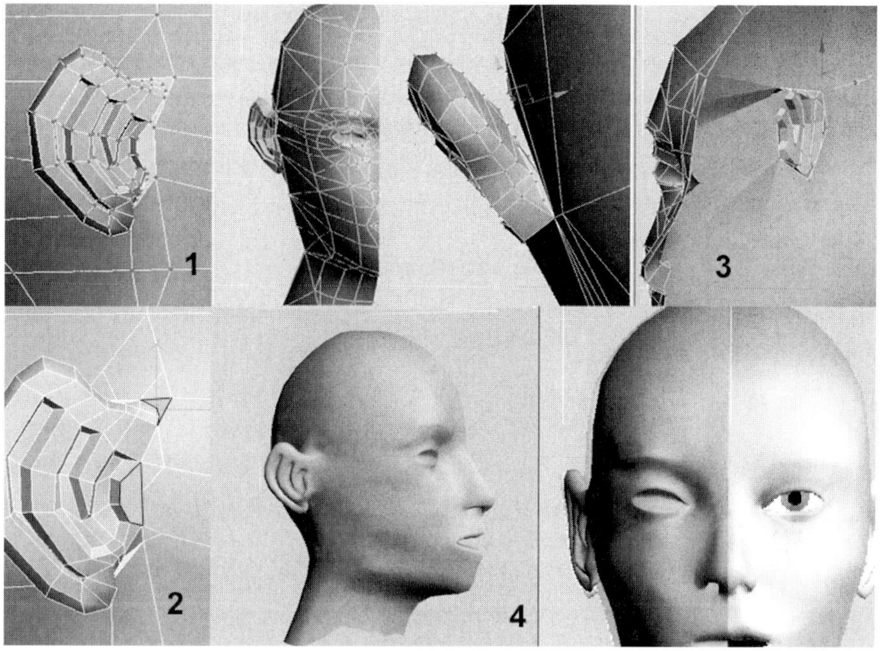

FIGURE 4.16 Collapse vertex pairs and create polygons to weld the ear on.

all the vertices around the front of the ear and the corresponding edge on the head. Then, double-click the last vertex to complete the polygon, as shown in Figure 4.16, example 2.

7. Work on the inside of the head to gain easy access to the ear vertices, as shown in Figure 4.16, example 3. Turn on Force 2-sided in the Viewport Preferences to help you see the surfaces correctly.
8. The ear will probably be positioned a little too far from the head when you are done attaching it. Select all vertices associated with the ear, and then move the ear closer into the side of the head.

ON THE CD

9. You will need to spend some time moving vertices around to attain the smoothest transition possible between the ear and the head. Apply MeshSmooth to see which areas around the ear need more smoothing work, as shown in Figure 4.16, example 4. You might need to do additional sculpting in the area around the eye if it has been distorted. If you had trouble, look at how the ear is attached in the sample Alien407.max file on the companion CD-ROM in the Chap04 folder.
10. Save your scene in your working directory as Alien407.max.

There is still a lot of work do to on the head, but it is a good time to get away from the head for a while and look at other areas of the model that need to be worked on. In the next tutorial, you will concentrate on building a hand with fingernails.

TUTORIAL 4.8

BUILDING THE ALIEN HAND

To build a hand:

1. Load the Alien407.max scene. Select the head mesh, enter the Modifier Stack, and Turn off MeshSmooth (click the Lightbulb). In Editable Poly > Sub-object > Polygon mode, go to the Edit Geometry menu and click Unhide All to unhide all of the body polygons. Change the left viewport to a top viewport.
2. In the top view, load the Alien_HandSize.tif image into the viewport background from the Chap04\Images folder on the companion CD-ROM. In the Aspect Ratio dialog area, be sure to turn on Match Bitmap, and Lock zoom/pan. Position the body mesh so that it matches the size of the body in the image. (Use Background Unlock Toggle – Ctrl > Alt > B.)
3. Ideally, the knuckles of the model's arm should lay on top of the knuckles of the hand in the background image, as shown in Figure 4.17, example 1. They probably don't because the arm was originally extruded straight. To make the model more realistic, the arm should be bent a few degrees at the elbow.
4. To bend the arm to match the background image, select the central elbow vertices, then turn on Soft Select and move the elbow area of the arm toward the back of the arm, and then move the wrist toward the front and position the palm of the hand and knuckles over the background image.
5. Select the knuckle vertices of the palm and scale them in the Y-axis to match the width of the palm at the knuckles in the background image, as shown in Figure 4.17, example 2.
6. To extrude four fingers out of the polygons at the end of the arm you must first subdivide the two existing polygons into four polygons, so that one finger can be extruded from each polygon. In the left view, select the polygons at the end of the arm and then Arc-rotate the mesh so that you can see the end of the arm at the knuckles.

ON THE CD

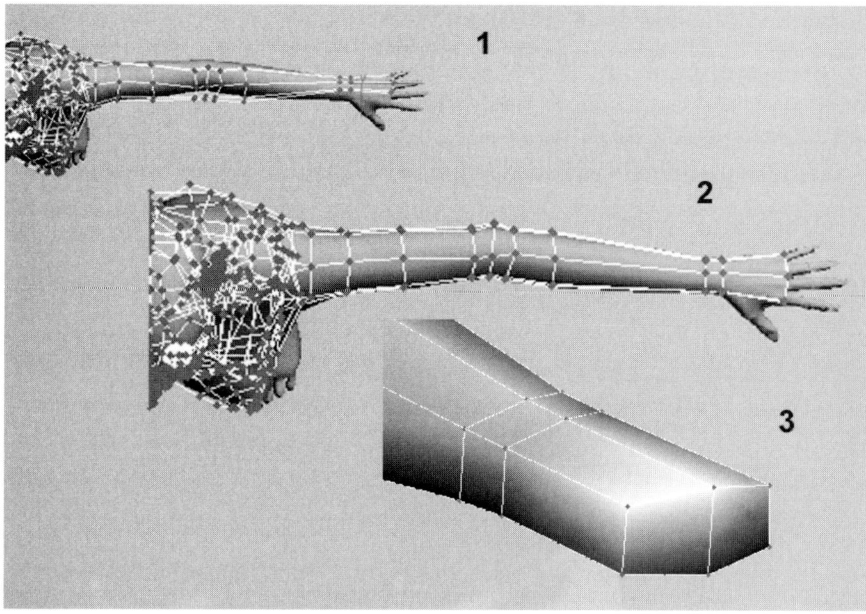

FIGURE 4.17 Preparing the model for building the hand.

7. Use the Editable Poly > Edit Geometry > Cut tool to add two more vertical divisions to the knuckle area, as shown in Figure 4.17, example 3. These will become the finger pads. Move vertices to make sure they are all rectangular and fairly equal in size.
8. Save the scene file as Alien408.max.

Continue on to the next tutorial to finish the fingers.

TUTORIAL 4.9

EXTRUDING THE FINGERS

To extrude the fingers:

1. Load the Alien408.max scene. In the front view, you should see the end of the arm at the knuckles. If not, Arc rotate the end of the arm at the knuckles so that you can clearly see the four polygons at the end of the arm.
2. The first step in modeling fingers is to extrude a separate finger pad for each of the four polygons at the knuckles. The angle of each of the four

polygons forming the knuckles should be curved slightly in the top view to make sure that the fingers will be spread out and not be parallel when they are extruded.

3. In Editable Poly > Polygon mode, select the polygon at the little finger position and then use the Bevel tool to extrude it out about .5 unit and scale it down about 15%. Repeat this procedure for each of the other three finger pads, as shown in Figure 4.18, example 1.
4. In the top view, you should still have the Hand_Size.tif background image loaded. Align the mesh to it and then Zoom in on the hand, as shown in Figure 4.18, example 4. The next step is to extrude all four fingers at once. A good technique is to extrude in a perspective view in the right side of the screen, and watch the size of the fingers in the top viewport on the left side of the screen. Select all four finger pads and lock the selection (spacebar).

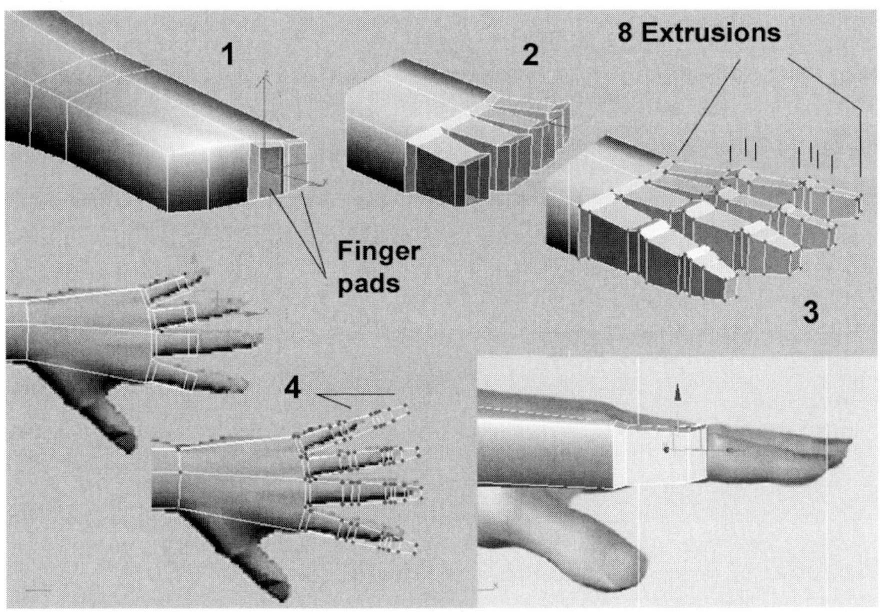

FIGURE 4.18 Extruding fingers and knuckles.

5. Click the Extrude tool and extrude the fingers out of the finger pads until they reach the first finger knuckles, as shown in Figure 4.18, example 2. Make sure that they are each pointed in the correct direction and are not parallel in the top view (see Figure 4.18, example 4).

6. To form the finger joint, extrude again a short distance in the front view, and then move the polygon finger ends upward a short distance to create the knuckle bulge on top and a v-shaped depression under the knuckle. Extrude again a short distance and then move the polygons downward to the original position in line with the upper finger bones, as shown in Figure 4.18, examples 2 and 3.
7. Extrude out again to the second finger bone knuckle and do two more short extrusions to create the knuckle, as shown in Figure 4.18, example 3. Extrude out once more as far as the top of the finger nail, and then scale down the polygons. Finally, extrude once more to the end of the finger and scale the end polygons down about 50% to form the fingertips.
8. All fingers are now the same size. Scale down the fingers relative to the middle finger to establish the correct sizes, using the top view background image as a guide, as shown in Figure 4.18, example 4.
9. Turn on MeshSmooth to see how the fingers look. Save the scene as Alien409.max.

Continue on to the next tutorial where you will create the thumb.

TUTORIAL 4.10 CREATING A THUMB

To create a thumb:

1. Continue from the previous tutorial or load file Alien409.max if necessary. To divide the palm of the hand you will use the new Quick Slice feature.
2. In the top view, select all the polygons of the hand (Ignore Backfacing should be off). Then, go to Editable Poly > Edit Geometry > menu in Sub-object polygon mode and click the Quick Slice button. Use the cursor to draw a line at right angles across the palm that divides it in half, as shown in Figure 4.19, example 1. Right-click to complete and turn off the command.
3. In the front view, use the Cut tool to cut a horizontal line across the side of the palm of the hand. This will become the edge that forms the web of skin connecting the thumb to the palm, as shown in Figure 4.19, example 2.
4. To extrude the thumb, select only the two large polygons of the side of the palm that are closest to the wrist. Use the Bevel tool to extrude out a pad for the thumb and scale it down by about 30%. Then, switch to the Rotate tool and rotate the polygons slightly so that they angle downward and

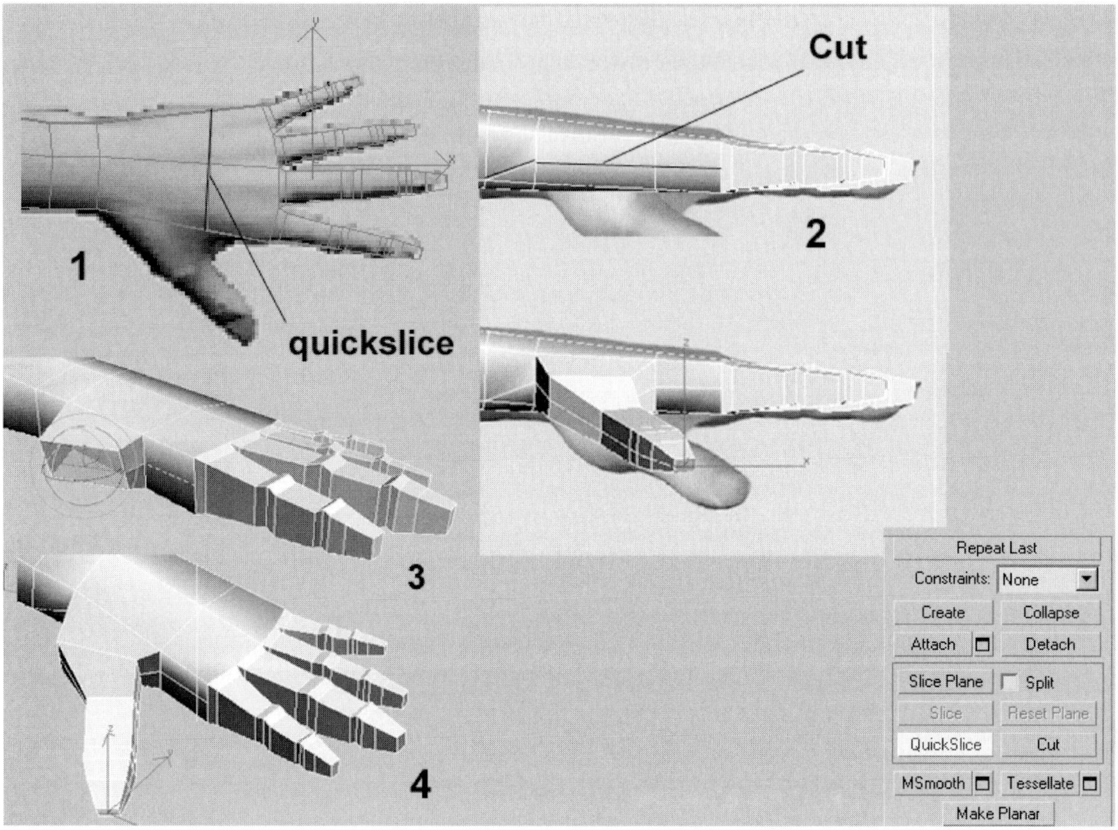

FIGURE 4.19 Extruding the thumb from the side of the palm.

forward so that they face the angle of the thumb, as shown in Figure 4.19, example 3.

5. Extrude the polygons at the end of the thumb stub a short distance to create the division for the thumb knuckle. Use Non-uniform scale to reshape the rectangular polygons into a square, and then move it downward and angle it to make sure it points in the direction of the thumb in the background image.
6. Next, extrude the first thumb bone, and its knuckle, followed by two more extrusions to form the top of the thumbnail and end of the thumb. Once you have the divisions, switch to Vertex mode and then sculpt the thumb into shape to match the background images of the hand, as shown in Figure 4.19, example 4.

7. The hand still needs additional sculpting before it is finished. The fingernails will be added in the next tutorial. Save the file as Alien 410.max.

In the next tutorial, you will finish the details of the hand. After the extrusion process, a fair amount of re-shaping and sculpting might be required to establish the correct proportions of the fingers and the hand.

TUTORIAL 4.11 SCULPT THE FINGERS AND ADD THE FINGERNAILS

To sculpt the hand and add the fingernails:

1. Load the Alien410.max scene.
2. Move vertices to sculpt the fingers and thumb to match the background image. Turn MeshSmooth on and off as you work using the Show End Result On/Off Toggle icon to see the effect of your changes.
3. Because the fingers are basically segmented rectangular boxes, they need to be cut along the top surface to increase the resolution of the mesh before making the fingernails. Cut along the top center of each finger starting with the end of the finger and cutting upward through the knuckle joint, as shown in Figure 4.20, example 1.

It always helps the Cut tool make cleaner cuts if you turn on 3D Snap, and then right-click and set Snaps to Vertex, Edge, Midpoint. Be sure to turn off Grid Points.

4. To start creating a fingernail, zoom in on the end of the middle finger in the top view. Then, select a vertex, and Arc Rotate Selected to tip the hand back so you can see the top as well as the tip end of the finger.
5. In Polygon mode, select the two polygons at the top of the fingertip, use the Bevel tool to extrude them down into the finger a short distance, and then scale them down about 15%, as shown in Figure 4.20, example 2. Then, scale the new fingernail longer by about 20% so that it protrudes a little out of the fingertip. Next, rotate it about 7 to 10 degrees so that the tip is higher than the upper end of the fingernail, as shown in Figure 4.20, example 3.
6. Move the fingernail upward so that the tip is above the edge below it, but not too much, and then select the central vertices of the fingernail and

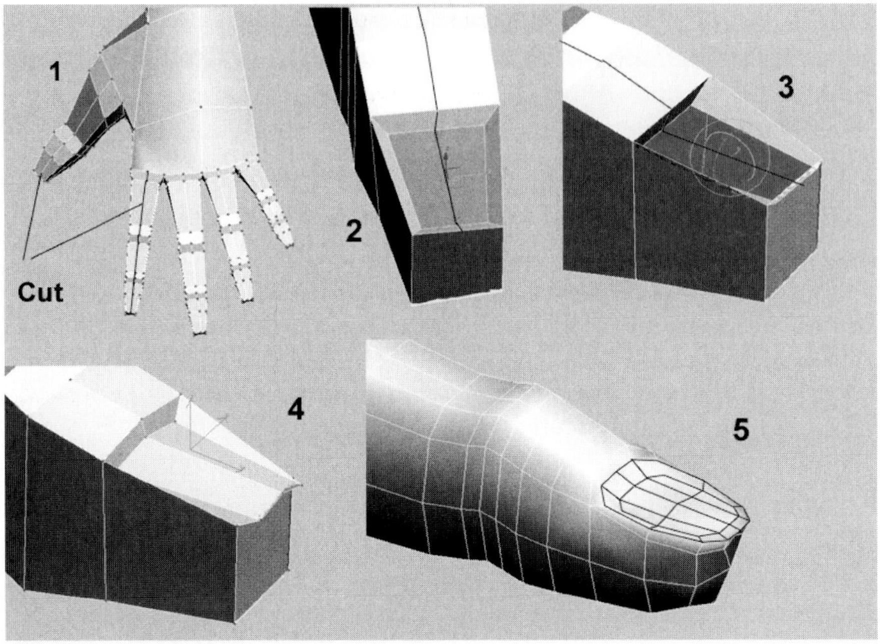

FIGURE 4.20 Cut the finger tops and extrude the fingernail.

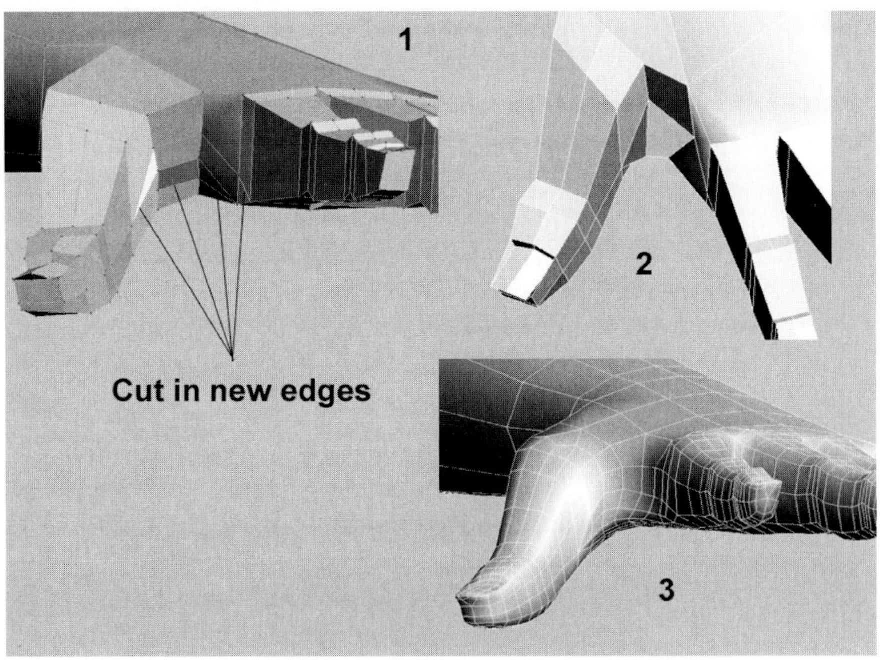

FIGURE 4.21 Cutting in new edges to create the web of skin at the thumb.

move them upward to arch the top of the fingernail, as shown in Figure 4.20, example 4.

7. Apply MeshSmooth to see how the fingernail looks. Then, continue and create fingernails on the other three fingers and the thumb.
8. To create the web of skin that goes between the thumb and the side of the hand, use the Cut tool to cut two lines across the faces parallel to the edges that connect the thumb and hand, as shown in Figure 4.21, examples 1 and 2.
9. Select the vertices of the original edges and pull them out to form the web of skin, as shown in Figure 4.21, example 2. Apply MeshSmooth to check for problems, and re-position vertices where necessary to get the results shown in example 3.
10. Cut additional lines across the knuckles and around fingernails to add creases and hollows to enhance realism.
11. Save the scene as Alien411.max.

In the next tutorial, you will finish the feet.

TUTORIAL 4.12 FINISH THE FEET AND LEGS

ON THE CD

1. Load the Alien411.max scene and change the Viewport Configuration to three views: a left, bottom, and front viewport. Select the model, run Zoom Extents Selected, and load new background images. In the left viewport background, load Alien_Fnt.tif; in the front viewport, load Alien_Sid.tif; and in the bottom view, load Alien_Foot.tif from the Chap04\Images folder on the companion CD-ROM.
2. In Polygon Sub-object mode, select all the polygons above the ankles, and in the Edit Geometry menu click Hide Selected. That should leave only the feet showing. Zoom in on the feet in all three views and position the mesh feet over the background images, as shown in Figure 4.22.
3. Move the vertices of the right foot to re-shape the foot outline to match the background image in the bottom view. Position the front end of the foot where the toes begin. To create the toes, you will cut the polygons at the end of the foot just as you did to create the finger pads in the previous tutorials.
4. In the front view, zoom in on the end of the foot. Make sure Ignore Backfacing is turned on. Move the centerline vertices toward the big toe to create

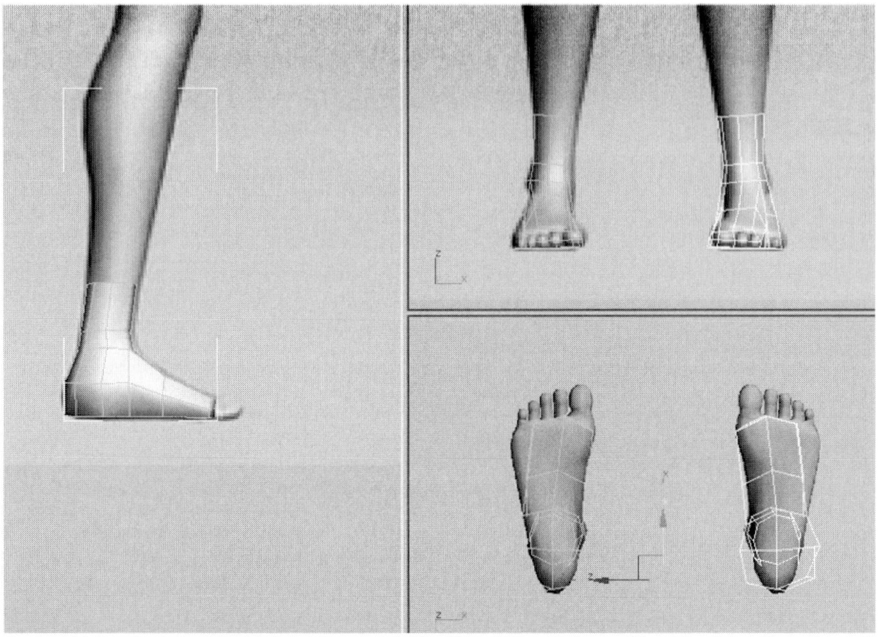

FIGURE 4.22 Model feet in position over the background images.

one large polygon for the big toe pad. Then, use the Cut tool to cut the remaining large polygon of the end of the foot three times to create polygons that will become the toe pads, as shown in Figure 4.23, example 2.

5. Change to Polygon mode, and with the Bevel tool extrude a small pad and scale it down 15% from the front of each of the five toe polygons at the front of the foot, as shown in Figure 4.23, example 3. Then, select the four small toe pads and extrude them out a short distance to make the toe bones. They should be quite short because the toe bones are very short.
6. Continue to Bevel-Extrude and scale the toe polygons until the four small toes are formed. They should be larger at the end joint than the thickness of the toe bones. Extrude the big toe and make the toe joint quite thick, as shown in Figure 4.23, example 5. Finally, create a toenail in the big toe in the same way you created fingernails for the fingers in Tutorial 4.11.
7. Turn on MeshSmooth to see how the toes look, as shown in Figure 4.23, example 6.
8. In Polygon mode, unhide all of the body mesh polygons. Save the scene file as Alien412.max.

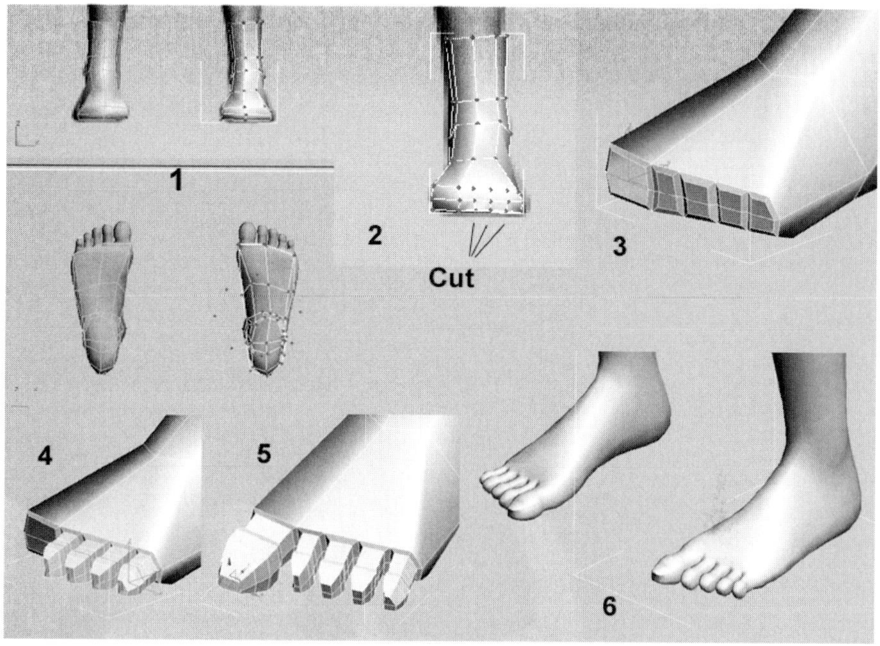

FIGURE 4.23 Extruding the toes from the end of the foot.

In the next tutorial, you will finish sculpting the model.

FINISHING XZULIXIA, THE ALIEN VAMPIRE CHARACTER

The construction of the model is nearly finished. Next comes the process of finishing the features, adding details such as additional musculature, lines and creases in the face and body, eyelashes, teeth, eyeballs, and tongue. In the next tutorial, you will adjust and fine-tune all the body parts.

TUTORIAL 4.13

FINISH THE HEAD AND BODY

To finish the head and body:

1. Load the Alien412.max file. In Customize > Viewport Configuration, click the Layout tab and choose two vertical viewports. Set one to Front and the

other to Left. In the viewport backgrounds, load Alien_Fac_Fnt.tif in the front viewport, and Alien_Fac_Side.tif in the left viewport. Be sure to set Aspect Ratio to Match Bitmap, and turn on Lock zoom/pan.

2. The head needs to be finished as much as possible before the two halves of the model are welded together. Position the model so that both views of the head fit their respective background images. Use the Background Lock-toggle tool and Ctrl > Alt > B, with Zoom and Pan.
3. Select the polygons of the back of the head in the left view and Hide Selected polygons. Zoom in close to the face in the front view. To correct the chin contour, select chin vertices beside the mouth and pull them wider. You will need to arc rotate the head quite often to make sure you are seeing the contours correctly, as shown in Figure 4.24, example 1.

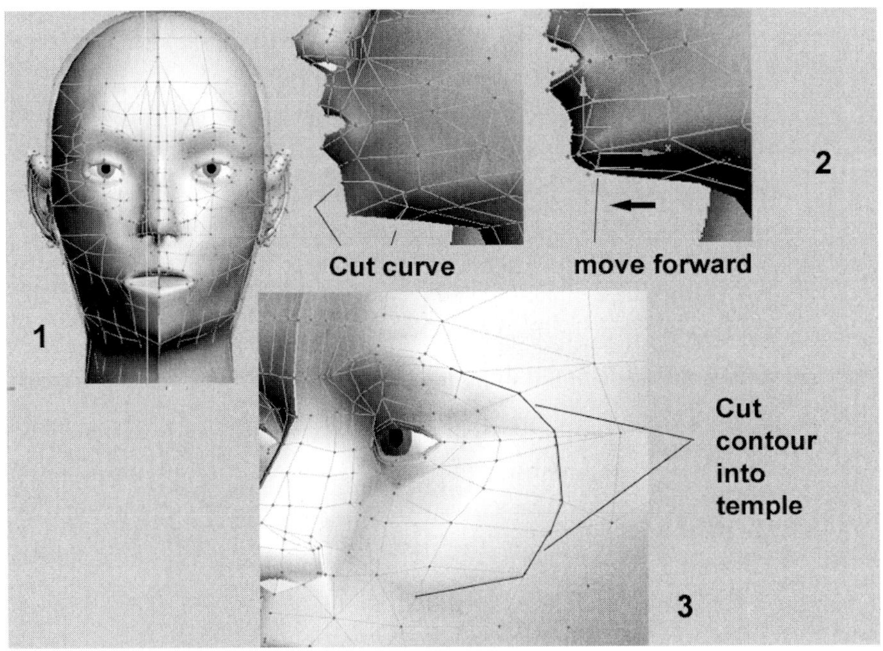

FIGURE 4.24 Adding cuts to help smooth contours of the face.

4. Cut a curve that defines a rounded chin into the model. This will help round the contours and preserve the shape when you apply MeshSmooth. Move the vertices of the new edges to round the tip of the chin, as shown in Figure 4.24, example 2. You might need to switch the left view to a right

view. To do so, press the V key, and then press R for a right view. The V hotkey for views is new in 3ds max 6.

5. The temple and cheek areas also need new curves cut into the surface to aid in smoothing the facial contours, as shown in Figure 4.24, example 3. Start at the outer corner of the eyebrow and cut a curve that flows downward smoothly through the temple and the cheek, and then curves across toward the corner of the nose. Adjust these vertices to improve facial contours.
6. Work on the corner of the mouth to make it V shaped and thin. Then, move the other mouth vertices to make the lips full and rounded. Cut a second line around the lips to make a crease at the edge of the lip, as shown in Figure 4.25, example 1. Cut another vertical line near the center of the lower lip down to the chin to help contour the lip.

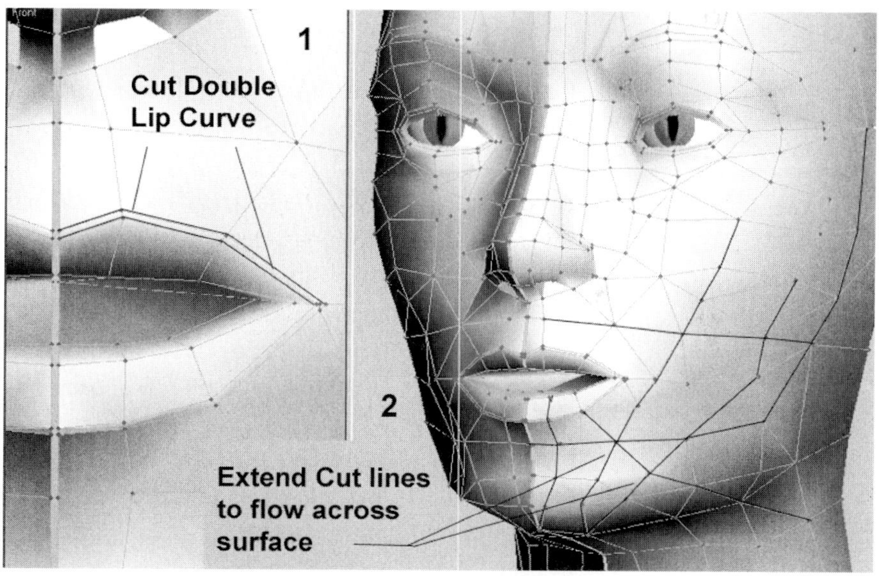

FIGURE 4.25 Cut additional edges to finish sculpting the face.

7. Use the Cut tool to extend all facial contour lines to make continuous flowing curves out of them, such as lines from the eye down to the lip and the chin line, as shown in Figure 4.25, example 2.
8. Adding resolution to these areas allows you to have enough points and contour lines to remove any unwanted folds, creases, hollows, or bumps from the surface. This is essential when you want to create a beautiful face.

9. Work on the rest of the body, adding new cut lines wherever you find it difficult to get smooth surfaces. Turn MeshSmooth on and off after each modification to see what else is needed. In Polygon mode, Unhide All polygons.
10. Finish the final contours of the body and head, and then save the scene as Alien413.max.

In the next tutorial, you will create a final mirror copy of the left half of the body and weld the two halves together.

TUTORIAL 4.14

Mirror Clone and Weld the Body

To mirror clone the body:

1. Load the Alien413.max file.
2. If you are satisfied with the level of detail you have attained in the body and face, you are ready to weld the two halves of the body together. Delete the Reference half of the body (on your left in the front view). Select the original half of the model and click the Mirror Selected Objects icon in the front view with Clone Selection set to Copy. Do not select Reference (a reference cannot be welded to an original mesh).
3. In Editable Poly, click the Attach button and click the other side to attach the two halves. They should be positioned so that the opposite centerlines match perfectly and are directly on top of each other.
4. Inspect the centerline edges. If they are not straight, or if the vertices are not together, you will have some difficulty welding them. You can use the Uniform Scale tool or the Edit Geometry > Collapse tool to pull pairs of vertices together to make the edges meet correctly, as shown in Figure 4.26, example 1.
5. To weld the two halves, turn off Ignore Backfacing, and then select all of the centerline vertices of both sides. Set the Weld threshold to .14 and click Apply. In shaded view, you will see the edge shift slightly and become smoother, as seen in Figure 4.26, example 2.
6. Inspect the seam area and smooth out any unwanted bumps or hollows in the model surface. If there are problems, you can apply a two-sided material to the mesh and put a free camera inside the mesh. Then, by looking at the inside of the mesh you can detect extra polygons, jumbled vertices, and holes. The back of the head will also need to be rounded more.

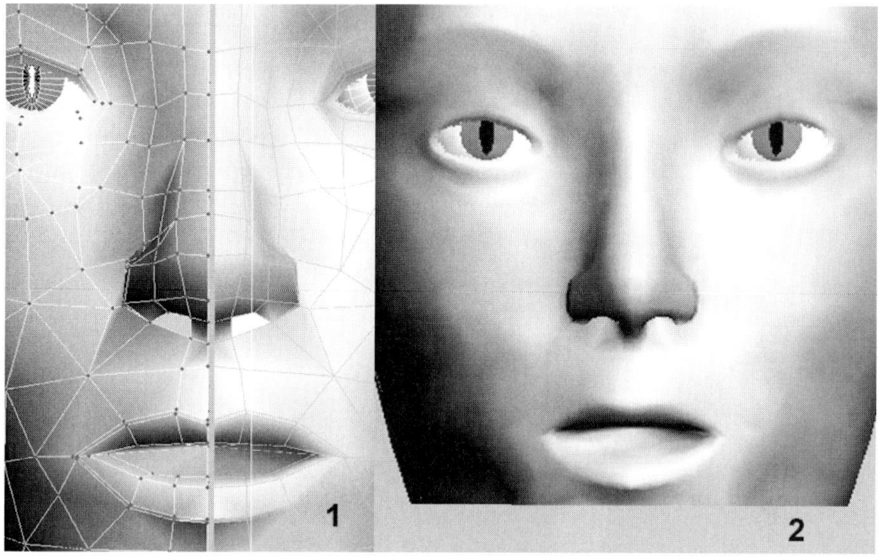

FIGURE 4.26 Welding the two body halves together.

ON THE CD

7. You will notice many distortions and problems in the mesh, and you will need to do additional sculpting to turn the model into a beautiful woman. To compare the author's finished version with your model, merge in the Body mesh from the scene file Alien 414.max in the Chap04 folder on the companion CD-ROM. Place that model inside your model and see how they differ. Modify your model to attain a more pleasing appearance. When finished, the Alien is ready for clothing.
8. To build detail items such as teeth, eyes, and eyelashes, refer to Chapter 6, "Finishing the Dr. Quin/Generic Man Patch Model." Save the scene file as Alien414.max.

In the next tutorial, you will create a simple form-fitting bodysuit using the Push Modifier.

Clothing can be made as external models that are fitted to the character, or by cloning the body mesh, which is then sculpted and modified to generate a piece of clothing. The next tutorial uses the second method. The resulting bodysuit can then be trimmed, sculpted, and extruded into many different articles of clothing.

TUTORIAL 4.15 CREATE A BODYSUIT FOR THE ALIEN USING PUSH

To create a bodysuit:

1. Load the Alien414.max file, and then in the front and left viewports, turn off Show Background. Before continuing, select the entire mesh and clone it using Edit > Clone. In the clone dialog, select Copy and click OK. Name the original mesh Body1 and name the cloned mesh Body2. Hide Body1. Use Body2 to make the clothing.
2. Select the model and open Editable Poly. In Polygon Sub-object mode, select all of the polygons of the head, arms, hands, and feet and delete them, as shown in Figure 4.27, example 1.

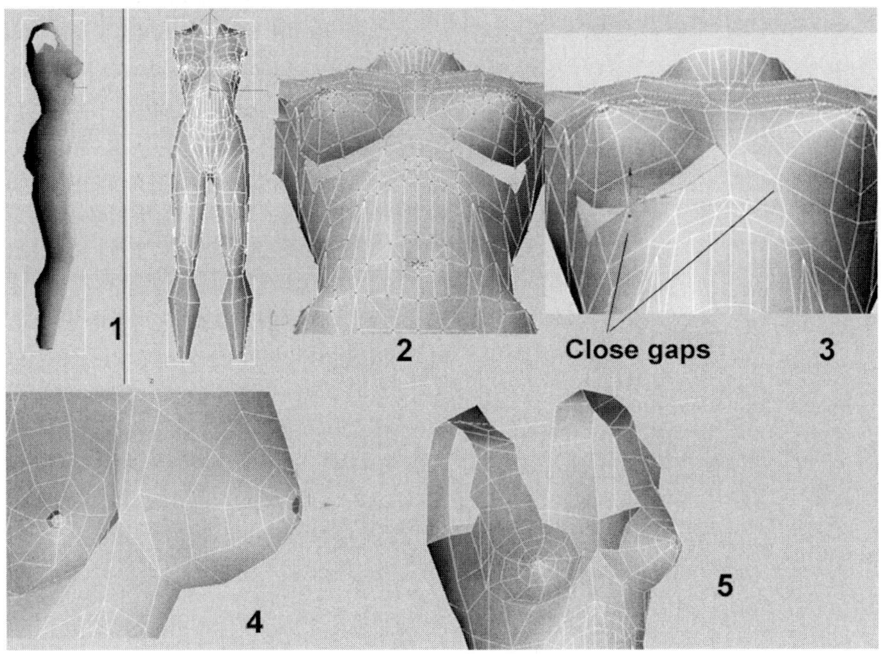

FIGURE 4.27 Creating clothing from the body mesh.

3. Apply the Push Modifier to the body to expand the surface along the direction of the surface normals. Caution: Do not use the Scale tools. That will distort the mesh and it will no longer fit the original model. To expand the mesh with Push, click Modifiers > Parametric Deformers > Push, and then in the Modify tab menu, set the Push Value to 1.35. This makes

the bodysuit slightly larger than the original skin, as shown in Figure 4.27, example 1.

4. To make the bodysuit you must trim the edges and remove as many of the body creases as you can. Smoothing the seams and creases of the cloned skin will make it look like a cloth bodysuit.

The best way to smooth out creases or folds in the skin is to delete the vertices in the skin crease, and then use the Editable Poly Vertex Collapse tool to draw together the edges across the gap and weld the vertices.

5. To remove the creases and smooth the mesh under the breasts, start by selecting and deleting the row or curve of vertices that are at the bottom of the creases under the breasts. If there are no vertices close to the bottom of the breasts, cut a line across under the breasts. Then, delete the vertices in the breast creases. This should result in having open areas with no polygons below the breasts, as shown in Figure 4.27, example 2.
6. To close the gaps, select the appropriate pairs of vertices across the gap from each other, and then click Editable Poly > Edit Geometry > Collapse. This will bring the vertices together and weld them. Close all the gaps under the breasts this way, as shown in Figure 4.27, example 3. Some gaps you will not want to collapse. Fill those areas by creating polygons.
7. Once the gaps are closed, use the Arc Rotate tool to roll the model around so you can look at the side of the gap area. Select vertices and move them around to smooth out the new seam. Remove the nipples from the breasts and fill the holes with new polygons, as shown in Figure 4.27, example 4. (Note: You will also need to remove the nipples from the body to keep them from protruding through the bodysuit.)
8. To remove the deep creases and smooth out the entire pelvic region and buttocks crease, repeat the same process by deleting the vertices inside creases and collapsing them to weld them shut.
9. To form the edges of the garment, delete extra polygons at the shoulders and neck, and then smooth the edges to simulate the lines of the pants cuffs, neckline, and arm cutout on the side, as shown in Figure 4.27, example 5. When finished, apply a two-sided blue material to the bodysuit mesh, and then unhide Body1.
10. The finished bodysuit fits over the original mesh, as shown in Figure 4.28. Save the scene as Alien415.max.

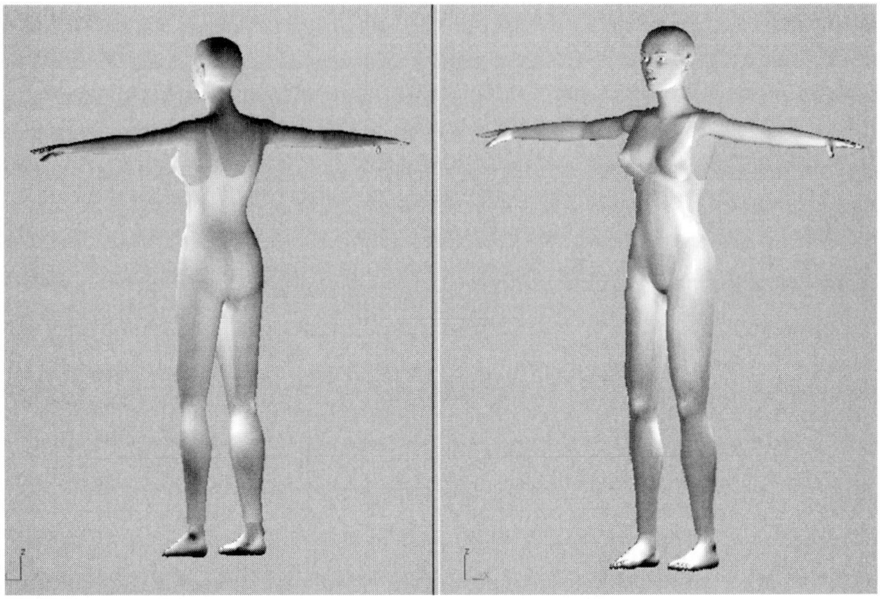

FIGURE 4.28 The finished bodysuit on the original body mesh.

To make it easier to animate the character and to eliminate the need for a cloth plug-in, all of the original body mesh that is covered under the clothing should be deleted. This will prevent the skin from penetrating the clothing when the body moves. Both the skin and the bodysuit will be bound to the skeleton so that they will move together. Make a duplicate of the model with different clothing shapes that will show different areas of the skin.

In the *Homing Instinct* film project, there are five different versions of this model, each with different clothing. One wears a powered armor suit that can fly. Three of them are set up with separate heads so that facial expression and lip-sync animation can be done with Morph Targets. The fourth version is a low-resolution model used in action sequences and distant shots with two different costumes. The fifth model is an unclothed model used for the scene where the Alien is rescued from her life support capsule.

The model is now ready to attach to a skeleton. The process of binding the Xzulixia skin to a skeleton is covered in Chapter 9, "Character Animation."

CREATING REALISTIC EYES

The quotation "the eyes are the windows to the soul" indicates how important eyes are to a character model. In the next tutorial, you will explore the creation of realistic eyes with depth, a transparent cornea, and liquid along the bottom eyelid. This tutorial explains how to make alien (cat) eyes for Xzulixia, and human eyes for the Dr. Quin character. The two different types of eyes used for the characters in *Homing Instinct* have the same basic structure, but each has a different shaped pupil. The alien pupil is an animatable vertical slit, whereas the human pupil is a scaleable round hole. For extreme close-up shots, the size of the pupil can be controlled by a slider or a custom attribute.

The eye is made in two layers. The outer layer is built by creating a spline cross-section and then revolving it with the Lathe Modifier. This generates the eye surface with a protrusion to form the cornea, and will be nearly transparent. The inner layer of the eye is a modified sphere that includes the pupil and the iris. A long reflective meniscus object that lies along the line formed where the surface of the eyeball meets the lower eyelid is added and raytraced to make the eye look wet. Eyelashes are made by cloning thin three-sided cones along a spline. They are attached to the mesh skin of the eyelids using the Sub-object Polygon Attach tool so that they will follow the eyelids closing and opening when using facial morph targets. The quality of the texture map for the iris must be very good to stand up to an extreme close-up shot, and looks best when taken from photographs of real eyes.

In the next tutorial, you will create a realistic two-layer eyeball. You will use the Layer Manager to organize the different layers and parts of the eye.

TUTORIAL 4.16 CREATING REALISTIC HUMAN AND ALIEN EYES

To create an eye:

ON THE CD

1. Load the RealEye_Start.max file from the Chap04 folder on the companion CD-ROM. The file contains the head of Xzulixia and two simple sphere eyes that were used during the creation of the Xzulixia model. Select one of the eyes, click Hide Unselected, and then click Zoom Extents All (press the Z key).

2. In the Front view, right on top of the existing eye, create a new sphere that has the same radius of 2.65 generic units. In the Sphere parameters, set Segments to 28. That makes one of the new sphere's segment rings the same size as the diameter of the iris in the modeling eye.
3. Place the sphere in a new layer by right-clicking the main toolbar and selecting Layers from the pop-up menu. In the Layer Manager dialog, click the Create New Layer icon, name the layer Inner Eye, and then click OK to include the sphere in the new layer, as shown in Figure 4.29, example 1.

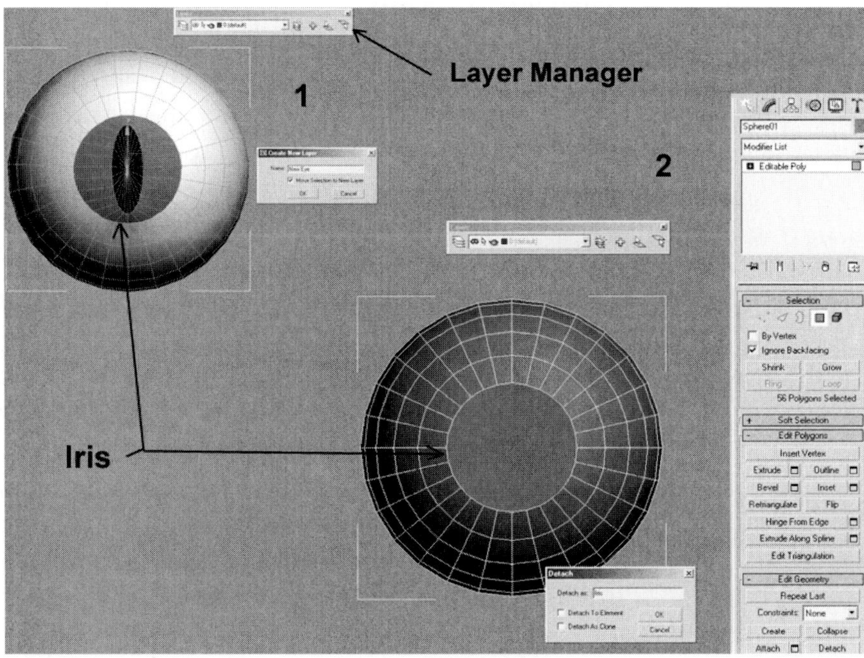

FIGURE 4.29 Creating the inner eye and placing it in a new layer.

4. In the Layer Manager, hide the original eye by clicking the small eye icon of layer 0 Default. Select the new sphere and convert to Editable Poly. Turn on Ignore Backfacing, and then click Sub-object > Polygon. Use the Circular Selection Region tool to select the two inner rings of polygons that will become the pupil and iris. Then, in the Edit Geometry drop-down menu of Editable Poly, click Detach as Object and name the new object Iris, as shown in Figure 4.29, example 2.

5. Select the new Iris object and in the Layer Manager, click Create New Layer. Name this layer Iris and click OK. You now should have three layers: 0Default, 1Inner Eye, and 2Iris.
6. In the left view, use the Mirror tool in the main toolbar to reverse the direction of the iris so that it goes in instead of out, and then reposition it so that its outer edge matches the hole in the inner sphere. It will now be transparent from the front view. Select the polygons, and then use the Edit Geometry Flip button to flip the normals so that the iris is visible from outside the eye. The next step is to create the outer eye. Switch to the top view and maximize it.
7. In the top view, draw a spline using Create > Shapes > Line and then select Creation Type: Smooth. Next, click a number of points around the eye to add extra points to form an enlarged "bump" where the cornea protrudes over the iris, as shown in Figure 4.30, example 1. The center of the eye sphere and the center point of the outer spline at the cornea should coincide, as shown in Figure 4.30, example 2.
8. Turn off Vertex Sub-object mode, click the Modifier button, and use the Patch/Spline Edit > Lathe tool to revolve the spline. By default, the center

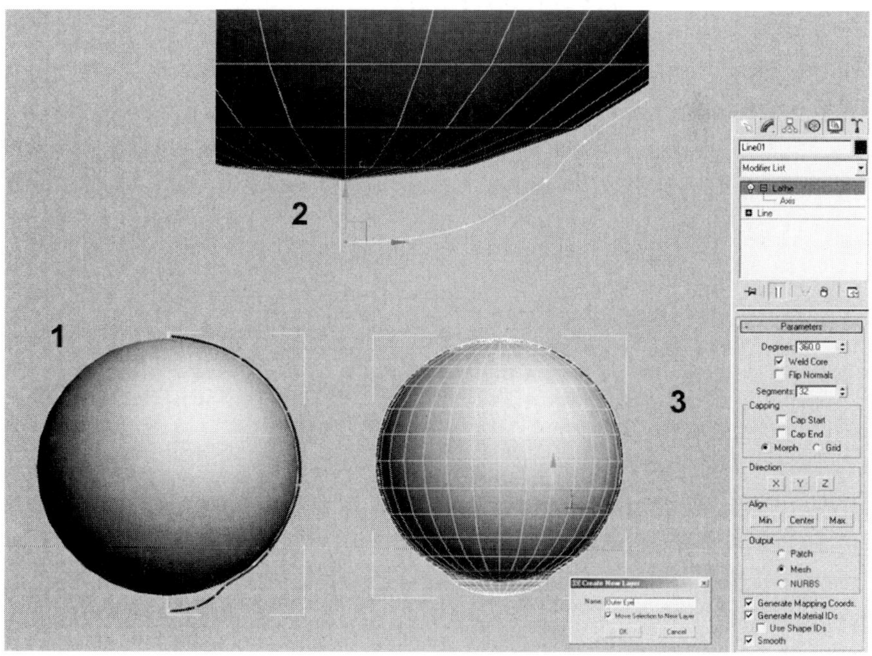

FIGURE 4.30 Creating the outer layer of the eye with the cornea.

will not be placed correctly. Go to the Modifier tab, select Lathe Tool Parameters, and click the Align > Min button. That should correctly form the outer eye, as shown in Figure 4.30, example 3.

9. Next, click the Weld Core button and turn lathe segments up to 32. Select Output > Mesh and turn on Generate Mapping Coordinates. Then, in the Layer Manager, click Create New Layer and name the layer Outer Eye.
10. Switch to four viewports and click Zoom Extents. Now move the center pivot of the outer eye using the Hierarchy tab > Pivot > Affect Pivot Only tool to center it over the eye's center point. In all views, move the new outer eye so that it is perfectly centered over the inner eye. Group the layers of the eye and name the group Eye Group.
11. That finishes the first stage of the eye's construction. Save the file as Eye416.max. and continue on to the next tutorial.

In the next tutorial, you will create the the meniscus object to make the eye look wet.

TUTORIAL 4.17 CREATING THE MENISCUS TO MAKE THE EYE LOOK WET

To create the meniscus:

1. Load the Eye416. Max scene if it is not already loaded. Unhide by name all objects in the scene except the XzuHead mesh. You should now see the new layered eye group and the two original eyes.
2. Select the Eye Group and position it over the original right eye. Then, delete the original right eye. Unhide the XzuHead mesh and position the new eye in the eye socket to your satisfaction. You are now ready to create the meniscus object for the lower right eyelid. In the front view, zoom in on the lower right eyelid, and use the Perspective view to see a tilted top view of the eyelid, as shown in Figure 4.31, example 1.
3. The meniscus object is created by snapping two NURBS curves on the eyelid and then using a two-rail sweep to generate the geometry. In the main toolbar, click the 3D Snap icon and right-click to view the Grid and Snap settings. Turn off Grid Points, and then turn on Vertex, Edge, Face, and Center Face. Close the dialog and then click Shapes > NURBS Curves > Point Curve.

4. In the perspective view, snap a point curve along the surface of the lower eyelid just in front of he eyeball, as shown in Figure 4.31, example 2. In the front view, snap a similar point curve, using the same number of points, along the surface of the eyeball just above the lower eyelid. Be sure to create both curves in the same direction or the surface will be twisted. Then, click the Modify tab and enter NURBS Curve > Point Edit mode and adjust the position of all the curve points to smooth the curves and make them parallel.

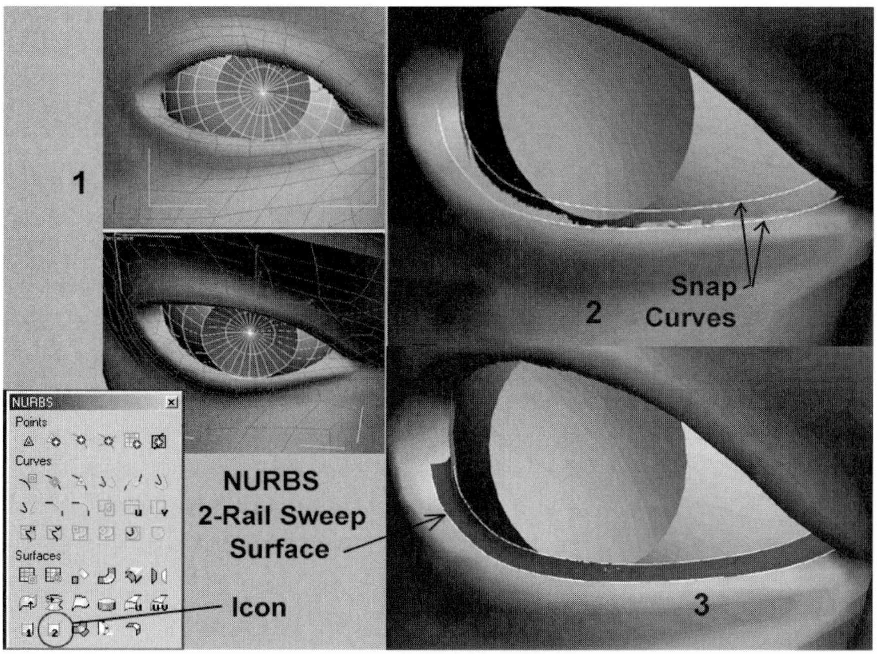

FIGURE 4.31 Creating the NURBS surface for the wet eye meniscus.

5. Exit the modifier and select the eyeball curve. Next, you will need to create one short cross-section curve to join the ends of the previous curves. It should be concave to form the characteristic meniscus surface as seen on the edge of water touching a glass. Snap a curve between the outer ends of the two curves. In the NURBS curve modifier, click Point > Refine, and add a point in the center of the curve. Then, pull it downward and inward slightly to make it concave, as shown in Figure 4.31, example 3.

6. In the NURBS modifier, make sure all of the curves are attached. Then, to generate the surface, select the Create 2-Rail Sweep icon in the NURBS floating menu. Click the lower eyelid curve, then the eyeball curve, and finally the short cross-section curve at the end. That will generate a NURBS surface, as shown in Figure 4.31, example 3. Flip the surface normals if the surface is transparent.
7. This finishes the basic construction of the realistic eye meniscus. However, the eye is far from being finished. Leave all the parts of the eye in separate layers for now.
8. Save the scene as Eye417.max.

Because animated controls and facial morphing to close an eyelid have not yet been covered, Chapter 9, "Character Animation," describes how to create an animated iris opening of the correct shape for each character, and how to create the eyelashes.

CONCLUSION

In this chapter, you completed the creation of an organic model of the Xzulixia character using Editable Polygons and the MeshSmooth Subdivision Surface Modifier. You worked with these tools to create the details of a human face. Then, you were introduced to a simple method of creating garments for the Xzulixia character In the next chapter, you will create a Generic Man using the Spline Patch modeling method.

CHAPTER

5

CONSTRUCTING THE GENERIC MAN CHARACTER

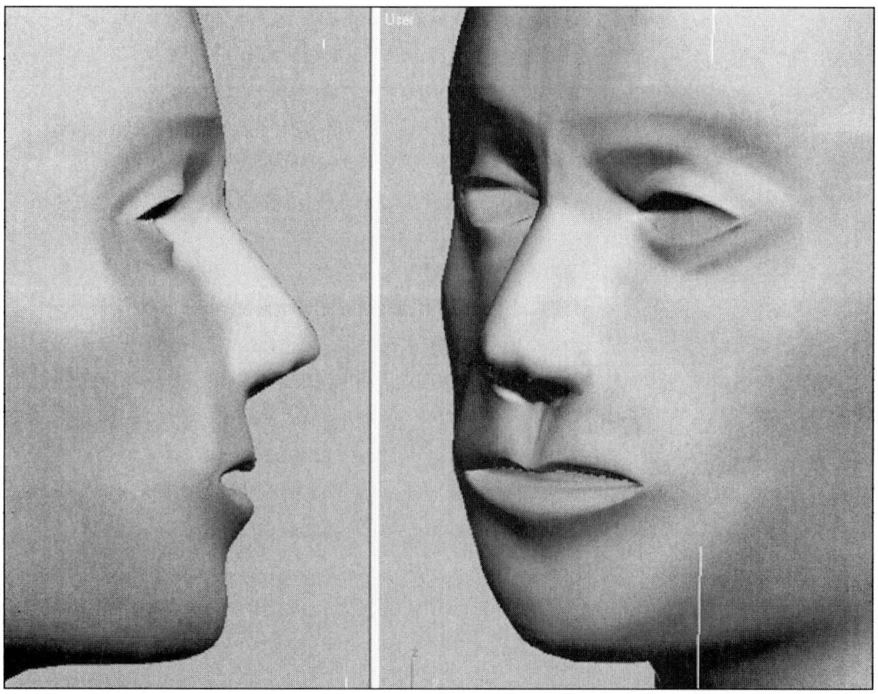

A number of male and female characters were needed for the *Homing Instinct* film project. The most important one was the Generic Man, from which all of the other male characters in the film were made. In this chapter, we explain the process of creating a generic man using the spline patch modeling method. This series of tutorials starts with the basics, so advanced users might want skip this chapter if they already know organic spline patch modeling.

BÉZIER SPLINE PATCH MODELING

A Bézier Spline Patch model is created by building a wireframe cage of splines and then applying the Surface Modifier to create a Patch surface over it, as shown in Figure 5.1.

There are many advantages to this type of model versus a conventional triangle mesh model. Features unique to patch models are variable resolution; a minimum number of vertices to create complex surfaces;

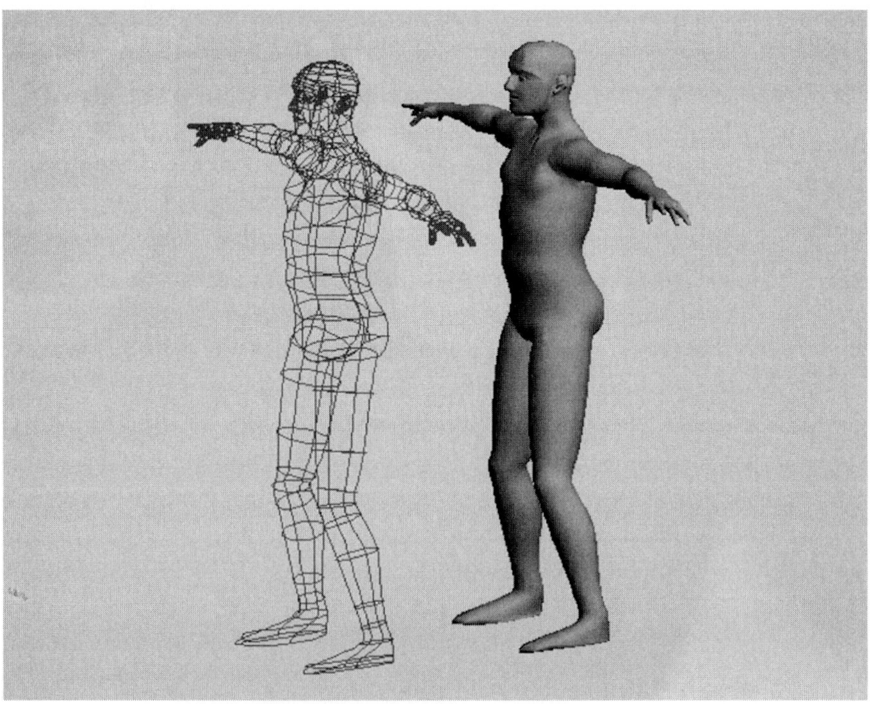

FIGURE 5.1 Spline Patch model of Generic Man.

surface smoothness is maintained all over the model even when distorted; patches are optimized for animation in 3ds max; and complex shapes can be built more quickly and with less work than triangle mesh modeling.

The Spline Patch modeling workflow consists of building up tubular torso, arms, and legs, and then connecting them smoothly together to form the character's body. Then the head is constructed as a separate spline cage and attached to the body. Finally, the entire model is skinned with the Surface Modifier.

ON THE CD

The first task in building a character is to draw front and side views of the character that can be scanned into the computer and placed in the viewport backgrounds. The companion CD-ROM contains images that have already been drawn for you. You will load them into 3ds max in Tutorial 5.1.

In the following tutorial, you will start modeling Generic Man by creating the torso.

TUTORIAL 5.1

BUILDING THE TORSO

To model the Generic Man character:

ON THE CD

1. Bring the Gman_Fnt.tif and Gman_Side.tif files from the Chap05\Images directory on the companion CD-ROM into your computer. The best place to put them is in your 3ds max\Maps directory.
2. In Customize/Viewport configuration, set the layout to two views: a front on the right and a left view on the left, as shown in Figure 5.2.
3. Click in the front viewport, and then open the Views > Viewport Background menu. Load Gman_Fnt.tif. Be sure to turn on Match Bitmap so that the images are not distorted. Repeat this for the left viewport, and load Gman_Side.tif.
4. Next, you will create a number of spline circles in the front view to construct the spline cage for the chest. Click Create > shapes > circle, and then click and drag to make a circle the same diameter as the width of the top of the leg, as shown in Figure 5.2.
5. Convert the circle spline to an editable spline and open the Editable Spline Modifier. To increase the number of vertices in the circle, select the Refine

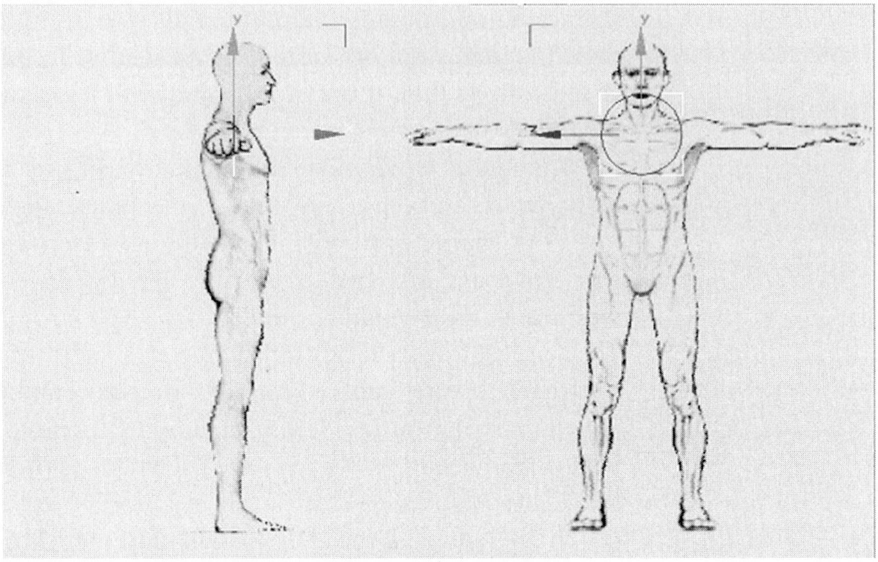

FIGURE 5.2 The background drawings of Generic Man.

tool, and then click the spline circle halfway between each existing vertex pair to make a total of eight vertices in the circle.

6. It is important to pre-shape the spline at this point. Study the left side of Figure 5.3. It shows the desired shape. Select the top vertex of the circle in the front view and move it downward a short distance until it forms a soft "V." This will create the area that corresponds to the depression of the backbone when this spline is finally rotated into a horizontal position and cloned. The torso is made from a stack of circular splines. You pre-shape them at this early stage so you don't have to sculpt them later.
7. Select Spline Sub-object, and then click on the spline circle. It should turn red. You are now ready to clone the spline circle. Hold down Shift and then click-drag the spline downward a short distance to create a second spline. Continue holding Shift and clone four more so that you end up with six spline circles.
8. Next, select them all and rotate them 90 degrees in the X-axis so that they appear horizontal in the front view, as shown on the right half of Figure 5.3. Position them vertically to match the positions of the circles shown. The top circle should be at the height of the shoulder joints, and the bottom circle should be at the height of the leg joints.

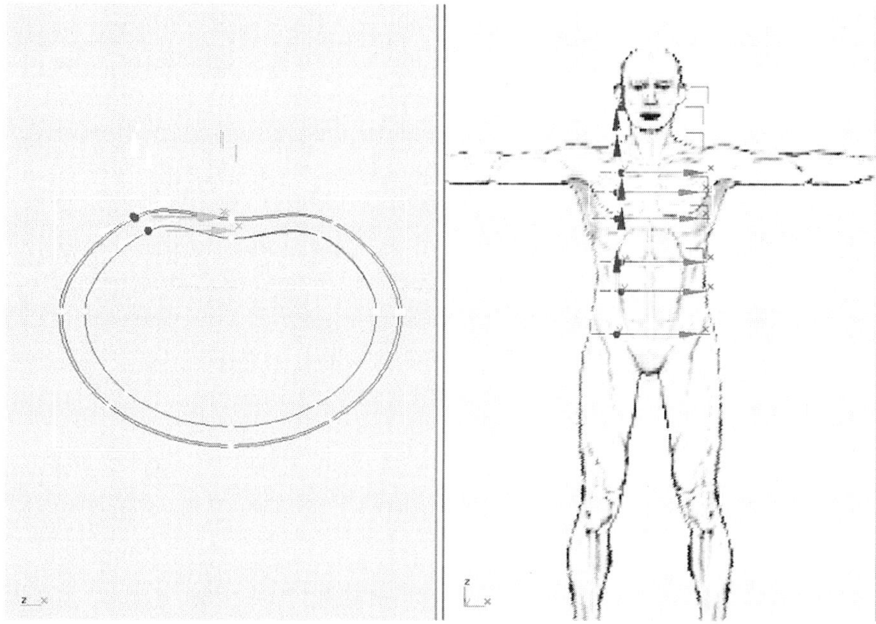

FIGURE 5.3 The top spline vertex is moved down to create the backbone depression.

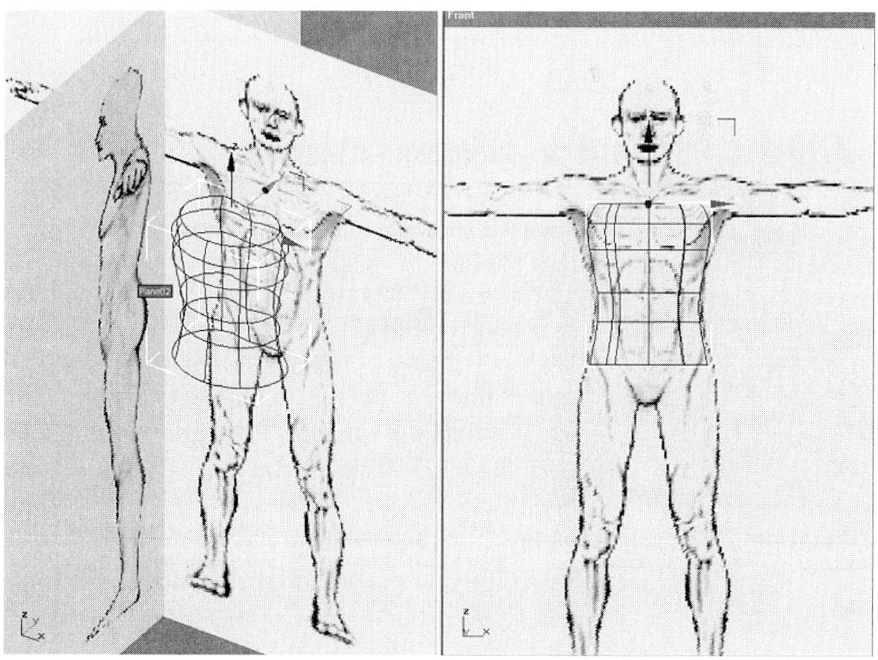

FIGURE 5.4 The Cross Section Modifier connects the spline circles.

9. Select and scale each circle spline to roughly follow the contours of the outline body drawing. Refer to Figure 5.4.
10. By cloning the splines at the Sub-object level, they are already attached. Now you can apply the Cross Section Modifier to create the spline cage. Select all of the spline circles, and then click Modifiers > Patch/Spline Editing > Cross Section. Vertical wires or splines should now be created connecting all of the circle splines, as shown in Figure 5.4.
11. In the Cross Section parameters, turn on Smooth. This makes the vertical splines smooth. Finally, select the entire spline cage, right-click, and convert it to Editable Spline. Save the scene as GenMan501.max. This forms the basis of the torso.

Because the geometry can easily slip out of locked alignment with the background image, you will need to use Background Lock Toggle repeatedly when you are building this model to fix the alignment. Use the hotkey, Ctrl-Alt-B, to unlock the foreground geometry from the background image. Then, use Pan and Zoom to realign and size them with each other. Caution: Never scale the geometry to fit the picture. Whenever you maximize the image, the geometry and the background image will slip out of locked alignment. This is normal behavior.

In the following tutorial, you will complete the top of the shoulders.

TUTORIAL 5.2

ADD THE SHOULDER SPLINE CAGE

To create the shoulder and arm spline cages:

1. Load the GenMan501.max scene file. The first step is to create the splines to form the top of the shoulders.
2. Look at left side of Figure 5.5. Notice the "roof-like" appearance of the splines that are attached to the top of the torso spline cage. To create this structure, start in the front view, and zoom in a bit on the shoulder area. Click the leftmost Snap icon on the top menu bar, and select 3D Snap. Right-click the icon, and in the Snap Settings pop-up menu, turn off Grid Points, and turn on Vertex. Close it.
3. Select the spline cage, and then select Vertex Sub-object mode. In the Editable Spline, Geometry menu, click Create Line.
4. Position the cursor over the upper-right corner of the torso spline cage. A blue Snap cursor should appear when the mouse is over the vertex. Click

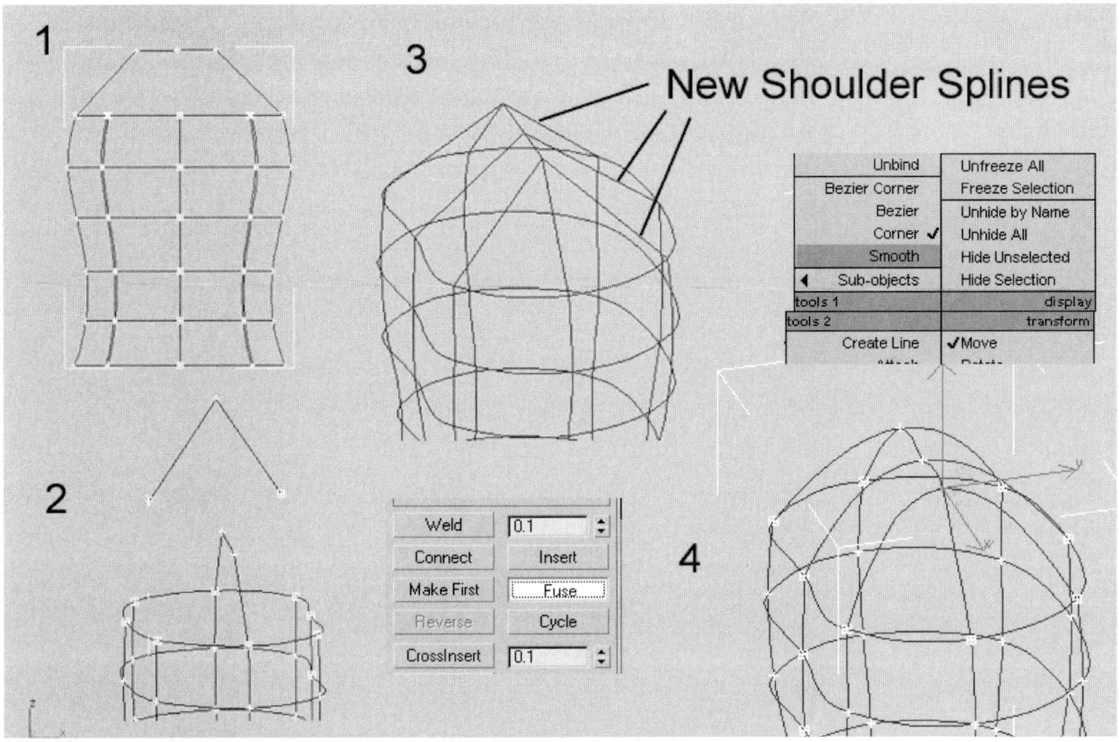

FIGURE 5.5 New splines snapped to the top of the torso to form shoulders.

there, drag the mouse to where the neck starts in the drawing and click to place a vertex, click again at the other side of the neck, and click again on the top-left corner of the torso spline cage. The line should snap to the vertex at the top of the torso spline cage.

5. You should now have a spline that resembles a "wire handle on a gallon paint can" running above the torso spline cage, as shown in Figure 5.5, example 1. The next process is to add three more splines to close in the top of the shoulders.
6. Use Arc Rotate to rotate the view to approximately an isometric view. Next, create three small splines that will go from the top of the torso vertex on the front side up to the neck, and then down to the top of the torso vertex on the back side. Examples 2 and 3 in Figure 5.5 illustrate where the splines should go. Again, use Create Line with 3D Snap turned on.
7. When finished, you should have a roof-like structure of splines on top of the torso. Look at the torso wire cage from all angles to make sure that the

3D Snapping worked. If any vertices are separated, you can select them both and click the Fuse command to bring them together. Note: You should always drag a selection marquis around any two points. Simply clicking on them never selects both points.

Do not weld these points. Welding averages the weight of all vertices on all connected splines. This will distort the spline cage and can ruin the curvatures of the model. As a general rule, never use weld when making a spline cage. Use the Fuse command instead, which does not average vertex weights. Fuse is the best tool for creating a stable, complex wire cage that will be skinned with the Surface modifier.

8. To smooth the curves on top of the shoulders, select two vertices that are together and then right-click. In the pop-up menu, select Smooth as the vertex type. This will result in rounded curves as shown in Figure 5.5, example 4.
9. Make sure that the contours of the spline wire cage match the shape of the torso in the drawings. Save the scene file as GenMan502.max.

In the next tutorial, you will create an arm for the Generic Man and attach it to the shoulder.

TUTORIAL 5.3

CREATE THE ARM AND ATTACH IT TO THE SHOULDER

To create an spline patch arm:

1. Load the GenMan502.max scene, and then maximize the front view. The torso wirecage and the Generic Man background drawing should be visible. Zoom in on the shoulders.
2. To begin the arm, create a Spline Circle right on top of the shoulder joint. It should be about the same diameter as the entire shoulder, as shown in Figure 5.6.
3. Convert the spline circle to Editable Spline, and then select the Spline Subobject mode. Hold Shift and move the circle to the right to clone a number of circles to create the cross sections of the arm in the following locations: shoulder 2, biceps 2, elbow joint 3, lower upper forearm 1, and wrist 2. Scale each circle to fit within the outline of the arm drawing as shown in example 2 in Figure 5.7.

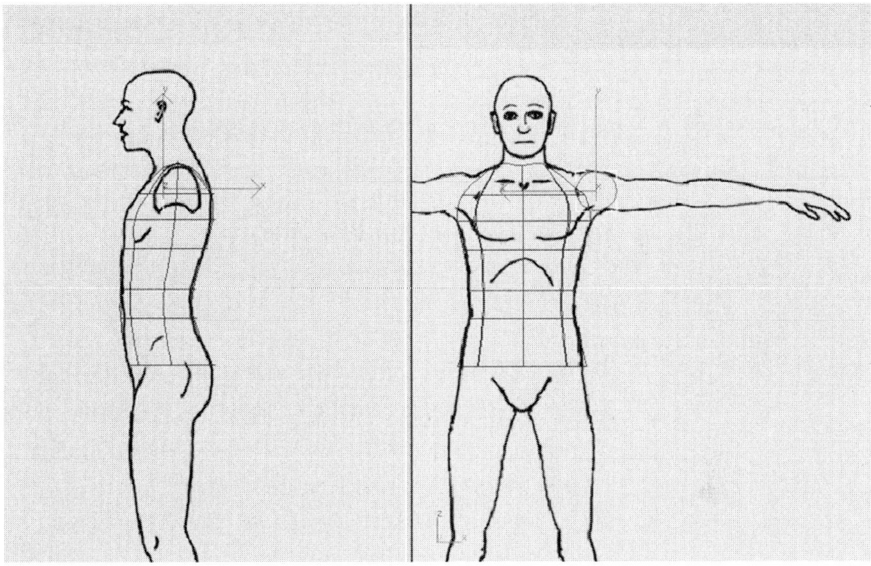

FIGURE 5.6 Spline Circle positioned at shoulder for creating the arm.

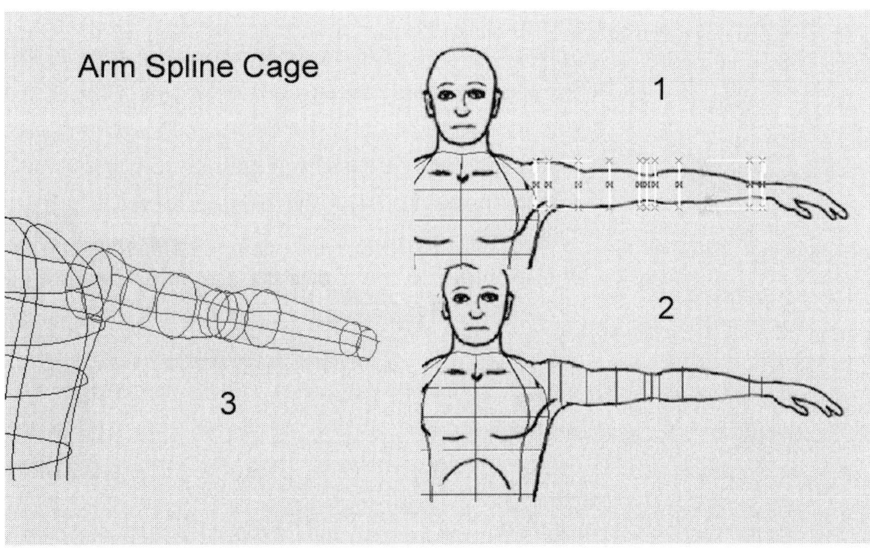

FIGURE 5.7 The arm circles are cloned, scaled to fit, and made into a wire cage.

4. There should be 10 circles.
5. All the circles should be automatically attached to the first circle you cloned. Select all the arm circles, and then make the wire cage by clicking

Modifiers > Patch/Spline Editing > Cross Section. Turn on Smooth in the Cross Section Parameters.

All of the patch objects, including arms, legs, hands and fingers, are built by creating and positioning spline circles in the front view, rotating them 90 degrees, and then Shift-Move cloning them to place in them in position over the background drawing. Then, their outside diameters are scaled so that they match the shape of the outline in the reference drawing. Finally, the Cross Section Modifier is applied to create a spline cage.

6. To attach the arm to the shoulder, you must first attach the arm to the torso. Select the arm wire cage, click the Modify tab, and in the drop-down menu select Attach. Then, click on the torso wire cage. They will become one object.
7. To prepare the shoulder to receive the arm, you must first delete a spline segment. In the left view, zoom in on the shoulder area of the torso. It is best to turn off the background display at this point. Use Arc Rotate to tip the viewport to a 30-degree angle, as shown on the left in Figure 5.7.
8. In Editable Spline > Segment mode, select the spline segment that corresponds to the vertical spline in the armpit. See Figure 5.8, examples 1 and 2. Delete that spline segment. Now select the bottom vertex at the armpit and fuse to the side of the body, as shown in Figure 5.8, example 3.
9. Next, you will create three splines to connect the arm to the shoulder. Click Editable Spline > Vertex, and then Click Create Line. Turn on the 3D Snap icon, and make sure it is set to Vertex only. Snap a line from the top of the shoulder to the top of the arm, then from the front of the shoulder to the front of the arm, and from the back of the shoulder to the back of the arm, as shown in Figure 5.8, example 4.
10. Finally, switch to Segment Sub-object mode, and select the three segments from the original shoulder that now lie inside the new shoulder splines. Delete them to clean up the shoulder, as shown in Figure 5.8, example 5.
11. The arm should now be smoothly attached to the shoulder with no extra spline segments inside the wire cage. To check for problems or unfused vertices, temporarily apply the Surface Modifier. Click Flip Normals if the surface looks inside out, and be sure to click Remove Interior Patches.
12. If the surface is missing anywhere, zoom in on the vertices and look for two that are not fused (located in exactly the same place, but not welded). Fix any points that are separated. The surface should now be smooth.

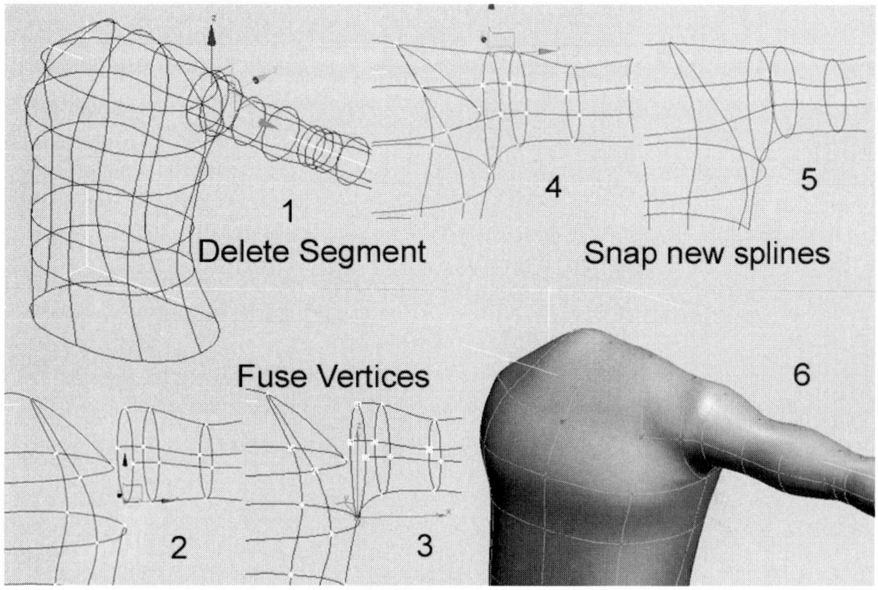

FIGURE 5.8 Attaching the arm to the shoulder.

13. Delete the Surface Modifier from the Stack, and save the scene as GenMan503.max.

In the following tutorial, you will create a leg and attach it to the torso.

TUTORIAL 5.4

CREATE THE LEG AND ATTACH IT TO THE TORSO

To create the leg:

1. Load GenMan503.max, and make sure the background images are loaded into the front and left viewports. Realign them if necessary by clicking Background Lock Toggle, Ctrl-Alt-B, and using Pan and Zoom to move and size them to each other. Do not scale the geometry.
2. In the front view, create a Spline circle that is the same diameter as the top of the leg. Position it over the leg joint, and then rotate it 90 degrees on the X-axis, and about 10 degrees on the Y-axis so that it is not quite horizontal. It should be tilted to face down the centerline of the leg, as shown in Figure 5.9, example 2.

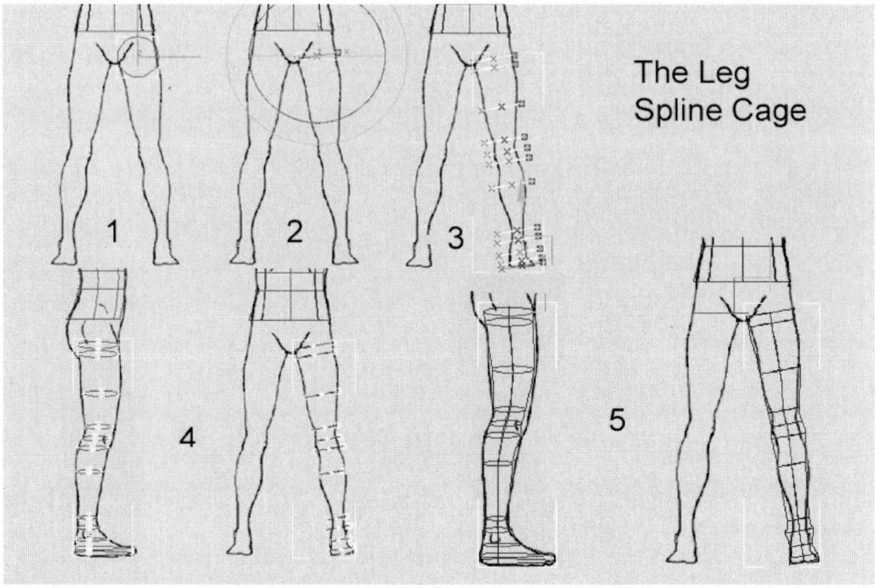

FIGURE 5.9 Creating a leg spline cage.

3. Convert the circle to Editable Spline, and then select Sub-object > spline mode. Select the top circle. It should be red. Use Shift > Move to clone 11 more Spline circles to form the leg. There should be two circles at the top of the leg, one in the middle of the thigh, three at the knee, one at the calf, two at the ankle, and three to form the foot, as shown in Figure 5.9, examples 3 and 4.
4. Next, uniform scale each circle to fit the shape of the leg in the background drawing. Then, switch to the left view and move the circles so they match the shape in the side view drawing of the leg, as shown in Figure 5.9, example 4.
5. Change to Vertex Sub-object mode, and in the left view zoom in slightly on the foot area and select the three vertices of the foot spline circles that face the toe. Move them out toward the toe until they match the contour of the foot drawing.
6. To create the leg spline cage, turn off Sub-object mode, and apply the Cross Section Modifier. Click Smooth in the Cross Section Parameters. Convert the spline cage to an editable spline to remove cross sections from the stack.

7. You are ready now to attach the leg to the bottom of the torso. Use the Editable Spline > Geometry > Attach command to attach the leg spline cage to the torso spline cage. Next, you must create a few new splines to form the connection between the leg and the torso.
8. In the front view, zoom in about 40% to focus on the hip area, or as close as you can without causing 3ds max to turn off the background display. The bottom of the torso is closed in the same way as the shoulders were made. In the front view, turn on the 3D Snap icon and make sure it is set to Vertex.
9. In the left view, turn off background display and use Arc Rotate to tip the spline cage so you can easily see the bottom of the torso and the top of the leg, as shown in Figure 5.10, example 2. Switch to Editable Spline > Vertex mode and turn on Create Line.
10. In the front view, click on the lower-right vertex of the torso wire cage, and then click the upper-right corner of the leg. Right-click to end the Create Line command and check to see that the line snapped to the correct vertex. If not, use the Fuse command to bring them together, as shown in Figure 5.10, example 1.

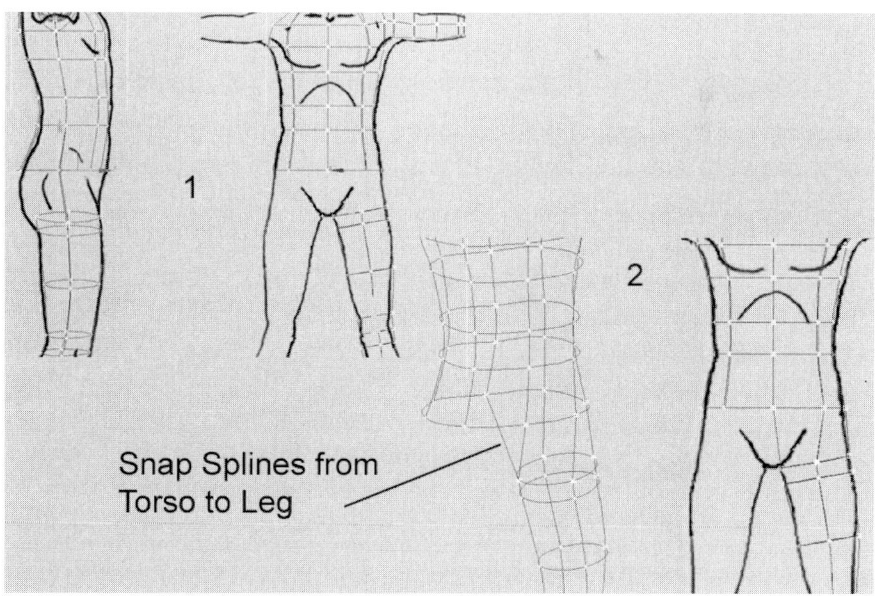

FIGURE 5.10 Snap splines from the bottom of the torso to the top of the leg.

11. Turn Create Line on again. Snap a spline from the top-front vertex on the leg to the corresponding lower-front vertex of the torso. Do the same for the top-rear vertex of the leg and bottom-rear vertex of the torso on the side where the leg is. Finally, do the same for the top inner leg vertex and the bottom center vertices on the front and back of the torso. You model should look like Figure 5.10, example 2.
12. Save the scene as GenMan504.max.

In the next tutorial, you will finish the pelvis area of the model and the neck.

TUTORIAL 5.5

COMPLETE THE PELVIS AND THE NECK

To complete the pelvis and the neck:

1. Load GenMan504.max, and then zoom in on the hip area of the model. The splines created to attach the leg in the previous tutorial are straight, which is fine for the side and front of the leg, but they need to be rounded for the crotch and the back of the leg. In addition, another spline needs to be added in the horizontal direction to smooth the crotch and buttocks.
2. In the front view, select the spline wire cage and click Modify > Editable Spline > Vertex mode. Click the Geometry > Refine button, and then in the left view (which should still be tipped at an angle from the previous tutorial), click the center of each of the five splines connecting the leg and torso, as shown in Figure 5.11, example 1.
3. To add a horizontal spline, turn off Refine and turn on Create Line, and click on the 3D Snap icon, setting it to Vertex. In the left view, snap a spline from the new front center vertex, then the front of the leg, the side of the leg, the back of the leg, and the center back of the buttocks. Then, right-click. Turn off Create Line and 3D Snap (Figure 5.11, example 2).
4. You can now pull the points on this new line around to sculpt the pelvis area into shape, but first you should smooth the splines. Individually marquis select each pair of vertices that you just snapped the spline to, and then hold down a right-click. From the upper-left Quad pop-up menu, select Smooth, as shown in Figure 5.11, example 3. That will smooth the pelvis area. Later, you will need to adjust the curves more precisely.

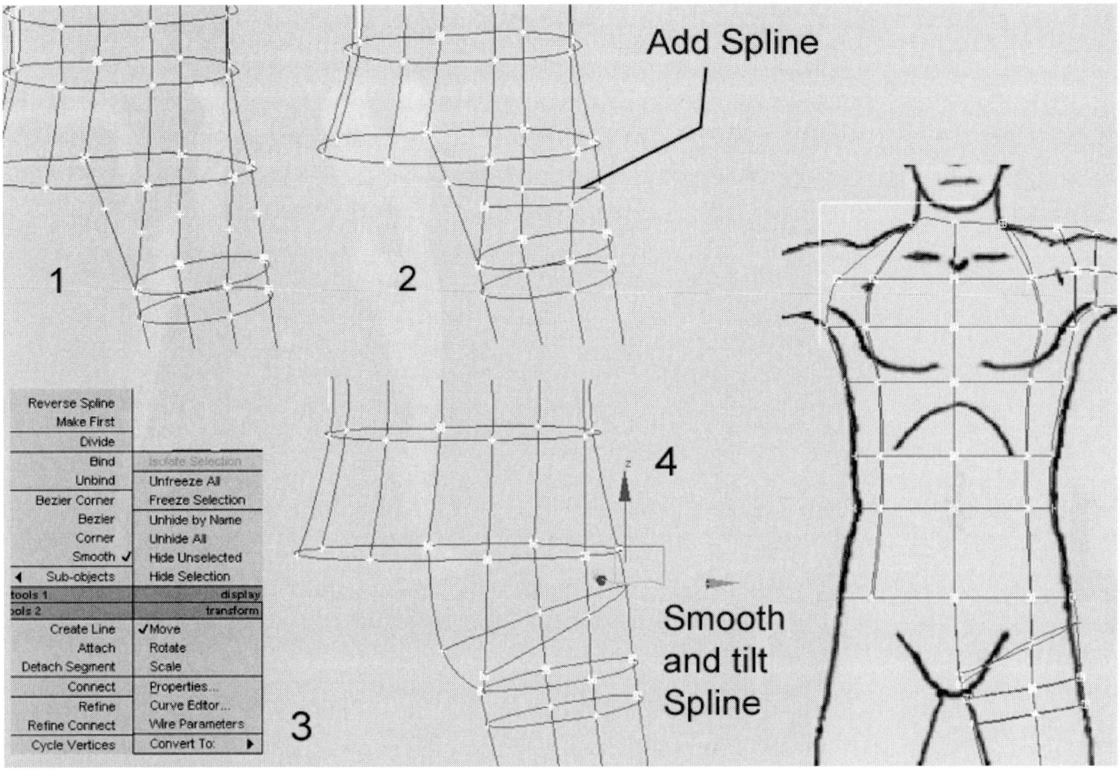

FIGURE 5.11 Refining the pelvis area using Refine, Snap, and Create Line.

5. Next, select and move the vertex pairs up or down as necessary to round the pelvis splines and to tilt the new spline you added as shown in Figure 5.11, example 4.
6. To add the neck to the shoulder area, zoom in on the shoulder area of the model in the front and left views. Select the Editable Spline > Vertex > Refine tool, and then in the left, tip the view so you can see the shoulder area from above. Click on the center spline of the neck in front and behind where the center of the neck should be, as shown in Figure 5.12, example 1.
7. Click Create Line, turn on 3D Snap, and snap all four vertex pairs to create a new spline that forms a "diamond" shape around the center of the neck, as shown in Figure 5.12, example 2. 3ds max will ask you if you want to close the spline. Click No, and then turn off 3D Snap and fuse any vertex pairs that are not together.

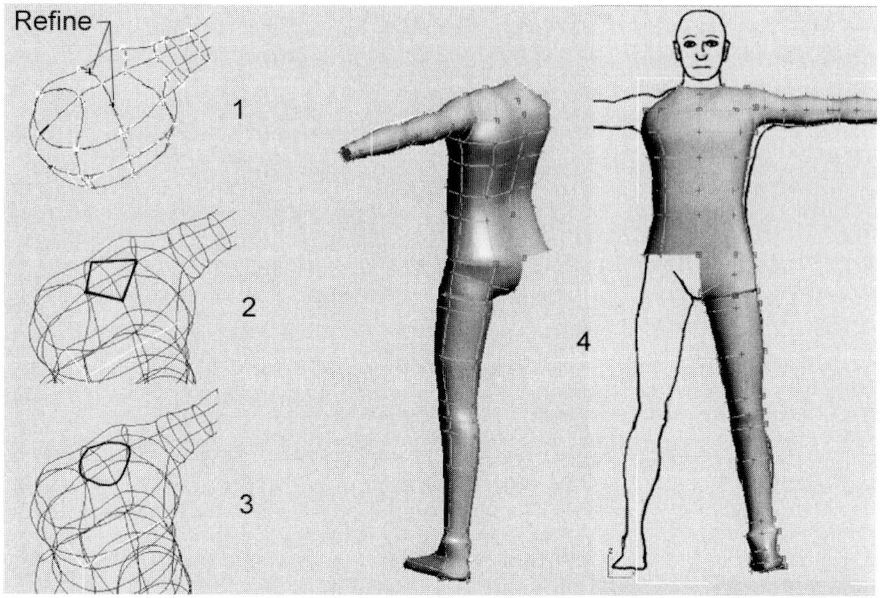

FIGURE 5.12 Inserting the neck spline circle into the shoulders.

8. Select the four pairs of vertices around the neck, right-click, and from the Quad menu, select Smooth as the vertex type. That should turn the diamond shape into a rough circle, as shown in Figure 5.12, example 3.
9. Select the segments that are now inside the neck circle, and delete them. Temporarily apply the Surface Modifier to see if any vertex pairs are not joined. Click Remove Interior Patches and, if necessary, Flip the Normals. The patch skin should be smooth with no unwanted holes, as shown in Figure 5.12, example 4.

To see the splines on the patch skin, select Editable Spline > Vertex, and then click the Show End Result on/off toggle.

10. Remove the Surface Modifier from the stack, and save the scene as GenMan505.max.

In the next tutorial, you will create the head for the Generic Man.

TUTORIAL 5.6 CREATE THE HEAD FOR THE GENERIC MAN

The wire cage for the head will be started using the same background drawings. However, after the initial structure is finished, the head will be removed from the body and placed in a new scene project where much more detailed background drawings of the head will be used to add all the features such as eyes, nose, mouth, and ears. By doing this, the structure is the correct size for the body, and the details can be done in a separate scene file without the body getting in the way of modeling the head.

To create the spline cage for the head:

1. Load GenMan.505.max, and then return the left and front views to their original state with both background drawings visible and the mesh aligned with the drawings. If you cannot see one of the images, click Views > Reset Background Transform, unlock the foreground and background with Ctrl-Alt-B, and then pan and zoom the mesh to the correct location. Lock the background by pressing the hotkeys again.
2. In the front view, create a Spline Circle the same diameter as the width of the neck in the background drawing. Position it where the neck meets the shoulders, and then rotate it 90 degrees on the X-axis so that it is horizontal, as shown in Figure 5.13, example 1.
3. To shape the head you will clone eight new spline circles, one for each major feature. Select the neck circle and Convert to Editable Spline. Select Sub-object > Spline mode, and then hold Shift and move the neck spline circle upward to just under the chin. Move it again to clone a spline circle for the chin, the mouth, the nose, the eyes, the brow, the forehead, and the top of the head. You should have eight new spline circles in addition to the first neck spline circle, as shown in Figure 5.13, example 2.
4. Keep the splines in the same vertical position. Move them horizontally to center them within the side view outline drawing of the head. Use Non-uniform Scale to scale the spline circles to fit the side and front views of the head, as shown in Figure 5.13, examples 3 and 4.

It is not necessary to close the spline circle at the top of the head. All the characters in the movie project will have hair, hats, or helmets that cover the head.

5. The bottom circle of the neck must now be modified to fit the neck hole in the top of the shoulders. To see only the spline segments around the neck,

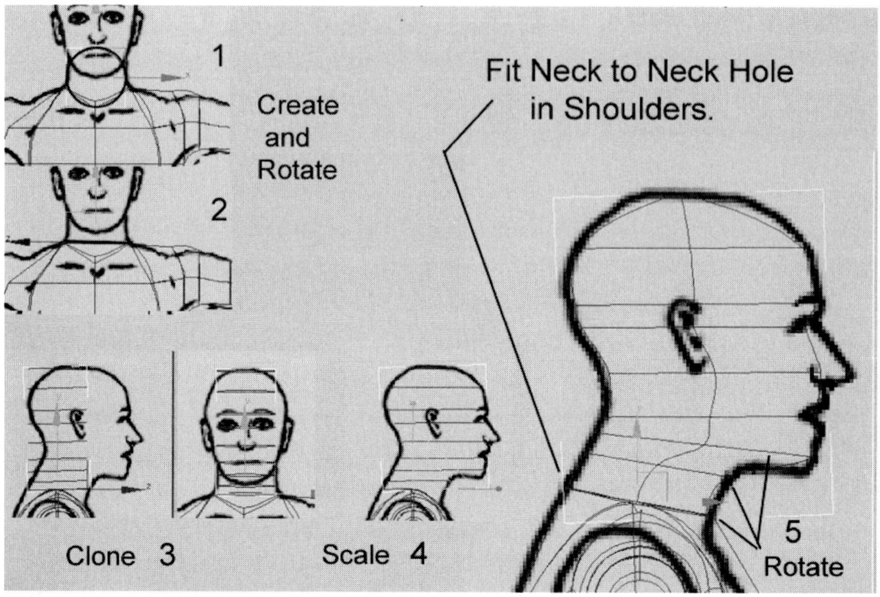

FIGURE 5.13 Building the basic spline cage for the head.

hide the body except for the top of the shoulders. To do that, go to Editable Spline > Segment mode, and then select the body spline cage below the arms. Scroll down into the Editable Spline > Geometry drop-down menu and select Hide. Most of the body should now be hidden, making it easier to work on the neck area, as shown in Figure 5.14, example 1.

6. In the side view, tilt the bottom three circles of the head about 10 degrees to match the angle of the neck, as shown in Figure 5.13, example 5.
7. In the left view, locate the spline circle that forms the neck hole in the shoulders. Lower the bottom spline circle of the neck until it touches some part of the neck hole in the shoulders. Now move the corresponding vertices of the neck hole upward to meet the vertices of the lowest spline circle in the neck. Eventually, these vertices will be fused to join the head to the body. Do not weld or connect them at this time.
8. Select all of the head spline circles, apply the Cross Section Modifier, and set to Smooth. Then, convert the head spline cage to Editable Spline. You model should now look like the example 5 in Figure 5.13. You might find it more convenient to use the built-in spline Connect tool, new in 3ds max 6 in the Editable Spline Modifier. It performs the same function as the Cross Section Modifier.

9. Save the scene as GenMan506.max. Now select the body and hide it. The spline cage of the head should be visible.

In the next tutorial, you will load the head spline cage only, and then create the facial features and details.

TUTORIAL 5.7

CREATE THE FACIAL FEATURES

ON THE CD

To create the facial features, follow these steps:

1. Load the scene file GenMan506.max. In the front viewport background load G_HeadFnt.tif from the Chap05\Images folder on the companion CD-ROM. In the left view, load G_HeadSide.tif. Be sure to turn on Match Bitmap and Lock Zoom/Pan in the Viewport Background dialog.
2. Use background lock toggle (Ctrl > Alt. > B) to unlock and reposition the Generic Man head spline cage so that it fits nicely over the background images, as shown in Figure 5.14, example 1.
3. Select the spline wire cage, and then click Modify > Editable Spline > Vertex. Select vertex pairs and re-adjust the spline cage to fit the Generic Man Head background images. Do not try to create the nose yet. It will be added later after you have added more splines. In addition, do not move any vertices in the lowest neck spline circle.
4. Hide the spline segments on the back of the head so that you don't accidentally select them when working on the face. Use Editable Spline > Segment > Geometry > Hide. Then, maximize the front view and re-align the wire cage with the background image. Use background lock toggle, Ctrl-Alt-B, and the Pan tool.
5. You will now create a spline that goes around the mouth. Go into Vertex Sub-object mode, and then click the Geometry > Refine button. Click on the spline segments above both corners of the mouth to add a vertex, and then add a vertex above and below the mouth.
6. To create the mouth outline spline, click the 3D Snap icon, set to Vertex, and then click Editable Spline > Geometry > Create Line. Snap a spline to the new points you made and create the mouth outline spline, as shown in Figure 5.14, example 2. Do not close the spline or weld points. Select the points above and below the mouth, and change the vertex type to Smooth to round the mouth spline.

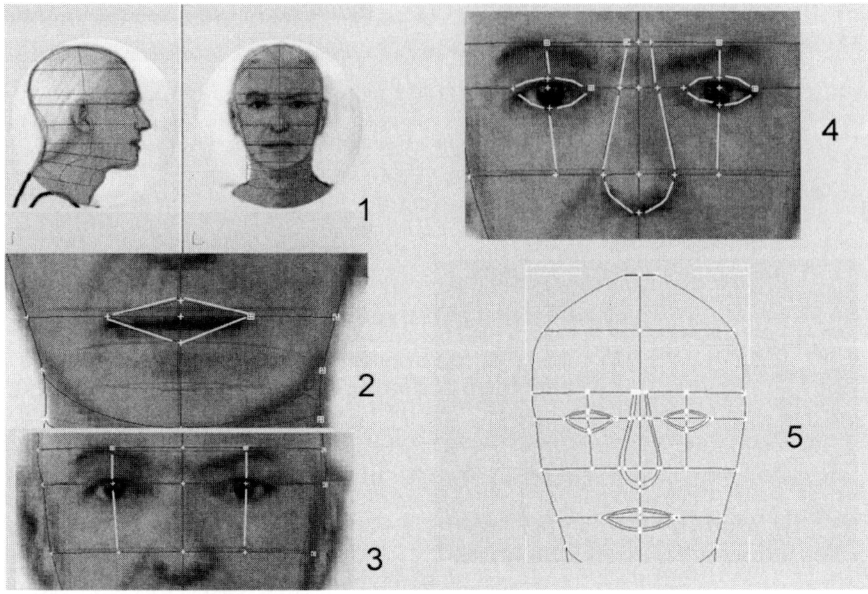

FIGURE 5.14 Creating the spline outlines for eyes, mouth, and nose.

The face will be worked on with both sides intact until all features are established. This makes sure the face will be symmetrical. Then, one half of the face will be deleted, as a reference mirror copy will be made so that your work on one half of the face will be mirrored on the mirrored reference half.

7. To create the eye outline splines, first use the Vertex Refine tool to insert vertices at the center of the eye, the eyebrow just above the eye, and in the cheek spline just below the eye. Then, turn on 3D Snap and create a spline that connects the new vertices, as shown in Figure 5.14, example 3.
8. Turn off Snap (the S hotkey). Use Refine to add vertices at the corners of the eye, and add one above and one below the eye. Turn on 3D Snap, and then Snap a spline around each eye. Select the eye vertices and set to Smooth type. Don't worry if they don't exactly match the picture; you will adjust them later.
9. To create the nose outline spline, use Refine and insert vertices on both sides of the centerline at the brow, the eyeline, and at the outer edges of the nostrils. Then add an additional point at the bottom of the nose on the centerline. Now, snap a spline that goes from the brow, around the bottom of the nose and back up to the brow centerline, as shown in Figure 5.14, example 4.

10. Create a second mouth, eye, and nose spline just inside the first ones you made by repeating the previous steps. Be sure to use Refine to insert vertices just inside the splines you already made, and snap new splines just inside the first ones, as shown in Figure 5.14, example 5. You might need to turn off viewport background display temporarily so you can zoom in on the eye area. Use the Fuse command to bring together any vertex pairs that did not snap together correctly, and then smooth the new splines.
11. Save the scene as GenMan507.max.

In the following tutorial, you will further refine the facial features, and then sculpt them into shape.

TUTORIAL 5.8 REFINE AND SCULPT THE FACIAL FEATURES

This part of the process is more complex. The care that you take in adding splines, positioning the vertices, and adjusting the Bézier splines handles will determine how good the facial features look. There are two sets of background images to use in this tutorial. The first two images are the Generic Man showing a man's face. The second group of images are of the head of another model called Generic Soldier, which displays the splines needed to create all of the features. These images are various close-up views of the model from different angles that provide you with multiple reference images to show exactly where the splines should be placed on your model. You should transfer them from the companion CD-ROM in the Chap05\Images\GenericSoldier folder to your 3ds max Maps directory before continuing with this tutorial.

ON THE CD

To refine and sculpt the facial features:

1. Load GenMan507.max, and then examine the left view and make sure that the spline segments that form the back of the head are hidden. Next, maximize the front view and turn on Display Background. If necessary, re-align the spline wire cage with the background image (use Ctrl-Alt-B background lock toggle hotkey).
2. Click File > View Image File, and then from your Maps directory (or from the companion CD-ROM in the Chap05\Images\GenericSoldier folder), load GenSolFacB.tif. To enlarge or reduce it, hold the Control key and left-click or right-click on the image. You can drag the corner to make it smaller, and position it on the left side of the front view so you can refer to it easily, as shown in Figure 5.15.

ON THE CD

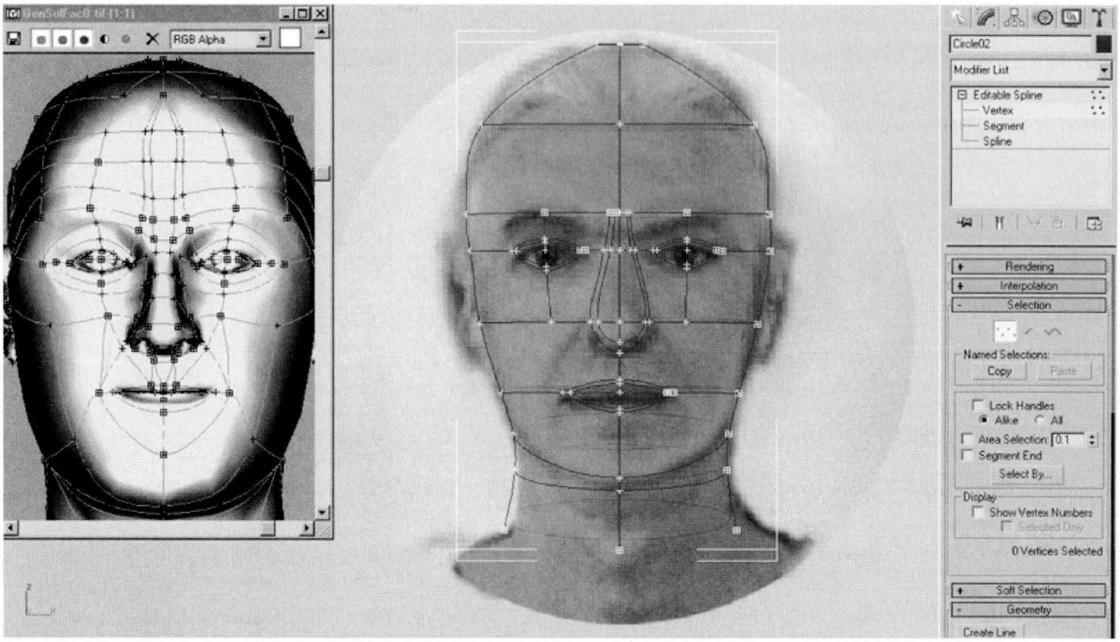

FIGURE 5.15 Reference image showing all splines needed for the facial features.

3. Next, you will add more splines around the nose and mouth to finish the lower face. Select the spline cage, and then select Modify > Editable Spline > Vertex. Next, click Refine in the Geometry drop-down menu and click the horizontal mouth spline to insert a vertex on either side of the mouth. Insert a third point below the mouth, as shown in the GenSolFacB.tif Reference image.
4. In the Geometry drop-down menu, select Create Line, and turn on the 3D Snap icon, set to Vertex. Click on one of the vertices below either eye on the nose line, and then click the new vertex on the same side of the mouth, then below the mouth, then the other side of the mouth, and finally back up at the vertex below the other eye. This should create a loop that runs from cheek to cheek under the mouth, as shown in the reference image in Figure 5.15.
5. Next, refine both the upper lip splines by inserting one vertex on either side of the upper lip centerline, for a total of four new vertices. Change to Create Line and Snap a spline from the center of the right cheek to the new top vertex on the upper-right lip spline. Repeat this for the upper-left lip and left cheek. Then, add the spline that runs from the nose line, to the

side of the mouth, under the mouth, back up to the other side of the mouth, ending at the nose line on the other side of the face.

Rather than read all of the instructions in this tutorial, it is much faster to simply add the vertices and copy the splines you see in Figures 5.15 through 5.18.

6. Before you start making new splines around the eyes, move the brow line up higher. Select the vertices on the brow line above the eyes and raise them as needed to form a "double arc" as shown in Figure 5.16. That will place the brow line a short distance above the eyebrows.

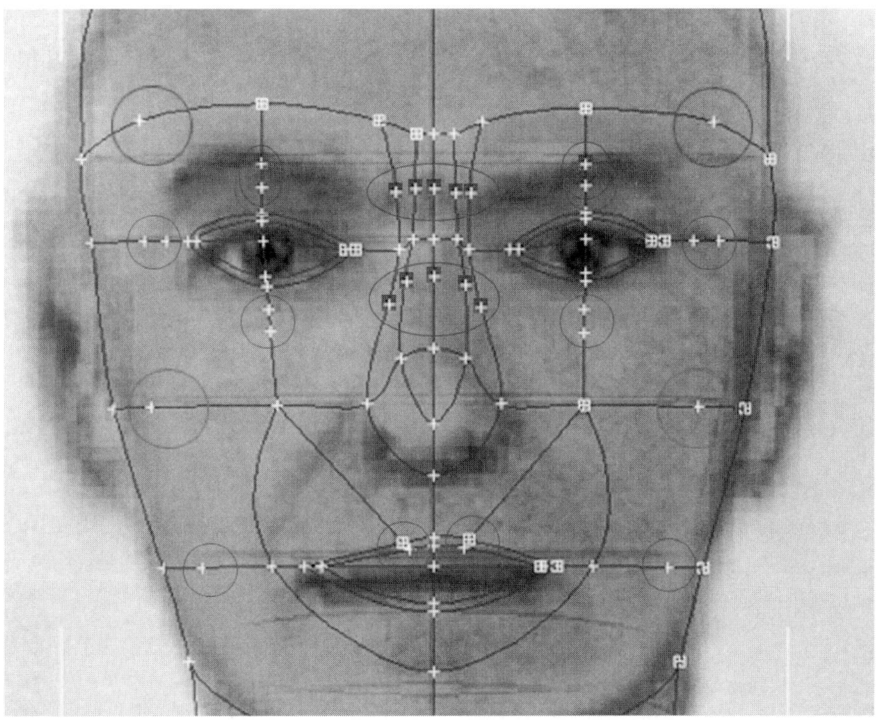

FIGURE 5.16 Use the Refine tool to insert new vertices into the splines at circled locations.

7. Zoom in on the nose and insert two new rows of five vertices across the bridge of the nose as shown in Figure 5.16. Notice that there is a centerline in the nose at this point. Leave it there for now. It will be deleted later, but you'll need it when you start working on only half of the face in the next tutorial.

8. Snap a spline all the way around the outer part of the face beginning and ending at the forehead line as shown in Figure 5.17, example 1. Then, snap a spline to the points spaced around the eyes to form a "mask" shape (example 2). Select all of the vertices at the sharp corners of your new splines and set them to Smooth type.

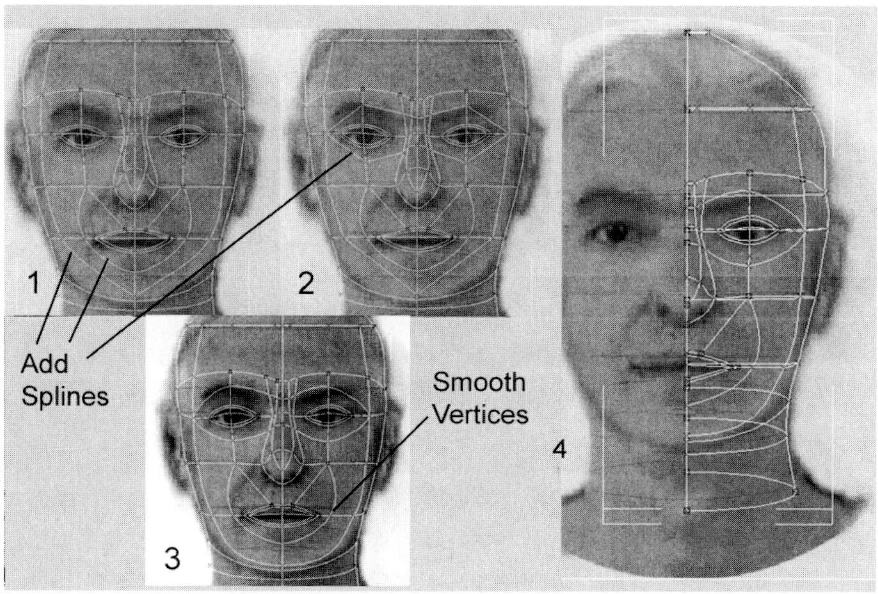

FIGURE 5.17 Adding facial feature splines.

9. Now that the major facial curves have been established, it is time to cut the face in half. Working on only half of the face or body saves lots of time. First, unhide all of the spline segments by clicking Editable spline > Segment > Geometry > Unhide All. Then, in the front view, select all the spline segments on the left side of the face, but not the centerline (example 3). Delete all of the left-side spline segments. You should now have only the right side, as shown in Figure 5.17, example 4.
10. Save the scene as GenMan508.max.

In the next tutorial, you will work on completing the features on the right half of the face.

TUTORIAL 5.9

COMPLETE THE RIGHT HALF OF THE FACE

To finish the right half of the face:

1. Load the scene file GenMan508.max. Work with the front and left views and re-position the spline wire cage over the background images as necessary. As in the previous tutorial, you should be using G_HeadSide.tif and G_HeadFnt.tif as background images.
2. Open the Editable Spline Modifier and select segments. In the left view, select and hide all of the spline segments at the back of the head. Then, switch to Vertex. In the front viewport, select all the vertex pairs that make up the end of the nose. Pull them outward to match the profile in the background photograph.
3. Pull the mouth into better shape to match the left-view background. Work with the vertices to make splines smooth around the nose and across the cheeks. In addition, adjust the eye socket splines.
4. More splines are needed around the nose and the eyes to form the eyelid surfaces. Make an eye sphere that is slightly larger than the width of the eye opening and place it in the eye socket. This will be a guide to help shape and round the splines of the eyelids.
5. Make the eye sphere semi-transparent by selecting the sphere, right-clicking, and in the Properties menu click See-through. In the left view, pull the inner and outer corners of the eyelid splines even with each other. Compare it to the example in the GenSolFacB.tif image, as shown in Figure 5.18.
6. In the front view, add additional splines around the eye. Temporarily apply the Surface Modifier to see how the spline cage is skinning. If patches are missing, make sure that all vertex pairs are fused together. The shaded patch surface will help you adjust the curvature of the splines so that the eye does not poke through the skin, as shown in Figure 5.19. To get this view, select Vertex Sub-object and turn on the Show End Result on/off toggle. For the next step, delete the Surface Modifier from the stack.
7. To finish the nose, refine the lower nose splines to add two vertices, and then add a spline running from the tip of the nose to the vertex next to the corner of the mouth. Figure 5.19 shows this spline but does not show the centerline spline of the face. This centerline is necessary for joining the two halves of the face. It will be deleted later.
8. Create a small spline circle with three vertices to use as the nostril hole. Then, snap a spline across two of the vertices of the circle. Place a vertex

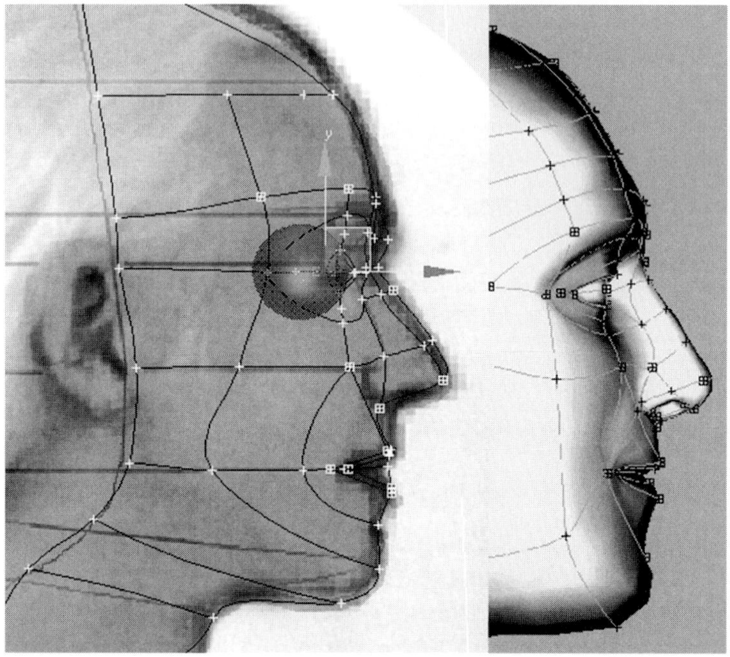

FIGURE 5.18 Pulling out the features.

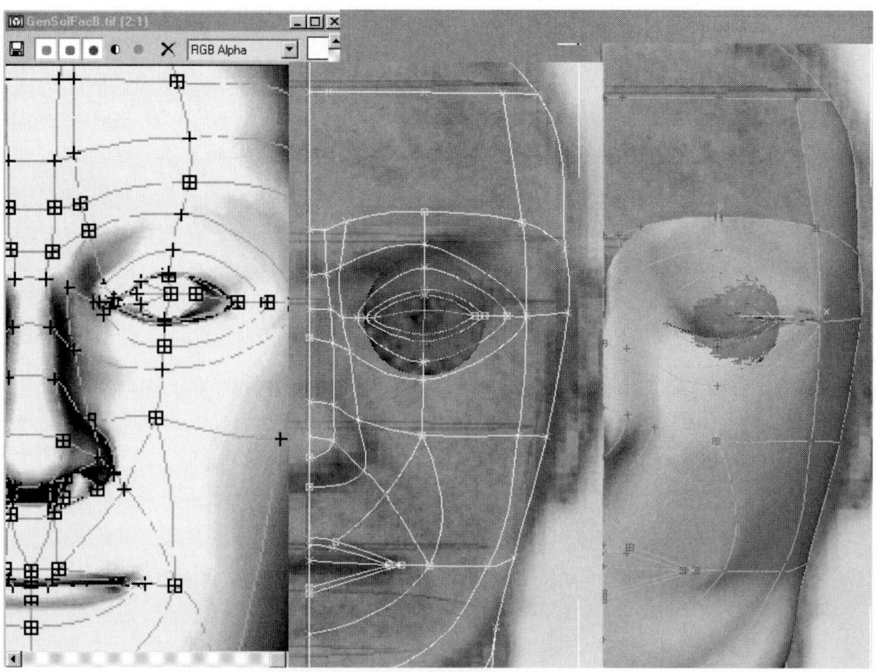

FIGURE 5.19 Add splines to the nose and around the eye.

in the center of that spline, and then snap from that center point to the third vertex on the circle. It should be a "Mercedes logo" shape. Fuse the center vertices together, and then select all vertices, right-click, and select Smooth. Move and rotate the finished nostril hole into position in the nose.

9. Zoom in on the nose of the Generic Soldier example image to see where the small nostril wing spline is placed. It should run from the upper corner of the nostril hole to the corner of the nostril wing part way up the side of the nose. Use Refine to add a vertex below the nostril hole on the lower nose spline. Then, snap one spline from there down to the upper lip point. Snap a second spline from the newest nose vertex down to the centerline vertex on the upper lip, as shown in Figure 5.20.

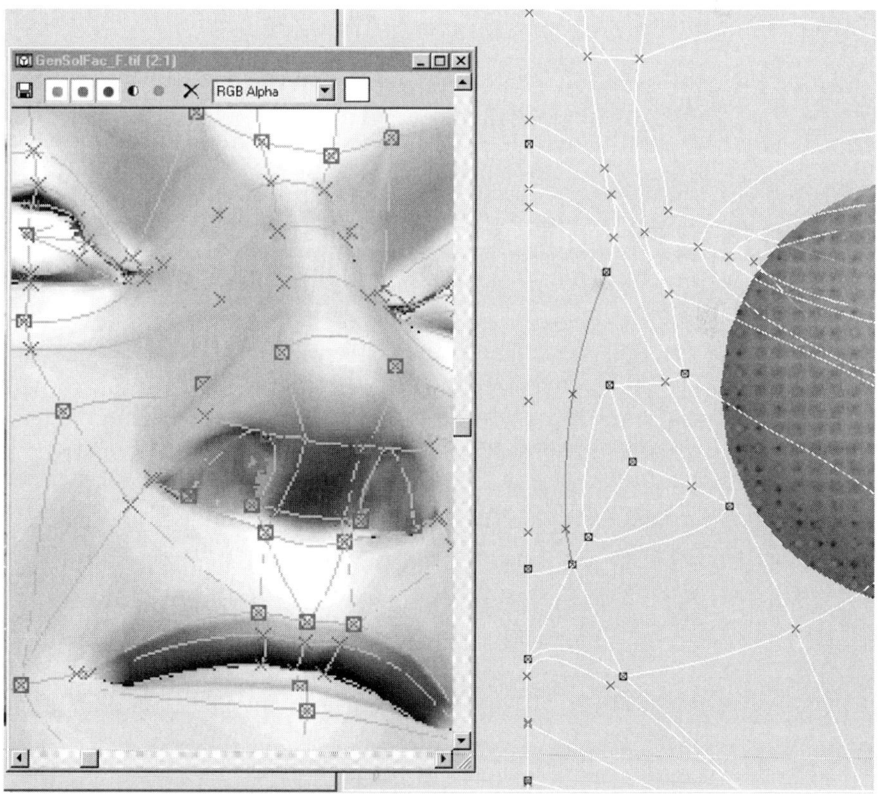

FIGURE 5.20 Finishing the nose splines.

ON THE CD

10. For a better view of the nostril area, load GenSolFac_F.tif from the Chap05\Images\GenericSoldier folder on the companion CD-ROM. Notice that three small splines connect to the corners of the nostril hole. To finish this area, first delete the curved spline segment that comes from the side of the nose tip to the centerline just above the nostril hole. Then, snap a new spline beside the nostril hole that connects the nose side tip spline with the two splines that run down to the upper lip, as shown in Figure 5.20.
11. To finish the nose, refine the last spline you added with two vertices near the nostril vertices. Also, refine the centerline. (The centerline will be removed after the two halves of the face are joined.) Snap splines to join these vertices to the corners of the nostril hole.
12. The last step is to select the center nostril vertex pair, and then in the left view, pull them up and into the nose to form the nostril hole. Save the scene as GenHead509.max.

In the following tutorial, you will finish the mouth.

TUTORIAL 5.10 FINISH THE GENERIC MAN MOUTH

To finish the mouth:

1. Load the GenMan509.max scene file, and zoom in on the mouth area. Load the example image GenSolFac_F.tif and drag its edges smaller to just see the mouth. You can enlarge it by clicking Control and then left-clicking the image.
2. The mouth splines need to be smoothed. Select all mouth vertices, and then right-click and select Smooth. If the outer corners don't smooth, you can select the offending vertex pairs and weld them. (As a general rule, don't weld the vertices on the rest of the face.)
3. To complete the mouth, change to Spline mode, and then select the inner lip outline spline. Scale-Clone it using Shift > Scale, reducing it by 15%. Then, re-position it so its ends touch the face centerline and it is inside the other two lip splines. Refine the centerline and the horizontal mouth line to provide attachment vertices, and then fuse the new inner lip spline to those points.

4. Select all the vertex pairs at the corners of the inner lip spline and pull them into the face a short distance in the left view. This will form the inner edge of the lips, as shown in Figure 5.21.

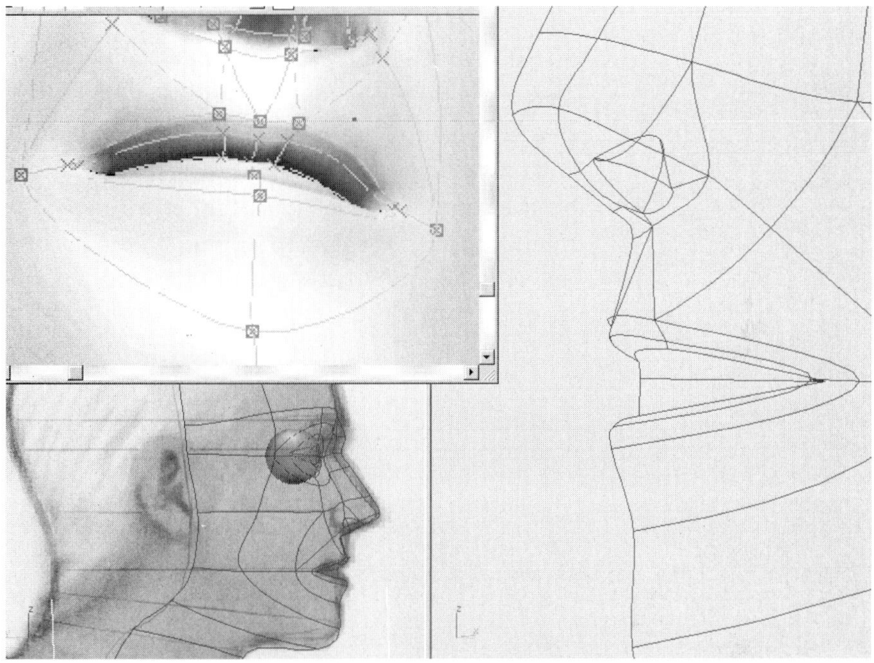

FIGURE 5.21 Finishing the mouth.

5. Add a spline to three vertices below the upper lip point. Select all the vertices of the mouth, right-click, and set them to Bézier. Use the Bézier handles to adjust the curvature of the lips until they look like the mouth in the example image GenSolFac_F.tif.
6. Cancel Sub-object mode, and then apply the Surface Modifier to check the face for skinning problems. At this point, you will probably have many problems, but do not worry. Don't spend too much time adjusting Bézier handles until you get the entire spline wire cage built and have cloned and joined both sides of the face.

Surface Modifier Patch Skin problems are almost always from four main causes: 1. Separated vertex pairs: Solution = Fuse the vertices. 2. Bézier handles pointing in the wrong direction: Solution = Move handles, or try switching to Smooth, then returning to Bézier. 3. Creases from Triangle Patches: Solution = Triangle patches (with only three vertices) should be avoided if possible. However, a few of them can be incorporated into the face around the nose or where you want a crease in the face. 4. 5-Point Patches: Solution = Add a spline to the patch to create one 4- and one 3-point patch.

7. Add a second spline along the outer edge of the nose to create a nice crease around the wing of the nostril. Add vertical splines in the forehead area to finish the top of the head. Extend the vertical splines at the brow line upward and join them to the horizontal spline near the top of the head, as can be seen in Figure 5.22. It is a good idea to insert another horizontal upper head spline to help round the head.

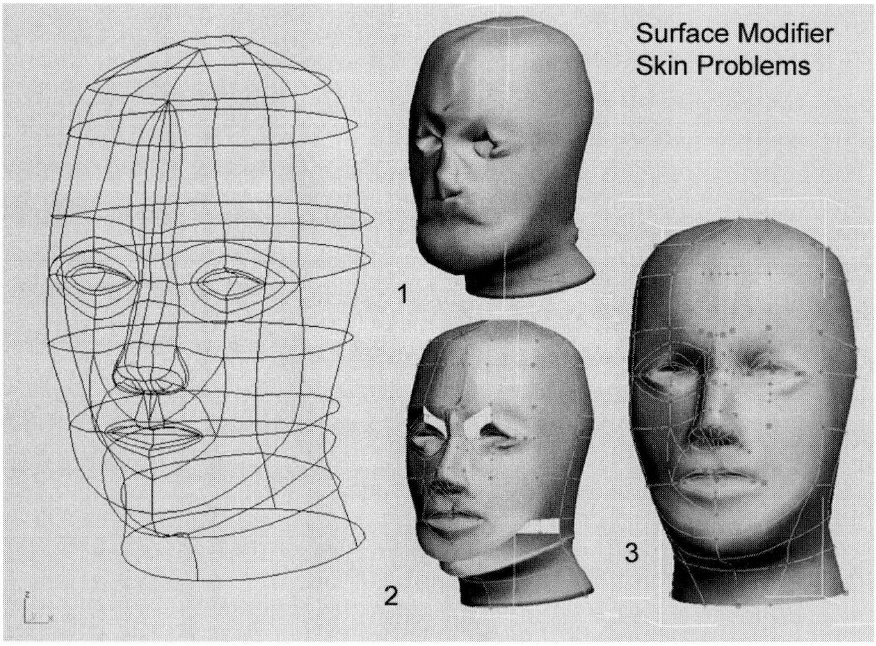

FIGURE 5.22 Mirrored spline cage with various Surface Modifier skin problems.

8. Next, you will Mirror Clone the spline wire cage to make the other side of the face. Delete the Surface Modifier from the stack if you haven't already done so. Make sure that the centerline is perfectly straight in the front view; otherwise, the two halves will not be easy to join. Exit from Modify mode, and then maximize the front view and hide the background image.

Select the spline cage, and then click the Mirror Selected Object icon. Click the X-axis and turn on Copy. The other side of the face should appear. Zoom in close to make sure they do not overlap but are very close.

9. Use the Arc Rotate tool to put the head at a slight angle to make seeing the entire centerline spline easier. There are now two copies of the centerline spline, one from each half of the face. Open the Editable Spline Modifier and use the Attach command to join the two spline cages. Change to Sub-object > Spline mode, and then click the rear centerline spline. Delete it. Click the front centerline spline and delete it. You should still have one complete centerline spline, as shown in Figure 5.22.
10. Zoom in on the spline cage, go to Vertex mode, and then select and fuse (merge) each pair of vertices at the ends of the horizontal splines that make up the cage. There will actually be three vertices at every merge point. Make sure you do not accidentally merge points in the back of the head with those in the front. Caution: Do not weld any of these points. If you do, it will change the curvature of any associated splines and you will have to re-adjust the splines.

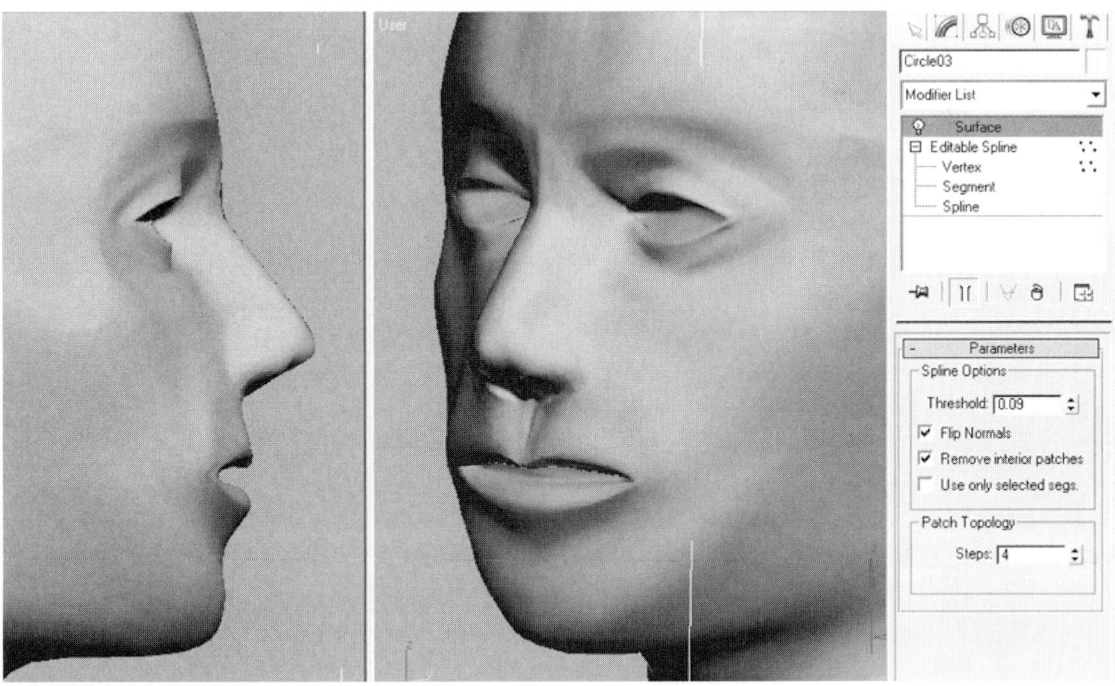

FIGURE 5.23 Setting the Surface Threshold and Patch Topology.

11. When finished, apply the Surface Modifier to see if there are problems. There usually are problems with some of the patches. Make sure to Flip Normals and Turn off Interior Patches in the Surface Modifier. It could still look wrong at the default Threshold setting, as shown in Figure 5.22, example 1. You might also find that you have holes from unfused vertices or 5-point patches, as shown in Figure 5.22, example 2. Figure 5.22, example 3 shows a problem with the Threshold and Patch Topology settings. The default settings do not work and should be changed to: Threshold = 0.09, and Patch Topology = from 4 to 12, depending on how tightly you want the shape of the skin to follow the splines, as shown in Figure 5.23.
12. Once all the splines are shaped correctly, and all pairs of vertices are fused, there should be no open or twisted patches, and you should have a basic smooth face, as shown in Figure 5.23. Save the scene as GenMan510.max.

In the next tutorial, you will build the ears for the head.

TUTORIAL 5.11 ADDING THE PATCH EARS

ON THE CD

To model an ear:

1. Load the GenMan510.max scene file. A patch ear is made by creating a set of semicircular curves that are positioned to create the inner and outer surfaces of the ear. These curves are difficult to describe in written text, so we have included them on the companion CD-ROM.
2. Merge in the EarCurves.max file from the Chap05\Ears folder. Position the set of ear curves at the correct ear position in the left view. Leave a space between the ear and the head, and then select the head model and hide it. You should now only see the ear curves.
3. The ear surfaces can be partially visualized by rocking them with the Arc Rotate tool (Alt-MMB). Rocking the ear curves around in the view helps you to see the curves. In the left view, select the smallest of the ear spline curves, the ear hole shape. In Editable Spline, click the Attach button and select the next largest ear curve on the inside of the ear. It is green, but it will flash white and then assume the color of the first spline curve. Continue attaching the next largest curve inside the ear all the way to the outer edge.

4. Continue around the edge of the ear to the outer surface curves. End with the last spline shape, the blue curve, which will become the point at which the outside ear skin meets the skin of the head.
5. Apply the Cross Section Modifier or use the spline Connect tool to create the spline cage, then turn on Smooth in the Cross Section drop-down menu to smooth all the splines, as shown in Figure 5.24, example 2. Convert the spline cage to an Editable Spline. Temporarily apply the Surface Modifier to make sure the patch skin works correctly. Flip the Normals if the surface looks reversed. Next, delete the Surface Modifier and unhide the Generic Head model. Turn off the Surface Modifier on the head.

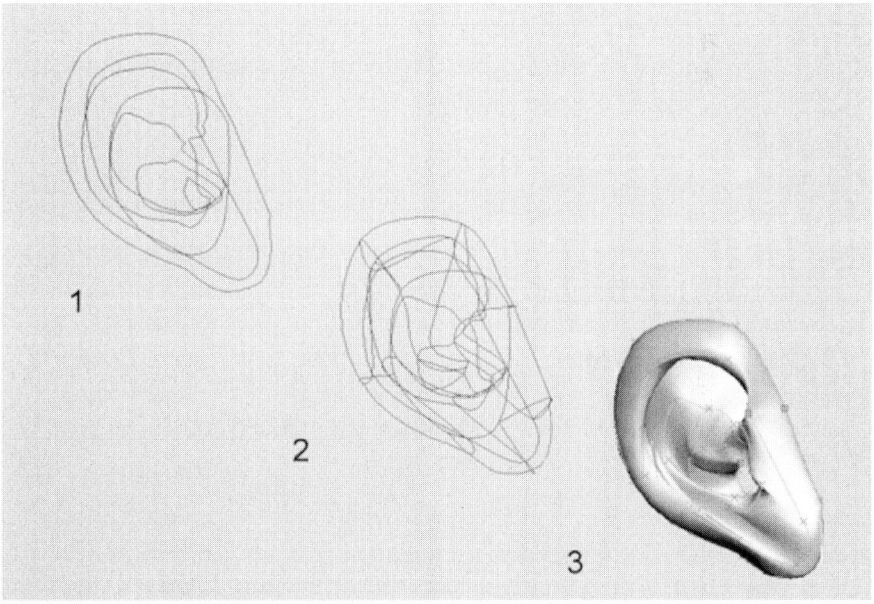

FIGURE 5.24 Attach curves and apply cross section to the ear splines.

6. Select the ear curves in the front view and Mirror-clone to create the opposite ear. Position the second cloned ear, and then hide it for now. Notice that the spline that forms the inner edge of the ear where it meets the head has five vertices. The side of the head does not have that many points near the ear for making a proper connection. Use the Editable Spline > Geometry > Refine tool to insert new vertices into the head as shown in Figure 5.24, example 1.

7. Turn on 3D Snap to Vertices, and use the Create Line tool to add a vertical spline to the side of the head to box in an ear attachment area, as shown in Figure 5.24, example 2. Repeat this on the other side of the head.
   With the head splines selected, click the Attach command, and then select the ear to attach it to the head spline cage.
8. You are ready to connect the ear vertices to the head points. Use the Fuse command to join the vertices on the inside ear spline to the vertices on the side of the head as shown in Figure 5.25. It will help to hide the spline segments on half the head. Then, look at the ear from the inside of the head to find the correct connection points.
9. When finished, select and delete the short spline segment that crosses the ear connection hole on the side of the head to prevent the formation of an unwanted inner patch, as shown in Figure 5.25. In the front view, finalize the ear position by selecting all ear vertices and moving them closer into the head if necessary.

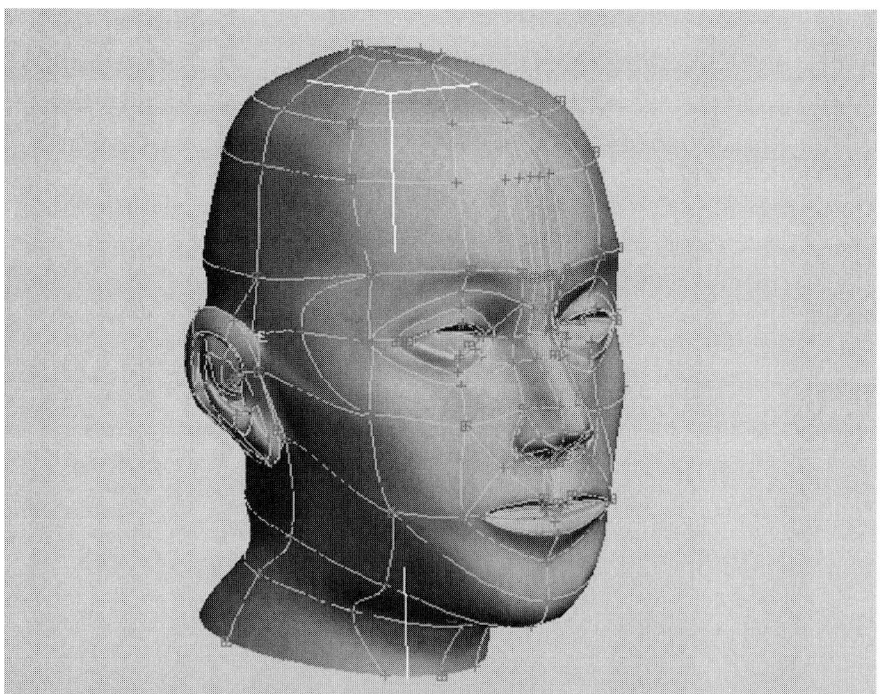

FIGURE 5.25 Connect the ear to the head with the Fuse command.

10. Unhide the other ear, and then repeat the previous connection steps to connect that ear to the head. When finished, turn on the Surface Modifier. Adjust the vertex positions and check for open patches. Alternatively, you could delete the opposite side of the head, leaving the half with the ear. Then, Mirror-clone the side with the ear attached, and reconnect the two head halves together using the Fuse command .
11. You can close the hole at the top of the head by snapping a spline across the opening at the centerline to create two 4-point patches. Save the scene file as GenMan511.max.

This completes Part 1 of the Generic Man construction.

CONCLUSION

In this chapter, you worked with spline patch modeling to create the body, face, and hands of a generic man, which will also be used as the Dr. Quin character. You used the Surface Modifier to generate a skin on the spline model and then worked on the head to create facial features. In the next chapter, you will continue with Part 2 of the Generic Man construction tutorials. There you will create the hand, attach it to the body, and then clone the body and fuse the two halves together. Then, you will finish the feet and the details of the face, torso, arms, and legs.

CHAPTER

6

FINISHING THE DR. QUIN/GENERIC MAN PATCH MODEL

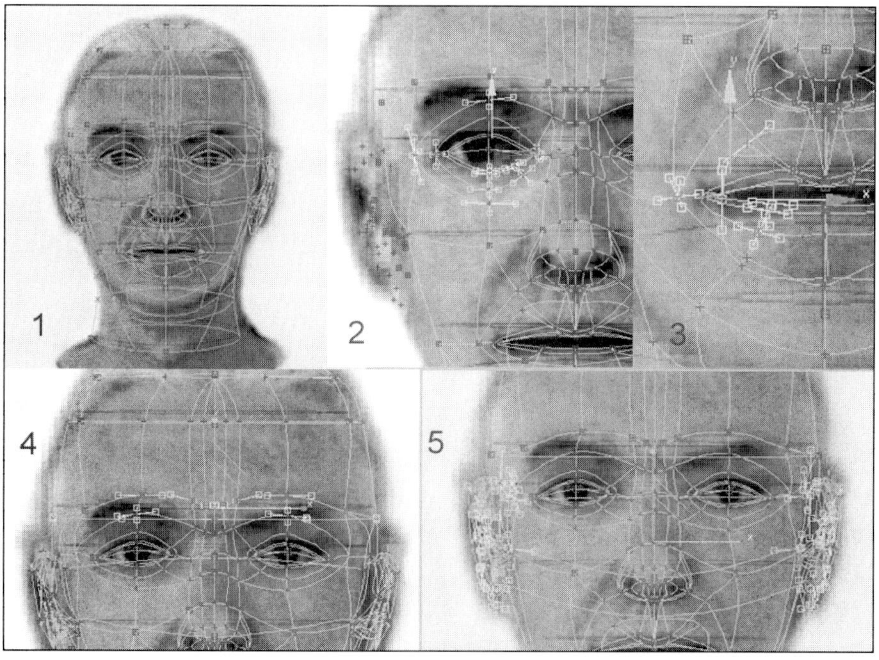

In this chapter, you will continue working on the Dr. Quin model, also called the Generic Man model. It is used as a basis for all of the other male characters in the film. A number of important structures must be completed before the character is ready to animate. First, you will create the hand and attach it to the arm; then, you will clone the body and fuse the two halves together. Next, you will finish the feet and adjust the shape of the legs, torso, and arms. Then, you will add teeth, and adjust the contours and details of the face (Figure 6.1).

In the first tutorial, you will create a patch hand for the Dr. Quin model by creating a spline cage and then applying the Surface Modifier to create the skin.

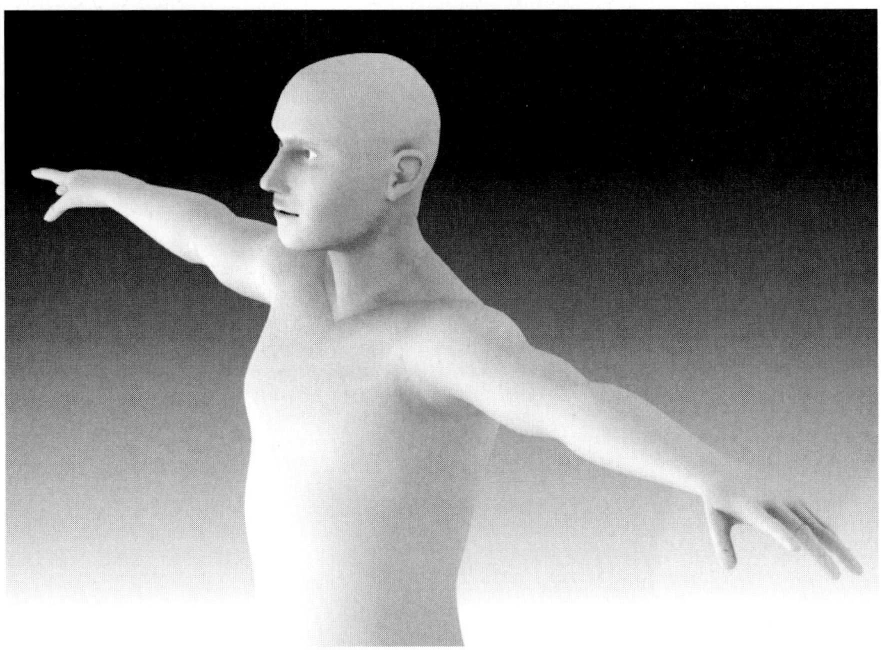

FIGURE 6.1 The finished Dr. Quin/Generic Man model.

TUTORIAL 6.1

Creating Patch Hands

To create a hand:

ON THE CD

1. Load the GenMan600.max scene from the Chap06 folder on the companion CD-ROM. This file contains a number of spline circles that you will use to build the spline cage. They are the correct size for the hand, as shown in Figure 6.2.

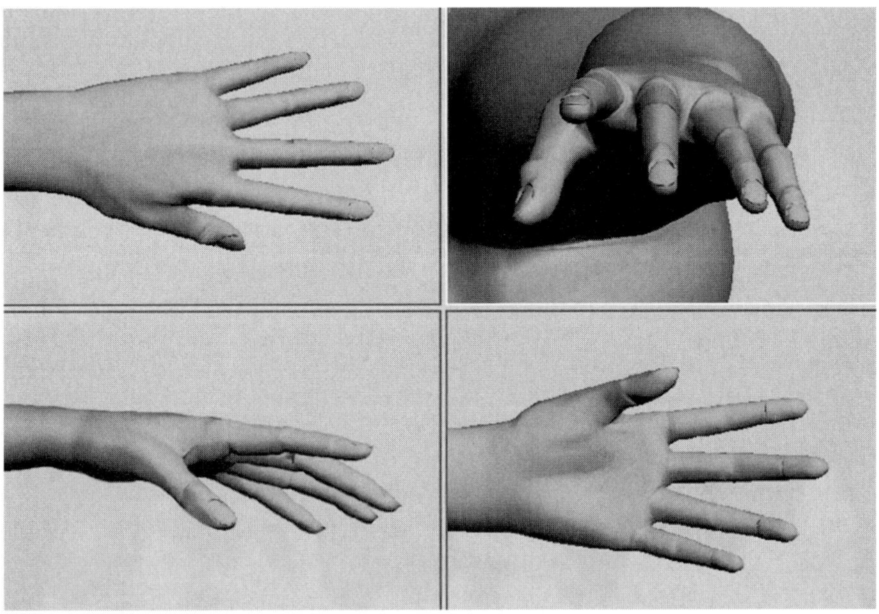

FIGURE 6.2 Four views of the finished Patch Hand.

ON THE CD

2. From the Chap06\Images folder on the companion CD-ROM, load the GenHandTop.tif image into the top viewport background. Using the Background Lock toggle command (Ctrl-Alt-B), re-position (Pan), resize (Zoom), and rotate (Arc Rotate) the spline cage circles until they align with the GHandTop image, as shown in Figure 6.3, example 1. Caution: Do not scale the spline circles; the fingers and palm are separate spline circle objects.

3. The first step is to turn the fingers into spline cages by applying the Cross Section Modifier to create long splines to connect the circular splines of the fingers together. This will create a spline cage for each finger. In the top view, click on the thumb splines. Then, click Modifiers > Patch/Spline Editing > Cross Section. Splines will be created to connect the thumb spline circles, as shown in Figure 6.3, example 2. You might find it more convenient to use the built-in spline Cross Section tool that is new in 3ds max 6 in the Editable Spline Modifier. It performs the same function as the Cross Section Modifier. Either tool will work.

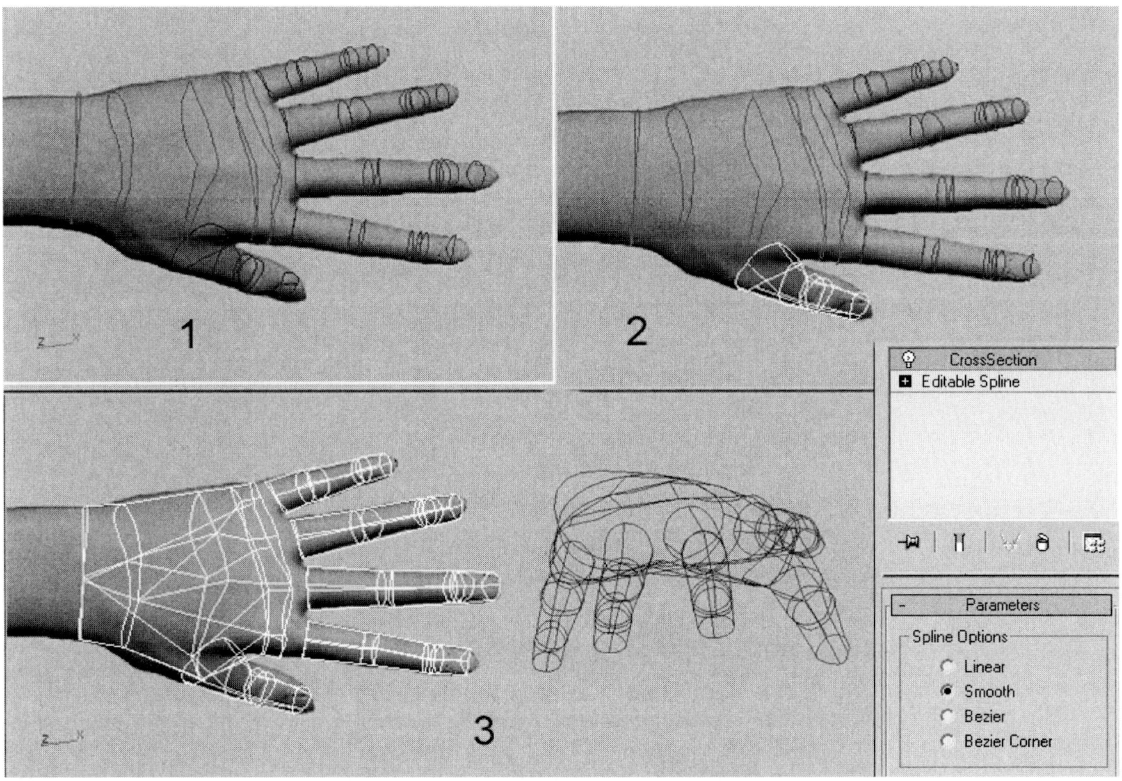

FIGURE 6.3 Apply the Cross Section Modifier to create the hand spline cage.

4. Select each finger and apply Cross Section to create all of the finger spline cages. Then, select the palm spline circles and apply Cross Section to create the palm spline cage, as shown in Figure 6.3, example 3. In the Cross Section Parameters, turn on Smooth. Now, select each spline cage and collapse them by converting them to Editable Spline. This removes Cross Section from the Stack.

When you apply Cross Section to circular splines of the palm of the hand, the number of vertex points changes on each spline circle from the wrist to the knuckle area. There are only 5 vertices at the wrist, but at the knuckles, the fingers need to connect to 10 vertices. The Cross Section Modifier automatically makes the transition from 5 to 10 vertex points by creating branching splines to connect the points of the palm splines circles to form a finished wire cage.

5. Right-click, and from the Quad menu select Unhide by Name, and then unhide the KnucklFRings object. This group of splines shows how the fingers are connected to the palm at the knuckles. In the perspective view, select the knuckle curves, and then zoom and Arc Rotate the object until you can see the individual splines that run from the finger end spline circles to the vertices of the palm at the knuckles.
6. Select the palm spline cage, then go to Editable Spline and click Attach to attach the knuckle curves to the palm. Next, click the finger spline cages to attach the entire hand together.
7. In Sub-object > Vertex mode, select the pairs of vertices at the base of the index finger where each of the small knuckle splines meets the large spline circle of the palm at the knuckles. Then, use the Editable Spline > Geometry > Fuse command to pull the spline ends to the knuckle spline circle, as shown in Figure 6.4, example 1. Do not weld these points.
8. Select the vertices of each finger base spline circle and move them so that they are contacting the vertices of the spline circles of the knuckles. Fuse these vertices. You will now have double circles at the base of each finger, as shown in Figure 6.4, example 2. Select and delete one of these spline circles for each finger, leaving only one spline circle at the base of each finger.
9. When finished you will notice that some of the vertices at the base of the fingers are not connected to splines. Turn on 3D Snap, set to Vertex Only, and then create small splines to connect these vertices to the corresponding vertices on the large knuckle spline circle using the Create Line tool, as shown in Figure 6.4, example 3.
10. Connect the base of the thumb spline circle to the closest palm spline. You will need to add two points to the long spline at the side of the palm using the Refine tool. When finished, examine all of the junctions between the long splines and the circular splines at the knuckles. Notice that many of the splines are curved under a bit. Use the Bézier handles to straighten out these splines so that the curves and the splines flow together nicely, as shown in Figure 6.4, example 4.

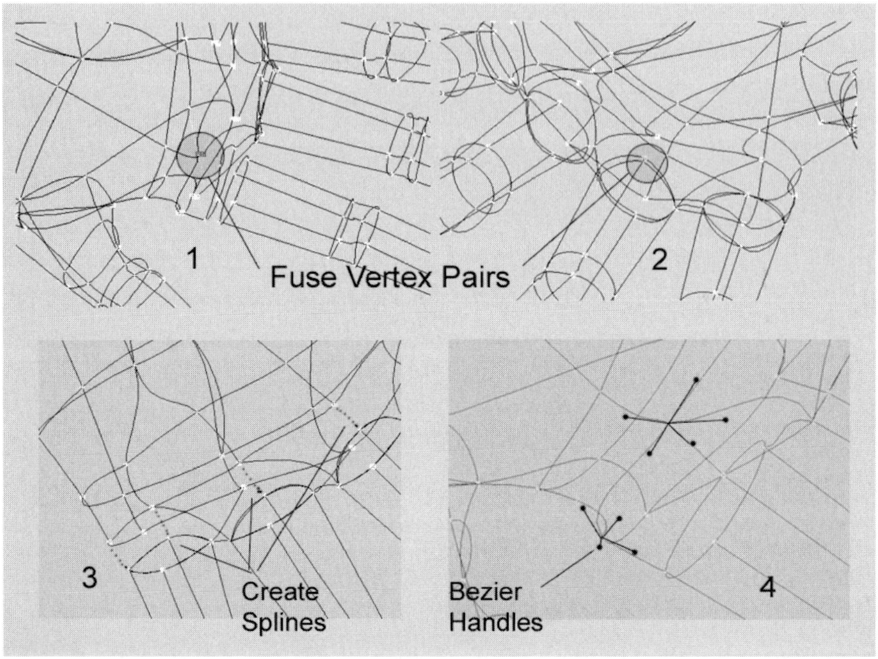

FIGURE 6.4 Fusing the finger splines to the knuckles.

If you do not see all of the Bézier handles, Marquis (rectangular) select the vertex, right-click, and in the Quad menu click Smooth, and then click Bézier. All of the handles should now be displayed for adjustment.

11. Save the scene as GenMan601.max.

In the next tutorial, you will add the fingernails.

TUTORIAL 6.2

ADD THE FINGERNAILS TO THE FINGERS

To add the fingernails:

1. Load the GenMan601.max scene. To see if there are mistakes in the spline cage, select the hand and then change the wire mesh color from dark blue to light blue. This makes it easier to see the surface. Turn off Edged Faces Display if it is on in any viewport.

2. Select the hand spline cage and click Modifiers > Patch/Spline Editing > Surface to create a skin on the hand. Notice that the hand is not skinning correctly, and a number of interior patches are visible, as shown in Figure 6.5, example 1.

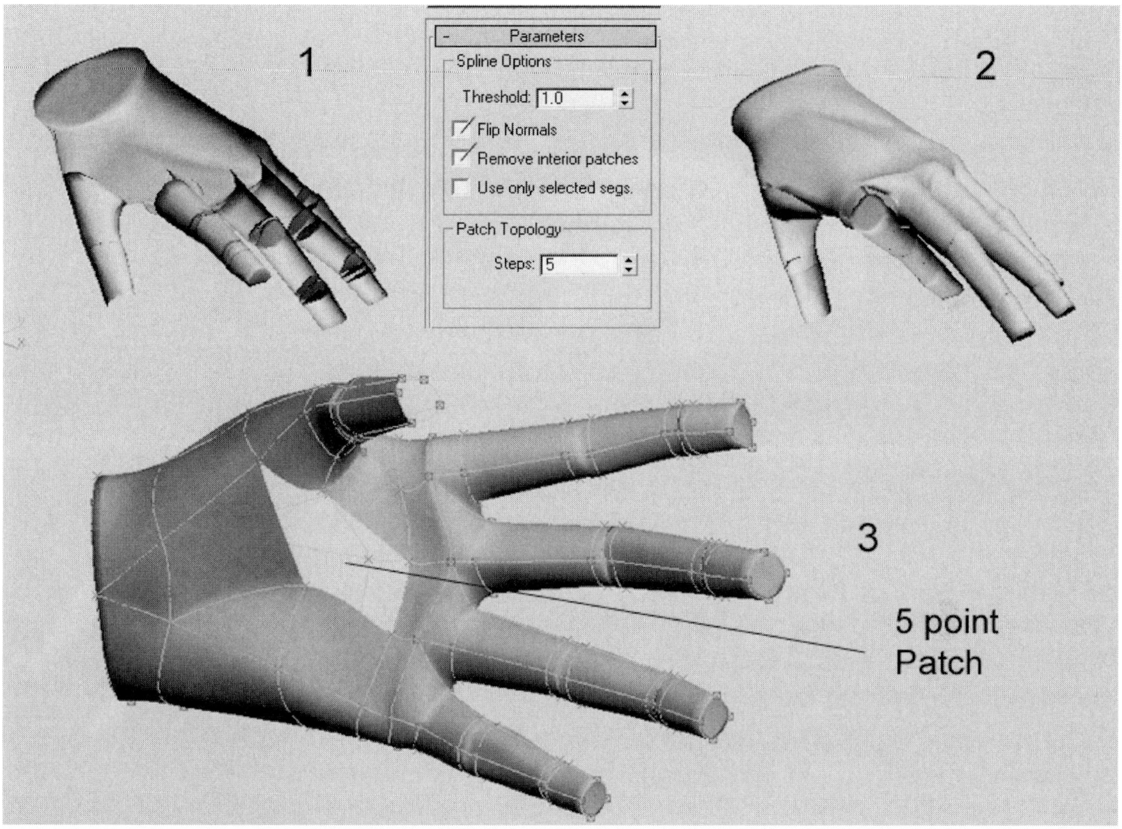

FIGURE 6.5 Correcting patch surface problems.

3. In the Surface Parameters, click Flip Normals and Remove Interior Patches. That will improve the appearance but, as shown in Figure 6.5, example 2, there could still be problems with the skin. Most skin problems are caused by pairs of vertices that are not properly fused together.
4. To fix the hand, click the Lightbulb icon in the Modifier Panel to turn off Surface. Then, check for 5-point patches that will not skin correctly. In addition, look for double splines at the edge of patches that can be removed.

The base of the thumb has a spline that was not removed when the thumb was attached. Select and delete the unneeded spline segments inside the base of the thumb, as shown in Figure 6.5, example 3.

5. When you have corrected these problems, turn on Surface again and inspect the hand. If it looks good, you're ready to add the fingernails. Delete Surface from the Stack and then right-click and select Unhide by Name. Unhide the object named Fingertip, as shown in Figure 6.6, example 1.

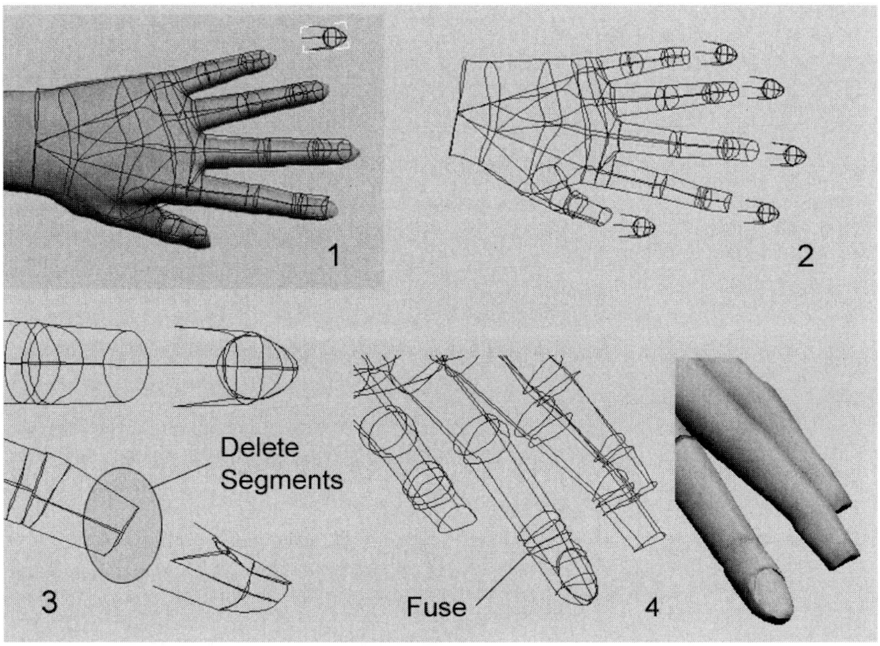

FIGURE 6.6 Putting the fingertips on the fingers.

6. The fingertip contains all of the curves necessary to build the fingernail and finish the end of the finger. Select and clone the Fingertip object and place a copy at the end of each finger, as shown in Figure 6.6, example 2. Starting with the middle finger, position the fingertip over the end of the finger spline cage. The last segments of the finger should be deleted to make room for the fingertip, as shown in Figure 6.6, example 3.
7. Position the fingertip on the end of the finger and make sure that the ends of the fingertip splines contact the vertices of the last knuckle spline circle,

as shown in Figure 6.6, example 4. When it is in position, select the hand, and then in the editable Spline menu, click Attach and then click the fingertip.

If you have difficulty aligning the fingertip to the finger, switch from the default View Reference Coordinates to Screen Reference Coordinates. Then, align the finger to the screen axis. You should be able to position the fingertips easily using Move in Screen mode.

8. Use the Fuse command to bring the corresponding pairs of vertices together. Avoid welding these points if you can. Welding causes the splines to re-adjust, changing the curvature of the spline cage, which wreaks havoc with the finger splines.
9. Repeat the preceding steps for each of the fingers and the thumb. You should Uniform scale the fingertips to fit each finger. When finished, reapply the Surface Modifier and use the Fuse command to fix any pairs of vertices that are not in contact. The hand should now look like the hand in Figure 6.2.
10. Save the scene as GenMan602.max.

In the next tutorial, you will load the Dr. Quin/Generic Man model from Chapter 5 and merge in the new hand. Then, you will mirror clone it, position it, and attach it to the arm.

TUTORIAL 6.3

Attach the Hand to the Arm

To attach the hand to the Dr. Quin model arm:

ON THE CD

1. Load the GenMan511.max file that you finished in Chapter 5, or load it from the Chap06 folder on the companion CD-ROM. This file should contain the unfinished Dr. Quin/Generic Man model with a partially finished body, a head and eyes, but no hands.

ON THE CD

2. Merge in L_HndPalm object from the GenMan602.max scene file, which you just finished, or merge it from the same file in the Chap06 folder on the companion CD-ROM. It will be approximately in the correct position at the end of the character's left arm.

3. In the top view, select and rotate the hand in the Z-axis about 8 degrees to align it with the end of the arm in the top and front views. Note: The arm is straight at this point. In a later tutorial you will bend the elbow a few degrees for fitting it on the skeleton, as shown in Figure 6.7, example 1.
4. With the hand selected, open the Modifier and remove Surface from the Stack, exposing the spline cage. Then, select the body spline cage and remove Surface from that Stack. Next, click Attach in the Editable Spline > Geometry menu and click on the hand spline cage in the viewport to attach the hand to the body, as shown in Figure 6.7, example 2.
5. To create the connection between the wrist of the hand and the wrist of the arm, maximize the top view and zoom in on the wrist area. Go to Vertex Sub-object mode and region select all the vertices of the last spline circle of the arm. Move it over to touch the wrist spline of the hand. You might need to re-position the arm vertices to match the location of the hand vertices at the wrist, as shown in Figure 6.7, example 3.

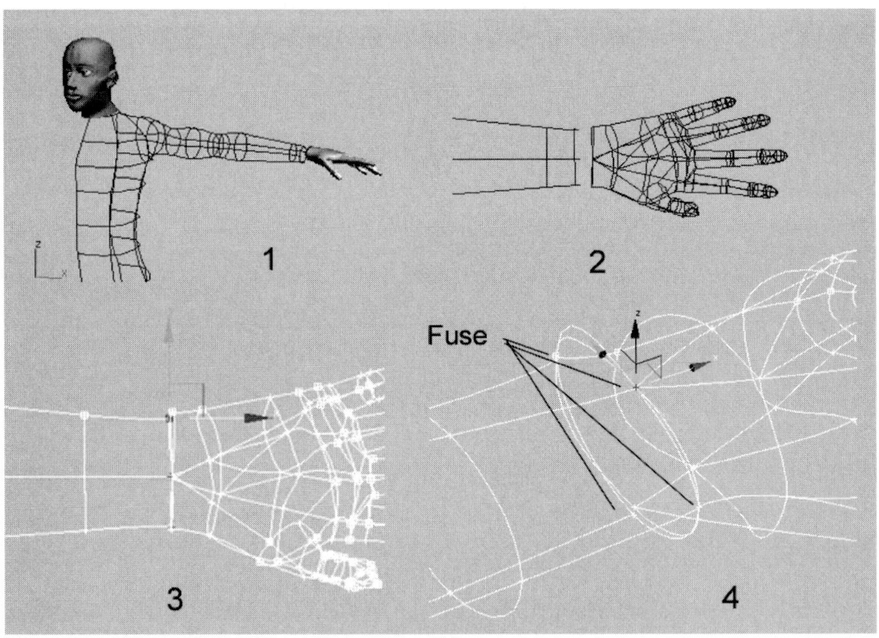

FIGURE 6.7 Merge and attach the hand to the arm.

6. Select and fuse corresponding pairs of vertices to complete the attachment of the hand, as shown in Figure 6.7, example 4. You now have two spline circles in the same location at the wrist. Select one and delete it.
7. Notice that the long splines that meet at the wrist are twisted at each of the four vertices. In Vertex mode, region select each pair, right-click, select Bézier from the Quad menu, and then use the Move tool to straighten out the Bézier handles and take the twist out of the splines. This will insure a smooth transition between the arm and the hand when you reapply Surface.
8. Re-apply the Surface Modifier to the body. The hand might look quite bad if the Surface > Parameters > Spline Options > Threshold is set to the default value of 1.0. If the fingers are missing, set the Threshold value down to .06. The fingers should now be visible. If the mesh looks hollow, click Flip Normals.

ON THE CD

9. Now that the hand is attached to the arm, you need to switch to the top view and bend the elbow of the arm. Maximize the top view and click Zoom Extents. The arm needs to be bent a few degrees at the elbow so that the skeleton will fit properly into the model. To do that, you will need to load a top view reference image of the body. Click Views > Viewport Background > Files, load the BodyTop.tif image from the Chap06\Images folder on the companion CD-ROM, and click Match Bitmap and Lock Zoom/Pan.
10. Position the background image to fit the snugly on the half of the body you have built, as shown in Figure 6.8, example 1. Then, select all the arm vertices from the wrist to the biceps and move them toward the back of the body. Next, select only the three rows of elbow vertices and move them backward until they are on top of the elbow in the background image, as shown in Figure 6.8, example 2.
11. Spread the vertices at the back of the elbow to make it a bit wider, and pull the center out farther to make the point of the elbow. Go over the arm and even up the vertex positions to match the background image shape. The arm should now be bent, as shown in Figure 6.8, example 3.
12. Save the scene as GenMan603.max.

In the next tutorial, you will clone the body to create the right half, and then fuse them together.

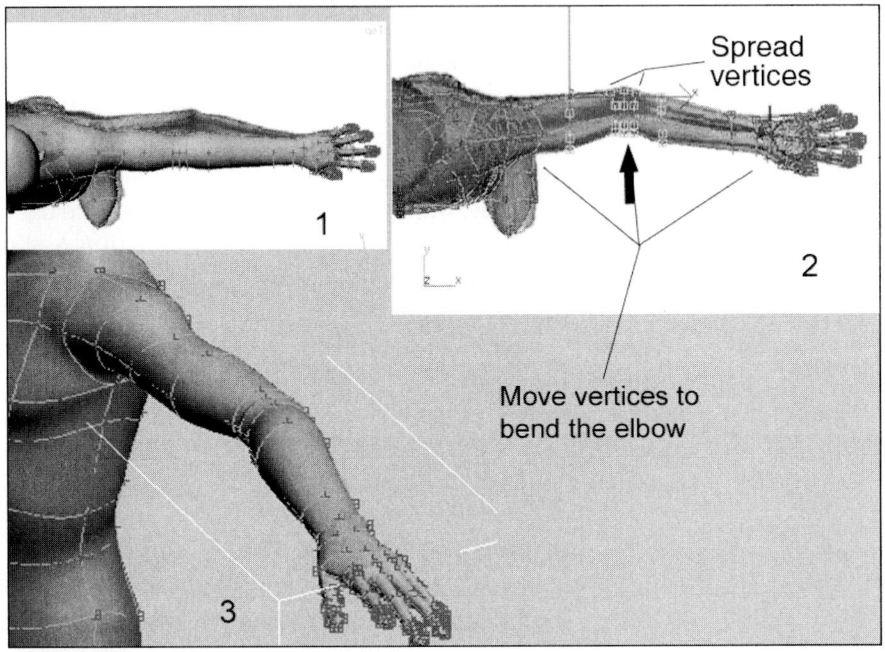

FIGURE 6.8 Bending the elbow by moving vertices of the arm.

TUTORIAL 6.4

MIRROR CLONE AND FUSE THE BODY

To mirror clone the body:

1. Load the GenMan603.max file. Make sure that all splines and spline segments are visible, and then select and hide the head and the eyes.
2. Maximize the front view and click Zoom Extents, and then select the body and open the Modifier Panel. Delete Surface from the Stack leaving only the spline cage.
3. In Editable Spline > Segment Sub-object mode, region select all the spline segments of the character's right side (on your left), but do not select the centerline spline, as shown in Figure 6.9, example 1. Delete these segments.
4. Examine the centerline, and move vertex pairs as needed to make sure that it is straight. This will insure that the two halves of the body meet properly. Turn off Vertex Sub-object mode in the Editable Spline modifier. The left side body half should now be selected.
5. Check to see if the XYZ gizmo is centered on the body centerline. If it is not, click the Hierarchy tab and Adjust Pivot > Affect Pivot Only, and then move the pivot point to the centerline.

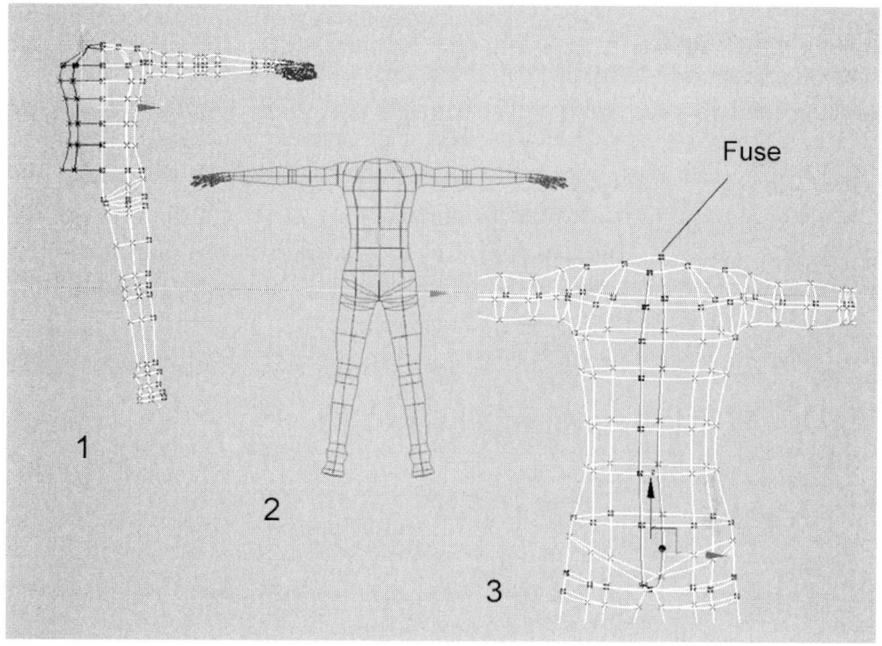

FIGURE 6.9 Mirror clone and fuse the body halves.

6. Click the Mirror Clone icon in the menu bar, and in the dialog box click Copy. The X-axis should be chosen by default. The right side of the body should now be visible, as shown in Figure 6.9, example 2. Open Editable Spline and click Attach. Place the cursor over the half of the body and click to attach it.
7. Zoom in and Arc Rotate the body a few degrees in the front view until you can easily see the entire centerline spline. You now have two centerline splines where the halves of the body meet. Select and delete one of these splines. It might be in separate pieces, so you will need to select all of the pieces to delete, leaving one complete centerline spline, as shown in Figure 6.9, example 3.
8. Use the Editable Spline > Vertex > Fuse command to fuse all of the corresponding pairs of vertices along the centerline (one pair at a time). Do not weld these vertices. To prevent the Weld menu from popping up, set the Weld Threshold to 0.0.
9. Re-apply the Surface Modifier. The surface might have problems such as the skin showing holes. Check around the holes to make sure that all vertex pairs are fused. In addition, inspect the Bézier handles in problem areas

or around unwanted creases. If any are folded under, select the Bézier handles and move them to straighten out the splines and restore the surface.

10. Unhide all, and save the scene as GenMan604.max.

In the next tutorial, you will finish the feet. This model is a generic man used to create many other characters. Shoes will cover the feet, so there is no point in making the feet realistic as no toes will be needed. The important thing is that the feet are shaped to simulate a human foot.

TUTORIAL 6.5

FINISHING THE FEET

To finish the feet:

1. Load the GenMan604.max file and zoom in on the feet in the front view. The feet are very simple and do not have much shape, as shown in Figure 6.10, example 1.

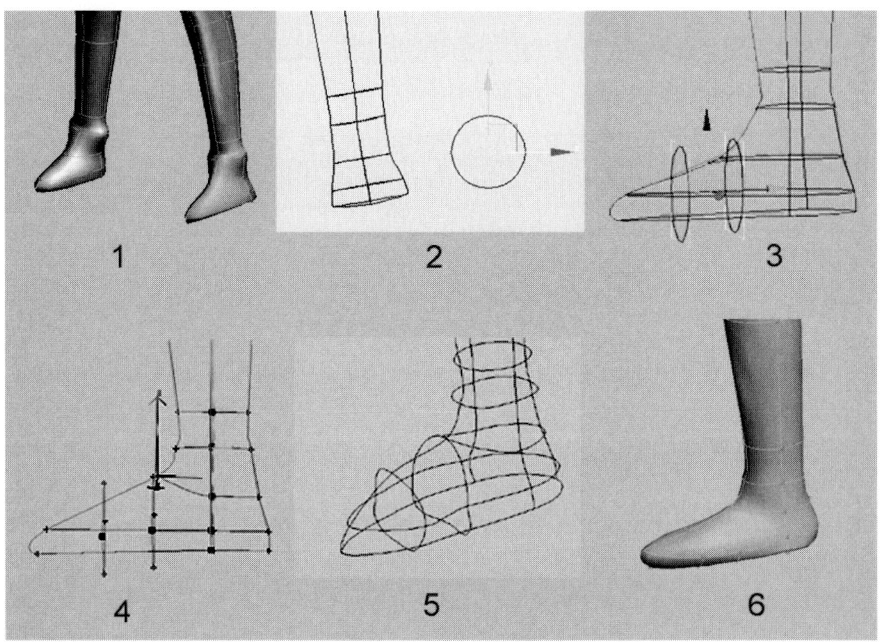

FIGURE 6.10 Finishing the feet.

2. To improve the feet and make them fit inside shoes, you will add two spline circles and sculpt the shape by moving vertices. Zoom in on the feet in the front view, and then select the model and turn off the Surface Modifier in the Stack.
3. Smooth the sides of the left ankle by moving vertex pairs, and then go to the Create > Shapes menu and click the Circle button. In the front view, click and drag to create a spline circle next to the character's left foot, as shown in Figure 6.10, example 2. Select and Move to copy this circle, and then move both circles over the foot. Switch to the right view (press V then R) and zoom in on the feet.
4. Select the body, and then select the Splines of the character's right foot and hide them using Editable Spline > Geometry > Hide. This will make it easier to work on the left foot in the left viewport.
5. Select and move the two spline circles so that one surrounds the ball of the foot and the other surrounds the arch of the foot, as shown in Figure 6.10, example 3. Use the Arc Rotate tool to tip the view slightly so you can look at a correct side view of the foot. Then, set the viewport Reference Coordinate System to Screen.
6. Select the body, and then in the Editable Spline menu click Attach and attach the two new spline circles to the body. Select the front vertex pair of the existing horizontal spline that forms the arch of the foot and raise it to meet the top vertex in the new arch spline circle you just added. Then, fuse the vertices, as shown in Figure 6.10, example 4.
7. You will need to refine the foot splines to add more points so that the new spline circles can be fused into the foot. Click the Editable Spline > Geometry > Refine button, and then click the original foot splines next to the new spline circles to add points. In addition, add points to the new spline circles to match the points you added to the foot. When finished, select and fuse corresponding vertex pairs to integrate the new splines into the foot, as shown in Figure 6.10, example 5.
8. Use the 3d Snap > Vertex and the Create Line functions to add a spline running under the centerline of the foot to connect the splines, the toe, and the heel. Then, select and adjust the positions of all the foot vertex pairs to sculpt the foot into a pleasing shape, as shown in Figure 6.10, example 6.
9. To make the other foot match, switch to the front view, unhide all of the splines, and then in Sub-object > Segment mode, select the revised left foot. In the Editable Spline > Geometry roll-out menu click Copy and Detach. Click OK in the Detach pop-up window, and then exit Editable Spline.

10. Click the H key (Select by Name), click on Shape 1, and click OK. Then, click the Mirror Clone icon and make a copy of the foot splines. The copy will appear next to the character's right foot. To finish, go back to Editable Spline > Segment, select the right foot splines up to the ankle, and delete them. Then, move the new cloned and mirrored foot into place and fuse the ankle spline vertices. You should now have two finished feet.
11. Save the scene as GenMan605.max.

In the next tutorial, you will begin the process of finishing all the details of the model starting with the head. The body, with the exception of the hands, is sufficiently finished to animate as it is because it will be covered with clothing. The head and face need additional work to correct errors in proportions and to smooth out surface irregularities.

This must be done before adding hair, texture maps, and clothing. The head of the Dr. Quin/Generic Man model will be left as a separate object to facilitate creating morph targets for facial expressions and lip-sync animation. The seam at the neck will be hidden by clothing such as a shirt collar. In a case where the neck would be shown, the seam can either be moved down to the shoulders or up under the chin and lower hairline to hide it.

TUTORIAL 6.6 FINISHING THE GENERIC MAN HEAD

To finish the head of the Generic Man:

1. Load the GenMan605.max scene file. Unhide All, hide the body and the eyes, and, in the front view, zoom in on the head. Select the head and in the Modifier Panel turn off Surface (click the Lightbulb icon) to display the spline cage.

ON THE CD

2. It is important to correct the proportions and placement of the features at this time. Load the reference image G_HeadFnt.tif from the Chap06\ Images folder on the companion CD-ROM into the front viewport background. Turn on Match bitmap and Lock Zoom/Pan. Then, align the head over the background image (use background lock toggle, Ctrl-Alt-B). Line up the eyes and the mouth, as shown in Figure 6.11, example 1.

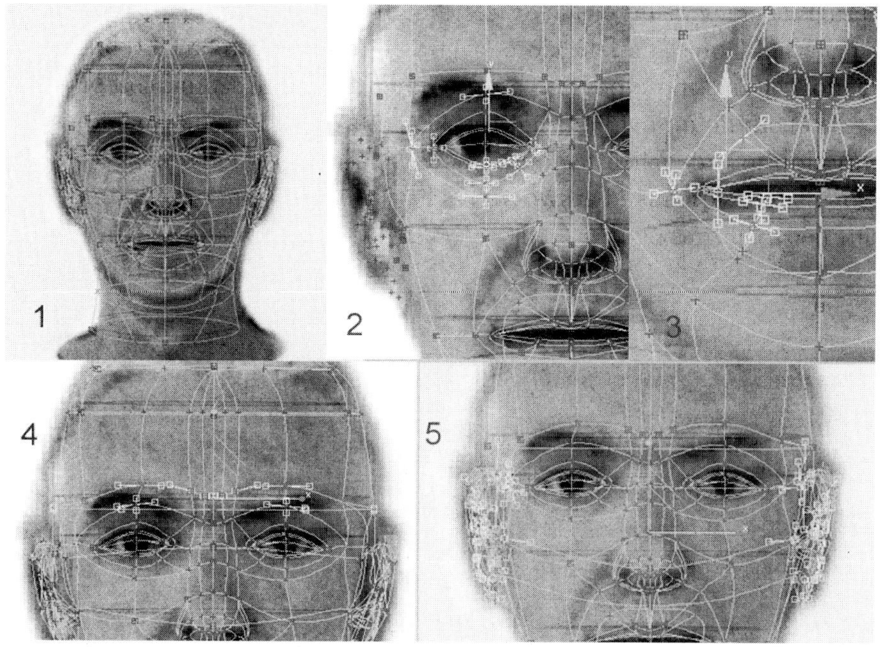

FIGURE 6.11 Adjust the facial proportions with the background image.

ON THE CD

After the eyes and mouth of your head model are aligned to the background image, you can adjust the rest of the head proportions to fit. For example, in the case of the GenMan605.max file from the companion CD-ROM, the head is distorted, the eyes are too narrow, and the mouth is too wide. Both the jaw and the cranium are too narrow and the nose is too long. The eye openings are too big and the brow area is too narrow. The width of the head is too narrow and the ears are too low. Facial proportions are very subtle and very important. Once you correct all of these problems, the head will look more realistic.

3. Hide the splines of the back of the head so you can work on the face with less visual confusion. Switch to the left view, and then in Editable Spline > Segment Sub-object mode, select all the spline segments of the back of the head including the ears. Then, in the Geometry menu, click Hide. Next, return to the front view. You might need to re-align the image with the background. The vertices of the ear will still be visible, but you will not be able to select those that are part of the back of the head, which is hidden.
4. The next step is to determine the final position and size of the eye openings. The vertical distance from the eye centers to the mouth center

should be maintained. In Vertex Sub-object mode, select all of the vertices of one eye, lock the selection, and move them to center them over the background reference eye. Repeat this for the other eye. Then, select and scale the eye openings to match as closely as possible the background image. Be sure to always lock the selection (spacebar) so you don't accidentally scale the Bézier handles instead of the vertices.

5. The eye opening might be too tall. If so, move up the vertices on the upper and lower eyelids as needed. In addition, check the width and the shape of the splines around the eye. Adjust the Bézier curve handles to shape the eye opening, as shown in Figure 6.11, example 2.
6. Zoom out a little and then select, move, and scale the lower part of the nose to match the background image. Select the corners of the mouth and position them over the mouth in the background image, as shown in Figure 6.11, example 3. Then, make sure the upper and lower lip splines match the background image lips.
7. At the outer corners of the nose, two lines run down to the sides of the mouth. Adjust their width to match the line that defines the lower edge of the cheeks above the mouth.
8. Go to Segment Sub-object mode and click Geometry > Unhide All to reveal all the spline segments of the head. You can now adjust the width of the head and jaw, and the placement of the ears. Select the line of vertices at the brow and scale them out as needed to make the width of the spline cage match the background image, as shown in Figure 6.11, example 4.
9. Select, re-position, and adjust the angle of the ears to match the background image, as shown in Figure 6.11, example 5. Once the major proportions look correct, turn on the Surface Modifier and make any necessary adjustments.

The positions seen in the front view will not be the same as the positions seen in the side view reference image. This should not be a problem. As long as the face looks correct from the front, it will look realistic in most of the close-up shots. You can go in and move some of the items around to find a best over-all compromise position for the ears by splitting the difference between the front and side views. This mismatch can happen when the front and side views were originally photographed with the head at slightly different angles.

10. Save the scene as GenMan606.max.

There is more smoothing and detail work to be done on the head before it is finished. In the next tutorial, you will work on the details of the lips and add an inner mouth cavity where the teeth and tongue will be added to facilitate lip-sync dialog animation.

TUTORIAL 6.7 REFINE THE LIPS AND ADD THE INNER MOUTH OPENING

To refine the lips:

1. Load the GenMan606.max scene file.
2. In the front view, turn off Display Background, and then select the head. In the Modifier Panel, turn off the Surface Modifier. Next, hide the spline segments of the back of the head as you did in the previous tutorial. Depending on what material or wiremesh color you are using, the splines might be hard to see. Apply a dark blue color to make the splines easily visible. This will make it easier to work on the mouth and reduce visual confusion.

The mouth was built with the minimum number of splines, and because of that the shape is symmetrical, but not very realistic. To improve it you will need to add additional splines to subdivide the lower lip. This will also give you two more attachment points inside the mouth where you will be adding the inner mouth surface and teeth.

3. Zoom in on the mouth, as shown in Figure 6.12, example 1. To refine the lower lip, go to Editable Spline > Vertex mode, and in the Geometry menu click Refine. Three lower lip splines run horizontally. Click all three splines to add a vertex in a vertical row one-third of the way over from the left corner. Then, do the same thing one-third of the way over from the right corner.
4. Now, continue the refinement down the chin on both sides, by clicking on each of the chin splines until you reach the neck, as shown in Figure 6.12, example 2. Next, you will create splines to connect the new points.
5. Click the 3D Snap icon, and then right-click it and select Vertex. Snap splines to the new vertices by clicking Editable Spline > Geometry > Create Line, and then clicking on each vertex in the vertical row of vertices on the right side of the chin. Repeat that for the left side. You should now have two splines running down the lower lip curves and down the chin to the neck, as shown in Figure 6.12, example 3.

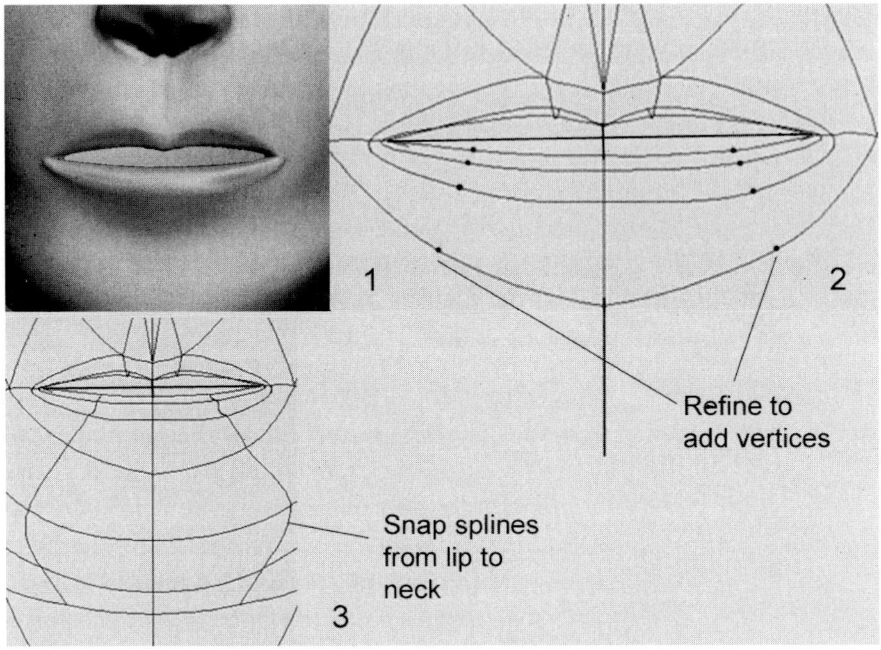

FIGURE 6.12 Refine the lower lip and chin.

ON THE CD

6. Next, select the two splines that can be seen crossing the center of the mouth and delete them to clear the mouth opening. Because of the complexity of explaining how to build the inner surface of the mouth, the necessary spline cage has been supplied for you on the companion CD-ROM.

ON THE CD

7. To load the Inner Mouth Surface into the scene, click File > Merge and then select the InnerMouth.max file from the Chap06 folder on the companion CD-ROM. In the Merge file dialog, click All and then click OK. The inner mouth object should now be in the scene, as shown in Figure 6.13, example 1. Notice that it looks hollow in a shaded view. The surface Normals are flipped inside so that the inner surface is visible and the outer is transparent.
8. If the inner mouth is not correctly positioned behind the lips inside the head, select and move it into position so that the back curve of the mouth matches the front curve of the inner mouth. Do not attach it to the head at this time. You will attach it later, after you fit the teeth into the mouth.

ON THE CD

9. Merge in the teeth and tongue in the same way you merged the inner mouth object by merging the TeethTongue.max scene file in the Chap06

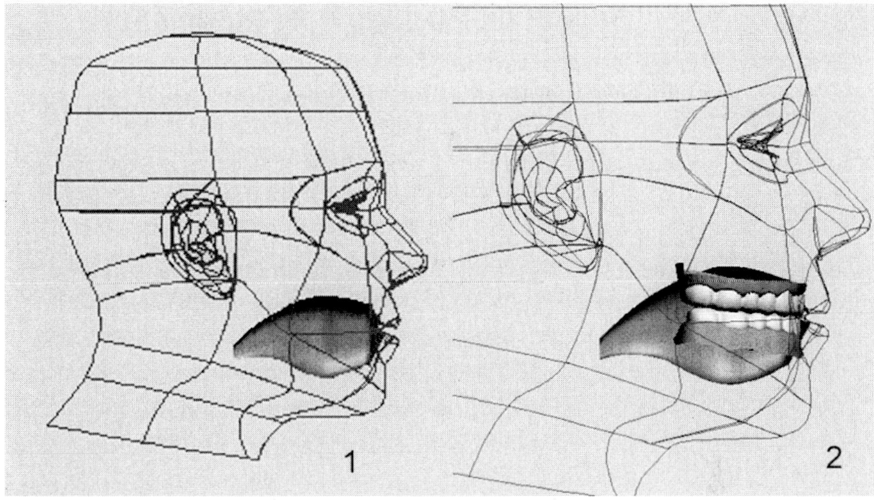

FIGURE 6.13 Merge the inner mouth surface into the head.

folder on the companion CD-ROM, as shown in Figure 6.13, example 2. In the File Merge dialog, select Teeth, which contains the teeth and the tongue, and then click OK.

10. Position Group01 inside the inner mouth, but do not attach them to the model at this time. They will be adjusted and linked to the skeleton in a later tutorial, when the model is prepared for lip-sync animation in Chapter 8, "Preparing for Character Animation."
11. Save the scene as GenMan607.max.

In the next tutorial, you will smooth the head and then re-position the neck seam.

To create the morph targets, copies of the head must be made. This is to enable the creation of Morph Targets for facial animation. That means that the head must remain separated from the body so it can be cloned. The problem is that the existing neck seam is too high up on the neck so it can be seen when the character wears an open-collar shirt or uniform. The solution is to move the neck seam downward by incorporating a new spline circle into shoulders, and then use that as the seam between the body and the head.

TUTORIAL 6.8

SMOOTH THE HEAD AND MOVE THE NECK SEAM

To smooth and adjust the head and body:

1. Load the GenMan607.max scene file. Unhide All objects and click Zoom Extents All. The head should be blue from the previous tutorial. Select the head, and then change the spline cage color (or the material color, if you have applied a material) to a flesh color to match the body.

ON THE CD

2. Turn on the Surface Modifier in the Stack to display the head surface. Locate the worst problems on the head surface. In the sample GenMan607.max file (on the companion CD-ROM in the Chap06 folder), the problems are very pronounced around the ear. You might have different problems with your model, but as an example of how to fix a Bézier handle problem you can load this file and see how we adjusted the Bézier handles to smooth the problem, as shown in Figure 6.14, example 1.

There are usually a number of irregularities that perturb a new spline patch model. One way to reduce these problems is to apply the Relax Modifier, but that only takes care of small problems. To completely smooth every irregularity in the head, you will need to spend time adjusting the Bézier handles at every problem point to achieve the smoothest surface you can. Welding the spline ends usually introduces additional problems, so that is not recommended; using the Fuse command is recommended instead.

3. To smooth the problem above either ear on the sample model, zoom in on the area and Arc Rotate the view until you can easily see the problem above the ear. There is a groove in the surface caused by an incorrect angle of one of the Bézier handles. Go into Editable Spline > Vertex mode, and turn on the Show End Result on/off Toggle button below the Stack window.
4. Select the vertex just above the ear, as shown in Figure 6.14, example 2. There should be five Bézier handles visible. If you only see two handles, place the cursor on the vertex, right-click, select Smooth, and then select Bézier from the upper-left Quad menu. That resets the handle display. Five handles should now appear. If you see four, one is probably hidden inside the surface.
5. By clicking Smooth, part of the problem has been corrected because the Smooth setting equalizes all Bézier handle angles where three or more splines come together at a vertex. However, there is still a large hollow area above the ear. To fix that, you need to move the handle that points down behind the ear.

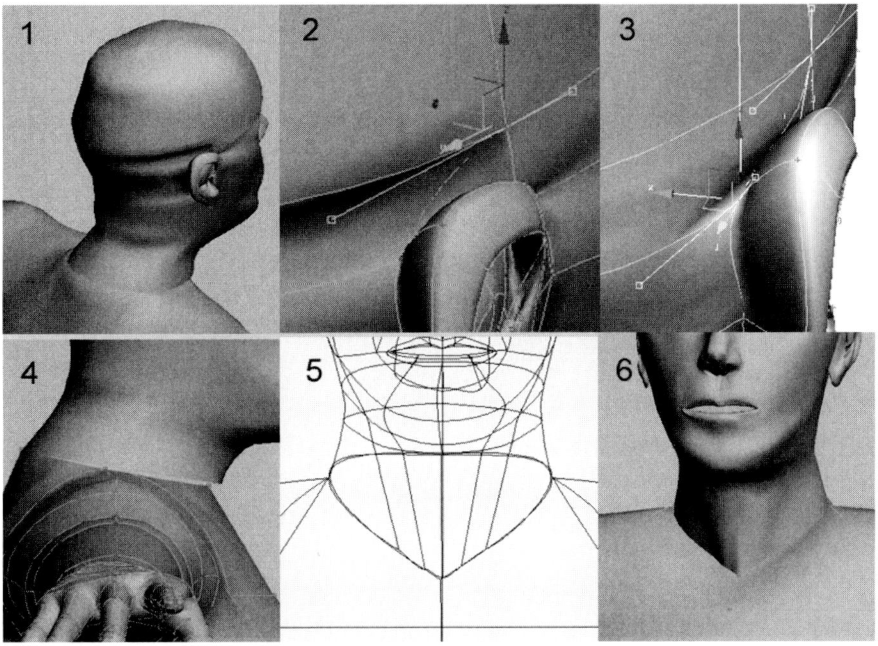

FIGURE 6.14 Adjusting the Bézier handles to correct surface problems.

The cursor will respond slowly with the Surface Modifier turned on. For quick action, turn off Surface and temporarily color the spline cages dark blue to see the splines in the viewport. The vertices will now move more quickly. When finished, turn on Surface and change back to the flesh color.

6. Try moving the handle by clicking and dragging it with the cursor. If it moves in the wrong direction, you can change the direction by pressing the F5, F6, F7, or F8 key. These keys control the axis constraints for X, Y, Z, and XY, respectively. The best guess is to try F8 (move in XY) first. If the Bézier handle still moves the wrong way, try each of the other hotkeys. One of them will let you move the Bézier handle toward the ear and minimize the hollow behind the ear. You will need to adjust the Bézier handles of the nearby vertices to help spread the curvature across a wider area of the surface, as shown in Figure 6.14, example 3.
7. Because the head will be cloned to create facial morph targets for lip-sync animation, the head and the body will not be attached. The original seam at the neck will be re-shaped and the seam moved downward to hide it below the level of the collar. Move the neck opening vertices of the head

to align with the neck opening of the body, as shown in Figure 6.14, example 4. On the head, select the five vertices at the front of the neck, pull them downward, and form them into a V-shape where the "pit of the neck" should be, as shown in Figure 6.14, examples 5 and 6.

8. Next, a new neck seam must be created that is farther down into the shoulder area, and the original neck seam must be fused together and smoothed. This is done by inserting an additional spline circle into the shoulders below the neck. To insert a new neck seam spline, refine each of the shoulder splines just below the neck opening to add a vertex, as shown in Figure 6.15, example 1. Turn off the Surface Modifier on the body. In Spline Sub-object mode, select and Shift > Move to clone the body neck spline and move it downward a short distance.
9. Select the new spline, and then Non-uniform scale it in the X-axis to double its width, as shown in Figure 6.15, example 2. Refine the new neck circle spline to add two points on each side, and then fuse its vertices to the new points you added to the shoulder splines, as shown in Figure 6.15, example 3. Re-shape the top of the shoulders and the neck to create a more natural athletic shape, as shown in Figure 6.15, example 4.

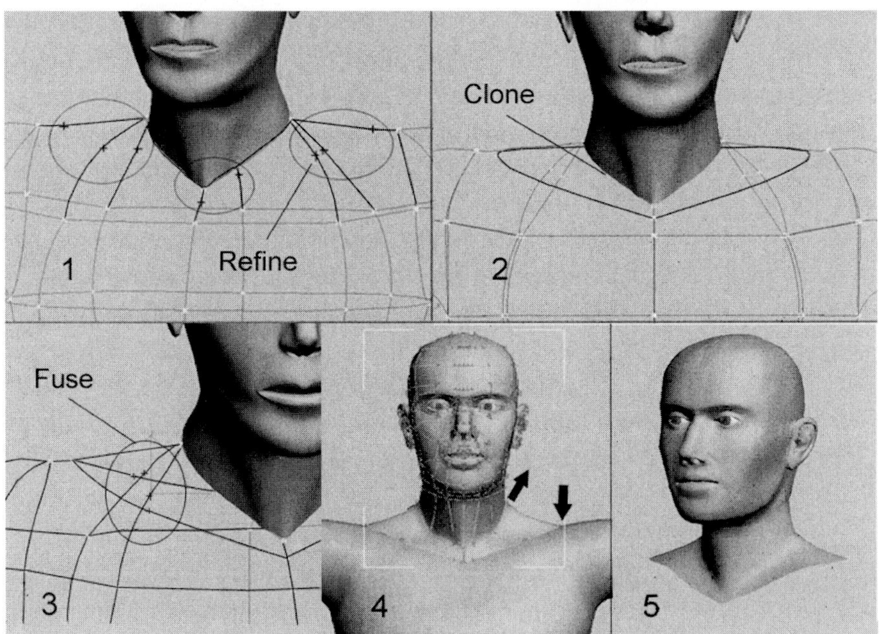

FIGURE 6.15 Moving the neck seam down.

10. Click the Attach button and temporarily attach the head to the body. Then, fuse the vertices of the original neck opening at the sides and back. In the front of the neck, use the Create Line tool and 3D Snap > Vertices to extend the bottom of the throat splines down to the new neck seam spline. Refine to add points to the spline and fuse them to it. Next, delete the second neck spline at the old seam.
11. The mesh is now one piece, but you must separate the head so it includes the new neck seam. To do so, create a clone of the new seam. Select and clone the new neck seam spline using the Edit > Clone command. This way, you will not move it, and the edges of the new seam will match perfectly.
12. Once the seam is cloned, select all of the spline segments of the head as well as the spline segments above the new seam, along with one of the new neck seams, and detach them using the Editable Spline > Geometry > Detach as Object command. Name the new object Head. You can then select and hide the body and you should see a complete separate head and upper shoulders, as shown in Figure 6.15, example 5.
13. Save the scene file as GenMan608.max.

In the next tutorial, you will finish the final contours of the face.

TUTORIAL 6.9 FINISHING THE FACE

To finish the face:

1. To determine what the face will look like when finished, apply the Relax Modifier to the top of the Stack above MeshSmooth. Relax is usually applied at the very end of the modeling process. It will make the surface contract slightly and remove small bumps and hollows. If there still are surface problems, they must be fixed at this point.
2. The lips and nose require careful adjustment to achieve softness and roundness. Zoom in close and Arc Rotate the view to look at the lip surface from every angle, as shown in Figure 6.16, example 1. It helps to toggle F3 on and off to be sure you are seeing all of the Bézier handles. In addition, toggle off the X key (display Gizmo) to make it easier to select and move the ends of the Bézier handles, as shown in Figure 6.16, example 2.

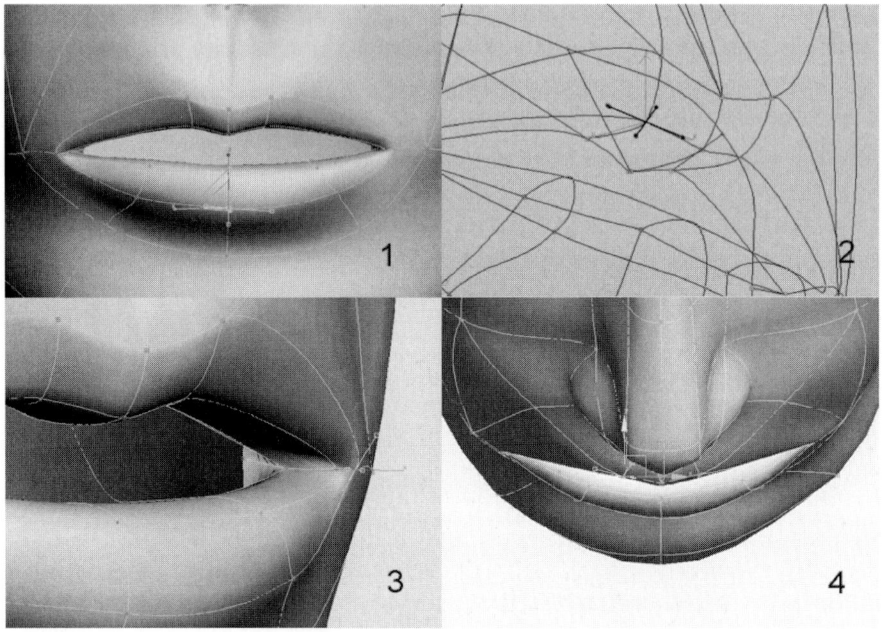

FIGURE 6.16 Adjusting the curvature of the lips.

3. The outer corners of the mouth need to be angles so that the lower lip lines are slightly farther in than the upper lip lines. Round the contours of the mid-lip splines, as shown in Figure 6.16, example 3. Check the overall curvature of the lips from the top to see how the contours are blending with the face.
4. If an area of the face is difficult to adjust, such as the cheek area beside the nose, add one or two more splines to refine the surface. If you want to put a crease in the face or make the edge of the lip sharper, add two splines that run side by side. This will create a crease in the surface, as shown in Figure 6.17, example 1.
5. Add additional splines to help refine the chin area under the jaw. In many cases, you will need to delete a spline segment and then add additional segments to extend a spline to create more flowing lines for the curves on the side of the head. Do this to the spline at the top of the neck to extend it below and up behind the ear, as shown in Figure 6.17, example 2.
6. The inner ear will need to be revised to create a more natural shape. Delete any segments that run in chaotic directions, and add new spline

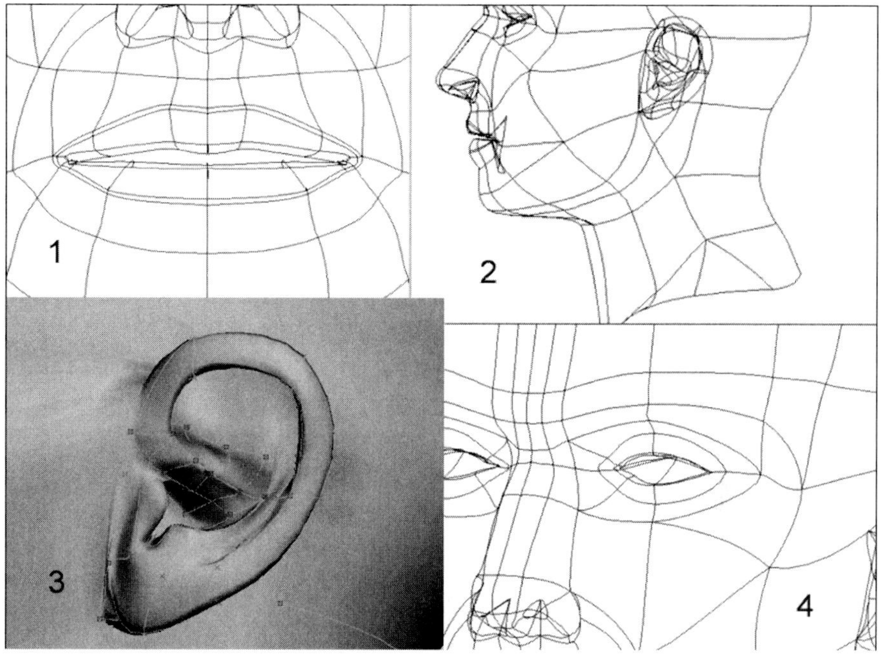

FIGURE 6.17 Adding splines to finish the face.

segments that help to create more smooth and flowing lines. The ear is complex and will require close study to make it more realistic, as shown in Figure 6.17, example 3.

7. The area around the eye and the temple should be enhanced by re-arranging the splines of the eyebrow and adding another spline above the brow. Two brow splines will improve your control over the contours, as shown in Figure 6.17, example 4. Since the face will be seen in close-up shots, the eye nose, and mouth area are very important to get smooth and correctly shaped.

The author used photos of his own features as references to shape the facial features, but instead of copying, he modified and enhanced them to make the face more generic and stronger. The final generic man face can be made to look like anyone.

8. Save the scene as GenMan609.max.

THE FINAL DETAILS

Finishing the face can take a considerable amount of time depending on how realistic you want your finished model to be. In the *Homing Instinct* project, this character is used as the basis of many other characters by modifying the shape of the splines and adding creases and other details to the face. A polygon mesh version of this mesh can be made by converting the surface to an Editable Poly or and Editable Mesh. This will allow you to more easily modify the shapes of the body by using the Soft Select tool. High-resolution spline patch surfaces tend to slow the screen refresh rate during animation. Editable Polygon was chosen as the standard method of creating low-resolution versions of all models in scenes where there are animated groups of people and crowds.

You can reduce the resolution of a spline patch model by changing the Patch Topology Steps setting in the Surface Modifier. The useable range is from 6 to 2. At 2, you will sacrifice much of the surface detail, but this will help to speed screen refresh time and make animation much easier. When the animation is done, you can raise the Patch Topology back up to 6 for the final rendering. The Level of Detail utility is used to switch between low-polygon and high-polygon models depending on how far away the camera is from the model. These concepts are covered in Chapter 10, "Scene Animation."

CONCLUSION

In this chapter, you finished the construction of the Dr. Quin/Generic Man spline patch model.

In the next chapter, you will create a skeleton to fit the model and rig it for animation. Then, in Chapter 8, you will add slider controls and clothing. In Chapter 13, you will add surface textures, and in Chapter 17, you will add hair using the Shag Hair plug-in.

CHAPTER

7

CHARACTER SETUP WITH BONES

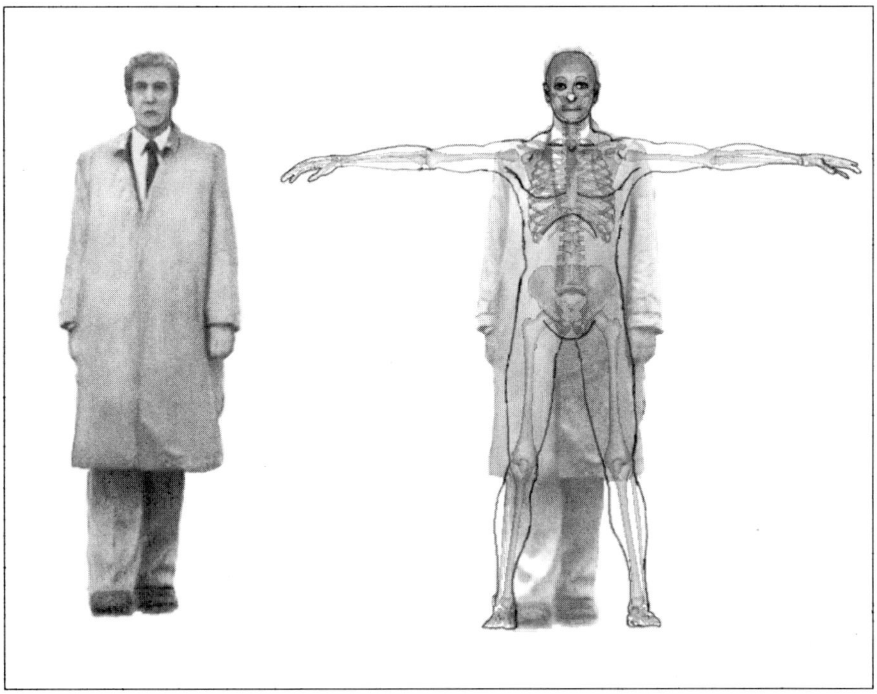

In the film *Homing Instinct*, animated characters are called on to perform a wide variety of motions, from fighting and stunts to complicated interaction with hand props and machinery. Bones in 3ds max have a number of special attributes that make them uniquely suited for character animation.

By using Inverse Kinematics (IK) and a slider to control the hand, a complex movement such as reaching out and picking up a cup of coffee becomes a simple proposition. If the same movement were animated using only joint rotations, you would find it difficult and very time consuming. IK is designed for making smooth, fluid movements, with automatic joint rotations distributed over many joints.

There are many different types of skeletons that you could build. A skeleton built mainly for walking will not work well for all types of action. In visual effects or stunt shots, special situations arise that require a more complex skeleton built specifically to perform the stunt. Therefore, when designing your skeletal rig, it is important to bear in mind the specific purpose of the skeleton. Each structure in the human body has its own type of movement. A person can move with grace, or be extremely awkward. If the character is strong or heavy, this should be reflected in his or her movements. The same idea applies to a weak or a fat character.

Three different examples of skeletal proportions have nearly the same sized cranium: an adolescent girl, a four-year-old child, and an adult male, as shown in Figure 7.1. The skeletons shown are from the program Poser 4. (See the appendix for details on programs used in the *Homing Instinct* project.)

CREATING A SKELETAL SYSTEM

A basic skeletal system in 3ds max consists of a bones hierarchy with IK applied to each limb and to the spine. For simulating human motion, a more sophisticated fully rigged skeletal system includes additional linkages, constraints, and control points that are designed to mix together the motions of multiple joints to create smooth coordinated movements in different areas of the body. The hand and finger motions, an important part of all gestures, are not operated with IK. Instead, they are controlled by a set of external slider controls that are wired to operate the appropriate finger and hand bones. The sliders let you close and open individual

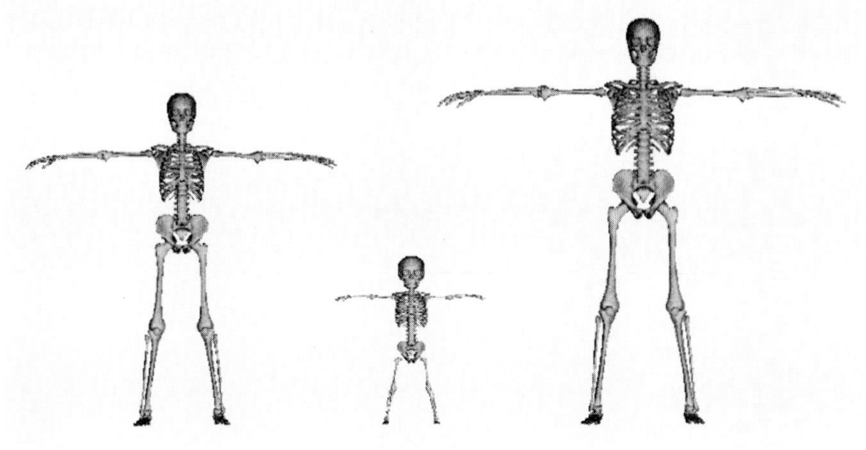

FIGURE 7.1 The different proportions of a girl, a child, and a man.

fingers and wave the hands without having to select the finger bones. Another set of sliders controls the jaw, facial expressions, eye, and eyelid motions. When the model is finished and ready to animate in a scene, a Look At constraint is applied to the eyes to make them point at a target point in the environment.

A skeleton called "the Acrobat" is the most elaborate one used in the *Homing Instinct* film project. It was designed to facilitate the animation of stunts and fights. It has extra controls added to the upper legs, upper arms, shoulders, hips, legs, and feet that make it easier to animate a kick, a spin on one foot, a flip, or multiple punches by moving sliders, as shown in Figure 7.2. For most character animation, a much simpler skeleton is adequate and will work very well. The skeleton on the right uses spline circles to control the skeleton in place of the box and cross style point helpers used to control the skeleton on the left. Many animators prefer the spline circle style rig because it looks less cluttered in the Max viewport and is easier for beginners to understand. However, both skeleton rigs work in the same way, and either can be used effectively once you become familiar with skeleton rigging.

CONSTRUCTING A SKELETON FOR A SPECIFIC CHARACTER

The first tutorial takes you through the process of building a basic human skeleton. Advanced users might want to jump to Tutorial 7.6,

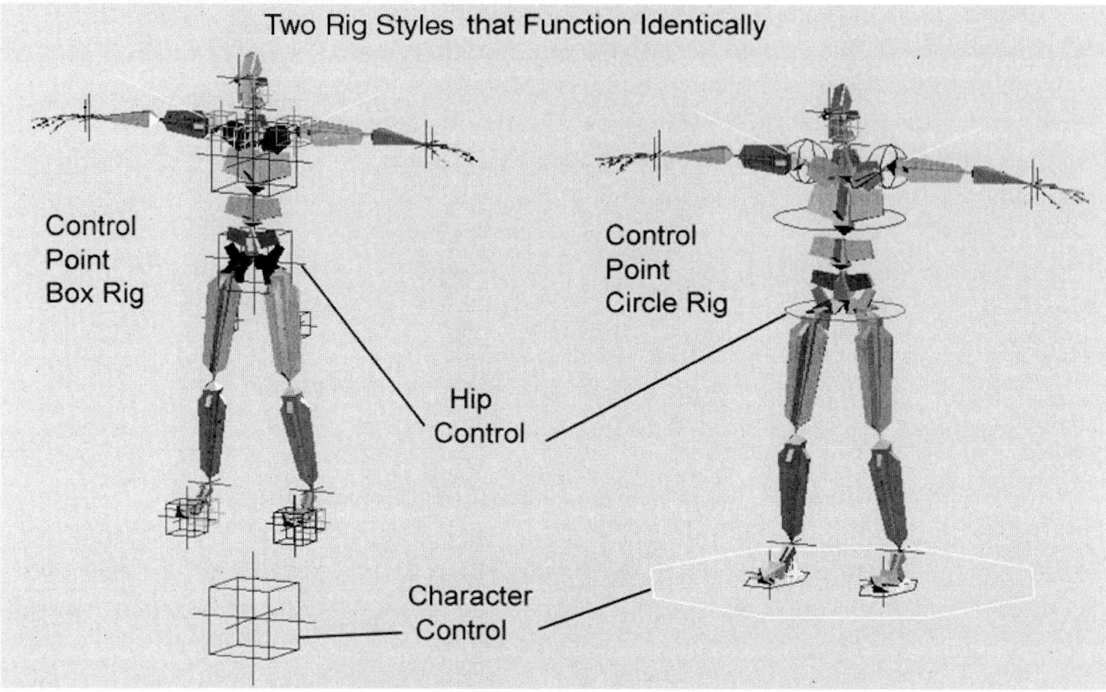

FIGURE 7.2 Two alternative styles of rigged skeletons.

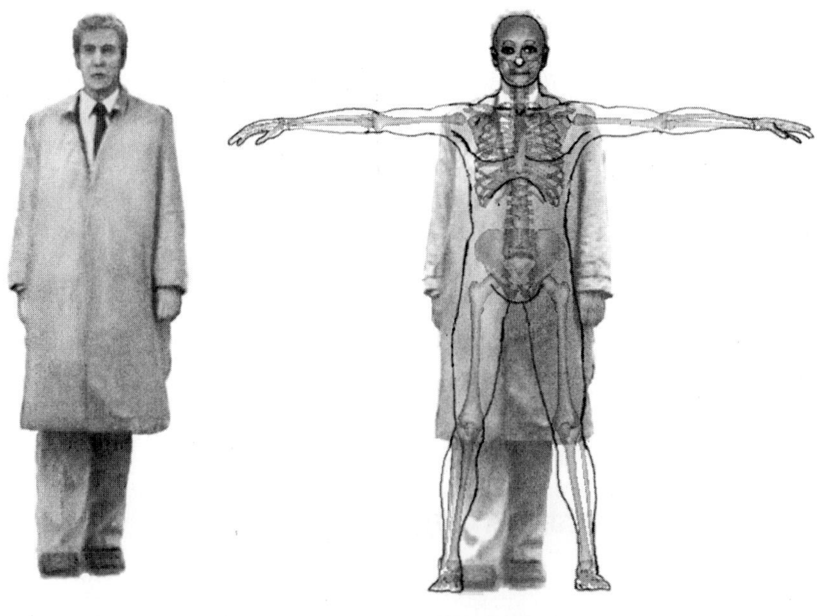

FIGURE 7.3 The Dr. Quin body outline with a skeleton in the Leonardo da Vinci Pose.

which describes the skeletal rigging. The Dr. Quin character, as shown in Figure 7.3, on the left, is one of the main characters in *Homing Instinct*. A body outline drawing with a skeleton in the Leonardo da Vinci Pose has been superimposed over it.

TUTORIAL 7.1

BUILD THE BASIC SKELETON

ON THE CD

To create a skeleton:

1. Load the Dr. Quin body outline images into the front, left, and top viewports from the Chap07\Images folder on the companion CD-ROM. Place the Gman_side.tif image in the left view, BodyTop.tif in the top view, and Gman_Fnt.tif in the front view.
2. Starting with the right view, create bones for the leg. Click Create > System > Bones and then click at the location of the hip, the knee, the ankle, the ball of the foot, and the toe, and then right-click to end bones creation. This completes a chain of bones, as shown in Figure 7.4, example 1.

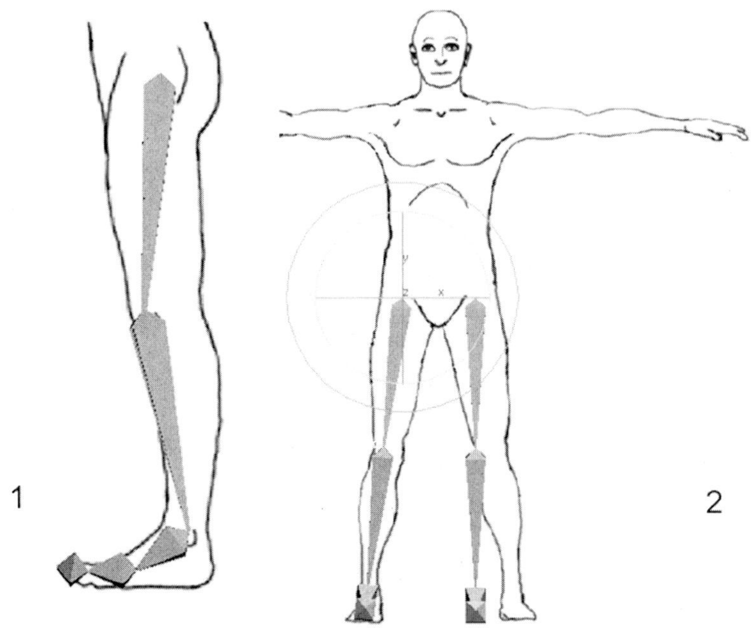

FIGURE 7.4 Creating the bone chains for the legs.

3. If one of the joints is out of position, click the Hierarchy > Adjust Transform > Don't Affect Children command in the Command Panel. Select the joint and move it to the correct location without disturbing the position of the other bones.
4. In the front view, double-click the top leg bone at the hip to select all the bones, and then Shift > Move it to one side to create a duplicate leg. In the Clone Options dialog, select Copy. Position each leg so that the top joint is placed in the location where a real leg joint joins the hip, as shown in Figure 7.4, example 2.
5. Position the leg bones with the legs spread outward about 15 degrees and centered in the legs of the background drawing, as shown in Figure 7.4, example 2.
6. To create the spine, move to the right view. Using the Bones tool, click in the center of the hip at the bottom of the spine, and then click four times, moving a short distance upward, to place four joints up to the top of the shoulder. Continue upward, clicking twice more for the neck bones, and once more at the nose.

Your spine should look like the spine shown in Figure 7.5. It might look a bit strange to have a bone sticking out through the nose, but this is done to allow an IK HI (History Independent) Solver to be applied to control the head and neck bones. The spine bones must form an "S" curve in the side view. A straight chain of bones will not work correctly with the IK HI Solver, which will be applied later in Tutorial 7.3.

7. The arms should be made with the elbows bent so that they will work correctly with the IK HI Solver. Switch to the top view, and then select and freeze the leg and spine bones. Using the Bones tool, click at the right shoulder, and then click at the elbow and at the wrist. Stop there because the hands will be made separately.
8. For the left arm, repeat step 7 on the other side as shown in Figure 7.6. Bones are always created on the construction plane, which is at the character's hip. Switch to the front view, select all the arm bones, and raise them up to shoulder level.
9. The next step is to create bones to link the arms and legs to the spine. Click Character in the menu bar and choose Bone Tools. Right-click the front view, and maximize it. Click the right upper arm bone, and then in the Bone Tools dialog, click Connect Bones, as shown in Figure 7.7. Drag the cursor over the lower chest bone and release the mouse button. This

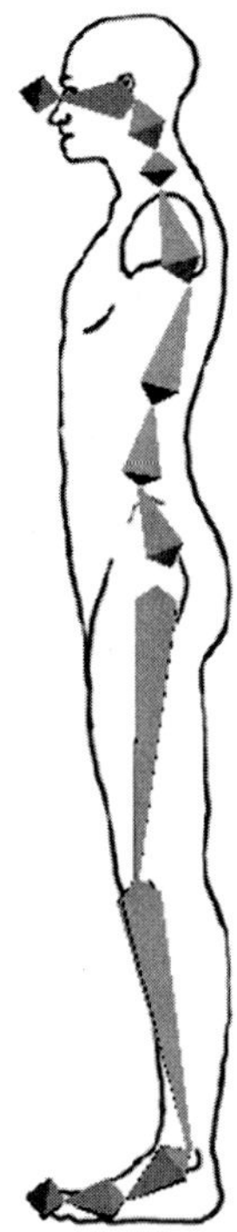

FIGURE 7.5 The spine is not straight, which allows the use of IK Solvers.

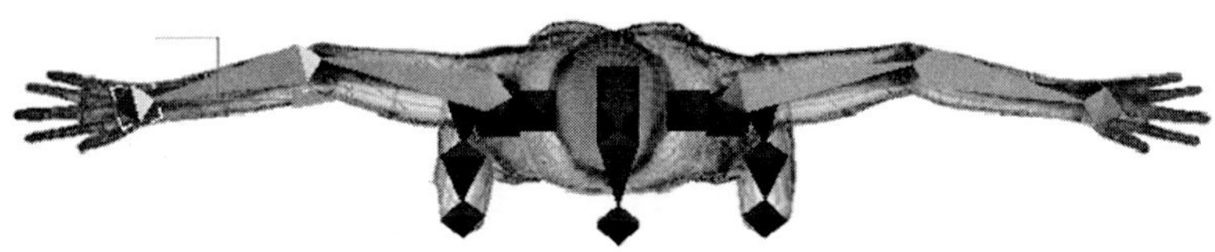

FIGURE 7.6 Creating the arm bones.

should create a clavicle bone connecting the arm with the top of the third spine bone. Repeat the operation for the other arm.

10. To connect the legs to the spine, there is one problem. If you try to connect the root bone of the leg to the root bone of the spine, 3ds max will try to connect it to the joint above the bottom of the spine. To work around this, select the second spine bone and click the Unlink icon to temporarily

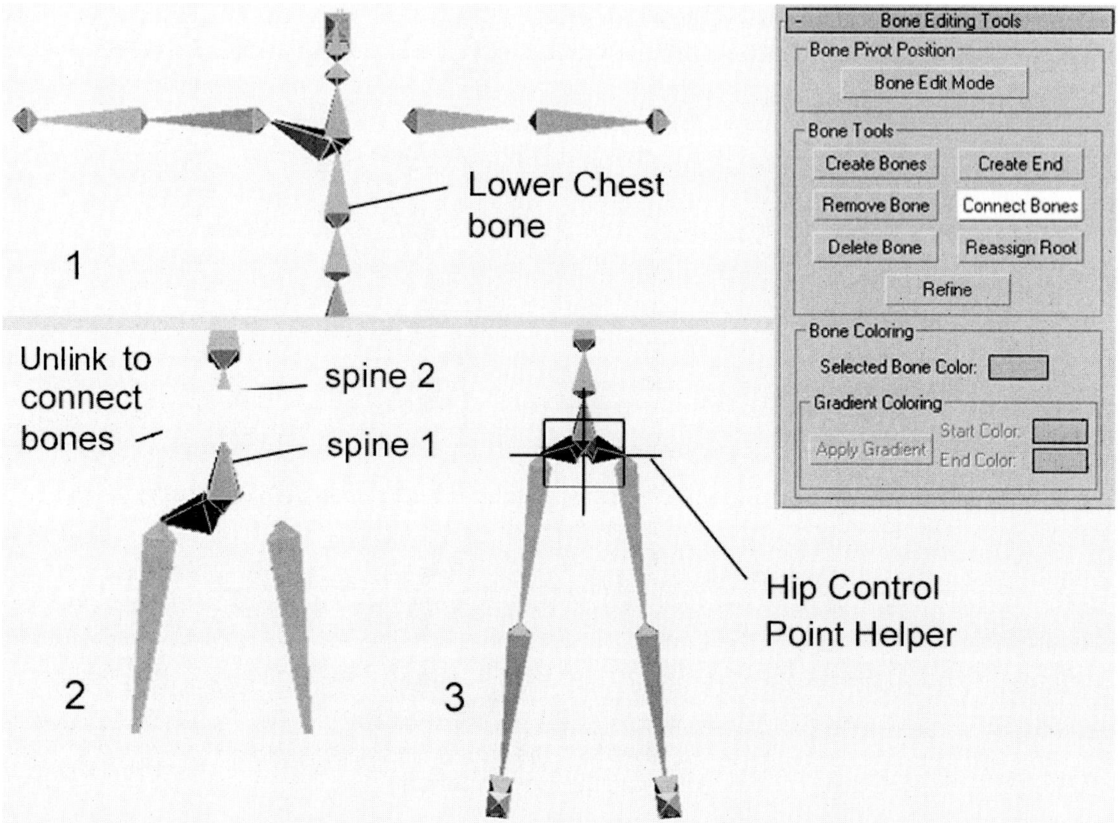

FIGURE 7.7 Arms and legs are connected to the spine using the Bone Tools Connect.

unlink the second spine bone from the root. Now you can successfully use the Connect Bones tool to attach each leg to the root spine bone.

11. Click the right upper leg bone, and then in the Bone Editing tools dialog box, click Connect Bones and click the root or bottom spine bone. A new bone will be created from the bottom of the spine to the top of the leg bone. Repeat this for the other leg. To finish, re-link the spine bones by selecting the second spine bone, and re-link it to the root spine bone.
12. Next, create a Hip Control point helper that runs through the upper joint of both legs bones, as shown in Figure 7.7, example 3. Click the Helpers tab in the Command Panel, select Point, and then click Cross and Box. Set the Helper Size to 60 units, position the mouse cursor over the bottom point of the root spine bone, and click to create the Hip Control. Move it

down slightly so it passes through the upper leg joint, not the lower spine joint. Check that it passes through the leg joints in the left and front views, as shown in Figure 7.7, example 3.

13. Finally, select and link the root spine bone to the Hip Control helper. Save the file as GenMan701.max.

In the next tutorial, you will create the bones of the hands.

THE HANDS OF THE DOCTOR

We'll begin building the hands by placing point helpers at each wrist and linking them to the arm end bones. These will become the Wrist Control points that will later be wired to sliders. Next, you will create the hand and finger bones and link them to the wrist control point. Do not link the hands to the arm IK chain's end effector.

The wrist is designed to simulate how the human wrist moves. The rotation point for the hand is at the side of the wrist, not in the center. The human hand rotates about the center of the ulna bone, the lower bone of the forearm, causing the hand to move in a 180-degree arc around the ulna in line with the little finger. The thinner radius bone, or upper forearm bone, which is in line with the thumb, moves back and forth across the ulna. When the skin is bound to the skeleton, you will be able to adjust the influence envelopes, allowing the forearm skin to stretch naturally with the rotation of the hand, just as it does in nature. Skinning will be explained later in this chapter.

TUTORIAL 7.2

CREATING THE BONES OF THE HAND

To create the bones for the hands:

ON THE CD

1. Continue with the previous file, or load GenMan701.max from the Chap07 folder on the companion CD-ROM. Maximize the top view with the background image displayed, and then zoom in on the character's left hand. The system will ask you if you want to display the background image even though it uses extra RAM. Choose Yes. Zoom out a little if it refuses to display at that size.

2. The arm ends at the wrist with a small bone called the end bone. This bone is necessary for proper IK arm functionality. Select and Uniform Scale the end bone down about 75% or until it quite small, but still easily visible. This will make more room for the construction of the new hand bones.

The bones of the hand are laid out in three branches: the thumb branch, the little finger branch, and the central branch for the index, middle, and ring fingers. This arrangement most closely resembles the way the human hand is built.

3. To create the hand bones, start with the central bone chain that runs from the wrist to the tip of the middle finger. Click Create>Systems>Bones, and in the Bone Parameters menu enter 1.6 in Width and 1.6 in Height. (Make sure your MAX Units are set to Generic. All tutorials in this book use Generic Units.) This will make thin bones. Next, click on the end bone of the arm, drag the mouse to where the bone branches, and click again. One bone is formed.
4. Click at the first knuckle position to create a second short hand bone, and continue clicking at two finger knuckles, and finally at the fingertip to complete the bones of the middle finger, as shown in Figure 7.8. Right-click to complete the bone chain. Keep the small end bone at the tip of the finger.

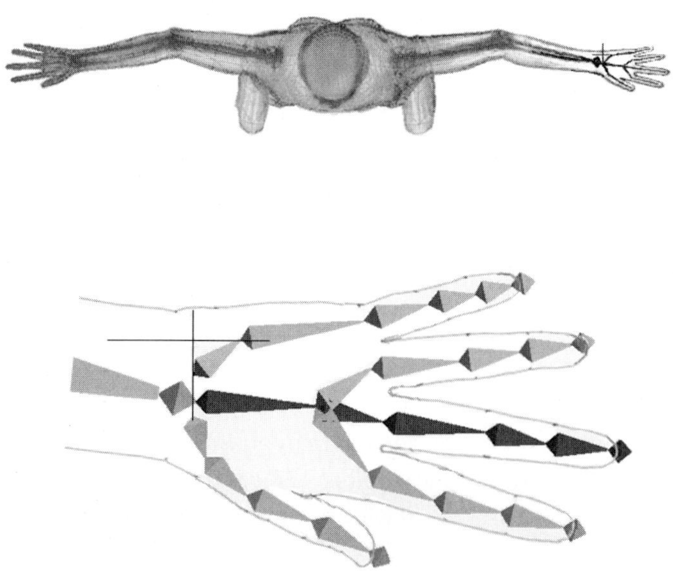

FIGURE 7.8 Construction of the hand bones in three branches.

5. Create the thumb, which should have a total of four bones plus the end bone. Then, create the little finger branch, which should have a total of five bones plus the end bone. You should have placed a bone joint at every corresponding finger joint.
6. Finish the fingers by clicking on the first bone of the central branch. That will attach a bone to the base of the next joint down the chain. Then, click each finger knuckle position to create the index finger, and then click the next knuckle positions until you reach the fingertip. Right-click to end the bone creation command. Repeat that action for the ring finger chain, as shown in Figure 7.8.
7. At this point, the hand bones are still not linked to the wrist. Do not link them to the wrist (end bone of the arm). Instead, you will create a point helper at the wrist and link the three hand bone branches to it. Create a point helper cross of about 20 units in size and position the cross as shown in Figure 7.8. That position corresponds to the true pivot point of the human hand, at the end of the ulna forearm bone.

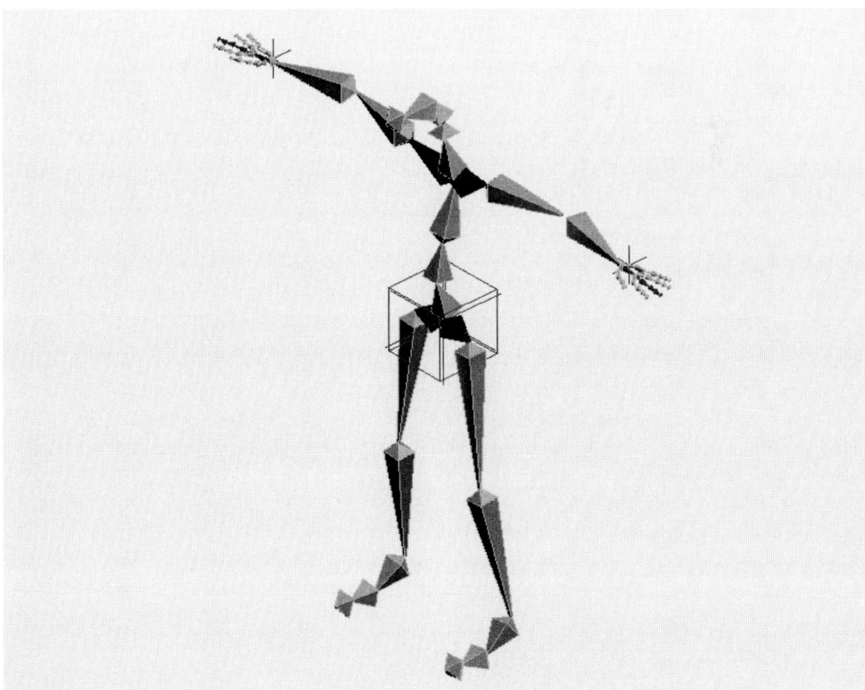

FIGURE 7.9 The bones of each hand are linked to the wrist control point helpers.

8. Select and link each of the hand bone branches to the new point helper. The ends of the bones at the wrist need not touch. If you look in another viewport, you will find that the hand bones have been created on the construction plain, which is level with the character's waist. In the front view, select and move the hand bones and wrist point helper up to the level of the wrist.
9. Create the right hand by cloning. Select all of the left-hand bones including the point helper. (Do not select the end bone of the arm.) Click the Mirror Clone icon, and Select Copy. A duplicate hand will be created on top of the original hand. Translate this new hand to the character's right wrist and position it there opposite of the left hand.
10. Finally, link both wrist control point helpers to their corresponding wrist bones (the end bones of each arm). The hands should now be linked to the skeleton as shown in Figure 7.9. Save the file as GenMan702.max.

NAMING THE BONES

ON THE CD

Before going to the next tutorial, all of the bones should be re-named. Chart 7.1 gives the names of the bones that will be used in all subsequent tutorials. It is assumed that you will re-name all bones, and that you will use the suggested bone names shown in Chart 7.1. (See the companion CD-ROM for the complete version of Chart 7.1, Chart7_1.doc in the Chap07 folder.)

Naming the bones is just about mandatory if you intend to use Wired Parameters to control the fingers. If you don't name them, you are bound to make mistakes when wiring bones together. If you want to paste the names on the selected bones, you can load Chart 7_1.doc into Notepad from the Chap07 folder on the companion CD-ROM. Then, with 3ds max open at the same time, you can select the names from the hierarchy list in Notepad, and paste them in the Object Name field in 3ds max.

CHART 7.1 SKELETAL HIERARCHY BEFORE RIGGING

DocCharacter Control Dummy
DocHip Control
DocRoot_Spine1
DocSpine2
DocSpine3
DocSpine4
Doc Neck1

```
                DocNeck2
                    DocHead
          DocRClavicle
                DocRUpperArm
                DocRForearm
                    DocRWrist
                        DocRHand
                          DocRFinger0  (thumb)
                              DocRFinger01
                              DocRFinger02
                        DocRFinger1   (index)
                        DocRFinger11
                            DocRFinger12
                        DocRFinger2   (middle)
                        DocRFinger21
                            DocRFinger22
                        DocRFinger3   (ring)
                        DocRFinger31
                            DocRFinger32
                        DocRFinger4   (pinky)
                        DocRFinger41
                            DocRFinger42
DocLClavicle
                DocLUpperArm
                DocLForearm
                    DocLHand
                    DocLWrist
                        DocLFinger0  (thumb)
                        DocLFinger01
                            DocLFinger02
                        DocLFinger1   (index)
                        DocLFinger11
                            DocLFinger12
                        DocLFinger2   (middle)
                        DocLFinger21
                            DocLFinger22
                        DocLFinger3   (ring)
                        DocLFinger31
                            DocLFinger32
                        DocLFinger4   (pinky)
                        DocLFinger41
                            DocLFinger42
        DocRPelvis
        DocRThigh
```

DocRCalf
DocRFoot
DocRToe1
DocRToe2
DocLPelvis
DocLThigh
DocLCalf
DocLFoot
DocLToe1
DocLToe2

The bone naming convention used for the models made for *Homing Instinct* generally matches the character studio biped bone names. The character identifier "Doc" at the front of each name is a variable that identifies each bone as part of the Dr. Quin model.

APPLYING INVERSE KINEMATICS SOLVERS

In 3D character animation, IK can be defined as an algorithm that calculates a mathematical solution for positioning all joints in a chain of hierarchically linked bones based on the position of the end effector. These IK algorithms are called IK Solvers.

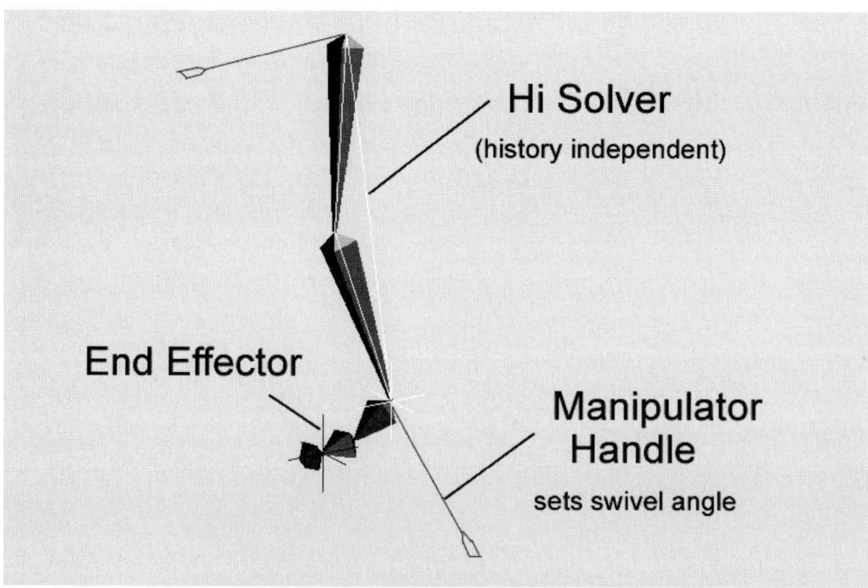

FIGURE 7.10 Leg bones with the IK HI Solver applied, showing a Manipulator handle.

There are four different IK Solvers available in 3ds max. The next tutorial will introduce the HI Solver, which is used for all of the human models. It is a versatile IK solver with a number of ways to align and control a hierarchical bone system's movement. It will be used to operate the doctor's limbs, spine, and neck. For a quick review, Figure 7.10 shows a leg with the HI Solver applied. The Manipulator handles, the IK end effector, and the rotating plane of the limb are labeled.

TUTORIAL 7.3 CREATING IK CHAINS WITH THE HI SOLVER

To apply IK HI Solvers to the spine, neck, legs, and arms:

1. Load the GenMan702.max scene file and maximize a right view of the skeleton (press V then R). Zoom in on the spine area. To simplify the view, select and hide the arm, hand, and leg bones, leaving only the spine showing.
2. To apply the HI Solver, click on the second spine bone from the bottom, DocSpine2. Then, in the Animation drop-down menu, click IK Solvers>HI Solver. Your cursor will now have a dotted rubber band line leading from the bone.
3. Click on the fifth bone of the spine, which is actually DocNeck1, the first bone of the neck. That will create the IK Chain and apply the solver to the spine. Figure 7.11 shows the triangular white outline of the IK HI Solver and its end effector displayed over the spine bones.
4. Test the IK control by selecting the end effector cross and then moving it down and back up in the Y-axis. Click Undo when you are finished.

This type of spine motion is called the "chest crunch," where the shoulders slump forward and the back becomes rounded. This motion is useful for creating unique postures that express fatigue, dejection, lack of energy, and relief.

Avoid straightening out the spine or any other IK chain. Once the end effector is moved away from the bones, the IK Solver can only point all bones toward the end effector, making the spine into a straight line. Human beings cannot straighten their spines, so a straight spine would not be valid for any human character.

5. Next, apply an HI Solver to the neck. Select the lowest neck bone, DocNeck1, and then in the Animation menu select IK Solver>HI Solver, exactly

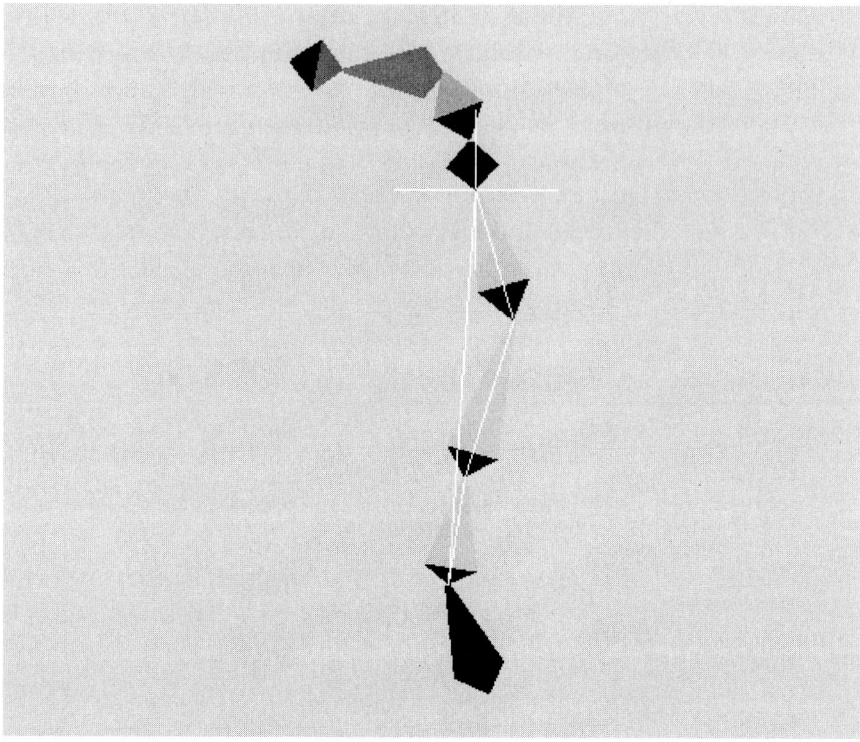

FIGURE 7.11 The IK HI Solver applied to the spine.

as you did in step 2. Drag the cursor to the nose end bone at the top end of the IK chain, as shown in Figure 7.12.

6. Un-hide the arm and leg bones, if you have them hidden, and switch to the top view to create the IK chains for the arms. To create the IK chain, select the left upper arm bone, apply the HI Solver as you did in step 5, and click on the left wrist bone, DocLWrist. Alternatively, if the wrist bone is too small to select, you can select it by pressing the "H" hotkey, which opens the Pick Object dialog, and then Select DocLWrist>Pick.
7. Repeat step 6 but apply a HI Solver to the character's right arm.
8. Switch to a right view and maximize. Region zoom in the leg bones, and then rotate the view using the Arc Rotate tool (V hotkey) so that you can see both legs, as shown in Figure 7.12, Leg IK. You will apply four HI Solvers to the leg bones.
9. To create the left leg IK chains, select the upper left leg bone, DocLThigh, and then click the HI Solver command. Drag and drop the cursor on the

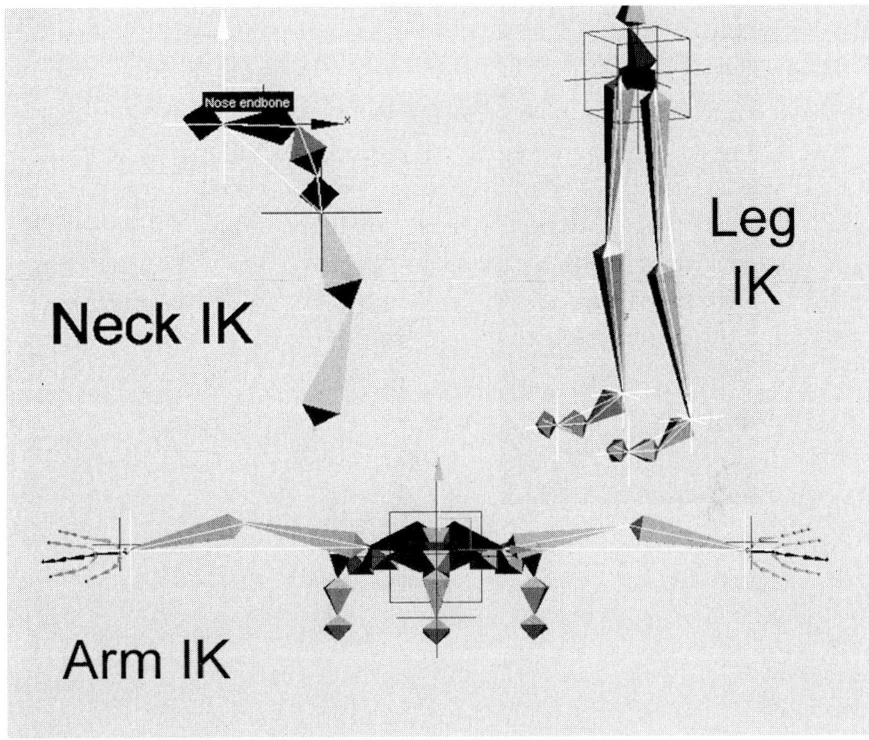

FIGURE 7.12 Applying IK HI Solvers to the neck, arms, and legs.

foot bone, DocLFoot. Re-select the foot bone, click the HI Solver command, and then drag and drop the cursor on the leg end bone, DocLToe2.

10. To create the right leg IK chains, select the upper right leg bone, DocL-Thigh, and then click the HI Solver command. Drag and drop the cursor on the foot bone, DocLFoot. Re-select the foot bone, click the HI Solver command, and then drag and drop the cursor on the leg end bone, DocLToe2.
11. All the HI Solvers should now be applied. Do not apply IK Solvers to the hands. They will be animated using sliders with wired parameters in a later tutorial. Be sure to save your files often. Save this file as GenMan703.max.

Phase One, the Basic Skeleton with IK, Is Finished

This finishes the construction of phase one of the basic skeleton with IK Solvers applied. At this point, the skeleton has become similar to a

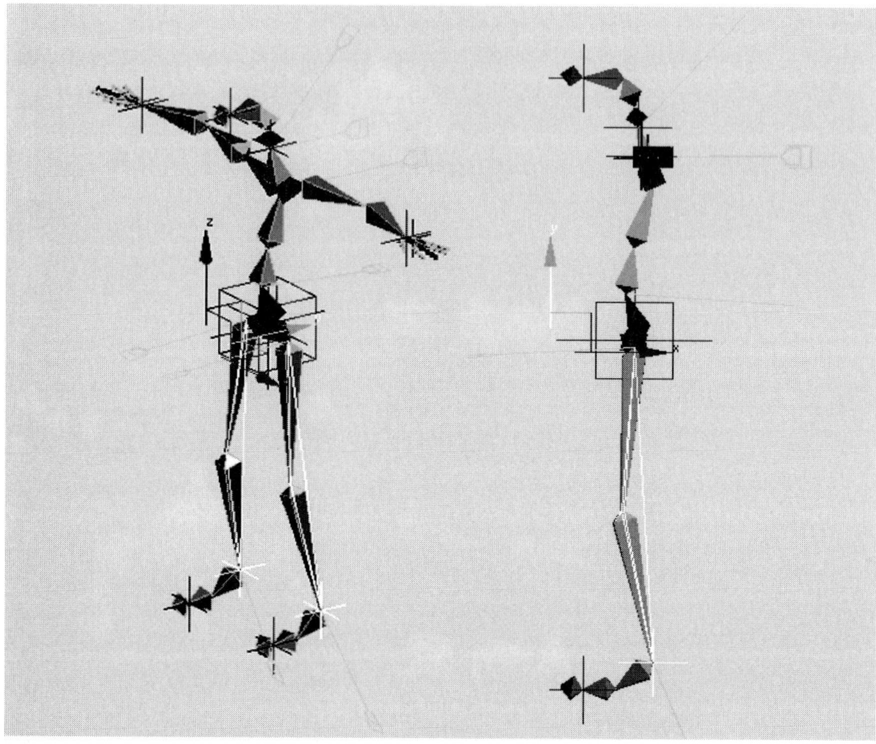

FIGURE 7.13 The basic skeleton with IK Solvers applied.

mannequin with its bones all linked together, as shown in Figure 7.13. However, it is not yet ready for character animation.

It is now time to think about fitting the skeleton into a mesh model. You could wait until after the skeleton is completely rigged, but you will find that the hands are hard to change once all the rigging and wired parameter slider controls are applied. It is better to fit the hand bones into the Dr. Quin/Generic Man model that you built in Chapter 6 at this time, before you have the hand controls on and it becomes difficult to change the length of the finger bones.

In the next tutorial, you will merge in the Generic Man model and fit the skeleton into it.

TUTORIAL 7.4

FIT THE GENERIC MAN ONTO THE SKELETON

To fit the Generic Man model onto the skeleton:

ON THE CD

1. Load the finished GenMan703.max scene, if it is not already loaded. Next, merge in your Generic Man model, GenMan609.max, or load it from the Chap07 folder on the companion CD-ROM (Figure 7.14).
2. Once the mesh is merged into the skeleton scene, you might notice that it is a different size. If it is, carefully scale it to fit the skeleton and align it with the skeleton in both the front and side views. (It is much easier to scale the mesh than the skeleton. If you need to scale the skeleton, select it all, and then group it first.) The skeleton and the Dr. Quin mesh should match well before beginning to work on the hands.

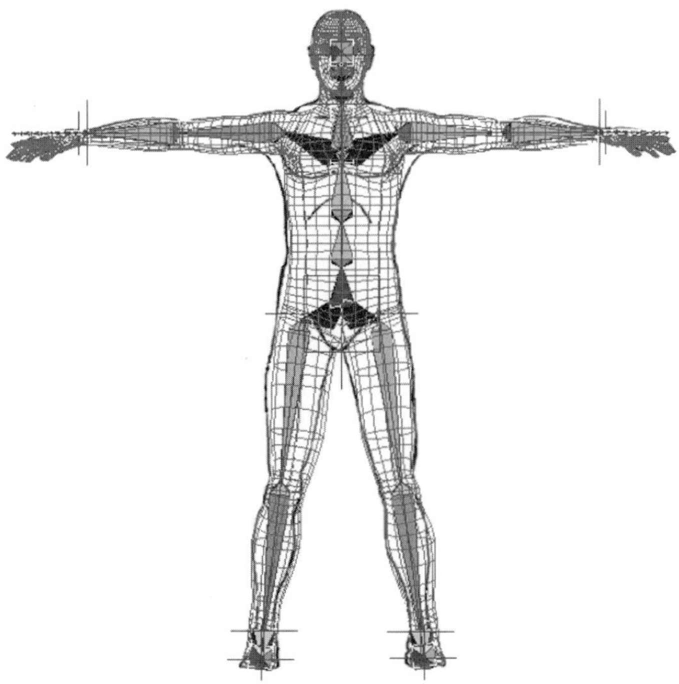

FIGURE 7.14 The Dr. Quin/Generic Man model fitted over the skeleton.

3. Re-configure the four viewports so that you have two top views side by side, and two front views side by side. Then, click Zoom Extents All, and Region Zoom in on the top and front of the character's left hand in your right-hand viewports, and the character's right hand in your left-hand viewports, as shown in Figure 7.15.
4. Select the left IK end effector and move it to center the wrist bone in the arm. Repeat that operation for the right wrist bone and arm. Then save the file as GenMan704.max.

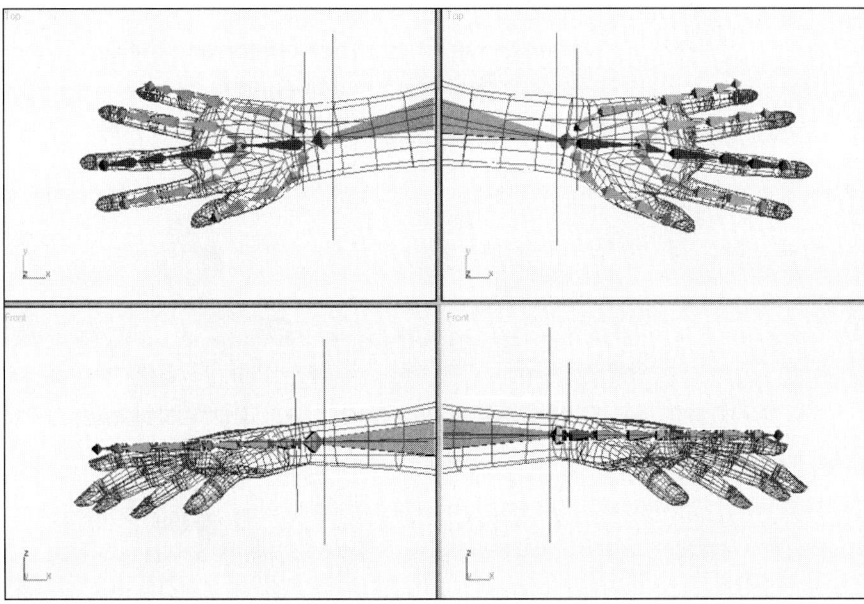

FIGURE 7.15 Aligning the bones of both hands in the top and front viewports.

TUTORIAL 7.5

POSITIONING THE HAND BONES

1. Load GenMan704.max. Notice that the finger bones are still on a flat plane.
2. Before starting to adjust their position, click the Hierarchy tab, and then select Don't Affect Children in the Adjust Transform rollout. This prevents a parent bone from moving a child bone.
3. In the top view, use the Move tool to position each bone joint approximately where the corresponding joint should be, as shown in Figure 7.16.

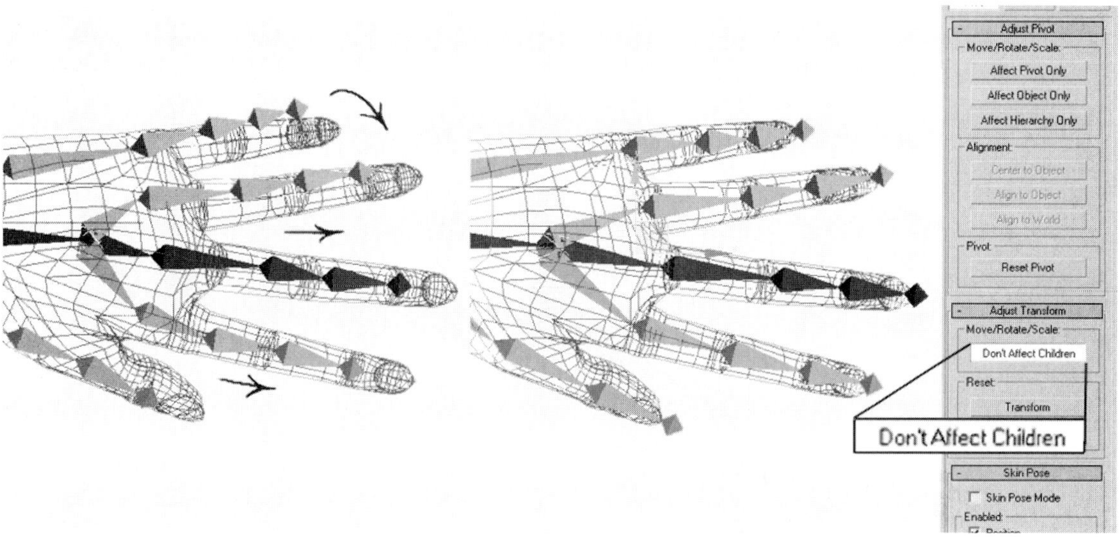

FIGURE 7.16 Moving the finger joints to the correct positions with Don't Affect Children.

4. Once the finger bones are centered over each finger of Dr. Quin's mesh hands, move to the front view, and translate the joints downward to follow the curves.
5. Use the Arc Rotate Selected (Alt-MMB) to rotate the viewport around the individual finger bones so that you can see along the side of a finger to tell if the bone follows it correctly, as shown in Figure 7.17.
6. After the joints are positioned, use the Rotate tool to inspect the hand from all positions, and then fine-tune the curvature of the finger bones. Ideally, the end bone of each finger should stick through the mesh fingertips, but all the other bones should be nearly hidden inside the mesh.
7. Repeat steps 5 through 8 to fit the left hand bones into the mesh. The hand and finger bones should be correctly positioned inside the mesh.
8. Take the time now to look at the rest of the skeleton to see if any joints in other parts of the body need to be re-positioned. If they do, fix them now. When finished, save the file as GenMan705.max.

In the next tutorial, you will begin rigging the skeleton. It assumes that the skeleton is now correctly positioned in the mesh.

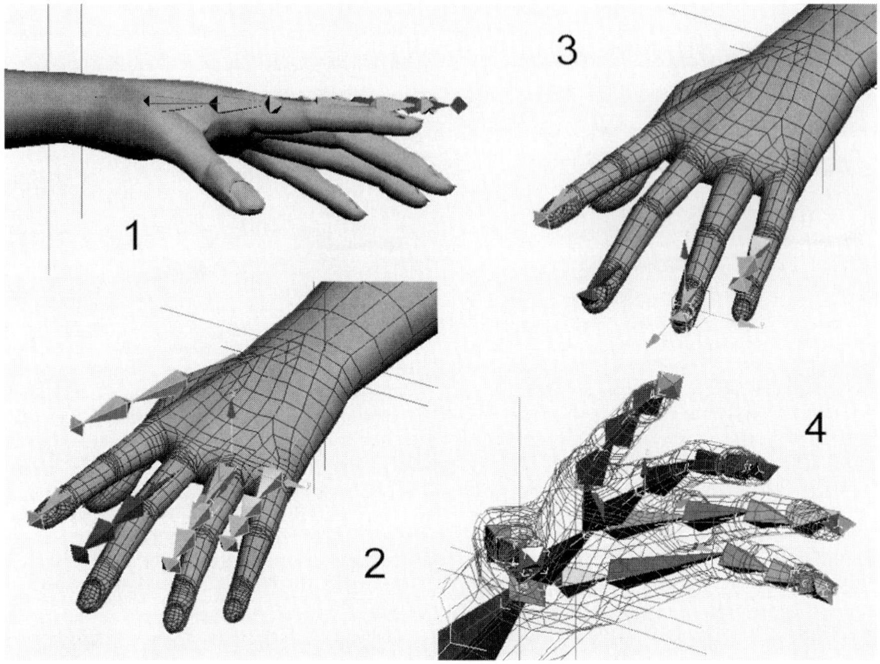

FIGURE 7.17 Fitting the finger bones inside the curve of the mesh.

WHAT IS RIGGING?

One of the main purposes of rigging is to combine multiple motions and move them together. Another purpose is to anchor or constrain part of a character to the world or to an object. A third purpose is to be able to manipulate or animate any part of a model using an external control, such as a slider. Ultimately, the goal of rigging is to speed the animation process, and allow the animator to do things that would be impossible any other way. Using what amounts to "tricks," rigging can give you control over very complex animations that simulate real life (Figure 7.18).

RIGGING THE DR. QUIN SKELETON FOR CHARACTER ANIMATION

In the next series of tutorials, you will build the skeleton rig by adding new links, control points, and offset centers and sliders. The basic skeleton will be set up so that the hands and feet are not parented to the pelvis, but instead are parented to the character Control object placed beneath the skele-

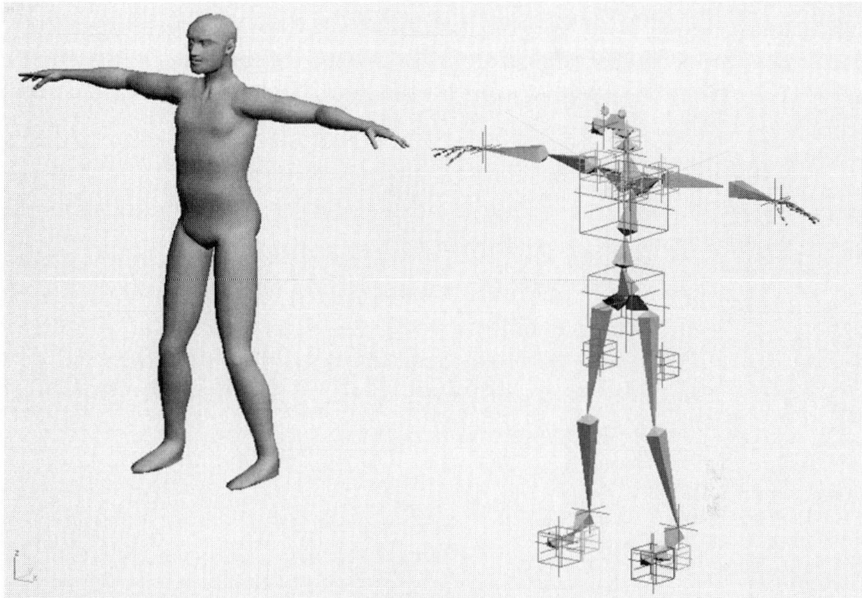

FIGURE 7.18 Skeleton rigged with animatable control points.

ton. This allows the torso to be moved up and down without moving the hands or the feet. This linkage setup has great advantages for re-creating human motions over the standard hip-centered linkage setup, which will be demonstrated in Chapter 8 during the Character Animation tutorials.

To begin rigging the Dr. Quin/Generic Man skeleton, start with the legs. The rigging process involves the creation of offset centers of rotation, and special linkages, which are designed to control and re-direct the path of motion of the spine, leg, or arm. The alterations are done to make the body move less like a set of rotating bones, and more like a living person. The rig is designed to allow animation using both IK, and Forward Kinematics (FK) at the same time. With this new level of control, the animator can accelerate his output and incorporate emotional tension, acceleration, weight, and body language into the animation performance.

To design how the character is going to walk, it is important to examine how the feet, legs, and hips move. The mechanics of the human walk cycle are well established, but each person or character has a unique way of walking. Factors such as the length of the legs, the size of the feet, and the thickness and weight of the character's legs introduce limitations on how the limbs will move.

The foot has limited movement in all rotation axes as it pivots around the ankle. The foot of your skeleton must mimic the same movement as a real human foot. During the walk cycle, the ball of the foot moves up and down as the character walks as it contacts and leaves the ground. The foot has limited sideways movement, with a sideways rotation range of about 15 degrees. The arch of the foot remains rigid when a person walks, but the toes constantly bend and flex to follow the contours of the ground surface. This helps keep the skeleton balanced while walking, running, and jumping.

The control points are actually new centers of rotation that are added at strategic locations around the skeleton. The heel and ball-of-the-foot control points are placed with their centers even with the ground plane. This helps you judge where the bottom of the foot contacts the ground during walk cycle animation. In most cases, you will be animating the skeleton without the mesh, so the axis lines of the control points are a handy way to indicate where the bottom of the shoes would be.

TUTORIAL 7.6

RIGGING THE FOOT AND LEG CONTROLS

To set up the rigging for the feet and legs:

1. Load the GenMan705.max file. In the front view, select and hide the body mesh. Then, select all of the character's right leg bones and hide them. The next operation is to create two point helpers that will become control point helpers for the foot.
2. Switch to the right view, and then zoom in on the lower left leg. Click Create>Helpers>Point, and then click on Cross and Box. Place the cursor at the back of the heel and click to create Point 1. Rename Point 1 to Heel Control. Set size = 17.0.
3. Next, in the Helper Parameters, set the Point Size to 36. Place the cursor directly below the toe joint on the same level as the bottom of the foot, and click to create Point 2, as shown in Figure 7.19. Rename Point 2 to Foot Control.
4. Switch to the front view and move the new points over until they are under the center of the foot, and then return to the right view.

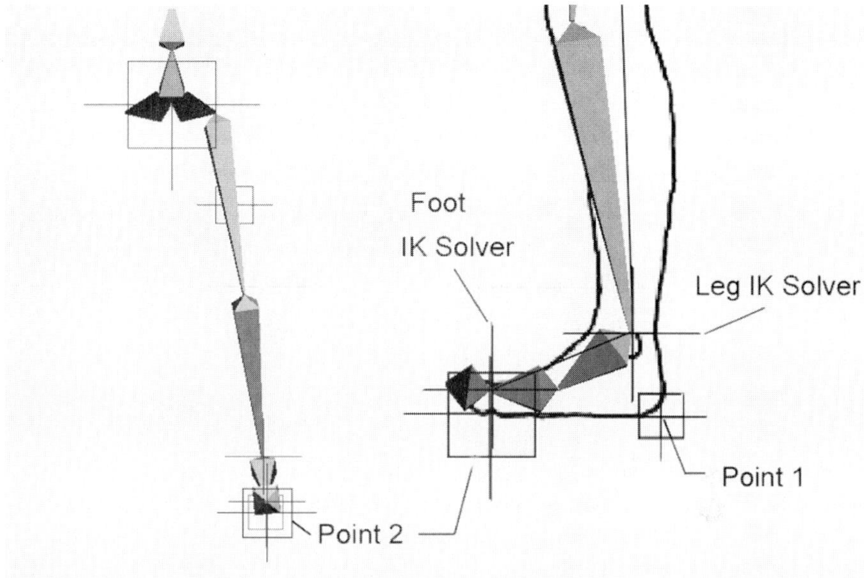

FIGURE 7.19 Two control point helpers added to the foot.

5. The next step is to link the end effectors. Click the Link icon, and then click and drag the link from the foot IK end effector to the leg IK end effector. Now when the ankle is moved, the foot will move with it.
6. To create a control that pivots the foot up and down from the heel, link the end effector at the ankle to Point 1, the Heel Control point.
7. Next, link Point 1, the Heel Control, to Point 2, the Foot Control, as shown in Figure 7.20.

With the ankle linked to the heel, and the heel linked to the ball of the foot, you are now able to select either control point and rotate the foot up and down. This action simulates the toe-pointing motion that is an important part of the walk cycle.

8. The leg control point helper mixes the motion of both foot controls, and is used to control the kicking motion. In the left view, place the cursor just behind and below the top of the upper leg bone, and create a third control point, Point 3, called the Leg Control. Refer to Figure 7.20 to check the correct location.
9. Link the Foot Control, Point 2, to the new Leg control, Point 3.

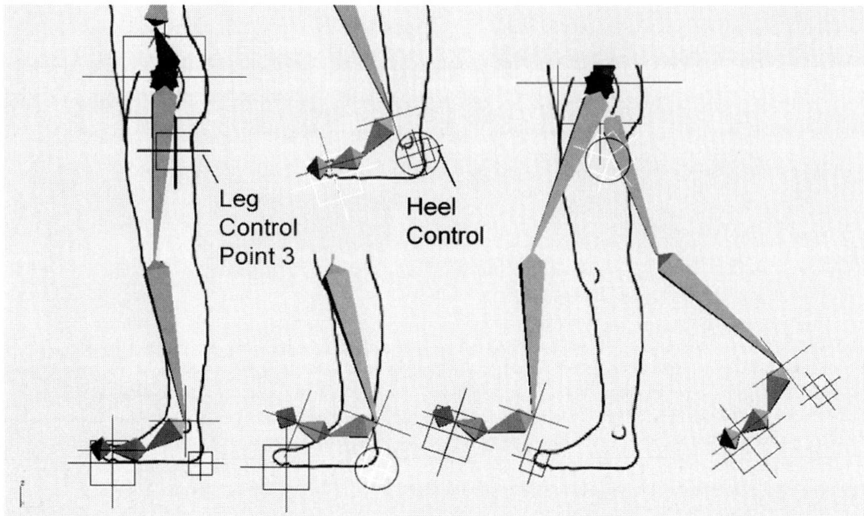

FIGURE 7.20 The foot and leg control points.

10. Test the control points by selecting them and rotating them in the Z-axis, as shown in Figure 7.20. Be sure to undo your actions so that the bones return to their original positions.
11. Now do the opposite leg. Freeze all of the left leg parts, and then unhide the right leg. In the left view, repeat steps 2 through 8 to rig the right leg, placing control points 4, 5, and 6.
12. Rename all the left leg control points L_Heel Control, L_Foot Control, and L_Leg Control. Rename the right leg points R_Heel Control, R_Foot Control, and R_Leg Control. Save the scene file as GenMan706.max.

The toes also rotate during a walk or run. However, they are not controlled with control points. Instead, you will control the toes with a slider. In the next tutorial, you will create the control points for the body, head, and arms.

Body, Head, and Arm Controls

The most interesting part of skeletal rigging is the hand-arm-head-shoulder-torso control system. These regions handle most of the expressive body language and are all linked together so that the upper skeleton can move as one unit, when bending over, for example. In this tutorial, you will be connecting all these body regions into a control system that allows the mixing of multiple movements. This mixing of motions gives you powerful ways to express the character's emotions, attitudes, and intent as revealed by body language. The arm motion multiplies the intensity of the body language messages we subconsciously send, especially in stressful situations.

TUTORIAL 7.7 RIGGING THE BODY AND HEAD CONTROLS

To create the body and head control points:

1. Load the GenMan706.max file. In the front view, select and hide both arms so that the spine will be easier to see in the side view. In the right view, Region Zoom to show the entire spine.
2. The next control point you will create is Point 7, which is called the Chest Control or the chest "cruncher." It will control the spine IK chain curvature. Place the cursor to the left of the spine, in the middle of the chest. It should be completely inside the rib cage area, as shown in Figure 7.21.
3. Click Modify, and set the size of the control point to 55 units so the ends of the XYZ handles will stick out of the body mesh, making it easy to select at any time.
4. The Chest Control is linked to both the end effector and the hip. First, link Point 7, the Chest Control, to the Hip Control, which surrounds the hip in Figure 7.21.
5. Next, link the spine end effector to the Chest Control. When you do this, you should see the IK Solver and the spine bones suddenly rotate 90 degrees. Do not be alarmed. This is normal behavior, and will be very familiar to you before the skeleton rigging is finished.

When any IK Chain is linked to a control point, it is likely to rotate 90 degrees because it is no longer linked to world space, and it gets its new axis orientation from the control point. To correct the IK Chain and rotate it back to its original position, turn on the Manipulator icon to show the manipulator handles. Then, switch to the view where the green spatula-shaped IK manipulator handles can be easily seen. Use the Move tool to drag the handle around to the original orientation it had before it was linked. You can read the exact angle in degrees in the Swivel Angle popup box. Do not skip this step, or the skeleton will become useless with IK chains twisted at right angles to the body.

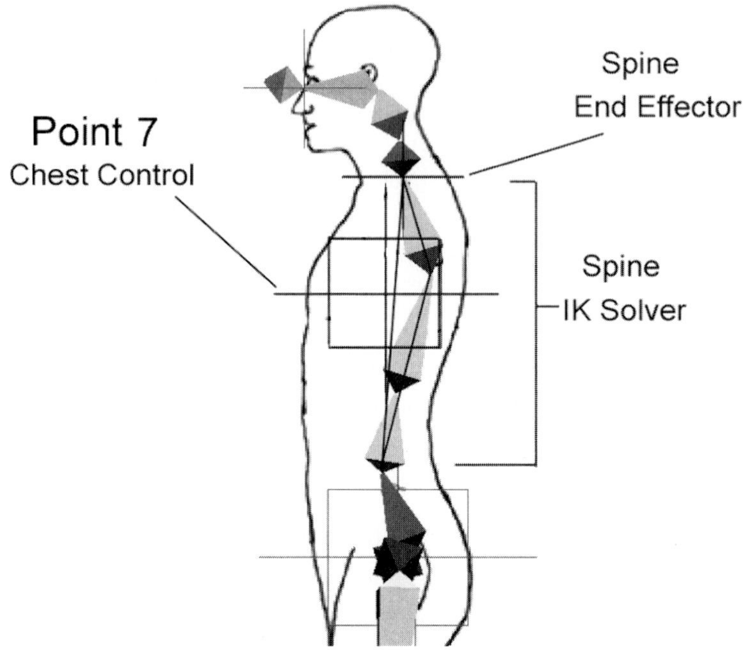

FIGURE 7.21 The Chest Control controls spine curvature and motion.

6. To correct the spine IK chain angle and return it to its original position, click the Manipulator icon, and switch to the top view. In the top view, click the Move tool, and then click and drag the green handle around so that the spine faces the correct direction again, as shown in Figure 7.22.
7. Switch to the right view after the spine faces forward again, and then place another point helper, Point 8, on top of the joint between the first and second neck bones. Rename it Head Control, and set its Size to 20 units.
8. Next, you will add two more links. First, select the Head Control, Point 8, and link it to the Chest Control, Point 7, as shown in Figure 7.23.
9. Select the end effector of the Head IK Chain and link it to the Head Control. If the Head IK chain rotates 90 degrees, switch to the top view, and turn on the Manipulator icon so that the manipulator handles are displayed. Use the Move tool to reposition the manipulator handle so that the head and neck bones are in their original positions.
10. Unhide all objects and save the scene file as GenMan707.max.

In the next tutorial, you will rig the Arm and Shoulder controls.

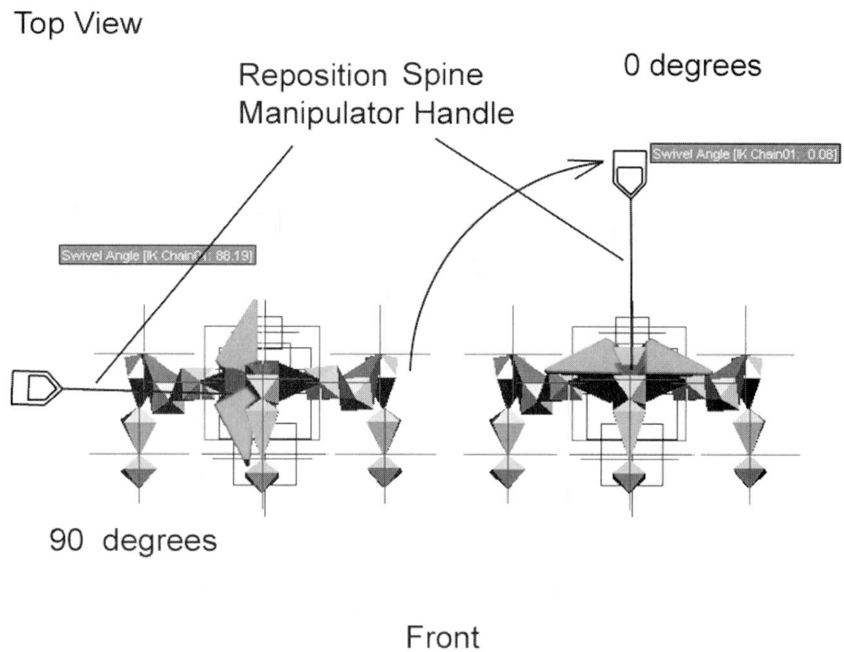

FIGURE 7.22 You must turn the IK manipulator handle to correct the angle of the spine IK chain after linking.

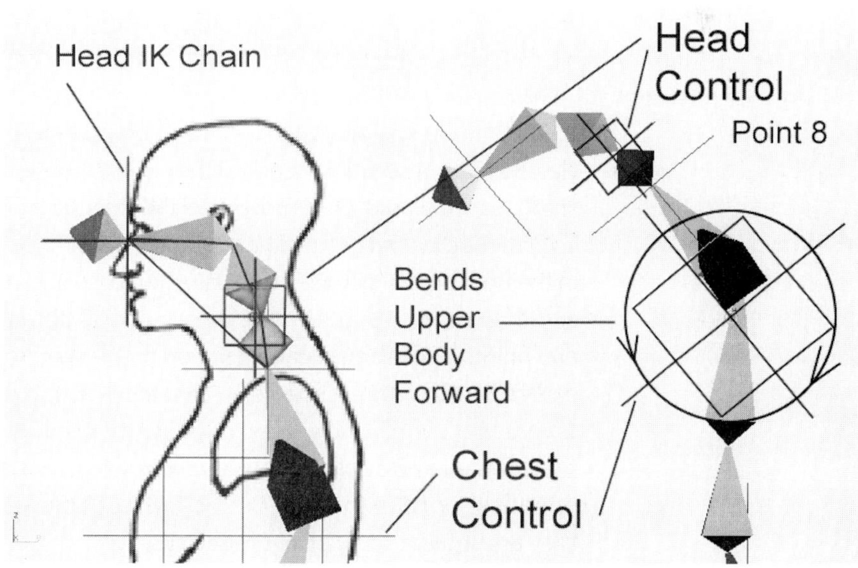

FIGURE 7.23 The Head Control is linked to the Chest Control.

TUTORIAL 7.8

RIGGING THE ARM AND CLAVICLE CONTROLS

To rig the arm and shoulder controls:

1. Load the GenMan707.max file. Maximize the front view, and then Region Zoom in on the shoulders and arms.
2. To make the Right Arm Control, click Create > Helper > Point, turn on Cross and Box, and place the cursor over the right shoulder joint. Click to create a point, and set the Size to 32 units.
3. Over the left shoulder joint, create another control point called the Left Arm Control. Right-click to end point creation. Remember to rename both control points.
4. To align the points, switch to the top view and zoom in close to the shoulder joints. Move both new control points to match the centers of their respective shoulder joints.
5. Return to the front view. Zoom in or out so you can see both blue arm end effectors at the wrists, as shown in Figure 7.24. Click the Link icon, and then select the right arm end effector and drag a link to the Right Arm Control point. Repeat the operation to link the left arm end effector to the Left Arm Control point.

The arms should now rotate up and down when you select one of the arm controls and rotate it. Remember to undo any test movements to return the skeleton to its original position. Do not change the links on the wrist control points; they are already linked to the wrist bones.

There are two more body control points that need to be created. The clavicle control points will control the clavicle bones to allow the character to shrug his shoulders, or to move one shoulder up or forward when reaching.

6. To create a clavicle control point, zoom in on the shoulder area of the skeleton in the front view. Place the cursor over the base end of the right clavicle bone, and then move it out from the center a small distance. You will be creating two points in the same location, so you must separate them a little so you can easily select the correct one when animating, as shown in Figure 7.25.
7. Create the Left Clavicle Control point by placing a second point at the base of the left clavicle bone. Move a small distance from the center in the opposite direction that you moved the Right Clavicle Control point so that they are separated by about four units.
8. Select and link the new clavicle control points to the spine bone below them, Spine3.

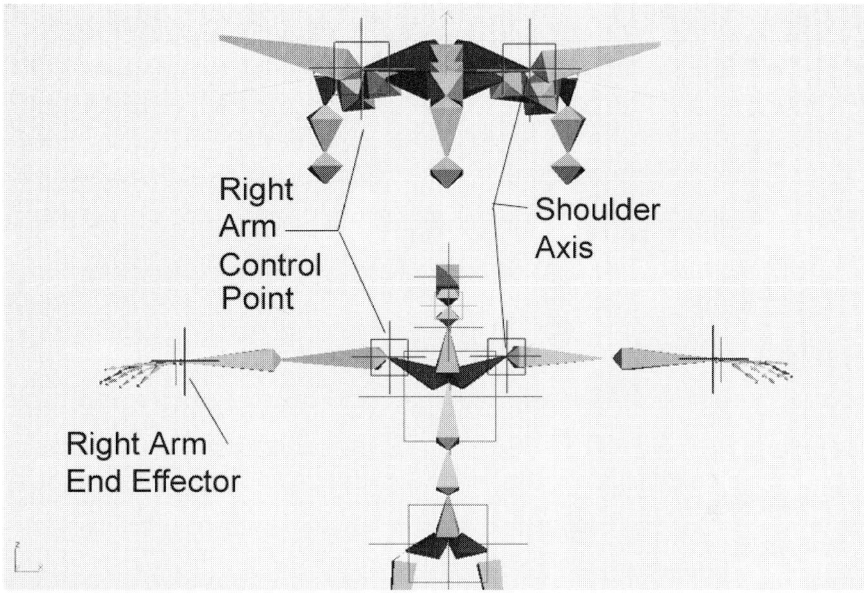

FIGURE 7.24 Linking the arm end effectors to the arm control points.

9. Next, select and link the Right Arm Control point to the Right Clavicle Control point. Repeat the operation to link the Left Arm Control point to the Left Clavicle Control point.

When you rotate the clavicle control, the arm control should move, but the upper arm bone will not follow it. To make the right clavicle bone follow the right shoulder when you rotate the clavicle control, you need to apply a Look At Constraint to the clavicle bone.

10. Select the right clavicle bone, and then click the Motion tab and open the Assign Controller dialog box. Select Rotation: Euler, and then click the Assign Controller menu icon. The Controller menu opens. Select LookAt Constraint and click OK.
11. The LookAt Constraint rollout menu will open. Click the Add LookAt Target button, and then in the front viewport, click on the Right Arm Control point. The name of the target will appear in the constraint target window, as shown in Figure 7.25. Now the clavicle bone and upper arm will move along with the Right Arm Control when you rotate the Right Clavicle Control point.
12. Repeat the process in steps 10 and 11 to create a LookAt Constraint for the left clavicle bone. You can rotate the Left Clavicle Control slightly to test the constraint. Be sure to undo any bone movements.

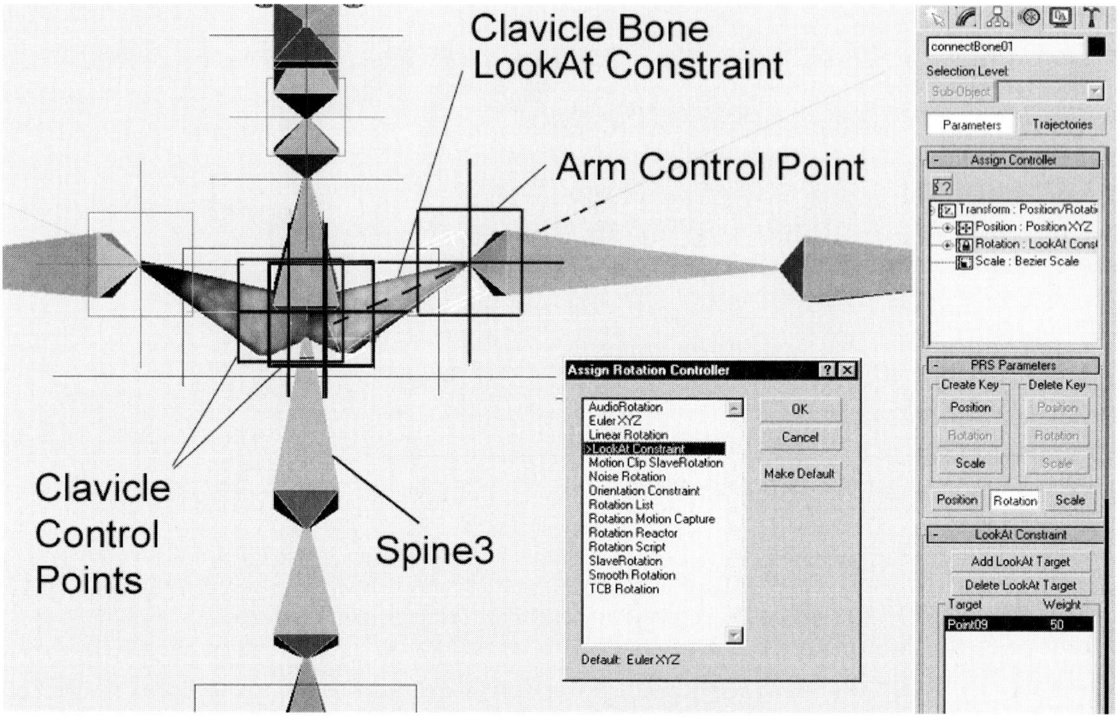

FIGURE 7.25 Creating the clavicle controls and applying a LookAt Constraint.

13. Below the feet, place another point helper. Set its size to 70.0, and then center it under the hip in the side and front views. It should be below the floor. Name it CharacterControlPoint. Link the hip control, and both the left and right leg controls, to this control point. Save the file as GenMax708.max.

CONCLUSION

This completes the major part of the skeleton rigging. In this chapter, you created a bones skeleton and applied IK solvers to arms, legs, and the spine. You worked through the skeleton rigging process and created control points. In the next chapter, you will add Fins to the bones and then bind the skin to the skeleton using the Skin Modifier. Then, you will add slider controls to operate the hands. When the hand rigging is finished, you will create facial morph targets. You will finish the model by texturing the skin, creating the clothing, and adding hair to the model.

CHAPTER

8

PREPARING FOR CHARACTER ANIMATION

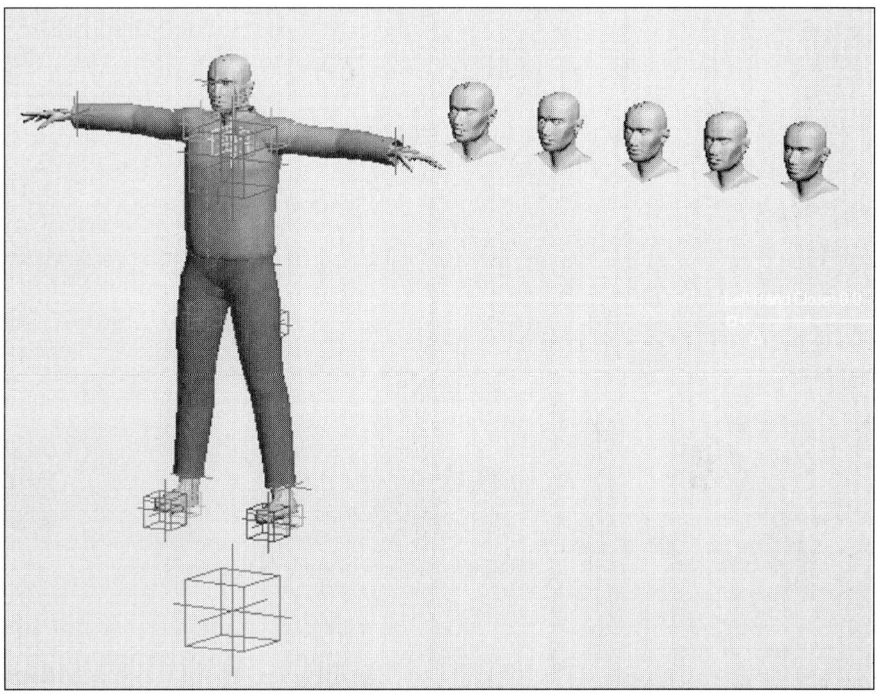

Dr. Quin is one of the central characters in the cast of *Homing Instinct*. The doctor is seen in most of the scenes, and is required to speak dialog, show emotions, and perform the functions of doctor, protector, and hero. In this chapter, you will finish the final preparations of the skin and the internal rigging of the character. When finished, the model should be capable of simulating all types of human actions (Figure 8.1).

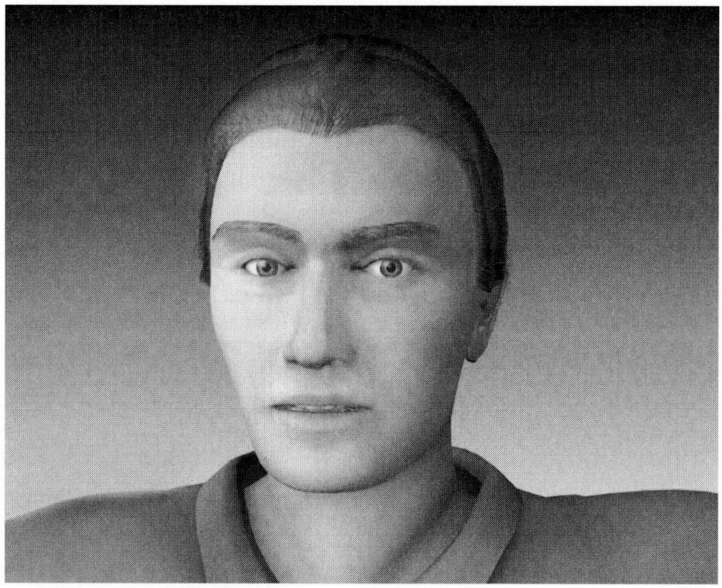

FIGURE 8.1 The finished Dr. Quin model.

The process of finishing Dr. Quin begins with preparing the skeleton for binding the skin to the bones using the Skin Modifier.

USING THE SKIN MODIFIER

The Skin Modifier is capable of binding a Triangle mesh, a Polygonal mesh, a NURBS surface, or a Patch surface skin to a skeleton by assigning the control of each vertex to the nearest bone. Skin creates a zone of influence over the skeleton called an influence envelope. This envelope can overlap other envelopes and allows adjacent bones to share influence over the skin so that the skin actually slides back and forth over the joints when the elbow or any other joint rotates.

The bone tools are a set of functions designed to make the management of bones and skeletons more efficient and easier. Fins can be created on the front, the sides, and the back of each bone. The size of these fins tells the Skin Modifier how large to set the influence envelope radius of each bone. 3ds max 6 bones have built-in fins that can be made to protrude from the bones to simulate the outside shape of the skin. For example, the upper leg the bone of the skeleton that you built in Chapter 7, "Character Setup with Bones," is much smaller than the outside diameter of the upper leg mesh. By increasing the size of the fins so that they just touch the patch surface of the leg, the Skin Modifier is given a reference dimension that it uses to pre-set the size of the skin influence envelope radius.

In the next tutorial, you will add fins to the bones to pre-set the influence envelope sizes for binding the skin.

TUTORIAL 8.1

ADDING BONE FINS

To add fins to the bones:

ON THE CD

1. Load the GenMan708.max scene file that you created in Chapter 7, or you can load it from the Chap08 folder on the companion CD-ROM. Maximize the front view. You should see the complete skeleton with its control points , as shown in Figure 8.2, example 1.
2. Unhide the head and body, and select all of the mesh. Right-click, and from the Quad menu, select Properties. In the Properties dialog, turn on See Through. If the body is still opaque, check the viewport Transparency setting. It should be set to Simple. You should see the bones and the control points inside the body, as shown in Figure 8.2, example 2.
3. In the Display tab, click Hide by Category > Helpers. Now only the bones should show inside the body. Select the body and head, and then Freeze Selection.
4. Zoom in on the legs, open the Fin Tools dialog by clicking Character in the menu bar, and then click Bone Tools > Fin Adjustment Tools to open the floating dialog box. Select the upper leg bone on the right. In the Fin Adjustment Tools dialog, click Fins > Side Fins, and set the size to 7.0. Fins

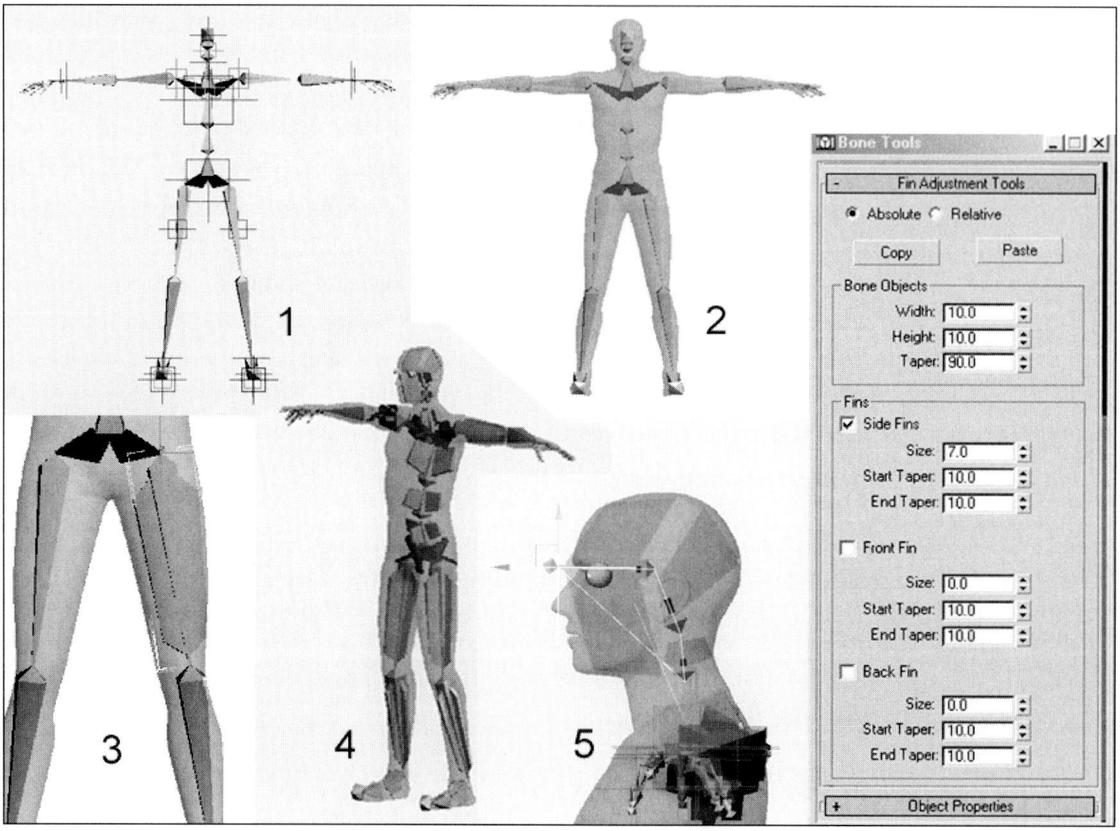

FIGURE 8.2 Adding fins to the bones.

should appear on both sides of the leg bone, as shown in Figure 8.2, example 3.

5. Arc Rotate the view so you can get a view of both the front and side of the leg bone. Turn on Front Fin and Back Fin. Set the front fin size to 5.0. In this model, the back fin is at the front of the leg. Set its size to 10. The fins should now approximate the shape of the upper leg.
6. In the Fin Adjustment Tools dialog, click the Copy button with the upper leg bone selected. Now click the other upper leg bone and then click the Paste button in the Fin Adjustment Tools dialog. Now both upper legs have fins.
7. Create fins on all the bones of the arms, legs, chest, neck, and head using the preceding steps, but only set the fin sizes that are appropriate for each bone, as shown in Figure 8.2, example 4. Examine the side view of the

head. The fins have been extended to give the last two bones of the head and neck IK Chain more control over the face. The width and height of the last head bone has been reduced, and the Start and End Tapers have been adjusted to extend the fins down into the chin and up to the top of the head, as shown in Figure 8.2, example 5.

8. Do not create fins on the wrist or in the palm of the hand. It is better to set those envelopes manually after the Skin Modifier has been applied. When all the fins have been created and adjusted, unhide the Helpers.
9. Save the file as GenMan801.max.

In the next tutorial, you will apply the Skin Modifier and bind the skin to the skeleton.

APPLY THE SKIN MODIFIER AND PAINT WEIGHTS

The Skin Modifier works with 3ds max bones to create skeletal deformation animation. Skin is a sophisticated system that includes deformation lattices for joints and morphing controls that can change the shape of the skin to correct problems or to simulate muscles as the angle of the arm changes. Painting weights is much improved in 3ds max 6, making it possible to paint the skin with the mouse cursor to adjust the influence of one or more bones over the mesh. A vertex weight chart similar to a spreadsheet enables you to adjust the skin weighting down to the individual vertex level.

TUTORIAL 8.2

BINDING THE MESH TO THE SKELETON WITH THE SKIN

To bind the model to the skeleton:

1. Load the GenMan801.max scene file and maximize the front view. Make sure that the IK end effectors, helpers, control points, eyes, inner mouth, and teeth are all hidden before applying the Skin Modifier. You should see only bones, the head, and the body in the viewport.
2. Inspect the mesh closely to make sure the skeleton and the bones of the hands are still aligned correctly. Correct any bone alignment problems, select both the head and body meshes, and turn off the See Through property.

3. Click Modifiers in the menu bar, and in the drop-down menu, select Animation Modifiers > Skin. The Skin Modifier will be applied to the skin and the Modifier Panel will open showing Skin in the Stack window. Then, click Add in the Skin Parameters drop-down menu, and in the Select Bones dialog, click the arrow in the Selection Sets window and select Bones All and click Select. The bones will load into the Skin Parameters window.
4. With the skin still selected, click Edit Envelopes in the Skin Parameters window. The skin will turn dark blue in the front viewport, and thin bone icons will be displayed on the surface of the blue mesh that represent the end joints of each bone. Click the Bone icon in the middle of the chest. A red color that turns to yellow at the edges will be displayed, as shown in Figure 8.3. This is the influence envelope of the third spine bone, DocSpine3, also called the Chest Bone.

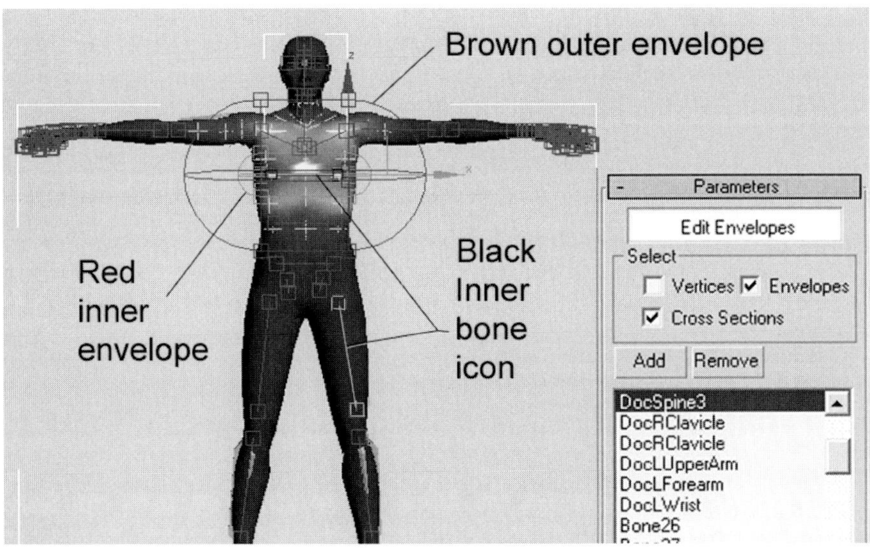

FIGURE 8.3 The skin envelope is displayed by clicking a bone icon.

PARTS OF THE SKIN ENVELOPE

The capsule-shaped influence envelope has three main parts: the black inner bone icon with a small box at each end, the red inner envelope, and the brown outer envelope, as shown in Figure 8.3. The black inner bone icon lets you change the length or angle of the envelope by clicking on either end and dragging it. The red inner envelope surrounds all the vertices that are influenced exclusively by the selected bone. The brown outer envelope shows the fall-off of the bone's influence and shows the vertices that are shared with adjacent bone envelopes. The small boxes that can be seen where the round end of the envelope starts are the adjustment handles. To set the size of the envelope, click on one of the small boxes. It will turn purple. Drag it with the Move tool to adjust its size, and watch how it changes the size of the bone's influence. Alternatively, you can use the Envelope Properties > Radius spinner to accomplish the same thing. When working in a User view, it is better to use the Radius setting to adjust the envelope.

You will find that it is of little use to adjust the envelopes with the figure standing still. The best strategy for testing and adjusting Skin envelopes is to temporarily animate the model bending, squatting, and moving its arms for about 30 frames. By scrubbing the Time Slider, you can easily see where the skin behaves correctly, and where the problems are. When you are finished with the adjustments, you can delete these temporary keys to restore the skeleton to its starting position.

5. To animate the character to help in adjusting the skin envelopes, first hide the skin. Then, unhide the control points by clicking Display > Hide by Category, and then turn off (uncheck) Helpers. The skeleton rig control point helpers should appear, as shown in Figure 8.4, example 1.
6. Select the Hip Control, and then turn on Auto Key. Move the Time Slider to frame 30, and move the Hip Control downward about –30 units in the Y-axis. That should bend the knees. (In this book, all tutorials' lengths and movements are measured in generic units.) Next, select the Shoulder Control Point on the right and rotate it downward 45 degrees. Select the Chest control and rotate it to the right in the Y-axis to twist the upper body about 20 degrees, as shown in Figure 8.4, example 2.
7. Turn off Auto Key and Scrub the Time Slider to watch the animation. Unhide the head and the body skin, and then Arc Rotate the viewport to look at all sides of the model. This motion will reveal most of the major problems of the skin envelopes.
8. Notice that the hands are the only bad problem areas of the skin, as shown in Figure 8.4, example 3. The rest of the skin works rather well as a result of using the fins to pre-set the envelopes. The other problem areas are the armpits and the backs of the legs.
9. Save the scene as GanMan802.max, and then continue on to the next tutorial to adjust the envelopes.

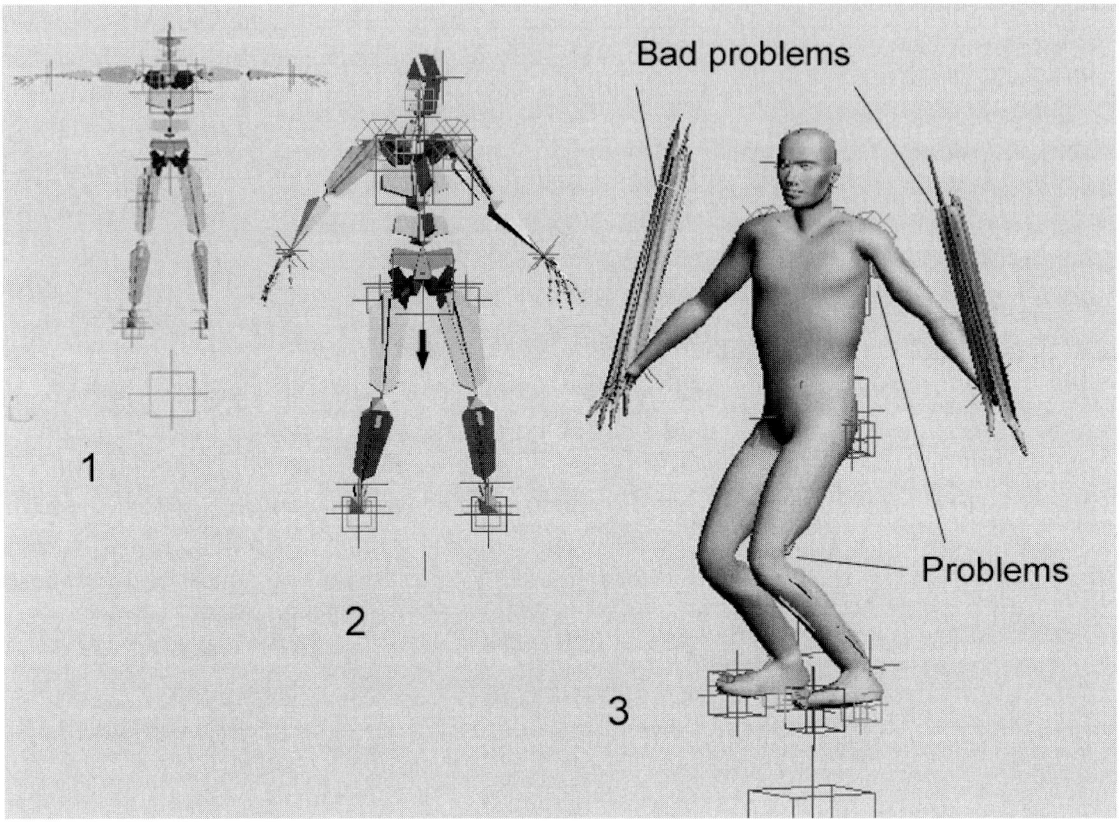

FIGURE 8.4 Animate the skeleton to see where the bad skin problems are.

In the next tutorial, you will adjust the envelopes and use the Paint Weights tool to correct the hands, armpits, and the backs of the legs.

TUTORIAL 8.3

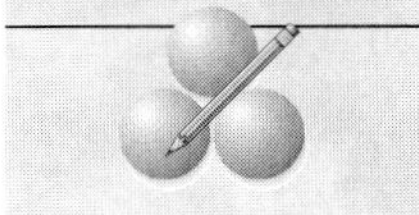

ADJUSTING THE SKIN ENVELOPE PROBLEMS

To adjust the skin envelopes:

1. Load the GenMan802.max file, if it is not already loaded. Zoom close to the left hand in the front view, and then move the Time Slider to frame 10. The skin should protrude up from the hand because the envelopes are not correctly adjusted.

2. To adjust the hand envelopes, Arc Rotate the view so that you can see most of the top of the hand, as shown in Figure 8.5, example 1. Click the Display tab and in the Hide by Category menu, click Helpers to hide the point helpers to give an unobstructed view of the hand. The skin is pulled away from the bones of the palm of the hand.

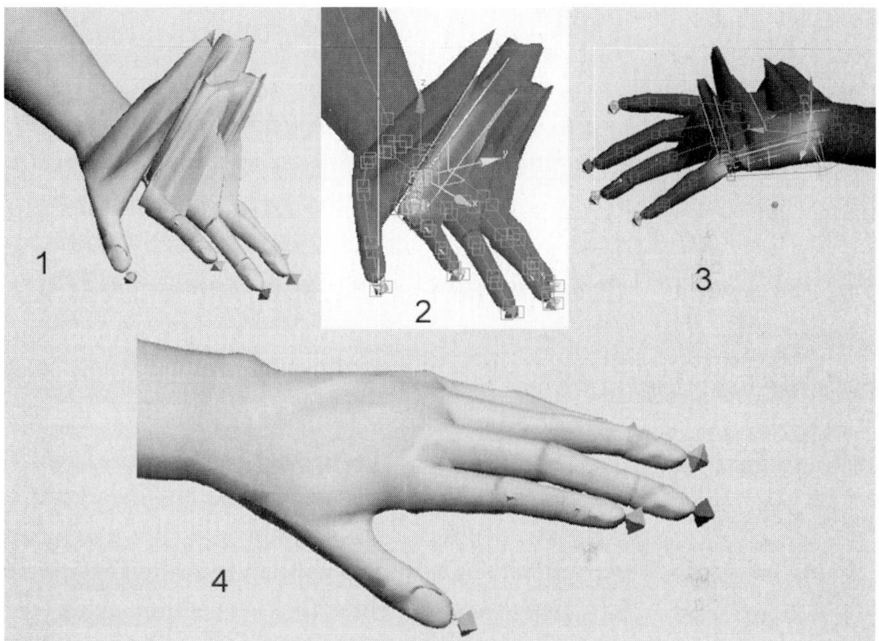

FIGURE 8.5 Adjust the Skin Modifier envelopes.

3. Select the skin, open the Modify Panel, and click the Edit Envelopes button. The skin will turn blue. Click the different bone icons of the palm of the hand until the orange color shows streaks rising up to the portion of the skin that has been left behind. This indicates that the skin envelope needs to be adjusted, as shown in Figure 8.5, example 2.
4. Select one of the envelope adjustment handles of the outer envelope and move it to enlarge it. Part of the skin that is sticking up should move down to the hand. Repeat this process for both ends of the skin envelope, and for every bone that influences the portion of the skin that is misbehaving.
5. Change the envelope radius by small amounts and spread the changes across adjacent bones to achieve the smoothest control over the skin. Use

Arc Rotate to roll the hand around and view it from all sides, as shown in Figure 8.5, example 3.

6. In this model, all of the skin problems were solved by selecting the outer palm and thumb bones and setting their envelope radius to 0.6 in the finger area and 1.2 in the palm, as shown in Figure 8.5, example 4. Adjust the envelopes on the other hand to tune the skin and get the envelopes working properly.
7. Save the scene as GenMan803.max and continue with the next tutorial.

In the next tutorial, you will adjust the armpit area, the backs of the knees, and the elbow skin.

TUTORIAL 8.4

ADJUSTING THE ARMPITS, KNEE, AND ELBOW SKIN ENVELOPES

To adjust the armpit skin envelopes, follow these steps:

1. Load the GenMan803.max scene file, if it is not already loaded. In the front view, zoom in on the upper chest and armpit area.
2. Move the Time Slider to frame 30, and then Arc Rotate the view so you can easily see the armpit, as shown in Figure 8.6, example 1. Notice that the armpit remains quite wide and rounded even though the arm is lowered. That means that either the chest or the clavicle envelope is too large and is fighting the influence of the upper arm bone envelope.
3. With the skin selected and the Skin Modifier > Edit Envelopes button turned on, select the Chest Bone icon (DocSpine3). Select the outer skin envelope handle, and then in Envelope Properties > Radius reduce the value. In this model, the value was 8.6. Reduce it to 7.0 and observe the behavior of the armpit skin. It should narrow and the gap should become smaller.
4. Next, select the Clavicle Bone icon (DocRClavicle), and select its outer envelope handle at the shoulder. Reduce its size. In this model, the radius should be changed from 5.0 to 4.0. Then, select the Upper Arm Bone icon (DocRUpperArm), and then select its outer envelope handle at the shoulder and reduce its radius from 5.14 to 3.0.
5. This combination of envelope adjustments reduces the size of the armpit opening to an acceptable level, as shown in Figure 8.6, example 2. Now, click Zoom Extents and in the left view, zoom in on the knees. You will

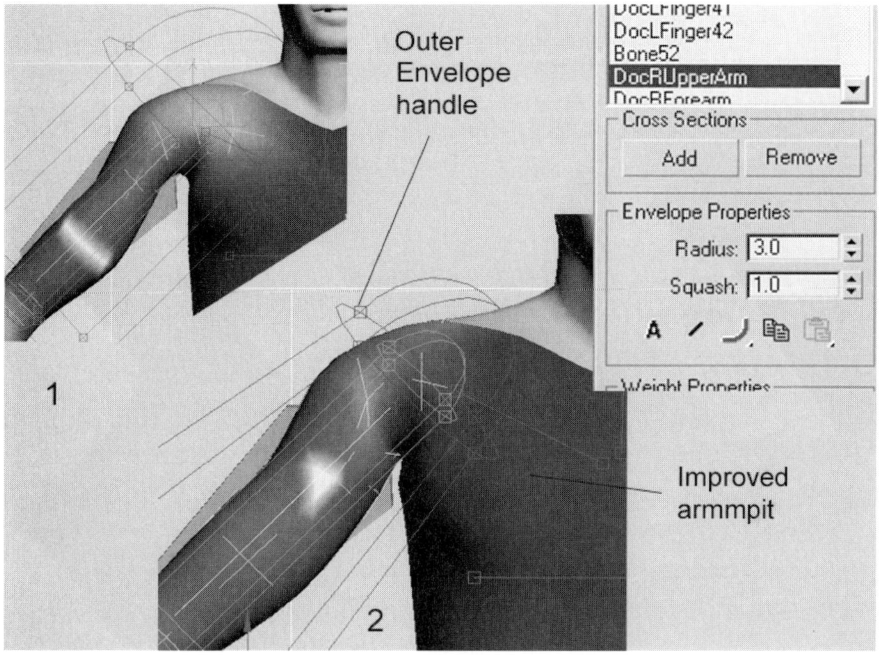

FIGURE 8.6 Adjusting the armpit skin envelopes.

need to hide the bones. Go to the Display tab and, in the small white window inside the Hide by Category menu, click Bone. The bones will hide. Now click the Modify tab again, and re-select Edit Envelopes.

6. The backs of the knees are too wide open and do not come together in a crease as they should in Figure 8.7, example 1. To correct this, select the right upper leg Bone icon (DocRThigh). This time, you will start by shortening the Bone icon. With the square end of the Bone icon selected, move it up the thigh about 10 to 15% above the knee. Notice that the back of the knee starts to close into a crease the moment you shorten the thigh skin envelope, as shown in Figure 8.7, example 2.
7. Next, the select upper leg outer envelope handle at the knee, and reduce the envelope radius from 7.0 to 6.0. This is sufficient to correct the back of the knee. Repeat this operation on the left knee.
8. Switch to the top view and click Zoom Extents. Set the Time Slider to frame 10. You will need to temporarily bend the arm to see how the elbow skin behaves. In the Display Panel, click Hide by Category > Helpers to unhide the control points and the IK end effector handles. Turn on Auto Key, and then select the blue IK end effector for the left arm. Move the wrist toward

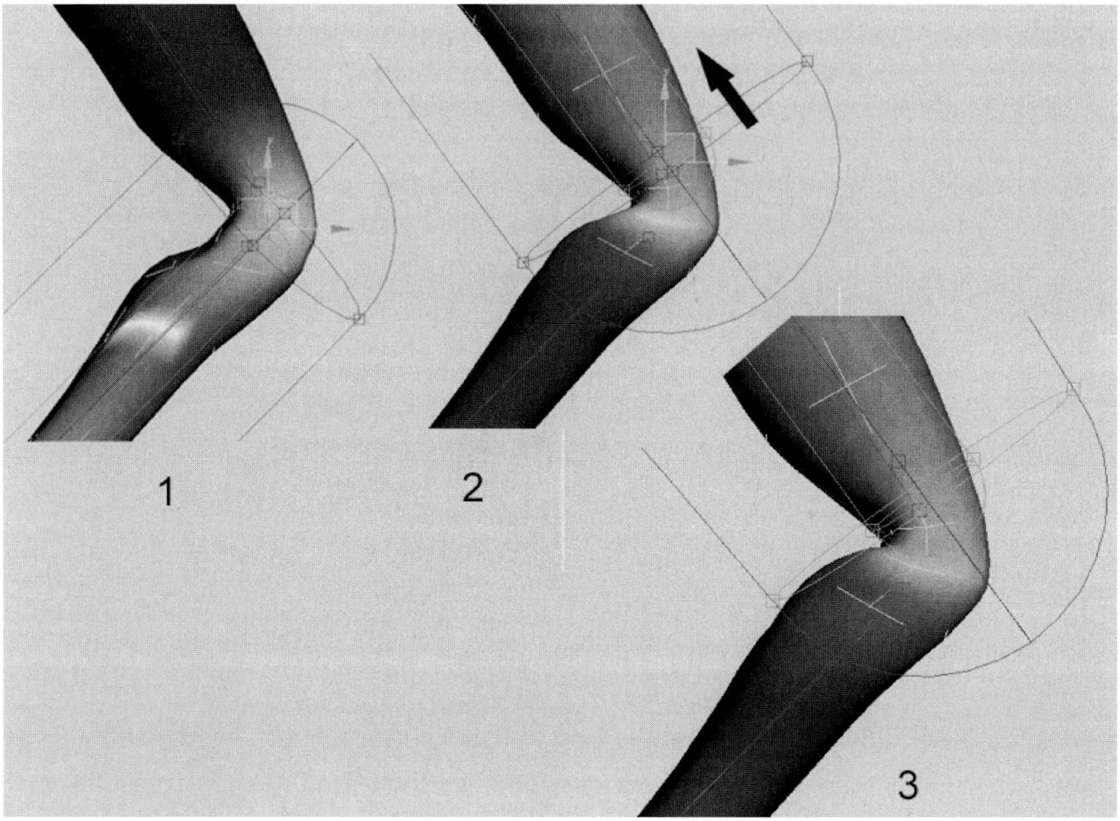

FIGURE 8.7 Adjusting the knee skin envelopes.

the body in the X-axis until the arm is approximately bent half way. Notice how the skin at the elbow forms a distorted wide loop instead of creasing as it should, as shown in Figure 8.8, example 1.

9. Select the skin and click the Modify tab, and then click Edit Envelopes. Click on the upper arm bone icon (DocLUpperArm). Select the square handle at the elbow end of the upper arm bone icon and move it up the arm, shortening it about 15% of its length, to reduce its influence over the elbow. The elbow relaxes a little, but not enough.
10. Click the upper arm outer envelope handle at the elbow, and in the Envelope Properties menu, reduce the Radius from 5.1 to 3.0. The elbow skin should now close the gap and crease more naturally, as shown in Figure 8.8, example 2.

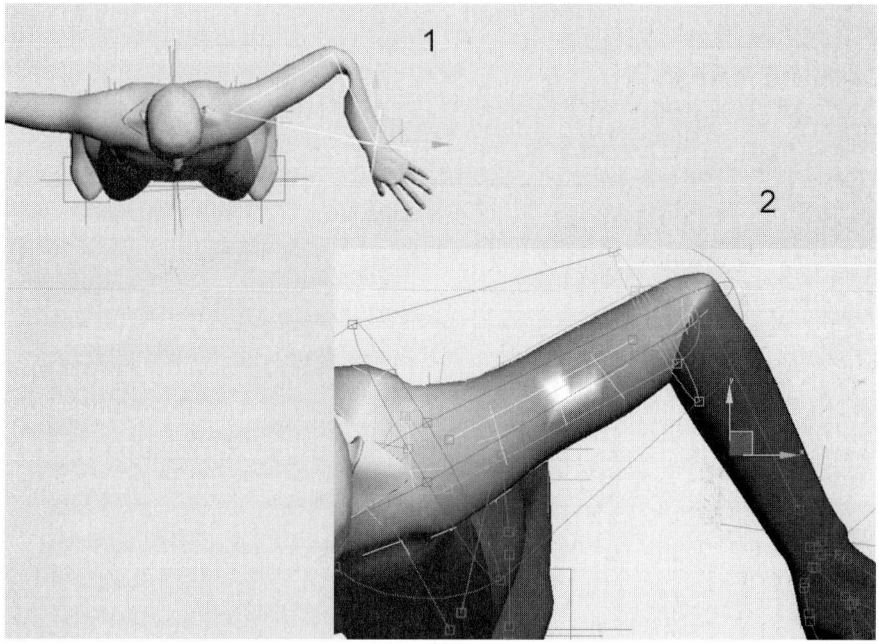

FIGURE 8.8 Adjusting the elbow skin envelopes.

11. Repeat this process to correct the elbow of the right arm, and then save the scene file as GenMan804.max.

At this stage of adjusting the model, there is no need to paint weights on the skin. When the model is actually animated in a close-up scene, any flaws or distortions become more obvious. Then, the ability to paint skin weights becomes more useful and important.

Mirror Skin Weights

A valuable new feature in 3ds max 6 is the capability to adjust the skin weights on one side of the model and then use the Mirror Skin Weights tools to apply those skin weight adjustments to the other side of the model. This is a tremendous time-saver when setting up a model, and this simple procedure can be used with the previous tutorial.

To see how this tool works, load the previous tutorial file and switch to the Front view. Then select the skin and open the Skin Modifier. Click the Edit Envelopes button. Next, select one of the Bone Envelope icons from the arm on your right (the model's left arm). The model skin should be blue, and the bone influence show green, red, and yellow color around the selected bone, as shown in Figure 8.9, example 1.

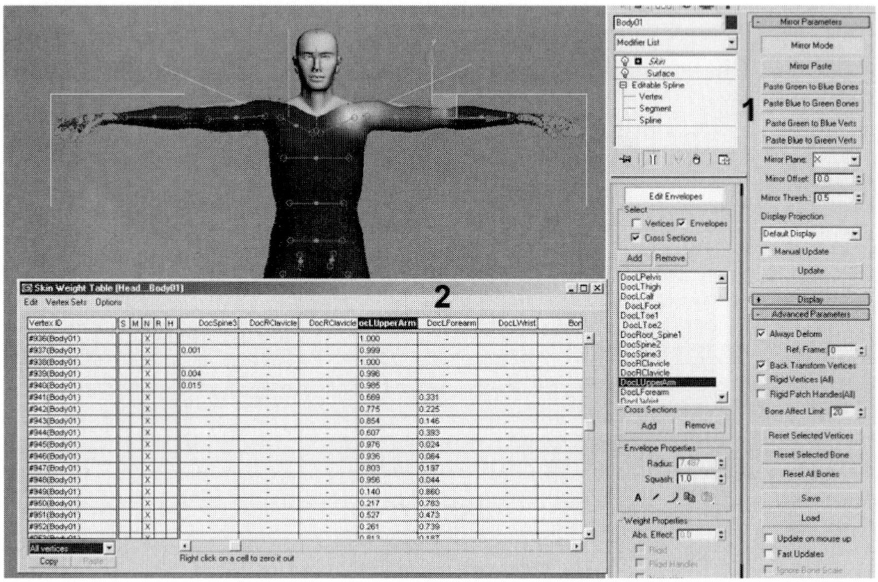

FIGURE 8.9 Using Mirror Skin Weights.

Now scroll the Skin Modifier window to locate the Mirror Parameters menu and click the Mirror Mode button. Notice that the bone icons will turn either red, or blue and green. Max is trying to decide for you which bones are on the model's left (blue) and right (green) sides of the X-axis line, which should now be visible down the middle of the model. However, if all the bone icons stay red, turn up the Mirror Threshold value to about 22. Now the bone icons on your right should be blue, and on your left (the model's right side) they should be green. The last step is to click the bone icon for the skin weights that you want mirrored on the blue side of the model, and then click the Paste Blue to Green Bone button. That will paste the skin weight values from the blue bones to the green bones. That's all there is to it. Repeat the process for any bones on which you want to mirror values.

If you open the Skin Weight Table by clicking the Weight Table button under Weight Properties, you will see a list of all of the vertices that are associated with the upper left arm bone, as shown in Figure 8.9, example 2. If, when you are done mirroring weights, you find that some of the vertices of the skin are not moving correctly, you can change their strength value in the Skin Weight Table. The normal vertex weight range is from 0.0 to 1.0. All skin vertices are numbered and are shown in this table with their associated bones and vertex weights for fine-tuning the skin.

In the next tutorial, you will create slider manipulators and wire the finger bones to open and close the hand by moving a slider.

SLIDERS AND WIRED PARAMETERS

A slider is a manipulator helper object that looks and acts much like a traditional volume control on a stereo radio, but instead of changing volume, it can be assigned to change any parameter or setting. A slider normally floats in the viewport at all times, but can be hidden or minimized. When used with wired parameters, the slider can be set up to control any object you want to animate with an external control. 3ds max enables you to create a physical connection between one parameter and another by "wiring" them together in the Wired Parameters dialog.

A wired parameter can be either a driver or a driven parameter. A slider is considered a driver object that controls a parameter of the driven object such as a finger bone. In this skeleton rig, the movements of the hand and fingers are controlled by the Y-axis Rotate parameter. To animate the hand or finger closing, you move the slider, which then changes the angle of the Y-axis. One of the fingers can be wired to control all the other fingers in a parent > child relationship. For example, when the index finger bends or closes, the entire hand can be made to close with it. Alternatively, if you want to control the fingers individually, you would create one slider per finger.

Note that many advanced users prefer to use custom attributes to control hands, feet, and facial expressions in their skeleton rigs. They work in much the same way as sliders do, but the setup and wiring of custom attribute controls can be more complex than sliders. Custom attributes are discussed in Chapter 12, "Advanced Animation."

In the next tutorial, you will set up a slider to control index finger movement.

TUTORIAL 8.5 CREATE A SLIDER AND WIRE IT TO A FINGER

To create a slider and wire it to control a finger:

1. Open the GenMan804.max. Before working on the hands, you must delete all of the animation keys you applied to the skeleton during the previous tutorials. Unhide the bones and the control points. In the Display > Hide By Category menu, uncheck Helpers, and then click the None button next to the small window where the word *Bone* is highlighted. The skeleton with its rig and control points should now be visible.
2. To delete the temporary animation keys, maximize the front viewport and then hide the body skin. Select the Hip Control. Two animation keys should be displayed on the time line: one at frame 0, and another at frame 30. Select the keys and then right-click. In the pop-up menu, click Delete Selected Keys. Repeat this operation for the keys on the Chest Control, the Shoulder Controls, and the Right and Left Arm IK end effectors. When finished, there should be no movement of the model when you scrub the Time Slider.
3. To create a slider manipulator, zoom in on the character's left hand in the front view. Next, open the Create > Helpers > Manipulator menu and click the Slider button. In Parameters, put a label on the slider before you create it. Label it: Left Hand Close. In Slider Parameters, leave Value = 0, and then set Minimum = 0 and Maximum = 1.0. Click in the lower-right corner of the viewport A new horizontal slider now floats on the viewport, as shown in Figure 8.10. Right-click in the viewport to turn off slider creation.

   The next operation will determine how the hand will work. The basic idea is to select the slider, right-click, and choose what parameter it will control. Then, select an object, such as a bone, right-click, and choose which bone parameter you will control with the slider. In this case, you want the slider to control bone rotation in the correct axis to close the finger.
4. During this operation, a floating window is going to cover part of the front view. Pan the view downward to leave room at the top. Select the slider, and then right-click. The Quad menu will pop up, as shown in Figure 8.11, example 1.
5. Click Wire Parameters. As soon as you click it, a small pop-up menu opens, as shown in Figure 8.11, example 2. If you are zoom in close to the hand, the menu will probably be over in the lower-left corner of the interface. In that pop-up menu, click Object (which refers to the slider), and then click Value.

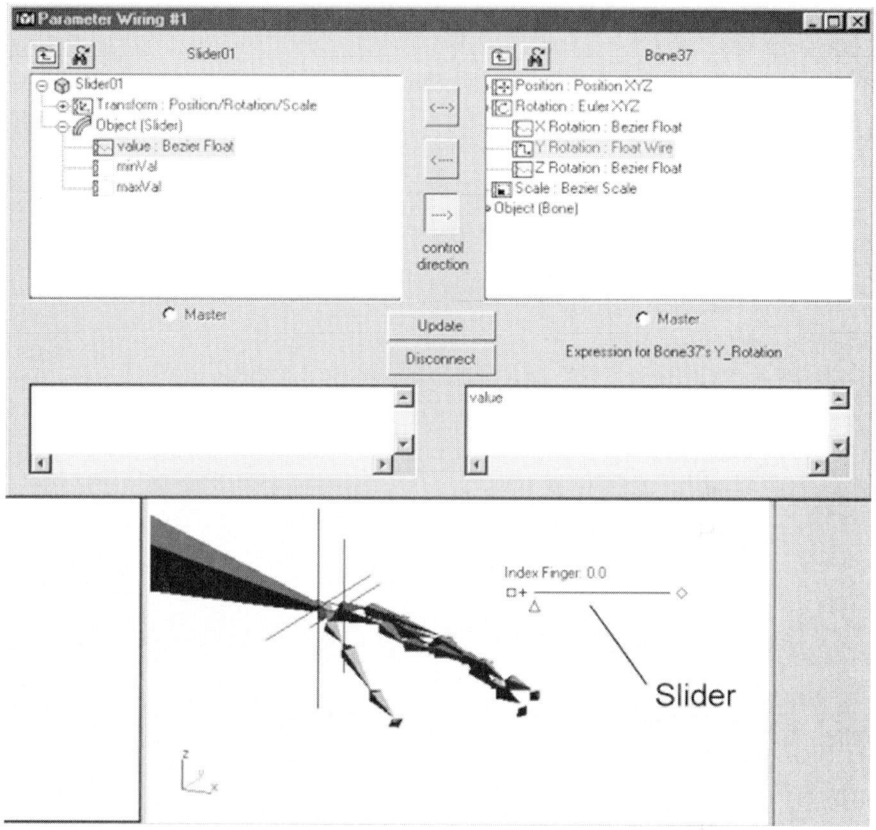

FIGURE 8.10 The Parameter Wiring dialog box where parameters are wired together.

6. Drag the cursor over and select the root bone of the Index Finger (DocLFinger01). A dotted line will follow the cursor. A second Parameter pop-up menu will appear for the finger bone. Click Transform, then select Rotation, and finally select Y Rotation. The large Parameter Wiring window will then open, as shown in Figure 8.11, example 3.
7. Notice that the slider is listed on the left with Value highlighted in yellow, and the finger bone is listed on the right with Y Rotation: Float Wire highlighted. In the center of the Wiring dialog box is a column of arrows. Select the arrow pointing from the slider side toward the Finger side. It will turn yellow to indicate the Control Direction, as shown in Figure 8.11, example 3.
8. Click the Connect button below the arrow to create a connection between the slider and the index finger Y-rotation axis.

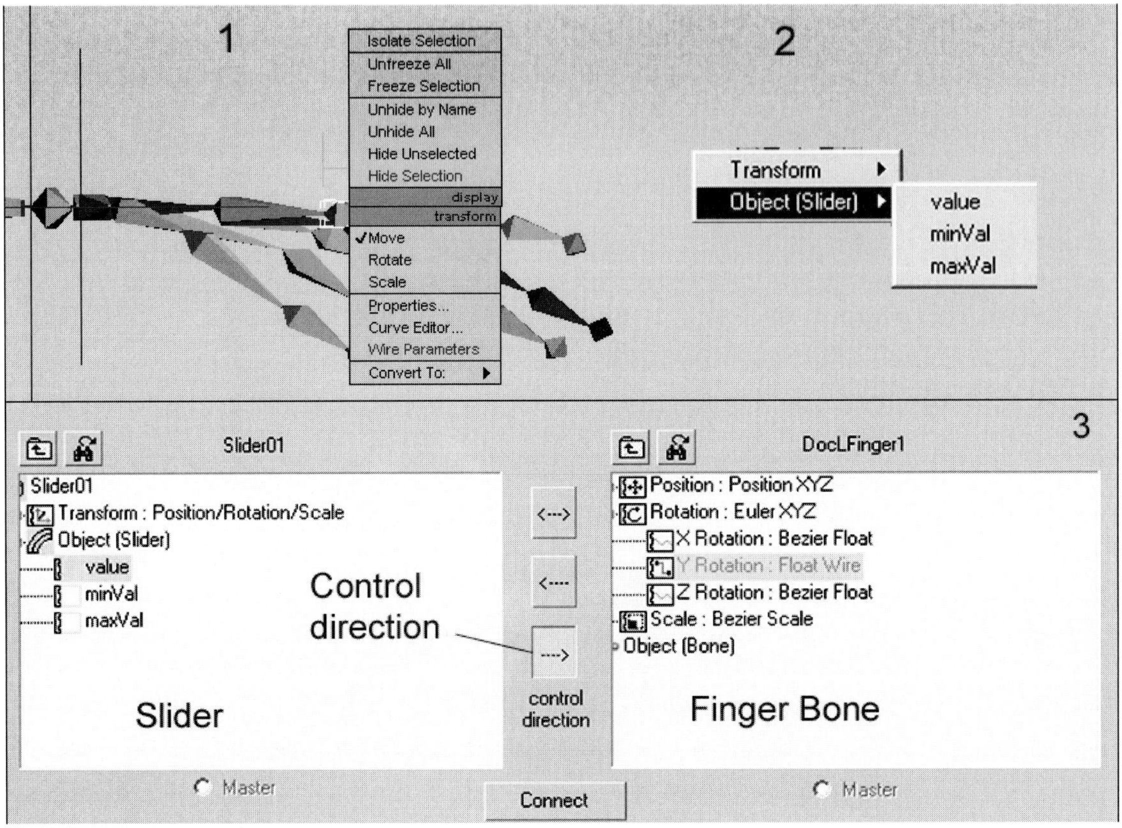

FIGURE 8.11 Connecting Wired Parameters from a slider to a finger bone.

9. To test the function of the new Left Hand Close Slider, click the Select and Manipulate icon in the Main toolbar (next to Move), and then click and drag the small triangle handle under the slider to the right and watch the finger move.
10. The finger bone should rotate down in the Y-axis. This completes stage one of wiring the hand. Close the Parameter Wiring window. Save the file as GenMan805.max.

In the next tutorial, you will wire the bones together so that the first bone of the index finger closes all of the bones of the hand into a fist. All of the other finger bones will be set up to inherit their rotations from the root index finger bone. For more flexible control of the hand, you can later wire the thumb to its own slider.

TUTORIAL 8.6

WIRING ONE FINGER TO CONTROL ALL OF THE FINGERS

To wire the left index finger to control all of the fingers on the left hand:

1. Load the GenMan805.max file if it is not already loaded. You should see the bones of the left hand and the Left Hand Close Slider.
2. Select the root bone of the index finger, DocLFinger01. The next step is to wire the Y-axis rotation of the second and third index finger bones to the Y-rotation parameter of the first or root index finger bone.
3. Press the RMB to open the menu and select Wire Parameters. The small wiring pop-up box appears. Click Transform > Rotation > Y Rotation, drag the cursor to the second index finger bone, DocLFinger02, and left-click the bone.
4. A second wiring pop-up will open. Select Transform> Rotation > Y Rotation. The Parameter Wiring window will open showing the two Rotation parameters. The left side is the driver, DocLFinger01, and the right side is the driven object, DocLFinger02.
5. In the center Control Direction area, click the arrow pointing to the right or the second driven bone, and then click the Connect button to wire the parameters together.
6. Test the wiring by turning on the Select and Manipulate icon, and then click on the triangle below the slider and slide it left and right with the mouse. The finger should change from straight to bent, and the second bone should inherit its Y rotation from the first finger bone, as shown in Figure 8.12.
7. Close the Parameter Wiring window and turn off the Manipulate icon. To wire the second index finger bone rotation, DocLFinger12, to control the rotation of the third index finger bone, DocLFinger13, repeat steps 2 through 6, but substitute the second and third bones for the first and second bones. All operations are the same.
8. Turn on the Manipulate icon and test the slider to make sure that all three bones rotate correctly and that the second and third bones inherit the rotation from their Parent bones.
9. To make the entire hand close when the index finger does, you will wire the first index finger bone to control all of the first finger bones in the rest of the hand. To do that, select the Index finger root bone, DocLFinger1, then RMB-click and select Wire Parameters.

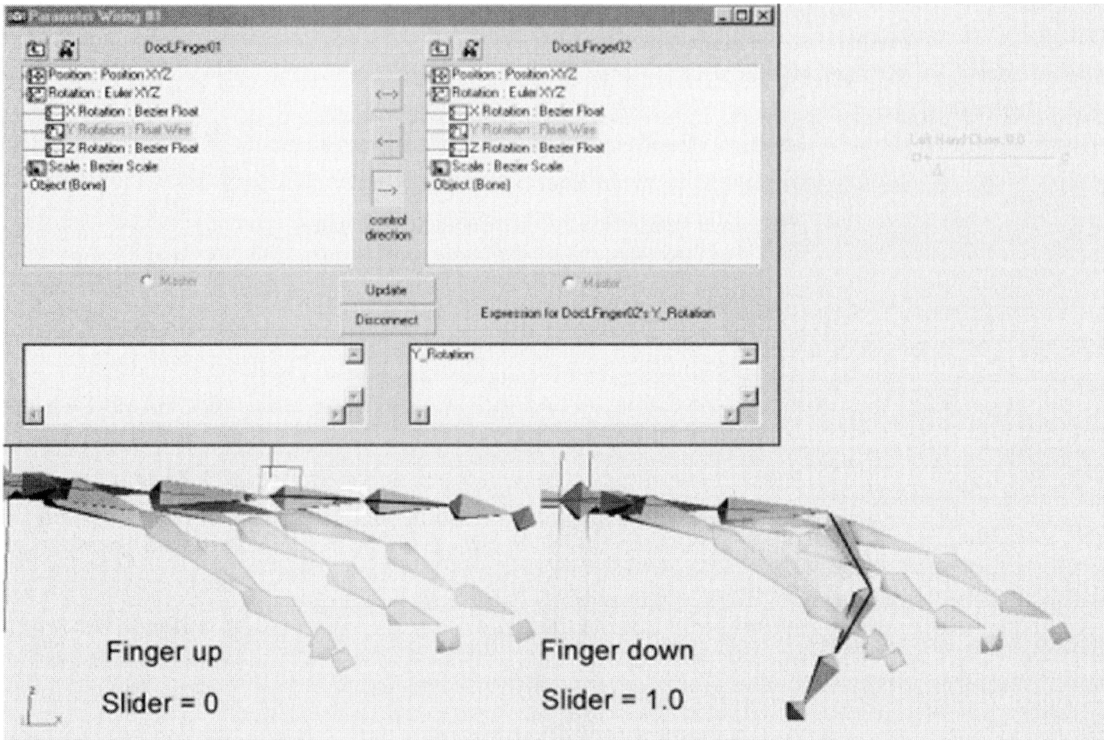

FIGURE 8.12 Wiring the first index finger bone to control the second bone.

10. Select Transform > Rotation > Y rotation, and then drag over to the root bone of the middle finger, DocLFinger2. In the pop-up box, select Transform > Rotation > Y rotation.
11. The Parameter Wiring window opens. In the Control Direction area, click the arrow pointing to the right so that Index finger bone 1 controls Middle finger bone 1. Then click connect to wire them together.
12. Test with the slider to make sure the middle finger now moves with the index finger. If that works, continue wiring the second middle finger bone to be controlled by the first middle finger bone. Then, wire the second to control the third bone, and so on.
13. Continue wiring all the bones of the hand in the same way you did the index finger. When finished, you should be able to move the index finger slider and cause all the other finger bones to move. This will allow you to close and open the entire hand by moving the slider, as shown in Figure 8.13. Save the file as GenMan806.max.

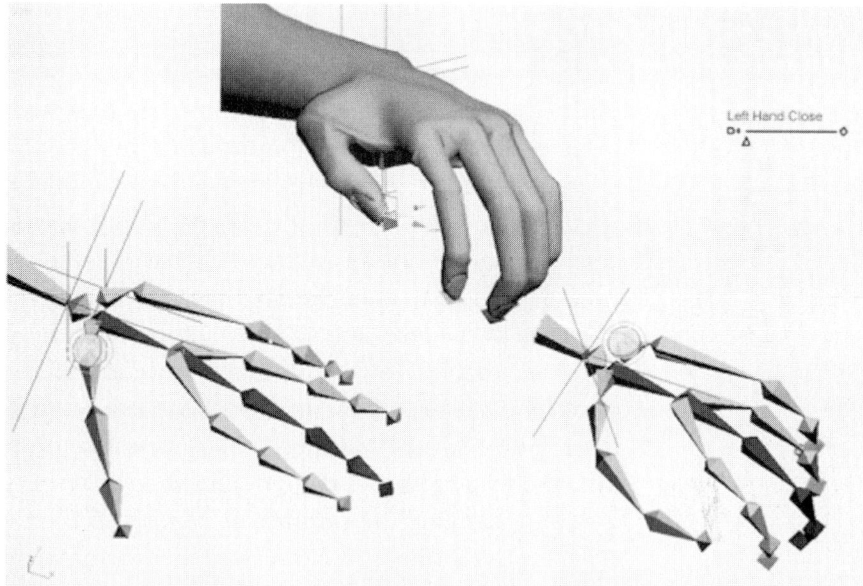

FIGURE 8.13 All the fingers are wired to and controlled by the root index finger bone.

The root bone of the index finger should be wired to control the root bones of all other fingers and the thumb, which is called DocLFinger0. This means that every bone in the hand inherits its rotation from the original index finger root bone, which is the only bone directly controlled by the slider. The angle of movement of the thumb might need to be adjusted by rotating its root bone axis so that it closes under the palm. For better control of the thumb, create a second slider that only operates the thumb.

Wiring the Right Hand

Wiring the right hand is essentially the same process as wiring the left hand. When the Generic Man is configured as Dr. Quin, the character handles props with his right hand and needs to have independent finger control. To wire the right hand, repeat the operations in the previous tutorials, but instead of creating one slider to control the entire hand, create five sliders and wire them to the individual finger. Each slider should only be wired to the root bone of its respective finger. All of the second and third finger bones should inherit their rotations from their first or root finger bones.

FACIAL MORPH TARGETS

In order to prepare the character to simulate human speech and emotion for the lip sync tutorial in Chapter 9, the head will need to be separated from the body and cloned a number of times so that facial morph targets can be made. The morph targets are then sculpted into different facial expressions and the shapes formed by the mouth during speech. The concept of facial morphing animation is based on the ability of the computer to move the vertices of the original face object around to match a modified copy of the face, and still have it bound to the skull bone of the skeleton. This enables you to make any variation of the expression or mouth shape and then have the original head assume that shape at a particular frame number that you specify by setting a keyframe. The basic idea is to take the original head, copy it, and then sculpt it into a new expression without changing the number of vertices in the new head so that it still matches the number of vertices in the original head exactly. If the number of vertices is changed, the new head will not work as a morph target, and will become invalid.

The morph target shapes that are needed range from a head with a closed mouth and open eyes, to a head with an open mouth and closed eyes. The second head could be used for a yawning face, for example. There are a few standard mouth shapes that are required to mimic human speech. These shapes are known as *phonemes*. These are the face shapes you will sculpt in. In order to create the morph targets, you will begin by separating the head from the body, and then cloning it five times. Each of these five clones will then be sculpted into one of the basic phonemes to create the speech morph targets. However, if elaborate dialog and expressions are required, additional morph targets will be needed. A minimum number of morph targets for both rudimentary speech and facial expressions would include about a dozen different shapes. These shapes would simulate the jaw movement for opening and closing the mouth during speech, and emotions such as the smile, anger, sadness, surprise, puzzlement, intense concentration, and concern. All of the expressions involve different movements of the eyebrows, the skin around the eyes, the cheeks, and the mouth. Many of these emotions include different eye shapes such as half closed, winking, or wide open. You will probably want additional morph targets that simply close and open one or both eyes. Potentially you could have 20 or 30 different facial targets: It is not uncommon in professional character animation to have a large number of different facial shapes that can be mixed together during animation. Stewart the mouse in the film *Stewart Little* had more than 80 morph targets to give it a full range of expressions and mouth shapes for dialog and different emotions. The management of a large number of facial targets in 3ds max is done in the Morpher Modifier, which can handle 100 facial targets, each with its own animation channel. The usual workflow in animating speech and facial expressions involves creating all the shapes, recording a soundtrack, and then matching the facial shapes to the sounds frame by frame to create the animation using the spinner dials in the Morpher Modifier Channel List window, as shown in Figure 8.14. You can also use slider manipulators to control the facial shapes. This will be discussed in Chapter 9, "Character Animation," where you will actually animate the face to create a lip sync animation.

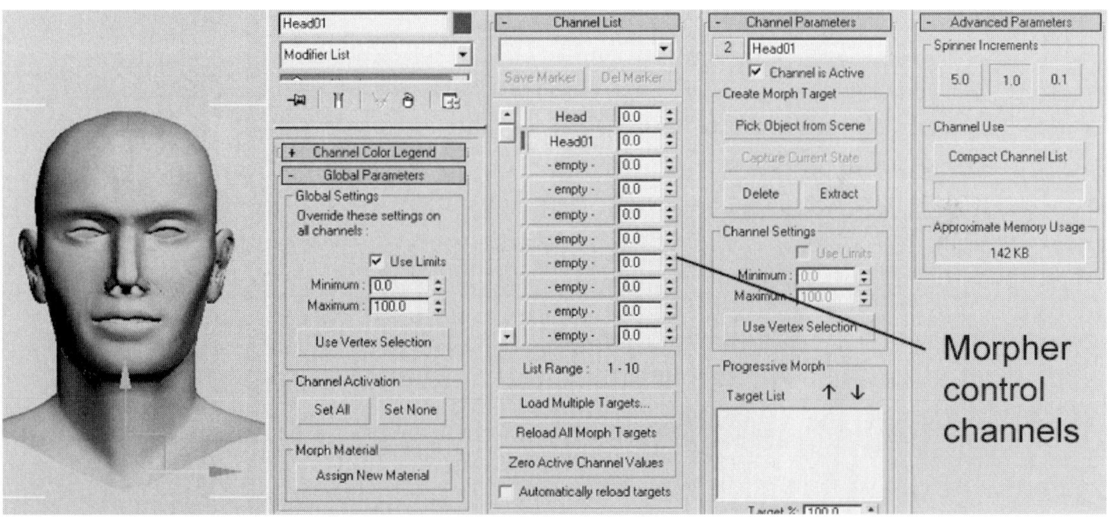

FIGURE 8.14 The Morpher Modifier Channel controls.

In the next tutorial, you will clone the head five times and then hide the clones. They will be used in a later tutorial to create facial morph targets.

TUTORIAL 8.7 CLONE THE HEAD FOR MORPH TARGETS

1. Load the GenMan806.max scene file, if it is not already loaded.
2. Select the head, then right-click, and in the Quad menu, select Unfreeze All. Then, select the head, right-click, and select Properties. In the Properties dialog, turn off See Through.
3. In the front view, click Zoom Extents (Z). Click Display and Hide Helpers.
4. With the head selected, locate its XYZ gizmo. If it is not centered on the head, move it to the head using the Adjust Pivot tool. To do that, click the Hierarchy tab, and then click Affect Pivot Only. When the Affect Pivot XYZ gizmo appears in the viewport, move it over to center it on the neck. Then, turn off Affect Pivot Only.
5. Clone five copies of the head. Use Shift > Move in the X-axis to drag five clone copies of the head to the right, spacing each about one head length farther over in the X-axis, as shown in Figure 8.15.

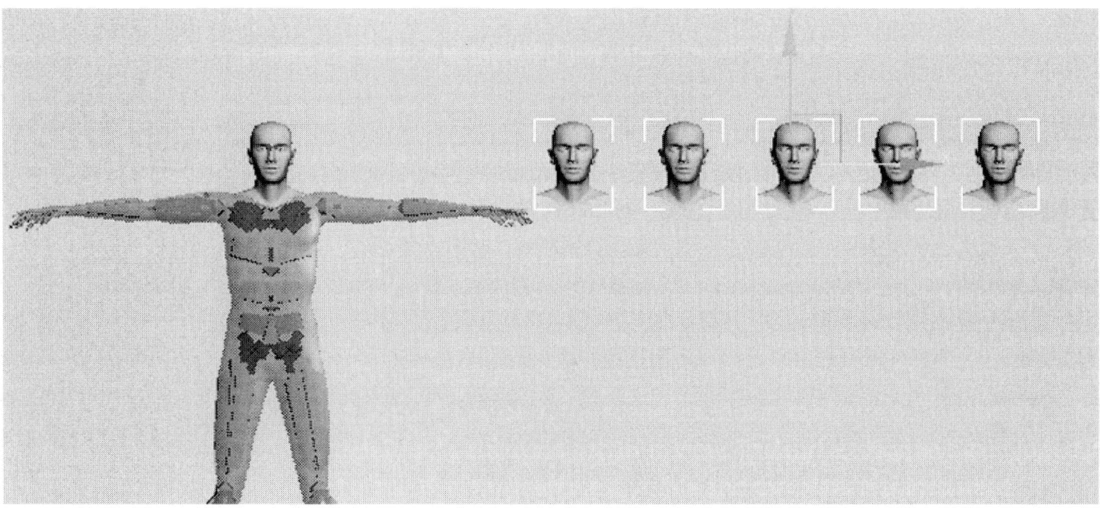

FIGURE 8.15 Five clone copies of the head.

6. Select all five clone copies of the head, and create a Selection Set called Morph Heads. To do that, click the Named Selection Sets window in the menu bar, type in Morph Heads, and press Enter.
7. Select each cloned head and remove the Skin Modifier.

8. Next, select all of the bones of the skeleton and create a Selection Set for them called Bones Only.
9. Select and hide the eyes, mouth, and teeth groups if they are not already hidden. You are now ready to apply the Skin Modifier to the model.
10. Save the file as GenMan807.max.

In the following tutorial, you will sculpt the five facial morph targets into four basic mouth shapes and one emotion. This will give you a starting point from which you can expand and create all the shapes you want to use.

TUTORIAL 8.8 SCULPTING FACIAL MORPH TARGETS

To sculpt a morph target, follow these steps:

1. Load the GenMan807.max scene file. Unhide the five morph target heads, and then select them and click Hide Unselected. Select one of the morph target heads, and then click Hide Unselected and Zoom Extents. You should see only one head in the front view.
2. To sculpt the face, click the Modify tab and go to Editable Spline > Vertex mode. Open the Materials Editor and apply a dark blue material to the head so that you can see the spine cage in the viewport more easily. Then, click the Show End Result on/off toggle to display the patch surface and the splines, as shown in Figure 8.16, example 1.
3. The first mouth shape you will create is the shape for the vowel "O." To see an example of the correct mouth shapes for simulating speech, open the 3ds max tutorial called Lip Sync > Lip sync and Facial Expressions with the Morpher Modifier, which can be found in 3ds max 6 tutorials. Scroll the window down until you find the image of the sergeant forming the "O" as in "other" mouth shape, as shown in Figure 8.16, example 2.
4. As the tutorial states, to form the "O" shaped mouth, "Pull the corners of the mouth in, indent the cheeks, move the upper lip up slightly. Move the lower lip and the chin and jaw down." To do that, you will use an Free Form Deformer (FFD) to select areas of vertices in the face and move them.
5. Before working on the face, it is a good idea to hide the back of the head so you don't accidentally select it. In the left view, select all the spline

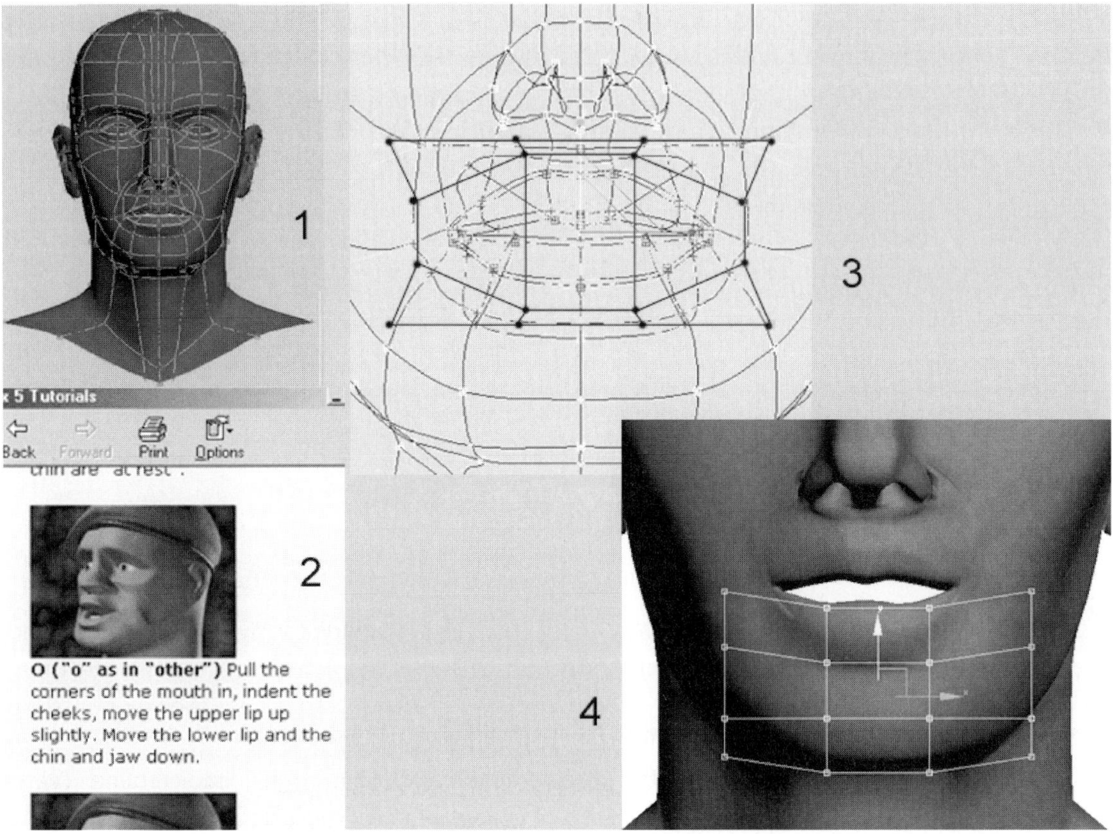

FIGURE 8.16 Sculpting a morph target head into the "O" mouth shape.

segments of the back of the head including the ears and hide them using Editable Spline >, and then return to the front view.

6. Region Select all of the vertices of the mouth and lips, and then apply an FFD. Click Modifiers > Free Form Deformers > FFD 4x4x4. A lattice will appear around the mouth. In the Modifier Stack, click the Plus next to FFD, and turn on Control Points. Select only the center two horizontal rows of control points, and then use Non-uniform Scale to narrow the mouth. Then, select the central control points and pull the mouth opening wider, as shown in Figure 8.16, example 3.
7. To remove the FFD lattice, but keep the new position of the mouth vertices, right-click the FFD Modifier in the Stack and select Collapse To. You will get a warning message saying that it will remove a portion of the

stack. Click Hold/Yes. The patch surface will be displayed with the new mouth shape, as shown in Figure 8.16, example 4.

8. Repeat this operation to move the jaw down, and then pull in the cheeks. When you have completed the creation of the "O" mouth shape, remove all FFD Modifiers from the stack using the Collapse To procedure, and then unhide all the head spline segments. That finishes the first facial morph target. Rename the head Mouth O, and then hide the finished morph target.
9. Unhide another morph target head and create the "M" mouth shape using the same procedure explained earlier. Then, create the "E" shape and the "T" shape. That will give you four mouth shapes that will get you started and will be sufficient mouth shapes to finish the Lip Sync tutorial in Chapter 9.
10. Sculpt the eyebrows up (Brows UP) shape into the fifth morph target head. When you are finished, select all the morph target heads and apply the flesh colored material to the heads.
11. Save the file as GenMan808.max.

In the next tutorial, you will create the clothing for Dr. Quin.

Creating Clothing for Dr. Quin with the Push Modifier

There are three methods of creating clothing. The simplest is to use the character's own patch surface and modify sections of it with the Push Modifier to become a garment. In this book, we'll call that type of clothing Push Clothing. The second method is to use box modeling methods and sculpt the clothing as a polygonal mesh. The third method is to use a plug-in program such as Stitch from Digimation to create patterns for the pieces of cloth that will form the garment, and then stitch them together. All three methods will yield good character clothing. The first method uses the original mesh to generate the clothing. This method makes it easiest to fit the garment to the character's body shape, and looks good in medium and distant shots. For the critical close-up scenes where the cloth must look soft and hang well on the body, Stitch will be used. The Stitch Tutorial can be found in Chapter 17, "Plug-ins."

Dr. Quin wears a light work jacket and a pair of pants for the Alien Ship Crash scene near the beginning of *Homing Instinct*. In the following tutorial, you will create a jacket and pants using the Push Modifier to modifying sections of the Generic Man body.

TUTORIAL 8.9

Creating Push Clothing for Dr. Quin

ON THE CD

To create Dr. Quin's clothing, follow these steps:

1. Load the Body_Only.max file from the Chap08 folder on the companion CD-ROM. This is a copy of the GenMan808.max file with the skeleton, morph target heads, and the Skin Modifier removed. This body and head will be modified into clothing.
2. In the front view, select the body and apply a dark blue material. Click the Modify tab, and then turn off the Surface Modifier. In addition, select the head and turn off its Surface Modifier. Then, in the Editable Spline > Modify menu, scroll down to the Geometry menu and click Attach. Next, click on the head in the front view. That will attach the head to the body. Turn off Attach.
3. With the body selected, select Edit in the 3ds max Main menu bar. In the drop-down menu, click Clone. In the pop-up dialog, select Object > Copy, and rename it Pants. Then, click OK. The copy will be modified into the pants later. Hide the copy named Pants.
4. Select the original body. It will now be modified into a coat. In the Editable Spline Modifier, go to Segment Sub-object mode. Select all the spline segments below the waist, and delete them, as shown in Figure 8.17, example 1. Make sure that you keep the spline that goes around the hip. Switch to the top view, zoom in on the right hand, and then select the spline segments of the hand and delete them. This should leave the wrist spline circles intact. Repeat this for the left hand.
5. In the front view, zoom in on the head. Select all the spline segments of the head, but do not include the neck. Delete the head. Use Arc Rotate to inspect the neck opening to make sure it is intact and that you have not left any extra spline segments. You should now have a spline cage object that resembles the shape of a tight shirt, as shown in Figure 8.17, example 2. In the neck area, delete the extra spline that runs around the shoulder where the original wider neck opening was. If you do not delete it, it will create unwanted twisting of the surface later. Also, fuse all the vertex pairs around the opening and delete the two small spline segments along with the extra vertices at the front of the neck.
6. Turn on the Surface Modifier. The Coat object should be smooth and have no holes in the surface. Rename the object Coat. Unhide the copy of the body you named Pants earlier. Select the object, and then in the Modifier Stack, turn on the Surface Modifier. Apply a flesh-colored material, as

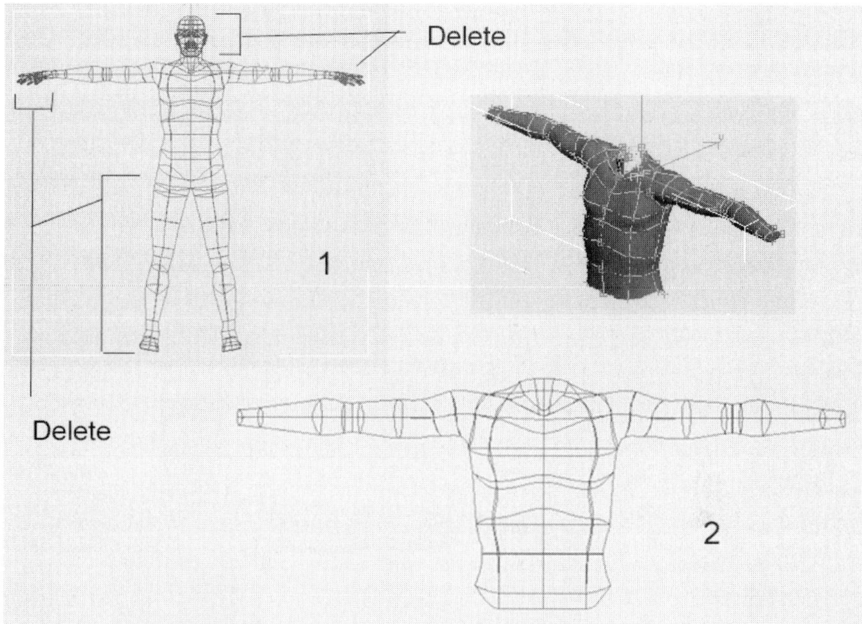

FIGURE 8.17 Preparing the mesh to create a coat.

shown in Figure 8.18, example 1. The new coat and the Pants object will occupy the same space.

7. Freeze the Pants object so that only the new coat will be unfrozen. You will now enlarge the new coat object about 15% larger than the original body. Select Modifiers in the Main menu bar, and then select Parametric, Deformers > Push. In the Push Modifier Parameters menu, set Push Value to 0.5, as shown in Figure 8.18, example 2.
8. In the Display tab, click Hide > Hide Frozen Objects. You will be collapsing the coat to an Editable Poly object, but first it needs to be modified to smooth the neck area, the waist, and the elbows. In the Stack, go to the Editable Spline > Vertex mode. Then, right-click the surface in the front view, and in the Quad menu, select Properties. In Properties, click See Through. You should now see the original unexpanded spline cage inside the new pushed out coat surface.
9. Zoom in on the left elbow. Select the vertices on the bottom of the elbow and pull them downward a short distance to straighten out the elbow surface. Repeat this for the top vertices of the elbow, as shown in Figure 8.19, example 1. Then, switch to the top view and straighten the back and the

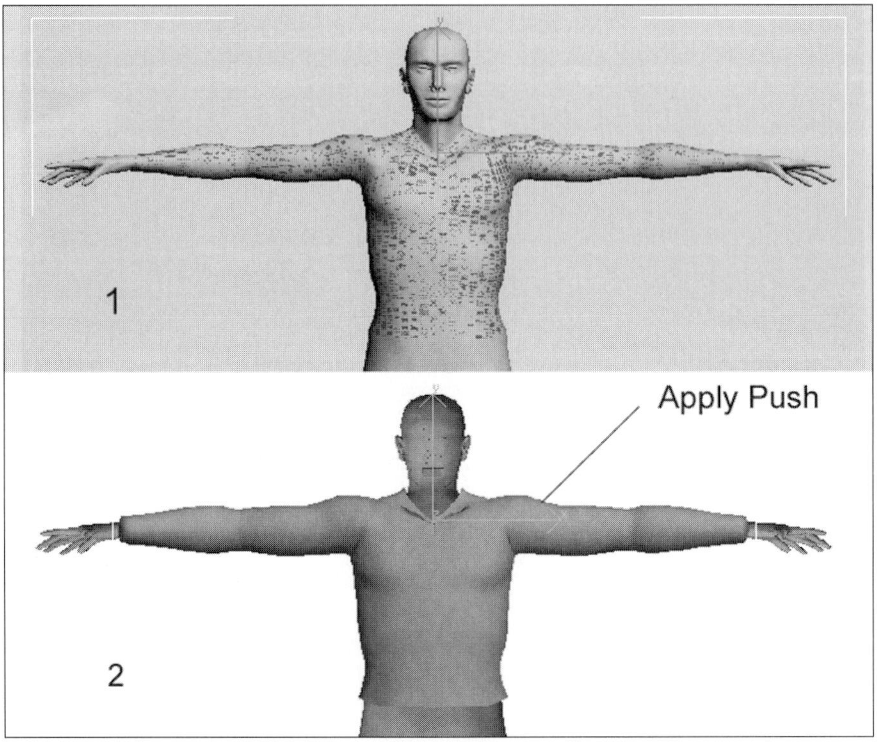

FIGURE 8.18 Apply the Push Modifier to expand the coat.

front of the elbow, as shown in Figure 8.19, example 2. Repeat this to straighten the other arm, and then straighten the lines of the shoulders and move the armpit area lower a small amount.

10. In the left view, pull down the vertices on the bottom of the coat to make it straight, and then pull out the area in the small of the back, as shown in Figure 8.19, example 3. Finally, convert the coat to an Editable Poly object. Hide the coat.
11. Unhide the frozen pants and unfreeze them. Create the pants in the same way as the coat, by deleting the upper body at the waist, and the feet below the ankles, as shown in Figure 8.20, example 1. Then, apply Push with a value of 0.35. Then, in Vertex Sub-object mode, straighten out the curves of the legs and at the back of the knees. Straighten the waist line, and then convert the pants to an Editable Poly object, as shown in Figure 8.20, example 2.
12. Save the scene as GenMan809.max.

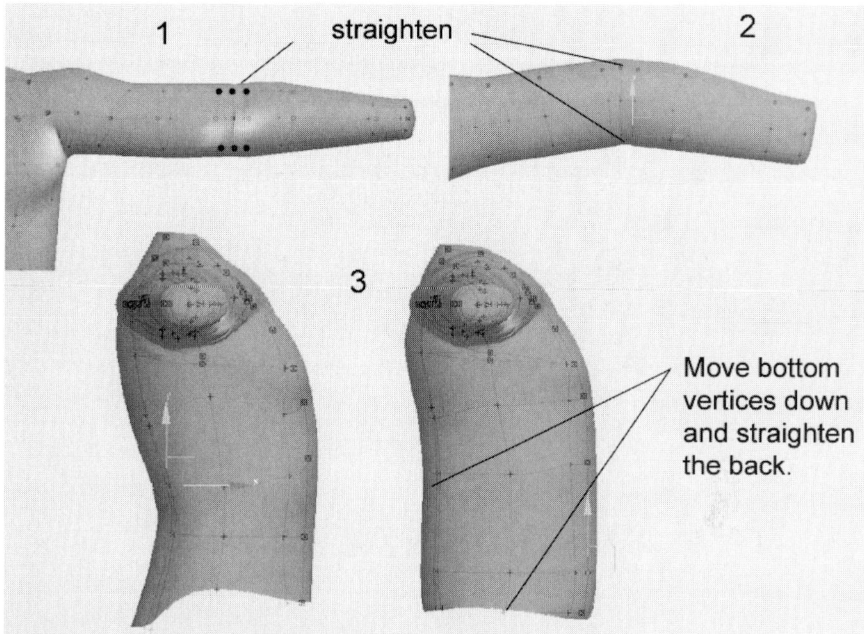

FIGURE 8.19 Straighten out the lines of the coat.

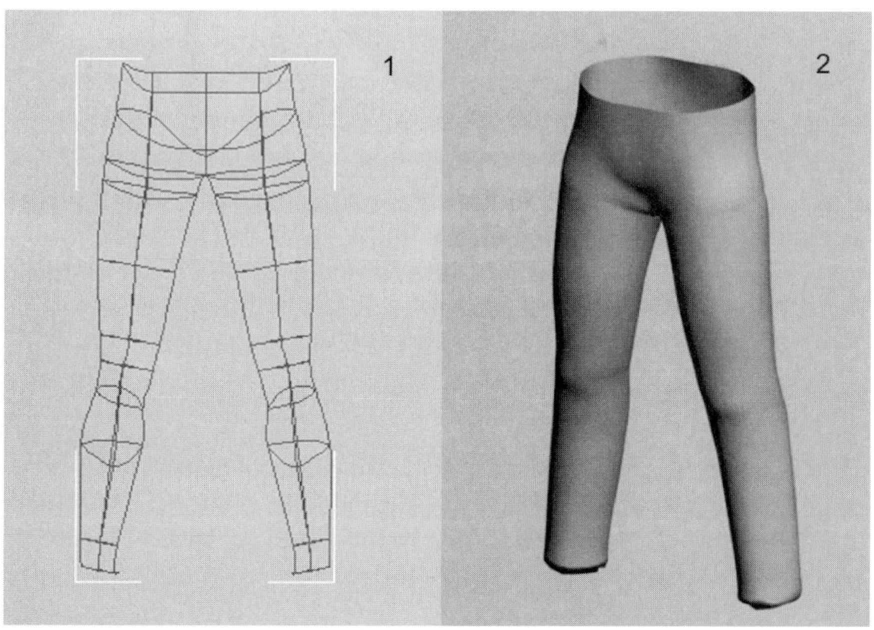

FIGURE 8.20 Creating the pants.

In the next tutorial, you will create a collar and cuffs for the coat and pants.

TUTORIAL 8.10 PUT A COLLAR AND CUFFS ON THE COAT AND PANTS

To create a collar on the coat:

1. Load the GenMan809.max file, and then select and hide the Pants. Change the blue color on the coat to a brown that is dark enough to see easily in the viewport.
2. In the front view, zoom in on the collar area. In Editable Poly, select Border Sub-object mode, and set the view to Smooth > Highlight > Edged Faces. Select the edge of the neck opening. It will turn red indicating that it is a Border of the object, as shown in Figure 8.21, example 1.

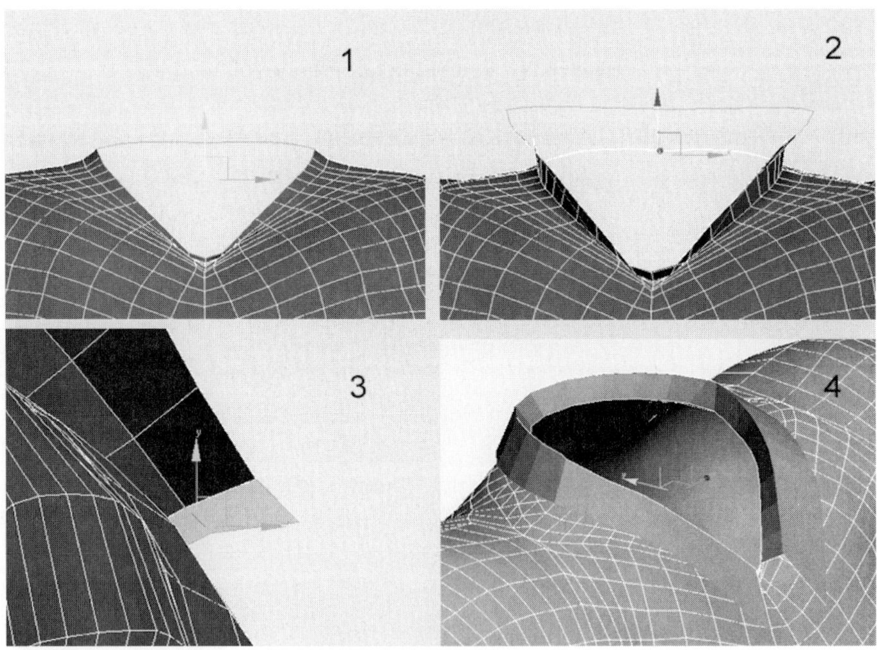

FIGURE 8.21 Extruding the collar for the coat.

3. In the Editable Poly > Edit Borders menu, locate the Extrude button, and then click on the small square icon directly to the right. It will open the Extrude Edges dialog. The Extrusion Height is set to 10 by default. Change

the Height to 0.8. The border of the neck opening should now be extruded upward a short distance. Click OK.

4. With the border still selected, switch from Border to Edge Sub-object mode. Then, click the Extrude button. A second extrusion will occur that moves sideways to spread out the collar. Now turn off the Extrude button, and in the viewport, move the new extruded edges up a short distance, as shown in Figure 8.21, example 2. You should now have a flaring collar area. Arc Rotate the coat to see it on all sides.
5. Switch to the left view. Zoom in on the front of the collar area and then select the four polygons at the front of the neck, as shown in Figure 8.21, example 3. Delete these polygons. Apply a brown two-sided material to the coat.
6. In the front view, select the border around the collar again, switch to Edges Sub-object mode, and de-select the edges at the front of the collar so that only the outer edge is selected. Move the edge down until part of it touches the shoulders, and then Non-uniform scale the edge to make it wider in the X-axis. In the left view, move the collar toward the front of the coat and lower it until it almost touches the shoulders, as shown in Figure 8.21, example 4.
7. To make cuffs at the ends of the sleeves, first select and delete the cap that was formed over the end of the sleeve before the coat was converted to Editable Polygons. Next, select a ring of polygons around the wrist area and extrude them a very short distance. That will raise a cuff around the sleeve at the wrist. Apply Uniform Scale to make the cuff slightly larger or smaller as you choose, as shown in Figure 8.22, example 1.
8. Select the small group of polygons at the front of the neck opening and delete them to open the collar area a bit, as shown in Figure 8.22, example 2. Then, select a vertical row of polygons that run down one side of center, down the front of the coat from the collar to the bottom seam. Extrude the row and scale them up a bit to overlap the polygons beside them, as shown in Figure 8.22, example 3.
9. Increase the resolution of the collar to match the rest of the coat by selecting all of the collar polygons, and then applying MeshSmooth. The collar will become more rounded and realistic, but the rest of the coat will not change.
10. Repeat the preceding process to create cuffs around the pants legs. To reduce the overall polygon count on the coat, apply the Optimize Modifier. Set the Face Threshold to 2.5 and set Max Edge Length to 1.2 units. That

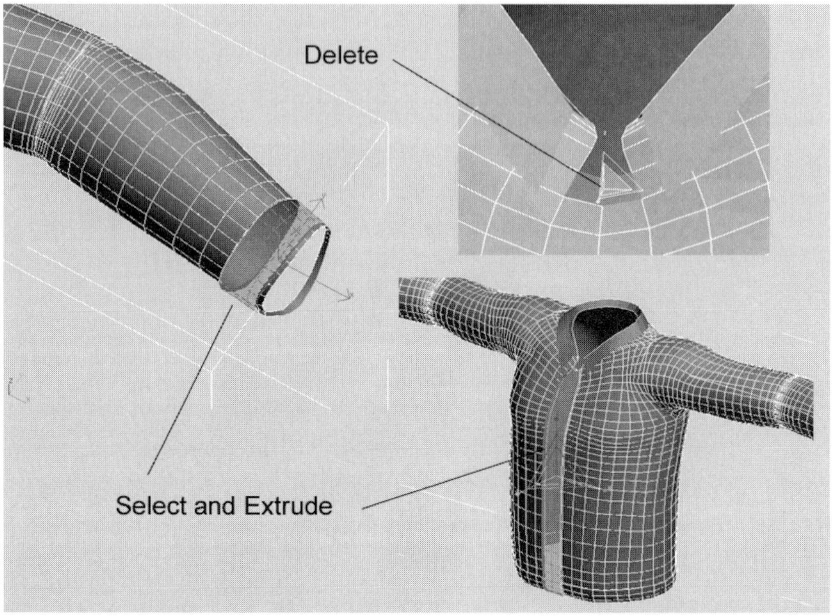

FIGURE 8.22 Creating the cuffs for the coat.

will reduce the resolution without making the coat look faceted. It is also a good idea to select all polygons, remove Smoothing, and then apply Auto-Smooth.

11. Save the file as GenMan810.

In the next tutorial, you will merge the skeleton and the finished skin into the scene file that contains the coat and pants.

TUTORIAL 8.11 MERGING THE CLOTHING, SKIN, AND SKELETON

To merge files:

1. Load the GenMan810.max scene. This scene only contains a coat and pants.
2. The GenMan808.max scene file contains all of the parts of the character, including the skeleton, the patch surface skin, and the morph target

heads. The Merge command will combine this file with the GenMan810.max file.

ON THE CD

3. Click File > Merge, find your GenMan808.max file, or you can merge it in from the Chap08 folder on the companion CD-ROM. When the Merge dialog box opens, click All, and then click OK. The body, head, skeleton, and the morph targets heads will load into the GenMan810.max scene, as shown in Figure 8.23.

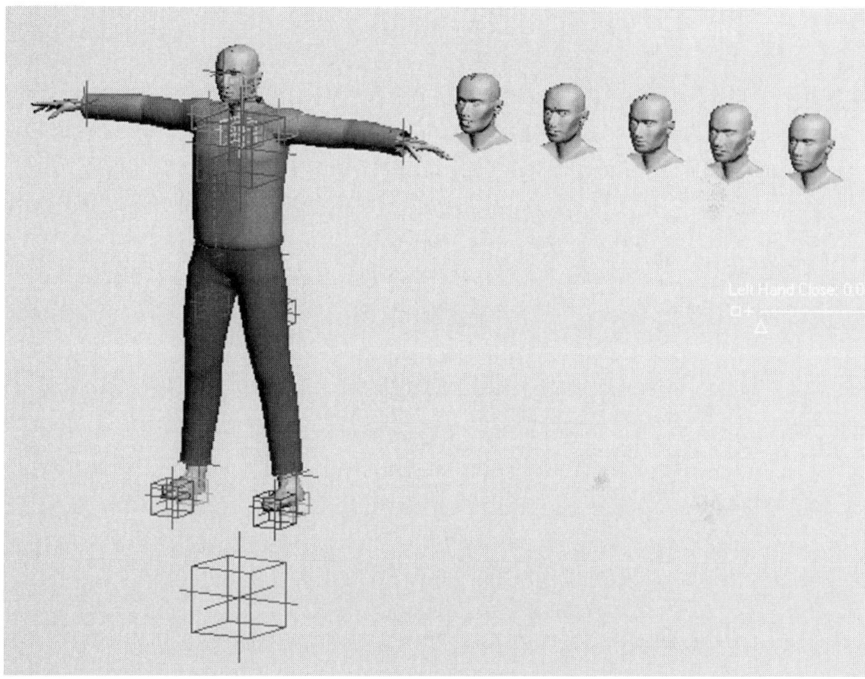

FIGURE 8.23 Merging in the Generic Man model, with the skeleton and morph heads.

4. Once everything has been brought together in one scene, save it as GenMan811.max.

To create hair for the Dr. Quin character, see Chapter 17, "Plug-Ins" for the Shag Hair tutorial.

The skeleton of Dr. Quin is based on a generic "normal" man, and therefore he does not have a heroic build. His shoulders are quite narrow, and in some circles he would be described as a "wimp," rather than a macho man. When you finish these tutorials, you might decide that you want a character with a more heroic build, such as wide shoulders and big muscles. To create that type of a character, see Chapter 12, "Advanced Animation," and go through the Major Black tutorial, which explains how to add controls to a skeleton for a fight scene. Major Black has a very wide-shouldered, athletic build with large muscles, and can be used for a superhero character.

SCHEMATIC VIEW TOOLS

The Schematic view will help you manage and organize your entire scene. The new node-based Schematic view has undergone a major revision in functionality and power for 3ds max 6 and can display all object hierarchies, modifier connections, constraints, and parameter wiring as colored wires in the view window.

The wires show dependencies. In a parent-child hierarchy, such as the skeleton and skin of the Dr. Quin character model, all of the child objects are dependent on their specific parent objects. Many operations can be performed on the objects in the hierarchy from within the Schematic view. The most common tasks would be to link or unlink hierarchies, or to create relationships such as wiring the parameters of two different objects together. Most operations can be done by selecting and then using drag and drop to modify dependencies.

All objects in the Dr. Quin model are indicated by node boxes. You will notice that things such as modifiers, materials, and cameras are also considered objects in Max. If you click on an object node and then right-click, you will get a Quad menu indicating all the possible operations you can perform. For example, if you right-click a bone and then select Edit Properties, you can make the bone transparent from within the Schematic view. The Skin Modifier and Bone relationships are indicated by the numerous yellow wires, as shown in Figure 8.24, example 1.

Next to the hierarchy is the Display floater, which is used to turn on the display of relationship wires, as shown in Figure 8.24, example 2. A very useful new feature is the Relationship viewer, as shown in Figure 18.24, example 3. It can be accessed by clicking List Views in the Schematic menu bar, and selecting All Relationships or Selected Relationships. The Relationship viewer shows direct object-to-object relation-

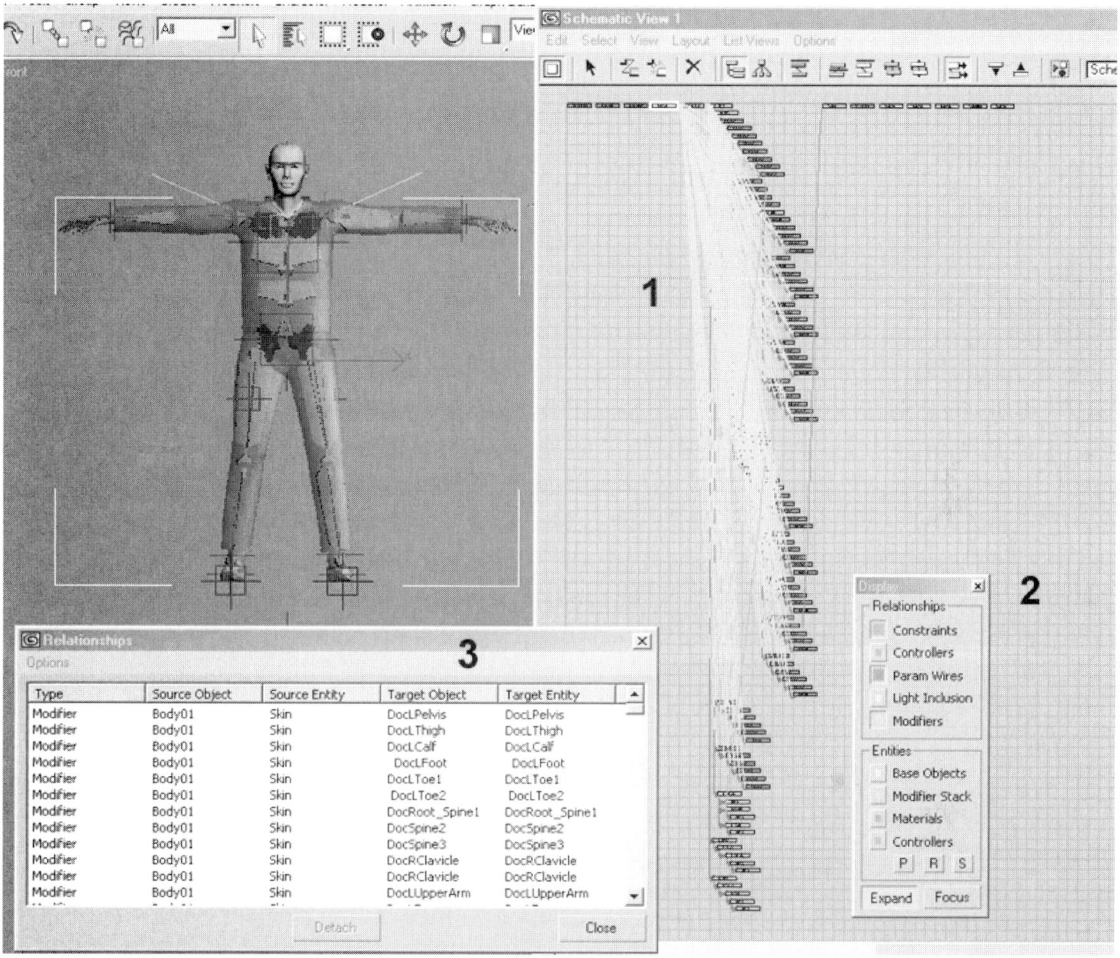

FIGURE 8.24 The Schematic view for Dr. Quin, showing all of the Skin Modifier dependencies in the model.

ships to help you make sense of all the wire connections indicated in the main Schematic View window. If you click on an individual wire, a small pop-up window will indicate what the wire is connected to.

Using the Schematic view will speed up your workflow. With the new functionality, the Max Schematic view now functions in the same way as the Maya Hypergraph and the Softimage XSI Schematic view, which means that users of those packages will find it easier to learn and use Max 6.

CONCLUSION

In this chapter, you finished modeling the Dr. Quin character. You bound the skin mesh to a skeleton using the Skin Modifier, and then you created five morph targets by cloning his head. You used the Wired Parameters tool to wire sliders to the fingers to control the hand. Then you created a coat and pants for him using the Push Modifier. In the next chapter, you will animate Dr. Quin's hand, arm, and body in an environment. Then you will animate a conversation using lip sync animation, and finally you will animate a walk cycle.

CHAPTER

9

CHARACTER ANIMATION

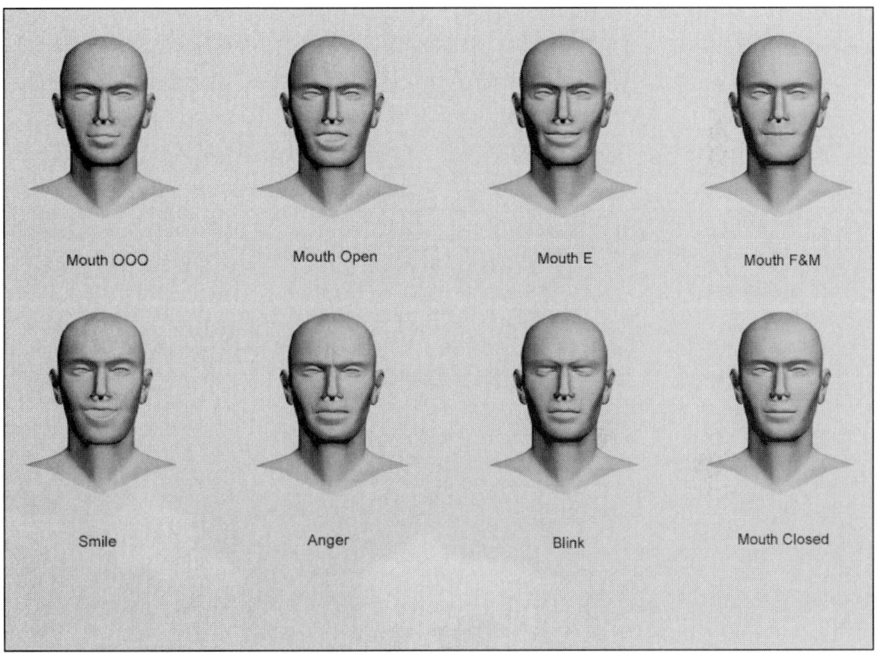

To test and troubleshoot the animation functions of the Dr. Quin skeleton rig, and to perform the final adjustments to the skin, it is convenient to begin with an animation that concentrates on the upper body motions. The first task will be to animate Dr. Quin sitting down in a chair and picking up a telephone, which is one of the scene actions he performs in the *Homing Instinct* film. To facilitate that, an office with a desk, a chair, and a telephone have been provided on the companion CD-ROM, which you will merge into the scene in the next tutorial, as shown in Figure 9.1. Only by animating the character will you discover what needs to be changed to perfect the skin behavior. This is also a good way to become familiar with the logic behind the design of the rig, and to discover what it is capable of, before launching into animating walk cycles.

ON THE CD

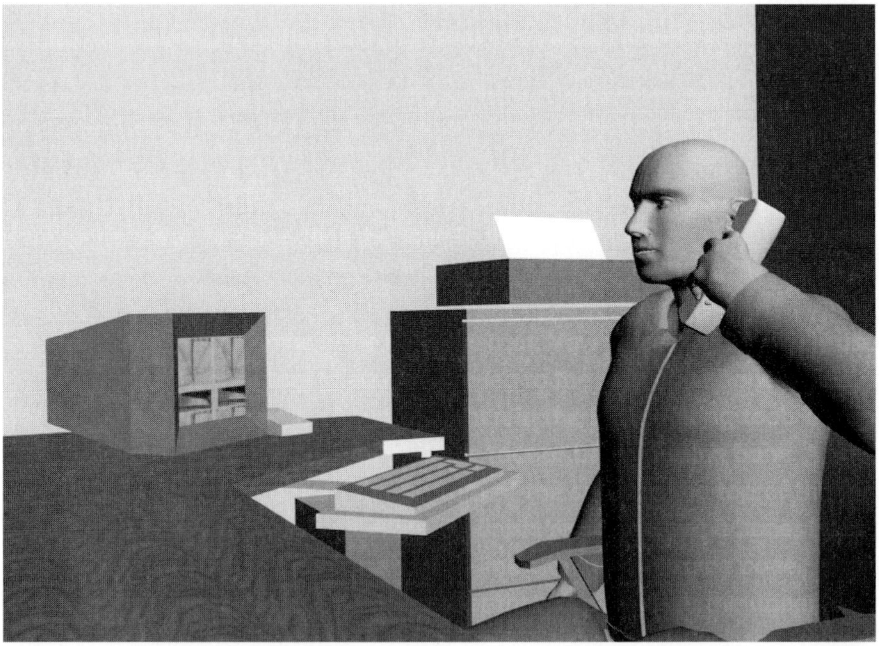

FIGURE 9.1 Dr. Quin's office setting.

UPPER BODY MOVEMENT AND GESTURES

Many of the scenes in which Dr. Quin appears include medium and close-up shots of his upper body, face, and hands. Even in the action scenes, the upper body is mostly on camera. The rigging on the arms of the Dr. Quin skeleton is very simple and is designed for multipurpose animation. That means that most of the arm action will be animated by selecting the arm IK end effector and moving the hand to a new position, or by selecting the Shoulder Control Point and rotating it to move the arm. That means that you will be using a combination of Forward and Inverse Kinematics.

The goal of the animation is to have the character interact smoothly and naturally with the objects in his environment. For example, he must pick up a telephone and put it up to his ear. That requires that an Animatable Link Constraint be assigned to the telephone so it can be attached to his hand when he touches it. He also must sit down in a chair and not pass through the surface. His arm must rest on the desk and not penetrate the top. All these considerations must be included in your thinking as you work with the model. In addition, he will be wearing the pants and coat, which are simply bound to the bones along with the skin. No attempt will be made to prevent the skin from penetrating the clothing because this is a pre-visualization model. The setting is Dr. Quin's office in the Xenobiological Research Center, on the planet-moon Titan, orbiting around the planet Saturn. His action is to answer a telephone call. This scene will be further developed with a soundtrack and dialog in the "Animating with Lip Sync" tutorial later in this chapter.

TUTORIAL 9.1

ANIMATE DR. QUIN SITTING AT A DESK AND ANSWERING A TELEPHONE

ON THE CD

1. Load GenMan811.max scene file, or you can load it from the Chap09 folder on the companion CD-ROM.
2. Select and hide the morph target heads. You should see the doctor standing there wearing his coat and pants.
3. Select the coat and pants, and then apply the Skin Modifier to them. In the Skin Parameters, click the Add button and then press the H key. In the Selection dialog, click the Selection Set window arrow in the lower-right cor-

ner, and select Bones All. Click Select. That will load the bones into the Skin Modifier and bind the coat and pants to the skeleton.

ON THE CD

4. The next step is to merge the doctor's office into your scene by clicking File > Merge, and on the companion CD-ROM, go to the Chap09 folder and select Dr_Office.max. In the Merge dialog, click All and then click OK. The office should load and be positioned as shown in Figure 9.2, example 1. Switch to the right view (V-R) and zoom in on Dr. Quin's pants. The front of Dr. Quin's legs should be just touching the edge of the desk. If it is out of position, select and move the entire office group to position it, as shown in Figure 9.2, example 1.

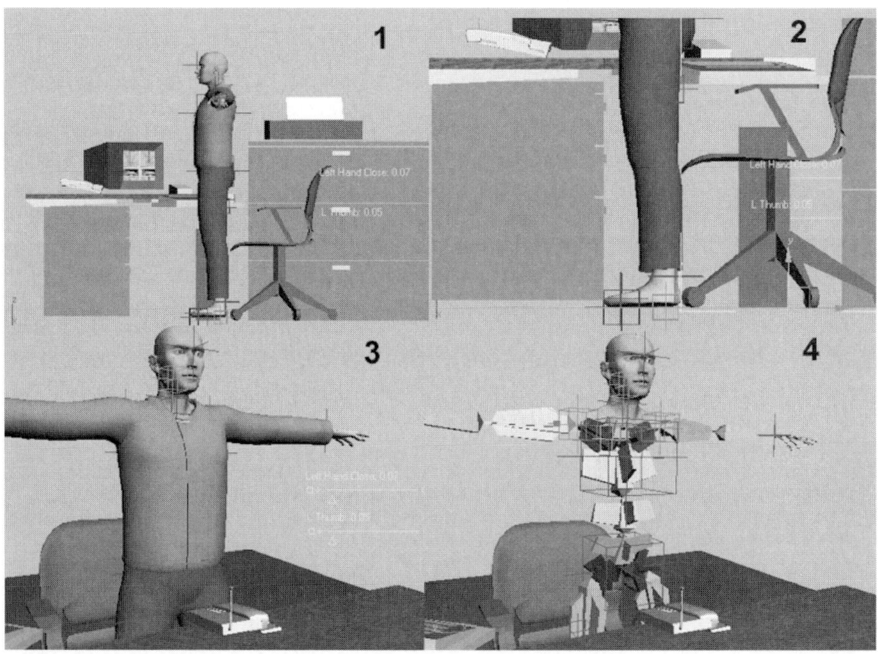

FIGURE 9.2 Doctor Quin ready to animate standing in his office.

5. Before you start the animation, you should move the office chair so that it is positioned right behind Dr. Quin. To do that, select the office group, and in the Main menu, click Group > Open. Next, move the chair closer behind Dr. Quin so that the front edge of the seat touches the back of Dr. Quin's legs, as shown in Figure 9.2, example 2.

6. Reposition Camera01 so that you get a good view of the doctor and the telephone sitting on the desk in front of him, as shown in Figure 9.2, example 3. In the Camera Parameters, set the Lens angle to 35 mm.
7. For the first part of the animation, hide the coat, pants, and the body so that you can see the skeleton and the rig control points easily, as shown in Figure 9.2, example 4. The first operation will be to sit the model in the chair.
8. To animate Dr. Quin sitting down, switch to the right view, and then zoom in so that the entire figure is centered in the viewport. Right-click the Play button, and in the Time Configuration dialog, set the Length of the animation to 400 frames.
9. Set the Time Slider to frame 60. Select the Hip Control, which is the box surrounding the hip bones, and then turn on the Auto Key button. Using the Move tool, click and drag the Hip Control down and to the right until he is sitting in the chair, as shown in Figure 9.3, examples 1 and 2. Scrub the Time Slider to watch the motion.
10. Switch to the front view. Select one of the Shoulder Control Points. Set the Time Slider to frame 60, and then with Auto Key on, rotate the Shoulder

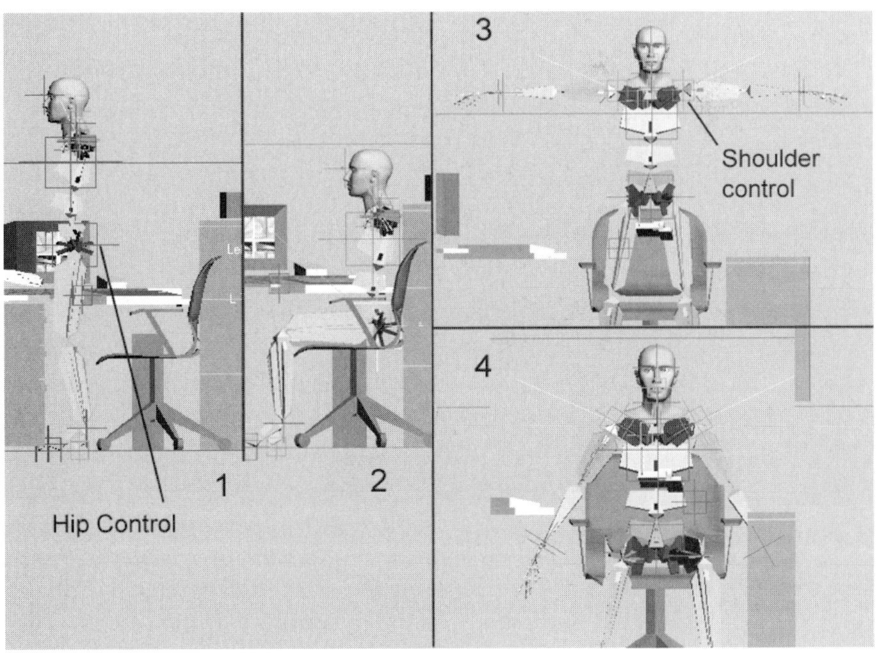

FIGURE 9.3 Animate the figure to sit in the chair.

Control to move the arm down 60 degrees. Repeat that for the other Shoulder Control Point, as shown in Figure 9.3, example 3. Now, turn off Auto Key, move the Slider back to frame 0, and click Play to watch the motion.

11. Save the scene as GenMan901.max.

In the next tutorial, you will animate Dr. Quin's arms, hand, spine, and shoulders.

The next operation is to move the hands into position for picking up the telephone and bringing it to the character's ear. It is important to add small secondary motions such as the bending of the spine and tipping of the head to make the motion more natural.

TUTORIAL 9.2

ANIMATING THE ARM AND HAND

To animate the arm:

1. Load the GenMan901.max scene, if it is not already loaded, and then activate and maximize the right viewport. Zoom in so that the left arm can easily be seen. The first step is to select the Left Arm IK Chain and move it up to position the hand over the telephone.
2. To animate the hand moving to the telephone, turn on Auto Key, and then move the Time Slider to frame 80. In the Named Selection Sets window, in the Main menu bar, click the arrow and select Left Arm IK. Now move the IK end effector (blue cross) up and position it near the telephone, as shown in Figure 9.4, example 1. You will not be able to actually reach the telephone until you animate the spine to lean forward.

The motions of the skeleton rig are designed to mimic the motions of the human body. There are two types of motions normally applied to the control points of the skeleton. Rotations can be applied to any control point. A move should normally only be applied to control points at the ends of the legs and to the Hip Control. The Hip Control is designed to be both moved and rotated. The Chest Control should only be rotated, since it controls the entire upper body. The human upper body cannot really stretch because it is limited by the spine. Therefore, do not raise it upward, because that will cause the shoulders and arms to rotate backwards at an unnatural angle. The Shoulder Controls should normally be rotated. However, if you want to raise the shoulder to create a reach or a shrug, only move the Shoulder Control a small amount. Then, return it to its starting position as soon as possible. The arms

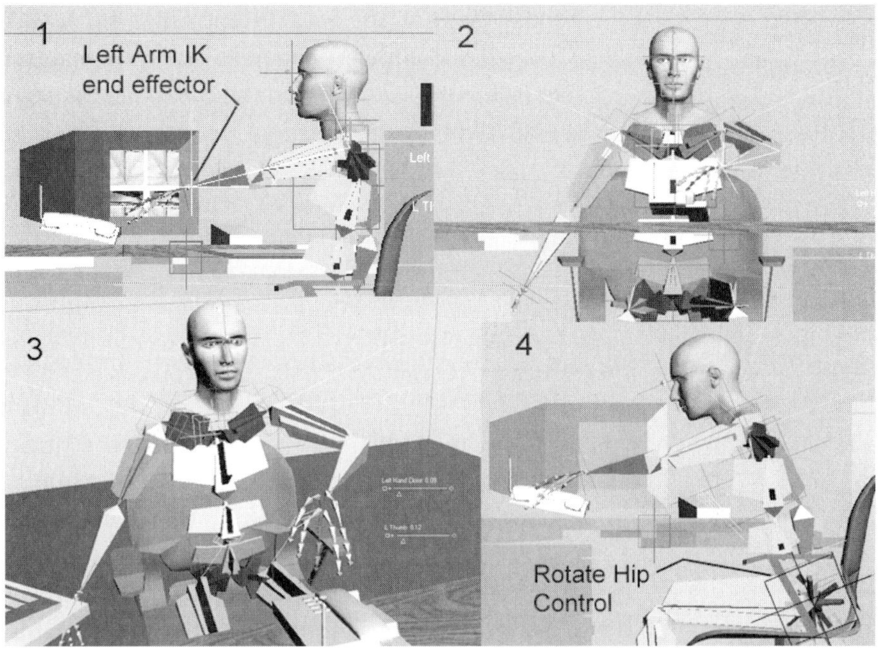

FIGURE 9.4 Raising the hand to the telephone and leaning forward.

are mostly controlled by moving the Arm IK end effector (blue cross). The Wrist Control Point is only for changing the angle of the hand and should only be rotated, not moved, because it will pull away from the arm.

3. Scrub the Time Slider. Notice that the arm now moves during the entire animation. The idea is to move the arm down, and then at frame 40, start moving the arm up toward the telephone. To do that, you will add another key. Go to frame 40, and with Auto Key turned on, lower the arm back down toward the chair armrest. Now, switch to the front view and maximize it to further tune the action.
4. Scrub the Time Slider and watch the arm move in the front view. To position the hand over the telephone, you must move the arm toward the center of the body. Select the Left Arm IK end effector, go to frame 80, and with Auto Key active, move the wrist so that it is over the telephone, as shown in Figure 9.4, example 2.
5. Switch to the Camera01 view and maximize it. Adjust the camera so that you see an image that includes the telephone, as shown in Figure 9.4, example 3. You should be able to see the two Slider Controls for the left

hand, which are labeled Left Hand Close, and L Thumb. These controls will be used in Manipulate mode to close the fingers around the telephone handset. Next, you will lean the body forward so that Dr. Quin can reach the telephone.

There are two ways to lean the body forward. One is to rotate the Chest Control, and the other is to rotate the Hip Control. The Chest Control is mainly for rounding the back to look down or to pick something up. The Hip Control gives a much greater degree of movement. In this case, use the Hip Control. For this animation, you should get used to switching views quickly as you animate. Use the hotkeys V-R to switch to the right view, and then use the C hotkey to switch to the camera view.

6. Switch to the right view (V-R), then with the Time Slider at frame 80, and Auto Key on, select the Hip Control. Rotate the Hip Control forward about 22 degrees, and then select the Arm IK end effector and move the hand upward until it is above the telephone, as shown in Figure 9.4, example 4. To make the character and its rig easier to see in the scene, select the computer monitor. Then, right-click and select Properties in the Quad menu. In the Properties dialog, click See Through. All of the office elements except the telephone and the chair should turn transparent gray. Now is a good time to turn on the motion trajectory paths.
7. To turn on trajectories, click the Motion Panel tab and then click the Trajectories button. A red dotted line will appear in the viewport showing the animation path of the Left Arm IK end effector. Move the Time Slider to frame 60. You need to add a key here to raise the arm higher quicker so that it does not hit the edge of the desktop as it reaches for the telephone. With Auto Key on, move the Left Arm IK upward so the fingertips are just above the height of the desktop. Scrub the animation. If the hand still collides with the table, raise it just a bit higher.

There are two ways to rotate the hand. The first is to use the Wrist Control Point. It is designed to create the side-to-side and up-and-down (waving) motion of the hand. This control point is not in the center of the wrist because it is designed to correspond to where the human hand rotation center point is. The hand rotates about the end of the ulna bone. The second method of rotating the hand is to use the wrist bone, the small bone at the end of the forearm beside the IK end effector. It is designed to rotate the hand axially to turn the hand over. By using a combination of these two methods, any hand motion can be simulated.

8. The next action is to rotate the wrist to align the fingers so they can pick up the telephone handset. Press C to switch to the camera view. Right-click and select Unhide by Name. Unhide Body01, the character's skin, to get a better idea of how the hand should be rotated to pick up the telephone handset, as shown in Figure 9.5, example 1. In the next step, you will rotate the Wrist Control and the wrist bone to create the correct motion of the hand for grasping the telephone handset.

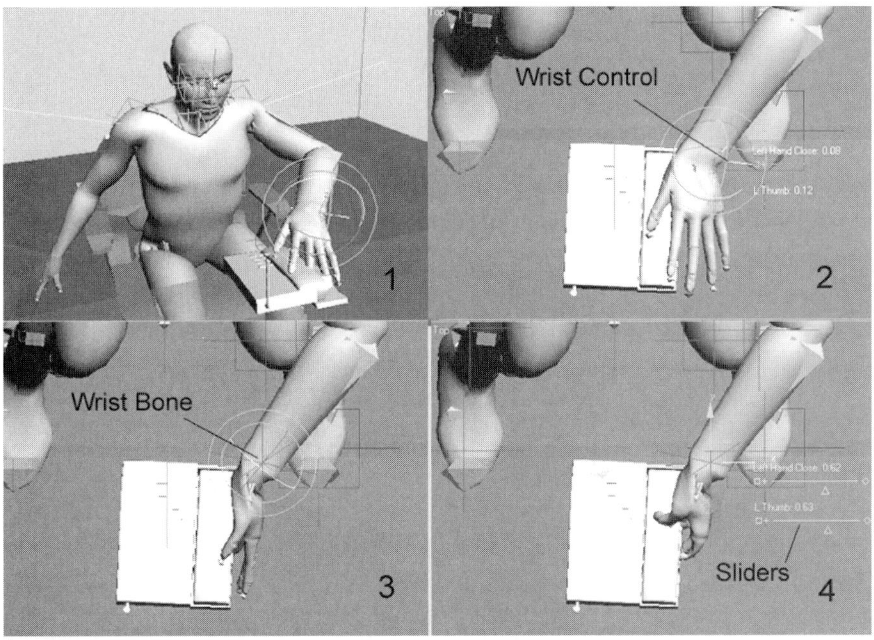

FIGURE 9.5 Bending the wrist and grasping the telephone handset.

9. To bend the hand to the correct position, start with the Left Wrist Control. Click the brown control point (cross) at the left wrist. Once you select it, you should create a selection set for it named Left Wrist Control. The grasping action starts with bending the hand back. Click Select and Rotate, and then set the Reference Coordinate system to Local. In the top view (T), zoom in on the left hand. Move the Time Slider to frame 80 and Turn on Auto Key.
10. Click the Y-axis ring (yellow) and rotate the hand upward about –35 degrees. Select the Z-axis ring (blue) and rotate the hand toward the little

finger 17 degrees, as shown in Figure 9.5, example 2. Then, press the H key, and from the Select by Name dialog, select DocLWrist. Create a selection set called Left Wrist Bone. Rotate it in the X-axis (yellow) to –76 degrees. That should place the fingers down along the side of the telephone handset, as shown in Figure 9.5, example 3.

11. To partially close the fingers, you will use the Left Hand Close Slider. In the Main menu bar, click the Manipulator icon (next to Move). The Sliders will turn green. Select Move, and then click and drag the triangle slide in the Slider to 0.62. That will curve the fingers under the handset. Now, move the thumb control to 0.63 to align the thumb to a better angle to grasp the handset, as shown in Figure 9.5, example 4.
12. Notice that the skin around the wrist is twisted. You will correct that in the next tutorial. Save the scene as GenMan902.max.

In the next tutorial, you will adjust the skin envelopes. The idea is to have the forearm skin twist naturally and remain smooth, and not be folded or distorted. Then you will apply a Link Constraint to pick up the telephone.

TUTORIAL 9.3

ADJUSTING THE WRIST SKIN ENVELOPES

ON THE CD

To adjust the wrist skin:

1. Load the GenMan902.max file if it is not already loaded, or you can load it from the Chap09 folder on the companion CD-ROM. Switch to the top view, maximize it, and move the Time Slider to frame 80. Auto Key should be off.
2. Select the Body01 skin, and then in the Skin Modifier drop-down menu, click the Edit Envelopes button. The skin should turn dark blue. Click the Bone icon for the forearm (DocLForearm). The area influenced by the forearm bone will turn red and you will see a red inner envelope and a brown outer envelope.
3. To smooth out the skin around the wrist, you must first shorten the forearm envelope to reduce its influence over the wrist area. In the top view, click on the central black bone icon at the wrist end. It should turn purple. Set the Reference Coordinate System to Screen, and then select and move the end of the Bone icon up the arm about half way. That will cause the

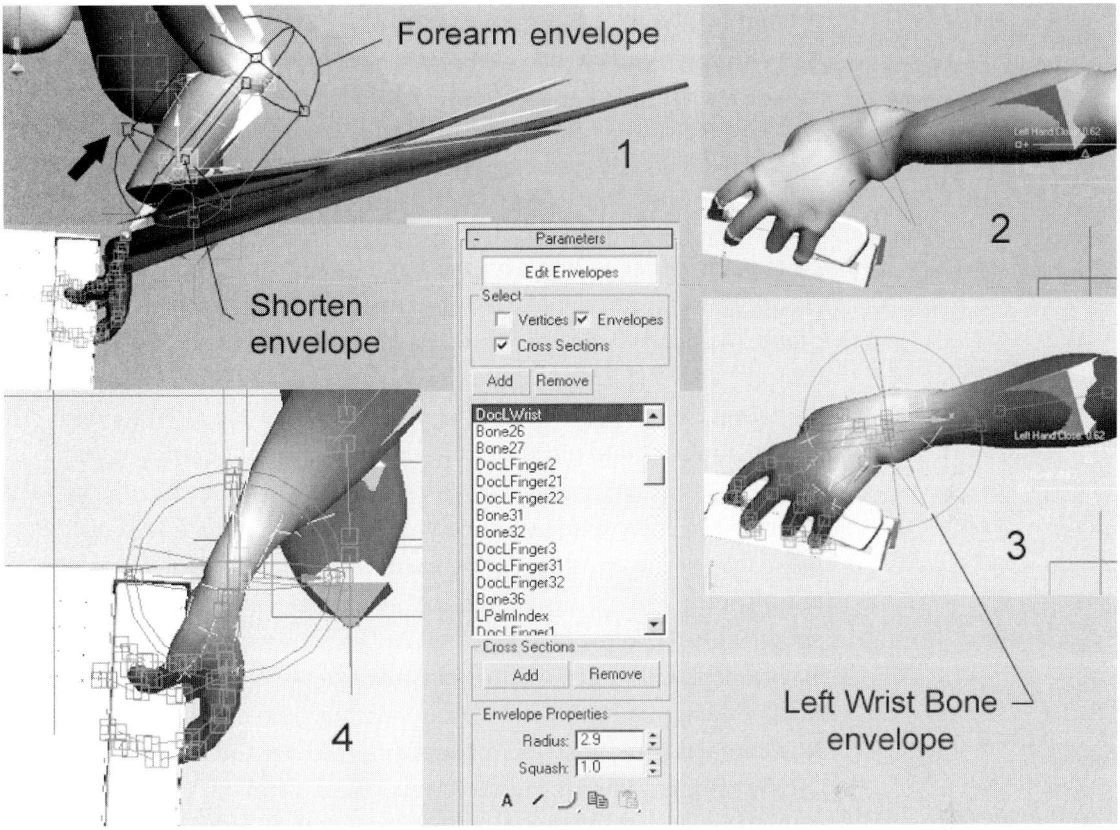

FIGURE 9.6 Adjusting the wrist and forearm skin envelopes.

wrist skin to temporarily shoot out away from the arm bone, as shown in Figure 9.6, example 1.

The method shown here is the simplest way to solve the wrist skin-twisting problem. Another way to solve the problem of twisting skin on the wrist and forearm is to use multiple twist bones and attribute controls to control the skin envelopes of the forearm, a topic beyond the scope of this book. To see the extensive character rigging tutorials in the 3ds max 6 tutorials help files, go to "Tutorials for Character Animation Professionals/Creating Complex Character Rigs/Rigging Wrist Twists."

4. Now, select one of the small box handles of the brown outer envelope on the wrist end, but don't try to move it. Instead, go to the Envelope Properties menu in the Skin Modifier and type in a Radius of 5.0. The end of the envelope will expand and pull in some of the skin back to the bone. Select

the handle of the red inner envelope and set it to a radius of 0.4. Do not try to pull all the skin in at this time. Go to the next step.

If your Units are set to Feet, go to Customize > Units Setup and change them to Generic Units International. All of the tutorials in Chapters 3 through Chapter 17 use 3ds max units, and do not use feet or metric measurements.

5. To make it easier to work on the hand, select the office and close the group. Then, ungroup it and hide all of the office except the telephone set group, the handset, and the chair. Next, re-select the skin, turn on Edit Envelopes, and select the Wrist Bone icon (DocLWrist). In Skin > Envelope Properties, set both of its outer envelope radii to 2.7. All of the arm skin should pop back into place, but the wrist will still not be smooth, as shown in Figure 9.6, example 2.
6. To finish the adjustment, you need to balance the other envelopes of the palm against the envelope influence of the arm. Select the upper thumb bone and increase its envelope to 1.0. Do the same for the palm bone above the little finger.
7. Slowly increase or decrease the Forearm and the Wrist Bone envelopes in small increments until you find the best balance between them so the wrist remains smooth as you move the Time Slider and the wrist is rotated and twisted, as shown in Figure 9.6, examples 3 and 4.
8. In this step, you add a Dummy to the hand that will be the point where the telephone handset is linked. In the right view, zoom in on the hand, and then select and hide the skin (Body01). Go to Helpers > Object Type and click on Dummy. Click and drag on the center of the palm of the hand to create Dummy01. In the top view, zoom in on the hand and move the Dummy so that it touches the bones of the hand, as shown in Figure 9.7, example 1.
9. Link the Dummy to the first middle finger bone (DocLFinger2). Move the Time Slider to frame 90, turn on Auto Key, and then select the Left Wrist Control. Rotate the control 8 degrees more to bring the palm of the hand in contact with the handset. Then, turn on Auto Key, as shown in Figure 9.7, example 2. Move the Time Slider to frame 0.
10. To animate the link of the telephone so it can be picked up, add a Link Constraint. Still in the top view, select the telephone handset. Click the Motion tab, and then click Parameters > Assign Controller. In the Controller menu, click Transform: Position/Rotation/Scale. It will turn yellow.

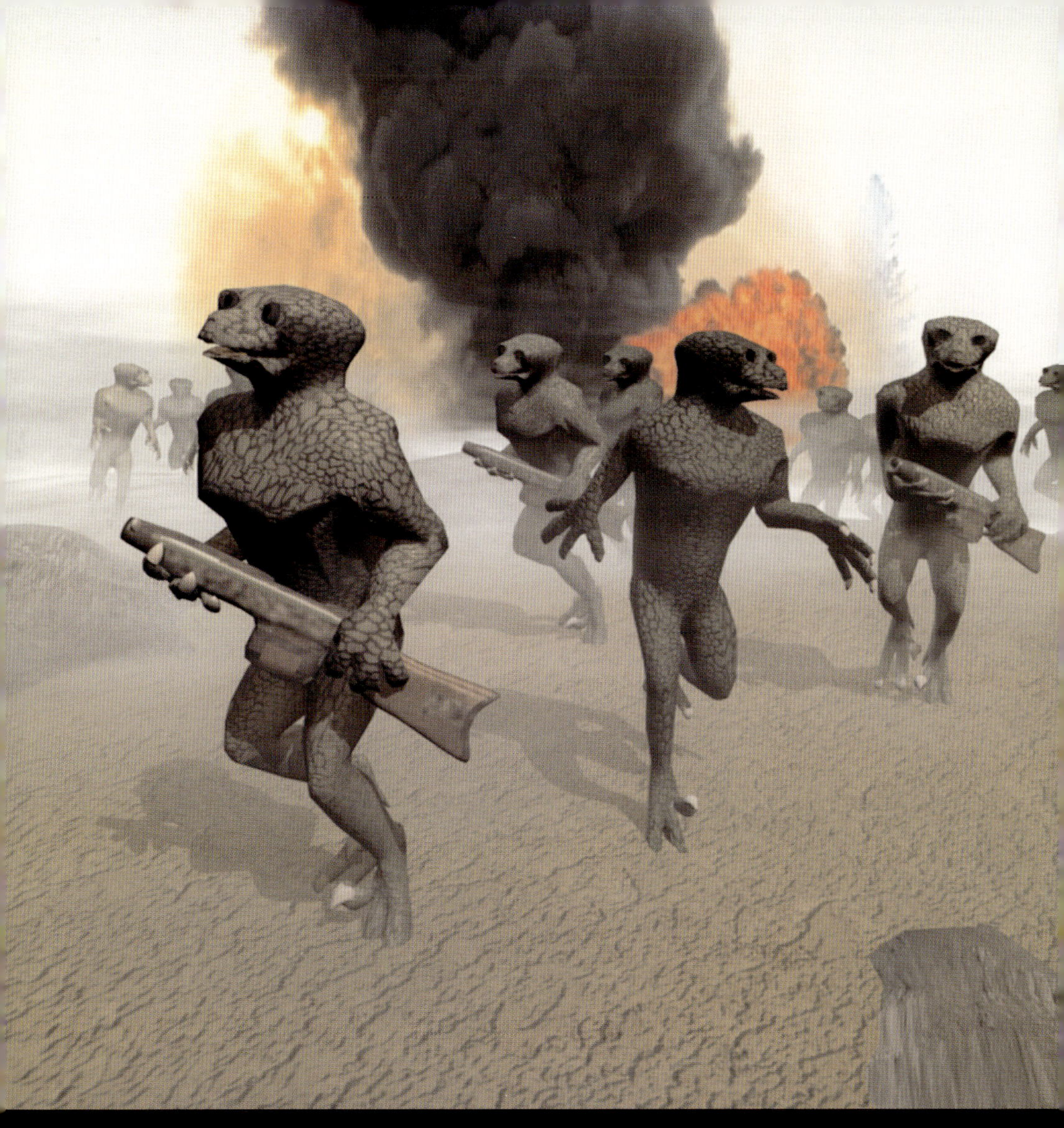

COLOR PLATE 1 Dinomen warriors raiding the Indigenous Food Distribution Center from *Homing Instinct*

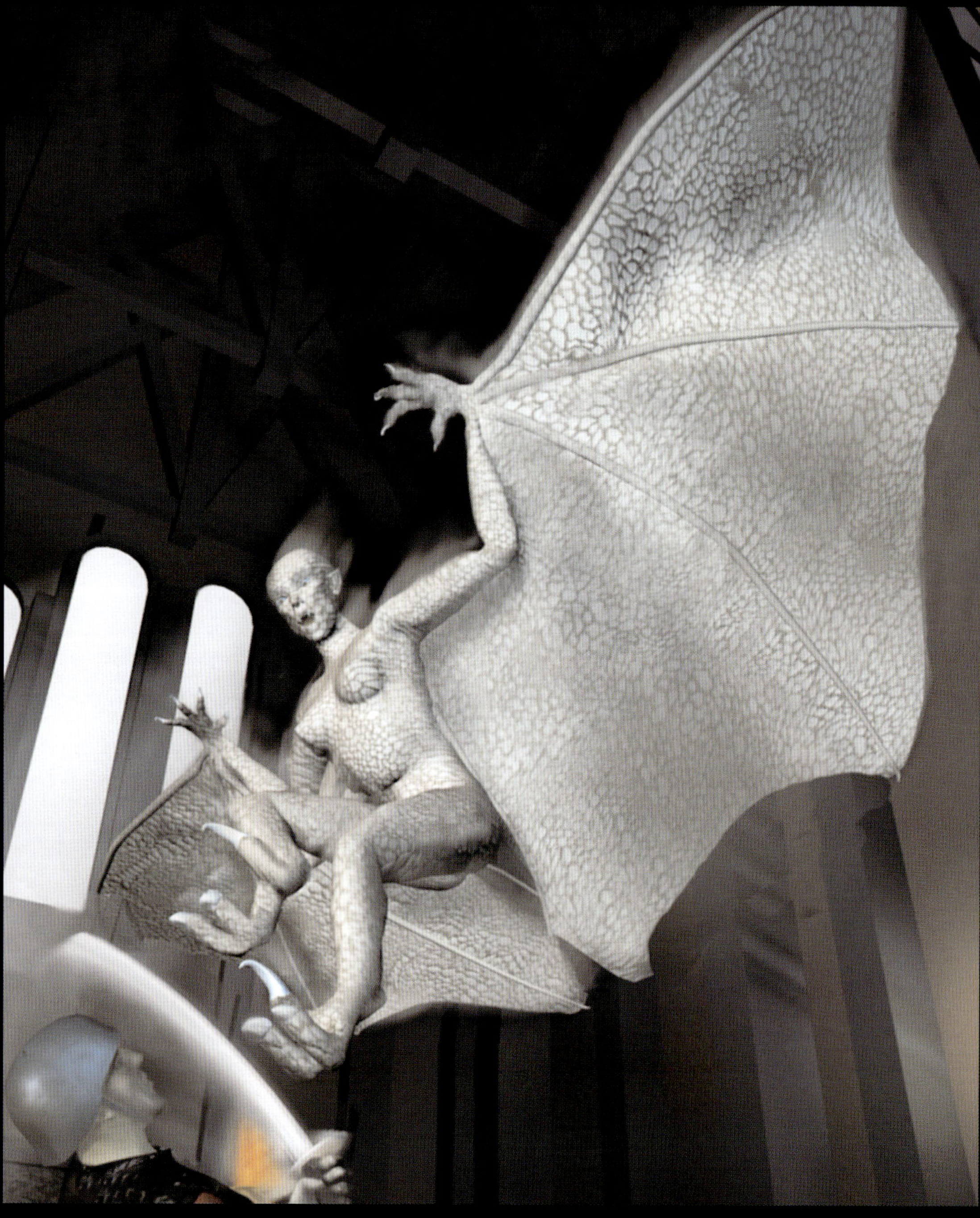

COLOR PLATE 2 Xzulixia in winged vampire form attacking Chris, the Vampire Slayer.

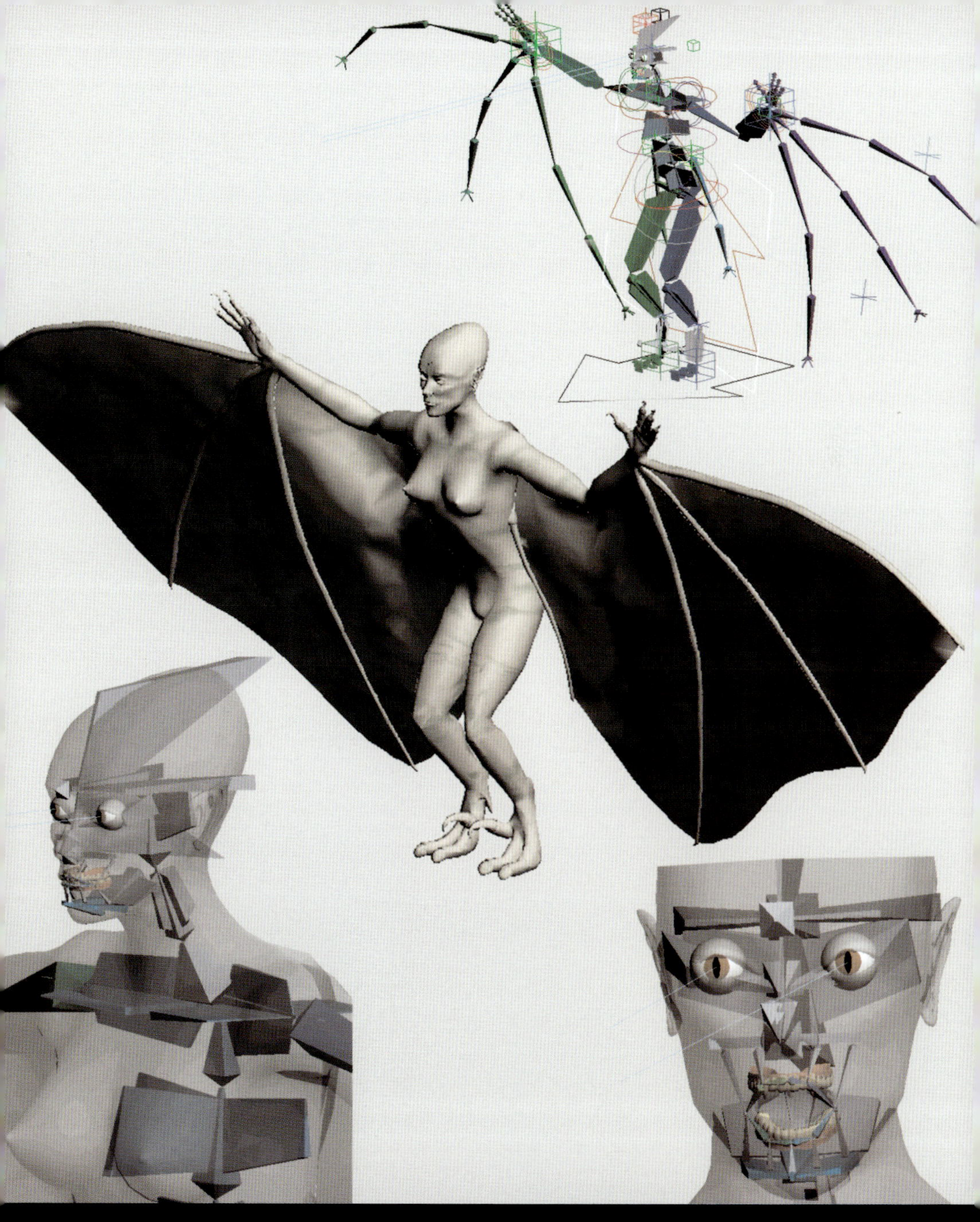

COLOR PLATE 3 The polygonal mesh body, Skeleton Rig, and Facial Bones of the Xzulixia Winged Vampire model.

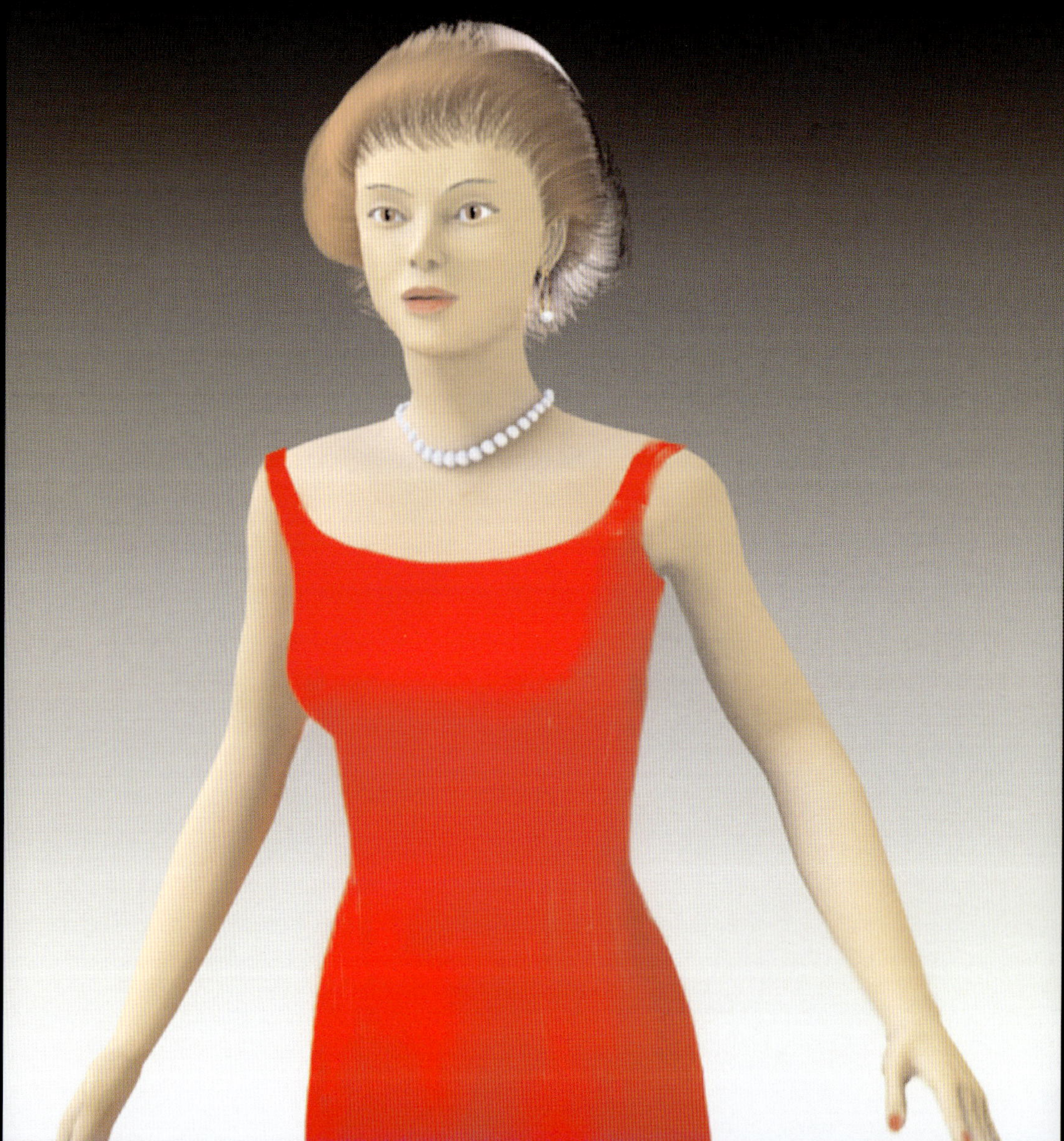

COLOR PLATE 4 Xzulixia the vampire in a dress made with clothfx from Turbo Squid, and hair done with the Shag Hair plug-in from Digimation.

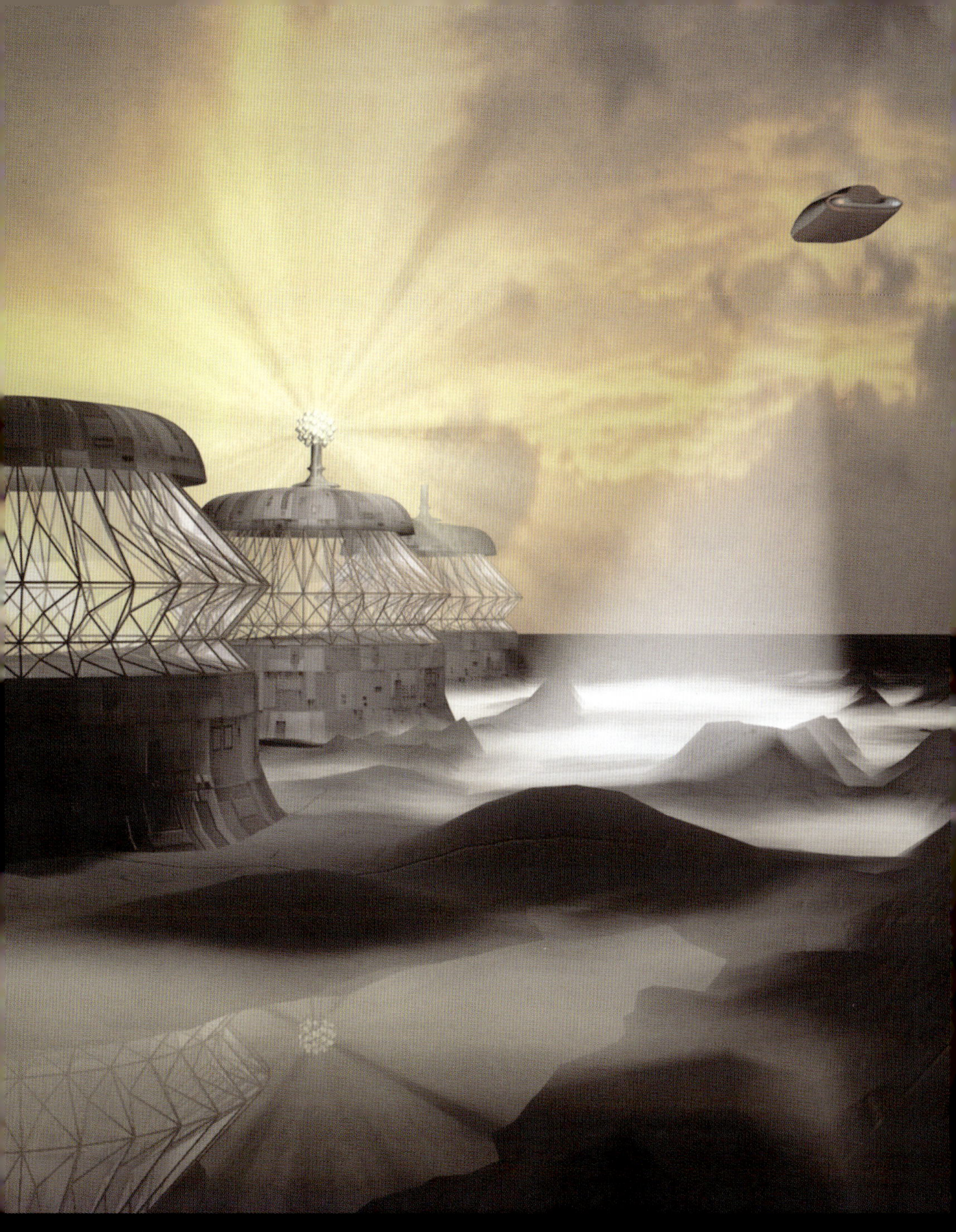

COLOR PLATE 5 The Titan Geothermal Power Station in the Great Northern Swamp from *Homing Instinct*

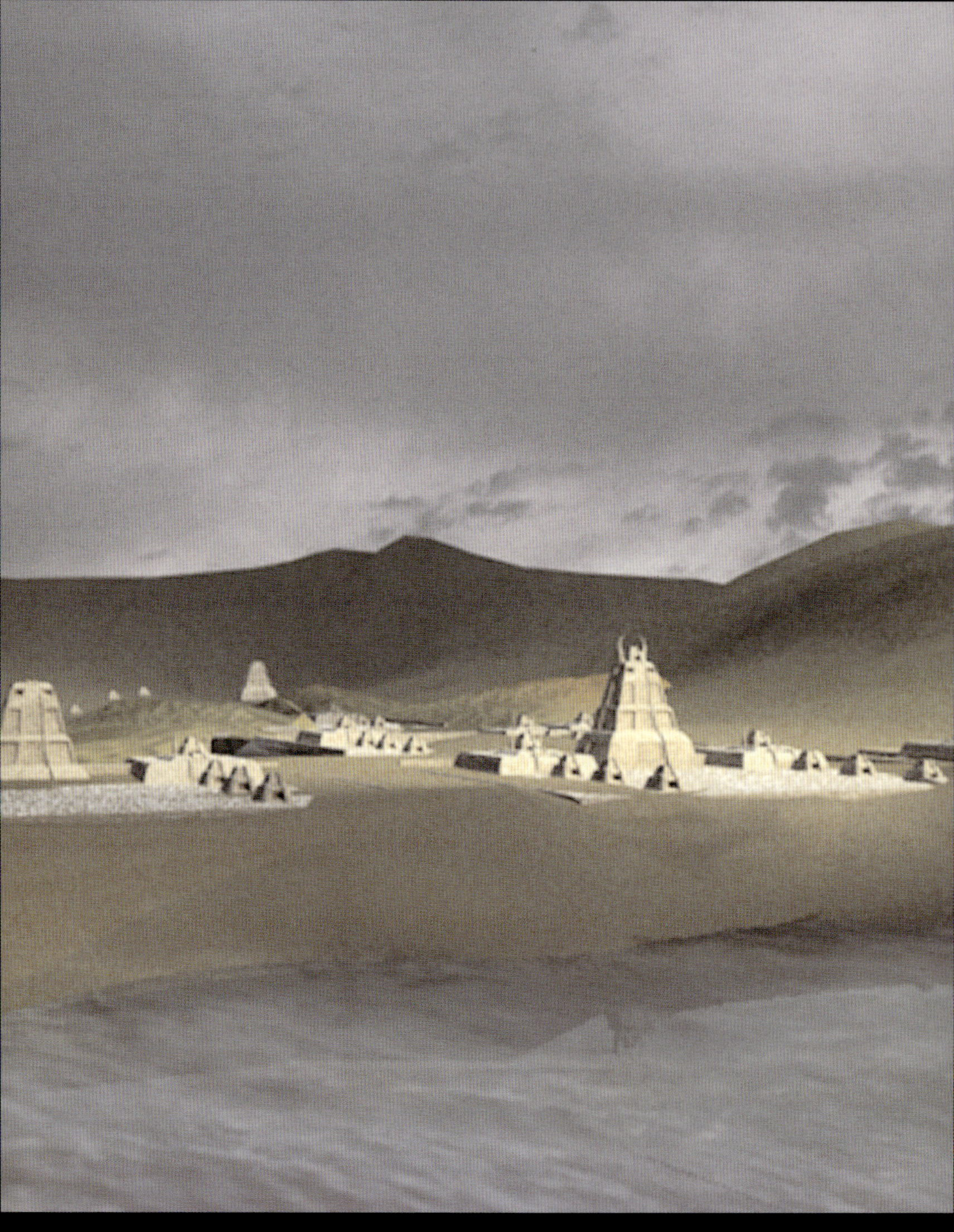

COLOR PLATE 6 Valley of the Vampire Temple Ruins from *Homing Instinct*.

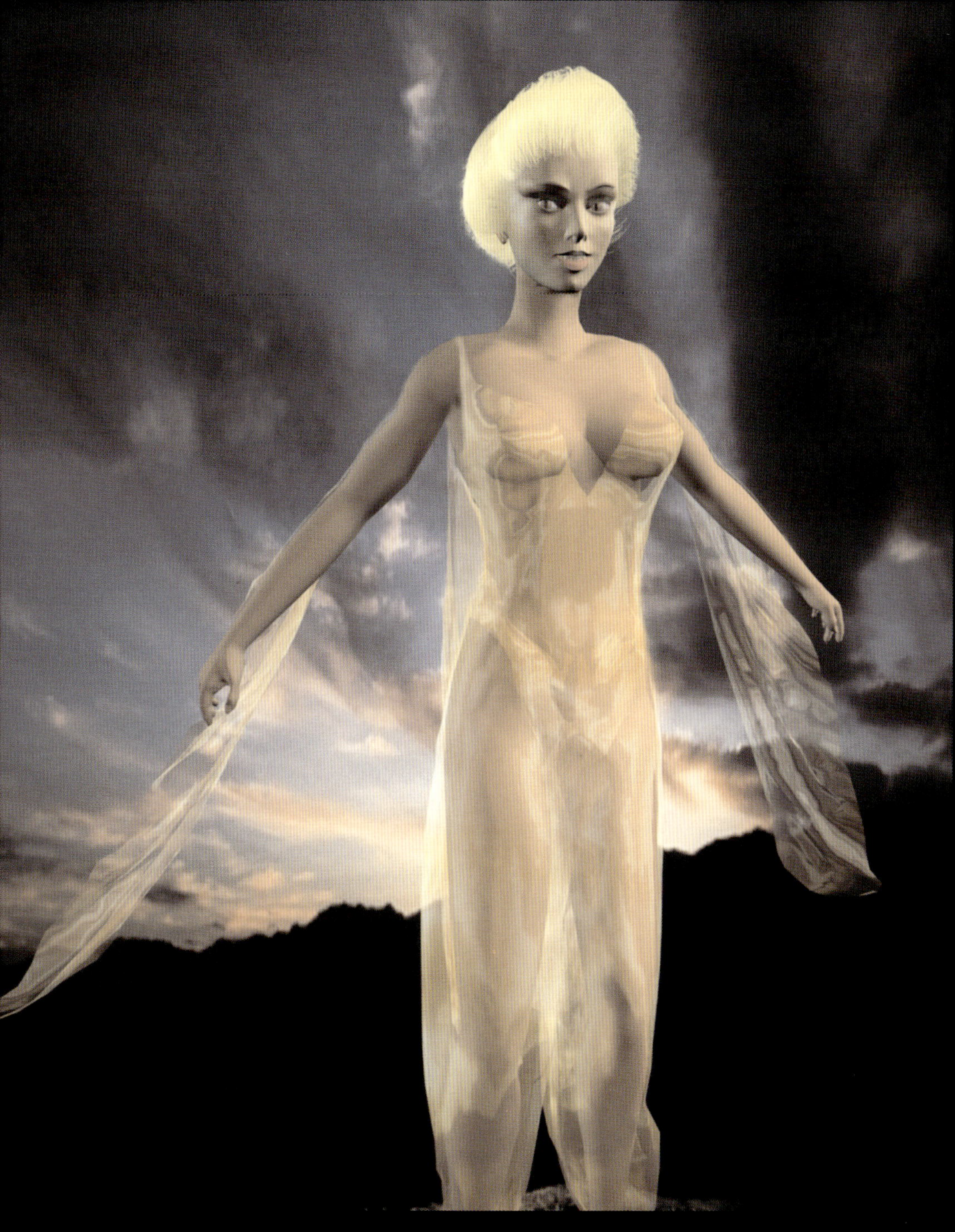

COLOR PLATE 7 Xzulixia performing as a dancer in a harem girl costume made with clothfx.

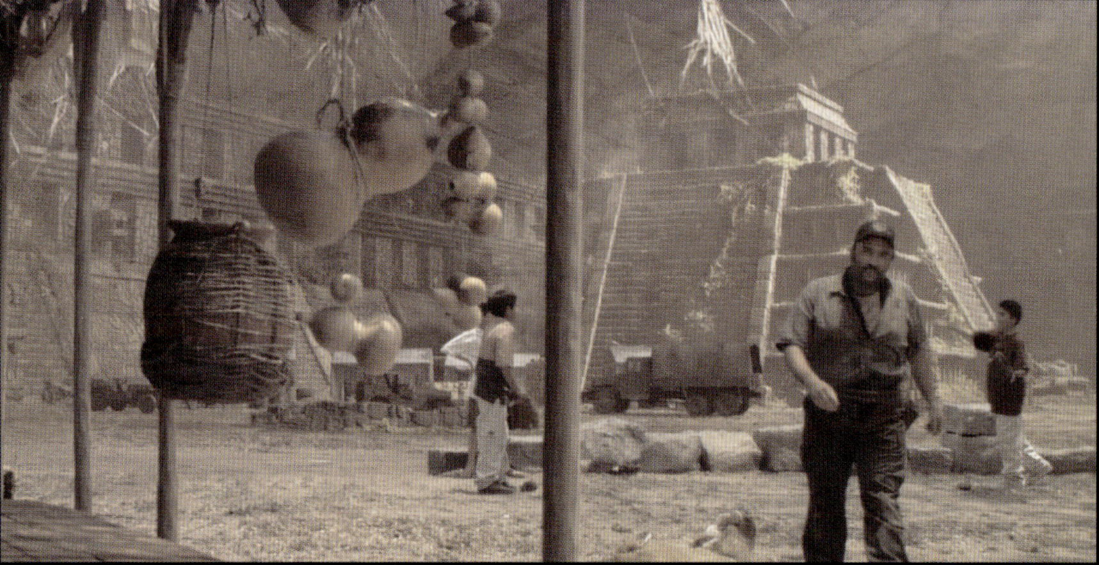

COLOR PLATE 8 3ds max visual effects: Maya temple cave from *Coronado*, courtesy of Uncharted Territory, LLC.

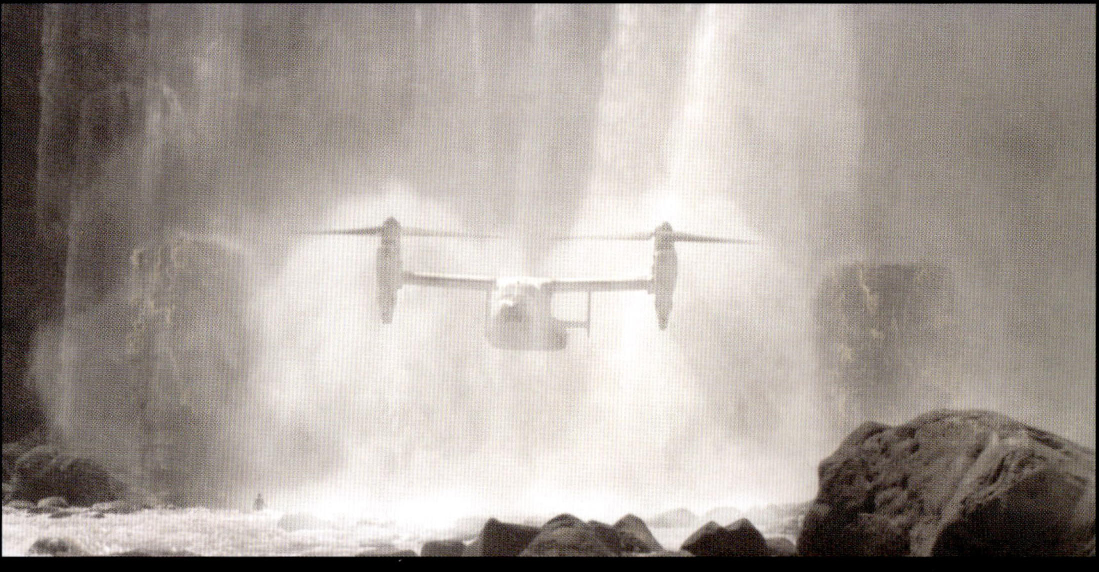

COLOR PLATE 9 3ds max visual effects: Osprey aircraft leaving secret cave base behind the waterfall from *Coronado*, courtesy of Uncharted Territory, LLC.

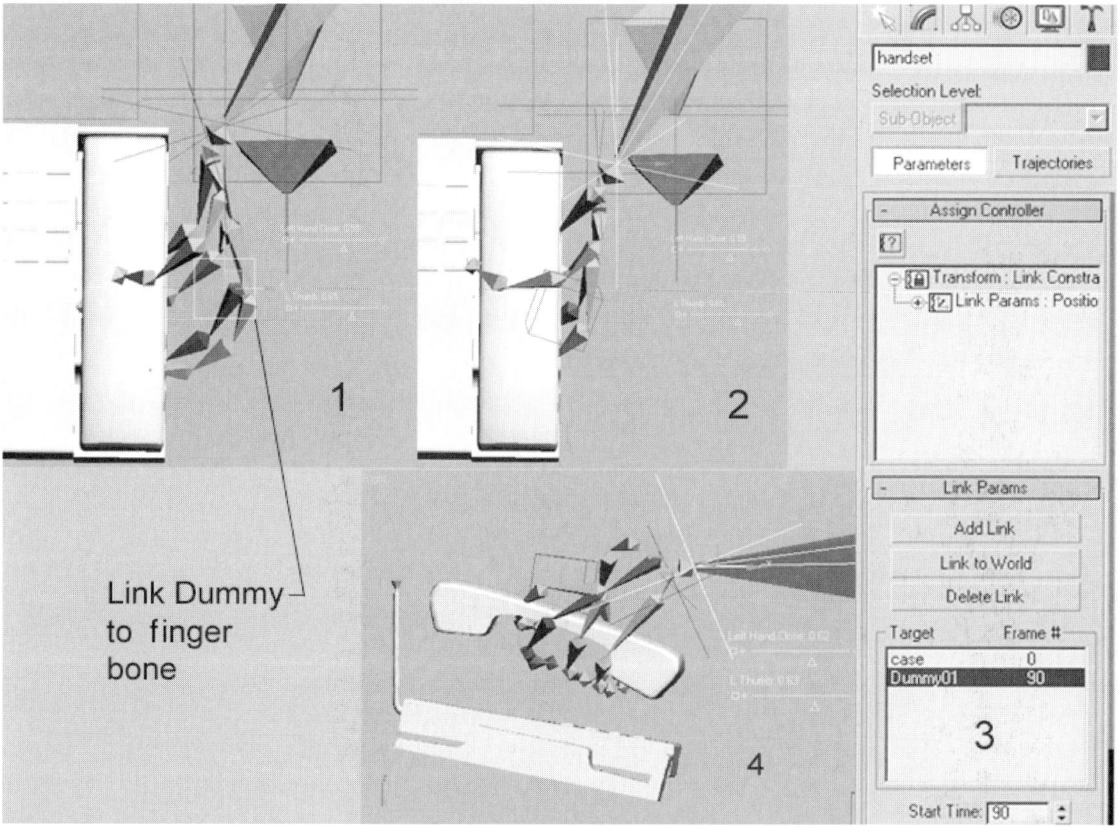

FIGURE 9.7 Apply an animated Link Constraint to the telephone handset.

Next, click the Assign Controller radio button (with the question mark) and open the Assign Transform Controller dialog. Select Link Constraint and click OK.

11. At frame 0, click the Add Link button in Link Parameters, and then select the body of the telephone case next to the handset. The word "Case" will display in the Link Params window. Now, move the Time Slider to frame 90. The hand will be next to the telephone. With Add Link still active, click on the new Dummy01 in the palm of the hand. The word "Dummy01" will display in the Link Params window, as shown in Figure 9.7, example 3. Click Add Link to turn it off. The handset will now stay on the telephone set from frame 0 to 90, and then follow the hand after frame 90.
12. To test the Link Constraint, move to frame 110. Switch to the right view, and then select the Left Arm IK end effector. Turn on Auto Key, and move

the hand up a short distance from the telephone. The handset should follow the hand, as shown in Figure 9.7, example 4.

13. Save the scene as GenMan903.max.

In the next tutorial, you will move the telephone handset up to the character's ear.

TUTORIAL 9.4 MOVE THE TELEPHONE TO THE EAR

To move the telephone to Dr. Quin's ear:

1. Load the GenMan903.max scene file. Unhide the skin (Body01), switch to the four viewport layout, and click Zoom Extents All.
2. Switch to the right view, maximize it, and then zoom in on Dr. Quin, as shown in Figure 9.8, example 1. The next step is to move the telephone handset to Dr. Quin's ear as he leans back in the chair. Move the Time Slider to frame 140, and turn on Auto Key.
3. Select the Hip Control, and then at frame 140, rotate the Hip Control –20 degrees until Dr. Quin is sitting straight in the chair. Go to frame 165 and select the Left Arm IK end effector. Move it toward the head until the wrist is just in front of the chin, as shown in Figure 9.8, example 2.
4. Switch to the top view, zoom in on the arm and hand, and select the Left Wrist Control. Rotate the X-axis 45 degrees, which will turn the palm facing downward. Then, rotate the Z-axis –45 degrees, and rotate the Y-axis 90 degrees to bend the wrist back and up. That should bring the handset to a vertical position, but it needs to be rotated in its long axis in the hand, as shown in Figure 9.8, example 3.
5. In the top view, select the Handset Dummy (Dummy01) and then rotate it a few degrees in the Y- and Z-axis to place the underside of the handset against the fingertips, as shown in Figure 9.8, example 4. Move to frame 180, and in the right view, pull the arm back so it brings the earpiece of the telephone handset next to the ear.
6. This movement causes the elbow to move up too high. To correct the angle of the elbow you will animate the Swivel Angle of the Left Arm IK Chain to lower the elbow. Switch to the front view and maximize. Click on

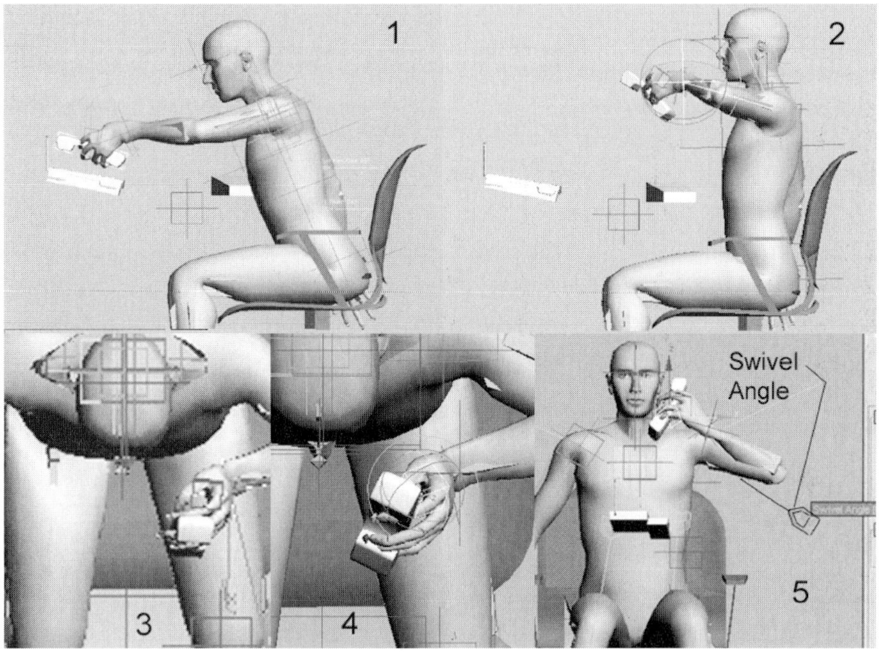

FIGURE 9.8 Moving the handset to Dr. Quin's ear.

the Select and Manipulate icon in the Main tool bar. You will see green Swivel Angle handles extend from all of the IK chains in the model.

7. With Auto Key on at frame 180, select the Left Arm Swivel Angle Handle and move it downward to lower the elbow from straight out to a new position pointing downward at a 30-degree angle, as shown in Figure 9.8, example 5.
8. Next, move back to frame 160, select the Swivel Angle Handle, and raise it back to the original position so it does not affect the movement of the arm at earlier keyframes. Scrub the Time Slider to check the earlier part of the animation to make sure you have not moved the Swivel Angle too far.
9. At frame 180, the telephone is next to the ear but still needs adjusting. Select Dummy01, and using Rotate and Move, reposition the telephone so it is in a natural position next to the ear. You might also need to adjust the wrist angle. Scrub the Time Slider to test the animation, and then create a Preview Animation. Turn off Auto Key.

10. To create a preview animation, click Animation in the Main menu and select Make Preview. In the display in the Preview box, turn off everything except Geometry. Set Custom Range to 20 to 190 and click Create. A low-resolution preview will render and play back repeatedly in the viewport.
11. Save the file as GenMan904.max.

In the next tutorial, you will use the Facial Morph Targets you made in Chapter 8 to create a lip-sync animation. Additional Morph Targets are used to create facial expressions as Dr. Quin talks and listens on the telephone.

LIP-SYNC AND FACIAL EXPRESSIONS

Good lip-sync and facial expressions are essential in realistic character animation. Close-up shots must communicate the emotional content of the dialog and the story. Mouth shapes can be mixed with facial expression Morph Targets to create a number of new Morph Targets, so that a handful of Morph Targets can yield a great number of expressions through mixing or blending the target weights. The different mouth shapes and facial expressions are mixed together in the Morpher Modifier control panel.

To accurately cover the full range of human emotions, dozens of facial Morph Targets would be needed. It is not uncommon in animated feature films for a main character to have 50 or more Morph Targets. However, in a semi-realistic film like *Homing Instinct*, each character is given his or her own attitude by using a specific set of facial expressions to express emotion. This limits the number of targets needed and simplifies the job of managing the Morph Targets while reducing the size of the scene files.

ON THE CD

A soundtrack and additional facial expression Morph Targets have been supplied on the companion CD-ROM to give Dr. Quin a wide range of facial expressions. They are the Smile, Anger, Smirk, and Blink.

In the next tutorial, you will mix mouth shapes and expression Morph Targets to create a lip-sync animation.

TUTORIAL 9.5 SETTING UP FOR LIP-SYNC FACIAL ANIMATION

To animate facial expressions, follow these steps:

1. Load your GenMan904.max scene file, or load it from the Chap09 folder on the companion CD-ROM. Maximize the front view, select the original head and eyes of the Dr. Quin model, and click Hide Unselected. You should now see only the head with no hair and the eyes.

ON THE CD

2. Unhide the selection set called Morph Heads, which should contain the mouth shape Morph Targets you made in Chapter 8. You can use your own Morph Targets. However, for the purpose of this tutorial it is recommended that you substitute the eight mouth shape and facial expression Morph Targets that are provided for you on the companion CD-ROM. You can retain all of your own Morph Targets and add the additional facial shapes to the scene.
3. To merge in the additional Morph Targets, Click File > Merge and go to the Chap09\Morphs folder on the companion CD-ROM. Select the 8_MorphHeads.max file and merge the Morph Targets into the scene. You might need to re-name some of the Morph Targets. Position them together in a group in the front viewport so that you can easily see them, as shown in Figure 9.9.

ON THE CD

4. Before merging in the dialog soundtrack from the companion CD-ROM, you will set up the Morpher Modifier. Select the original Dr. Quin head, and then click the Modify tab. You should see a Stack, as shown in Figure 9.9, example 2. There are two issues to consider here. First, the Morpher must be inserted into the Stack below the Skin Modifier. Skin will create unpredictable behavior if it is below Morpher. Second, the UVW Mapping Modifier must be right above the Surface Modifier, or the face texture material will not stick to the face when you animate and expression.
5. To insert the Morpher into the Stack, click the UVW Mapping entry in the Stack, click Modifiers in the Main menu bar, go to Animation Modifiers, and select Morpher. The Morpher will be inserted in the Stack above UVW Mapping and below Relax, as shown in Figure 9.9, example 2.
6. The next step is to load all of the Morph Target heads. Select the Morpher in the Stack, and then in the Channel List drop-down menu, click the Load Multiple Targets button, as shown in Figure 9.9, example 3. A Selection dialog will open showing you what Morph Targets are valid and can be loaded into the Morpher. Select them all. They will be loaded and their names will be displayed in the Channel List.

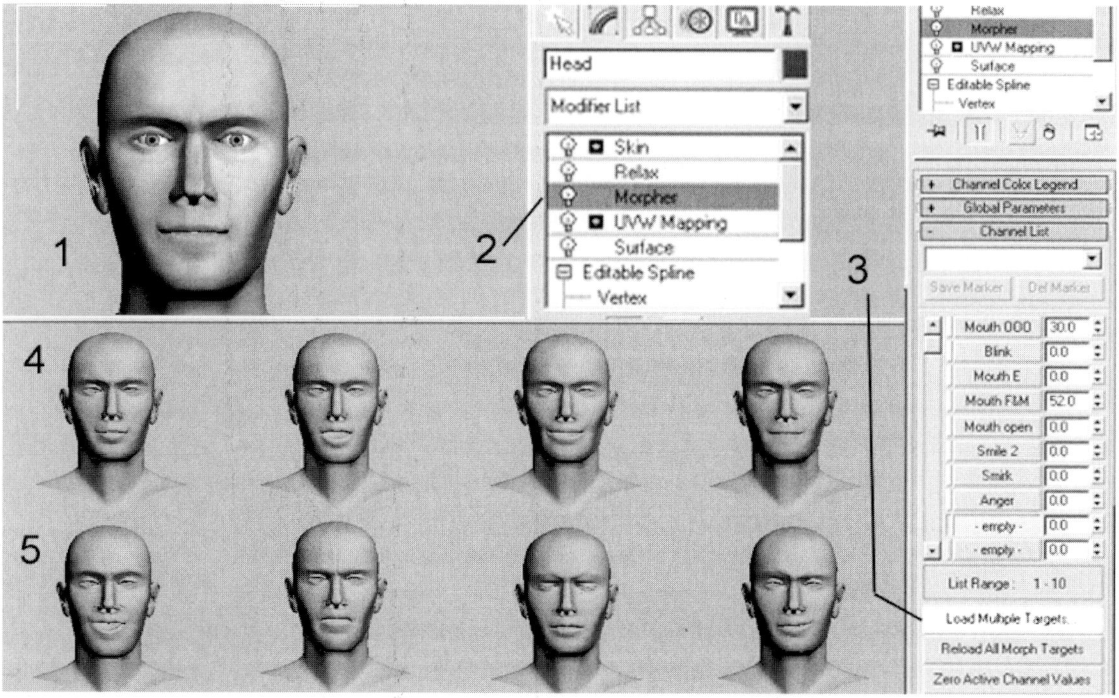

FIGURE 9.9 The original head of Dr Quin, the Morph Targets, and Morpher Controls.

If some of the Morph Targets you made do not show in the Selection dialog, it is most likely that you have distorted the morph head copies in some way. If you push the Spline Patch Control Points too close together, it will change the resulting surface tessellation and give that head a different number of faces than the original head. Each head must have exactly the same number of vertices and faces as the original head, or it cannot be loaded into the Morpher.

ON THE CD

7. To check a Morph Target head that will not load into the Morpher to see if it has the correct number of faces, open the Polygon Counter. In the Utilities tab, click the More button, and then select Polygon Counter from the list. It will float in the viewport. Select each Morph Target individually to see what its polygon count is. They all should have 16,310 faces. If they do not, you might need to re-create the Morph Target. All of the targets in the Chap09\Morphs folder have 16,310 faces. If your original head has a different count, delete it and load the head from the GenMan904.max scene file in the Chap09 folder on the companion CD-ROM. You can test the Morpher by clicking any of the Morph Channel Spinners to the right of a chan-

nel and raising the percentage value. The original head should respond by changing expressions. If it still will not load, check the File > Summary Info to see the vertex count, which should be 8220.

8. When you move the Time Slider, the original head will move out of view in the viewport. To keep the head centered in a viewport, you will create a camera and link it to the head bone of the skeleton so that the camera always looks at the face no matter where it moves in the scene. (You cannot link the camera to the head.) In the front view, center the original Dr. Quin head. Unhide the skeleton by going to the Selection Set window and selecting Bones All. In the Command Panel, click the Create > Camera icon and then click the Free button. Click the head. A camera will be created on top of the head in the viewport, as shown in Figure 9.10, example 1.

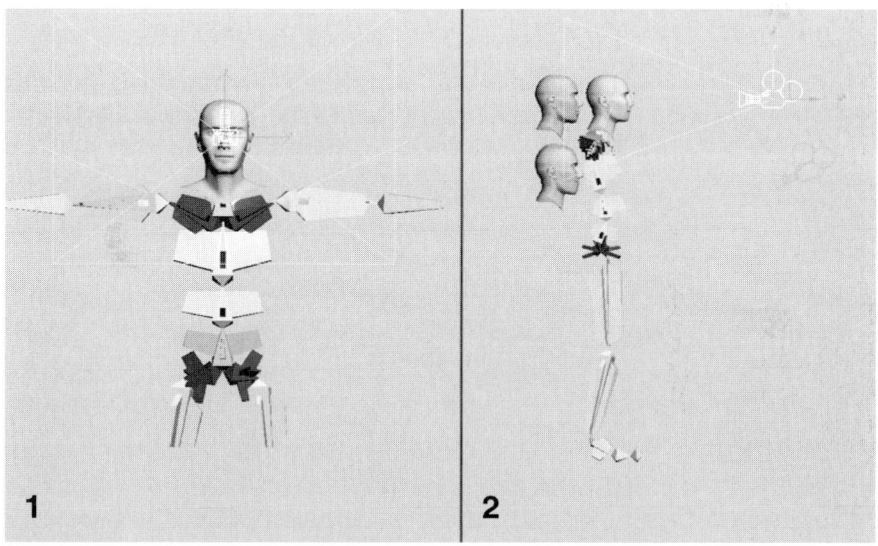

FIGURE 9.10 Link the camera to the head bone to follow the face.

9. Press the C key to change to a camera view. You will now be looking at the inside of the head. In the navigation controls at the lower-right corner of the interface, click the Dolly icon (small red arrow), and then click and drag downward in the camera view to dolly back until you can again see the face. Switch to a left view. Zoom out until you see the camera and the head, as shown in Figure 9.10, example 2. Select the camera and link it to the DocHead bone of the skeleton. Press C and scrub the Time Slider. The

head should not move, but the bones do. The camera is following the head and keeping it centered in the viewport as you scrub the Time Slider. This makes it much easier to animate the facial expressions and lip sync.

ON THE CD

10. The soundtrack is loaded next. To load the dialog soundtrack, first copy the Phone.wav sound file from the Chap09\Sound folder on the companion CD-ROM, and paste it into the 3ds max Sounds directory on your hard drive. To load the soundtrack into the scene, open the Track View Curve Editor. Locate the word "Sound" at the top of the Track View Hierarchy window. Select Sound, right-click, and then select Properties. The Sound Options dialog will open. In the dialog, select the Choose Sound button. The Open Sound dialog will open, as shown in Figure 9.11.

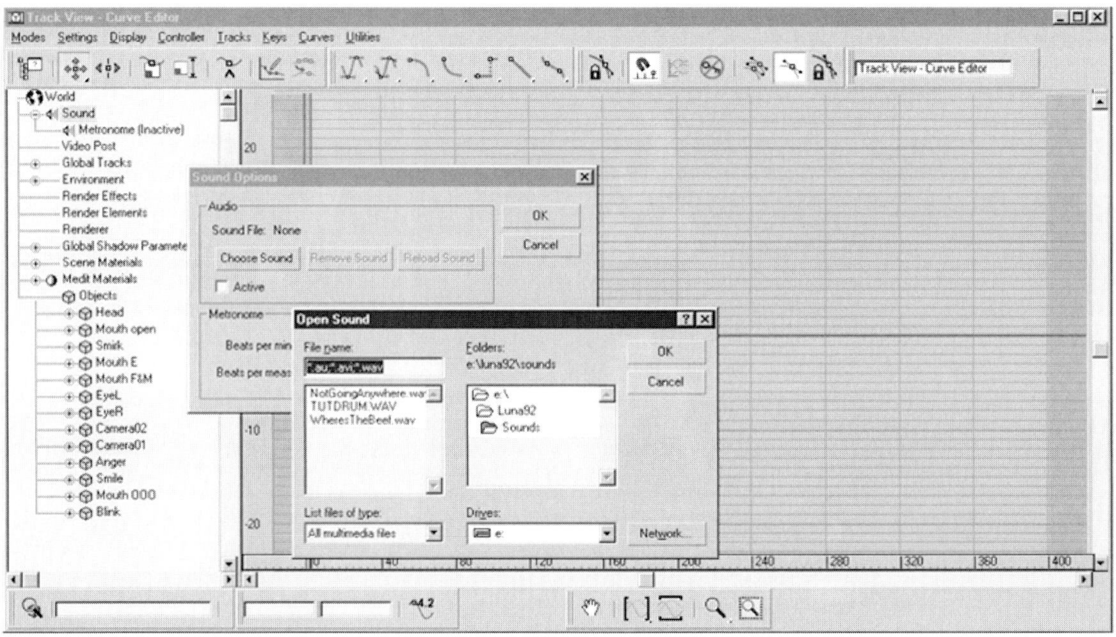

FIGURE 9.11 Loading a soundtrack into the track view.

11. Go to the 3ds max\Sounds directory and select the Phone.wav file. Click OK. The Open Sound dialog will close. Next, click OK and the sound will load into the Track View—Curve Editor. Click the small Plus sign (+) next to the word "Sound," and then click Waveform to display it in the track view.
12. Save the scene as GenMan905.max.

Recording the Soundtrack

In nearly all animated films, the dialog is recorded first. For lip-sync animation, the dialog must be available before the facial animation is done. However, some of the general animation can be completed first, such as bringing the character into the environment where he will speak. Recording the dialog is done with an eye toward getting a performance from the voice actors that will bring the characters to life. The voice actors are often videotaped to aid the animators in re-creating the gestures and expressions, and the proper physical timing that match the dialog. The following text is a scene from the *Homing Instinct* script.

> A telephone conversation takes place between Dr. Quin, a noted Xenobiologist, and Major Black, who controls access to the Alien Archeological sites where Dr. Quin does his research on alien life forms. Dr. Quin is just leaving his office to attend an important meeting when the telephone rings.
> Interior Shot: Early evening in Dr. Quin's office.
> Dr. Quin
> Hello?
> Voice
> Is Dr. Quin there?
> Dr. Quin
> I'm sorry, the office is closed.
> Voice
> This is Major Black. I need to speak to Dr. Quin.
> Dr. Quin
> Major Black? This is Dr. Quin. Why are you calling now?
> Voice
> You must attend the council meeting tonight.
> You are avoiding your responsibilities.
> Dr. Quin
> I already planned to attend the meeting!
> Voice
> See that you do.
> Voice
> I'm on my way now. Goodbye!
> Dr. Quin hangs up.

In the recording, Dr. Quin's voice is normal, while Major Black's voice has been run through an Echo Delay processor to make it sound like he is talking on a speaker phone. This scene is part of the personality conflict between Dr. Quin and Major Black that runs through the entire film. Their conflicts grow in intensity as the story progresses. In the next tutorial, you will load the pre-recorded soundtrack. You will animate a short section of the dialog.

Before the character speaks, time must be allowed in the soundtrack for Dr Quin to sit down and pick up the telephone. The soundtrack includes a telephone ring sound effect that is added to fill in the time before Dr. Quin picks up the telephone and speaks. When doing lip-sync animation, you will need to watch the waveform of the soundtrack, the facial animation, and manipulate the Morpher Modifier spinners all at the same time. This is accomplished by displaying the track view with the sound waveform as a floating window over the scene with the Morpher Modifier Channel List open.

The animation is at a very early stage, and can only be used as a pre-visualization of the action and timing. It is far from finished. There are numerous details yet to be worked out on this character, such as perfecting his clothing and textures, refining and smoothing out his actions, finishing the environment with props and textures, and adding lighting before the scene can be used in the film. The best use of this scene is to establish the timing of all the events and to synchronize them with the dialog track.

Before the soundtrack was recorded, a rendered preview animation was done of Dr. Quin sitting down and picking up the telephone. When the first rough recording was made, a countdown from 10 to 1 was spoken with the word "Mark" at frame 0 when the video preview playback was started. This spoken Mark was used as a synchronizing "pop" or slate clapper sound to synchronize the start of the animation with the dialog. A rough recording of the entire dialog was then prepared while watching the preview animation play. That recording was then transferred to a multitrack recorder where the sound effect and the other character's voice speaking over the telephone were added to Dr. Quin's dialog. In that way, the soundtrack maintained the correct length, and the action would be correctly synchronized with the sound effects.

In the next tutorial, you will create a lip-sync animation of Dr. Quin answering the telephone.

TUTORIAL 9.6 ANIMATING WITH LIP SYNC

To animate Dr. Quin's conversation:

1. Load the GenMan905.max scene file, if it is not already loaded. To save time when doing test renders, be sure to hide everything except the original Dr. Quin head, the eight Morph Target heads, the telephone, and the eyes.
2. To set up the viewport for lip-sync animation, click Customize > Viewport Configuration, and in the dialog click the Layout tab. Select the viewport with three windows—a long window on the top and two smaller ones below (second from the left in the lower row of layouts)— and then click OK. Next, right-click the lower-right view and make it the Camera02 view. On the lower left, make it a front view. Click the Track View icon, and then position the Track View—Curve Editor over the top window, as shown in Figure 9.12.

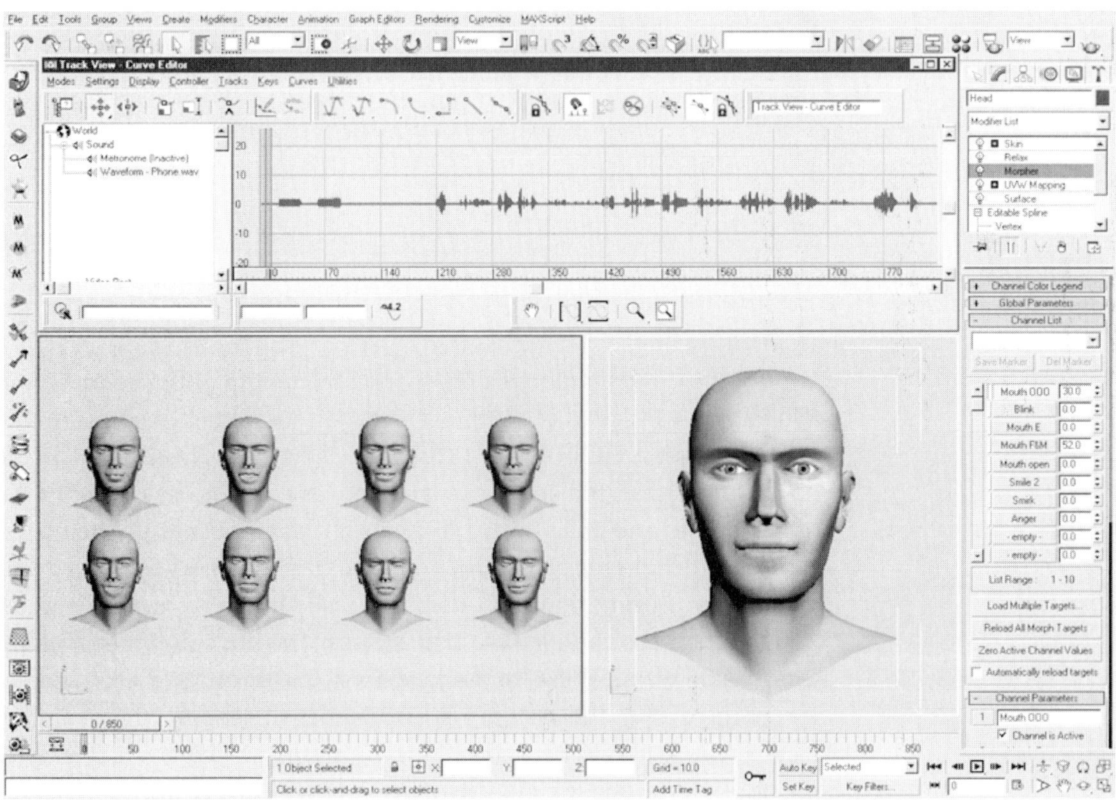

FIGURE 9.12 The interface ready for lip-sync animation.

3. Click the original Dr. Quin head in the Camera02 view, and then click Modify. In the Stack, select Morpher to display the Morph Channels List. To get an undistorted view of Dr. Quin's face, select Camera02, set its lens angle to 135 mm, and then dolly in on the face. It will no longer be distorted, as shown in Figure 9.13.

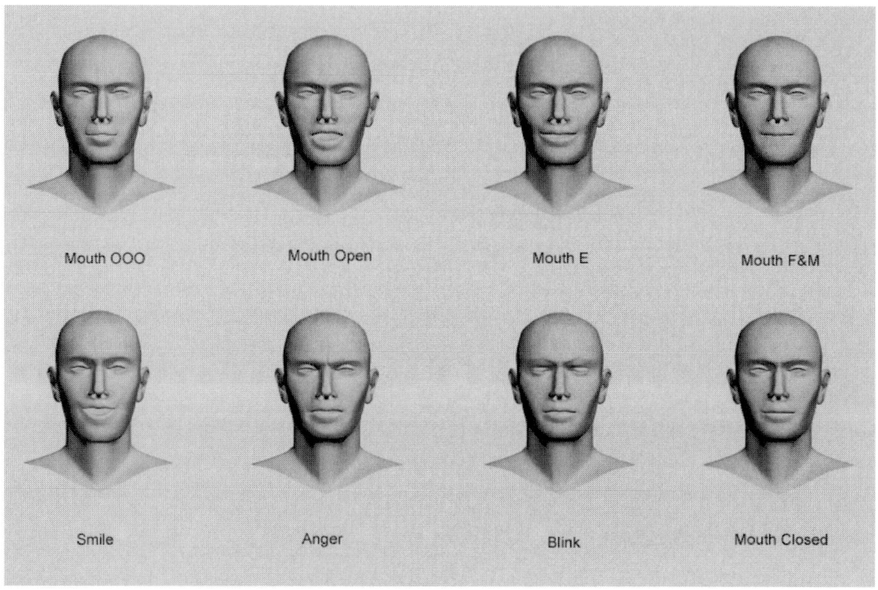

FIGURE 9.13 The eight Morph Target heads.

4. In the Time Configuration dialog, change the length of the animation to 850 frames, which is the length of the dialog soundtrack. Make sure that Playback is set to Real Time at 1X, or you will not hear the sound. You are now ready to start the lip-sync animation. Turn on Auto Key, save the file using Save As, and press the "+" to create an incrementally numbered file. When you do lip-sync animation, you should save a new file with a different name every time you add a phrase in case something goes wrong.
5. Play the sound by clicking Play. You will hear two rings, and then after Dr. Quin sits down and picks up the telephone, you will hear "Hello" and the rest of the dialog. The system will skip frames to keep up with real-time playback at 30 frames per second (fps). This is normal behavior. The faster the display card, and the more memory your system has, the fewer frames

that will be skipped. Stop Play and scrub the Time Slider. Sound will only play forward, not backward.

6. You will set the first key at frame 0. In the Morpher, move the Mouth Closed spinner to a value of 100.0. Then, move the Slider to frame 200, which is just before the first word of the dialog. Move the Mouth Closed spinner down a little and back up to 100 to create a second key. Additionally, set a key at frame 200 for the Mouth OOO target with a value of 0.0, and for Mouth E with a value of 0.0.
7. At frame 208, move the Mouth E value to 65, and the Closed value down to 0. At frame 213, raise Mouth OOO to 70, and lower Mouth E to 0. At frame 222, lower Mouth OOO to 0.0, and raise Mouth Closed to 100. This should animate the mouth to form the word "Hello," as shown in Figure 9.14.

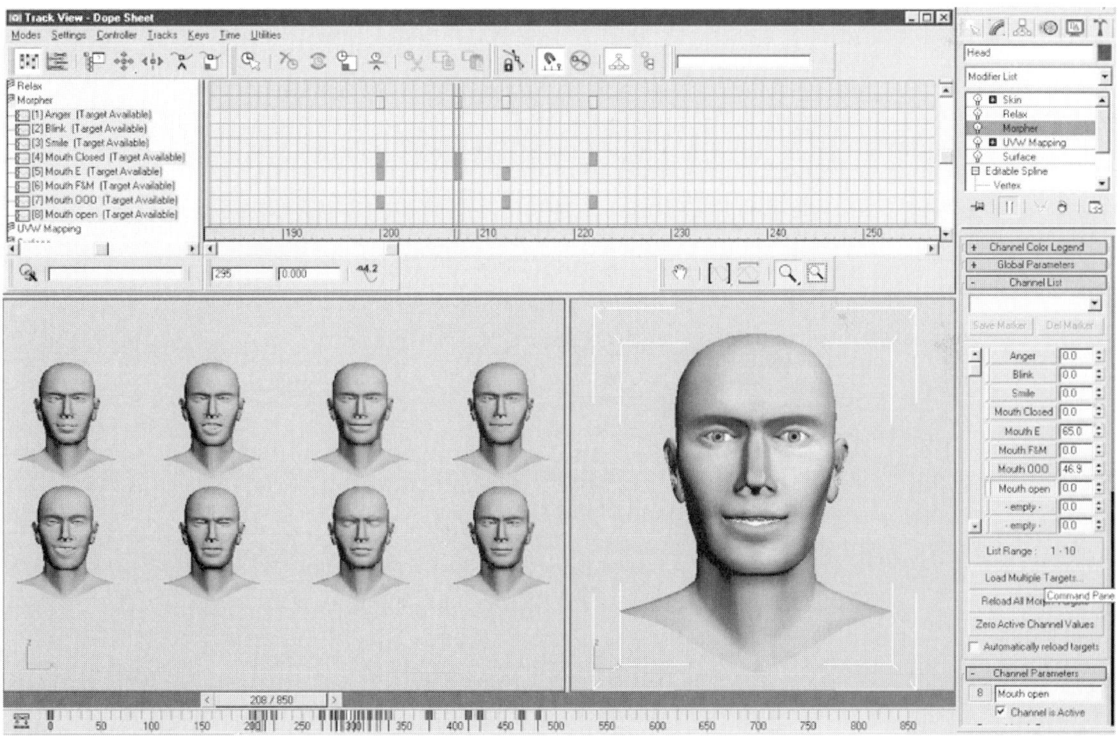

FIGURE 9.14 Setting Morph Target keys for the word "Hello."

8. Test the lip-sync animation by rendering a short section of frames from 190 to 230, and play it back to see how it works. Create a QuickTime movie (.mov) using Sorenson Color compression set to 30 fps with a resolution of

320 x 240. Play back the rendering and make any changes you think are necessary. Then, continue on to the next line that Dr. Quin speaks, which is "I'm sorry, the office is closed."

Nudging is the technique of clicking and moving a Morph Target value spinner up slightly and then lowering it back to 0.0 to set a 0.0 value key. This blocks any key interpolation from an earlier key so that the movement will not start until after the 0.0 key. These nudged or "blocking" keys are necessary if you want to animate lip-sync accurately. From this point forward, this process will be referred to as nudging.

9. While Dr. Quin is listening to his old enemy Major Black, he becomes a little unhappy. To change his emotional state from relaxed to angry, go to frame 269 and nudge the spinners of the Anger and Blink Morph Targets to set 0.0 value keys, and then go to frame 278 and set Anger to 24 and Blink to 100. Advance to frame 283, reduce Blink to 29, and raise Anger to 36. Next, to animate the second phrase in the dialog, go to frame 284, and nudge the Mouth Open spinner to set a 0.0 key. Also nudge the Mouth Closed spinner to set a key with a value of 100. Then, at frame 288, set Mouth Closed to 0.0 and Mouth Open to 32. At frame 290, set Mouth Open to 0.0, Mouth F&M to 40, and Mouth Closed to 50. At frame 295, set Mouth F&M to 0.0, Mouth Closed to 0.0, Nudge Mouth E to 0.0, and set Mouth OOO to 60. At frame 301, set Mouth E to 34 and Mouth OOO to 0.0. All of the preceding keys are necessary to animate the lips to say the phrase "I'm sorry, " and to change Dr. Quin's facial expression.
10. To form the words "the office," go to frame 305 and nudge Mouth Open to 0.0, and set Mouth closed to 100. At frame 310, nudge Mouth E to 0.0, set Mouth OOO to 100, and Mouth Open to 20. At frame 315, set Mouth Closed to 0.0, and Mouth Open to 16. At frame 317, set Mouth Closed to 40, Mouth F&M to 0.0, Mouth Open to 0.0, and Mouth OOO to 0.0. At frame 323, set Mouth OOO to 20. At frame 327, set Mouth Open to 18, Mouth OOO to 100, and Mouth Closed to 0.0. At frame 335, set Mouth OOO to 0.0, Mouth Open to 0.0, and Mouth Closed to 100 to form the word "closed."
11. Render a QuickTime movie of the scene from frame 190 to frame 355 to see how the lip-sync animation works with the soundtrack. After you view the results, make any necessary changes to and continue animating the rest of the Dr. Quin dialog. When you are finished animating with the Morph Targets, unhide the teeth. Animate the lower teeth with the Jaw Control to follow the up-and-down movement of the chin.

ON THE CD

12. You can see a sample rendering of the preceding steps 6 through 10 by viewing the PhoneAnim.mov movie in the Chap09\Images folder on the companion CD-ROM. Save the scene as GenMan906.max.

In the next tutorial, you will load a different file and explore the creation of a walk cycle using the Dr. Quin skeleton rig.

ANIMATING A WALK CYCLE

The way a character walks reveals many things about his or her personality, age, attitude, and athleticism. Physical problems, such as a limp, contribute to creating a unique personality for a character. For example, a pirate with a peg leg would not walk like a human being with two natural legs. The walk contributes to the overall posture that creates a unique physical presence on the screen. Walk cycles can show a character's different moods and energy levels ranging from elated excitement to dejected fatigue. Understanding the differences between walks and how to create them with the standard rigged skeleton will be explained in the tutorials that follow.

Many factors can be varied to create a personalized walk, such as the length of the stride, the springiness of the body, or lack of it, and the roll or swagger of the walk. When the character becomes tired, drunk, or sick, his walk is severely affected. When he is agitated or in a hurry, additional stiffness is added along with a quicker pace.

BODY LANGUAGE

Body language is one of the animator's most powerful behavioral tools. Body language is a very powerful form of nonverbal communication. One classic example of the use of body language is the story of the pretty girl sitting on a bench. An unattractive boy walks toward her with the intention of asking her out on a date. She sees him coming and does not want to talk to him, so she turns her back on him, crosses her legs, and clamps her arms tightly around her body. As the boy comes up to her, she turns her head away and refuses to look at him. The boy waits for a moment, and then walks away with his head hanging, shuffling his feet.

A few important rules to keep in mind:

- The pelvis is the center of all motion, so it is a good idea to animate its motion first, or at least very early in the animation process.
- Human motions are round, not linear. Try to move hands in an arc whenever you animate a gesture.
- Hips and shoulders always counter-rotate during a walk or a run, which helps maintain balance.
- When the left foot is forward, the right arm is forward.
- The spine is always flexing during any movement and should not be left rigid.
- When moving, center of weight of the body is shifted in the direction of travel. Walking or running is controlled falling.
- Human beings always anticipate a turn by looking in that direction before they make the turn.
- The hip moves up and down with each stride.
- A human being endeavors to keep the head centered even though the body moves side to side during a walk or a run.
- All motions should include anticipation and follow through.

The skeleton rig that you are working with can be divided into zones of body motion. They are the legs, the torso including the hips, spine, shoulders, the arms (which can include the shoulders), and the head (which can include the shoulders).

CHARACTER ASSEMBLY NODE

All parts of the skeleton are controlled by the skeleton rig control points, which are linked to the hip and foot controls. The hip and the feet are, in turn, linked to the Character Control, which is a control point below the character that looks like a box with a cross. Inside the Character Control box is a Character Assembly Node, which is represented by a small round icon surrounding a picture of a man, as shown in Figure 9.16. The Character Assembly Node is a new feature of 3ds max 6. The purpose of the Character Assembly is to contain all of the parts of a character, and allow you to merge animation data from other models with the same skeletal setup and names. This enables you to paste poses from other animations to create new animations.

Breakdown of the Walk Cycle

The walk cycle movement can be broken down into parts. There are general terms used in the animation field to describe each part of a walk. In this book, we will use the terms *Point, Contact, Plant, Support, Lift,* and *Passing* to describe the movement and rotation of the feet and legs during the walk, as shown in Figure 9.15.

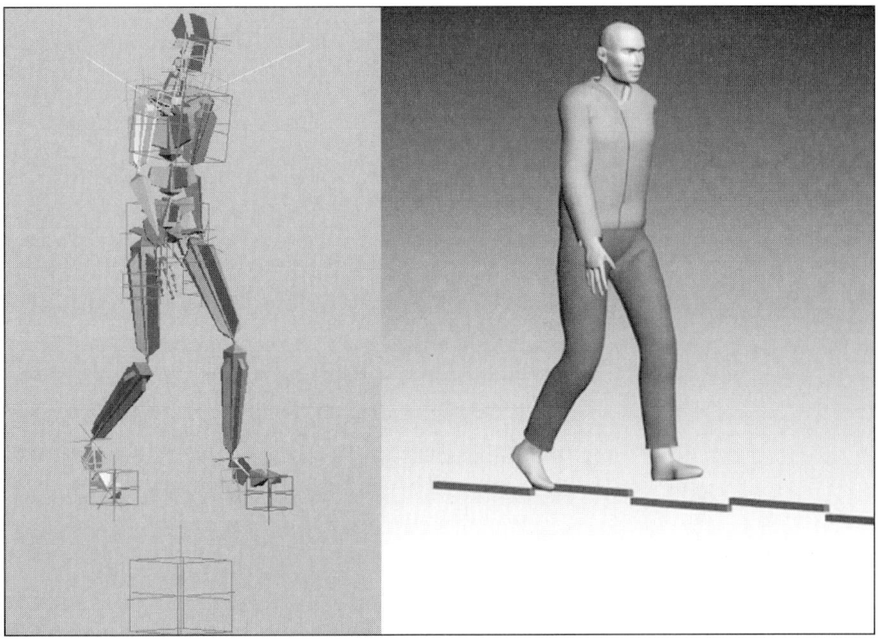

FIGURE 9.15 The 30-frame Slow Walk Cycle repeats each motion every 60 frames.

Skeletal Structure and Linking

It is important to note that the hip and the feet are linked separately to the Character Control below the figure. This allows the hip and upper body to be moved around while the feet stay on the ground. When you want to move the character forward, you do not move the hip. Instead, you move the Character Control box and animate the feet moving according to stride length. In essence, the character walks in place while the Character Control is moved forward. This type of character animation rig is very versatile and allows a greater ability to simulate human motions than other types of rigs. When you get used to this skeleton rig, you will find it is very fast and easy to animate realistic human motion with it.

While animating this skeletal rig, the idea is to use Forward Kinematics rotations to move most of the control points such as the head, shoulders, and hip, and use Inverse Kinematics to move the feet and wrists. Do not try to move the bones directly. If you do, the function of the skeletal rig will become unpredictable. This tutorial is set up so that the character will take one stride every 30 frames, which corresponds to a slow walk.

In the following tutorial, you will work with the skeleton to create a walk cycle. All distances are measured in Generic Units.

TUTORIAL 9.7

ANIMATING A WALK CYCLE

ON THE CD

To animate a walk cycle:

1. Load the GenMan811.max file from the Chap09\Images folder on the companion CD-ROM. This file includes the Morph Target heads, but does not include the Dr. Quin office. To animate the walk cycle, you will work with the main skeleton control points and the arm IK end effectors. Caution: Do not move the foot or the ankle IK end effectors (blue crosses). If you move them away from the control points, you will degrade the function of the skeletal rig and make it unpredictable.
2. Click the Select by Name icon in the Main menu. When the dialog opens, click Display Subtree to display the hierarchy of objects. Notice that "(Character01)" is at the top of the hierarchy, as shown in Figure 9.16. This is the Character Node icon. You use it to move the character. The best way is to select and freeze the Character Control Dummy, and then select only the Character Node (Character01) when you are animating the skeleton. It is the parent of the entire figure and all of the data is grouped in the Character Node.
3. Select Body01, Coat, and Pants, and then hide them so you only see the bones and the skeleton rig. Select and hide all of the geometry so that you can only see the bones and the helpers or control points. In the Named Selection Sets window, many of these items are selectable.
4. The first task in animating the skeleton is to set the stride length. Maximize the left view. Click Zoom Extents (Z) and position the model so you can see

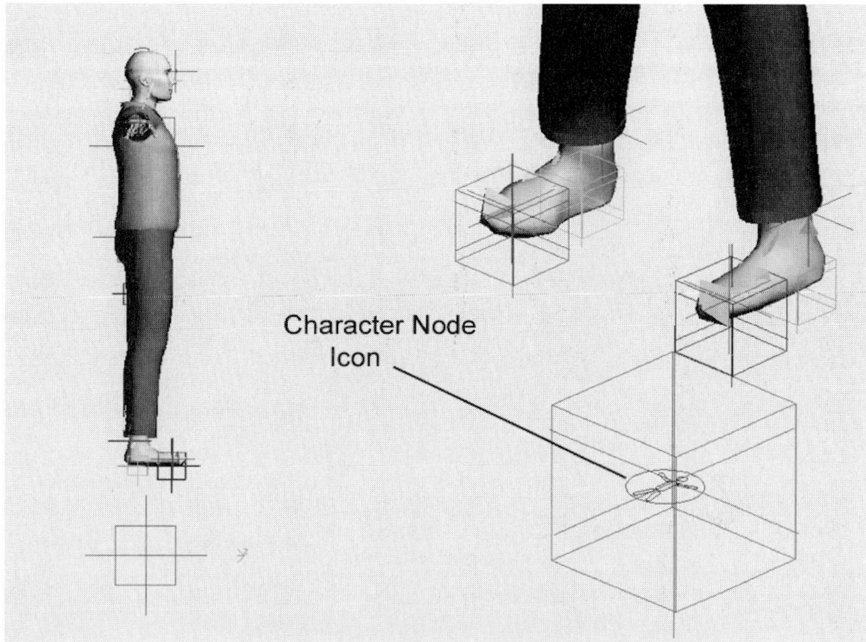

FIGURE 9.16 The Dr. Quin/Generic Man character with the Character Node.

the entire skeleton and the Character Node below it. Turn on Auto Key, and then select the Hip Control (point helper box) and move it downward −12.0 units in the Y-axis. This will bend the knees slightly to make sure that the IK solvers of the legs are not stretched beyond their extension limit when you move the feet apart to set the stride length.

5. Surrounding each toe is a control point. They are named LFoot Control and RFoot Control. To determine the correct stride length, move the feet. Select the LFoot Control and move it forward (to your right) slightly less than the length of the foot. Then, select the R Foot Control and move it backward (to your left) about the same amount. There should now be a space between the left heel and the right toe of about one foot length, as shown in Figure 9.17, example 1.

A Stride Marker is used to determine the distance the character will move at each step so that four strides will move the Character Control four stride-lengths forward.

6. Create a narrow Stride Marker box by clicking Create > Box, and then click and drag from the center of one foot control to the center of the other foot control, as shown in Figure 9.17, example 2. The Stride Length box should

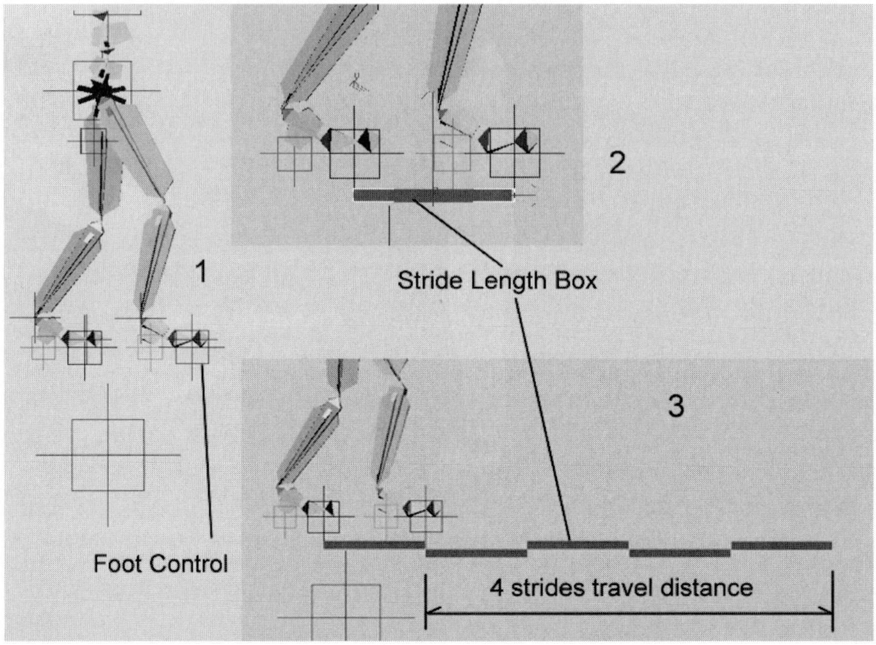

FIGURE 9.17 Setting the stride length and character travel distance.

measure about 90 Generic Units from toe to toe and about 3 units on the other sides. This becomes a Stride Marker.

7. To copy the Stride Marker, Shift > Move it to the right and then line up its back end with the front end of the original box, as shown in Figure 9.17, example 3. In this way, you create a row of markers set end to end that can be used to create a motion path. They show where the character will walk, and the points where the heels will strike the ground. Make at least five Stride Markers.
8. Now that the Stride Markers are in place, the next step is to move the character forward one stride length for every 30 frames. The idea is to move the Time Slider, then move the character one stride length, and set a key. Do this now. Set keys at 0, 30, 69, 90, and 120 frames. The character's feet should straddle a Stride Marker correctly every 30 frames, as shown in Figure 9.18.
9. The next operation would be to reverse the feet every 30 frames. That will be covered in the next tutorial. Save the project as GenMan907.max. Continue with this same scene file to the next tutorial to animate the legs, arms, and feet.

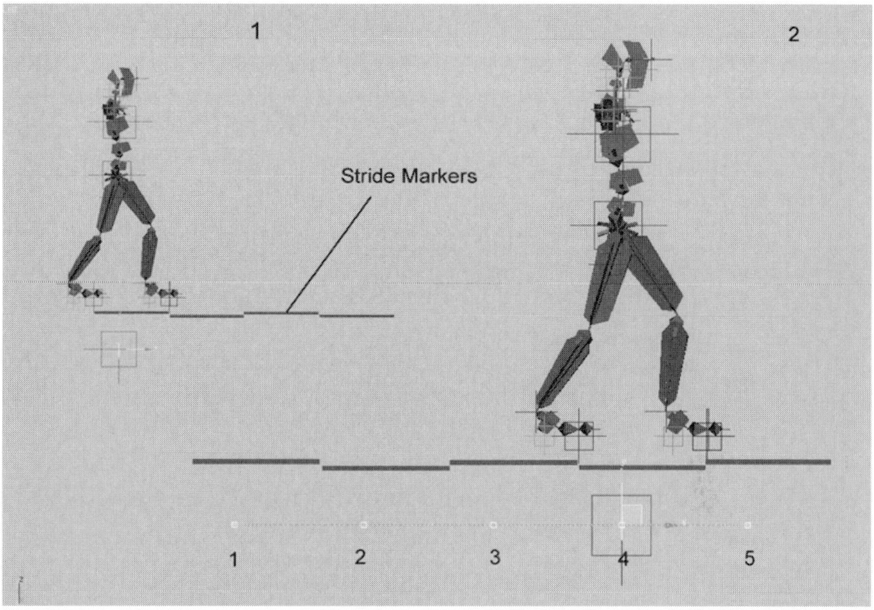

FIGURE 9.18 Moving the character forward every 30 frames to match a new Stride Marker.

FOOT MOVEMENT CONCEPTS

The terminology of the foot movement is as follows: The walk cycle consists of a first pair of motions that consist of pointing the right heel toward where you are going to step. The goal of the heel is the point where it will Touch the ground as the body moves forward. After the heel contacts the ground, the ankle is rotated to Plant the bottom of the foot flat on the ground. Immediately afterward, the Left foot lifts from the ground and Moves or Passes by the Right foot. This is accompanied by a shift in the weight of the body so that it is centered over the right foot. This is called the Support position of the foot. During the continuation of the step, the left foot is moving forward to the next point where you will step. The sequence of movements and rotations is repeated on the opposite side of the body as the heel of the left foot makes contact and rotates down, taking on the weight as it transfers from the right foot to the left foot. Finally, the right foot comes off the ground and passes by the left foot, and so on.

Establishing the basic procedure of moving and rotating the foot, leg, and arm controls to create a smooth walk cycle will help you later when you use these and other rigged skeletons in your animations. The design of this skeleton rig has a few rules that should be observed for the best results. For example, the foot is controlled by two control points, one at the ball of the foot or toe and the other at the heel. The IK end effectors are not used to control the foot. The rotation of the foot up and down when walking is done by rotating the Heel Control. Do not rotate the Toe Controls. The rotation of the feet using only the Heel Controls helps simplify foot animation, as shown in Figure 9.19. The movement and the rotation animation tracks of the feet have been separated into one for each heel and one for each toe, or ball of the foot, to make it easier to edit the foot animation tracks later. In the text, we will refer to the Foot Control as being the "toe control" that actually rotates around the ball of the foot as we go through the tutorials. Strictly speaking, we actually mean the "ball-of-the-foot control." In these animations, the toe bone rotation is always left unanimated until after the entire walk cycle is finished.

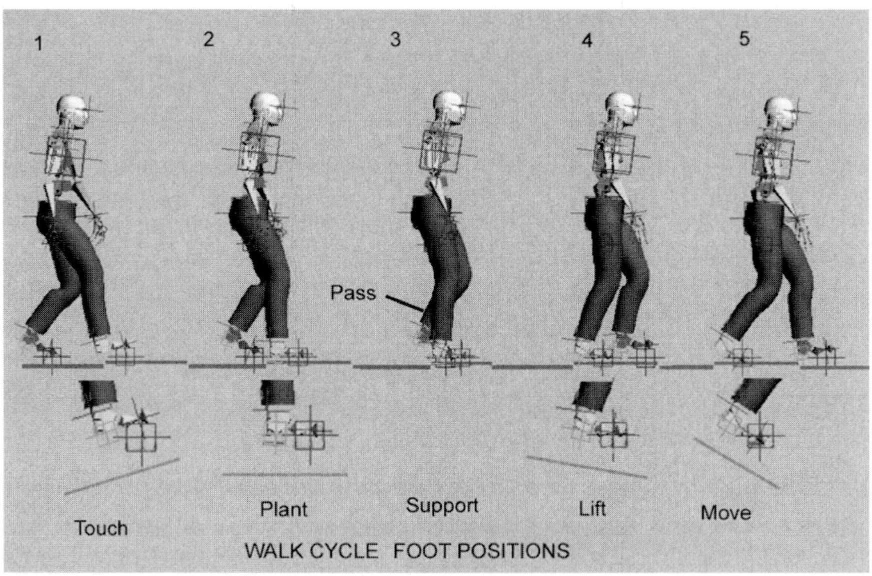

FIGURE 9.19 Foot movement during the walk cycle.

Hip and shoulder counter-rotation is another important part of the walk cycle process. The body shifts and twists constantly as you walk to maintain its balance and an even distribution of weight. Arms and legs should move in arcs, not in perfectly straight lines, and the body must shift its weight from side to side to indicate when the weight shifts from the left leg to the right leg. Head movements in anticipating direction changes, along with spine and shoulder flexibility and gestures, can give the spark of life to an otherwise stiff animation.

These factors are all important in creating a convincing and realistic walk cycle. They also apply equally to the jog cycle and the run cycle. In fact, counter-rotation and the shifting of weight with a flexible spine are universal attributes that should be applied to all character and animal animations, even those with four legs. In the next tutorial, you will continue with the Generic Man walk cycle animation.

TUTORIAL 9.8 ANIMATE THE FEET, LEGS, AND ARMS IN A WALK CYCLE

To animate the feet:

1. Load the GenMan907.max scene file if it is not already loaded.

Foot animation is a complex task that is hard to describe in words. The best approach is to learn by studying and copying a movie of a walk cycle. There is a reference walk cycle movie on the companion CD-ROM in the Chap09/Images folder called GenManWalk.avi. It is designed to be loaded into the left viewport background and played as a reference animation to show how the skeleton rig should be animated in a walk cycle. Note: The movie will not play at full speed in the viewport backgrounds and can only be advanced one frame at a time. Use the "<" and ">" keys to move forward and back. Hold either key to move continuously.

ON THE CD

2. To load a reference movie into the left viewport background, click Views > Viewport Background > Files, and load the GenManWalk.avi movie from the Chap09\Images folder on the companion CD-ROM. Turn on Match Bitmap, Lock Zoom\Pan, and Animate Background. Then, click OK to show the movie in the left viewport.
3. In the left view, use Background Lock Toggle to position the skeleton of the Generic Man model to match the starting position and size of the skeleton in the background movie at frame 0. Turn on Auto Key, and then move the Time Slider to frame 30. Your character should advance forward one stride length since you animated the Character Node in Tutorial 9.7.

4. The next step is to reverse the feet every 30 frames. Turn on the Auto Key button. Then, at frame 0, select the LFoot Control. The left foot should be in the forward position and the right foot should be back, as shown in Figure 9.20, example 1. Move the Time Slider to frame 30. The front foot should now be moved back to its original position, and the back foot should be selected and move forward to match the next Stride Marker position, as shown in Figure 9.20, example 2.

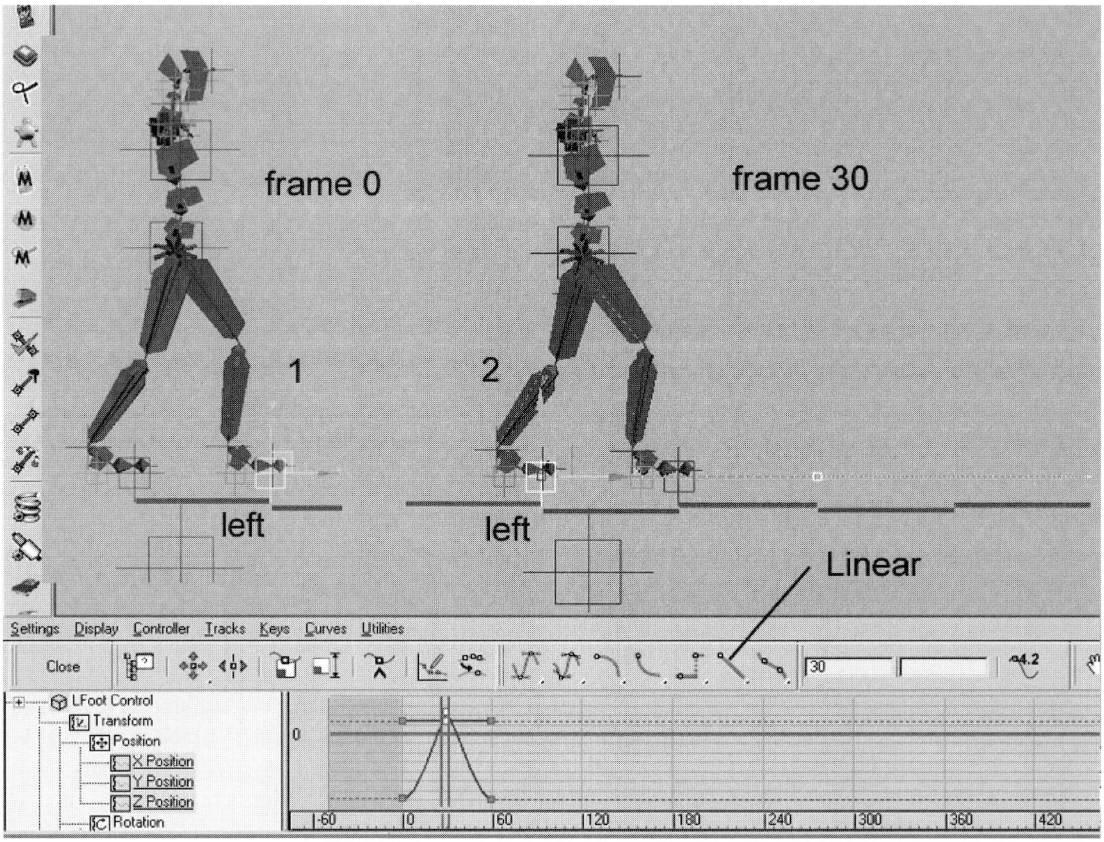

FIGURE 9.20 Reversing the foot animation.

5. The foot will slide unless you set linear key transitions. To make the key at frame 30 linear, open the Trackbar, then at frame 30 select the key for X Position of the LFoot Control, and click the Set Tangent to Linear button, as shown in Figure 9.20. This will make the foot stay there without sliding. Repeat this process for each new stride.

6. The author prefers to set the computer to Linear tangents for all keys, which is very helpful when animating intricate character motion. This is set by clicking Customize > Preferences > Animation tab > Controller Defaults – Set Defaults > Bezier Float > Set... . Click the In and Out tangents to Linear and click OK, then click OK and close the dialog. Now, all your motions will stay exactly where you put them. You can convert them to smoothed or Bézier later when you need smoothed motion.
7. Use the reference video to apply rotations to the Heel Control to rock the foot between heel and toe during the walk cycle. As shown in Figure 9.19, the foot goes through the Touch, Plant, Support, Lift, Move, and Pass motions for each stride.
8. Copy the motion of the legs, feet, hips, shoulders, and arms in the reference movies to animate the character.

Remember these rules as you work: The hip moves up and down and rotates side to side with the Hip Control. The Chest Control rotates the shoulders and upper body to create hip-shoulder counter-rotation. The Shoulder Control points are used to swing the arms down, forward and back, and the Wrist end effectors are used to bend the arms. The Heel Control is used to rotate or rock the foot angle. The Foot Control is moved to advance the foot forward or raise it up. Do not animate the Foot IK Chain or the Leg IK Chain end effectors. The skeletal rig will become unstable if you move them. Do not use the Kick control boxes in the normal walk animation. Hide the Leg IK.

9. When you have animated four strides, save the scene as GenMan908.max. Load the author's version to see an example.

ACROBATIC MOTION OF THE SKELETON

The skeleton rig is capable of doing many acrobatic motions. The rig rotation points can be modified or augmented with additional points to accomplish a wide variety of mixed motions that involve many bones at once (Figure 9.21).

If you want to have the character jump up and hang by its hands, you need to add another control point above the body, and then unlink the Foot Control points from their linkage to the lower character control box. This is re-rigging the skeleton for special purposes. Another alternative is to use FK_IK to constrain the hands temporarily to an object in the

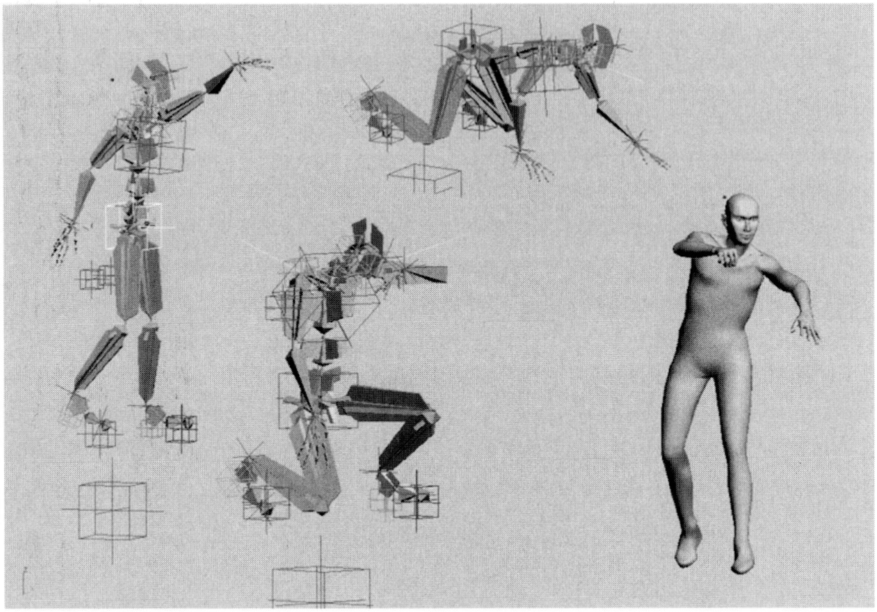

FIGURE 9.21 Various motions with the skeleton rig.

environment so that the model appears to be moving the object. When the animated point constraints for the wrists are on, the wrists can be made to snap to an object such as a shipping crate. The crate is pre-animated to move as if it was pushed by the character. After the crate is moved, you turn off the constraints and the hands will appear to pull away or let go of the object. The character can then walk away. The Link Constraint, which you worked with in Tutorial 9.3, is used to pick up and drop things, and is not considered FK_IK.

The Kick Controls behind the legs can be used in a number of ways. Similar linkages can be applied to the arm to create an automatic reach-and-return arm motion controller that is positioned near the biceps of the arm. This point would rotate the arm IK end effector on a diminishing radius relative to the shoulder joint.

The hip is a very good place to start when trying to master a new character rig. It is the center of all body motions and the center of the weight when the body is in motion. If you select the Hip Control and move the hips around, you will discover very quickly how easy it is to find a realistic pose for the skeleton. Try lowering the hip to bend the knees, and then add a rotation to twist the torso slightly and more evenly distribute the weight over the feet. These motions are very realistic when combined with hand and arm gestures. Moving the head is accomplished with the Head Control. Notice that its movement is more like leaning than turning. It is not well suited to swivel the head, but it does work well during physical motion where the head is not turning too drastically. You can change the centers of rotation or add more of your own to extend the rig's capabilities.

Putting the Xzulixia Model on the Dr. Quin Skeleton

Now that you have animated the Dr. Quin model answering the telephone and walking, you will want to put the Xzulixia Alien Vampire model on a skeleton so it can be animated. Since the process for fitting the Xzulixia model to the skeleton and binding it to the bones with the Skin Modifier is the same process used for the Dr. Quin model, the Skin instructions will not be repeated here. Only a few things need to be done to re-size the Dr. Quin skeleton to work in the Xzulixia mesh.

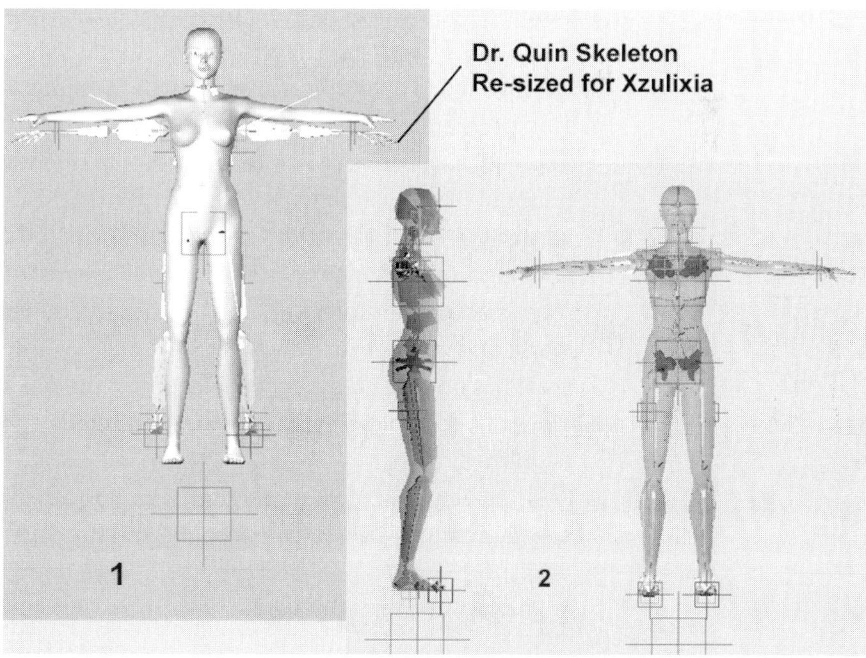

FIGURE 9.22 Resizing the Dr. Quin skeleton to fit the Xzulixia model.

The first thing to understand is that the models have different proportions. Dr. Quin is a Generic Man with average proportions in every way. Xzulixia is proportioned after the Anime characters with proportions that are more heroic. Her legs are much longer proportionately than are Dr. Quin's, and her neck is longer. In addition, her arms are a bit shorter and her hands are smaller. When the Xzulixia mesh is superimposed over the Dr. Quin skeleton, you can readily see the differences, as shown in Figure 9.22, example 1. With some careful scaling and moving of joint centers, the Dr. Quin skeleton will fit nicely into the Xzulixia mesh, as shown in Figure 9.22, example 2.

In the next tutorial, you will fit the Xzulixia mesh on to the Dr. Quin/Generic Man skeleton.

TUTORIAL 9.9

RESIZE THE GENERIC SKELETON TO FIT XZULIXIA

ON THE CD

To resize the skeleton:

1. Load the Skel_XzuMesh.max file from the Chap09 folder on the companion CD-ROM.
2. Position the torso. Center the torso of the Xzulixia model exactly on top of the torso of the Generic Man skeleton, as shown in Figure 9.22, example 2.
3. Remove the IK chains from the arms and the legs and feet.
4. Turn on Hierarchy tab > Pivot > Adjust Transform > Don't Affect Children. You can now move joints that were part of an IK Chain. You can scale bones to fit them in or to shrink them to match the length of the arms and legs of the new model. The bones at the ends of an IK Chain such as the fingers can sometimes get twisted if you try to use Don't Affect Children to reposition them. Moreover, don't rotate the bones when using this command or it will separate them.
5. Scale the bones and move the joints to fit the skeleton into Xzu.
6. Move the control points for the feet and hands into their new positions.
7. Align the fingers.
8. Re-apply IK solvers to legs and arms. Re-link all of the IK chains to their respective control points to restore the skeletal rig hierarchy.
9. Apply the Skin Modifier and then adjust the bone influence envelopes by animating the model. Save the file as Xzu_onskel909.max.

ADDING SWIVEL ANGLE TARGETS

IK solvers can flip if they are moved beyond their center point. This is seen when the hip is lowered and the leg slues unnaturally to one side. It means that the swivel angle is now reversed. To control the swivel angle during animation, an aiming target is created outside the model (Figure 9.23). It becomes the reference point for the swivel angle handle at the top of the IK Chain. With these targets, you can get a great deal of freedom of motion before the arm will flip. By animating the target you can completely eliminate IK Chain flipping and stabilize the entire animation.

To set this system up, you first must establish point targets by making four control points, two to control the knees and two to control the elbows.

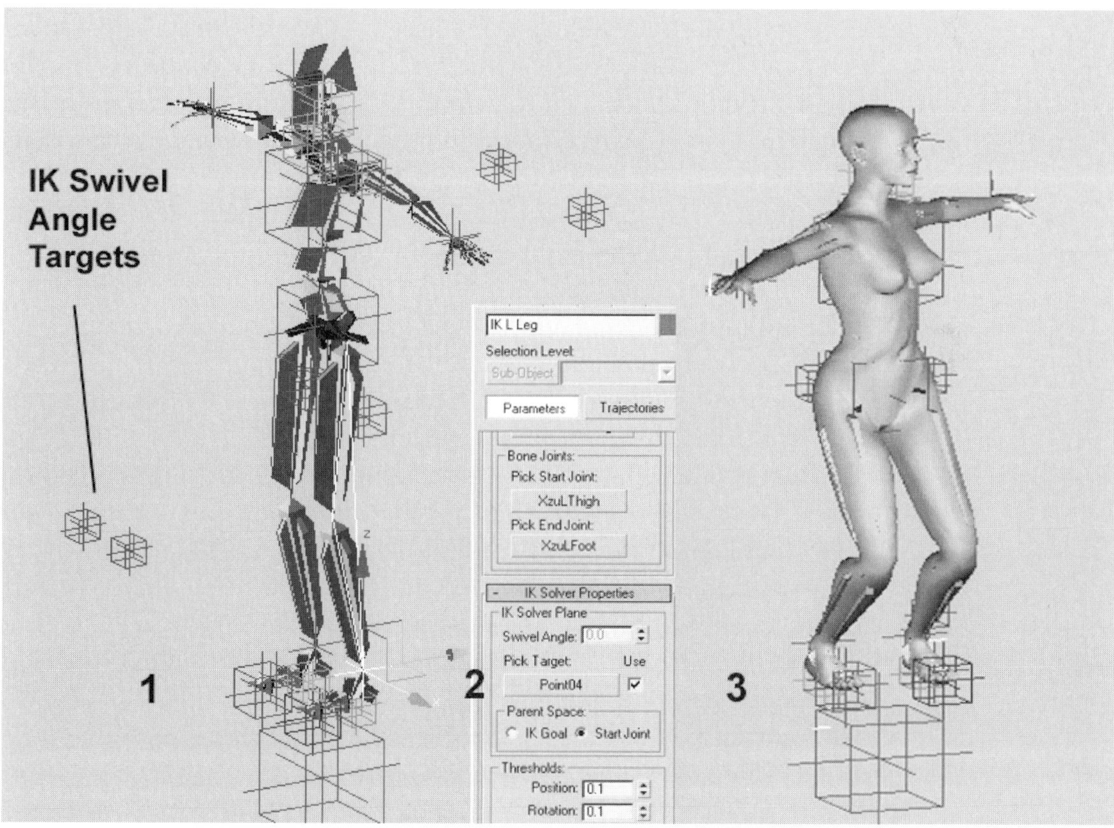

FIGURE 9.23 IK swivel angle targets are used on the Xzulixia character.

The linkage to the targets is applied by selecting the IK end effector, and then clicking the Motion tab. In the IK Solver Properties menu, click the Pick Target (none) button, and then select the target point you placed outside the model. Now when you move the arm, the IK swivel angle of that arm always points toward the target. The target should be linked to the character control Dummy below the model. The Dummy is a good place to link the target point because it moves along the same motion direction as the model.

ANIMATING THE IRIS AND EYELASHES OF A REALISTIC EYE

In Chapter 4, "Finishing the Alien Vampire Character," you modeled a realistic eye for Xzulixia, but did not set it up for animation. In the next tutorial, you will finish the iris and eyelashes and set them up for animation. Two types of iris shapes are used in *Homing Instinct*. The standard round pupil iris is used for all human characters, and the vertical slit cat-eye iris is used for all of the Alien Vampires and the Dinomen. Because there are many close-up shots of eyes in various scenes, the iris is animatable in all major characters. This is accomplished by making the iris and pupil as a spline patch surface, and then converting it to an editable patch surface. Once converted, the inner edge of the circular patch can be animated to stretch or scale as needed. The same surface can easily be scaled to form an animated circular human pupil, or narrowed to a fine point at the top and bottom to create a cat-eye pupil.

After the animated iris is finished, we will look at eyelashes. You can make two kinds of eyelashes. The simple type is a nearly flat planar surface that is all one piece and is curved to simulate eyelashes. It is textured with a picture of eyelashes and an alpha channel or a mask to make only the eyelashes show when rendered. The author chose to use a more complex and more realistic method, which is to create individual geometry eyelashes by snapping a spline along the eyelid, and then make one eyelash out of a three-sided cone. This cone is then animated to move along the spline, first scaling up, then down. When animated satisfactorily, the Snapshot tool is used to create copies of the eyelash that are spaced evenly along the spline, as shown in Figure 9.24.

When all eyelashes are in place, they are attached to the mesh as subobjects so that when the eyelid is closed by using an eye-close Morph Target, the eyelashes move with the skin. If they are linked only to the eyelid mesh, they will not work with Morph Targets.

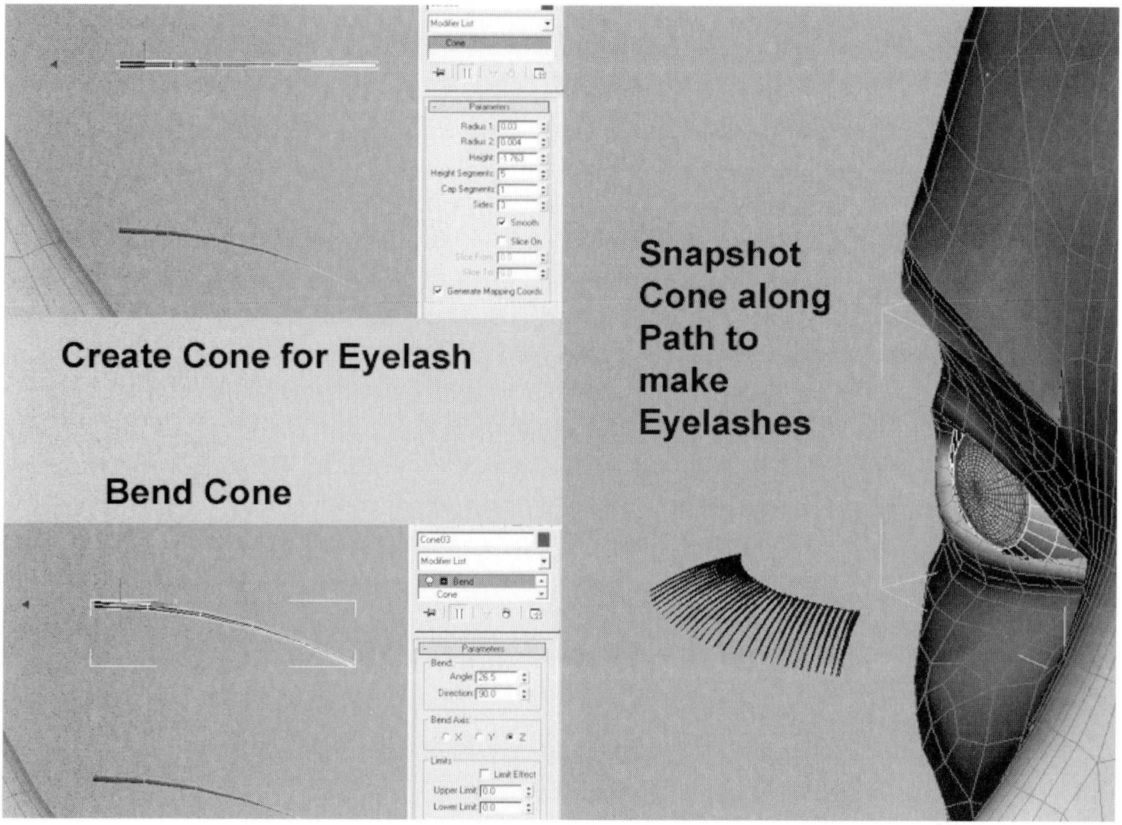

FIGURE 9.24 Curved cones used as eyelashes made with the Snapshot tool.

TUTORIAL 9.10 CREATING AN ANIMATED IRIS FOR A REALISTIC EYE

ON THE CD

To create an animated iris:

1. Load the Eye417.max file from the Chap09 folder on the companion CD-ROM. The file contains the head and shoulders portion of the Xzulixia model, with one realistic right eye, and one low-detail modeling eye, as shown in Figure 9.25, example 1.
2. Select the iris of the multilayer eye and then click Hide Unselected. Then, in the Front view, click Zoom Extents all (Z), turn on Shaded view, and show Edged Faces (F4). You will now build a new iris from splines. Click the 3d Snap icon in the main toolbar, and then right-click and select Vertex in Grid and Snap settings. The idea is to first build a round outer circle with six points using a smooth spline.

3. To create a spline, click Create > Shapes > Line and select Smooth > Smooth in Creation Method. Snap a point to the topmost vertex of the polygonal iris in the Front view. Then continue snapping points at the 10 o'clock position (going counterclockwise), 8 o'clock position, and so on, back to 12 at the top of the iris. Then click Yes to close the spline. It will not yet be round.
4. Turn off snap, right-click, and then convert it to an editable spline. To make the spline round, change all the vertices to Bézier type and adjust the handles until the spline matches the outside of the iris. Select the poly iris and click Freeze Selected. Then select the spline, change to Spline Sub-object mode, and Shift-Scale it 50 percent smaller, which will clone it, as shown in Figure 9.25, example 2.
5. In the Geometry rollout menu, click the Cross Section button, click on the outer spline circle, and then on the inner one. That will create new splines that connect both spline circles together to create a spline cage, as shown in Figure 9.25, example 3. Now exit Sub-object mode. You are ready now to apply the surface.

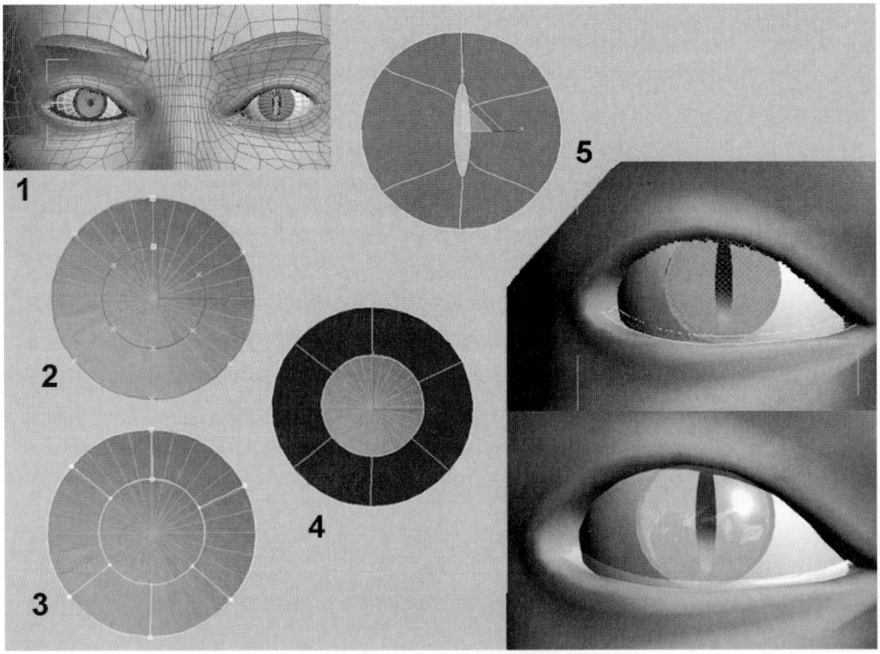

FIGURE 9.25 Creating the animatable patch surface iris.

6. Click Modifiers > Patch/Spline Editing > Surface. A surface will be formed. If it is not a circle with a hole (it might be a distorted square), adjust the Surface > Parameters > Threshold lower until it looks like a smooth round ring (doughnut). Threshold = 0 worked for the author, as shown in Figure 9.25, example 4. Then right-click and convert to an editable patch.
7. Max 6 enables you to delete members of groups. Unfreeze and delete the poly iris. To test how the iris can be animated, switch to Editable Patch > Sub-object > Edge mode and select all of the inner edges of the pupil opening in the patch iris. Then turn on Auto Key, move the time slider to frame 30, and uniform scale the selected edges smaller. Scrub the Time Slider to see the animation.
8. That is fine for the human eye. To create the alien or cat iris with a vertical slit, delete the previous scale key. At frame 0, non-uniform scale the pupil edges narrower in the X-axis, and taller in the Y-axis. You will get a very nice vertical slit pupil, as shown in Figure 9.25, example 5. Again, you can animate the pupil edges to make the slit wide or narrow. You can also clone the animatable patch iris and use it in either type of eye.
9. To see the results, Unhide all. Before rendering the eye, create a semi-transparent Blinn material and apply it to the outer eye. Usable settings are Opacity = 5, Specular = 127, and Glossiness = 47; and add a reflection map with a strength of 29 using Mountains.jpg from the 3dsmax\Maps\Backgrounds folder. Apply a white material to the inner eye, and then apply a material to the iris.
10. A very important step before rendering is to translate the outer eye backward into the head a small distance while maintaining the position of the iris and inner eye surface. This action will result in only the raised cornea section protruding from the surface of the inner eye sphere. That way, the sclera, or white part, of the eye will be a simple white material, and the clear cornea portion of the outer eye will protrude, showing the reflection and highlight.
11. Save the file as Eye910.max. Continue on to the next tutorial to create the animatable eyelashes.

In the next tutorial, you will create eyelashes that can be animated using eye-close/open facial morph targets.

TUTORIAL 9.11 CREATING EYELASHES FOR MORPH-ANIMATABLE EYELIDS

To create eyelashes:

1. Load the Eye910.max file if it is not already loaded. Next, you will merge in two small cones that will be used to create the eyelashes.

ON THE CD

2. Click File > Merge and then open the Eyelashes.max file in the Chap9 folder on the companion CD-ROM. Select All and click OK. You should now see the eyelash cones positioned in front of the right eye in the left viewport, as shown in Figure 9.26, example 1.
3. Select the eyelash cones, and then click Group > Ungroup in the main menu bar. You now have an upper and a lower eyelash cone. To generate the complete set of eyelashes, you will animate these cones along two splines and use the Snapshot tool to clone them. To do that, you must first snap splines to the upper and lower eyelids where you want the eyelashes to be attached. Hide the eyelashes for the moment.

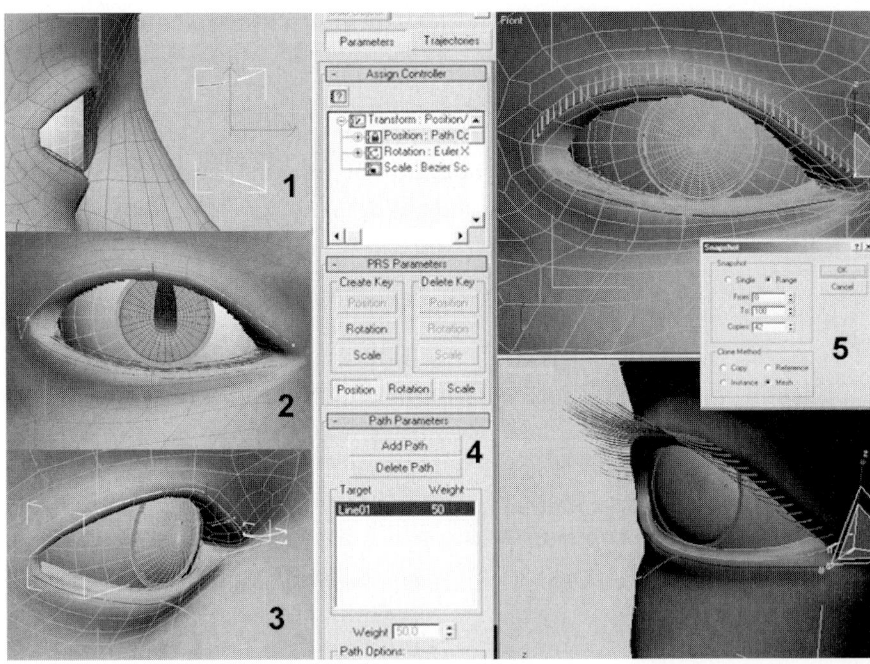

FIGURE 9.26 Creating the eyelashes.

4. Maximize the front view and center Xzulixia's right eye so you can see all of the eyelid geometry. Turn on Smooth and Highlight and Edged Faces. Then turn on 3d Snap, and in Grid and Snap settings, turn off Grid, and turn on Vertex, Edge, Face, and Center Face. Close the dialog. Next, click Create > Shapes > Line, and select Smooth > Smooth in Creation method.

You will notice that the geometry of the eyelids of the Xzulixia head are not highly detailed. The eyelid geometry does not perfectly fit the eye, and there is no tear duct. Total realism is not an issue here. You can revise the Xzulixia eyelids to make them more realistic before continuing if you want. This head model conforms to the "semi-realistic" style, which is the level of detail chosen by the author for the characters in Homing Instinct. Once the eyelashes are attached, the eye will look quite realistic as it is.

5. Click on the mesh above the inner corner of the eye to start the upper spline. Continue clicking six or seven times to create a spline that runs across the width of the upper eyelid. Then repeat the process for the lower eyelid. You should now have two splines snapped to the edges of the eyelids, as shown in Figure 4.26, example 2.
6. Select and freeze all geometry except the two eyelashes and the two new splines. The easiest way to do that is to select the items you do not want frozen, and then click Edit > Select Invert. Then right-click and select Freeze Selected. With the head frozen, it is much easier to work on the eyelashes. The next step is to animate the eyelash cones moving along the eyelash splines.
7. You will use a path constraint to animate the eyelash. Select the upper eyelash, scale it down about 50%, and then translate it to the beginning of the upper eyelash curve in the corner of the eye, as shown in Figure 4.26, example 3. Then click the Motion tab and open the Assign Controller drop-down menu. In the controller window, highlight Position: Position XYZ, and then click the open menu button (the square button with a question mark on it) to open the list of available controllers.
8. Select Path Constraint. Then, in the Path Parameters, click the Add Path button, and click the upper eyelid spline, as shown in Figure 4.26, example 4. Now you can move the Time Slider, and the eyelash will move along the length of the eyelash spline in 100 frames. Turn off the Add Path button. The next step is to add three scale keys to the eyelash cone to make it

short in the corner of the eye, long when it is above the center of the eye, and short again when it gets to the opposite corner of the eye.

9. Turn on Auto Key, select Uniform Scale, and click on the eyelash. Scale it down slightly to set a scale key at frame 0. Move the Time Slider to Frame 50, and scale the eyelash up about 40 to 50% to set a second scale key. Move to frame 100 and set a third scale key to reduce the eyelash to the same size as at frame 0. Now scrub the Time Slider and the eyelash should scale up and down. The next step is to snapshot copies of the eyelash all along the eyelash spline.
10. Click Tools > Snapshot, and in the Snapshot dialog, turn on Range. Set Number of Copies to 42 and press OK. You should now see 42 eyelashes evenly spaced along the upper eyelid, as shown in Figure 9.26, example 5. The last step is to delete the original eyelash, and then repeat Steps 7–10 for the lower eyelash spline. Make the lower eyelashes slightly shorter than the upper eyelashes.
11. When all eyelashes are done, unfreeze the head mesh. In order to animate the eyelid closing with the eyelashes, you must attach all of the eyelashes to the head mesh. Only then can you create a Morph Target of the head

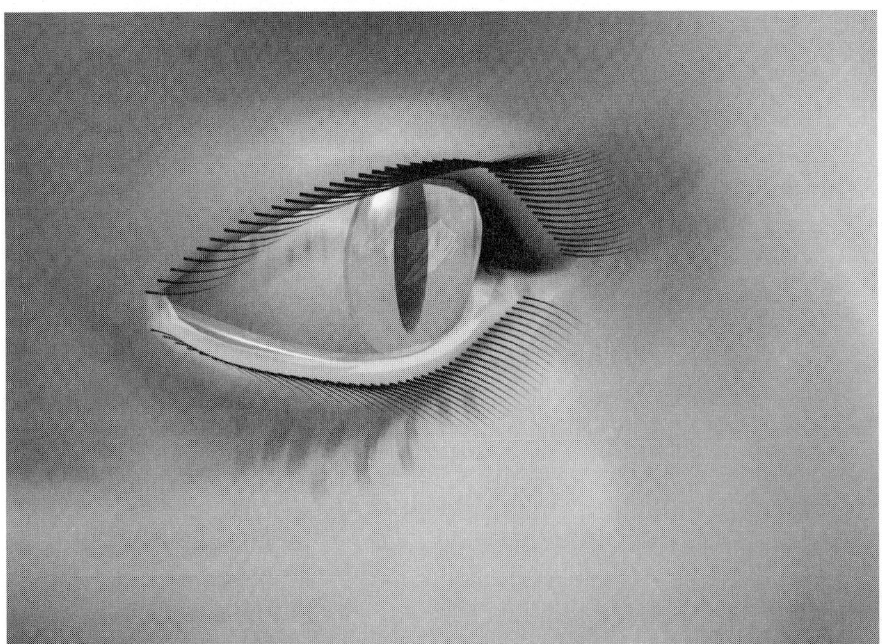

FIGURE 9.27 Rendering of Xzulixia eye with eyelashes.

that will move the eyelashes. All Morph Targets must include all of the eyelashes in order for this process to work correctly, as shown in Figure 9.27. For information on making morph target heads for closing the eye, see Chapter 8, Tutorial 8.8, "Sculpting Facial Morph Targets."

12. Save the file as Eye911.max.

ON THE CD

To see the results of this tutorial, load the XzuEyeBlink.avi movie from the Chap09\Extras folder on the companion CD-ROM. This model would be appropriate only for close-up shots. You could reduce the number of lashes and increase their thickness to reduce the polygon count. There is no reason to use this many individual eyelashes on a model that never gets closer to the camera than a medium or distant shot. For a lower-resolution model, use a flat, mesh plane eyelash object mapped to a picture of eyelashes, and use only upper eyelashes.

Conclusion

In this chapter, you animated the Dr. Quin model sitting at a desk and answering the telephone. You created a lip-sync facial animation using facial morph targets that were synchronized to a dialog soundtrack. You animated a walk cycle with the Dr. Quin model, and then re-sized the same skeleton and bound the Xzulixia model to it with the Skin Modifier. Then you created a realistic eye for Xzulixia. In the next chapter, you will integrate characters into a pre-built scene, animate the character, and add particle and atmospheric visual effects.

CHAPTER

10

SCENE ANIMATION

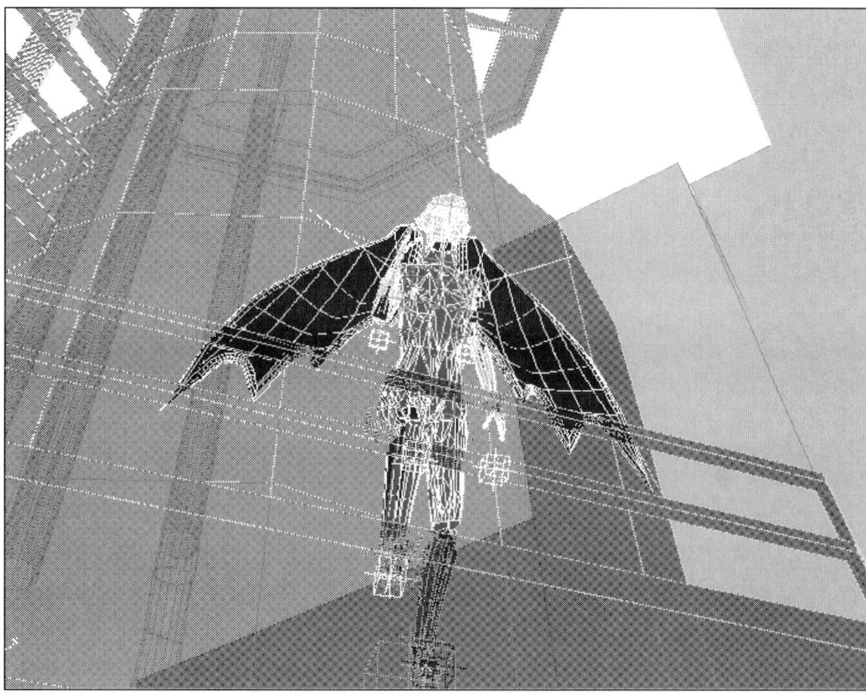

The process of bringing together your models and characters with the environments to create a complete scene is complex, but satisfying. In this chapter, you will animate a character in a scene. However, the environment does not need to be complete or finished before you animate. In fact, it is usually more convenient to bring in only the bare essentials of the environment until the animation is nearly finished. That way, you only have to deal with those things that are most important to the scene. Once the character is animated, you can merge in the rest of the environment and the props to complete scene. Then it will be ready for lighting and rendering.

This chapter is a bit different because it is part tutorials and part overview of the animated filmmaking process. A number of explanations take you through the workflow used to animate the characters in an attack-and-chase action scene. Tutorials are placed at important points where a simple explanation does not cover the topic.

The scene discussed here is an excerpt from the *Homing Instinct* script. It is a sequence called the Vampire Ambush and Chase. The action starts with an ambush where Dr. Quin and Xzulixia are cornered in an alley by vigilante assassins. During the attack, Dr. Quin is injured and Xzulixia is forced to flee. Then, the scene turns into a chase that moves down the back alleys and ends in a chemical refinery. The climax comes as Xzulixia escapes and the refinery explodes. The environment for the Vampire Ambush and Chase sequence is an industrial section of Titan City consisting of a number of industrial buildings with narrow streets and alleys, and a chemical refinery, as shown in Figure 10.1.

The industrial buildings for the chase scene were built from box primitives that have been texture mapped, with only a few doors to keep the polygon count as low as possible. The chemical refinery is a modified version of the stock model called Piping.max that comes with your copy of 3ds max 6 on the second CD-ROM entitled "Training and Learning." It can be found in the Model Library\Misc folder. It has been simplified and incorporated into the setting, and then scaled to match the buildings constructed by the author and the vampire character model. The helicopter is a stock model from an earlier version of the Model Library that shipped with 3ds max 2.5, and has been extensively modified to modernize it, change its profile, and add a spotlight and a machine gun. The streets of the surrounding area are made from plane primitive objects.

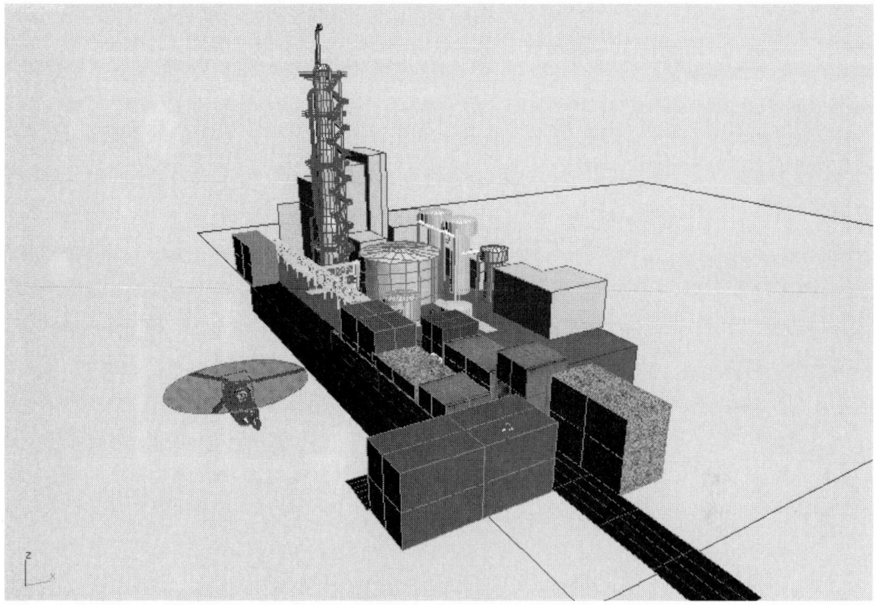

FIGURE 10.1 The environment for the Vampire Ambush and Chase sequence.

To see the action from different viewpoints as you animate, a number of cameras have been placed in the environment for you, as shown in Figure 10.2. Because it is an action sequence, a number of quick camera cuts and close-up shots will be most effective to maintain a high level of visual excitement, and to show the best views of the visual effects. The Video Post module in 3ds max is used to switch between cameras during the rendering of the scene. Switching cameras is discussed in Tutorial 10.2.

The entire scene including the model of the vampire contains just over 70,000 polygons (faces). This means that the scene will be comparatively easy to handle in 3ds max, and should not slow down your computer too much. When a scene contains upwards of 150,000 to 350,000 polygons, and includes cloth, hair, particles, transparency, fog, and Radiosity, as many of the other scenes in *Homing Instinct* do, computer performance is noticeably slower. Many scenes are so large that they must be broken into smaller sections, and then animated and rendered as separate layers. They can be put back together later by compositing.

If you were to try to animate the Vampire Ambush and Chase scene in its high-resolution version with clothing, hair, and all of the props, it is likely that the Time Slider would be very sluggish and perhaps not move.

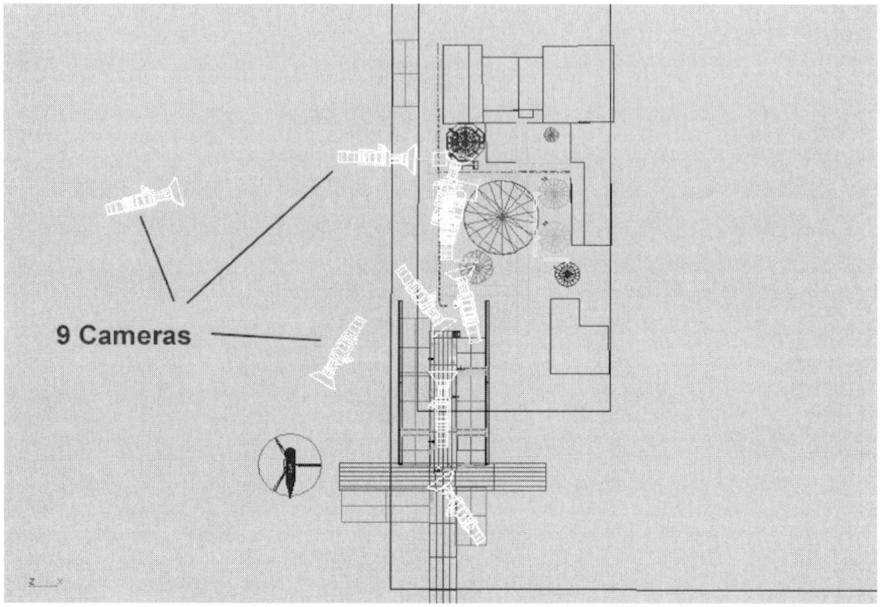

FIGURE 10.2 Many cameras are used to follow the action.

The computer refresh seems to freeze while it calculates a new change, and you must wait while 3ds max finishes calculating. If you don't wait, and try to force 3ds max to finish, you risk a nonrecoverable crash. If you can afford it, get the fastest computer available loaded with RAM, or learn to be patient. You can always go get a cup of coffee while you wait for the system to refresh.

Making a Low-Resolution Proxy Skin for Xzulixia

If you want to use your own models in the scene, here are some guidelines on how to create a low-resolution Proxy skin for the characters. There are a couple of ways to make a low-resolution version of the Xzulixia character body mesh. The simplest way is to turn off the Mesh Smooth Modifier, which results in a low-resolution mesh. The problem with that is that every time you re-load the scene, it comes in with MeshSmooth turned on again, and you are still using RAM calculating the Skin joints and deformations. Another way is to make a snapshot of the high-resolution model and then cut it into smaller sections that are then linked to the skeleton as if they were primitive objects. The advantage of this method is that the character looks a lot like the finished version, yet it uses a minimum of computer resources and moves quickly in the viewport. This is because the Skin Modifier is removed and is not making any calculations or binding the skin to the bones. All of the characters in *Homing Instinct* were animated with this type of Proxy skin mesh.

To convert your skin mesh to a cut-up Proxy skin: Open your model in a front view. Select the Xzulixia body mesh in the bind pose. Use the Tools > Snapshot command to clone the mesh. The result is an editable mesh with all of the modifiers removed, and it is in the same position as the original skin. Once that is done, delete the original skin. Next, the Snapshot clone body is cut into pieces so that all the mesh in the joint areas can be removed, which is done by selecting and deleting rings of polygons, as shown in Figure 10.3, examples 1 and 3.

This results in an number of sections of the model. These sections are then detached as separate pieces and re-named. For example, the upper leg piece is named XProx RUpleg. The skeleton is unhidden, but the Helpers (control points) are hidden. The finger sections and hand are replaced with very simple capsule primitives so that the hand could be seen

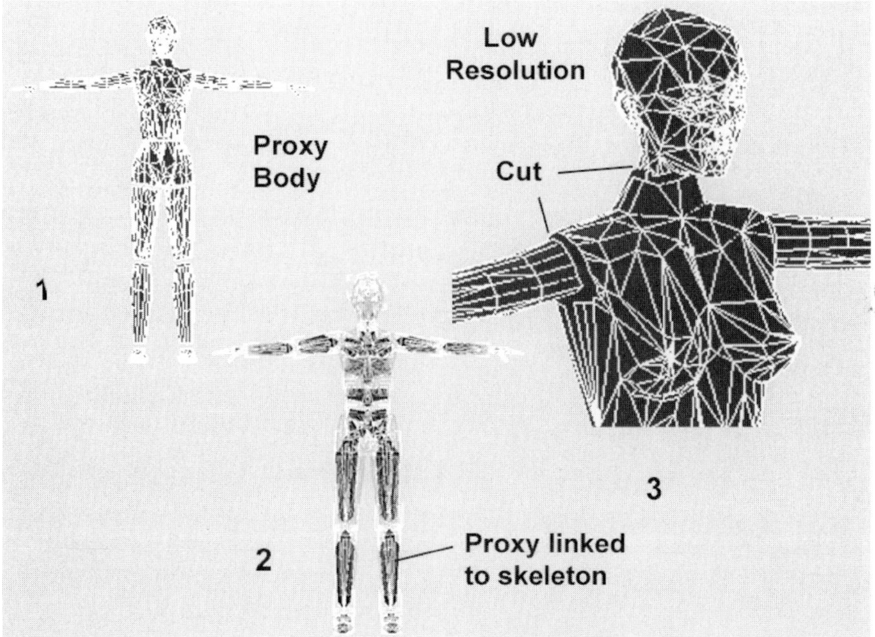

FIGURE 10.3 Linking the low-polygon Proxy body to the skeleton.

in the render. This form of hand is called a "Tootsie Roll™" mesh because it resembles the famous candy. Finally, the pieces of the mesh and the finger capsules are linked individually to the appropriate bones of the Xzulixia skeleton, as shown in Figure 10.3, example 2.

Once the Proxy body is linked to the skeleton, it can be animated easily as long as you keep the original body mesh hidden at all times. The polygon count for the original mesh is 12,520. The Proxy body polygon count is 9,524, which is not much lower. However, the real saving in speed and memory comes from the fact that the Proxy body does not require any Skin calculations, while still giving you the illusion that the body is there. You can tell more about how the character moves when you can see some type of body, rather than simply moving bones.

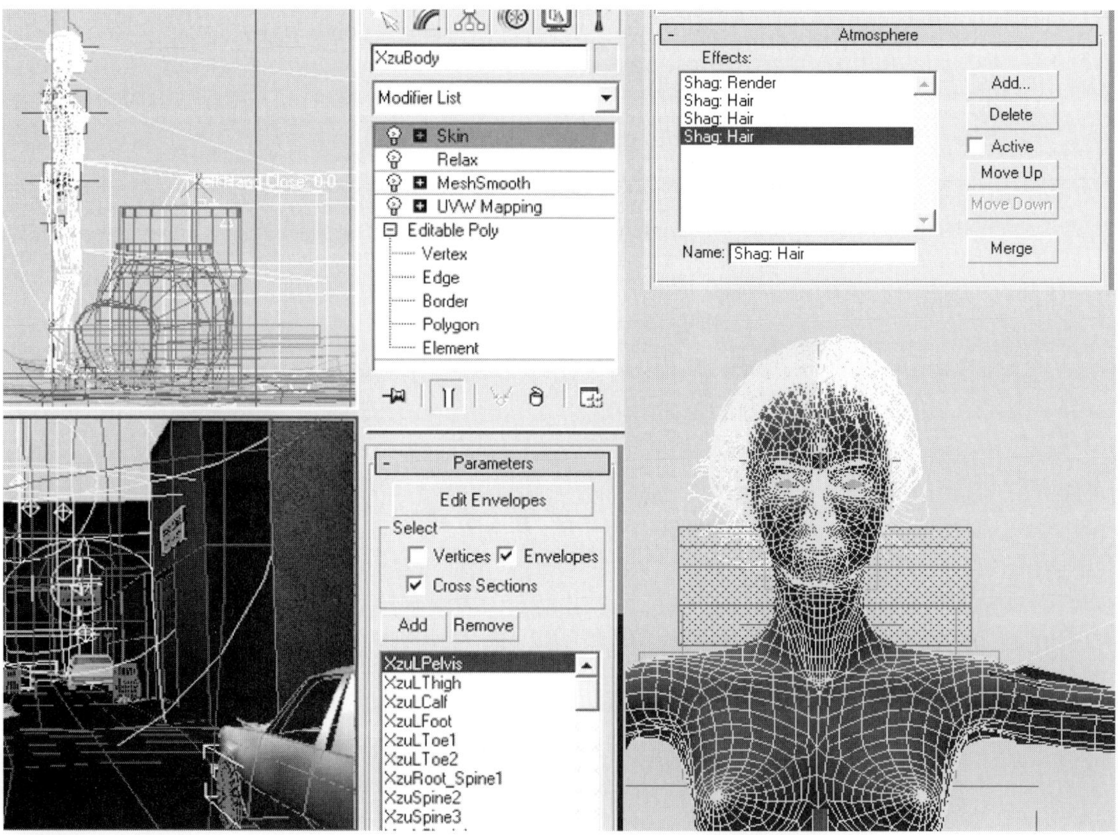

FIGURE 10.4 Remove Shag Hair entries and collapse the Stack to remove Skin.

A very important saving in computer resources comes from temporarily deleting the Shag Hair Renderer and Shag Hair emitters, as shown in Figure 10.4. Shag Hair takes a substantial bite out of the computer speed, so it is best to delete it, not just turn it off, while doing the animation. As long as you keep the scalp emitter, the model hairs, and record any special settings in a previous file, you can easily restore it later by merging them into your current file. When you work on this scene, which is meant to be a pre-visualization scene of the animation, you should not have any memory-intensive plug-ins running.

THE STORY

Homing Instinct is a vampire film, and true to that genre, during the story the frightened citizens send vigilante assassins to attack the vampire and kill it. However, Xzulixia, the beautiful female vampire, is also an alien with her own high-tech weapons, and is harder to kill than the traditional vampires seen on TV or in old Dracula movies.

Presented here is an excerpt from the *Homing Instinct* script that covers the alley attack and the explosion of the chemical refinery. To get an idea of what will be needed in the way of visual effects, read this excerpt from the *Homing Instinct* script before doing the tutorials in Chapter 11, "Visual Effects."

Excerpt from the *Homing Instinct* script:

Homing Instinct: Vampire Ambush and Chase

By Sanford Kennedy

Exterior – Night – A back alley in an industrial section of Titan city.

A taxi turns the corner and enters a small alley, coming to a stop by a lighted door beneath a sign that reads "Land Skimmers." Dr Quin and Xzulixia get out and pay the driver. At they turn toward the door, the taxi backs up quickly, and speeds away. Dr. Quin watches it in puzzlement.

Dr. Quin

That's strange.

They go up to the door and knock, but nobody answers.

Dr. Quin

Something is wrong. Boyd is supposed to be here. Let's go.

They turn and start to walk out of the alley, but two men enter the alley and start to walk toward them. Then, a car appears and screeches to a halt, blocking the entrance to the alley.

Xzu

Quin... trouble.

The two men stop walking. One of them holds up a large cross on a chain and yells.

Assassin

Abomination!

Both men start firing automatic machine pistols. Xzu and Dr. Quin dive to the ground and take cover behind a dumpster and a collection of trash cans. The assailants move into the alley firing bursts. One throws a hand grenade that blows a number of trash cans into the air, lighting the dumpster on fire.

Behind the dumpster. Doc is hit in the forehead by flying fragments and blood runs down his face. He falls back unconscious.

Xzu lets out a cry of anguish, then begins to morph into her Vampire form. As her face changes shape, she pulls out her tube beam weapon and enables it.

She rolls out from cover and shoots the closer of the two men in the stomach as he is about to throw another grenade. It goes off in his hand as the beam cuts him in half with a puff of steam, removing his middle. The other one yells.

Assassin

My God, Billy!

He dives for cover in the space between two buildings. He emerges and screams in rage.

Assassin

I'll get you!

He starts spraying the alley with bullets.

Xzu dodges behind the burning dumpster, slides the control on her beam tube to full, it beeps, and she fires. The whole corner of the building where the gunman was hiding disintegrates with a loud crackle as part of the concrete wall falls on him.

Sirens can be heard drawing closer and a helicopter comes swooping in overhead with a spotlight. Xzu, now in her full demonic vampire form, bends over and starts to lift the unconscious doctor up onto her shoulder. Suddenly, the door opposite her opens and a big man steps out. He points a shotgun at her and fires, hitting her in the back. She drops Dr. Quin and faces her assailant. He shoots her again in the stomach. Xzu is forced to flee. She snarls at the man and sprints away down the alley. He shoots again and misses.

The helicopter searchlight catches her as she runs. A machine gun shoots at her from the helicopter, but Xzu is too fast and escapes down another alley running toward the gate at the end that leads to Titan Chemical Refinery.

The helicopter follows close behind. She stops at the gate just long enough to tear it from its hinges, and then sprints past the startled security guard as the helicopter gives chase. The helicopter almost catches her, but has to pull back because of the wires and chimneys of the refinery.

Xzu enters the maze of tanks and pipes, then slumps to the ground to rest and look at the wound in her stomach. It is already starting to heal. After a moment, she hears yelling coming close, and the barking of dogs. She is troubled. She gets up, runs along one of the maintenance roads between the massive chemical tanks, and then turns down a smaller path that leads toward the Cracking Tower

A moment later, six armed men and three leashed dogs emerge and stop where she rested. The dogs let out a howl and strain to be let loose.

Leader

They got the scent. Let 'em loose!

The dogs yelp and bay as they are released to dash off after Xzulixia. The men run to follow with their guns drawn.

As Xzu runs, she begins to hear the sound of the dogs baying behind her. The expression on her face changes and her eyes change from blue to reddish-yellow. She begins to morph again as she runs. The strain of shape changing is sapping her energy, but she is desperate. She heads toward metal stairs leading up the side of the Cracking Tower.

She bounds up the stairs to the first landing, and then rips off her shredded blouse. She flexes her shoulders and takes a deep breath. A bulge appears behind her shoulders as she rapidly changes shape. Her shoulders extend higher, her chest grows deeper, her legs shrink, and dark wings unfold from her back. She is panting hard trying to force the change. She tears away more of the cloth on her body and we see that even her skin is changing from pink skin to a scaly gray hide.

The three dogs sprint around the corner of the tank below her and streak for the stairway where she is standing. She looks down at them and they see her. She growls at them and they go mad with barking, coming after her. She turns, flaps her wings twice, and then dives off the landing and into the air.

The dogs reach the landing as she takes flight. One of them is so excited that it falls off. The men come around the corner in time to see the dog falling. The owner of the dog curses and yells.

Gunman

My dog!

Another gunman points to the shadow shape wheeling out of sight among the tall pipes of the Cracking Tower.

2nd Gunman

There it is!

The first gunman raises his assault rifle and fires a sweeping burst. The bullets ricochet from the pipes and spray in all directions. The gunmen duck to avoid being hit. Many bullets have pierced the tanks and pipes around them, causing steam and liquids to start pouring out.

Too late, the leader slaps down the rifle.

Leader

No! you idiot. That's gasoline!
This whole place will blow up!

At that moment, a low rumble and a heavy whomp! comes from the Cracking Tower. A ball of fire rises followed by a dozen spouts of flame spewing from the bullet holes. A thin stream of fire and raw gasoline sprays from a bullet hole in the tank next to them.

Leader

Run!

Suddenly, the tank erupts in a huge explosion and fireball, and engulfs the men.

From a distance, the tanks and towers of the chemical plant explode, lighting up the night sky and narrowly missing the helicopter, which veers away wildly.

In a close slot of a dark cloud we see Xzulixia emerge from the smoke, coughing and flapping her wings laboriously, working hard to stay aloft and escape. She passes the camera and heads out into the darkness toward the distant moon that is just rising above the peaks of the mountains, outlining her as a dark silhouette.

End of scene.

SETTING UP A SCENE

The first tutorial deals with the Vampire Chase sequence. We pick up the chase at the point when Xzulixia, now in her flightless demon vampire form, is fleeing down a back street from a helicopter with a searchlight and a machine gun. Bullets strafe the alley behind her as she sprints around a corner and heads down another alley. At the end of the alley is a tall gate made of steel bars that leads to the Maintenance Section of the Titan Chemical Refinery. In the distance is the massive Cracking Tower where gasoline and fuel oil are made.

She enters the refinery, and finds a place to rest to induce the shape change to her winged vampire form. This change involves a morph of the body mesh from human to semi-bat-like through a shape change, growing wings. The climax comes after she climbs the Cracking Tower and tries to fly away.

The first storyboard image shows Xzulixia running in the helicopter searchlight beam with bullets hitting the ground behind her heels, as shown in Figure 10.5.

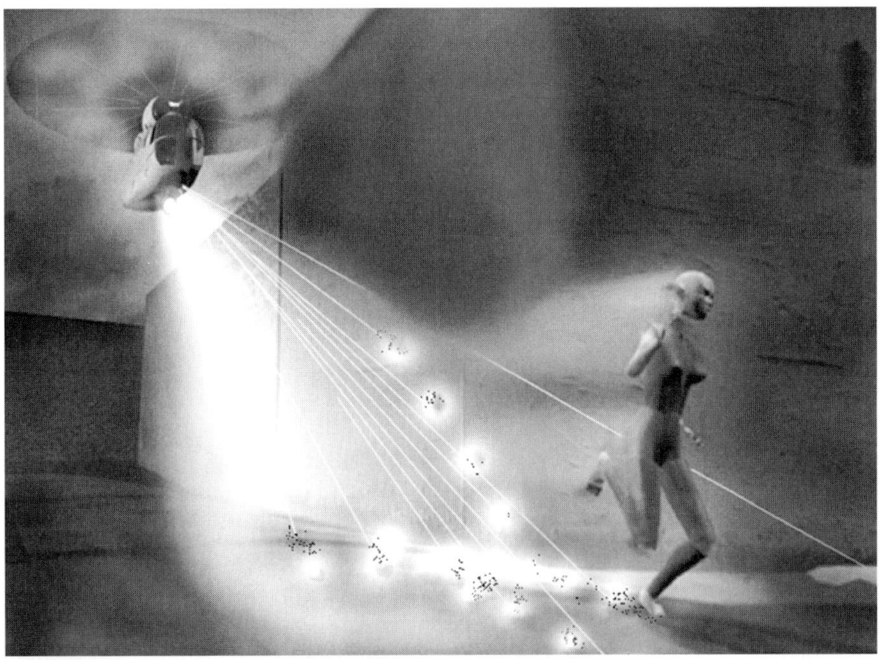

FIGURE 10.5 Storyboard for the Vampire Chase sequence.

The first task in building the scene is to animate the Xzulixia Vampire model running along the alley to escape the pursuing helicopter (Figure 10.6).

To plan the running gate and to insure that the feet do not slide on the ground, stride length boxes are used to plot the footfalls of the character motion (Figure 10.7).

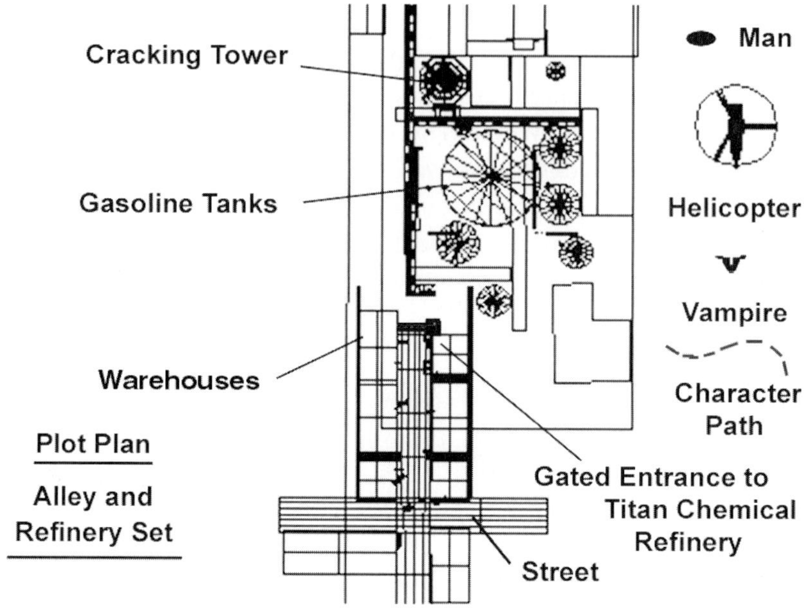

FIGURE 10.6 The plot plan of the virtual set.

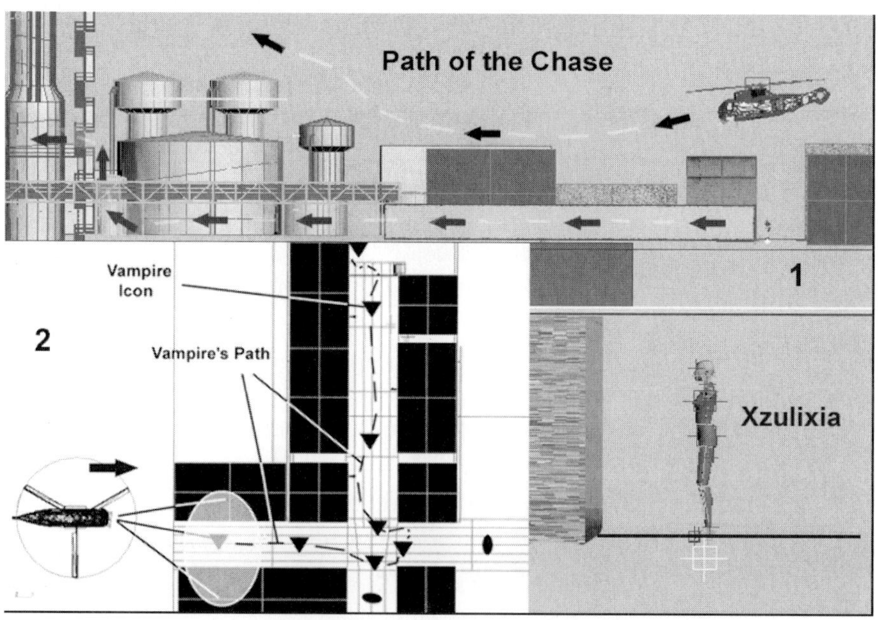

FIGURE 10.7 Left view of the refinery set with two planned motion paths.

THE FIRST ANIMATION

A spline is drawn first to plot the footfalls of the run. Use the running stride length boxes to measure a string of strides along the vampire motion path. Then, the stride lengths are put on the path according to the changes in speed and direction of the running character. The gait is the type of movement it is. For instance, a running gait would have the weight shifted forward, as shown in Figure 10.8. This position can be called controlled falling. The body falls forward and the legs stride forward to keep the body upright. The angle of the torso helps the viewer anticipate the direction of the character.

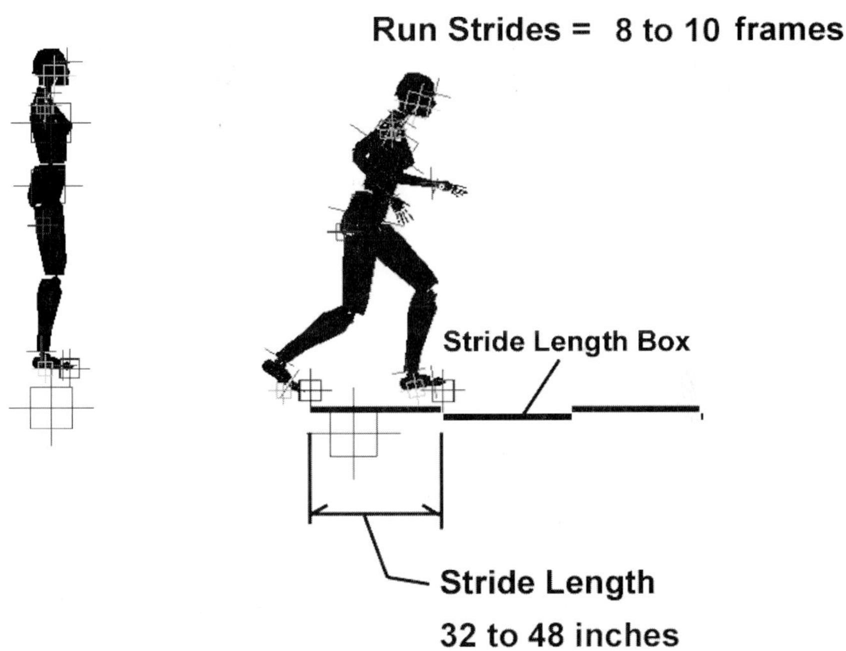

FIGURE 10.8 Determining the stride length of the run.

Each type of run is different. A specific manner of running can indicate the emotional and physical state of the character. The level of the emergency in the stride can also supply information about the character fatigue, or whether it is wounded. The aim is always to portray the emotion of the moment in the character's reactions. The run stride length is approximately 32 to 48 inches from front toe to back toe, or 3- to 4-foot lengths.

This project has been scaled to about 4.7 times life size to get better control over hair and cloth, so dimensions in the tutorial will not match the real world without the multiplication factor applied.

Body language, poses, and arm gestures have become the primary method of getting a performance even when the character is running for its life. Using the character rig, which can be modified to mix subtle movements, you can gain detailed control over the animated performance. By paying continuous attention to the curve and the angle of the spine, you can read a person. By simulating foot weight, body mass, flesh jiggle, and weight compression of the skeleton, you can duplicate all of the body's movements. When this happens, the audience will recognize a familiar motion, which will result in making the character look real, even if it is shaped like a dinosaur with wings.

The path that Xzulixia follows takes her into different alleys where men confront her with shotguns. She dodges away with a burst of speed and gets past them, and then heads down the alley that leads to the refinery. The helicopter tries to stop her, but misses with the machine gun.

The plot plan of the Running Vampire's path can be printed out in duplicates for plotting moves with a pencil, as shown in Figure 10.9. The paper is then trimmed to fit a Wacom 6 × 8 inch tablet, and inserted under the acetate paper guard of the Wacom tablet. The stylus is used to trace the path into 3ds max.

To create the stride length markers for the run path, the vampire run path drawing was loaded into the top viewport background with the alley warehouses and the Vampire model. Then, the background image and the alley model were aligned. Next, the alley set was hidden, leaving only the Vampire model and a few stride length markers, as shown in Figure 10.10, examples 1 through 4. At this point, you are ready to create the actual stride path by cloning markers that follow the drawn motion path.

Laying out the path with alternating left and right stride markers allows you to plan the move and know exactly where each footfall will be placed. You cannot simply clone the run cycle keys, because the vampire is being shot at and she has to bob and weave. Using the same type of gait for all strides would look very artificial. This is especially true in the cor-

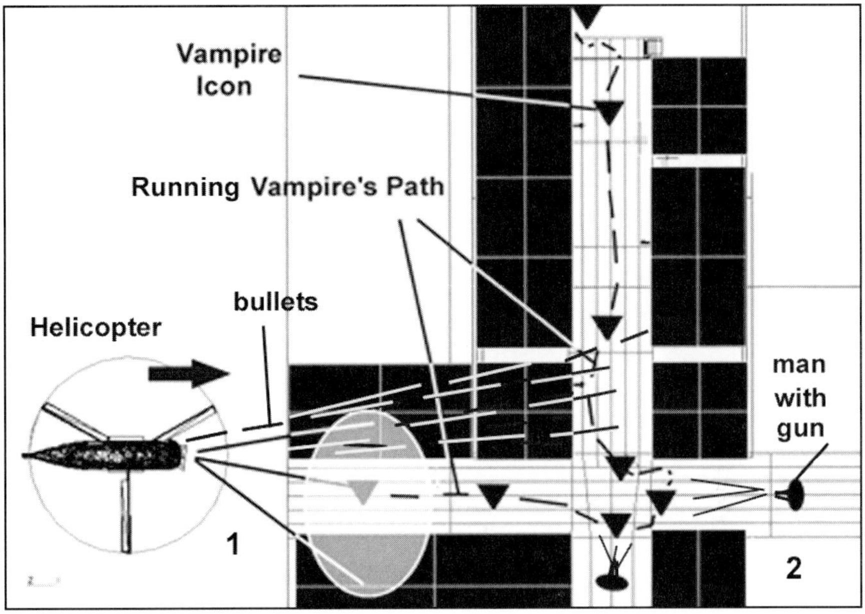

FIGURE 10.9 The run path on the plot plan with gunmen blocking the alleys.

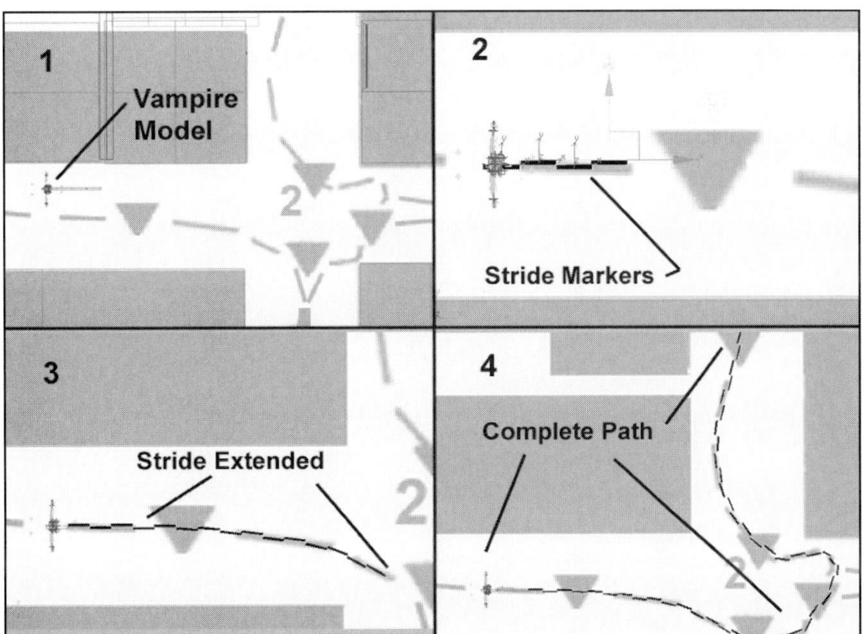

FIGURE 10.10 Path image in viewport background ready for stride length markers.

ners where she reverses direction and her stride length changes. Therefore, while the "pasting pose to pose" animation concept is very useful in theory, where the run is frantic and her direction is varying wildly, pose to pose is not the correct choice. You will have to animate every stride. However, you can successfully paste the keys that apply to the joint rotations of the rig to save a considerable amount of animation time.

To animate the rig in the run cycle, you need to pay attention to a number of joints, control points, and end effectors. This is not a difficult process once you understand the logic of the foot and ankle movement, and the counter-rotation of the hips and shoulders. In the following tutorial, you will animate the Xzulixia skeleton rig in a fast run cycle.

TUTORIAL 10.1

ANIMATING THE SKELETON RIG IN A FAST RUN CYCLE

To animate a run cycle:

ON THE CD

1. Load the Alien1000.max scene file from the Chap10 folder on the companion CD-ROM. Maximize the left view.
2. Turn on Auto Key and Animate the Character Control in the left view to move forward one long running stride length every nine frames, as shown in Figure 10.11. Make sure you align the toe control point centers with the ends of the stride markers to lock in the foot positions.
3. Set the computer Key to Key transition type to Linear to prevent the feet from sliding. Do that by clicking Customize > Preferences > Animation. Then, in Controller Defaults, click Set Defaults > Bézier float, and when the Bézier Default Key Values dialog opens, click and hold the left mouse button and select Linear for both In and Out key transitions, as shown in Figure 10.12. Then click OK, and OK. Now no keys will be averaged, and every control point will go exactly where you put it. You can smooth selected keys later.
4. Translate and rotate the character control in the top view to keep the model centered on the stride markers and headed down the path. Then, create the first part of the stride animation by reversing the forward and back foot positions on every stride. This will create alternating foot keys at every stride. After you do all of the foot reversals, go back over all of the rear foot positions and add the heel lift and rotation, and set the Support Position keys so that the feet do not slide once a key has been set. If you

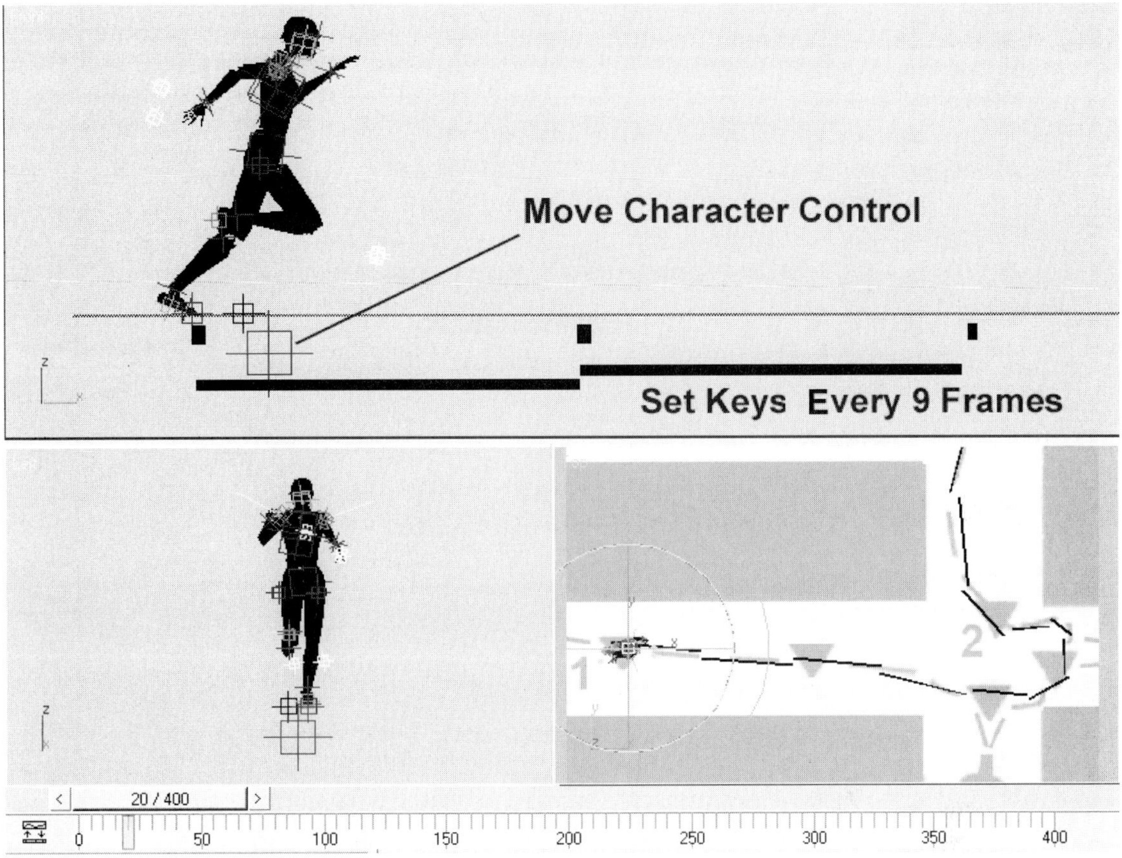

FIGURE 10.11 Setting basic stride keys.

need to review setting these foot keys, see Tutorial 9.7, "Animating a Walk Cycle" in Chapter 9.

5. Turn on Motion > Trajectories to see the path of any selected object. Then, animate the Hip control so it moves up and down every 4 to 5 frames—down when one leg is passing the other and up when the feet are spread apart the farthest from each other, as shown in Figure 10.13.
6. For a better-looking run, narrow the width between the feet so the ankles almost touch as they pass each other, turn off Auto Key, and then, looking at the front of the model, move the LFoot Control and the RFoot Control closer together, as shown in Figure 10.14.
7. Add hip and shoulder rotations that move the opposite of each other to maintain balance. Animate the arm rotations so they swing far backward

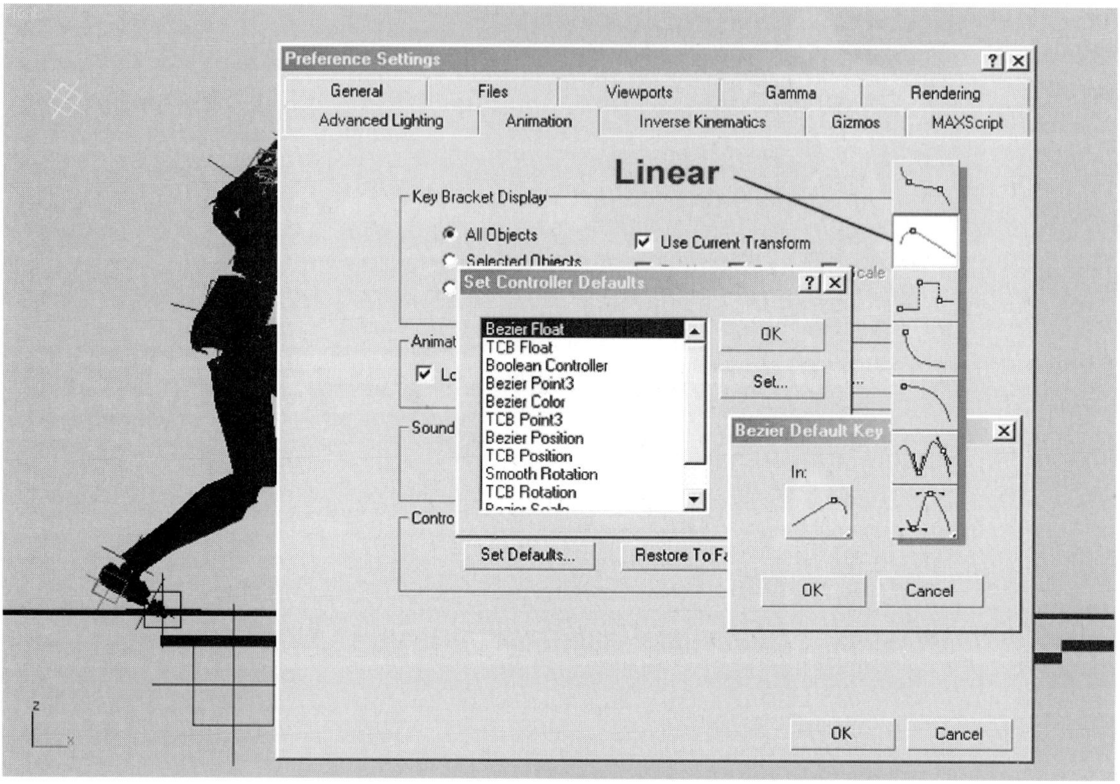

FIGURE 10.12 Setting the default Bézier Animation Controller to Linear type key transitions.

and forward. The top of the forward swing of the hand should be quite high, which will streak when motion blur is applied, and is meant to indicate the speed of a sprint, as shown in Figure 10.15.

8. Add body bob and compressions with each footfall by using the Chest Control to move the chest and shoulders down each time a foot hits the ground, and then move them back upward when the thrust occurs for the next stride. This helps give the body the illusion of weight.
9. Add head movement to anticipate change of direction (looking into the curves), and then lean the body into the direction of motion and turns, as shown in Figure 10.16.
10. Add a reaching forward motion to the shoulders by animating the clavicle bone of the leading shoulder. The arms are thrown high during this type of sprint and pump like pistons when going at top speed. The shoulders must be also affected to look natural.

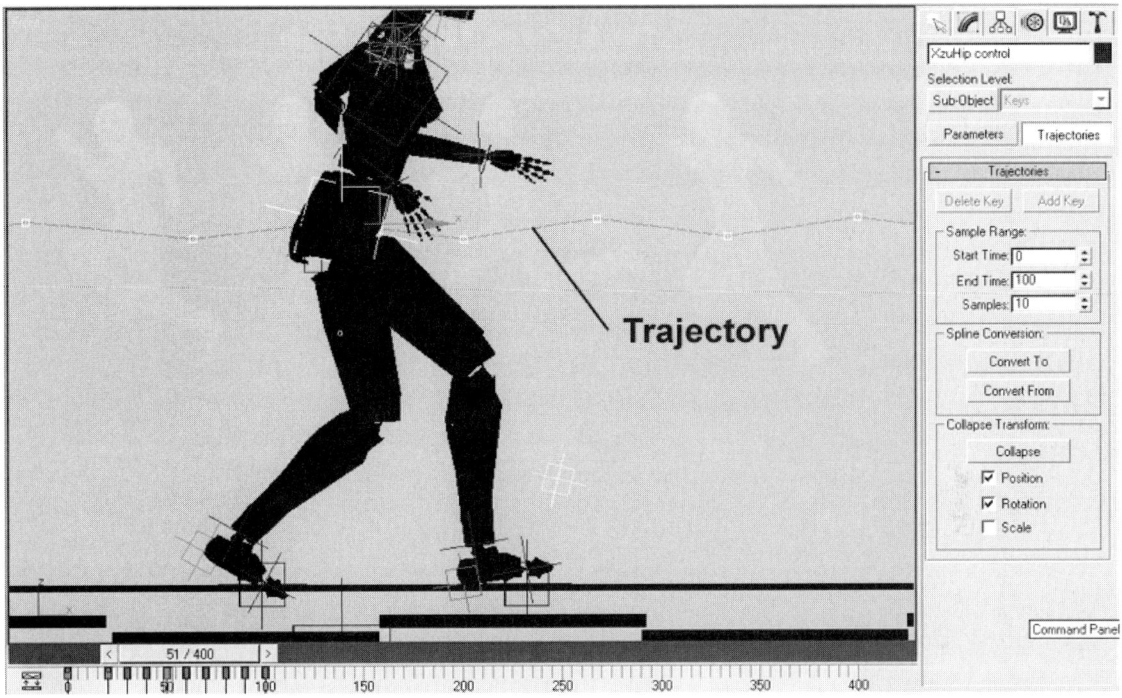

FIGURE 10.13 Animate the hip up and down for every stride.

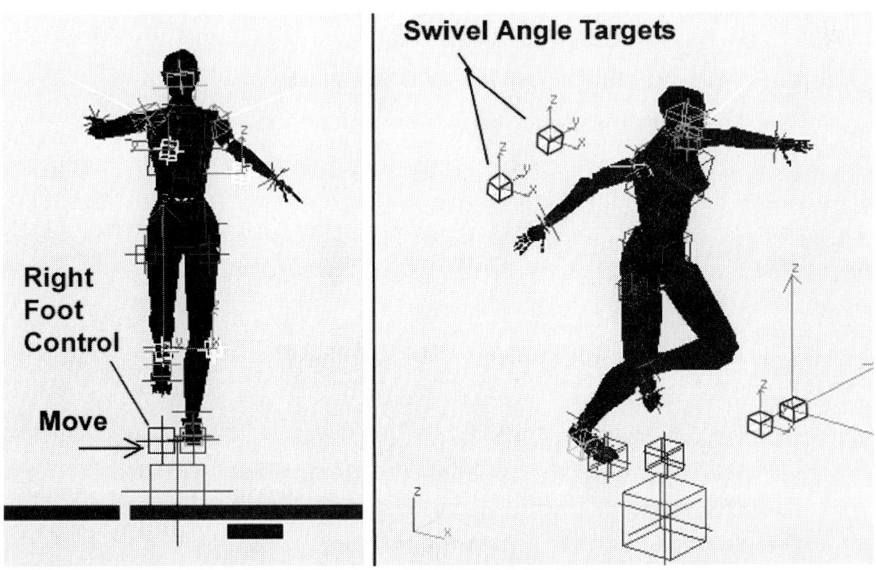

FIGURE 10.14 Adjust distance between the feet and adjust swivel angle targets to control knees.

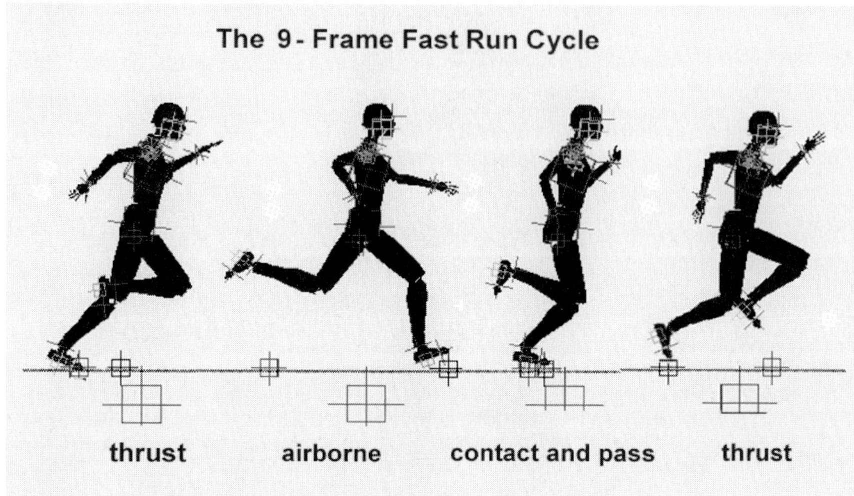

FIGURE 10.15 Adding arm rotations and hand movement.

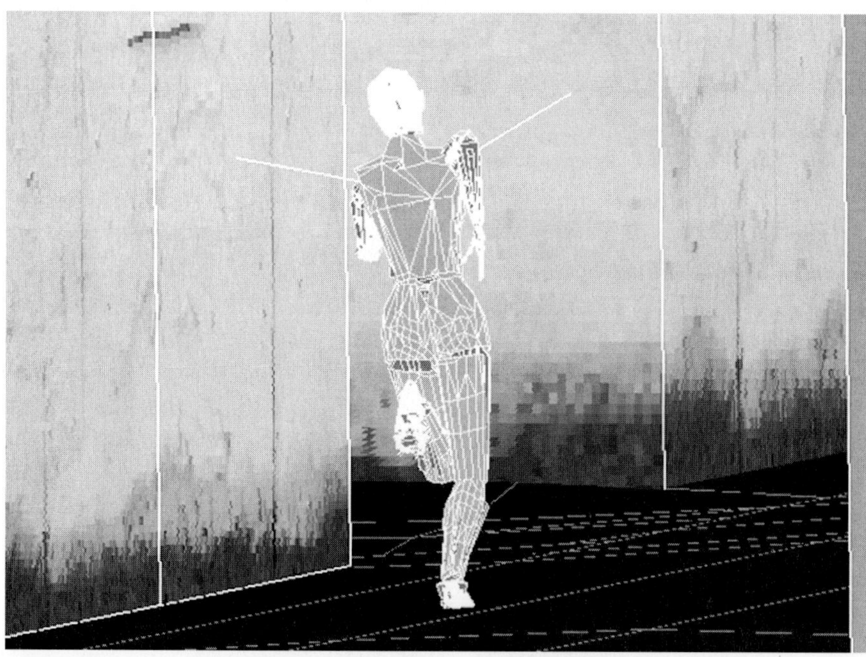

FIGURE 10.16 Leaning the body in the direction of motion and turns.

11. Add hand gestures such as raising both hands in front of the face whenever the character needs to react to a new threat or obstacle in the path. Other gestures would occur when changing balance, or tripping on something, as shown in Figure 10.17.

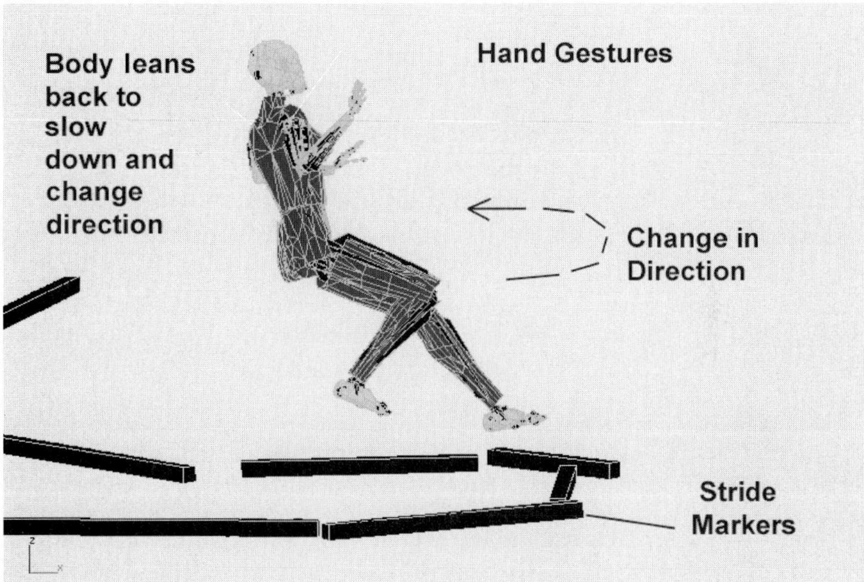

FIGURE 10.17 Hand gestures react to changing balance, surprise, or a barrier.

When a running character encounters a barrier, or in this case, a dangerous threat, the hands will fly up to guard the body and face. The spine will arch back to reverse the direction of the weight. Then, the runner can change direction, as shown in Figure 10.17.

12. A number of cameras are set up to capture the action from the most interesting angles during the chase. Quick cuts between different angles and close-ups are the best way to film a panic flight scene like this one, as shown in Figure 10.18.

Part of the tuning of the action should be done while looking through one or more cameras positioned as they will be when you are going to film and render the scene. If you just animate it and assume it will be okay, you might get an unpleasant surprise later. The lens angles used on the cameras control how much foreshortening and distortion is tolerable in the character. In wide-angle close-up shots, you might get a lot of distortion that will ruin the look of the action. Always set up some cameras and check out how it looks before you finish animating, as shown in Figure 10.18.

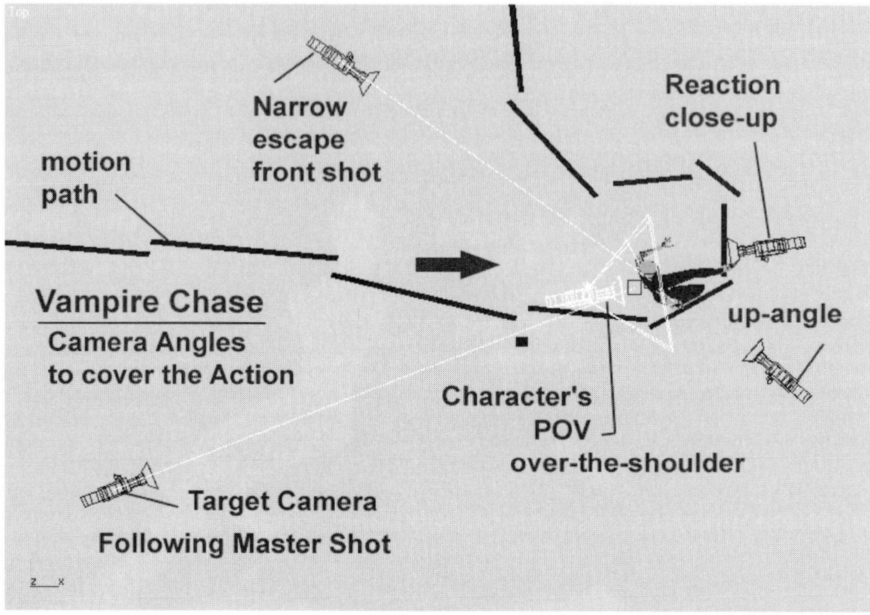

FIGURE 10.18 Setting up cameras to capture the best action and the turning points.

13. Add Image Motion Blur, and then do test renders from different camera angles. Save the scene as Alien1001.max.

This tutorial has brought you to the point where you can add the visual effects to the scene, and then synchronize the character's reactions to the effects and the soundtrack. The sequences are designed to be very fast and violent with maximum impact. This means that there must be a threat that is equal to the fear of the character. That threat comes from assassins in the streets with guns, and a helicopter overhead with a searchlight and a machine gun.

A lot of time is spent planning the scenes. In a visual effects scene like the chase of the vampire into the chemical refinery, it is impossible to choose the best camera angles and moves ahead of time. For this reason, many scenes are pre-visualized to decide how they should be shot. Many of the preferred camera angles are blocked by the buildings along the narrow streets. Camera placement is a real problem in this case because you really can't remove the buildings to get a good camera angle if you want the results to look realistic. However, the scene still has to be exciting to hold the audience's interest, and only by experimentation can you determine how best to place the cameras to shoot it.

MULTIPLE SCENE FILES

There is no advantage to making one continuous long animated scene—that would be a waste of time. The efficient way to make a film is to create everything as separate shots, only building and animating what will be seen and nothing more. Hopefully, you will be able to re-use objects and setups from earlier shots to save time. This is the efficient way of working. It is said that Hollywood is really just hollow building fronts with nothing inside. That is true of most of the stage sets we see in movies. The same concept can be used to save time in computer animation. In *Homing Instinct*, there is a separate scene for the gate-opening sequence, a separate scene for the shape-changing scene, that only contains a piece of the refinery with two tanks, and a separate scene where Xzulixia flies off of the Cracking Tower that does not contain the helicopter or the industrial buildings.

In the next tutorial, link the target of the light to Xzulixia who is trying to get away from the helicopter. Then, you will add cameras to cover the action. You will work with a short section of the helicopter's flight that has previously been animated, along with a sequence strides of Xzulixia sprinting along the street, trying to escape.

TUTORIAL 10.2

HELICOPTER CHASE

ON THE CD

1. Load the AlienCopter.max scene from the Chap10 folder on the companion CD-ROM. Click Unhide All to see the helicopter, which is already animated to move along the street above the vampire Xzulixia. Switch to the front view and maximize the viewport as shown in Figure 10.19.
2. The helicopter should chase the vampire down the street, following close above her. Move the Time Slider to frame 50 where Xzulixia is running. The helicopter should be just above her. Create a target spotlight by clicking on the front of the spotlight mounted on the bottom of the helicopter, and then drag the cursor down to Xzulixia's character control box, as shown in Figure 10.20.
3. Link the target spotlight to the spotlight housing on the helicopter. Link the spotlight target object to the Character Control dummy under Xzulixia. Now the spotlight will follow her.

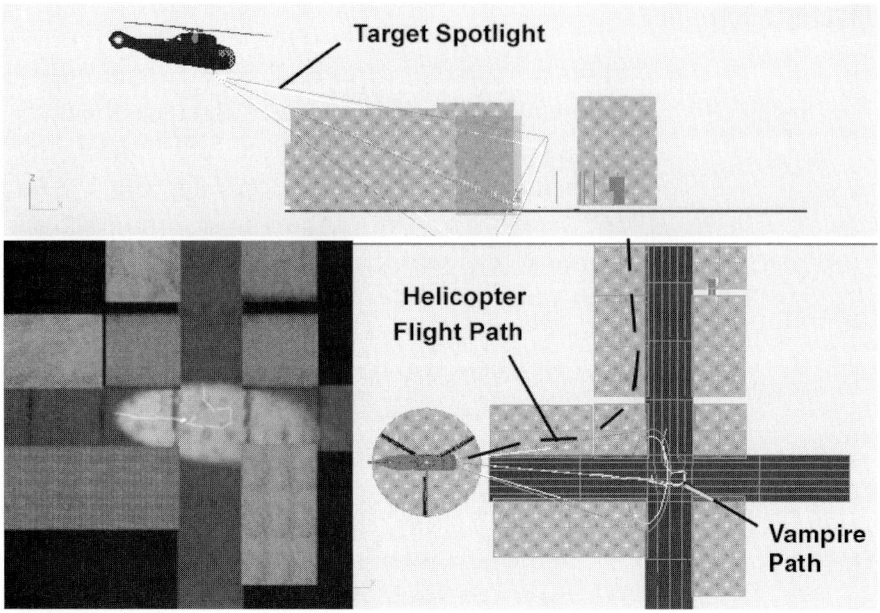

FIGURE 10.19 Flight path of the helicopter.

4. The light direction is now automatically controlled to follow her, but the target spotlight target object should be animated to make it veer away from the vampire for more realism, and give the feeling that she might get away if she can dodge the light.
5. Unhide all of the cameras in the scene. Notice that the cameras have every angle covered. In action sequences, many short cuts between cameras are used. Add a target camera above the helicopter to show a master shot of the character running, and then add a free camera that is linked to the character control dummy, and position it for a close-up of Xzulixia's face so you can cut to a close-up shot for the facial expressions. This should be camera05. You can also add another camera to cover her feet, and hand gestures.
6. Select camera01, which is positioned along the vampire's path. Then, press the C key to switch the viewport to the camera01 view. You should see the vampire running toward you with the helicopter above her. Scrub the Time Slider to see the best frame range to use for this camera angle. The author chose frame 24 to frame 48.
7. Switch to camera02, camera03, camera04, and camera 05 to see how each view has been composed, and to see which frame ranges would work best

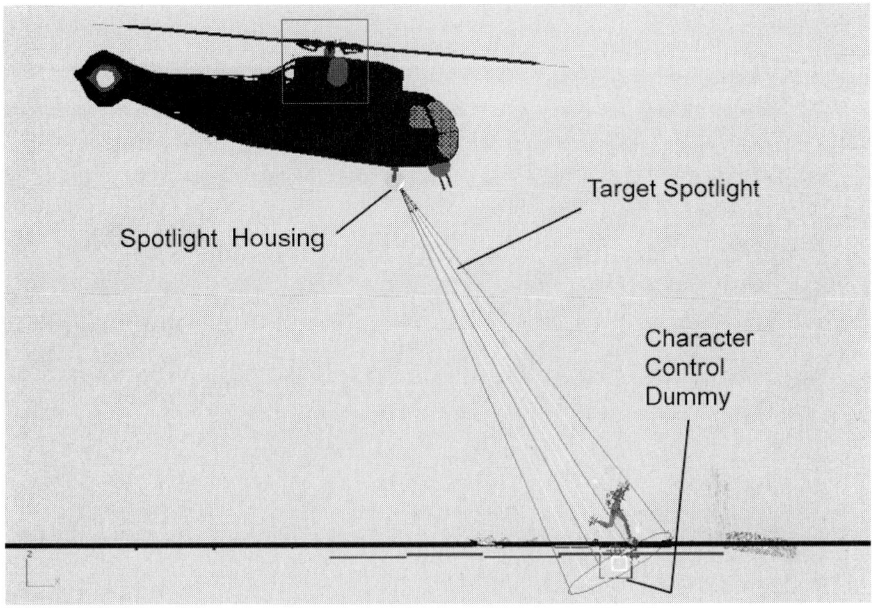

FIGURE 10.20 Adding a target spotlight to follow Xzulixia.

for each camera to make the shot flow with quick cuts of the action. The author chose the following: camera 05 = frame 49 to 60, camera 02 = frame 61 to 78, camera 03 = frame 79 to 94, and camera04 = frame 95 to 115. Enter these frame ranges for each camera in step 9.

8. Test render the scene using Video Post to cut from one camera to the next. To do that, click Rendering > Video Post. The Video Post dialog window has a timeline display with range bars and on the left is the shot Queue. In the row of command icons above the timeline, select the blue Teapot icon to load a camera view, as shown in Figure 10.21, example 1. The range should be automatically set to 400 frames to match the scene.
9. Next, load camera02, 03, 04, and 05 into the video post Queue. Next, select and move camera05 so it is just below camera01 in the Queue. Once all of the cameras are loaded you can set the range of frames that each will use during the test render. In the Queue, click camera01, and then select the Edit Scene Event icon, which is the fourth icon from the left in the video post tool bar. The Edit Scene Event dialog will open.
10. In the Video Post Parameters menu, shown in Figure 10.21, example 2, set VP Start Time to 24 and VP End Time to 48, and then click OK. This is the slow way to set the ranges. Now use the fast way. Select the left end of the camera02 range bar and move it to frame 61, which is shown by the small

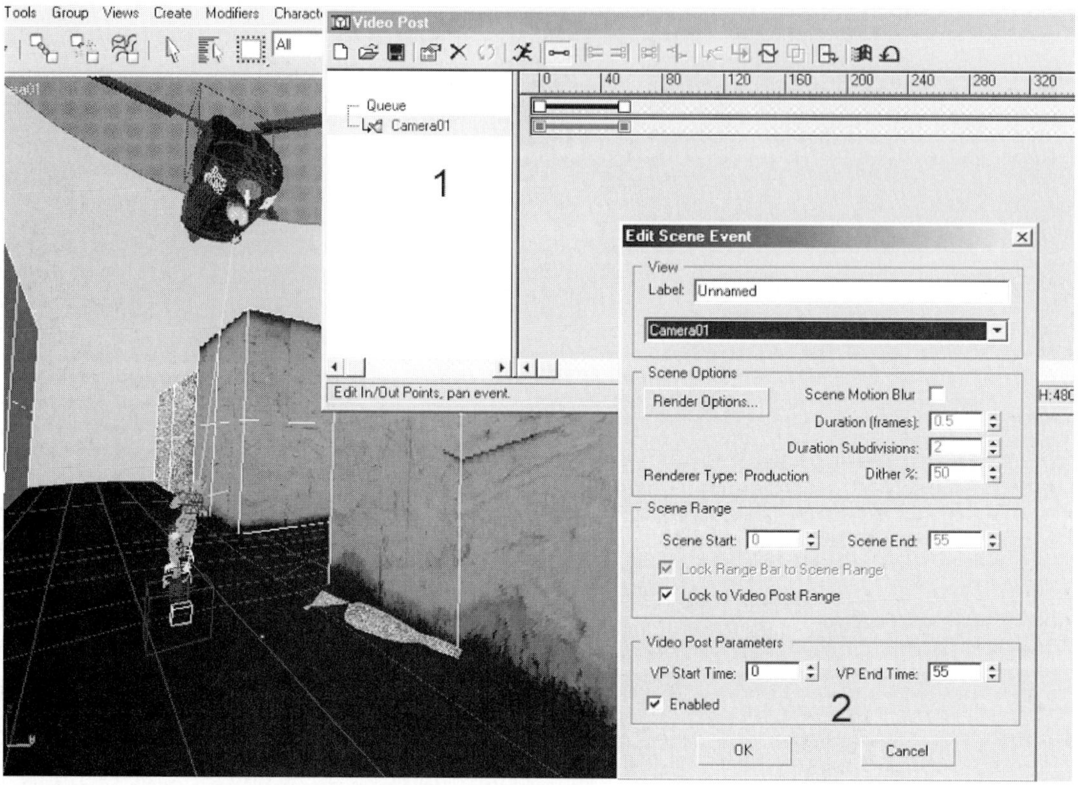

FIGURE 10.21 The Video Post dialog with camera01 in the queue.

window labeled "S:" at the bottom of the video post dialog. Then, select the right end of the range bar and move it to frame 78, which is shown in the small "E:" window.

11. Slide the ends of the range bars for cameras 03, 04, and 05 to the frame numbers as follows: 03 = 79 – 94, 04 = 95 – 115, 05 = 49 – 60, as shown in Figure 10.22, example 1. Next, make sure that no cameras are selected, and then click the Add Image Output Event icon in the video post toolbar, which is the last yellow icon to the right.
12. In the Add Image Output Event dialog that opens, click the Files button, as shown in Figure 10.22, example 2. In the Select Image File for Video Post Output dialog, choose MOV QuickTime File (*.mov) as the Save As type. Then, either select the 3ds max 6 Images directory, or one of your own choosing where you want the text render to go, and then name the file TestRend01.mov, as shown in Figure 10.22, example 3. This will open the Compression Settings dialog, as shown in Figure 10.22, example 4. Select Sorenson Video, with Quality set to Medium, and click OK.

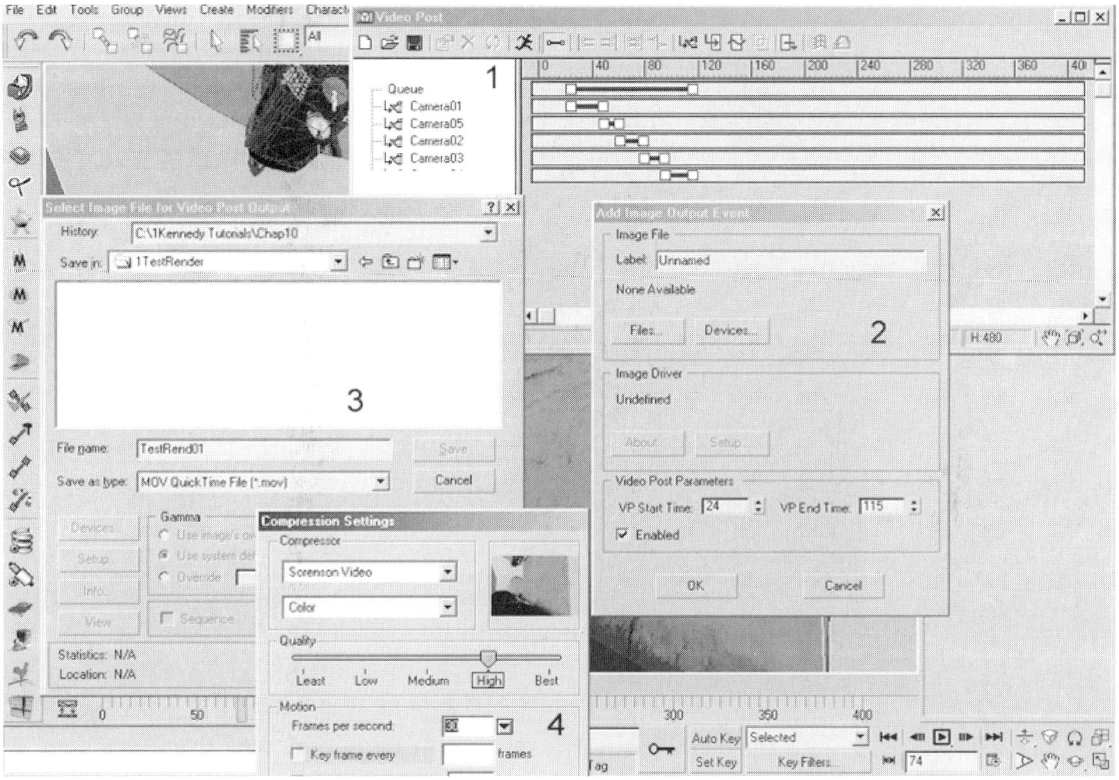

FIGURE 10.22 Setting up the Image Output Event.

13. The name of the output file will now show in the video post queue. To render the camera cut sequence, click the Execute Sequence icon (the running man), and in the Execute Video Post dialog, click Range, as shown in Figure 10.23, example 2. It should automatically show 24 to 115. Then, select 320 × 240 or 640 × 480 if you want a bigger image, and click Render. The sequence will render, switching from camera to camera seamlessly.
14. Play back the TestRend01.mov file by clicking File > View Image file. Each time you adjust the cameras or the animation, re-run the test render to see how it looks. Change things around and change the camera angles to improve the flow of the camera cuts. When you are satisfied, save the file as AlienCopterEnd.max.

The next discussion is an overview of how the remainder of the animation was set up and animated. This entire scene as shown in this chapter is a low-resolution pre-visualization of the final scene animation and

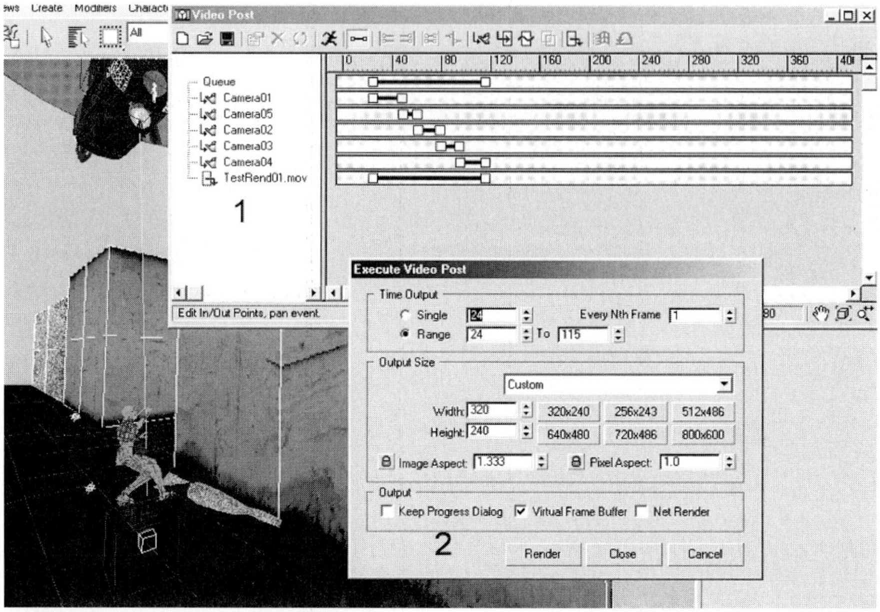

FIGURE 10.23 Test rendering setup to see the multiple camera cuts.

rendering, which will be done at a later time using the high-resolution versions of the models.

Entering the Refinery

When the helicopter chases Xzulixia into the refinery, it has to stop and draw back for fear of hitting some of the power lines or the refinery structure with its rotor. It swoops in at Xzu, but then at the last minute it pulls up and hovers above the tanks, trying to find her with the spotlight, as shown in Figure 10.24.

This setting gives you good opportunities for interesting lighting and structural details, especially when using the Skylight and Light Tracer Global Illumination solutions. A refinery is a place of poison and volatile danger, which raises the tension level. Toward the end of the chase, Xzulixia is cornered and is forced to change shape again. The shape-changing sequence involves a morph animation of the body mesh. For information on the vampire shape change morph animation, see Chapter 12, "Advanced Animation."

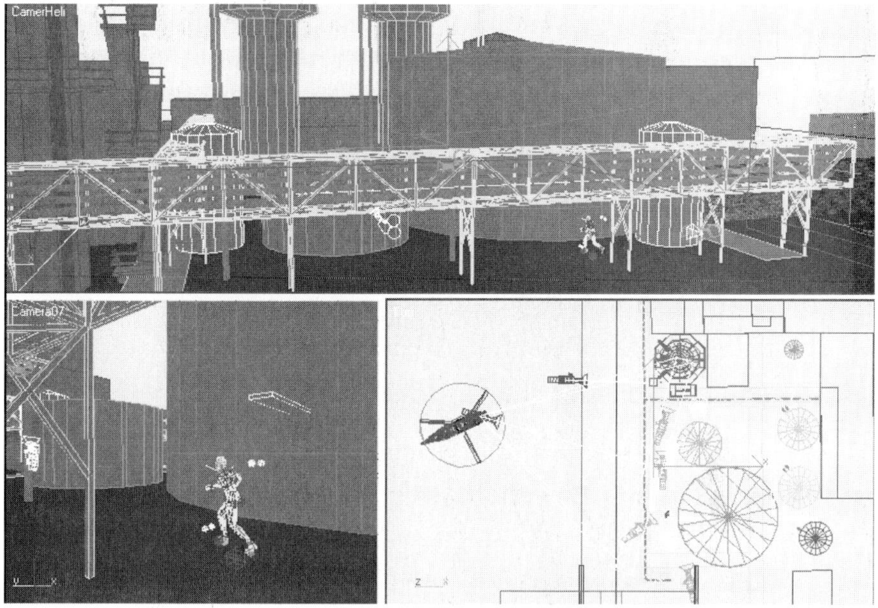

FIGURE 10.24 Xzulixia running between the tanks while being chased by the helicopter.

USING CHARACTER STUDIO

Adding the gunmen to the scene is done by using the character studio 4 plug-in program to create bipeds. A character studio biped is a skeleton that has its own internal rigging with variable centers of rotation, and can be driven by Motion Capture data. The main use of the biped is to re-create realistic movement of all of the secondary human characters in the film, as shown in Figure 10.25. The only characters who were animated by hand in this scene were Xzulixia and Dr. Quin, which use the skeletal rigs. The killers were animated with motion capture data and layer animation. For more information on character studio 4, see Chapter 15, "character studio 4."

ADDING ADDITIONAL CHARACTERS

Working with the character studio biped is quite different from animating a bones skeleton rig. The biped is generally animated either by pasting footsteps, or by loading pre-animated .bip motion files or motion capture data. The .bip files can be edited into sequences using the Motion Flow tools. Another animation alternative is to modify a .bip motion file using the character studio Layer Animation tools. This puts keys on top of the

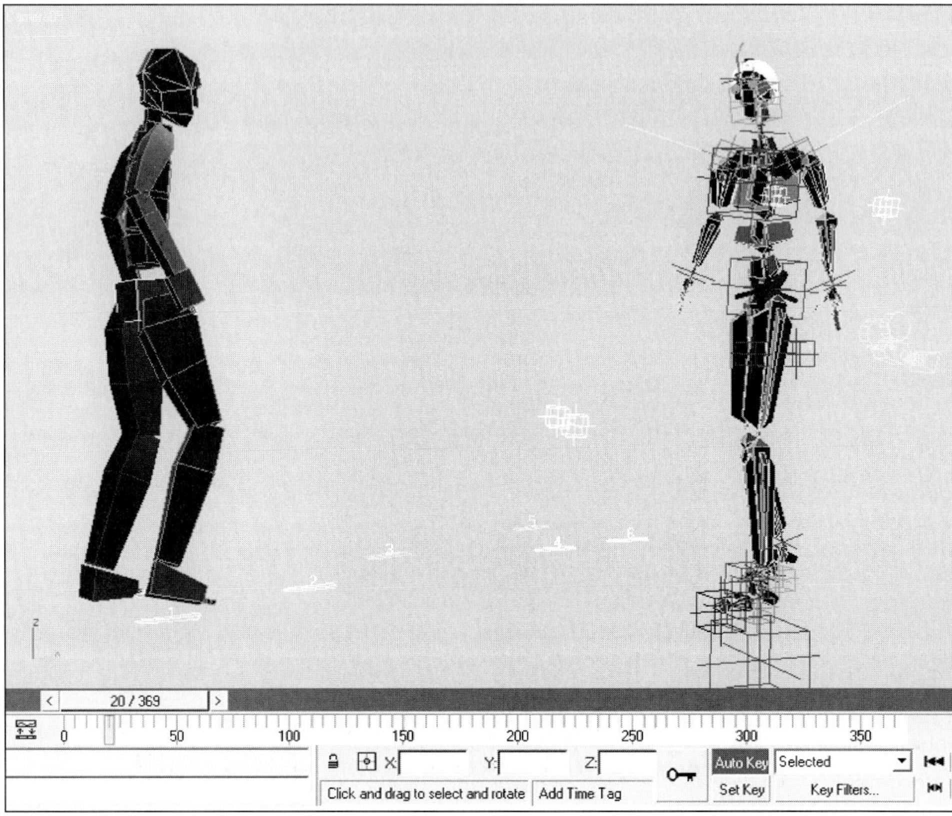

FIGURE 10.25 Bringing in character studio skeletons for gunmen and the dogs.

Motion Capture moves and allows you to change them or add to the end of the motion.

The 3ds max bones skeleton rig is animated either by hand, or by using video rotoscope images as a reference. A third way is to use the Mimic method, where a motion-capture-driven biped is used as a reference to animate the 3ds max bones skeleton rig.

During the pre-visualization of the Cracking Tower escape sequence that is depicted in Figures 10.26 and 10.27, the action of the vampire was worked out by trying different motion paths and camera angles. The camera angles that were finally chosen show the point of view of the vigilante killers looking up at her. As she is about to fly, her wings have not yet morphed large enough, as shown in Figure 10.28. She must wait until her wings expand more, which gives the dogs time to run up the Cracking Tower stairs after her. When she finally takes off, her wings are still expanding, and are barely large enough to support her body size, indicating that they are still growing as she flies away, as shown in Figure 10.27.

During the vampire's escape, the vigilantes fire at her and hit the pipes and the side of the Cracking Tower, as shown in Figure 10.27. To create the effects of bullets piercing the Cracking Tower and releasing steam, a particle system was used that can generate either steam or smoke. For more information on creating steam with particle systems, see Chapter 11, "Visual Effects."

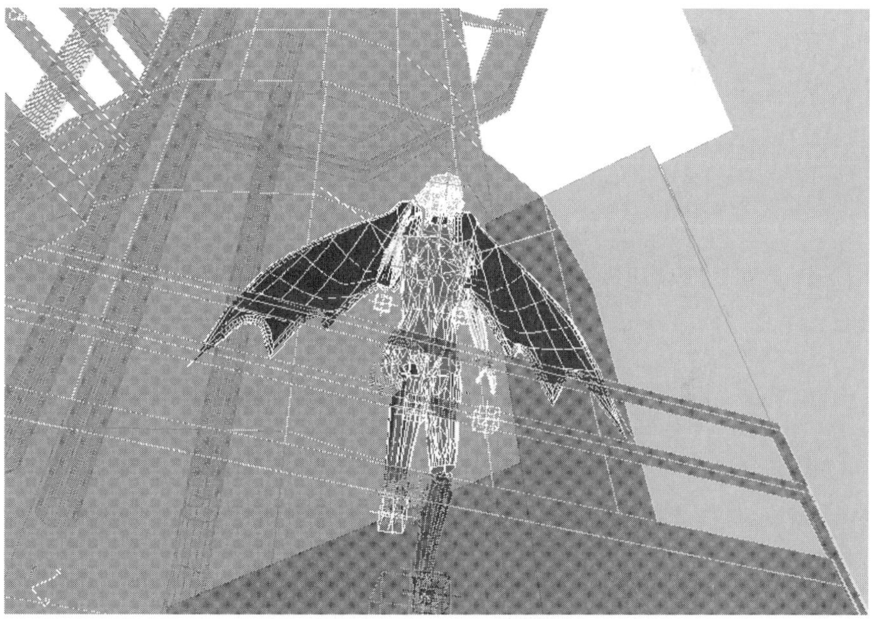

FIGURE 10.26 Pre-visualization of Xzu as seen by one of the men as she is about to fly.

Level of Detail and X-Refs

When a scene becomes heavy with numerous characters, buildings, landscapes, and details, it is important to be able to use low polygon or low face count models when they are not close to the camera. Otherwise, the system can bog down when trying to refresh the screen. A large number of unneeded polygons can make animation a frustrating experience

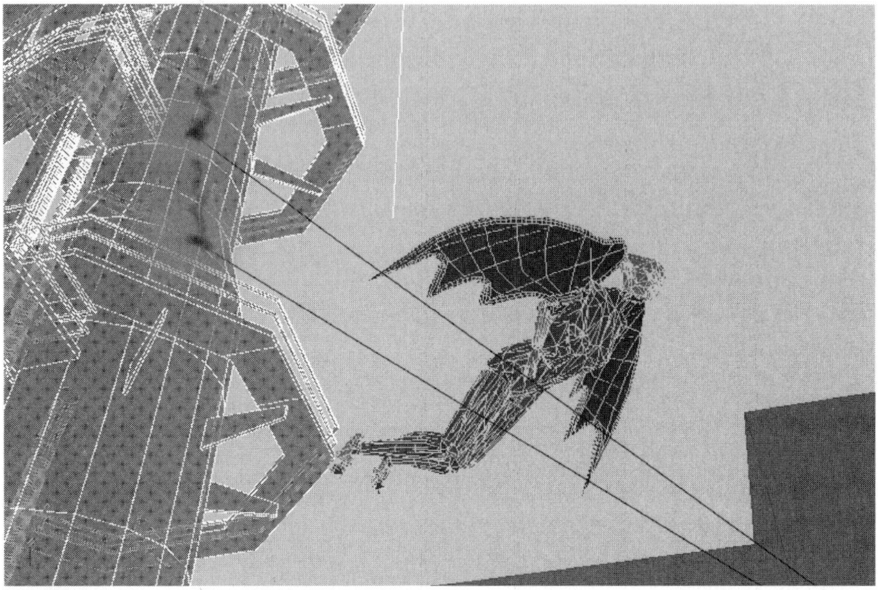

FIGURE 10.27 Pre-visualization of bullets fired at Xzu hitting the Cracking Tower as she escapes.

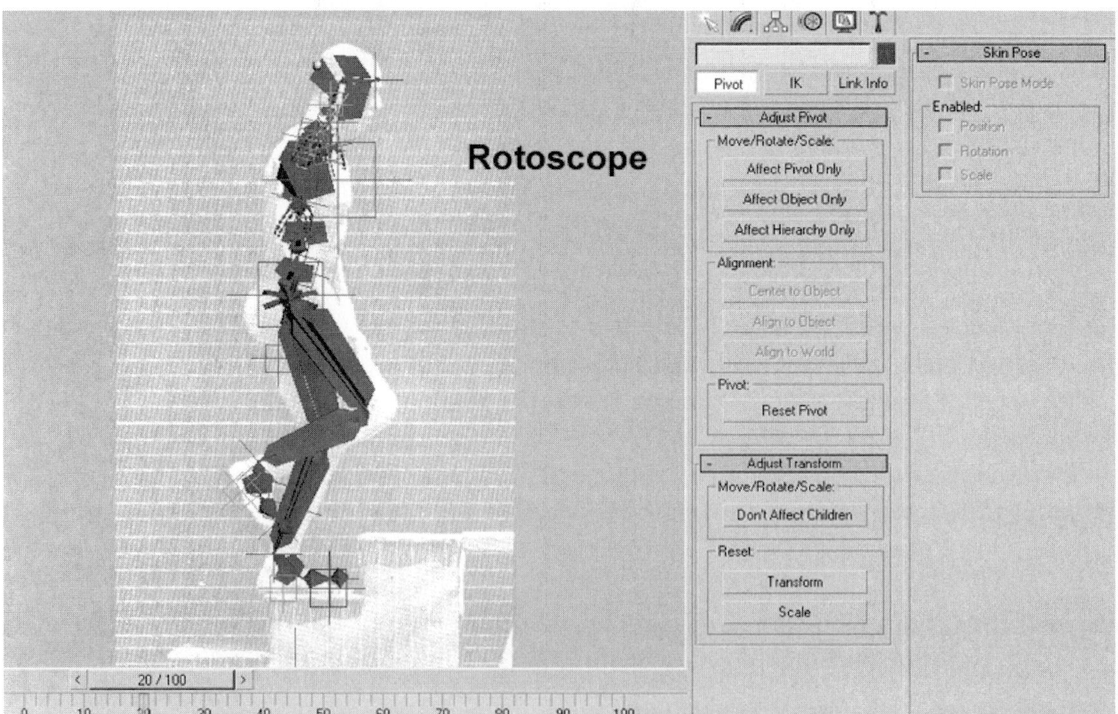

FIGURE 10.28 The model is aligned with the background movie for doing Video Rotoscope animation.

when the system requires three or four minutes of calculating to refresh each time you try to move the Time Slider. This commonly happens when your scene face count exceeds 200,000 faces. In production, this can affect the production pipeline and cost the studio valuable time.

One of the ways to deal with this problem is to cut the scene in pieces and only work on partial scenes. Another technique is to use the Level of Detail utility, commonly called the LOD, which enables you to group together model versions of different resolution, and then automatically substitute low poly meshes and materials for the high-detail ones by setting a threshold distance from the camera. The third possibility is to use Externally Referenced objects, or X-Refs, to substitute extremely low polygon stand-in proxy versions in place of the high-resolution models in the scene during animation, and then switch to the high-resolution models for rendering.

Video Rotoscope for Scene Animation

Using rotoscope techniques, you can act out a scene on film or video and then import it into your computer to use as a background reference image when animating the scene. Video movies in the .mov or .avi format, as well as image sequences, can be loaded into the 3ds max viewport background. You then position your set and your models over the background and animate the scene. This technique works very well when you want to animate a complex scene in a crowded area where different characters are moving about, and blocking each other from the camera's view. Instead of trying to work it out in the animation, it is much faster to simply direct the scene with real actors or some other animators. Once it looks like what you want, you can rapidly approach the animation of the scene in 3ds max. This technique was used extensively in the production of the recent animated hit film *Ice Age*.

Many motion pictures have been animated this way instead of using motion capture, including films like *Hollow Man* from Sony Pictures. It is an effective, if slightly inaccurate, method of creating life-like human motion in digital characters. Its detractors point out that you cannot see the motion of the arm on the back side of the body. Modern full-body motion control is superior, especially when animating many people fighting in a scene. However, it is also expensive compared to Video Rotoscope. If you can afford it, multiple character motion capture would be the fastest way to animate complex scenes. This technique has been used to animate the fight scenes in sequels to *The Matrix*. In *Homing Instinct,* video rotoscope techniques were used to block out and animate some of the more difficult scenes at the cost of a few cassettes of Hi-8 videotape.

In 3ds max, all viewports are capable of displaying different frame sequences or animated movies, so you could see the motion from more than one angle, thus eliminating much of the error inherent in the video rotoscope method. A side view camera and a front view camera are up to tape the action. A movie clapper can be held in front of the cameras and closed to make a visual and audio mark that is used to synchronize the images, The action is then taped, and the results are put into combustion 2 or any other video editing program to trim both movies so that they start from exactly the same frame.

Once trimmed and synchronized, the movies are rendered as black-and-white QuickTime movies (.mov) to reduce video display memory requirements when played in 3ds max. They are then loaded into the front and the left viewport backgrounds of 3ds max, ready for rotoscope animation, as shown in Figure 10.28.

CONCLUSION

In this chapter, you animated a character being chased by a helicopter, and then you added a target spotlight that tracked the character. You performed a test render of the scene that cut between different camera views using the Video Post tool. In the next chapter, you will add particle system and explosion visual effects to the Vampire Chase scene.

CHAPTER

11

VISUAL EFFECTS

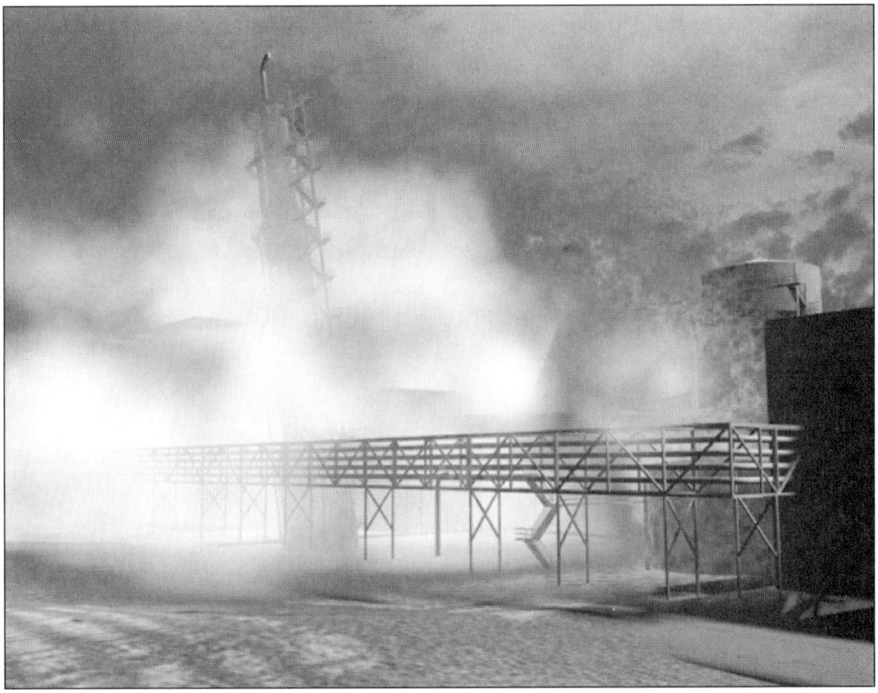

Six types of visual effects can be done in 3ds max 6: Particle, Dynamic, Atmospheric, Morphing and Transform, Compositing, and Rendering effects. A very popular compositing visual effect is the process shot or blue screen shot used to insert actors, animated creatures, exploding props, or vehicles into photographic or digital backgrounds. This type of effect can be seen in the battle scenes and the exotic planet environments of *Star Wars: Attack of the Clones*. In this chapter, you will explore the processes involved in creating different types of particle and atmospheric visual effects. The new event-driven particle system for 3ds max 6 is called *Particle Flow*. You will be introduced to this powerful new particle tool in a tutorial that explains how to use event-driven particle systems to spawn particles on impact and generate atmospheric effects such as dust raised by a character's foot hitting the ground.

Dynamic animation is explored in Chapter 12, "Advanced Animation." Morphing is explained in Chapter 12, and in Chapter 9, "Character Animation." Rendering effects are explained in Chapter 14, "Lighting and Rendering," and compositing effects are explained in Chapter 16, "combustion 2.1, Compositing and 2D Visual Effects."

PARTICLE EFFECTS

One of the most useful types of computer-generated visual effects is the particle effect. Particles can be used to simulate manmade phenomena such as explosions, object fragmentation or disintegration, machine-gun fire, fields of marching soldiers, flights of helicopters or bombers, spurting molten metal from a cutting torch, aerosol spray, bouncing ball bearings, and much more. A large number of natural phenomena can be simulated with particles such as rain, clouds, hail, smoke, fire, water, dust, tornadoes, flowing liquids, flocks of birds, bats, or butterflies, leaves falling from a tree, bubbles, schools of fish, and water spray, as shown in Figure 11.1.

Coronado, the action adventure movie produced by Uncharted Territory, LLC., in Los Angeles, is due to be released in 2003. It has 615 visual effects shots, many of which were done in 3ds max. The author interviewed the filmmakers: Volker Engel, CEO of Uncharted Territory, LLC, who won an Academy Award as the visual-effects supervisor on *Independence Day*; and Marc Weigert, COO of Uncharted Territory. Both also share credit as visual effects supervisors on *Coronado*. Brandon Davis, the

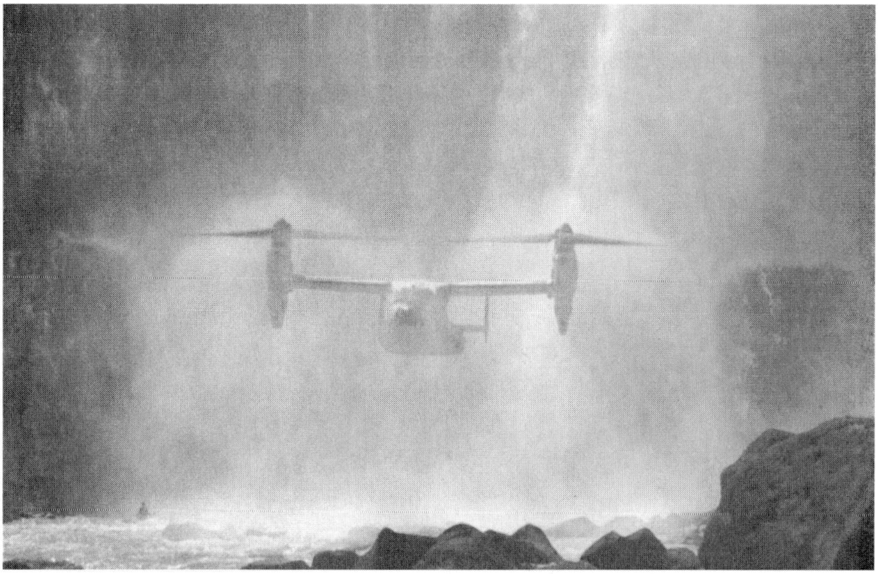

FIGURE 11.1 3ds max particles used to simulate spray from Osprey aircraft blades in a waterfall from the motion picture *Coronado*, Courtesy of Uncharted Territory, LLC.

lead supervising animator, described some of the fine points of using 3ds max particles for visual effects.

Davis explained that the particle effects in the scene with the Osprey aircraft flying out through a waterfall was accomplished by compositing real footage of a waterfall shot in Vera Cruz, Mexico, with 3ds max particle systems. The waterfall was extended in size by compositing cloned portions of the original waterfall footage. Brandon Davis explained that they added 3ds max water elements to the scene to create the illusion that the CG Osprey was interacting with real water. Particle mist and spray was used to make it look as though the waterfall was interacting realistically with the rotors of the aircraft, as shown in Figure 11.1.

See the Color Plate section in this book for a color image of this particle effect.

To understand how 3ds max particles are used for visual effects, we will start with a basic particle emitter and explore some particle features. The PArray particle emitter is very versatile, but looks deceptively simple, as shown in Figure 11.2.

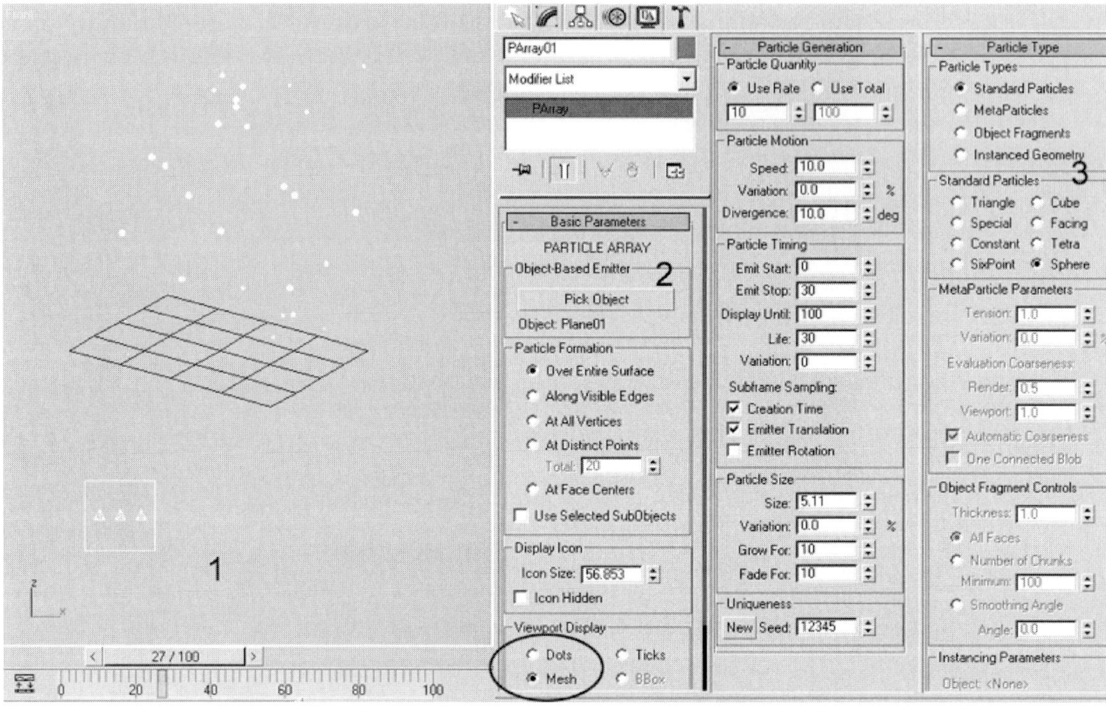

FIGURE 11.2 The PArray icon, a particle emitter object, and the PArray control panel.

In the next tutorial, you will set up a PArray particle system with gravity and a deflector. Then, you will apply motion blur to create a particle rain effect.

TUTORIAL 11.1 SETTING UP A PARRAY PARTICLE RAIN EFFECT

To set up a particle system:

1. Reset 3ds max, click Create > Standard Primitives > Plane in the main menu bar, and create a small plane primitive object in the top view. Right-click the Play icon and in Time Configuration set Animation > Length to 400. Click OK.
2. Next, in the main menu bar, click Create > Particles > PArray. The Particle Systems menu will open with PArray highlighted. Click and drag in the front viewport to create a PArray icon, as shown in Figure 11.2, example 1.

3. Select the PArray icon, and then click Modify. Place your cursor on the left edge of the menu and drag it left to expand the Command Panel menus. Open the Particle Generation, and the Particle Type menus. In the Basic Parameters menu, select the Pick Object button, as shown in Figure 11.2, example 2, and click on the plane object in the viewport. Scrub the Time Slider to see it emit particles from frame 0 to 30.
4. In the Particle Type > Standard Particles menu, select Sphere. Then, in Basic Parameters > Viewport Display, turn on Mesh and set Percentage of Particles to 100%. To make them display longer, go to the Particle Generation menu and set Emit Stop = 400, Display Until = 400, and Life to 60. Set Particle Size to 2.0. The particles travel in all directions by default.
5. To make the particles fall down, you will create a gravity spacewarp. In the top view, click Zoom Extents, and then in the Command Panel, click Create > Space Warps. Select Gravity, and then click on the center of the viewport and drag to create a gravity spacewarp gizmo.

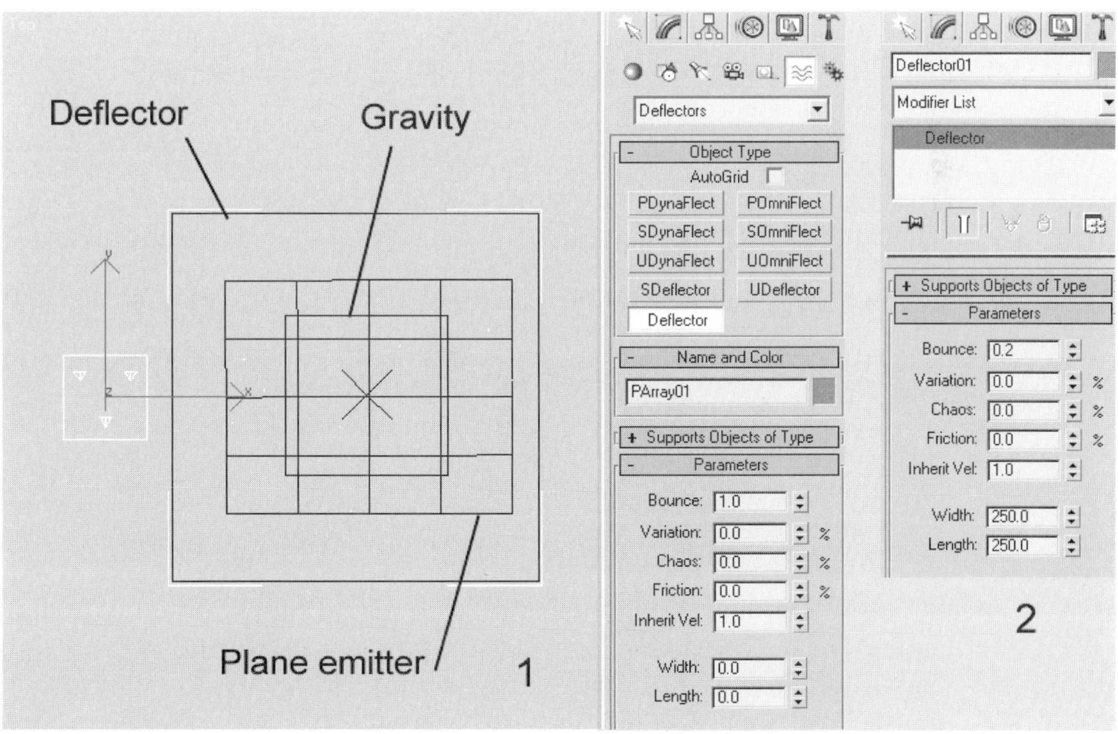

FIGURE 11.3 Setting up the particle deflector.

6. Also in Space Warps, create a deflector. To do that, click Forces in the white Object Type menu box and select Deflectors from the list. Click the Deflector button, and then in the top view, click the upper left and drag to the lower right to create a deflector gizmo, as shown in Figure 11.3, example 1.
7. Select the Deflector and click the Modify tab. In Parameters, set Bounce = 0.2, as shown in Figure 11.3, example 2. Then, switch to the front view. Everything is on the construction plane. Select the plane particle emitter and move it up so it is above the gravity and deflector gizmos. Then, select the deflector and rotate it in the Z-axis about 15 degrees, as shown in Figure 11.4, example 1.
8. To activate the gravity and deflector, bind them to the PArray icon. Click the Bind to Spacewarp icon in the main toolbar, as shown in Figure 11.4, example 2, and then click the H key. The Select Space Warp window will open. Select Gravity01 and Deflector01, and then click Bind. Scrub the Time Slider to see the particles fall downward and bounce off the deflector.

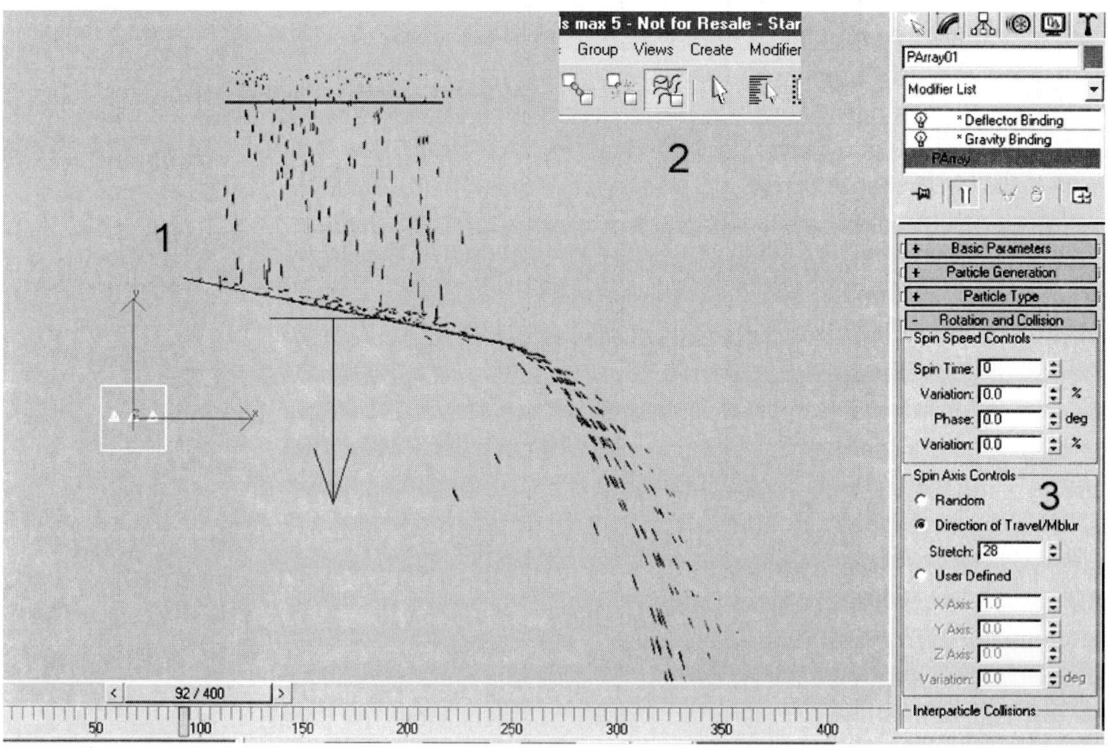

FIGURE 11.4 Binding the particle system to the space warps.

9. The last step is to set up particle motion blur. Click the PArray icon, and then in the Modify Panel, go to the Modifier List window and click PArray. In the Particle System menus, scroll up until you find the Rotation and Collision menu. In Spin Axis Controls, turn on Direction of Travel/Mblur, and set Stretch = 28, as shown in Figure 11.4, example 3. You should now see streaked raindrops in the viewport.
10. To render, first apply a light blue material with Specular Level = 50 to the PArray icon. Then set the environment background color to medium gray. You can add a Spotlight with cast shadows turned on for an more interesting appearance. Save the file as Rain.max.

OBJECT FRAGMENTATION PARTICLE EFFECTS

Object fragmentation PArray particle effects are used when exploding objects to break them up into fragments that have thickness, rotation, and impact detection. This effect was used in *Homing Instinct* to create a dense explosion in the chemical refinery in the Vampire Chase scene you animated in Chapter 10, "Scene Animation." In the next section on creating explosion effects, you will work with that scene again and use the PArray Object Fragment capability.

THE HOLLYWOOD EXPLOSION

One of the most common visual effects in films today is the explosion. In real life, however, many explosions are not always spectacular, and are over very quickly. Because they are usually obscured by smoke, accidental explosions look somewhat boring and anti-climactic. Fabricated explosions can be tailored to create any effect, from lots of smoke to no smoke with a large fireball. The high-rise building demolition explosion is spectacular, but carefully controlled. Film producers know that a real explosion that lasts two seconds would never bring people into the theaters.

Multilayered time-stretched explosions are used as the visual effects in *Homing Instinct*. The vampire pursuit ends in multiple explosions that occur in rapid succession, followed by a huge blast that nearly destroys the Titan Chemical Refinery, as shown in Figure 11.5.

Companies such as Art Beats offer stock explosions on CD-ROMs filled with different practical real explosions staged by pyrotechnicians

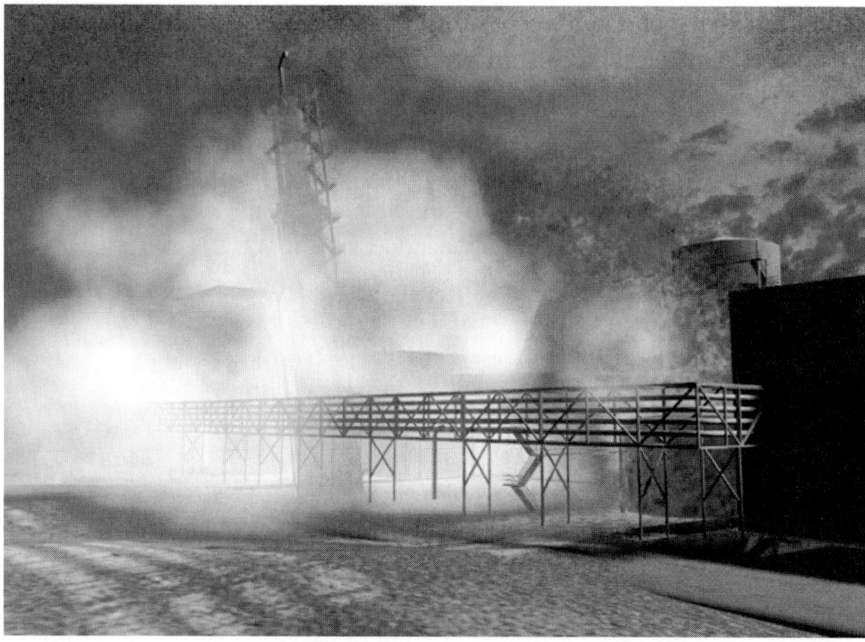

FIGURE 11.5 The exploding refinery.

that were shot on film. Sets of sequential mask images are supplied on the second CD-ROM, Training and Learning, that came with your copy of 3ds max, in the Textures directory. You can composite these explosion images with the explosions in your scenes. They are intended to fatten up a digital explosion to give it more detail and density. They can be used by themselves to save producers the cost of hiring a pyrotechnician to stage an explosion. The same type of effect can be accomplished in combustion 2 by using its particle system to generate dense 2D explosions, as shown in Figure 11.6.

In the early days of Hollywood, the explosion become a type of performance piece that built up and then peaked in a massive flaming crescendo, usually accompanied by flying bodies, cars flipping over, and debris raining down. Today's audiences are no different, and to satisfy the audience's thirst for excitement, visual effects pyrotechnicians in Hollywood have developed a dense explosion that is a mixture of a gel-like thickener for the gasoline and sawdust. This volatile mixture yields a much thicker and voluminous fireball with flying sparks and less obscuring smoke.

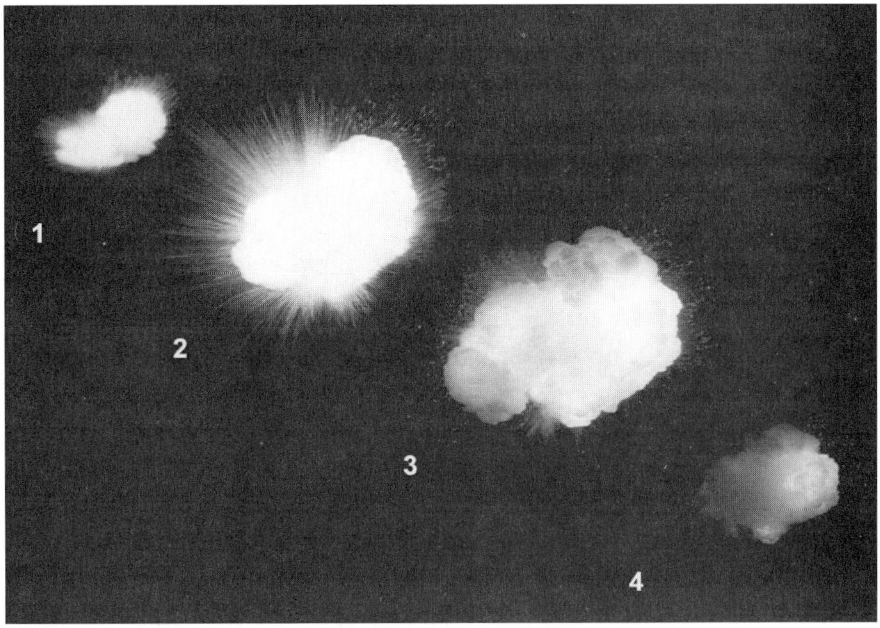

FIGURE 11.6 2D explosion image sequence created in combustion 3.

To further enhance their impact, most movie explosions are shot with high-speed cameras to slow the expanding fireball and increase the screen time to many seconds. With the advent of computer graphics, computer-generated explosion and fire effects add even more detail and excitement. Digital visual effects have not completely taken over the creation of explosion effects, but in most cases, live action explosions you see in films are digitally enhanced in some way.

CREATING AN EXPLOSION IN 3DS MAX 6

Explosions in 3ds max 6 are done as combinations of three or more different effects to give the explosion enough density to look like a real explosion. In the next tutorial, you will create an explosion that destroys part of a chemical refinery, as shown in Figure 11.7.

The explosion you will create is comprised of three Fire Effect atmospheric explosions that go off in sequence. An object fragmentation particle system is used to destroy the Cracking Tower and two tanks, and then volume lights are added to enhance the excitement of the scene. A

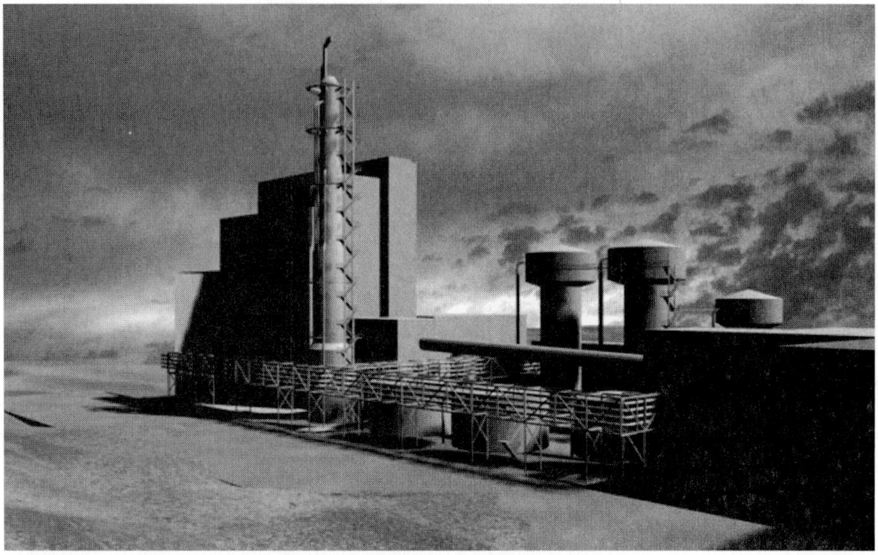

FIGURE 11.7 The chemical refinery before the explosions.

deflector is set at ground level to prevent the object fragments from passing through the ground plane.

In the next tutorial, you will create a sequential digital explosion.

TUTORIAL 11.2

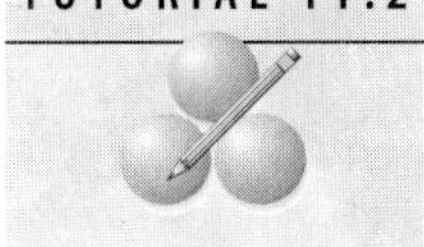

CREATE A DENSE EXPLOSION

To create an explosion:

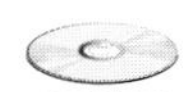

ON THE CD

1. Load the Refinery01.max scene file from the Chap11 folder on the companion CD-ROM. Render the camera01 view to see the scene before the explosions are applied. There are a number of cameras in the scene set at different viewpoints.
2. To set up the first explosion, switch to the top view and maximize the view. In the Selection set window in the menu bar, select Explode Objects, and then click Hide Unselected. Next, click Zoom Extents (Z). You should see three round objects, two tanks and the Cracking Tower, as shown in Figure 11.8.
3. The first step is to place a PArray Particle system icon next to each object. To do that, click Create in the Command Panel, open the Particle System

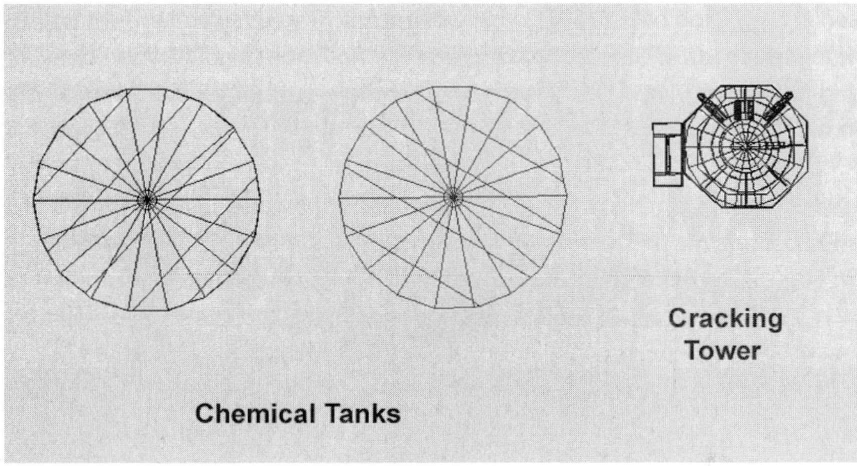

FIGURE 11.8 The three objects to be exploded.

menu, and click on PArray. Click and drag next to the left tank to create the PArray icon. Then, duplicate the icon by pressing Shift and then Click, and drag the icon twice and drop it next to the two other objects, as shown in Figure 11.9, example 1.

4. Click the first icon, and then click Modify, which will reveal the Particle Array menu. To better see the Particle menus, drag the right edge of the viewport two increments to the left, and then expand the Particle Generation and the Particle Type menus, as shown in Figure 11.9, example 2. Select Object Fragments as the Particle Type, also shown in Figure 11.9, example 2.
5. In the Particle Generation, Particle timing menu, set Emit Start = 70, Display Until = 400, and Life = 400. Then, go to the Basic Parameters menu. Click the large Pick Object button and select the Tank01 object next to the first PArray icon in the top view. Then, scroll the menu to find Viewport Display. Turn on Mesh Display so that the object fragments show in the viewport.
6. Now, select the second and third PArray icons and apply the same settings listed in steps 4 and 5 with the following exception: for Tank02, set the Emit Start = 80, and for the Cracking Tower, set Emit Start = 90.
7. Move the Time Slider to see that all of the objects generate fragments. Notice that the original objects remain in place. PArray makes copies and fragments them. You will need to apply visibility keys to hide the original objects after they explode.

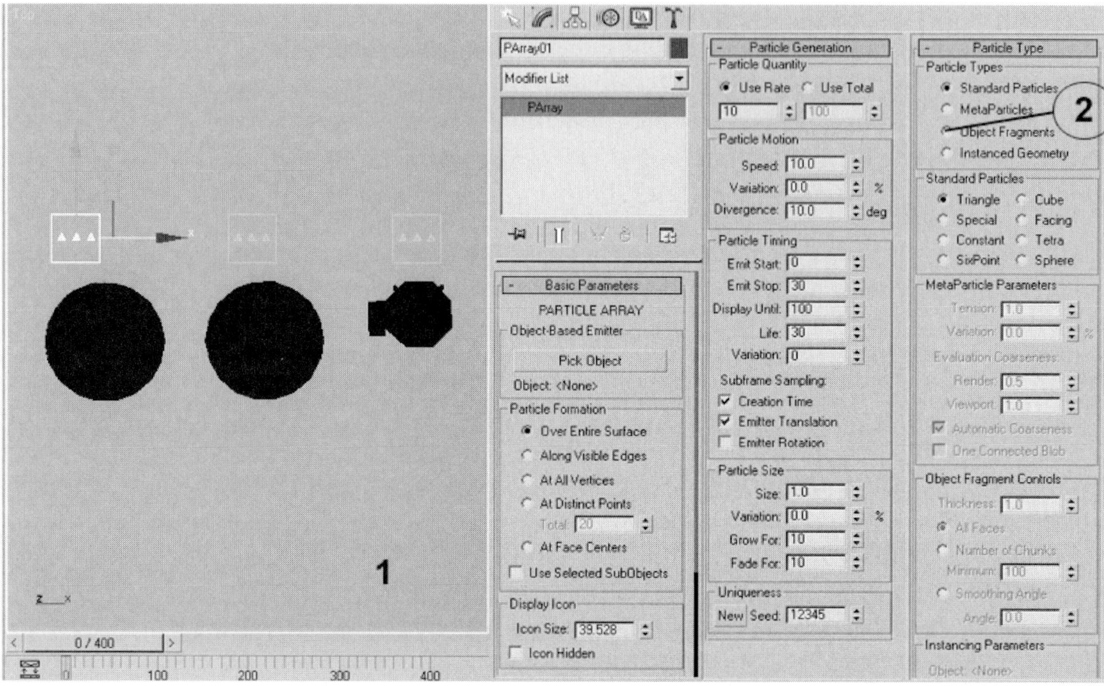

FIGURE 11.9 The expanded PArray menus.

8. To set visibility keys, open the Graph Editor menu and select Track View—Dope Sheet, as shown in Figure 11.10. Expand the track view so you can see the tracks easily. Then, select the Cracking Tower in the top view. In the Dope Sheet, select the name "Cracking Tower" in the Hierarchy list, and then in the Dope Sheet menu bar, click Tracks > Visibility Track > Add. A new visibility track will appear below the Cracking Tower.
9. Now you must add visibility keys to hide the objects at the correct frame. In the Dope Sheet menu, select Keys > Add Keys. The cursor will change to a Create Key icon. Click on the track at frame 1, then again at frame 90, where the tower should be hidden. Then, right-click on the new key to open the Key Transition Dialog box, as shown in Figure 11.11, example 1. Select both transition types and set them to Square for the first and second visibility keys. Then, set Value = 0.0 for key 2, and Value 1.0 for key 1.

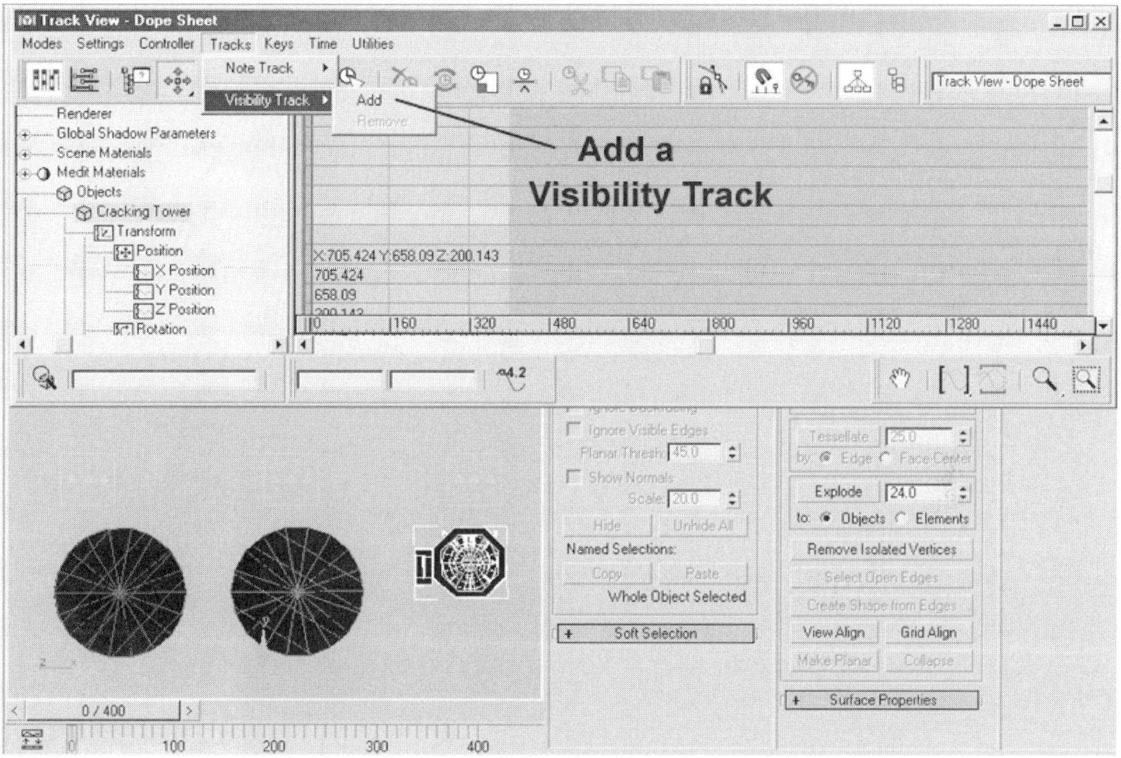

FIGURE 11.10 Adding an object visibility track.

10. Next, repeat steps 8 and 9 for the other two objects, setting Tank01 to disappear at frame 70, and Tank02 to disappear at frame 80. Close the Dope Sheet and test the visibility keys by moving the Time Slider, as shown in Figure 11.11, example 2. You might need to reset the Emit start times to 70, 80, and 90 so that it all works.
11. Save the file as Refinery02.max.

In the next tutorial, you will continue setting up the explosions by adding the atmospheric explosions.

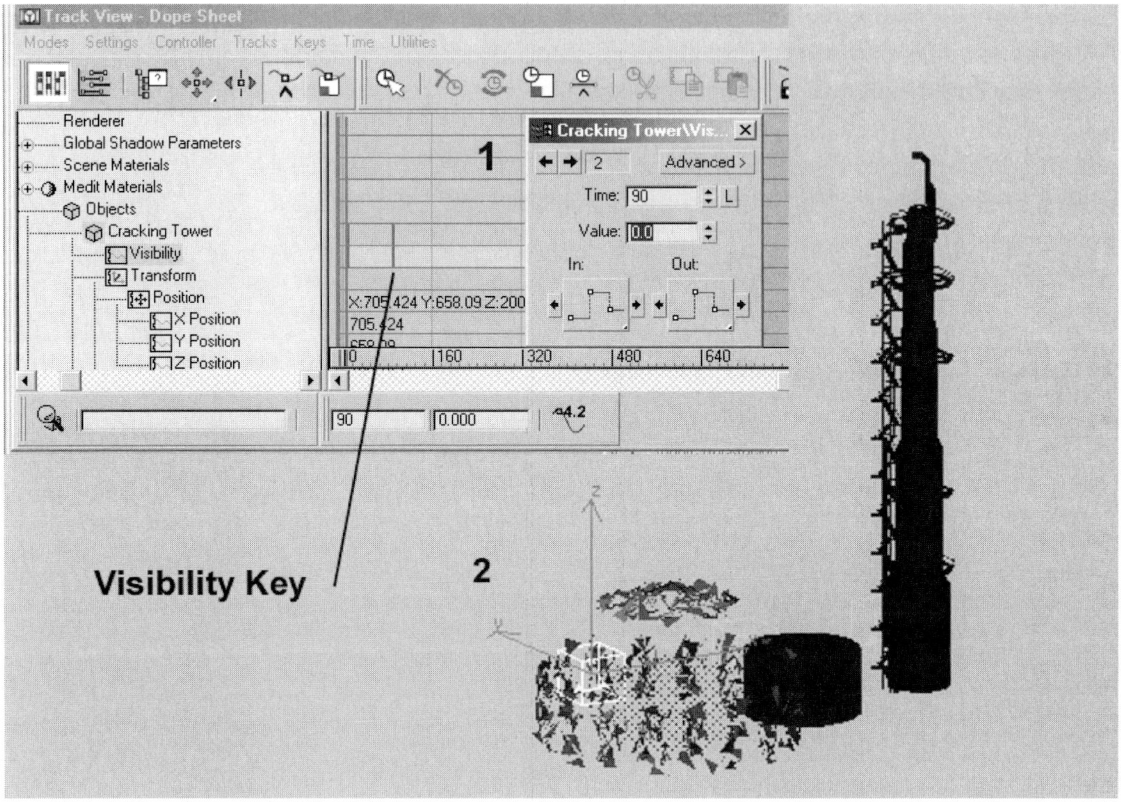

FIGURE 11.11 Create visibility keys and set them to Square transitions and a Value of 0.0 for Invisible.

TUTORIAL 11.3

SET UP ATMOSPHERIC EXPLOSIONS

To set up atmospheric explosions:

1. Load the Refinery02.max scene file if it is not already loaded. Maximize the top view and click Zoom Extents. Next, you will add four Spherical Atmospheric Apparatus gizmos to contain the atmospheric explosions.
2. To create the four Atmospheric gizmos, click Create > Helper, click Standard, and in the drop-down menu, select Atmospheric Apparatus. Next, select SphereGizmo and then click and drag on top of Tank01 to create a gizmo slightly larger than the tank, as shown in Figure 11.12, example 1. Place another on top of Tank02, and two more on top of the Cracking Tower.
3. Switch to a maximized front view, click Zoom Extents, and then select one of the two Sphere gizmos and raise it halfway up the Cracking Tower. Non-

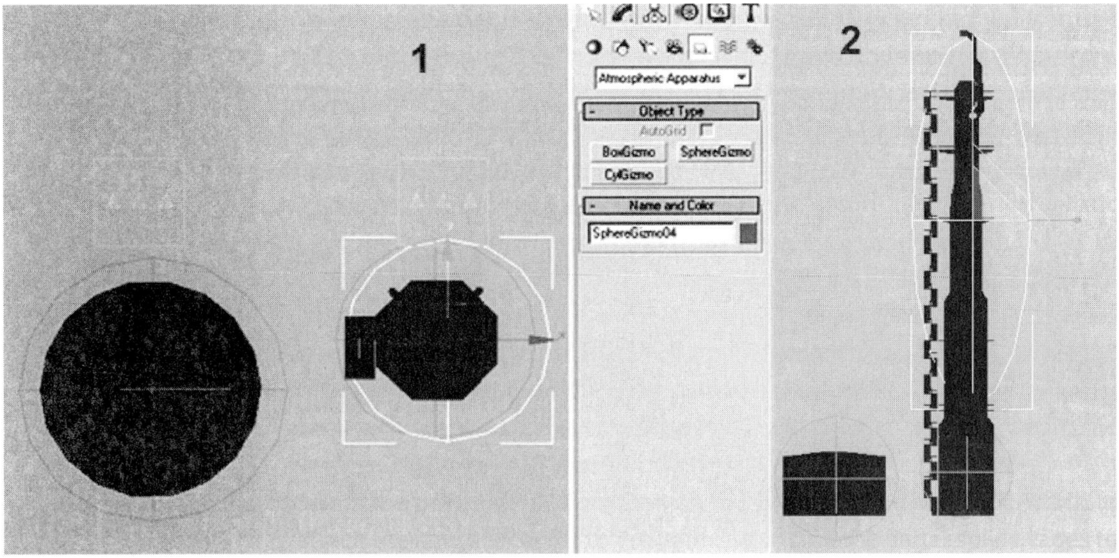

FIGURE 11.12 Placing the Spherical Atmospheric Apparatus gizmos.

uniform scale it in the Y-axis to make it half as tall as the tower, as shown in Figure 11.12, example 2.

4. Open the Rendering > Environment > Atmosphere menu. In the Effects window, you will add four Fire Effects to create the explosions. Click the Add button to the right of the Effects window, select Fire Effect, and click OK. Repeat that three more times, as shown in Figure 11.13, example 1.
5. Next, select each of the Fire Effect entries, and in the Fire Effect Parameters, click the Pick Gizmo button. Select one of the Sphere gizmos in the scene, as shown in Figure 11.13, example 2. Next, scroll up the Fire Effect menu, and in the Explosion menu, turn on the Explosion switch and click the Setup Explosion button, shown by the circled number 3. In the Setup Explosion Phase Curve dialog, shown by the circled number 4, set the Start Time to match the start time of the particle fragment effect for the associated object. For example, Tank01 will fragment at frame 70, so set the Fire Effect explosion Start Time = 67, End Time = 167. It should start three frames before the particle fragmenting starts to give the fireball time to start building in size, and last 100 frames. Repeat this step with the appropriate Start Time and End Time for all Fire Effects.
6. Since the explosion created by the Atmospheric Apparatus does not throw light, you will need to add four Omni Lights inside each Sphere gizmo. In the left view, Click Create > Lights > Omni, and then click at the

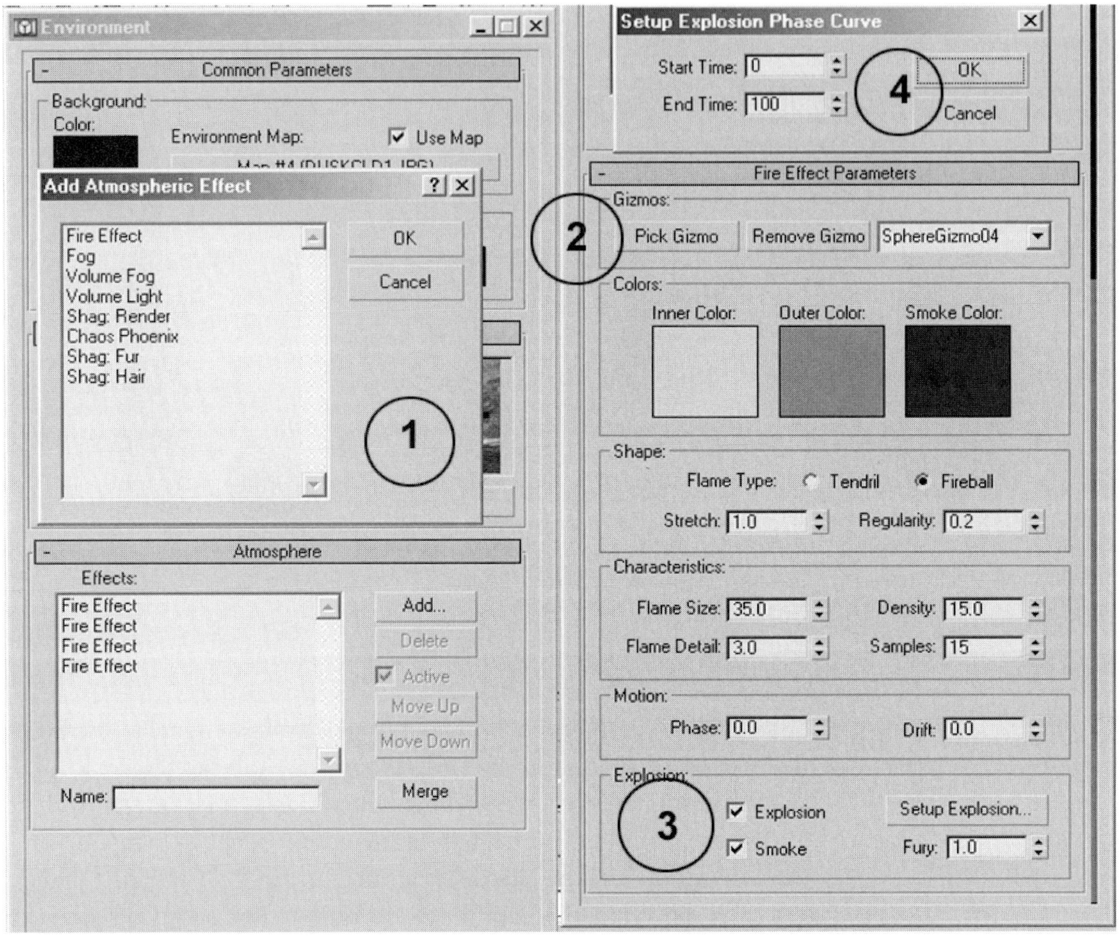

FIGURE 11.13 The Fire Effects Explosion Settings menus.

center of each Sphere gizmo to create an Omni Light for each. Next, you will set keys to turn the lights on as each object explodes to enhance the overall effect and throw light and shadows on the surrounding structure.

7. Select the Omni Light you placed inside the Sphere gizmo surrounding Tank01, and open the Modify Panel. In the Light Parameters, turn on Cast Shadows. Then, at Frame 0, turn on Auto Key. In the Intensity/Color/Attenuation menu, reduce the Multiplier value to 0.0, as shown in Figure 11.14, example 1. Next, move the Time Slider to frame 71 and set the Multiplier to 7.0. Then, set Far Attenuation to Start = 80, End = 200, and click Use and Show, as shown in Figure 11.14, example 2.

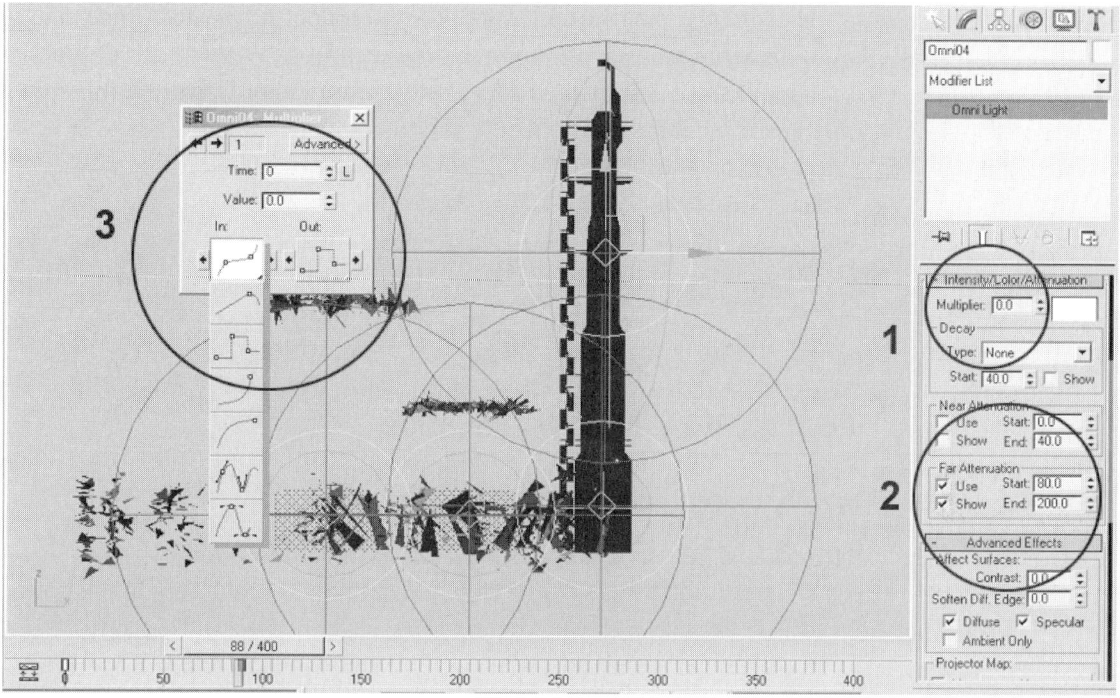

FIGURE 11.14 Set the Omni Light values and Multiplier Keys in the Light Modify panel.

Notice that when you move the Time Slider, the value of the Light Multiplier slowly ramps up or interpolates from the key at frame 0 to the key at frame 70. To correct that and make the light not turn on until frame 70, you will change the Key Transition Type.

8. To prevent the light from turning on until frame 70, go to the time line and right-click the Key. In the pop-up menu, click Omni01: Multiplier. The Key Parameters dialog opens, as shown in Figure 11.14, example 3. In that dialog, click and hold the icon labeled "In." A list of Key to Key transitions will drop open. Select the square-shaped icon with three dots. This is the "switch" transition type, which will cause the state of the key to change value abruptly at that frame.
9. Set both In and Out key transitions to Switch type, and repeat for the key at frame 1. Finally, set the Value setting at frame 1 to 0.0, and the Value at frame 2 to 0.7. 0.0 means that the light is off, and 0.7 means that the light is on and set to three-fourths of its full intensity. Now, move the Time

Slider to test that the light Multiplier value does not switch from 0.0 to 0.7 until frame 70.

10. Repeat steps 7 through 10 for the other omni lights, setting the light in Tank02 to turn on at frame 80, and the omni lights in the Cracking Tower to turn on at frame 90.
11. Save the scene file as Refinery03.max.

Continue on to the next tutorial to finish the explosion.

TUTORIAL 11.4

ADD A VOLUME LIGHT TO THE EXPLOSION

To make the final adjustments:

1. Load the Refinery03.max scene if it is not already loaded.
2. Next, you will add a Volume Light effect to the Omni03 light at the bottom of the Cracking Tower to create rays of light when it explodes. Select Onmi03, then in the Modify Panel, scroll the menu to find and open the Atmospheres & Effects dialog window. Click the Add button, select Volume Light from the list, and click OK. Now select the word "Volume Light," and click the Setup button. The Environment window will open.
3. In the Volume Light Parameters menu, change Density to = 2.0 for the first test explosions. You are ready for a rendered test of all of the lights and effects.
4. At this stage, the setup of the scene is almost done, but there is a lot of testing, adjusting, and re-rendering before you can get results that look realistic and spontaneous, as shown in Figure 11.15.
5. Render the explosion and then try different settings for the color and density of the Omni Volume Light. Change the camera angles and alter the timing of the Fire Effects.
6. You will have to devote some time to trying different settings before you can expect to get good results. It helps to change the speed of the explosion to add more animated debris flying into the air to give the explosion more density. However, triangles don't look good, so you want to avoid exploding an object as faces. It should be set to Chunks with a minimum of 40 to get big pieces that don't look like triangles. Increase the thickness of the object fragments and set their spin to 20.

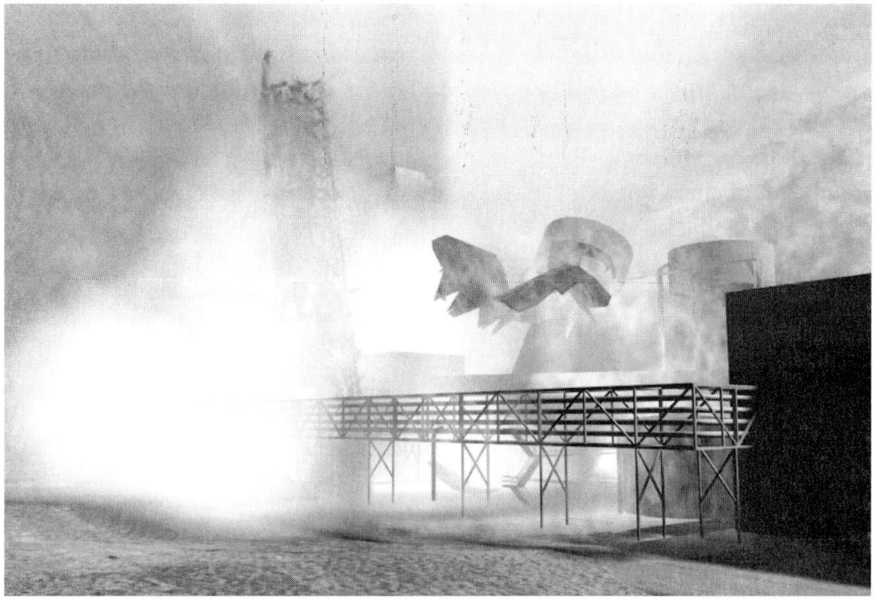

FIGURE 11.15 Final explosion of the refinery.

7. Add Image Motion Blur and then put Object Motion Blur on the fragments of the foreground tank.
8. When you have the results you want, save the scene as Refinery04.max.

More effects could be added, like particle sparks, to enhance this scene, including putting the helicopter in the scene with the explosion and having it crash. Xzulixia could also be placed above the fireball, flying away to make her escape. You will have to see the film when it is finished to see all of the elements working together. In the meantime, look at the RefineryExpl7.mov movie in the Chap11\Images folder on the companion CD-ROM.

ON THE CD

Instanced Geometry Particle Effects

Instanced geometry particle effects are very powerful for creating multiple animated objects, like fields of marching soldiers or a flight of butterflies. The process starts the same way as in Tutorial 11.1, "Setting Up a PArray Particle Rain Effect." The difference is that you add an animated geometry object to the scene that will take the place of the particles. In the next tutorial, you will use the file Rain.max that you saved from Tutorial 11.1, and change the particles from raindrops to instanced geometry butterflies.

TUTORIAL 11.5

INSTANCED GEOMETRY PARTICLE EFFECTS

To create instanced geometry particles:

ON THE CD

1. Load your Rain.max scene file, or you can load it from the Chap11 folder on the companion CD-ROM. When the file is loaded, maximize the front view, click Zoom Extents, and set the Time Slider to frame 0.
2. Next, you will Merge in an animated low-resolution butterfly has been created for you to use. Click File > Merge, and from the Chap11 folder on the companion CD-ROM, select the Butterfly.max file. In the Merge dialog, select Box01, which is the name of the animated butterfly object, and then click OK. The butterfly will appear in the scene, as shown in Figure 11.16, example 1.
3. Now you need to modify the particle system to handle instanced geometry type particles. First, select the gravity and the deflector and delete them. You will not be using them. Next, move the plane emitter object down even with the butterfly.
4. Select the PArray icon and go to the Modify tab. You should only see PArray in the Modifier List. Go to the Particle Generation menu and change the settings as follows: set Particle Quantity to Use Total and enter 100. Change Particle Motion > Speed to = 3.5 and Divergence = 40 degrees. Set Particle Size to Size = 0.4, as shown in Figure 11.16, example 2.
5. Move to the Particle Type menu. Change Particle Types to Instanced Geometry, scroll the menu, and in the Instancing Parameters submenu, click the Pick Object button. Click the butterfly in the viewport. Then, in the same menu, change Animation Offset Keying to Random and set Frame Offset = 4, as shown in Figure 11.16, example 3. This will make each butterfly birth happen at a different time and make each move slightly differently from all the others. This gives a natural or organic look to the animation.
6. Scroll to the Rotation and Collision menu, and then in the Spin Speed Controls submenu, set Spin Time = 200, as shown in Figure 11.16, example 4. Click Play. You should see a flight of butterflies rise up from the plane

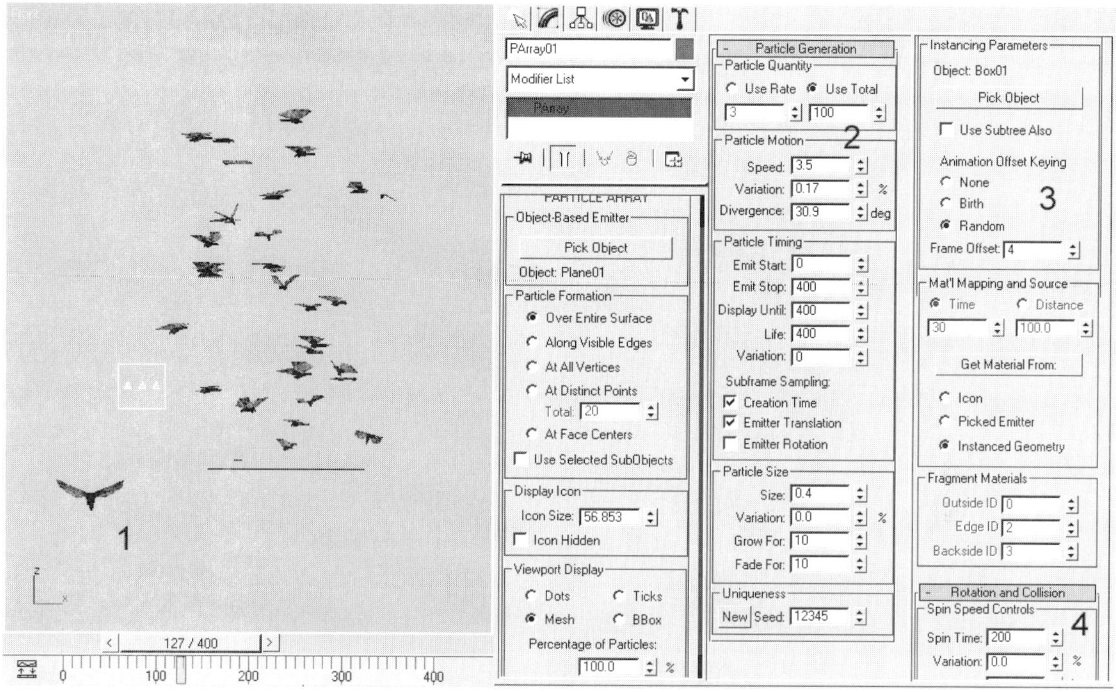

FIGURE 11.16 PArray particle system menus with butterfly merged into scene.

emitter in a random pattern, flapping their wings. They should all be moving slightly differently.

7. Change the view to Perspective and arc rotate the view to get a better angle on the flight of butterflies. Hide the original butterfly that you merged in, and load a background image into the Rendering > Environment > Environment such as the Lake_MT.jpg from the 3ds max\Maps\Backgrounds directory. Then, render a movie of frames 270 to 350 to see the final effect.
8. Save the file as Instance.max.

When you want to create instanced objects that are emitted once, and remain at a location, such as an animated soldier walking on a vertex of a plane, set Particle Generation > Particle Motion > Speed to 0.0, and limit the total number of particles generated to the number of soldiers you want. The idea then is to have two planes, one on top of the other. The top plane is the surface of the ground, and the plane just below it is

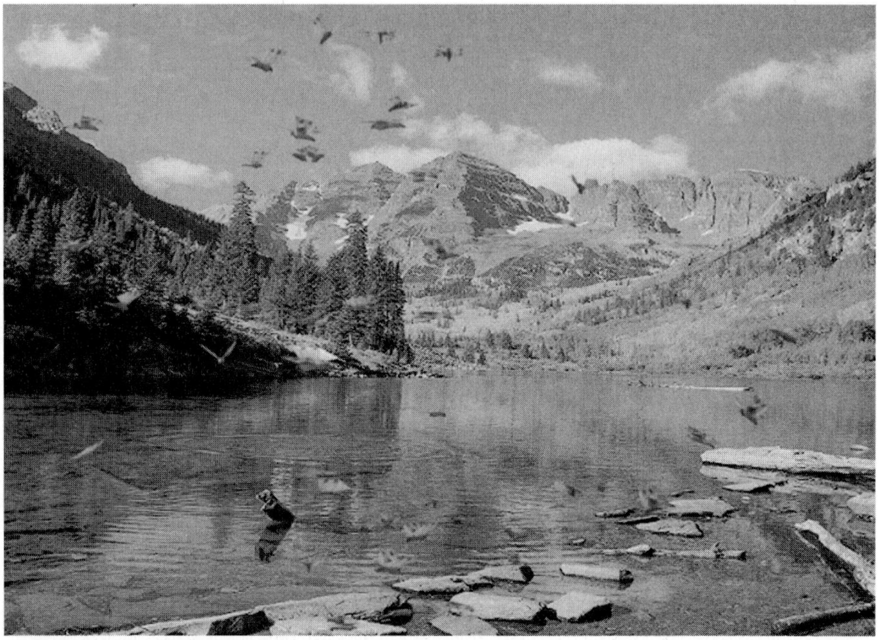

FIGURE 11.17 Final image of butterflies at a mountain lake.

the emitter plane that generates the instanced geometry particle soldier. To animate them marching forward, you translate the emitter plane in the direction and at the speed at which the soldiers are walking.

Facing Particle Effects

During the Vampire Chase in Chapter 10, "Scene Animation," the vigilantes fire at her and hit the pipes and the side of the Cracking Tower. To create the effects of bullets piercing the Cracking Tower and releasing steam, a particle system was used that can generate either steam or smoke. The steam particle effect used a Super Spray emitter that emits Facing type particles, also know as Sprites, which will always face the camera. They were mapped with a smoke image material made from a black-and-white radial opacity gradient that is applied to the particles as a face map. The ambient and diffuse colors are set to white, and specular and base opacity are set to 0. Create a radial gradient for the opacity map channel and set the opacity map strength to 5. To make the steam travel to the side, a Wind Space Warp is applied with a strength of .05. This makes them move gently to the left, as shown in Figure 11.18.

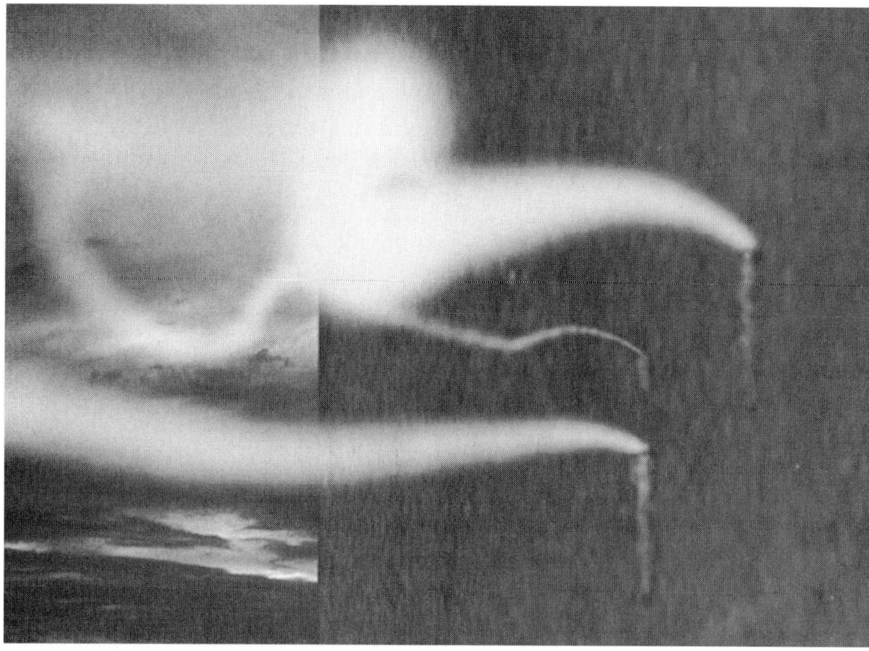

FIGURE 11.18 Facing particles simulate steam leaking from bullet holes in tanks.

To add liquid coming out of the hole, a Metaparticle system could be added to each hole. The drawback with Metaparticles is they are slow to render when you use enough particles to make a realistic flowing liquid. For realistic flames other than something like a candle flame or an explosion, it is better to use a plug-in like the Phoenix fire plug-in from Digimation. For a realistic squirt of burning liquid, you can create a morphed stream of liquid made from geometry. Then, you apply the Phoenix plug-in to emit flames all along the stream, simulating a squirt of gasoline that is on fire. Phoenix flames also emit light, giving you more realism than the 3ds max built-in Fire Effect, which does not emit light. For a tutorial on using Phoenix, see Chapter 17, "Plug-Ins."

USING PARTICLE FLOW FOR VISUAL EFFECTS

The new Particle Flow particle system in 3ds max 6 is an event-driven system that uses operators and tests to program the flow of particle events. The events are arranged in a vertical top-to-bottom flow diagram called the *Particle View*. The Particle View window contains four work areas, as shown in Figure 11.19. The upper left window is the Event Display, where the events and particle operators, called the *flow,* are edited and displayed as wired event nodes. On the lower left is the Depot, where you select the operators, tests, and other functions, and then drag them into the event nodes to assemble events. When you click on an action, operator, or test in an event, its parameters appear in the window on the upper right. To add a test or an operator to an event, you select what you want in the Depot, and then drag the item into the Event box. A blue line will appear in the box. When the line is positioned where you want the new operator to be, release the mouse and the event will appear. In this way, you can build complex events. To delete an event or test, select it, right-click, and then click Delete in the pop-up menu.

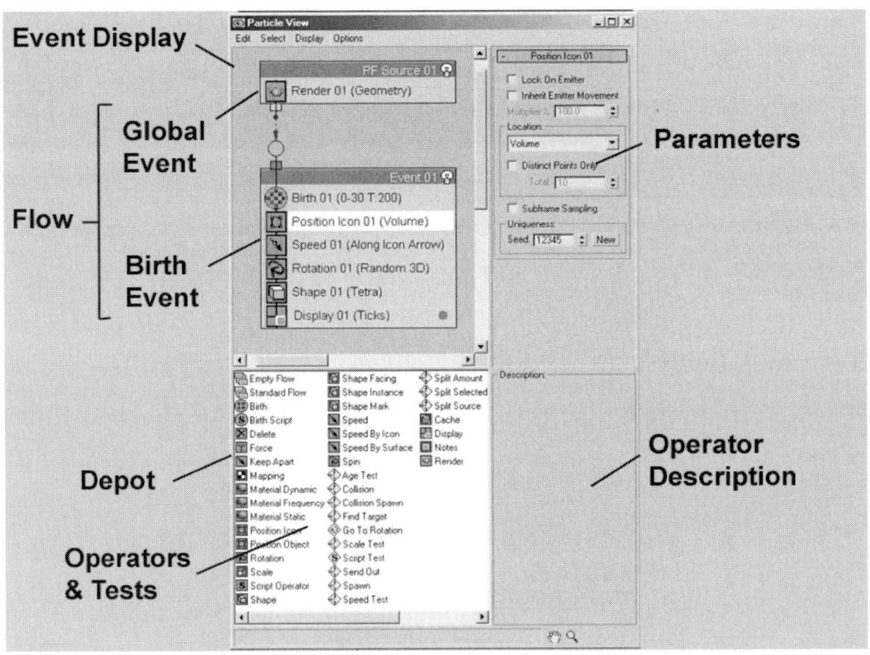

FIGURE 11.19 Particle events in the Particle View workspace.

The logical flow of a Particle Flow system runs from top to bottom, much like a logic ladder. However, because Particle Flow is event-driven, you can also set up a nonlinear progression of events that can branch to parallel events using tests, such as the Collision Spawn test, to create parallel or looping events. What is a test? A test is a kind of operator that applies a set of rules to an event in a particle flow. For example, a test can measure the age of a particle. When it reaches a certain age and the specified conditions are met, the test is considered "true." At that point, the particles are allowed to pass to the next event through an external connection, shown as a wire in the Event Display window.

Creating Dusty Footsteps

There is a major battle scene in the film *Homing Instinct* where an army of Dinomen warriors charges down a hill to attack the human colonial occupation forces that are positioned around an alien ruin. The attacking warriors raise dust as they run. If you had used the standard Max particle systems, this scene would have been a very tedious undertaking because where each footstep was going to impact the ground, you would need an individual particle emitter. Each emitter's timing, speed, and birth parameters would need to be adjusted manually for each emitter because Max standard particle emitters cannot be triggered by collisions. With Particle Flow's event-driven system, the dusty footsteps can be created automatically for all of the footsteps by making the ground a common deflector and making the soles of the soldiers' shoes into collision objects that spawn particles every time they collide with the ground deflector. Wind and gravity are then added to give the dust a more realistic behavior and direction.

The next tutorial describes how to make dust fly up as a Dinoman warrior runs down a hill.

This tutorial uses custom attributes to animate the angle of the feet. Before loading DinoWarrior.max file for this tutorial, you must place the Modifier-AttributeHolder.ms script into your Stdplugs (Standard Plugins) directory in the stdplugs\stdscripts folder. If you do not, you will get an error message and foot animation will not function correctly. The Modifier-AttributeHolder.ms script can be found in the 3dsmax6\scripts\PluginScripts folder in which you have installed max 6. This is a widely used script that enables you to store custom attributes in skeletal rigs. A tutorial covering custom attributes and this script can be found in Chapter 12, "Advanced Animation." The file used in the next tutorial is the DinoWarrior.max file from that tutorial.

TUTORIAL 11.6 CREATING DUSTY FOOTSTEPS WITH PARTICLE FLOW

ON THE CD

To create footsteps:

1. Load the DinoWarriorPF.max file from the Chap11 folder on the companion CD-ROM. If you get an error message, see the preceding note and install the Modifier-AttributeHolder.ms script. In this scene, you will find an animated Dinoman warrior with its skeleton rig and a ground plane that forms the hill terrain. Linked to the feet of the Dinoman are boxes that will be used as the particle emitters.
2. Start by creating a Particle Flow Source icon in the front view. To do that, click Create, Standard Primitives, and from the drop-down menu, select Particle Systems. Then select PF Source. Click and drag in the Front view to create a Particle Flow Source icon, and then click the Particle View button in the Setup drop-down menu. This will open the Particle Flow Event Display dialog. A default flow is displayed consisting of two boxes: PF Source01 and Event 01. Move the Particle view to one side so you can see the Dinoman in the Front view.
3. For this tutorial, two flows are needed, one for each foot. Create a second Particle Flow Source icon in the front view next to the first. You should now see a second flow appear in the Event Display, as shown in Figure 11.20. Right-click to complete PF Source icon creation. If you don't see them both, click the Zoom Extents icon in the lower right corner of the Particle View dialog. The next step is to change the operators in Events01 and 02.
4. To delete unwanted operators, go to Event01, select all of the operators except Birth 01 and Display 01, and delete them (right-click and select Delete). Move over to the other event, Event 02, and delete the same operators. Then, in the Depot window, select Position Object and drag it into the Event 01 box.Position it under Display 01 and release the mouse. A blue line will appear at the bottom of the event box as you do this. If the line is red, move it down a little. Next, select Collision Spawn from the Depot and drag it into Event 01, placing it below the Position Object operator. You should now have four operators in Event 01. Repeat the same process for the other event, Event 02.
5. Rename both events. Select the word *Event 01* at the top of the event box and then right-click and select Rename. Name this event Right Foot. Then select Event 02 and rename it Left Foot, as shown in Figure 11.21, example 1.

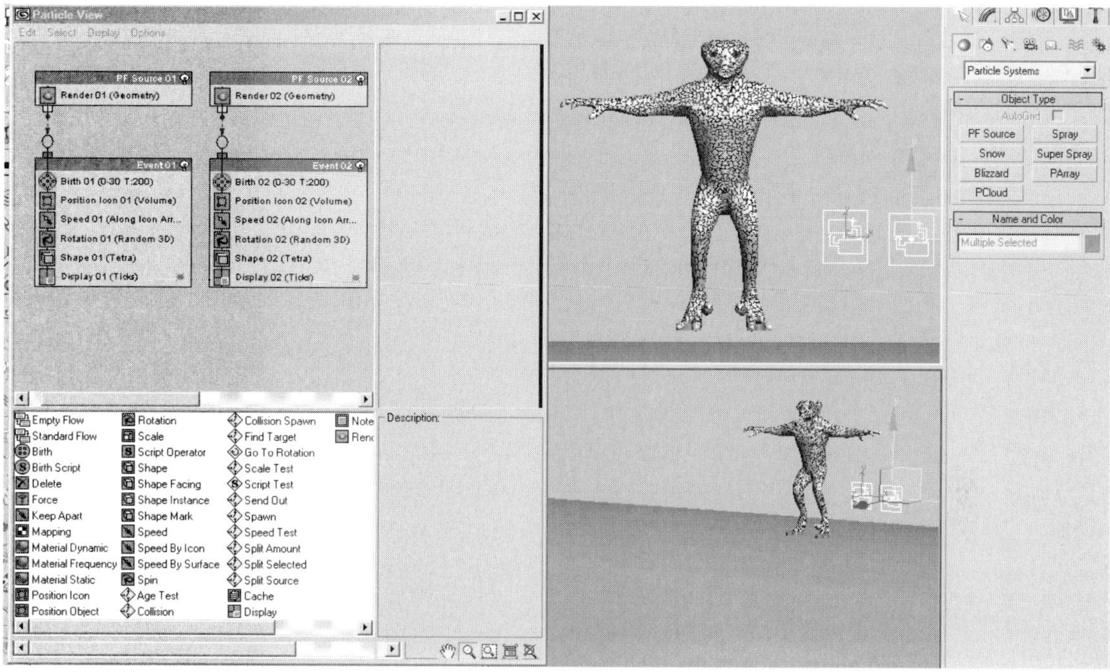

FIGURE 11.20 Using two Particle Flows for the right and left footsteps.

Notice that the Collision Spawn operator has an external connection at the left side of the event box. This is used to pass particles on the next event in the flow. The next event will be an output event that is capable of handling multiple inputs. Both the right and left foot particle spawn events will be wired to the output event that you will create next. In this way, the flow can be simplified so that both foot emitters use the same output event.

6. To create the particle output event, go to the Depot and select the Speed operator. Drag it into the empty part of the Event Display window just below the Right Foot event box. A new event box will be created that contains Speed 01 and Display 03. Rename this event Output Speed. Center this event below the Left and Right Foot events, as shown in Figure 11.21, example 2. Next, you will connect the output of the Right Foot event to the input of the Output Speed event.
7. Place the cursor over the output pin of the Collision Spawn operator. The icon will change to four arrows. Click and drag down to the input ball on top of the Output Speed event and drop it. A black wire should appear

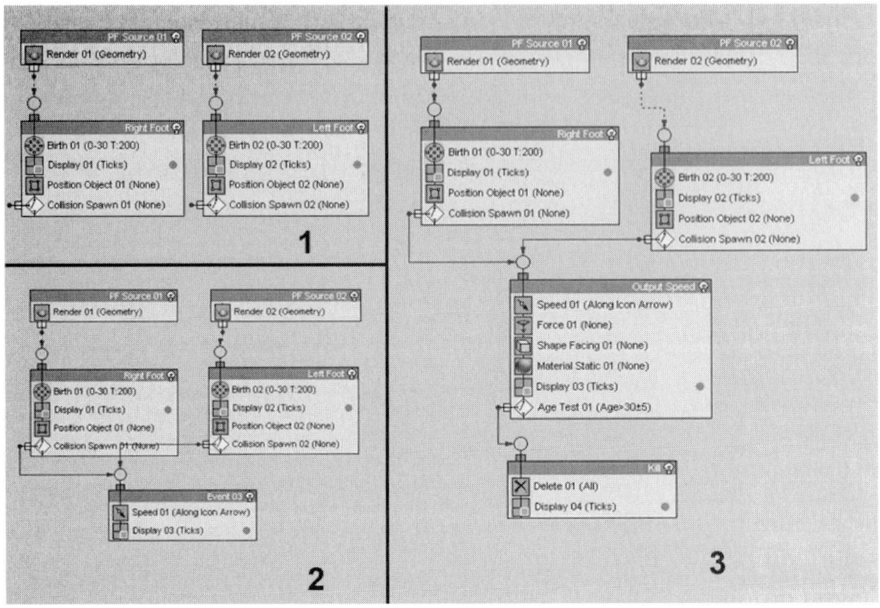

FIGURE 11.21 Adding new operators and events to a flow.

connecting the two events. Repeat this operation for the Left Foot event. You now have two flows with outputs wired into one output event, as shown in Figure 11.21, example 2.

8. Select the Left Foot event box and drag it down a little so that the connection wire runs just below the box and does not cover one of the spawn operators. You will now add additional operators to Right and Left Foot flows. In the Depot, select the Force operator and drag it to the Output Speed event box. Place it below Speed. Now select a Shape Facing operator and place it just below Force 01. Then select a Material Static operator and place it below Shape Facing. Finally, select an Age Test and place it below Display 03, as shown in Figure 11.21, example 3.

   The first five output event operators are designed to control the behavior and appearance of the particles. The last operator is an Age Test that is designed to test the age of a particle. In this case, we want to turn off each particle after a specified number of frames so that the dust cloud generated by the footstep will dissipate and dissolve. To do that, one more event is needed that will delete or kill each particle of a specified age. That requires a Delete operator. You will wire the output of the Age Test to the input of the Delete event to kill the particles.

9. To create the final Kill event for the system, go to the Depot and select the Delete operator. Drag it into the empty space below the Output Speed event box. It will contain the Delete operator and another Display operator. Delete the Display operator from the event. Rename the event as Kill, which is appropriate, as it will kill all particles beyond a certain age. Next, wire the external output pin of the Age Test operator from the Output Speed event to the input ball on top of the Kill event, as shown in Figure 11.21, example 3.
10. To make room in the event boxes for the names that will be added later to the operators, click the right edge of the events and drag the boxes a bit wider, as shown in Figure 11.21, example 3. This completes the basic event assembly for the right foot and left foot. Save the scene file as Pflow116.max. Then, continue on to the next tutorial to enter the settings that will make the Particle Flow events work.

In the next tutorial, you will enter the settings for all of the Particle Flow operators and set up the scene for animation.

The most realistic dust is made with facing particles. As mentioned earlier in this chapter, a facing particle is actually a small bitmap applied to a single square polygonal face that is generated by a particle emitter. These faces can be set to always face the camera. Almost any kind of atmospheric effect can be simulated with facing particles, including flames, bubbles, dirt, dust, smoke, and spraying water.

TUTORIAL 11.7 SETTING UP THE PARTICLE FLOW TO GENERATE DUST

To set up the flow:

1. Load the Pflow116.max file if it is not already loaded.

If you get an error message when you load the file, you will need to install the Modifier-AttributeHolder.ms script to enable the custom attributes. To do this, follow the instructions in the NOTE at the beginning of the previous tutorial.

2. You are now ready to enter the settings for all of the operators and tests in both Particle Flows. To do that, select one of the PF Source icons in the front view. Then, in the Command Panel Modifier menu, click the Particle

View button. You should now see the Event Display window, with the Right and Left Foot events side by side. Select the Birth 01 operator in the Right Foot event, and in the Parameters window, enter Emit Stop = 0 and Amount = 800, as shown in Figure 11.22, example 1. Repeat these settings for the Birth operator in the Left Foot event.

3. The foot emitter objects are hidden objects. Unhide them by first right-clicking in the viewport. From the Unhide by Name dialog, locate them quickly by typing an L or an R in the top white box of the dialog. That will highlight anything in the main list that starts with that letter. Select and unhide LParticle Box and RParticle Box. In the Right Foot event box, select Position Object 01. In its parameters, find the Emitter Objects menu and click the By List button. From the Select Object pop-up dialog, select RParticle Box. Next, select the Position Object 02 operator in the Left Foot event, and select LParticle Box as its emitter. Then turn on Lock On Emitter for both right and left Position Object operators, as shown in Figure 11.22, example 2.
4. Click the Collision Spawn 01 operator in the Right Foot event and locate the Deflectors menu. Click the By List button, and from the list select UOmniFlect01. This is the ground surface particle deflector. In the Spawn Rate and Amount menu, click Spawn On Each Collision, and set Until # = 7, Offspring # = 2, and Variation % = 10.0. Set Sync By to Particle Age. In the Speed menu, set Variation % = 10, and Divergence = 40, as shown in Figure 11.22, example 3. That setting will spread the spawned particles that will be generated when the foot impacts the UOmniFlect01 deflector. Repeat these settings for the Left Foot Collision Spawn operator.
5. To set up the Output Speed event operators, click Speed 01. In its parameters, set Speed = 80, Variation = 10, and set Direction to Inherit Previous, and Divergence to 50. Then select the Force 01 operator. In the Force Space Warps menu, click the By List box and select Gravity 01. Reduce Influence % to 150.0, and in the Offset Influence menu, set Sync By = Particle Age, as shown in Figure 11.22, example 4.
6. Before setting up the facing particles in the Shape Facing operator, you must first unhide camera02. To show all cameras, go to Control Panel > Display tab, and in the Hide by Category menu, turn off the Cameras check mark. You should now be able to press the H key (Select by Name) and see camera02 in the list of objects. In Size and Width, set Units = 4. Now, in the Output Speed event box, select Shape Facing 01, and in Parameters, click

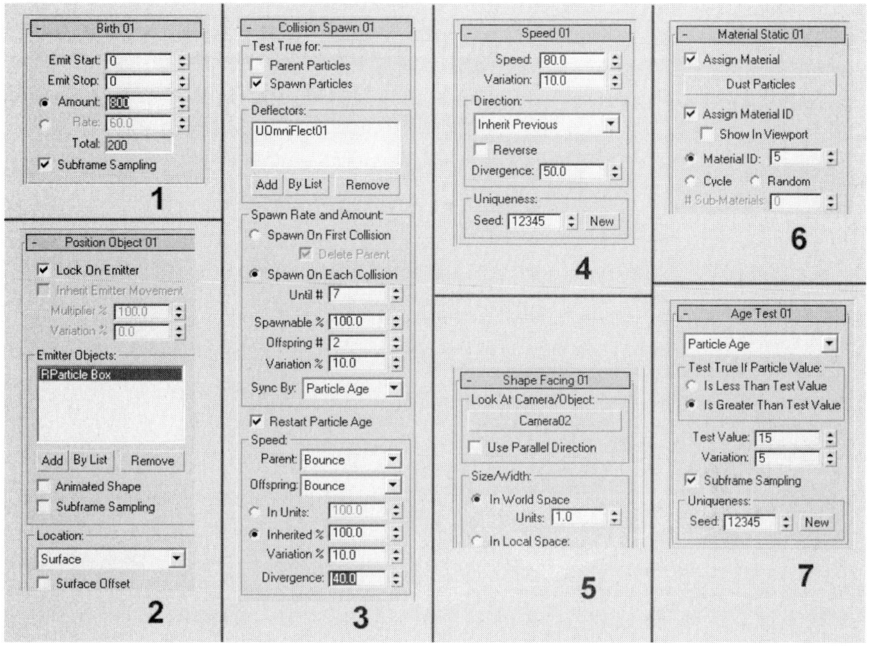

FIGURE 11.22 Entering the parameters for the event operators.

the None button under Look At Camera/Object. Press H and select Camera02, as shown in Figure 11.22, example 5. Now the dust particles will always face that camera.

7. A dust material has been made for you called Dust Particles, and can be found in the Materials Editor by clicking the M key. This material uses Material ID 5, with a radial gradient mask in the Opacity materials channel set to 16. Opacity is set to 0. In the Speed Output event, select the Material Static 01 operator. In its parameters, click the None button and when the Material/Map Browser opens, click Materials Editor. Select Dust Particles from the list. Then, back in Material Static 01 parameters, turn on Assign Material ID, and set Material ID = 5, as shown in Figure 11.22, example 6.
8. Next, set up Display and the Age Test. Click Display 03, and in its parameters, set Type = Geometry. Now select Age Test 01, and in its parameters, set Test Value = 15, as shown in Figure 11.22, example 7. Now move to the final Kill event and select the Delete 01 operator. In its parameters, set All Particles, which is the default setting, as shown in the finished Particle Flow in Figure 11.23.

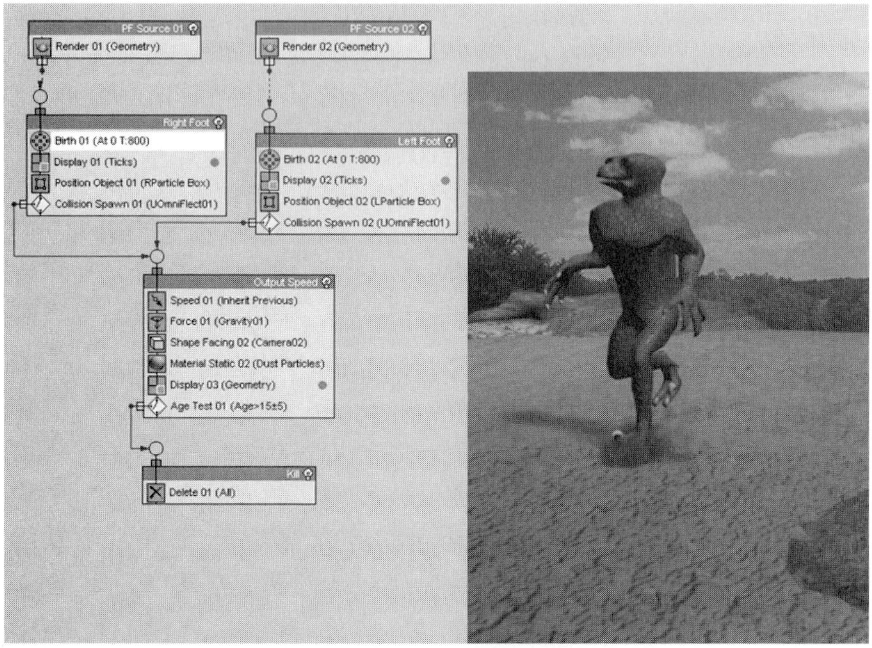

FIGURE 11.23 The finished Particle Flow for dusty footsteps.

9. Test the operation of the particle system by maximizing the Camera02 viewport and clicking Play. The Dinoman should now generate plumes of dust particles that are nearly invisible in shaded mode each time its feet collide with the surface of the ground. Render a movie to see the final results. To check the correct settings, you can open another instance of 3ds max 6 and load the Pflow 117.max file from the Chap11 folder on the companion CD-ROM. Then you can open its Particle Flow window and compare your settings with the finished file.

ON THE CD

10. Adjust the height of the dust plumes by changing the Force 01 Gravity Influence % setting. Save the file as Pflow117.max. This concludes the Particle Flow tutorials.

The same Dinoman Warrior file you have used in this chapter is used again in Chapter 12, "Advanced Animation," in the tutorial covering custom attributes.

Metaball Liquid Animation in Particle Flow

The BlobMesh Compound Object is new for 3ds max 6 and replaces the old Metaparticles blobby particles that did not perform well. BlobMesh works with both particles and mesh objects and can create metaball spheres around mesh vertices or particles. A metaball surface is created when the spheres come close enough to each other to blend together like liquid mercury. The resulting BlobMesh is good for simulating everything from weird amorphous creatures and worms to thick liquids and viscous flowing substances such as lava or soapsuds. When applied to a mesh object such as a sliced editable mesh tube primitive, it can be used to create smooth structural elements, such as the pipes shown in Figure 11.24.

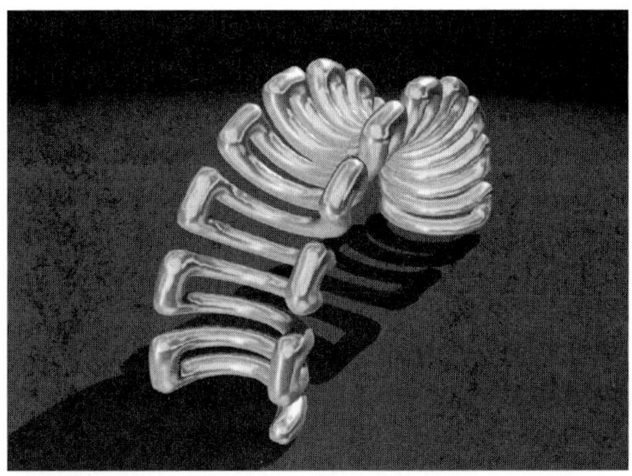

FIGURE 11.24 BlobMesh metaballs used to create smooth pipes from a mesh primitive.

ON THE CD

You can find the metaball pipe file, Blobpipes.max, in the Chap11 folder on the companion CD-ROM. The range and scope of objects that can be made with BlobMesh is limited only by your imagination. As an experiment, try placing three or more different primitive objects in an overlapping group and then apply BlobMesh to them. Another interesting example is to create a Torus Knot and try different combinations of blob size and knot parameters. You can also create ray-traced BlobMesh structures through which you can fly a camera to get outstanding surrealistic animations.

CONCLUSION

In this chapter, you worked with particle systems to create rain, blow up a chemical refinery, and create a flock of instanced butterflies. You worked with the PArray particle system to explode and fragment objects, and you created flames and smoke using the Fire Effect atmospheric explosion. You added a Volume Light to enhance the realism of the explosion. Then you used Particle Flow event-driven particles to add dusty footsteps to a running Dinoman Warrior animation. In the next chapter, you will work with advanced animation techniques to create other types of visual effects.

CHAPTER

12 ADVANCED ANIMATION

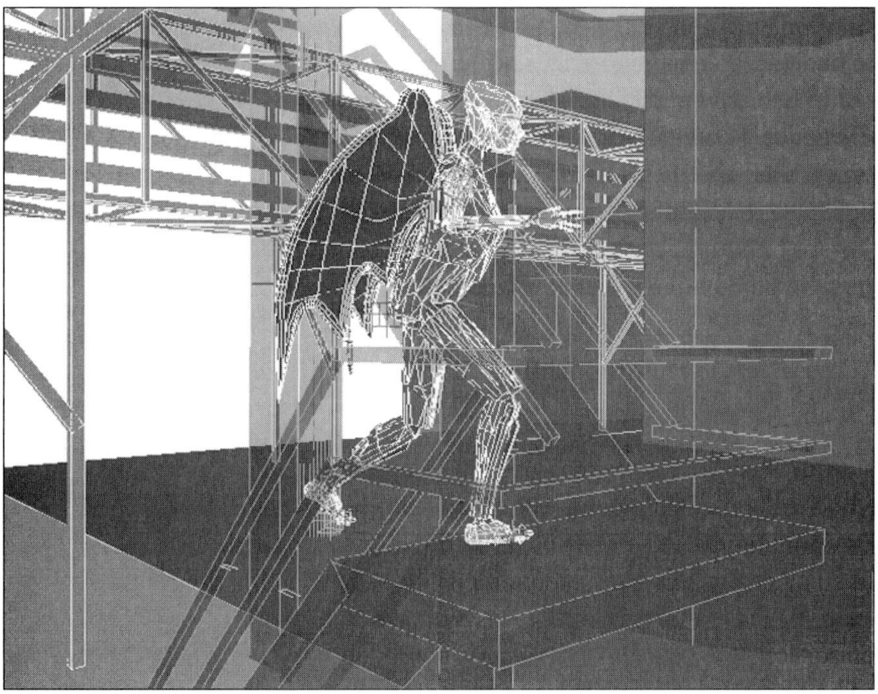

In this chapter, we introduce you to some of the advanced animation capabilities built into 3ds max 6. These features automate animation tasks that would be difficult or impossible to do by using only the mouse and keyframes. We will begin with the application of an mathematical expression to automate part of a walk cycle. Then we will explore the object collision and impact detection capabilities of Reactor 2 as they apply to character animation. Next, we will explore the exciting, new Rag Doll dynamic character animation capabilities, which enable you to create stunts such as falls and bodies impacting objects. Following that, you will be introduced to Reactor Cloth. Other advanced features covered are animating a character with custom attributes, using a facial bone network, and scripting.

EXPRESSIONS

In character animation, it is often convenient to animate a 3ds max bones skeleton rig by moving the feet, and assign an expression controller to move the body. The expression controller maintains the hips of the character centered halfway between the feet. That means that when you advance a foot to the next stride marker position, all of the bone chains linked to the hip will move in that direction so that the hip remains centered above both feet.

An expression can be defined as a mathematical function that returns a value.

The following is a standard expression for keeping one object centered between two other objects:

(Position1 + Position2) / 2

where Position 1 and Position 2 are the Position controllers of two objects.

The divisor 2 constrains the third object to always remain halfway between the two other objects.

In the following tutorial, you will learn how this expression is applied to a character animation walk cycle. The character you will use is the Generic Man skeleton circle rig with the circular control handles, which is referred to as the "circle rig," as shown in Figure 12.1.

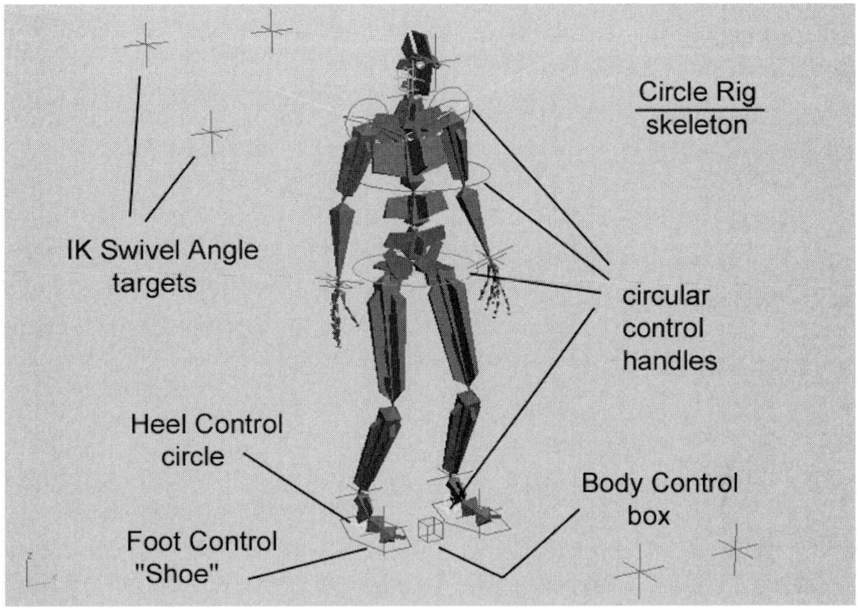

FIGURE 12.1 The skeleton rig is animated with an expression controller.

The skeleton with the circular joint manipulator handles is functionally the same as the skeleton rig with box manipulators, which is the type of skeleton rig you built in Chapter 7, and animated in Chapters 8, 9, and 10. The circle rig uses spline circles instead of helper points and boxes for the animation. Many animators prefer this type of rig because they think it is easier to understand, and it is less complex visually.

TUTORIAL 12.1

ANIMATE A WALK CYCLE WITH AN EXPRESSION CONTROLLER

To animate the walk of the skeleton rig with an expression:

ON THE CD

1. Load the Expression.max file from the Chap12 folder on the companion CD-ROM. Maximize the perspective view. You should see the circle rig skeleton standing on a flat plane. Click F4 to display edges.
2. Between the feet is a small box called the body control. The hip control circle and the entire upper body are linked to this box. You will apply the expression controller to this box. The foot control shoes are not linked; they are in world space. Select the body control box, as shown in Figure 12.2,

example 1, and then click Graph Editors > Track View – Curve Editor. The Curve Editor will open.

3. Zoom out and pan the skeleton down to the lower-left corner of the perspective view. In the Curve Editor hierarchy window, the Body Control should be highlighted because it is selected, as shown in Figure 12.2, example 2. Below Body Control is the track called Position. Click on Position.
4. In the Trackview menu bar, click Controller > Assign. The Assign Position Controller menu will open, as shown in Figure 12.2, example 3. Select Position Expression and click OK. The Expression Controller : Body Control\ Position dialog window will open.

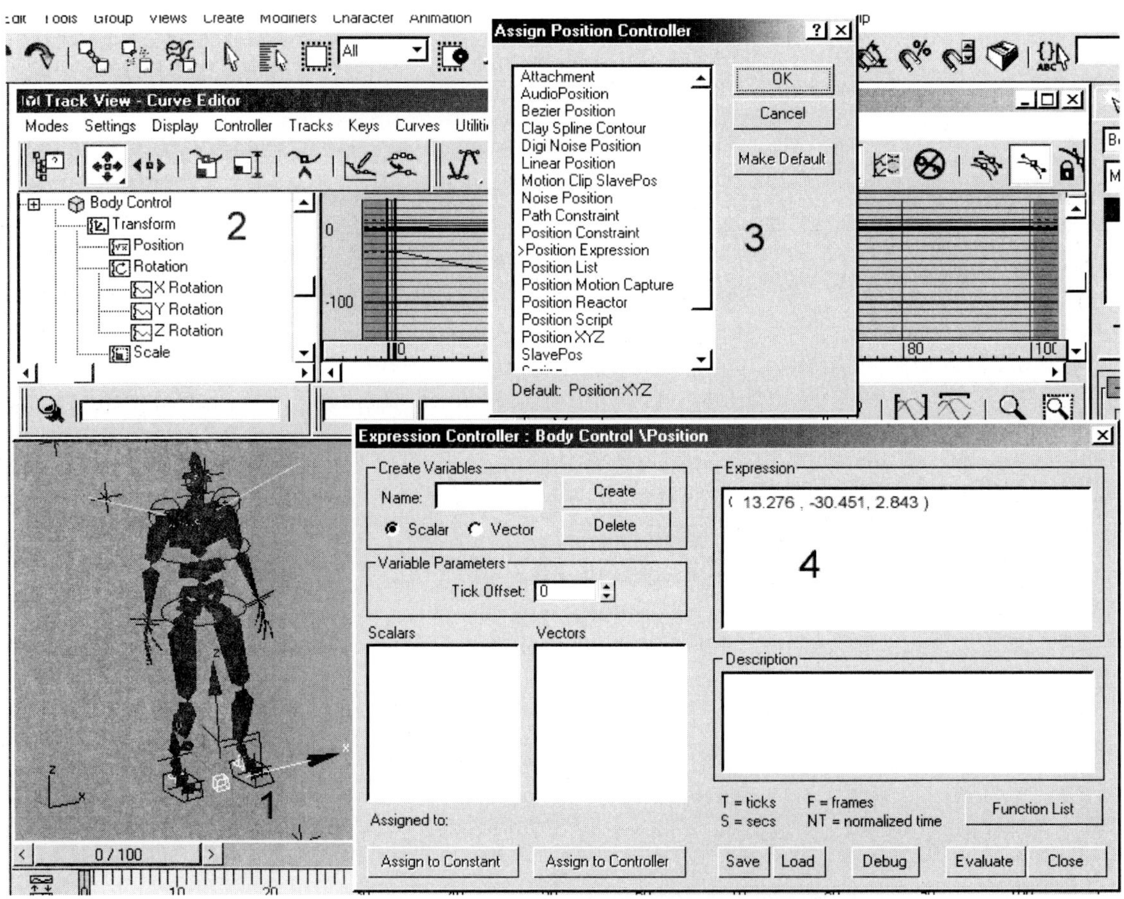

FIGURE 12.2 Steps to assign a Position Expression to an object in the Track View–Curve Editor.

5. When the Expression Controller dialog opens, you will see some data in parentheses in the Expression window, as shown in Figure 12.2, example 4. This is the X, Y, Z position of the body control box. Select and delete this data, and type in the following expression: (position1 + position2) / 2. To make this expression work, you will assign a vector variable named position1 to the left foot control, and the variable named position2 to the right foot control.
6. To assign the variables to the feet, enter the name position1 in the Name data field in the Create Variables section of the Expression Controller dialog, and then turn on the Vector switch, as shown in Figure 12.3, example 1. Next, click Create. Always turn on Vector before clicking Create. The name position1 will appear in the Vectors window, as shown in Figure 12.3, example 2. Repeat that for the variable named position2.
7. Click the Evaluate button. If you have typed everything correctly, you will not get an error message. To see if the expression is working, go to the Perspective window, turn on Auto Key, go to frame 12, and select one of

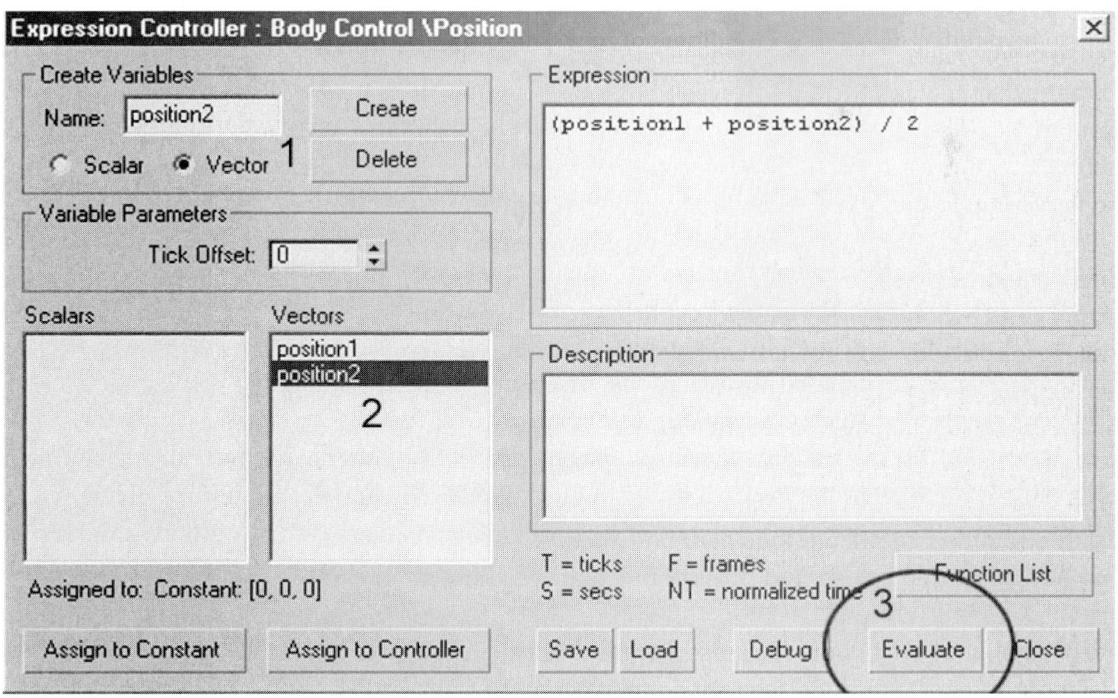

FIGURE 12.3 Assign the position variables to the feet in the Expression Controller dialog.

the Foot Control shoes. Move it forward one-half step. The body of the skeleton should respond and move as well.

ON THE CD

8. You are now ready to animate the feet in a walk cycle. If you had any trouble and you would like to see the skeleton taking a few steps, you can load the finished Expression01.max file from the Chap12 folder on the companion CD-ROM.
9. Save the file as Expression01.max.

In the next section of this chapter, you will explore the impact detection and collision detection capabilities of Reactor.

USING REACTOR 2

Reactor 2 works by putting objects in collections, similar to putting variables into an expression. The collection contains all of the objects that will react to each other. It can contain rigid bodies, soft bodies, cloth objects, or constraints. To create a rigid body dynamic effect, you must first create a Rigid Body (RB) Collection. Rigid bodies are objects that do not change shape. The basic workflow is as follows: First, you create an RB Collection icon in the viewport, and then add objects to the collection. Next, you assign which objects will become collision pairs. Then, you open the Utility > Reactor menus and set the physical properties of all objects. Finally, you run a simulation to see how the objects behave.

One of the unexpected characteristics of Reactor is that even though the character is part of the RB Collection, it will only detect collisions when is it moving very slowly. If the velocity of the character is much more than 0, the collision no longer works, so a work-around had to be devised for situations when the character is moving fast, such as in the Alley Chase scene.

Notice the large sphere surrounding the lower body of the character in the lower-left side of Figure 12.4. This standard primitive object is used as the character collision object. It is animated separately and given an initial velocity so that it meets the garbage cans at exactly the same time as the running character. Spheres will react to collisions regardless of the velocity, so the sphere has been made into an invisible proxy collision object and included in the RB Collection. When you render the scene, you get the effect of solid body collisions, but it is really the sphere proxy that is doing the work, not the surface of the character mesh. This limitation makes it more time consuming to set up collisions, but since it works well, this method has been used for almost all of the collisions in *Homing Instinct*.

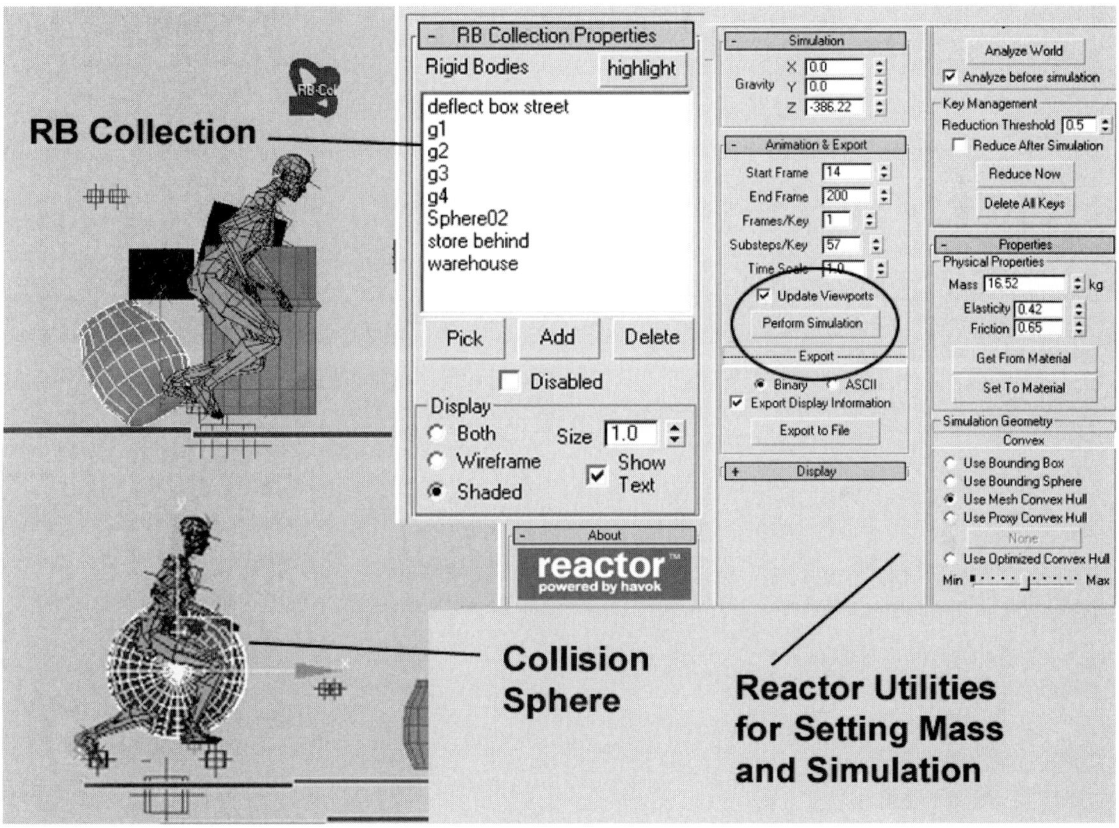

FIGURE 12.4 The Reactor interface and creating an RB Collection.

In the next tutorial, you will explore Reactor 2 Collision Detection and work with an RB Collection.

TUTORIAL 12.2

DYNAMIC COLLISIONS WITH CHARACTERS

ON THE CD

To animate dynamic collisions:

1. Load the Dyn_FX1200.max scene file from the Chap12 folder on the companion CD-ROM. If your Reactor menu bar does not show in the 3ds max interface, you can display it by clicking Customize > Load Custom UI Scheme and selecting reactor_light.ui. That puts the menu bar at the left of the screen.
2. The scene is a short running sequence. Xzulixia runs into the stack of rubbish. To set up the collision of the character with the trash cans, you first must create an RB Collection icon in the viewport. Click the RB Collection icon at the top of the Reactor menu bar, and then click and drag in the left viewport, as shown in Figure 12.4.
3. To create the RB Collection, select the RB icon, and then click the Modify tab. In the RB Collection Properties menu, click the Pick button. Select one of the garbage cans, and then click the Add button. From the list, select the objects named G1, G2, G3, G4, and G5, which is the Collision Floor object. You do not need to include the XzuBody character mesh because you will be using a proxy object in its place.
4. If you want to exclude any of the objects, you can click Advanced > Define Collision Pairs. For this tutorial, use the default setting of Common Collisions. Now, click the Utility Tab icon, and in the Utilities list select "reactor." (All discreet products, including reactor by Havok, have lowercase names. Do not confuse this with the 3ds max "reactor controller," which works like wired parameters and has completely different capabilities.)
5. To set up the objects for collision, they must either have mass or be unmovable (0 mass). Open the Utility > Reactor menus to set the physical properties of all objects. The two menus that you are interested in are Physical Properties and Animation & Export. In Properties, set the mass of G1 = 36, G2 = 16, G3 = 10, and G4 = 10. G5 is the Collision Floor or deflector object positioned on the same plane as the alley surface. It should be set to G5 = 0. "0" means that the object has infinite mass and is therefore immovable, and is not affected by gravity. Anything with more than 0 mass will be affected by gravity and impacts.
6. So far, there is nothing to impact with the objects. The next step is to set up the proxy object to create the character impacts. Unhide the object named CollisionSphere. It should be positioned around the lower body of

the Xzulixia model at frame 0, as shown in the lower-left corner of Figure 12.5. You will animate it by giving it an Initial Velocity. Set its opacity to 0.0.

You can use keyframes that were set before the Dynamic Simulation to give objects an Initial Velocity that will create impacts with stationary objects. For example, if you wanted a cannonball to knock over a brick wall, you would animate the cannonball to move a fairly long distance from frame 0 to frame 40. Its motion would be aimed directly at the brick wall. Then, that object is added to the existing RB Collection. You must also set its mass to a high number and increase the Friction. This gives it a greater effect on the objects it hits. The simulation is set to run starting at frame 44 or later. That way, the system will not overwrite the keys already applied to the cannonball. Reactor will include its current velocity in the total dynamic simulation.

7. Maximize the left view and position the character and the garbage cans so that you can see them both. To create an Initial Velocity for the collision sphere, select the sphere at frame 1. Turn on Auto Key, and then move the Time Slider to frame 18. Now, move the sphere in the X-axis so that it again covers the lower part of the body of the character. Turn off Auto Key and

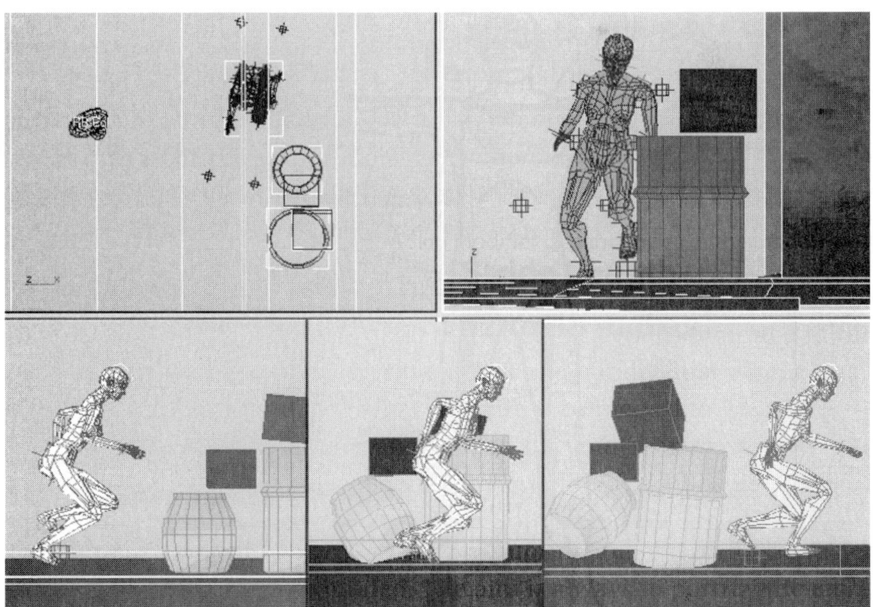

FIGURE 12.5 Trash cans and boxes reacting to collisions.

slide the Time Slider. The sphere should move with the character as it runs, but stop on frame 18 without hitting the garbage cans. You are now ready to add the sphere to the RB Collection.

8. Select the RB Collection icon, and click the Modify tab. In the RB Collection Properties menu, click the Add button to add the collision sphere to the list. Next, open the Reactor Utilities menu. Select the collision sphere and set its Mass to 100.0. You are now ready to try a simulation. In the Reactor Animation & Export menu, set Start Frame for the simulation to 18, and set End Frame = 80. Do not start it at frame 0. Click the Perform Simulation button and watch the system calculate the dynamic animation.
9. Now, hide the collision sphere and watch the animation. The garbage cans will settle a bit, and then they will be hit and thrown up and back by the collision sphere when it hits them. At the same moment, the Character model will hit them, as shown in Figure 12.5. Even though the character has no impact detection, the illusion will be created that the character is impacting the objects because the collision sphere is invisible.
10. This simple collision system is pretty much fool-proof and can be used to knock over or impact anything in your scenes. It also works well with constrained objects that need to be impacted to make them move. You might need to change the Elasticity if your objects bounce too much. You can also reduce the mass of the collision sphere.
11. Try setting the Friction to higher values to modify the collision behavior. Set the Substeps/Key to 50, and the Time Scale to .4 to slow the simulation and make it more accurate. You usually don't need to bother deleting keyframes between simulations. Perform Simulation overwrites the old keys each time you re-run it.
12. Save the scene as Dyn_FX1201.max.

Deformable meshes that use Physique do not provide high-speed collisions when used with Reactor 2. The workaround is to use primitive objects to act as proxy collision objects for the skin. Instead of firing a sphere at objects you want to collide with or knock over, you can link standard primitive objects such as cylinders or small spheres to the legs, body, and arms of your biped or 3ds max bones skeleton, as shown in Figure 12.6.

You include the proxy objects in the RB Collection to obtain a collision solution between the character and the objects with which it collides. To hide the proxy primitives, apply a 100% transparent material with no specular highlights.

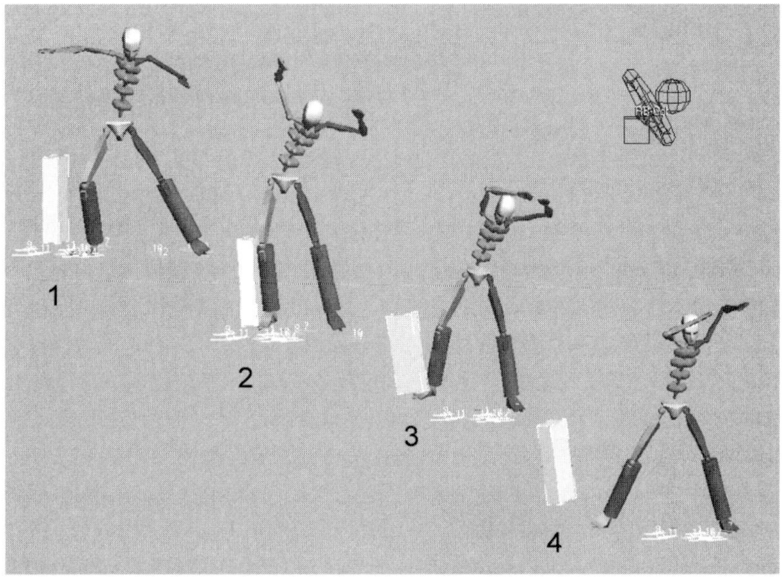

FIGURE 12.6 Primitive cylinders must be used as proxy collision objects when using Physique with Reactor.

Performing Stunts with the Reactor 2 Rag Doll

One of the most exciting and useful new features in Reactor 2 is the Rag Doll stunt skeleton, which will be referred to as a *stunt double* because that is what a stunt man is called in the motion picture industry.

A Rag Doll stunt double skeleton can react to physical forces such as impacts with objects. When it moves in a simulation, it obeys the physical laws of gravity, mass, inertia, friction, and weight. The Rag Doll constraint system enables you to create a skeleton and set up its properties to simulate the actual physics of human motion, which are impossible to animate realistically using manual keyframing methods.

By using a Rag Doll stunt double in Reactor 2, a character can be made to do stunts such as falling over when shot, tumbling down stairs, or being blown up into the air. The Rag Doll creation and conversion script, which is called rctRagdollScript.ms, can be used create a Rag Doll from a biped skeleton, or it can be used to create a stand-alone skeleton, as shown in Figure 12.7. The script automatically creates all the necessary constraints, plus a Rigid Body Collection, and a Constraint Solver.

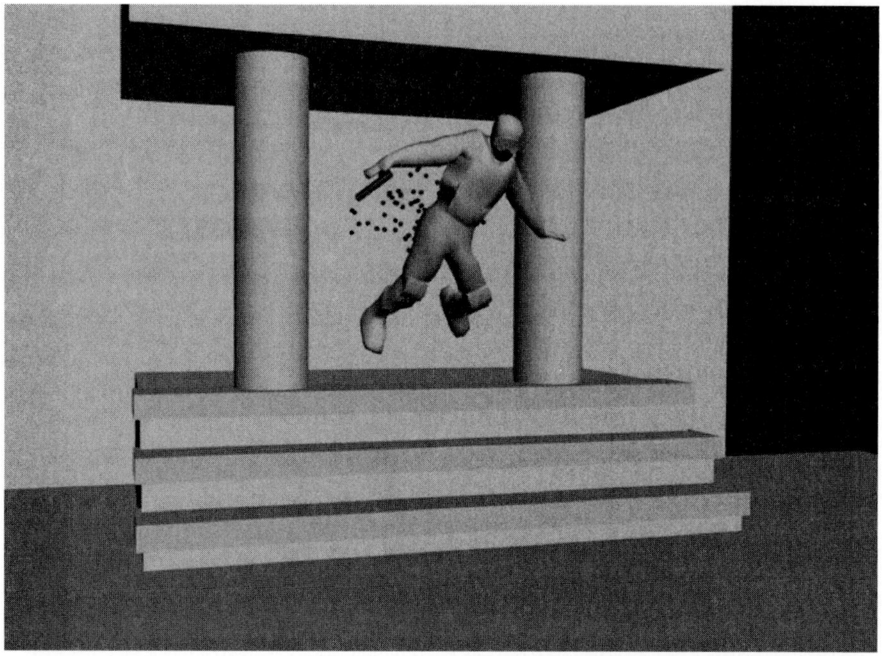

FIGURE 12.7 The character falling after being shot is a Rag Doll stunt double.

The next tutorial uses one of the Rag Doll soldier models that ships with the 3ds max 6 Reactor 2 tutorials. However, the stunt described here does not appear in the 3d studio max 6 tutorials. You are going to shoot and kill the Rag Doll, and then run a simulation to make him collapse and fall down the steps of a temple. The first part of the animation has already been done for you, but the simulation has not been prepared. You will set up the scene and work with a Constraint Solver, a Rigid Body Collection, and gravity to create the fall.

In the next tutorial, you will simulate a Rag Doll character performing a stunt.

TUTORIAL 12.3

SHOOTING A RAG DOLL

To perform the Rag Doll stunt:

ON THE CD

1. Load the ShootRDoll.max file from the Chap12 folder on the companion CD-ROM. The file should contain a Rag Doll skeleton, a soldier mesh, a

temple with two pillars, and steps. Also included is a simple Particle Flow particle system with a Gravity Space Warp to simulate the bullet exiting the back of the soldier when he is shot. The bones of the skeleton have already been set to have a mass of 10, which means that gravity will affect them. The floor and temple steps have 0 mass, which means that gravity will not affect them and they will not move during the simulation.

If you move the Time Slider, you will notice that the character is animated from frame 0 to frame 38. At frame 39, we will set up the simulation to do the rest of the animation and cause the character to fall down the steps. This is a low-resolution model for learning the principles of Rag Doll simulation and is not textured or finished. The blue icons that you can see at every joint indicate that each joint already has a Hinge constraint or a Rag Doll constraint applied to it. The Hinge constraint allows one axis of movement. The Rag Doll Constraint allows two or three axes of movement, with limits.

2. To set up the simulation, you will first create a Rigid Body Collection that includes all the objects that will collide with each other. The quickest way to do that is to hide everything that will not be a collision object. Select and hide the brown temple and the brown porch objects. Do not hide the gray steps, the floor, or the character. Next, in the main menu, click Reactor > Create Object > Rigid Body Collection, and then click and drag in the front view above the character to create the RB Collection icon.
3. Select the RB Collection and open the Modifier panel. You will see the RB Collection Properties window. Click the Pick button and click on the Floor. Then click Add, and in the Select Rigid Bodies dialog, select everything except the skin. It will include the floor, the steps, and all of the Rag Doll skeleton, as shown in Figure 12.8.
4. Next, create a Constraint Solver. In the main menu, click Reactor > Create Object > Constraint Solver, and then click and drag in the front view to the left of the RB Collection icon to create the C Solver icon. Next, open the Modifier panel. In the CSolver Properties menu, click the RB Collection button, and then select the RB Collection icon in the front view. Click the Pick button and select one of the Hinge Constraint icons at the character's feet. Finally, click the Add button and select all of the constraints listed in the Select New Constraints to Add dialog, as shown in Figure 12.9. You should now see hinges 1–8 and Rag Doll 1–8 in the Constraint Solver window.
5. The next step is to open the Reactor Utility menus. Click the Utilities tab in the Command Panel and then click Reactor. The menus will expand, but to

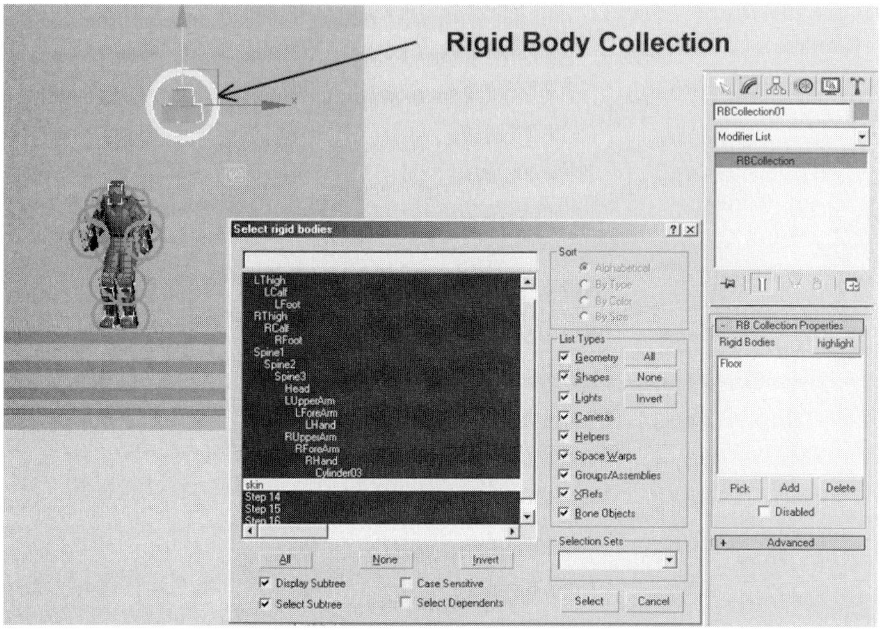

FIGURE 12.8 Creating a Rigid Body Collection.

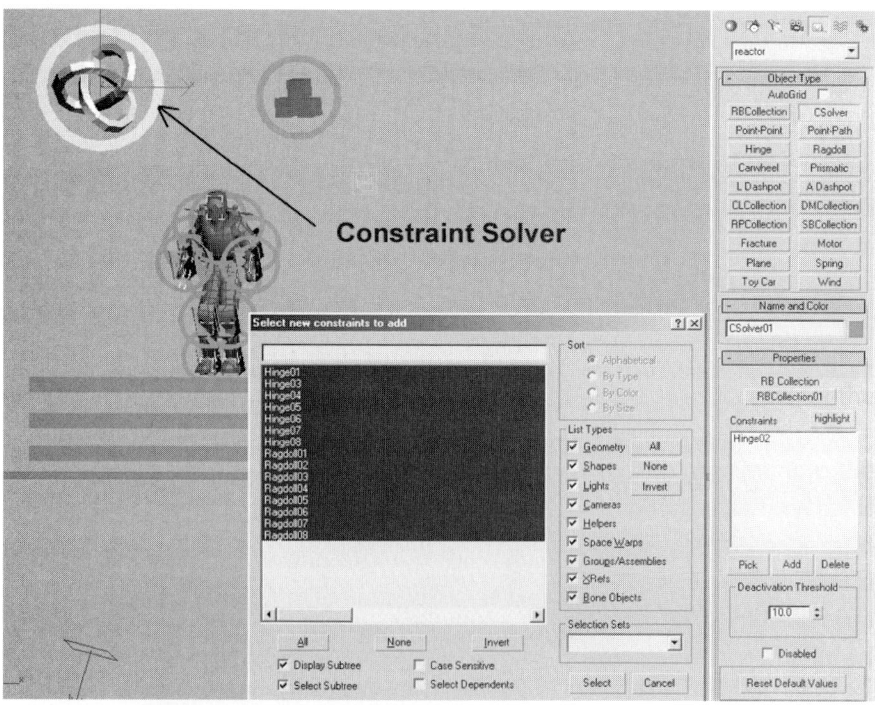

FIGURE 12.9 Creating a Constraint Solver.

see them all you must click and drag the right edge of the viewport toward the left. Expand it to three columns. Now, manually click each menu bar to expand it and open all of the reactor menus. Now run the Analyze World utility. This utility will look at the scene and indicate whether anything is wrong with the scene that will prevent the simulation from working.

6. The analysis shows that boxes that form the skeleton of the Rag Doll are interpenetrating, as shown in Figure 12.10, example 1. This will cause the simulation to act strangely. Reactor will try to solve the simulation problem by continually trying to move the bones apart while the constraints try to pull them together. This will cause the character to fall on the ground and jitter and jiggle continuously. (You probably don't want this effect unless you are depicting convulsions.) To solve this problem, you must disable the bone-to-bone pair collisions.
7. To disable bone pair collisions, go to the Reactor > Collisions drop-down menu. In the Global Collisions section, click the Define Collision Pairs button. The Define Collisions dialog will open and you will see all of the colliding objects listed in the Entities window. Select only the objects that are part of the skeleton, and then click the Double Arrow buttons next to the Disabled Collisions window. They will move and appear in that window for

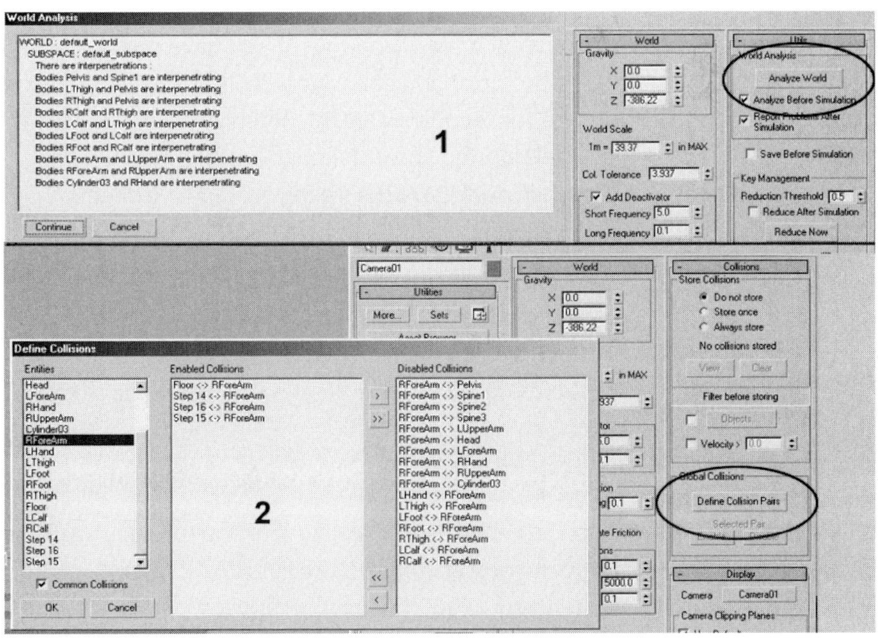

FIGURE 12.10 Use the Analyze World utility, and then correct collision problems.

only a moment. Then, to test whether the collisions are correct, select any of the bones in the skeleton, such as RforeArm. In the Enabled Collisions window, you should now see only four entries: the floor, Step 14, Step 15, and Step 16, as shown in Figure 12.10, example 2. All other collisions with this bone have been turned off.

8. You are now ready to simulate. Before you run the preview simulation, you must have a camera. However, in this scene, camera display is turned off. Go to the Control Panel > Display tab, and in the Hide by Category menu, turn off the Hide Cameras switch. Then go to the Utility > Reactor > Display menu, click the Camera button, and select Camera01.
9. Next, go to the Reactor Preview & Animation menu. Set Start Frame to 39 and End Frame to 250. Be sure that your Animation End Time is also set to 250 in the main Time Configuration dialog. Then, in the Reactor Preview & Animation menu, click the Preview in Window button. A window will open over the viewport and you will see the Rag Doll standing, pointing his gun at the top of the steps. Now press the P key to see the preview simulation. The Rag Doll should start reacting and then fall down the steps and onto the floor of the temple building. Press P to stop or close the window. The pistol will not follow the hand in Preview mode.

ON THE CD

10. If you are satisfied, you can now press the Create Animation button, but be aware that if you want to change anything, you will need to re-simulate with each set of changes. If you have problems, you can compare your file to the finished version called ShootRDoll123.max in the Chap12 folder on the companion CD-ROM. When you are ready to render, be sure to hide the skeleton but leave the pistol visible.
11. When done, save the file to your working directory as ShootRDoll123.max.

ON THE CD

To see a finished animation, load the RagDollShoot.mov movie file from the Chap 12\Images folder on the companion CD-ROM.

In the next section, you will explore how Reactor 2 was used to set up the dynamic effects for a battle scene in the film *Homing Instinct*.

Creating a Battle Scene with Reactor 2 Rag Dolls

Since the beginning of the motion picture industry, films have shown battle scenes staged with explosions, men behind barricades firing machine guns, and charging armies. *Homing Instinct* contains an extended battle sequence in which the indigenous Dinomen, who are the remnants of a long dead civilization, rise up against their human masters. The battle takes place at the entrance to an alien temple where two human guards are attacked and quickly killed by Dinomen snipers with a rocket-propelled grenade, as shown in Figure 12.11.

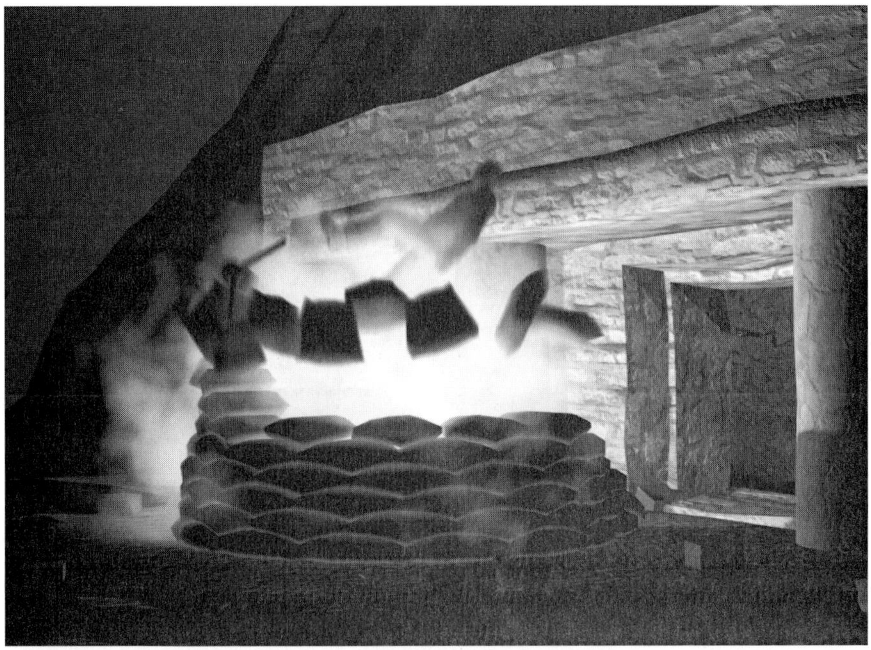

FIGURE 12.11 A rocket-powered grenade explodes during an attack on a machine gun nest.

This battle scene is quite complex and has a number of different effects. To enhance and support the dynamic physical effects done with Reactor 2, there are a number of visual effects.

The character animation for the battle scene was done with character studio 4 bipeds using motion originally derived from motion capture files. Two Rag Doll stunt doubles were used with the bipeds to simulate one soldier being blown into the air, and another soldier being shot. The explosion hits the machine gun, throwing sandbags in all directions. A particle system was used to enhance the explosion with smoke, and a fire effect was added to thicken the explosion. Particles were also used to add tracer bullets to simulate gunfire.

The "Shooting the Rag Doll" stunt from the previous tutorial has been incorporated into this battle scene. The Rag Doll that is shot is standing near one of the pillars at the entrance to the alien temple, as shown in Figure 12.12.

In the next tutorial, you will learn how the effects were set up and how all of the effects work. This is an exploratory tutorial. You are not expected to do anything beyond reading through the explanations of how everything was set up. You might want to modify the scene or add events to the battle scene when you are finished reading the tutorial.

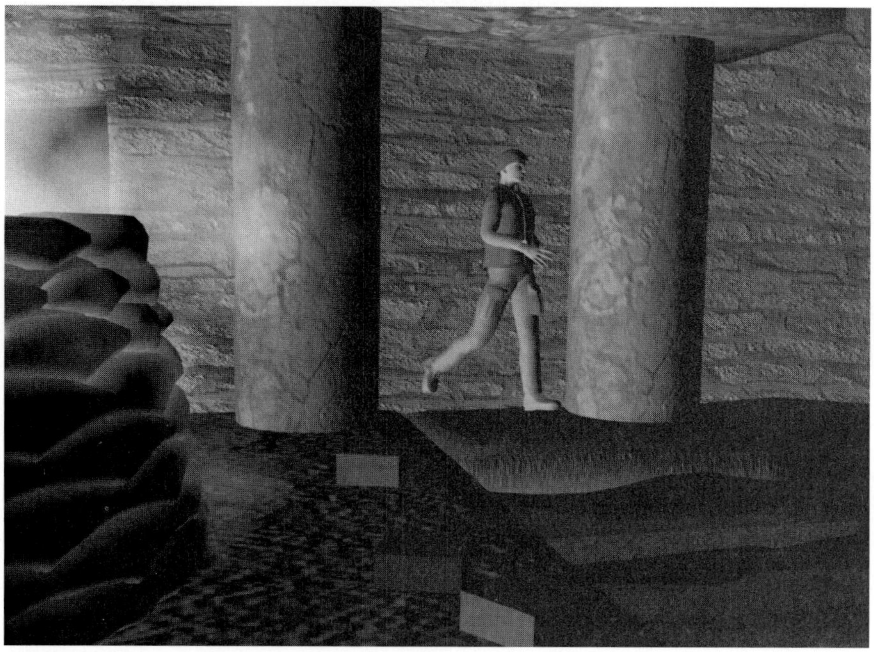

FIGURE 12.12 A more realistic soldier model set up to perform the same "Shooting the Rag Doll" stunt from the previous tutorial is included in the battle scene.

TUTORIAL 12.4

SETTING UP A REACTOR 2 BATTLE SCENE

To learn how the scene was set up:

ON THE CD

1. Load the Battle_Start.max file from the Chap12 folder on the companion CD-ROM into 3ds max 6. When you load the file, you might get a "Biped Obsolete File" warning. This is normal because max 6 uses character stu-

dio 4.2, and the battle scene was created with character studio 4.0. Simply click OK and ignore the warning.

ON THE CD

The GetPunched.bip motion file was chosen from the collection of over 100 Footstep motion files that ships with character studio 4.0. If you have not purchased the full version of character studio 4, or if Max tells you that it cannot find the GetPunched.bip motion file, you can find it in the Chap12\Extras folder on the companion CD-ROM.

2. When you first open the file, you will see a transparent soldier model with a biped inside. The rest of the objects have been hidden. The soldier you see actually has two skeletons: a Rag Doll stunt double skeleton and a biped skeleton, one inside the other. This is the way a biped must be set up if it is going to be used for a dynamic animation in Reactor 2. The Rag Doll skeleton is created by a script called: rtcRagdollScript.ms that can be found in the 3dsmax6\Scripts directory.

Warning! Do not run the script on either of the bipeds in the battle scene. The script has already been run on both bipeds, and both already have Rag Doll stunt doubles attached to them. This tutorial is designed only to inform you of what was done to each part of the scene. Do not do anything other than read the steps and examine how the scene was created until after you read the entire tutorial.

3. To create a Rag Doll stunt double for a biped, you must first select a biped center of mass (COM), which is usually called Bip01, unless the biped has been renamed. Then the script is run by clicking MAXScript in the Utility panel. In the MAXScript rollout, click the RunScript button and then navigate to the 3dsmax6\scripts directory and select: rtcRagdollScript.ms. A dialog box will open in the viewport and you can then select the lower window. Turn on all the switches you find in the lower menu to generate a Rag Doll, the Hinge and Rag Doll constraints, a Constraint Solver, and a Rigid Body Collection, and then click OK, as shown in Figure 12.13, example 1.
4. The script will clone the biped and transfer the body mesh binding from the biped to the newly cloned Rag Doll skeleton. Caution: Only skin can be used with Reactor 2. Physique will not work and the body mesh will not be transferred to the Rag Doll. Always bind the body mesh to the biped with the Skin Modifier whenever you create a biped animated model for use in Reactor 2.
5. The Rag Doll bones are automatically linked to the biped, so they inherit the biped motion and move along with the biped animation until you run

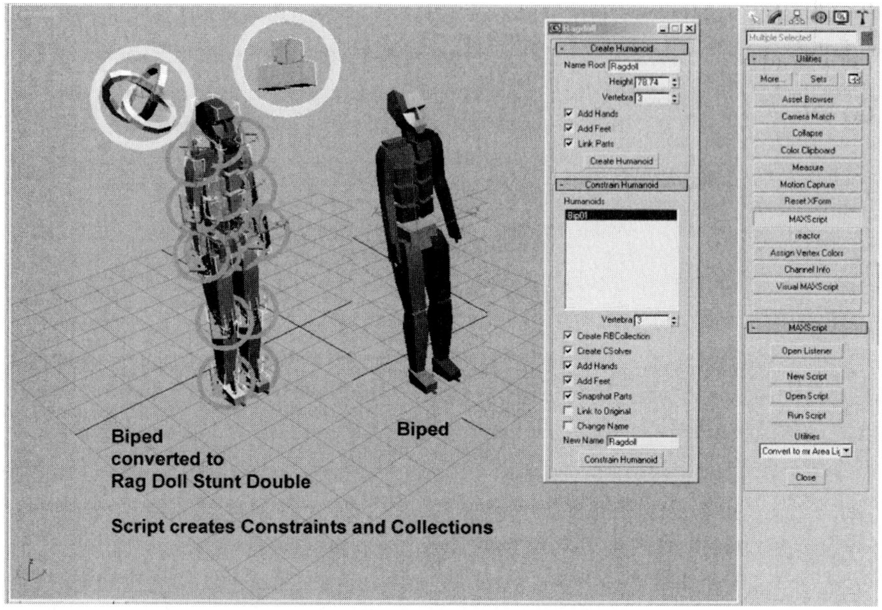

FIGURE 12.13 Creating a Rag Doll from a biped using MAXScript.

the Reactor 2 simulation. Once you run the simulation, the Rag Doll will separate from the biped and move off on its own, taking the skin with it. Then it will perform whatever dynamic stunt you have set up.

6. To see how the battle scene is set up, click Unhide All. You will see the temple, the ground and the cliff behind it, and the machine gunner, as shown in Figure 12.14, example 1. The machine gunner in the Camera02 view has been set up so that the motions of the GetPunched.bip motion file fit in with the action of the battle scene.
7. At this point, you might want to look at the finished animation, which can be seen by loading the Battle.mov movie in the Chap12\Images folder on the companion CD-ROM. Notice that the sandbags and the Rag Doll are impacted at the same time and thrown into the air. That is because they are all part of the same Rigid Body Collection that will be impacted by the catapult sphere.

ON THE CD

8. The biped motion file called GetPunched.bip animates the biped. Because the bones of the Rag Doll are linked to the bones of the biped, it inherits the motion. At the point when the machine gunner is to be blown up, the biped animation has reached its last keyframe. When the Rag Doll dynamic simulation takes over, the Rag doll is catapulted upward by an in-

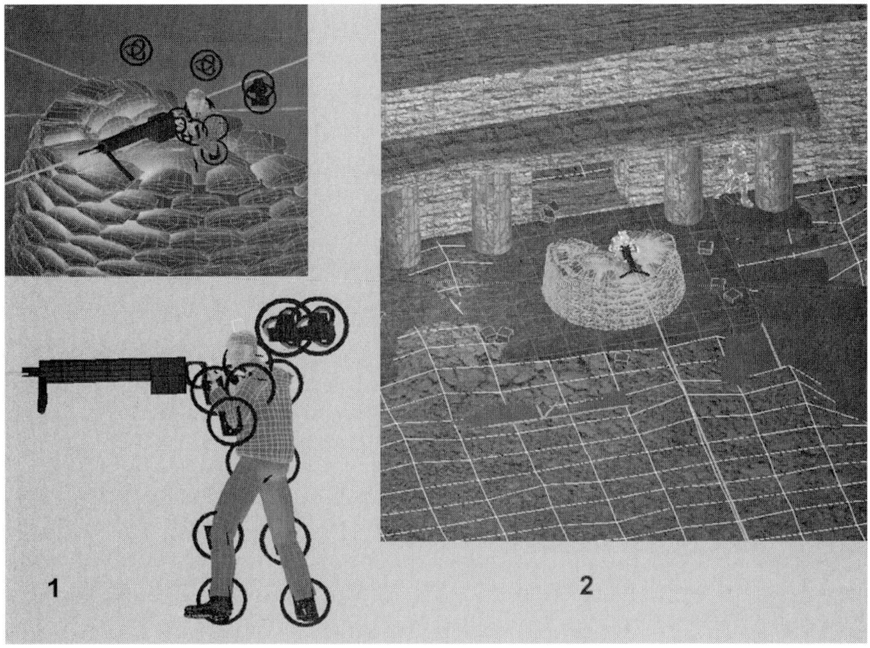

FIGURE 12.14 The temple setting and the machine gun nest.

visible moving sphere that hits it from below, as shown in Figure 12.14, example 2.

9. The machine gun nest explosion is a combination of effects, which include multiple dynamic collisions, a particle system, animated lighting, multiple sandbag collisions, and an atmospheric fire effect, as shown in Figure 12.15. The machine gun is actually a collection of parts (one of which is a small box used as a particle emitter) that are grouped so that Reactor will treat them as one object.
10. The sandbag wall was composed of 90 copies of one modified box primitive that has been mesh-smoothed. There were two problems with the sandbag wall. First, because the top two or three rows of sandbags are collision objects, they cannot be touching or interpenetrating during the simulation. That means a fairly wide space must be between all of the upper sandbags when the simulation starts. Any light from the three omni lights that create the flash from the explosion is going to shine through those spaces between the sandbags. The second problem is that because of the spaces that must be maintained, you can see the soldier standing behind the wall of sandbags. That was unacceptable. The solution was to add a

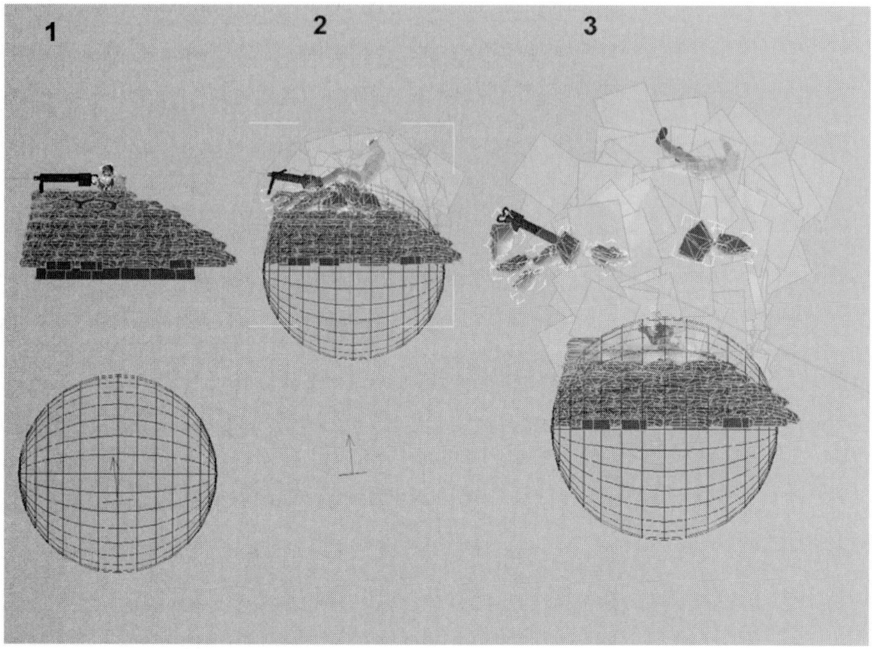

FIGURE 12.15 Setting up the sandbags and the catapult sphere to hit the soldier.

cylinder that runs up through all of the sandbags and acts as a light block. It was not part of the simulation, so it did not interpenetrate the active sandbags. A visibility key was added to the cylinder to hide it at the moment of the explosion, as shown in Figure 12.15.

The Reactor 2 Utility panel enables you to set the exact frame on which the dynamic solution will begin. The scene can be checked and previewed in the Reactor 2 utility before it is finally simulated and rendered, as shown in Figure 12.16. The mass of the large catapult sphere required adjustments to get both the Rag Doll and the sandbags to behave correctly. The sandbags were supposed to be heavy and fly up only a few feet before arcing out in all directions. However, if the mass or the velocity of the catapult sphere was set too high, it would knock the sandbags straight up out of the frame. Setting the mass and determining how fast the catapult sphere should go required numerous tests.

11. Max standard particles were used for the rising smoke effect with facing particles. Particle Studio can also be used for this, but for a simple effect like this one, Max standard particles often take less time to set up. A PArray particle system used the surface of a hemisphere inside the machine gun

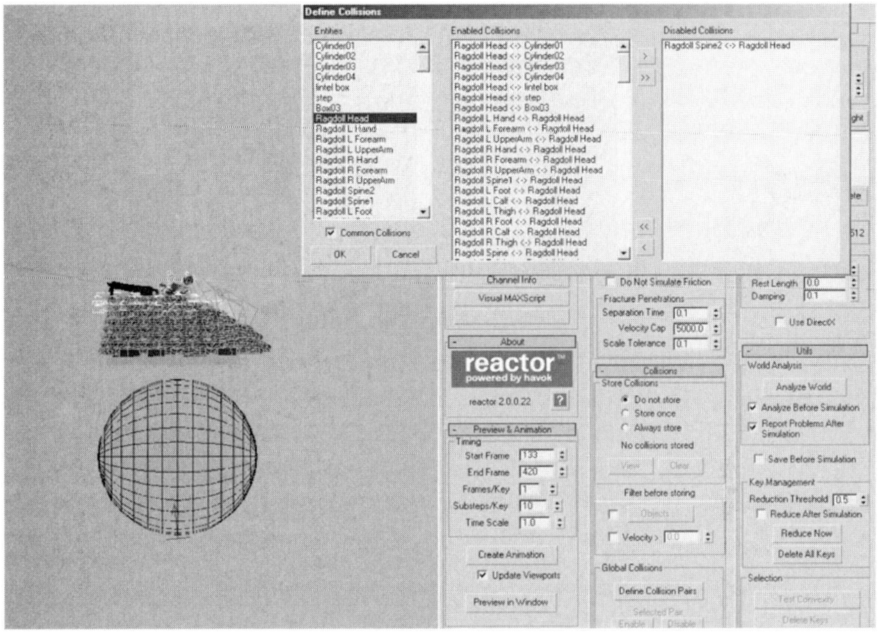

FIGURE 12.16 The Reactor 2 utility in which the explosion was previewed.

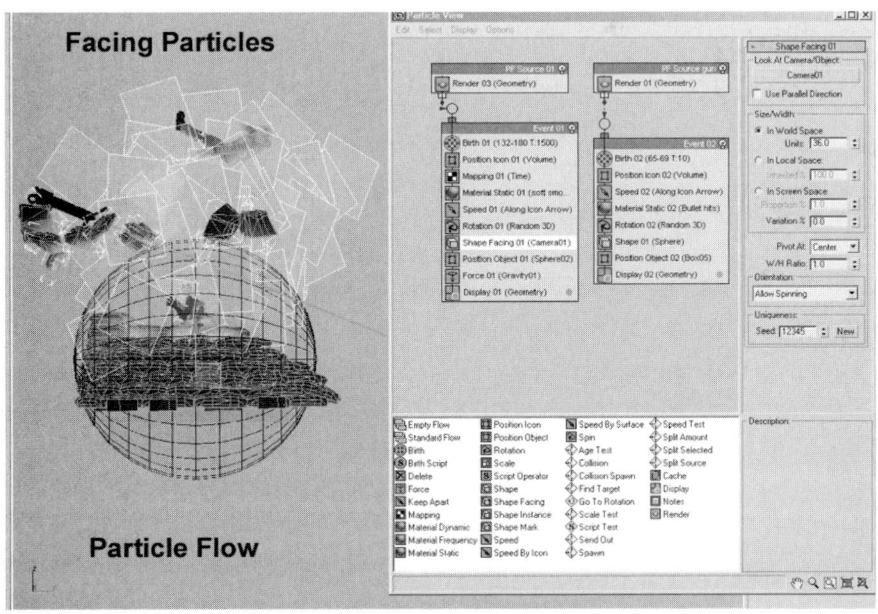

FIGURE 12.17 Smoke was created using facing particles.

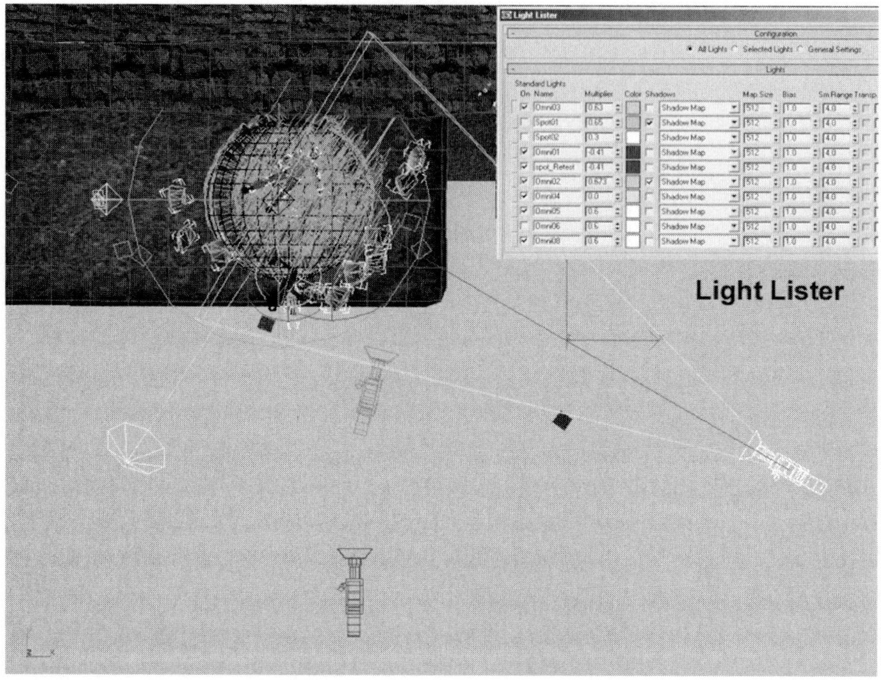

FIGURE 12.18 Attenuated and animated lighting for the scene.

nest as an emitter to generate the facing particles. A gravity space warp set to –0.4 was used to move the particles upward after the explosion, as shown in Figure 12.17.

12. The last task was to set up the cameras and the lighting. The lighting for the scene was designed to simulate a night attack. To accomplish that, almost all of the lights used far attenuation. The inner and outer range limits for each light can be seen in the viewport. The size and range of the attenuation fall off is animatable, and the outer, black range indicator tells you where the light will fall to black or no illumination, as shown in Figure 12.18. Negative lights were used to remove the light from inside the temple entrance. See the Battle.avi movie in the Chap12\Images folder on the companion CD-ROM.

ON THE CD

This was a complex scene, but what you have looked at was only the beginning. Other parts of the battle sequence show an army of Dinomen running down a hill to attack. A multitrack soundtrack was created in 3ds max 6 using the Sound Trax and the Foley Studio plug-ins for Max. For information on those plug-ins, see Chapter 17, "Plug-Ins."

In the next tutorial, you will add custom attributes to the ankles of a Dinoman skeleton rig to control the rotation of the feet as it runs down a hill.

ANIMATING A SKELETON RIG WITH CUSTOM ATTRIBUTES

Character rigs vary greatly in complexity and function. Most rigs are built with a specific purpose in mind. This book contains five different character rigs, each of which is configured differently. One of the most advanced rigs in the book is the Dinoman rig, shown in Figure 12.19.

The Dinoman character rig is a more sophisticated rig than the one you built in Chapter 7, "Character Setup with Bones." The Dr. Quin/Generic Man rig is very basic and does not have the detailed enhancements that many of the professional animation studios expect in their rigs. The full Dinoman rig is a step beyond the Dr. Quin rig and has additional controls for operating the feet, hands, face, and upper body. It also uses the more popular circle shapes as joint manipulator handles, instead of the simple point

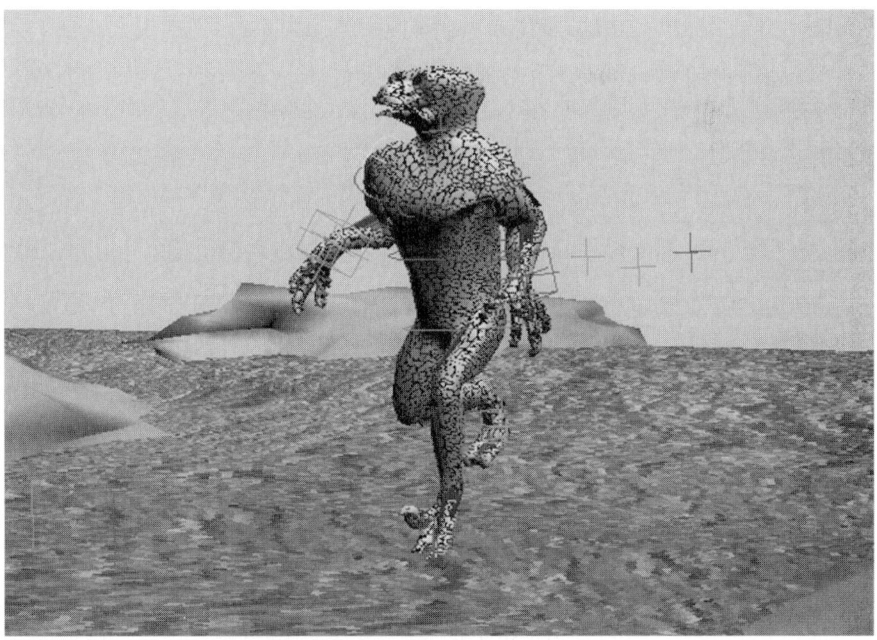

FIGURE 12.19 A Dinoman Warrior animated with the Dinoman skeleton rig and custom attributes.

helpers and boxes used in the basic Dr. Quin/Generic Man rig. Custom attributes are used in place of slider manipulators because they can be kept off the screen and grouped together in the Attribute Holder Modifier panel, which creates a kind of channel box in the Control Panel. Each attribute is shown along with its data entry window and a spinner for creating animation keys. This is very similar to the channel box that you find in Maya.

The Dinoman hands and feet are not linked directly to the arms or legs. Instead, they are constrained to a box helper object, or joint manipulator handle. The blue end effector for the leg's IK chain is linked to the box helper. The box helper then becomes the Leg Control handle. The same setup is found on the arms. To attach the foot to the leg, the root bone of the foot is constrained to the Foot Control with a Point constraint, as shown in Figure 12.20, example 1. This arrangement allows the feet to remain planted flat on the ground as the hips are moved from side to side, as shown in Figure 12.20, example 2. If they were linked directly to the IK chain, the feet would rock or tip when the hips or body

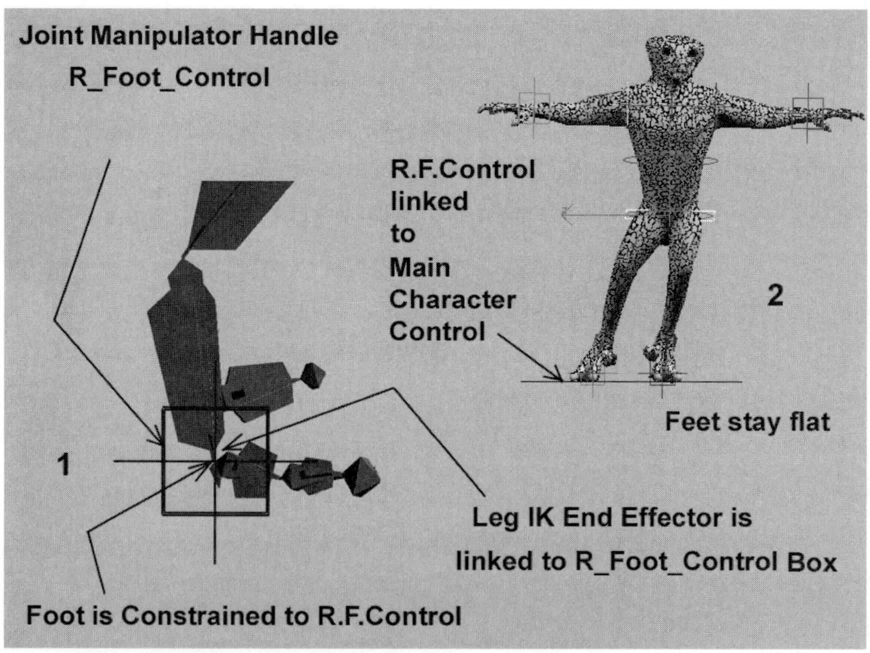

FIGURE 12.20 The feet and hands are attached using Point constraints and are not linked to the skeleton.

were moved from side to side, This rocking motion looks very unnatural in a human, a bird, or a creature such as a Dinoman, and can be avoided using this method.

Another advanced feature of the Dinoman rig is the shoulder, or clavicle, control handle, which gives you an easy way to animate the shoulders to counter the rotation of the hips. It can also moderately raise or lower the chest. This expansion and contraction can be used to indicate that the character has weight, that it is breathing hard, and that its spine is flexible. This helps bring the character to life when it walks or runs.

INSTALLING THE ATTRIBUTE HOLDER MODIFIER SCRIPT

The next tutorial explains how to use custom attributes to animate the rotation of the feet with each footstep. Before loading the DinoWarrior.max file for this tutorial, you must place the Modifier-Attribute-Holder.ms script into your Stdplugs (Standard Plugins) directory in the c:\3dsmax6\stdplugs\stdscripts folder. This script is part of 3ds max 6 and comes on your installation disk. After you install the script, you must restart Max, which will automatically load the script and create the Attribute Holder Modifier in the Modifier list. This action is required before you can load files that use custom attributes. If the script has not been run, you will get an error message, and foot animation with attributes will not function. This is a widely used script in many skeletal rigs.

In the next tutorial, you will add custom attributes to the feet of the Dinoman rig.

TUTORIAL 12.5

CONTROLLING THE FEET WITH CUSTOM ATTRIBUTES

To add custom attributes:

ON THE CD

1. If you have not done so already, load the Modifier-AttributeHolder.ms script into your 3dsmax6\stdplugs\stdscripts folder, and then restart Max.
2. Load the DinoWarrior_Start.max file from the Chap12 folder on the companion CD-ROM. You will see a Dinoman mesh, the bones, and the helper objects of the Dinoman skeleton rig, plus a terrain mesh that represents a hill and three rocks. Select the terrain and click Hide Selected.

3. Maximize the Camera03 view. It shows you a close-up shot of the feet. Camera03 is linked to the Main Character control so it follows the model as it runs. This camera makes it easy to follow and animate the feet of the moving character. You will see that there is a box point helper object around each ankle of the Dinoman, as shown in Figure 12.21, example 1. These boxes are called R_Foot_Control and L_Foot_Control. They are also known as *joint manipulator handles* and are used to animate the feet. If you create and wire up the custom attribute now, the foot bone is likely to rotate out of position and either stick up or point down at an odd angle. There is a way to prevent this, however, and force it to maintain the same angle as you apply the wired parameter. To stabilize the foot, you must first assign a Rotation List controller to the root foot bone, and then place both a Rotation TBC controller and then a Euler XYZ controller in the list, as shown in Figure 12.21, example 2.
4. Notice that the Rotation List controller has already been placed on the root bone of each foot for you. Look closely at Figure 12.21, example 2, and notice that the Assign Controller list contains two main entries under

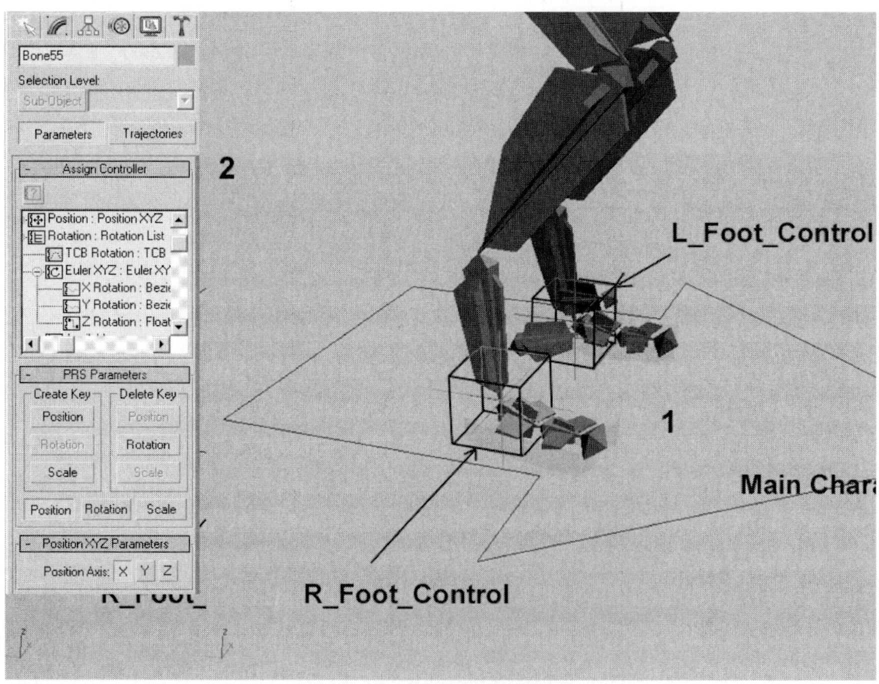

FIGURE 12.21 The Foot control boxes.

the heading called Rotation – Rotation list. The first entry in the list is the TBC Rotation controller. The second entry is the Euler XYZ controller. In the Euler XYZ list, the Z-axis is a float wire type. That is because this foot bone was already wired up to test this file, and then the wiring was removed so you could do it yourself in this tutorial. The Z-axis is the rotation axis of the foot bone.

5. Select the Right_Foot_Control box, and then click the Modify tab. Click the Modifier List arrow, and scroll down the modifier list to find Attribute Holder. Select it and add it to the stack. This modifier will hold the rotation data that you will be controlling with the custom attribute.
6. You are now ready to create the custom attribute for the right (green) foot. To do that, select the Right_Foot_Control box (if it is not already selected), and then in the main menu bar, click Animation > Add Custom Attribute. Expand all the submenus in the Add Parameter dialog. Now give the attribute you are going to create a name. In the Attribute Style > UI Type window, select the default name and type in RfootZ, as shown in Figure 12.22, example 1.
7. In the Float UI menu, go to the Range section and enter: From = –26, and To = 20. Then, in the Finish menu, locate the Add Attribute to Type window, select Object's Current Modifier, and click Add. You should now see the name RfootZ appear in the Modifier list of custom attributes in the

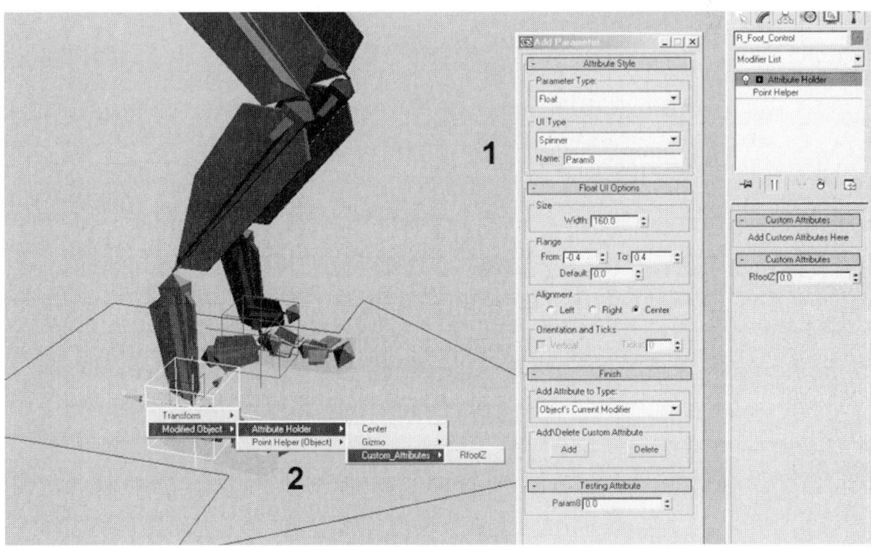

FIGURE 12.22 The Add Custom Attribute menu and parameter wiring pop-up menus.

Command Panel. Next, you are ready to wire the attribute to the Z-axis of the foot bone.

8. To wire up the custom attribute, select the Right_Foot_Control box, right-click in the viewport, and select Wire Parameters from the quad menu. A small pop-up window will open. Select Modified Object > Attribute Holder > Custom_Attributes_RfootZ, and then drag the cursor to the root bone of the foot and click it, as shown in Figure 12.22, example 2. A new, small window will open. In that window, Select Transform > Rotation > Euler XYZ > Z Rotation. The Parameter Wiring dialog will open.
9. The Parameter Wiring dialog contains four windows. In the lower right window, you should see the name of the custom attribute RfootZ. Select the name and type in the expression DegtoRad(RfootZ), as shown in Figure 12.23. This expression will convert degrees of rotation into radians, which the software can understand. On the upper right window, you will see the name of the bone with Z Rotation highlighted; and in the upper left window, you will see the name Right Foot control. The center contains a vertical bar with three arrows. Click the arrow pointing Right (from the Right Foot control to the Bone) and then click the Connect button, as shown in Figure 12.23. The attribute should now be wired to the foot bone.
10. To test the custom attribute, go to the Modifier Panel > Attribute Holder menu, and click the up-down spinner arrows of RfootZ. The foot bones should rotate up and down. To wire up the custom attribute for the left

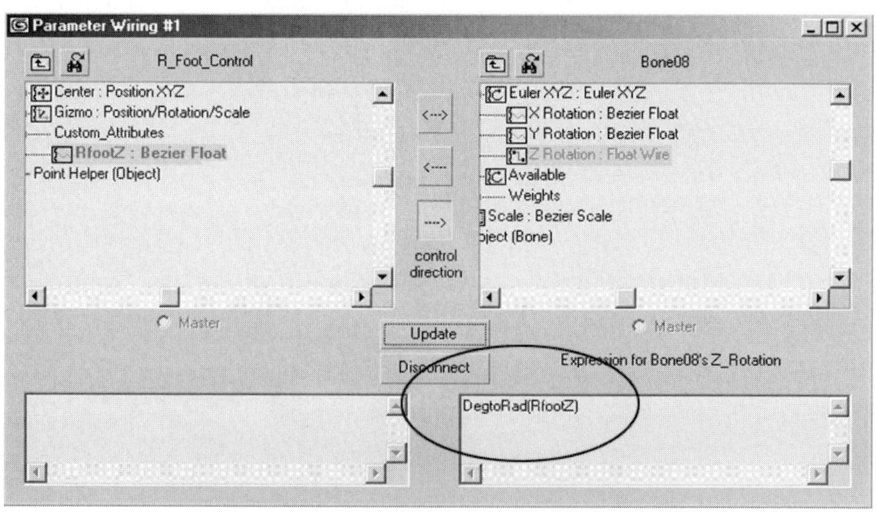

FIGURE 12.23 The Parameter Wiring dialog.

foot, repeat the previous steps but substitute the Left Foot control, and name that attribute LfootZ. Unfortunately, custom attributes cannot be edited, but only replaced. If you do not like the range of rotation, delete the attribute and re-apply a different setting under the same name. To do that, select the Right or Left Foot Control box, go to the Animation menu, and click Add Custom Attribute. Then open the Finish menu and select Delete. A list of all attributes will open, as shown in Figure 12.24. Click Delete Selected. That will remove the attribute. Now you can re-enter new From-To values and rewire the the attribute to the bone. That's all there is to it.

11. Save the file as DinoAttrib125.max. You can now animate the foot rotations so that the feet do not sink into the ground as the Dinoman runs. To look at the finished scene with the feet animated, load the DinoWarrior125.max file. That concludes the custom attribute tutorial.

    The Foot Control boxes and the Arm Control boxes on the wrists can hold several custom attributes. If you want to set up the hands with custom attributes, you can have one for each finger, and then wire the finger bones to close progressively, similar to what was shown in the tutorial on controlling hands with a slider in Chapter 8, "Preparing for Animation." After you have worked with custom attributes for a while, you will find

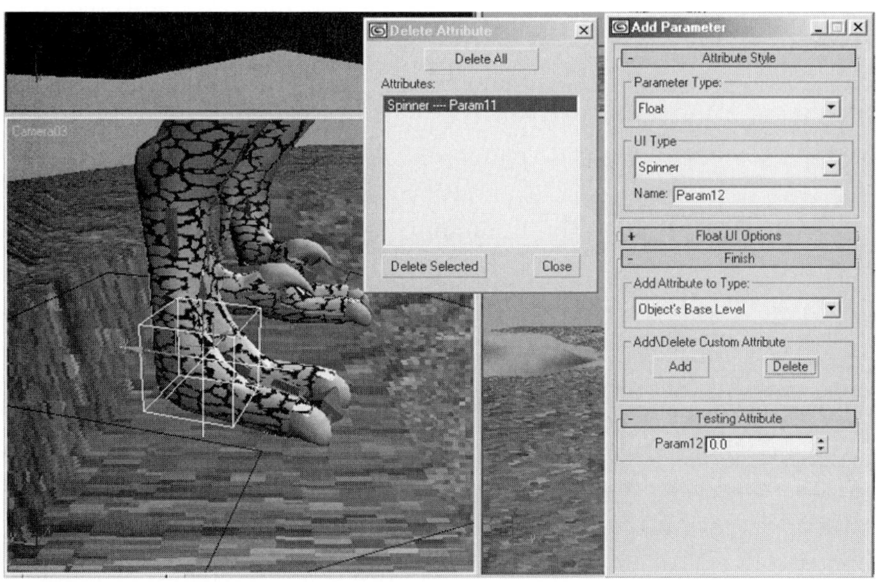

FIGURE 12.24 Deleting a custom attribute.

that they are much more convenient to use than multiple sliders, and they don't clutter up the viewport. Remember that you can float the Command Panel and drag it anywhere you want to bring the custom attribute spinners closer to what you are animating.

In the next tutorial, you will learn how to set up a facial bone network.

Using a Facial Bone Network

The Xzulixia Dancing Character Rig is a hybrid rig that combines a basic skeleton rig with a set of animatable facial bones called a *facial bone network*. This combination enables you to open and close the character's mouth for better control over facial expressions and lip sync than you would get by using facial Morph Targets alone. It also creates realistic facial stretching, as shown in Figure 12.25, example 1.

You might decide that you want more control over the face than what is afforded by using facial Morph Targets. You can achieve additional control over the cheeks, jaw, eyebrows, and smile muscles by using a network of small facial bones that are linked and constrained to the head and the main jaw operator bone. These small bones can change the shape of the cheeks as the jaw is lowered to increase the realism of facial expressions. The arrangement of these bones is shown in Figure 12.25, example 2.

The challenge is to determine first where the facial bones should be anchored; and second, how to connect them so that they follow the general movements analogous to human face muscles. A circular muscle around the mouth helps form our expressions. The ring of bones in the lips are meant to simulate that muscle. You can set up more control points so that the whole lip assembly is a child of external control points. That way, you can tip or twist the mouth for different facial expressions.

This model is not finished, so there are some problems with the lower lip skin weighting and other details. You can ignore this. It will not affect this tutorial.

In the next tutorial, you will explore how a facial bone network is created.

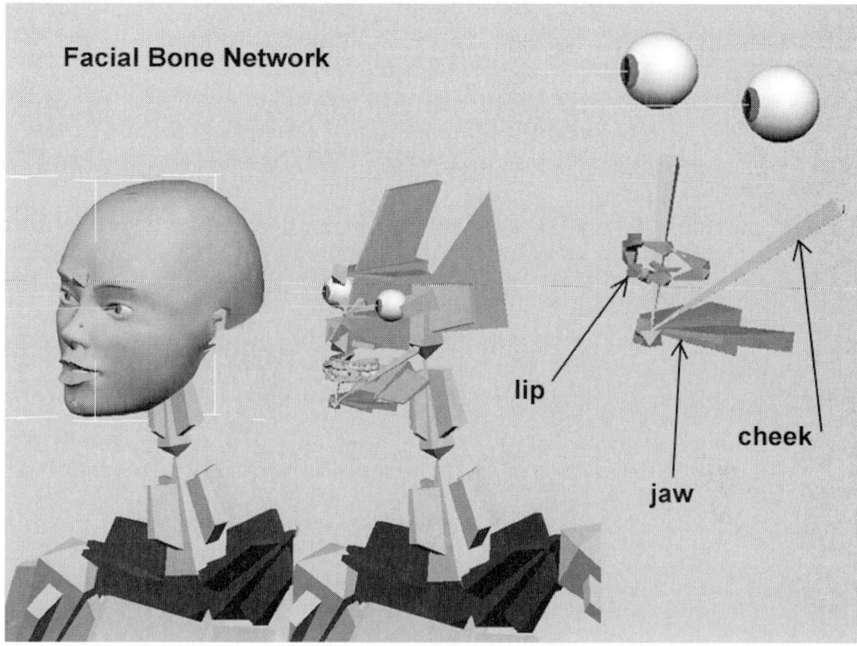

FIGURE 12.25 Xzulixia with a facial bone network.

TUTORIAL 12.6

CREATING A FACIAL BONE NETWORK

To create a facial bone network:

ON THE CD

1. Load the Xzu_FaceBones.max file from the Chap12 folder on the companion CD-ROM. The file contains the Dancing Xzulixia character, which has a fairly advanced skeleton rig that combines a facial bone network with a skeleton rig. Go to the Display tab and turn off Hide Helpers. You will see a large number of sliders that nearly cover the active viewport. To hide them, go to the Named Selection Set window and select Sliders. Then click Hide Selected, and hide the Xzulixia head mesh.

Xzulixia's head is separate from her body to allow for facial morph animation. In addition, five facial Morph Targets have been used to animate the facial expressions. To see them, go to the Named Selection Set window and click Morph Heads. Select Xzulixia's head to access the Morpher Modifier. These items should remain hidden for this tutorial. They are there for you to work with later to animate Dancing Xzulixia as you wish.

2. As the jaw opens, all of the skin and muscles of the face from the eyes downward should stretch. Therefore, the bones and their vertex envelopes must stretch too, and move along with the jaw. Notice the ring of eight bones around the mouth, as shown in Figure 12.26, example 1.

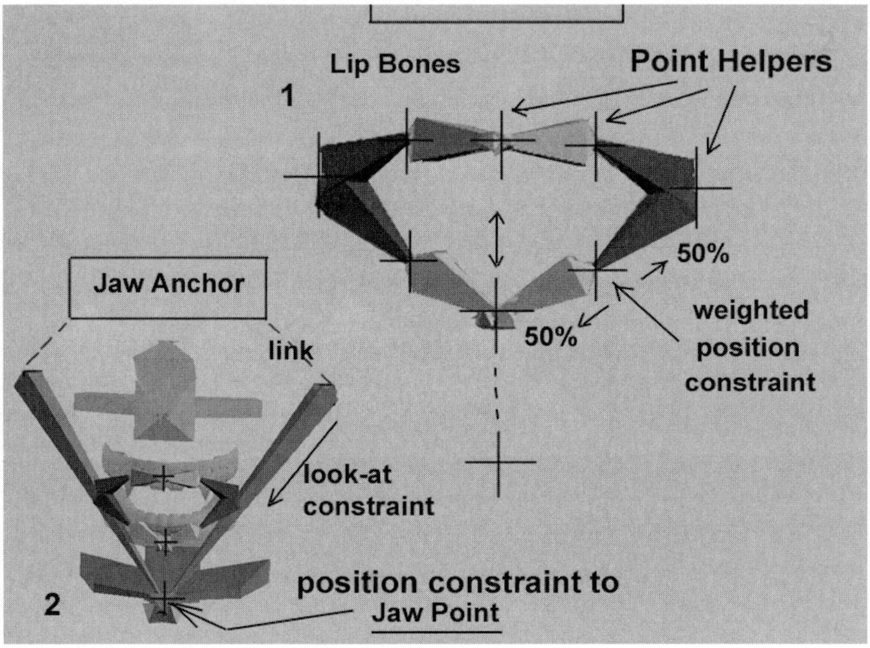

FIGURE 12.26 A combination of links and constraints causes the bones to stretch the skin.

3. The bones around the mouth are connected to point helpers with Links and Position constraints to make the lips flex and stretch as the jaw opens. Eight point helpers (green crosses) are distributed around the mouth. Scrub the Time Slider between frames 140 and 175. You will see the mouth open and close, and all of the bones of the mouth and jaw move and stretch somewhat. The bones are linked and/or constrained to these points.
4. Position constraints can be weighted, which means that if you have a row of three points, and the center point is constrained to both of the outer points with a weight of 50%, when you move one of the outer points up or down, the center point will maintain its position halfway between the two outer points, no matter where you move them. This is how the midpoints in the upper and lower lips are designed to work.

5. The two long cheekbones are constrained at one end and linked at the other end, as shown in Figure 12.27, example 2. Consider just the left cheekbone. It is linked at its upper end to the Jaw Anchor Dummy. This is a large dummy object that is linked to the main head bone. The left cheekbone has a Look-at constraint that forces it to point toward the jaw point helper at all times. There is also a Position constraint applied to the end or nub bone at the lower end of the cheekbone. The nub is constrained to the point helper at the center of the jaw called the *jaw point*. When the jaw opens, this arrangement causes the cheekbone to stretch.

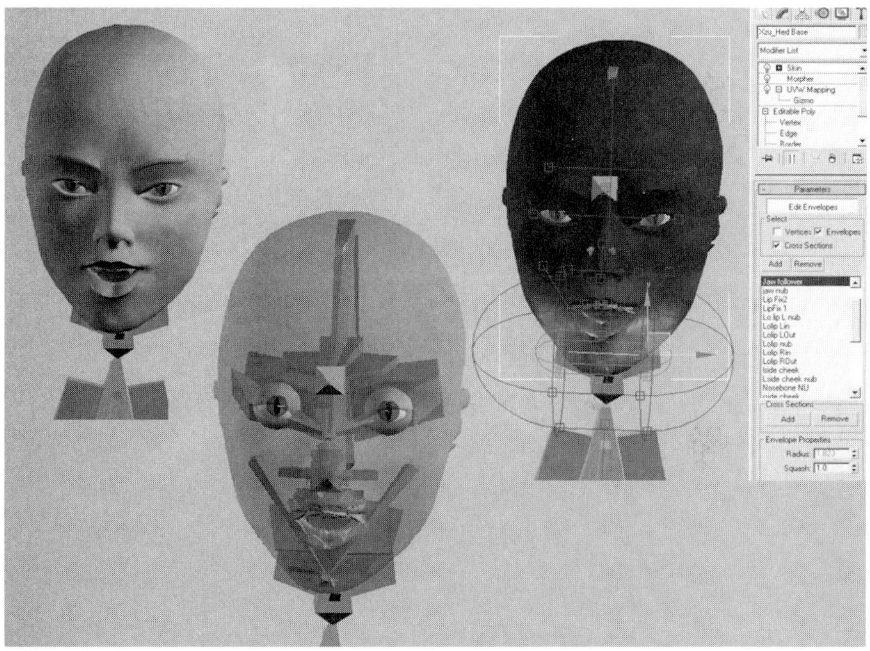

FIGURE 12.27 A combination of jaw movement and facial morph target animation is used to animate Xzulixia's face.

6. The character's face mesh is bound to the bones with the Skin Modifier. Each bone has influence over a certain area of vertices in the mesh. All of the vertices controlled by the skin envelope must stretch if the bone stretches, causing the face to stretch as well, as shown in Figure 12.27.
7. The face is animated with five facial Morph Targets. Opening and closing the jaw will not conflict with the Morph Targets except where the strength of the Morph Target it set too high. In that case, there might be a problem

with the skin envelopes, such as in center of the lower lip on this model. If you turn the strength of a Morph Target up all the way, it will cause the lip to pinch. The idea is to find a balance between the jaw movement and the Morpher animation to obtain the best results with this model, as shown in Figure 12.28.

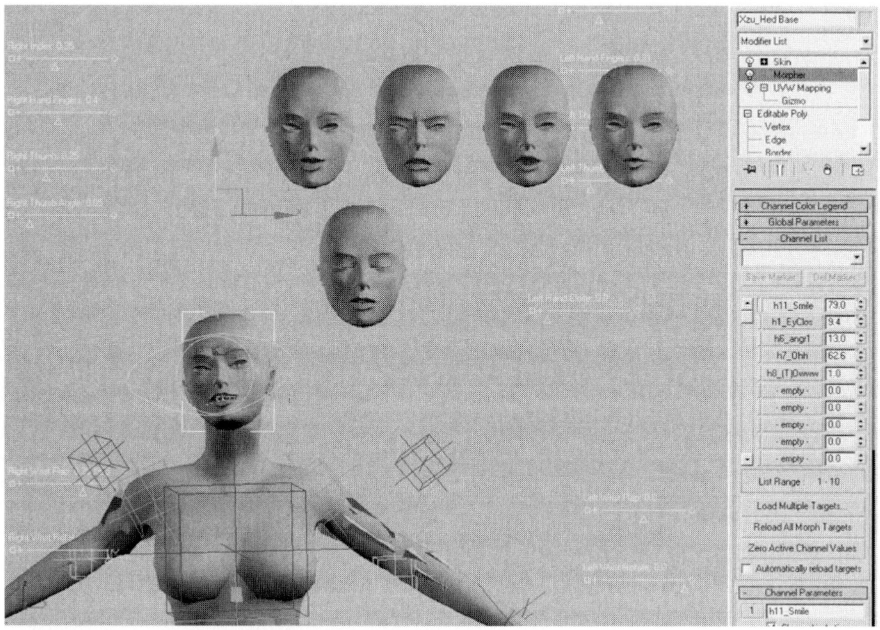

FIGURE 12.28 A wide range of expressions is possible with a facial bone network and Morph Targets.

8. This concludes the facial bone network explanation tutorial. By taking off the Skin Modifier and unlinking the dummy that connects the bone network to the head bone, you can use the entire assembly with another model on another rig.

   Facial bone networks are used for high-end, animated characters for motion pictures as well as for games. Bone stretch is useful in many situations where you need close control over the behavior of the skin, or where you want to do a squash and stretch animation using a skeleton rig. Facial bone networks, combined with facial Morph Targets, unlock the full potential of rigging to create lifelike character expressions.

In the next tutorial, you will learn how the Dr. Quin/Generic man model was modified to become Major Black.

Modifying Dr. Quin into Major Black

There are many ways to rig a skeleton and animate a character. The basic Generic Man skeleton is adequate for many of the characters, but when the characters need to run up the side of buildings, perform outrageous stunts, or fight six assailants at one time, the Generic Man skeletal rig is inadequate. In larger studios, special skeleton rigs designed to do a specific job are built for each character. Of course, big studios have the luxury of abundant manpower. *Homing Instinct,* however, was done by a very small studio, and there was no time or extra manpower to create special, elaborate rigs dedicated to only one or two scenes. It was very important to find ways to re-purpose rigs and make them able to do special kinds of motions.

The same re-useable concept was applied to the character meshes. In reality, only one male human character was made for *Homing Instinct*. All of the other characters were made by modifying the basic Dr. Quin/Generic Man spline patch model to turn it into all kinds of characters—from soldiers, grocery men, and old fat fishermen, to vampires and flippant punk teenagers.

In this section, you will explore the transformation of the mild-mannered Dr. Quin into the overmuscled, aggressive, and abusive Major Black, who is a fifth-degree black belt in Jeet Kwan Do martial arts. Major Black tries to solve every problem by force, and ends up in a number of fights. Major Black was made by modifying Dr. Quin to give him a square jaw, broad shoulders, and massive muscles, as shown in Figure 12.29.

Once the modification of the skin was finished, the Dr.Quin skeleton rig had to be modified to fit. Then, additional controls, rotational points, and manipulator handles were added to enable motions such as flipping over, hanging from the hands, standing on one toe, delivering a series of rapid punches, and spin-kicking six men in the head. The next tutorial shows you how it was done, and explains some of the specific modifications that were done to the skeleton rig to get it ready for the action animations.

In this tutorial, you will see how the transformation progressed from a basic character model and skeleton rig to a much more complex fighting rig modified to fit Major Black.

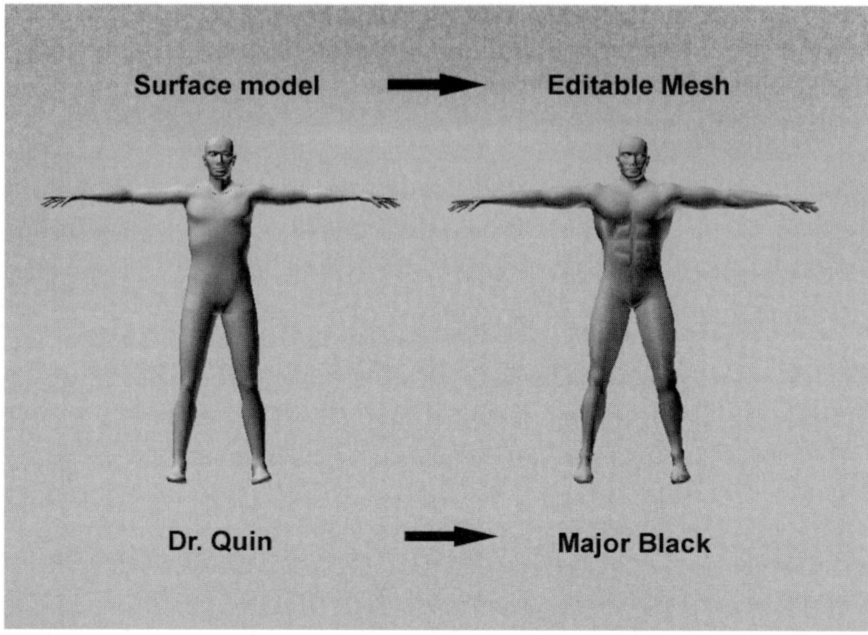

FIGURE 12.29 The conversion of Dr. Quin into Major Black.

TUTORIAL 12.7

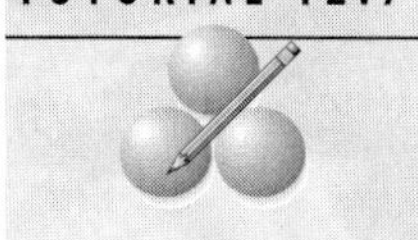

CONVERTING DR. QUIN INTO MAJOR BLACK

ON THE CD

To convert Dr. Quin to Major Black:

1. Load the Quin2Black.max file from the companion CD-ROM. You will see two models: the beginning Dr Quin patch surface model and the final Major Black editable mesh model, as shown in Figure 12.29.
2. The Dr. Quin patch was first converted to an editable poly by first selecting the surface and then going to the Surface Modifier to turn down the Patch Topology Steps (resolution) to a setting of 1. Then, the surface was converted to an editable poly mesh. This created the lowest possible resolution poly mesh. The same thing was done for the head, which is separate from the body so that it can be used to create facial Morph Targets.
3. Once that was done, the body was split down the middle and the left half was deleted. Then, the Mirror Clone tool was used to create a reference mesh that would mirror any changes done to the original side, as shown in Figure 12.30. The head was not split.

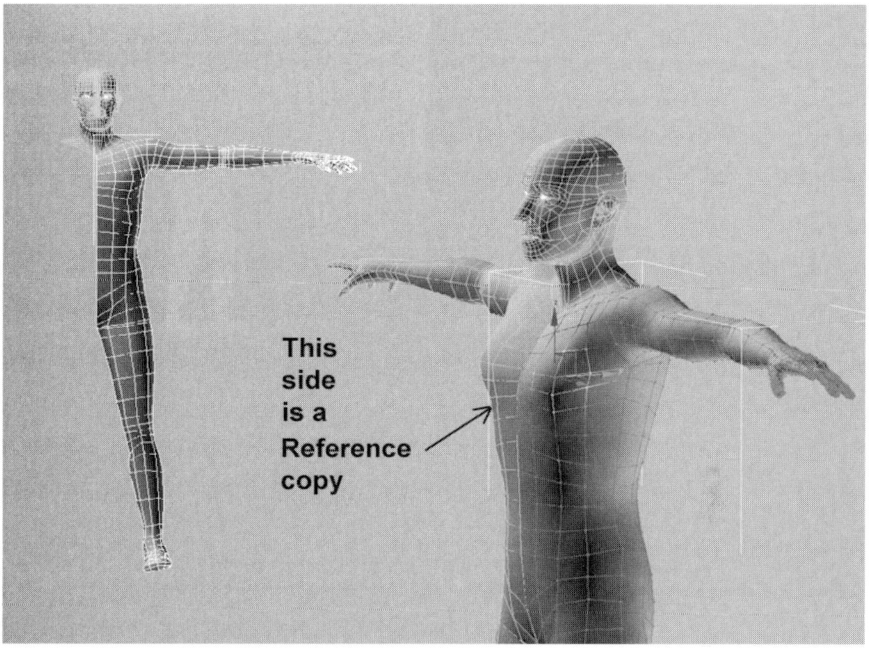

FIGURE 12.30 The first stages of the model conversion.

4. The chest was modified to have larger pectoral muscles. The Cut tool was used on the chest, shoulders, and stomach to build up the muscle shapes. The new muscle shapes were sculpted by pushing and pulling vertices using the Editable Poly > Soft Selection tool. Once the re-sculpting was done, the reference half of the body was deleted, and a mirror copy was made and attached to the original. Finally, the center seam was welded to rejoin the two halves of the body.
5. The head and neck was modified using the Soft-select tool in the Editable Poly Modifier. The nose and jaw were widened and made more prominent, and the overall size of the face was enlarged slightly to give it a more massive look. Additional work was done on the waist and hips to narrow them, and then the shoulders and arms were selected with Soft select and pulled out to widen the upper body and chest, as shown in Figure 12.31.
6. Next, the generic skeleton rig was modified to fit Major Black. The polygonal model was still in its position over the skeleton rig. Because it was derived from the original Dr. Quin model in the same pose, the skeleton did not need to be resized drastically except to accommodate the widening of the shoulders and the slight change in the angle of the legs and arms.

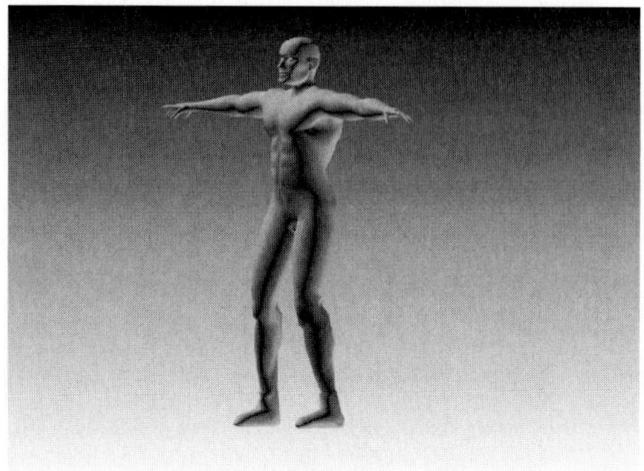

FIGURE 12.31 Final sculpting of Major Black.

7. The shoulder joints were widened. This was done by removing the links and constraints of the shoulders and arms. In addition, the Look-at constraints on the clavicles were removed by temporarily replacing them in the Assign Controller dialog with Euler XYZ controllers. One clavicle rotated around on its own, but it was restored to its correct position using Local rotate. Then, by selecting the shoulder joints one at a time, and turning on the Hierarchy > Adjust Transform > Don't Affect Children button, the joints were moved outward, as shown in Figure 12.32. Finally, the shoulder control boxes were moved outward to match the new shoulder joint location, and the elbow joints were moved slightly to restore the arm proportion. The hands still matched up well with their original position once the arms were modified. The linkages were then restored between the wrists and the shoulder controls, and the shoulder controls and the upper chest bone. Then, the Look-at constraints were restored to the clavicles. For a review on how to set up the shoulders, see Chapter 7, "Character Setup with Bones."
8. Next, the new fighting control points and auxiliary body rotation points were installed in the rig. The first new control was the arm punch rotation point that is linked to the Shoulder control. The Wrist end effector is linked to the Punch Control pivot, which sits quite a ways above the character. It looks a bit awkward up there, but when you want to throw punches, it is easy to select and rotate. It is placed a long distance above the arm so that the arc of rotation of the punch will be fairly flat, as shown in Figure 12.33. The Kick control works the same way. An auxiliary pivot point is put behind the upper leg, and linked in between the Foot control and the Main

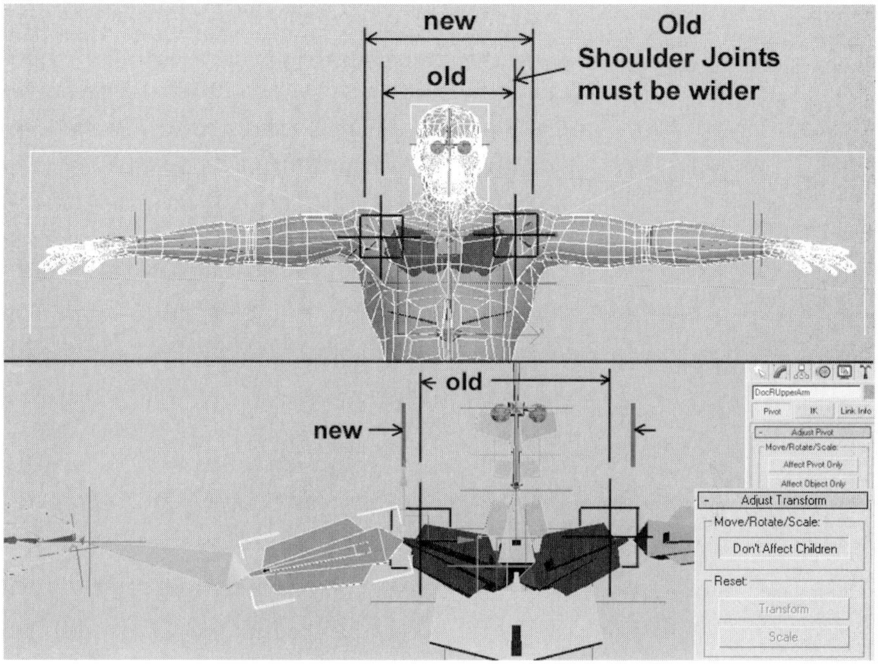

FIGURE 12.32 Modifying the location of the shoulder joints for the wider upper body.

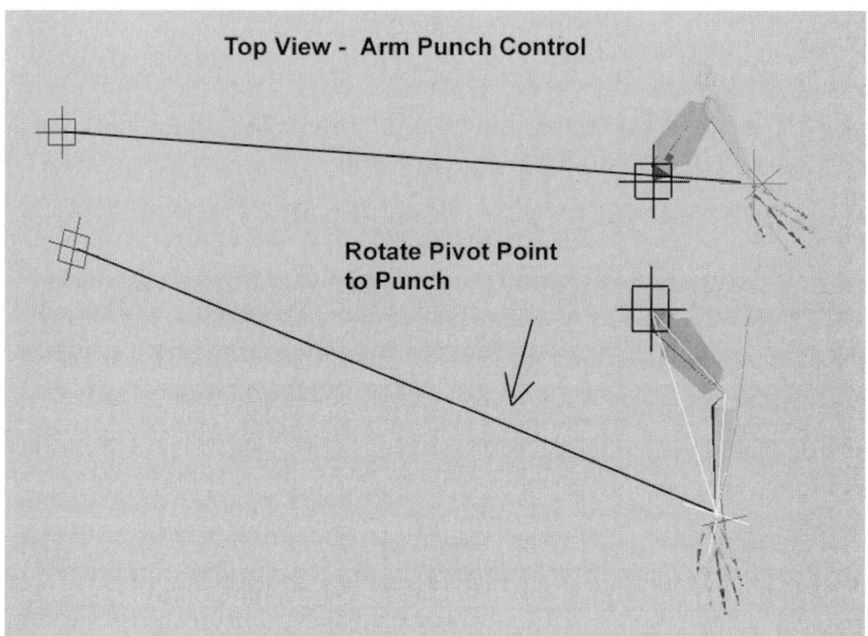

FIGURE 12.33 Adding Punch and Kick controls.

Character control. The only time it is used is when you want the character to deliver a fast arcing kick.

9. Two remaining important controls are the Body Spin and Flip controls, which function as new pivots for the Main Character control. Because everything in the character is linked to the Main Character control, you can flip the character by rotating it. Human beings rotate about their center of mass when they flip, so this point needs to go somewhere around the middle of the stomach, as shown in Figure 12.34.
10. Any number of additional points can be added. A point below both feet that enables the character to pivot around the ball of the foot is a great help when trying to choreograph a fight. By using a combination of these points, nearly any human motion can be recreated. The body moves by rotating its joints. The skeleton rig can be made to do the same thing. The finished rig is ready for a stunt or a fight, as shown in Figure 12.35.

In the next section, you will explore some of the features of MAXScript.

SCRIPTING

MAXScript is an extremely powerful tool for those who are willing to take the time to learn scripting. MAXScript has gone through a major revision for max 6 to provide access to all the new particle, modeling, animation, material, and dynamics operations that are now possible. For example, an entirely new set of script commands for Particle Flow gives you access to the metaball functions that are available when you use particles with the BlobMesh modifier to simulate liquids. Another interesting area that has expanded is access to the new Shell Modifier, Unwrap UVW, and the Skin Modifier. Some tools available in MAXScript are not available through the Max general user interface. The new Mental Ray section of MAXScript gives you access to hundreds of new Mental Ray data classes with which you can create custom shaders and control the renderer.

A MAXScript can be written so that when it is run, it looks for specified objects in the scene and then applies a selected operation to those objects. Alternatively, a script can be interactive so that a certain event triggers a script execute command. The possibilities are nearly endless, ranging from creating objects, building dialog boxes and spinners, and

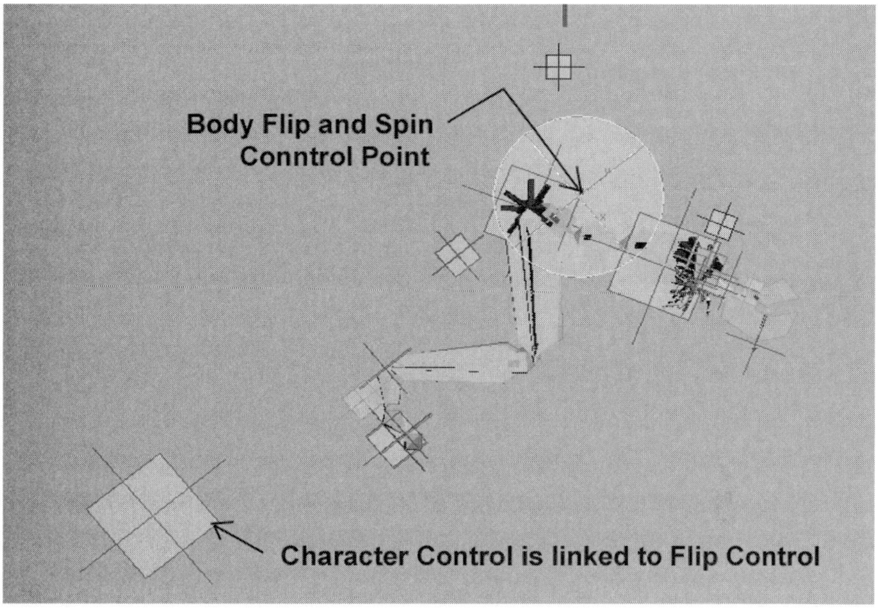

FIGURE 12.34 Adding the Body Spin and Flip control point.

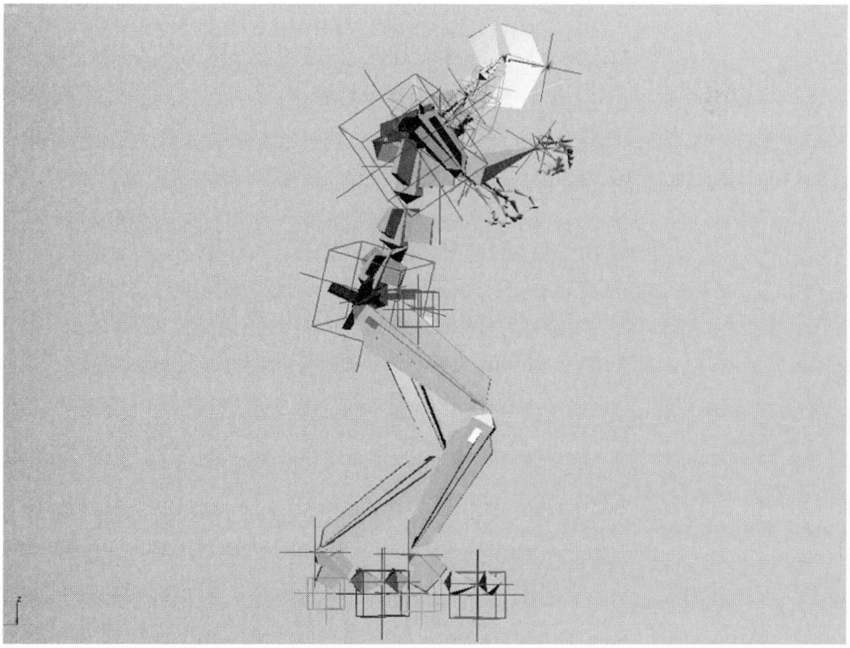

FIGURE 12.35 The Major Black rig, ready for a fight.

pre-rigging character skeletons to controlling the angle of a character's feet so that they match the angle of the surface of the ground. The last function would be very valuable if you had a crowd of 100 warriors charging down a hill and you had to align all of their feet to the surface.

What can a nonscripter do with MAXScript? A nonscripter can use MAXScripts without knowing anything about writing scripts. If you go to the Utility tab, click the MAXScript button, and then select Run, you can navigate to the C:\3dsmax6\Scripts\Examples directory, which contains a very interesting group of scripts. For example, double-click on the BoxArrayAnimation.ms script. The script will execute and a group of interconnected animated boxes will appear, moving in the viewport. You can open the script in the script listener and read the descriptions of what the script does. It is a good idea to open all of the scripts in the listener and read the descriptions. You will probably find something you want to use.

The *macro recorder* will help you create a recording of what you have done with your mouse. It looks like a script chunk because it is. The only thing the macro recorder will not save is what you do in Sub-object mode, as shown in Figure 12.36.

A very good tool to help you learn scripting is the Visual MAXScript utility. To open Visual MAXScript, click the MAXScript > Visual MAXScript Editor. Without knowing anything about MAXScript, you can use the interface to create dialog boxes and windows with various functions, and assign names to buttons, sliders, and spinners. It is well worth exploring if you intend to seriously pursue MAXScript (see Figure 12.37).

It is beyond the scope of this book to explain how to write a MAXScript. Excellent MAXScript tutorials come with 3ds max 6 if you are serious about learning to write MAXScripts.

In the next tutorial, you will use the Reactor 2 Cloth to simulate hair for a character.

Using Reactor 2 Cloth to Simulate Hair

You can create simulated hair by using Reactor 2 and Reactor Cloth. It will not be realistic hair, but if you are careful in modeling, and you have a good hair texture map with a suitable mask or alpha channel, it can look good. On a nonrealistic cartoon character, this hair will work great, as shown in Figure 12.38.

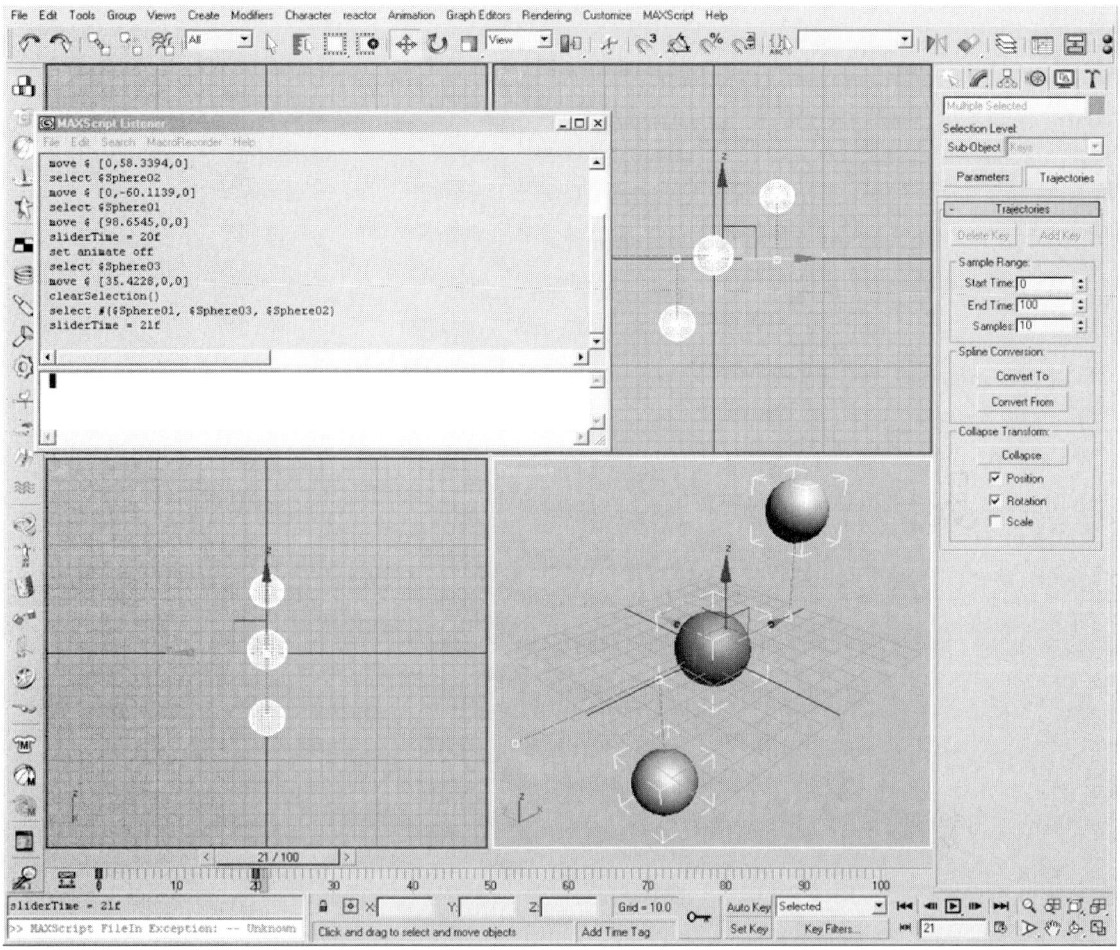

FIGURE 12.36 A typical MAXScript chunk in the Listener window, created by using the mouse to create three spheres and animate them in 3ds max 6.

To use Reactor 2 Cloth, you start by applying the Reactor Cloth Modifier to the geometry that is meant to simulate hair. Then you create a Cloth Collection and make the hair geometry part of the Cloth Collection. The head, if it is animated, must be part of a Deforming Mesh Collection. The character head mesh acts as a collision object. Once the Cloth Collection and the modifier solver are set up, the next task is to select a few vertices at the top of the hair geometry and attach them to the top of the head using the Attach to DefMesh constraint in the Reactor Cloth Modifier.

In the Reactor utility, you enter settings for the density of the cloth, and accept everything else at the default settings. Next, you preview the

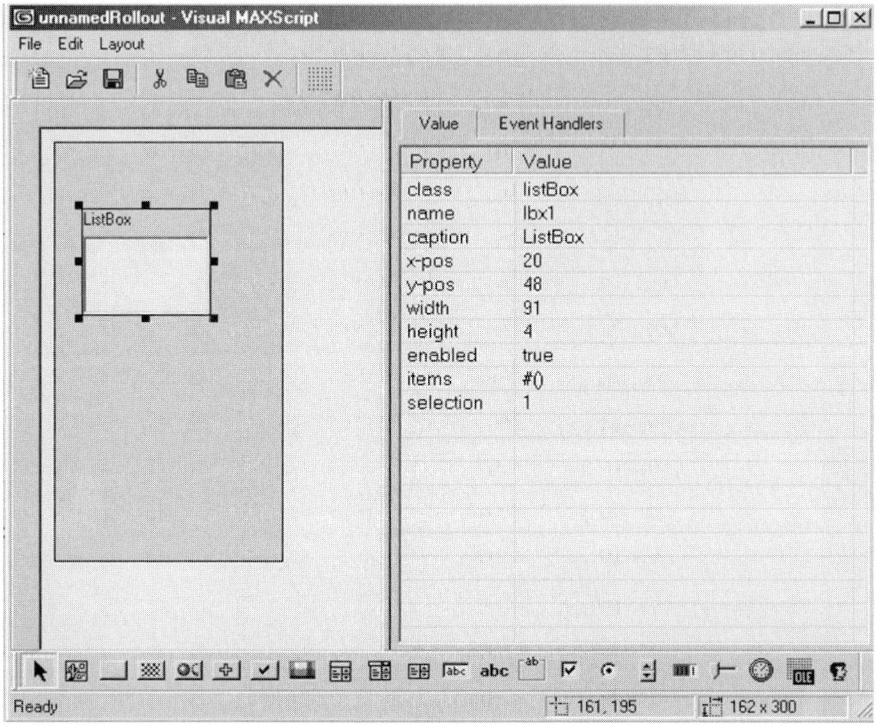

FIGURE 12.37 The Virtual MAXScript Editor dialog enables you to drag and drop to create dialog boxes and windows.

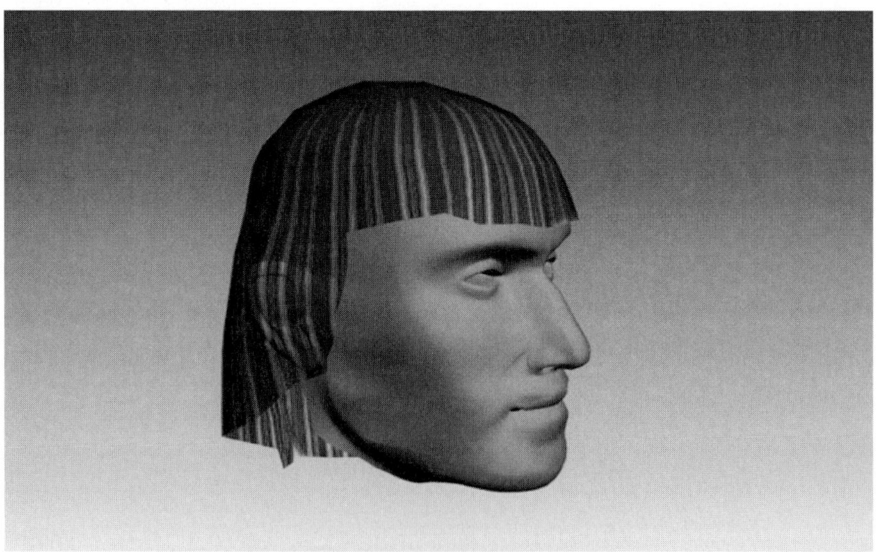

FIGURE 12.38 Reactor 2 Cloth, used to simulate hair.

simulation in the Preview window. You will see the cloth fall slowly onto the head and mold itself to the head's contours. If that condition looks good, you tell Max to update, which causes the cloth to keep that shape at frame 0. Then the animation simulation can start from frame 0, with the cloth already in the correct shape and position.

A very simple hair material can be created by creating a map in Adobe Photoshop, or by rendering an image of thick brown or black radiating splines in Max, and then reversing the colors and background to create a mask from the same geometry. The reverse image is made to create white lines on a black background. This becomes the opacity mask that causes only the black lines to show when it is rendered in 3ds max 6. You can make hair maps of any color as long as you can make a good, high-contrast opacity mask that will work in Max's opacity map channel. You can also use an alpha channel matte. However, you cannot use any specular highlight on the hair because the entire surface of the panel will show, and ruin the transparency illusion.

Admittedly, this method does not result in photo-realistic hair. For that, you need to use the Shag Hair plug-in that is described in Chapter 17, "Plug-ins." Flat geometry cloth hair is meant to be used when you want to simulate simple usable hair on characters. It is adequate if the characters will be seen only in the middle ground or background. Therefore, if your project is not meant to be realistic, this hair will work fine, as it is soft and flexible, and it moves naturally when the character's head moves. For a more realistic look, you can create a sculpted mesh that is already shaped like a hair style, and then add the Reactor 2 Cloth Solver to make it soft and flexible.

In the next tutorial, you will set up and simulate hair using Reactor 2 Cloth.

TUTORIAL 12.8

USING REACTOR 2 CLOTH TO SIMULATE HAIR

To simulate hair with cloth:

ON THE CD

1. Load the Hair_Cloth_Start.max file from the Chap12 folder on the companion CD-ROM. You should see a head mesh and a hair-shaped mesh positioned above the head.

2. The Reactor Cloth Modifier, the Cloth Collection, and the Deformable Mesh Collection have already been set up and applied for you. Select their icons to see their parameters in the Modifier Panel. You will be attaching the hair geometry to the head and running the simulation.
3. To attach the hair geometry to the head, select the hair geometry in the top view. Click the Modify tab to open the Reactor Cloth Modifier. Drag the right edge of the Command Panel to the left to expand it to two columns so that you can see all of the menus. Now go to the Vertex > Sub-object level in the Reactor Cloth Modifier.
4. To attach the vertices of the hair geometry to the head, you first create a constraint. In the Constraints menu, click the Attach To DefMesh button. The Attach To DefMesh constraint will appear in the Constraints list box, and a second small menu will open for the DefMesh constraint. Click the None button and then click the nose of the head in the top view to select the head.
5. Next, highlight the Attach to Deformable constraint, and then highlight the vertices you want constrain. Pick a small circle of vertices at the very top of the head. Remember that any vertices you constrain will no longer move, so don't make the selection too large. Lastly, select the Attach to DefMesh constraint again, as shown in Figure 12.39.

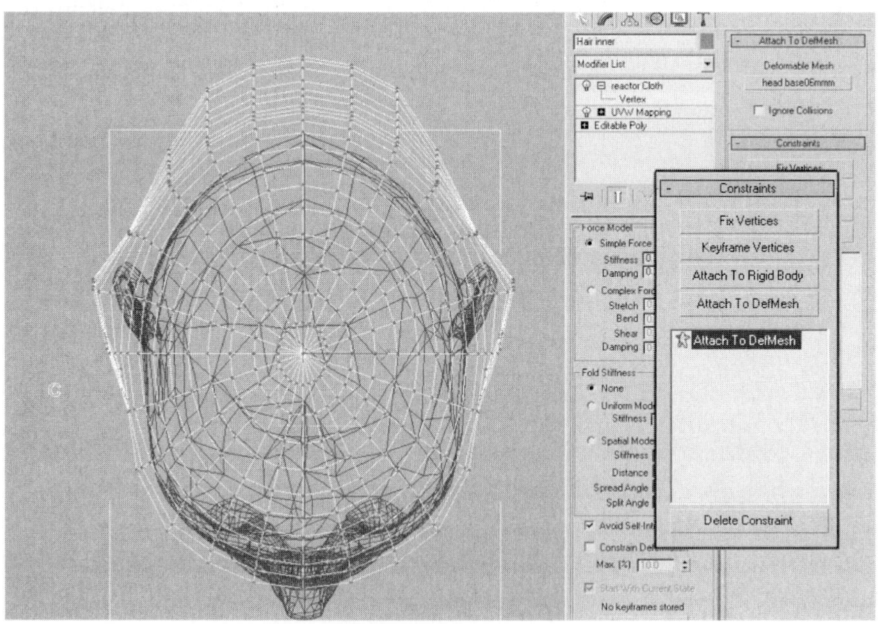

FIGURE 12.39 Using the Attach to Deformable Mesh dialog.

6. Open the Reactor 2 utility. Click the Utility tab and then click the Reactor button. The menus will open but they will be compacted. Drag the right edge of the viewport to the left to make three columns and then open all of the Reactor drop-down menus. Switch to the Camera01 view, as shown in Figure 12.40. Select the hair geometry, open the Properties menu in the Reactor utility, and under Physical Properties, enter Mass = 2.0. The cloth has to have mass or it will be unmovable.
7. To see if there are any problems with the simulation, click the Analyze World button in the Reactor utility > Utils menu. It will calculate for a little while and then it should display a message that says "World Analysis gave no warnings." Click OK. Now you are ready to run the preview simulation. First, however, go to the Reactor > Display menu and make sure the Camera button says Camera01. Save the file at this point so you don't lose your work if the simulation fails. Sometimes Max crashes when a simulation fails.
8. Now go to the Preview & Animation menu and click the Preview in Window button. The preview window will open with an option to press "P" to play the preview. Press the P key on your keyboard and the preview

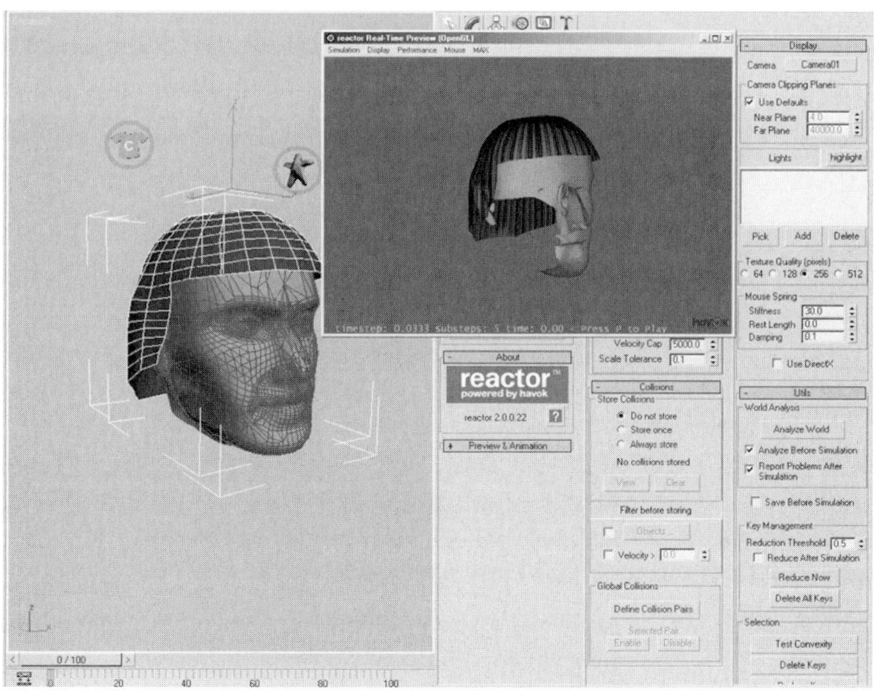

FIGURE 12.40 Setting up the simulation in the Reactor 2 utility.

simulation will start. If all goes well, the cloth will settle down over the head as the head moves around slightly. Press P again to stop the simulation after a minute or so.

9. If the preview was successful, you will want to perform the Update Max function so that the cloth will be updated at frame 0 in the "cloth settled" condition. To do that, make sure you stop the preview by pressing P at the point where you like the way the hair looks. Then, in the menu bar at the top of the preview window, click Max and then click Update MAX.
10. It will take a while to calculate the update, but after a bit, you can close the preview window and the hair object will update and assume the settled state in the viewport. You are now ready to run the final Create Animation simulation. To do that, click the Create Animation button. It will warn you that you can't back up, but in reality, if you don't like the animation, just run it again and it will overwrite the previous one.
11. That completes the Reactor Cloth Hair simulation. Save the scene file as Hair_Cloth128.max.

Reactor Cloth can be used for many different effects by mapping mesh objects with different bitmaps having an alpha channel or an opacity map. It has been used successfully as a distortion plane placed in front of an object to generate the look of heat waves. The cloth should be almost transparent with low specularity, and a weak wind should be applied to make it ripple. Then the scene camera looks through the cloth at the scene over which you want the rippling heat waves. You can also apply a map to the cloth with an image of fire or rain, or other interesting effects.

In the next tutorial, you will explore how to use a full body morph to transform Xzulixia from her human form to her vampire form.

FULL BODY MORPHING

During the vampire chase scene that you worked on in Chapter 10, "Scene Animation," the script called for the vampire Xzulixia to go through a shape change from her human form to her full alien winged vampire form. In this section, you will explore some of the issues and problems associated with this type of drastic body shape change. You can find a color image of Xzulixia in her winged vampire form in the Color Plate section of this book.

In the next tutorial, you will examine a full body morph and animated parametric objects that are scaled to change the size of wing bones in the vampire character.

TUTORIAL 12.9 VAMPIRE SHAPE CHANGE BODY MORPH

To explore the shape-change process:

ON THE CD

1. Load the AlienMorph.max scene file from the Chap12 folder on the companion CD-ROM. Maximize the front view. This file is not animated, but it contains pre-built body morph targets for Xzulixia.
2. Zoom in on the largest of the bodies, which is the original unmorphed Xzulixia mesh. Select the mesh, and then open the Modify Panel. Notice that Skin is on top of the Stack, and that Morpher is right below it. Click the Morpher in the Stack to open the Channel List menu, as shown in Figure 12.41.
3. There are three body morph targets loaded into three channels: 1/3 Vamp, 2/3 Vamp, and Full Vamp. Notice that the legs on the final vampire shape are much smaller than the original. This is to make the final silhouette of the model resemble a bat.
4. If you click the Full Vamp spinner and raise its strength to 100, you will see the original Xzu mesh morph into the Full Vampire shape.

The problem at this point was what to do with the arms. Should they become wing bones, or should they be hidden? It was decided to hide them and create additional bones to simulate the arm and hand bones that would grow into wing bones.

5. Set the Time Range to 800 and move the Time Slider to frame 620. The simulated arm bones are animated to grow and move as the Time Slider moves. This would correspond to a section of a scene where the hands turn into wings. To complete the effect, a NURBS skin membrane is attached.
6. Many problems can occur and a lot of time can be put into a complex effect such as this. The best solution is to use cut-away shots and not show the entire seamless morphing in one long shot because it is not practical to build the model to do that. It is far better to build three models that represent different stages, and cut from one to the next.

ON THE CD

7. This scene has not been finalized, but you can view an animation of the test human-to-vampire morph. To see the animation, click File > View Image File, and then from the companion CD-ROM, load the VampMorph.avi movie from the Chap12\Images folder.

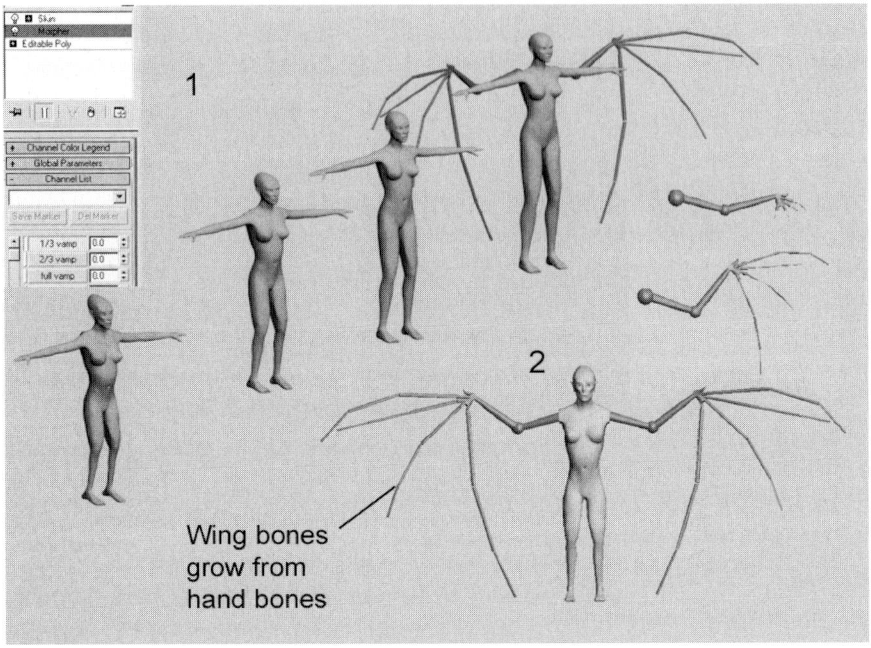

FIGURE 12.41 Xzulixia shape-change morph targets and hand bone extensions.

The final concept of filming the vampire morphing sequence involves Xzulixia hiding among the pipes near the Cracking Tower where she undergoes the shape change. This would be a static scene where the people looking for her cannot locate her until the morph is complete. The audience would see only parts of the morph, and then the camera would cut back to the men. When she emerges in the full vampire shape and takes to the air, the dogs would find her, and the man would fire, causing the pipes to explode. An early pre-visualization version of the model is shown in Figure 12.42. See the Color Plate section of this book for the final version of the vampire.

Secondary Motion

Secondary motion is an important concept to master in professional character animation. An example of secondary motion is the shaking of the flesh of a fat person, an elephant, or a dinosaur when they move. This kind of animation effect can be accomplished in two ways: You can use Reactor 2 soft-body dynamics or you can use the Flex Modifier. Flex is

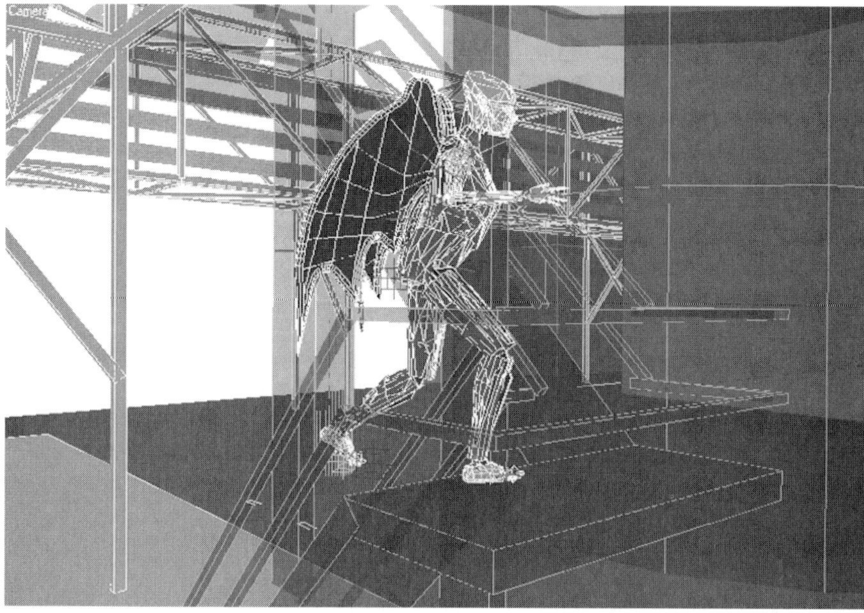

FIGURE 12.42 Pre-visualization model of the vampire running up the stairs.

the easiest method to use because it is simple to set up and works well with the Skin Modifier and Soft Selections. However, it does not perform nearly as well as Reactor 2, and can be considered a memory hog that will slow your computer. Be sure to add the Point Cache Modifier whenever you animate with Flex.

Point Cache

The Point Cache Modifier is a necessary part of dynamic simulations in Reactor 2, Flex, Reactor Cloth, and particle system animations. The purpose of the Point Cache Modifier is to enable you to maintain real-time playback speed in simulated scenes that would normally play back slowly or not at all in the viewport. A Point Cache can maintain a reasonable viewport refresh speed even though there might be thousands of points moving one time in a scene. Multiple Point Caches can used to record, store, and play back the point position data in large scenes with hundreds of objects, such as a battle scene or the dynamic simulation of water's surface in a storm.

A point cache is created by first running the simulation and then placing the Point Cache Modifier on top of the stack to record the point key positions over time. At that point, you turn off the simulation modifier that generated the simulation (click the lightbulb in the stack), such as Flex, and let the point cache provide the data as you scrub the Time Slider. Because the points are being animated with stored point cache data from memory, the computer does not need to calculate every frame, and the Time Slider can be moved normally.

When you save the scene file, the point cache data is saved along with the scene. Many plug-ins that perform simulations of some kind have built-in point cache systems.

We have explored just a few of the advanced animation features available in 3ds max 6. The techniques you learned here are used daily in professional animation studios around the world.

CONCLUSION

In this chapter, you worked with an expression controller to help create an interactive walk animation, and then you applied Reactor dynamics to a character for impact detection and collision. You also worked with the Reactor 2 Rag Doll stunt double. Then you examined how a battle scene was set up with two stunt doubles. Next, you looked at the setup for a facial bone network, and then learned how to apply custom attributes to animate hands and feet. You used Reactor 2 to make simple simulated hair for a character, and were introduced to using MAXScript. Finally, you explored the full body morphing procedure used to change Xzulixia into a winged vampire. In the next chapter, you will create layered and procedural materials and explore some of the new materials available in 3ds max 6.

CHAPTER

13 MATERIALS AND TEXTURES

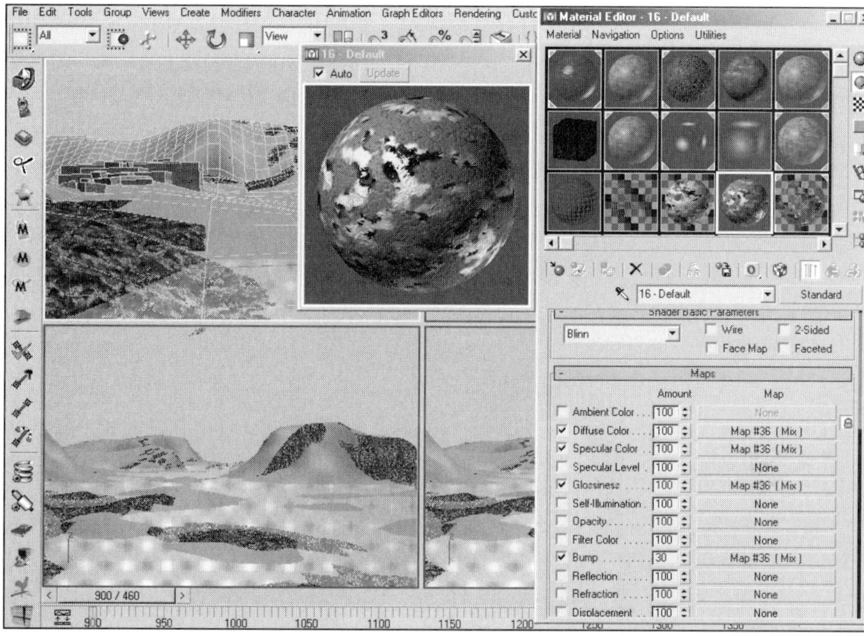

In this chapter, you will explore the approach taken in the design and creation of materials and mapping objects in *Homing Instinct*. You will apply a map to the Dr. Quin model to create a facial texture. To help apply textures to organic models, you will work with the UVW Unwrap Modifier. You will look at the new *architectural textures,* and then you will explore the *shaders* available when you choose Mental Ray as your renderer.

SEMI-REALISM

There was a conscious decision made to keep the style of the film *Homing Instinct* semi-realistic. This meant that everything should look anatomically correct, but no time should be wasted trying to disguise the fact that it was computer generated. The story line was filled with scenes of armed conflict, visual effects, and drama, so an effort was made to avoid cartoonishness. The final look combined smooth and often simple surface textures on man-made objects, with fairly complex organic textures in the environments, as shown in Figure 13.1. All water and glass surfaces were raytraced to create realistic reflections, and atmospheric fog was added to give

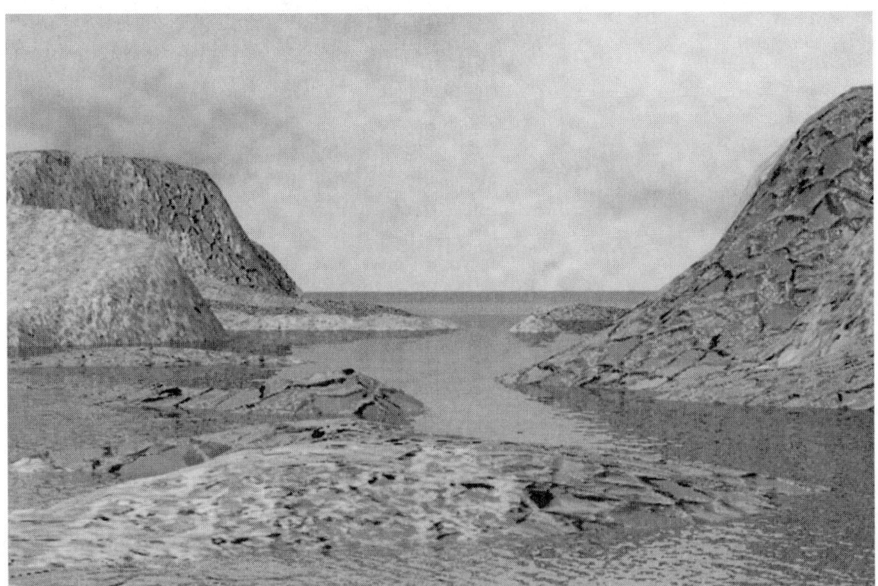

FIGURE 13.1 The environment with the Mix material includes the Cellular texture.

the scenes depth. The goal was to suggest that the environments, vehicles, and equipment depicted could really exist in a future world.

Nearly all of the environments were textured with materials that consist of two or three layers. The procedural texture map Cellular was used as the base layer of most organic materials. It was found that if the same texture map was placed in the diffuse, specular, bump, and glossiness material map channels, the organic appearance of a material was enhanced, as shown in Figure 13.2.

The Mix map is a very versatile map type and can contain nested layers of texture maps that are themselves composed multilayered maps. Cellular mixed with Noise is the author's favorite texture map combination, and was used for everything from concrete walls to the faces of characters. Cellular provides three intermixed regions within one map

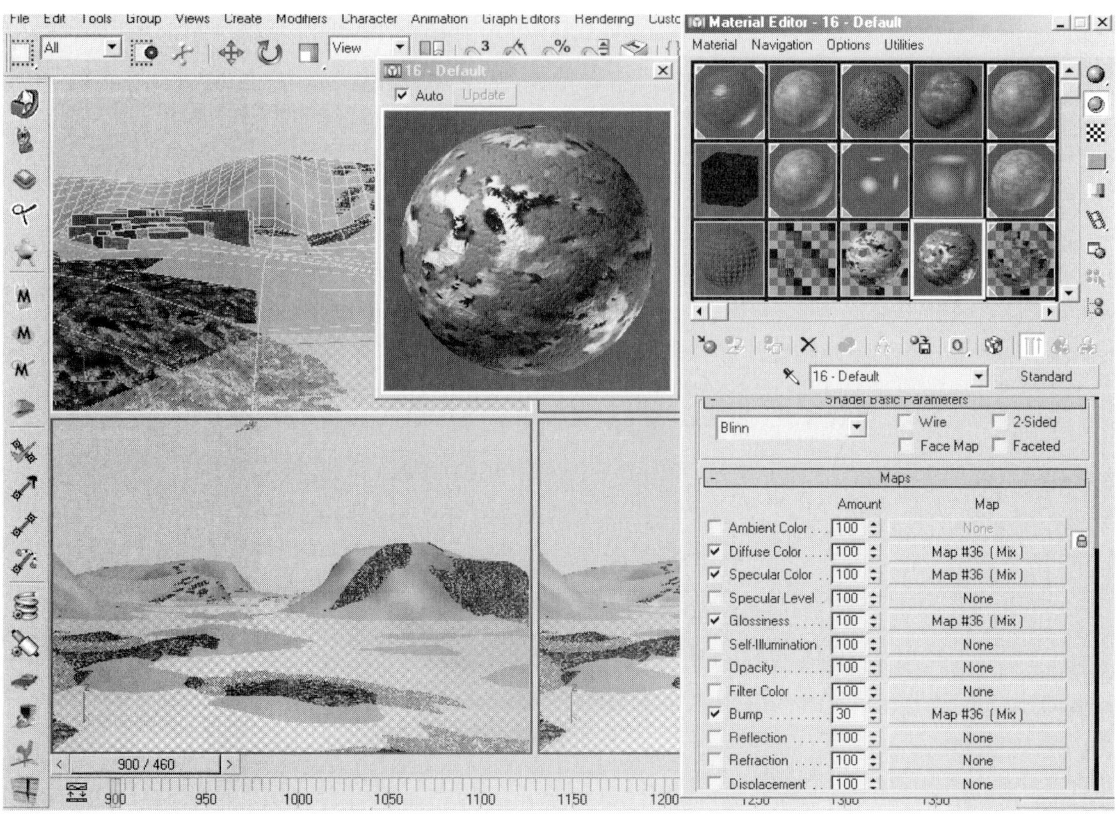

FIGURE 13.2 The Mix material is copied into additional map channels.

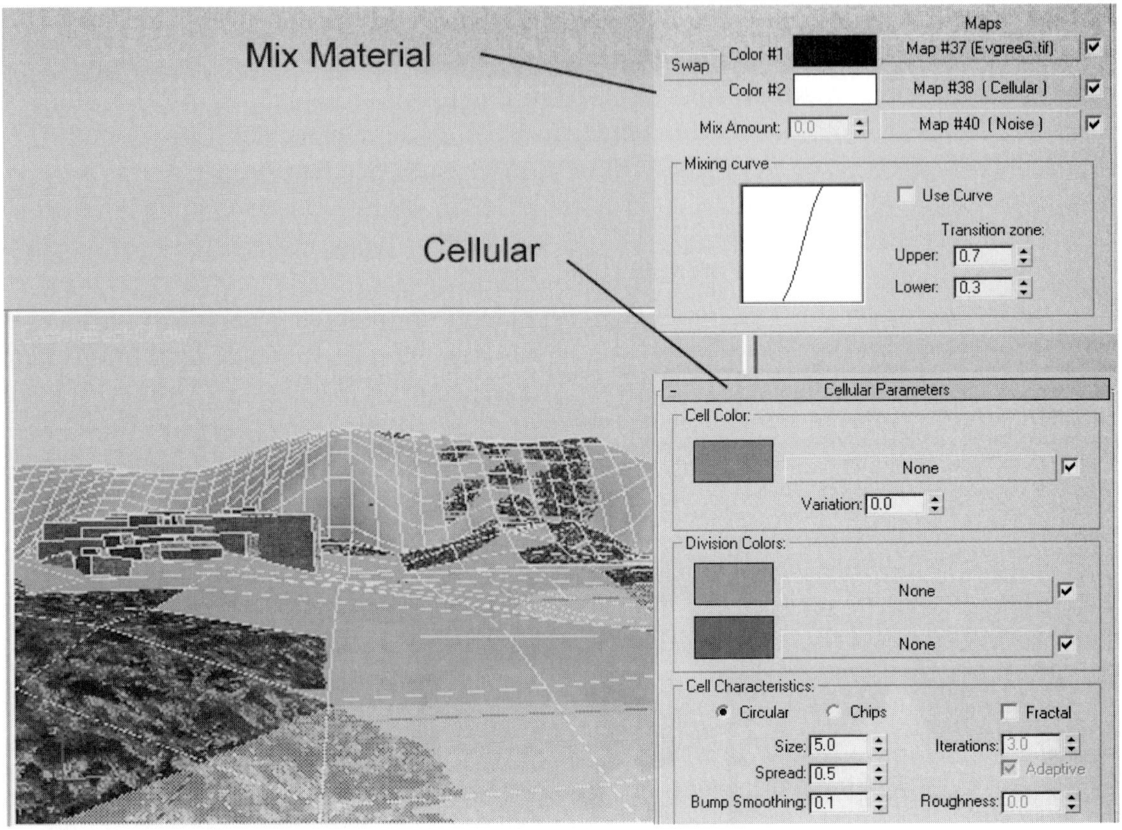

FIGURE 13.3 The Cellular map can be a mixture of three colors or three maps.

consisting of cells created from one color or texture map, outlines between the cells of a different color, and the edges of the outlines a third color, as shown in Figure 13.3.

You can also replace any of these colors with a bitmap, or you can put another Cellular or Mix map into one of the three Cellular map slots, which would give you six or more maps mixed together to make the one Cellular map.

The Mix material allows you to use two maps with a third map as a mask to reveal parts of a background map layer through openings in the top layer, as shown in Figure 13.3. In this case, a Noise map is used to open holes in the top map layer bitmap, Evergreen.Tif, of the Mix map, which reveals the bottom layer, Cellular, through the openings made by the black areas in the Noise map mask. This multilayer map material is the most common material used in *Homing Instinct* and can be seen in all of the environment images in this book and the color plates where it is applied to the objects in the valley of the temple ruins.

In terms of organizing the texture files, much time was spent making sure that all materials were properly named, and that all of the files associated with each model were kept together. The same material was used for many different models, such as the basic gray metal material. A central server computer was set up with a master directory of all materials and texture maps. To manage the materials files, the 3ds max 6 Asset Browser, which can be found in the Utility panel, proved an invaluable tool. It generates a thumbnail image that allows animators to look in any directory on any computer in the network to locate files, or to identify where duplicate files with different names were stored.

Because the textures used in *Homing Instinct* are meant to be semi-realistic, some photos of real surfaces became the basis for many of the materials used on vehicle models. The Composite material is made up of layers, which can themselves be made up of layers. Photographs, bitmaps, and other materials can be combined with animated bitmaps to create a wide array of interesting textures. Materials using a movie as a surface texture were used for effects such as water running over the surface of an object.

PUTTING A FACE ON DR. QUIN

A skin material must be applied to the character to make it look more like a living person. Each character in the *Homing Instinct* film should have believable textures. The flesh color that has been used on the model is uninspiring and drab. A real human face has a number of different colors on the surface and below the skin. Once you apply finished textures to the model, the lighting becomes more important. Lighting can make a texture look bad or good depending on how you position the lights and how bright they are. It is a good idea to use this rule: less light is more dramatic. Often, in motion pictures, three colors of light are projected on an actor's face: red on one side, blue on the other side, and white light on the front of the face and the outer edge of the hair, called a Hair light. The red and blue lights are called Modeling lights because they give shape to the face and help to separate the character from the background. They also make the character look good on camera. This same three-color lighting is used for all the character faces in *Homing Instinct*. In the next tutorial, you will create a face material with maps in the diffuse and bump map channels.

TUTORIAL 13.1 APPLYING A TEXTURE TO DR. QUIN'S FACE

To apply a material to the face:

ON THE CD

ON THE CD

1. Load the GenMan811.max scene file from the Chap13 folder on the companion CD-ROM. Maximize the front view.
2. Select the head, and in the Modify Panel, turn on Skin and Relax. Then, apply cylindrical mapping. Click Modifiers > UV Coordinates > UVW Map, and in the Mapping Parameters rollout menu select Cylindrical. It will be lying horizontal. In the map Alignment Parameters, select the X-axis, and then click the Fit button, as shown in Figure 13.4, example 1.
3. Open the Materials Editor (M). Select an unused material sample slot, and then click the Add Map button next to the Diffuse color swatch in the Blinn Shader Basic Parameters menu. In the Material/Map Browser, go to the companion CD-ROM, and in the Chap13\Images folder, select DrQuin-Face.tif. The map will load into the Diffuse map channel.

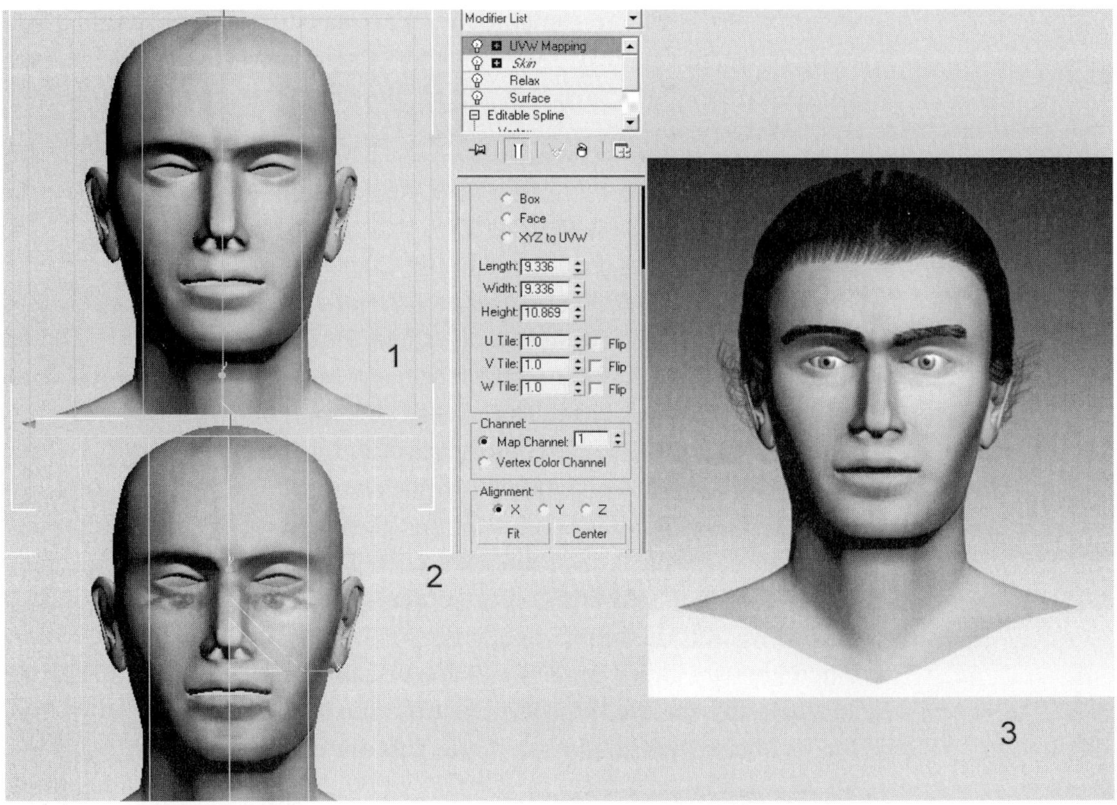

FIGURE 13.4 Apply the mapping and the material to Dr. Quin, showing him with Shag Hair.

4. Apply the material to the head. Click Assign Material to Selection, and then click the Show Map in Viewport icon. The map appears on the face, but it is too wide, distorted, and not positioned correctly. To correct these problems, go to the Modify Tab Panel and find the Width parameter in the UVW Mapping Parameters menu. Increase the Width amount to about 25.6, or until the eyes of the texture map are aligned with the eye sockets in the head, as shown in Figure 13.4. example 2.
5. The eyes and mouth will probably still be too low down on the face. To fix that, go to the top of the Modifier Stack, and click the Plus (+) button in UVW Mapping. Then, click the mapping gizmo. It turns yellow. Now, use the Move tool to raise the cylindrical mapping gizmo a bit until the eyes are aligned vertically with the eye sockets.
6. Adjust the Height and Length parameters to position correctly so that the lips and the eyes of the map are aligned with the head. Then, click UVW Mapping in the Stack to turn off the gizmo.
7. Test render the face until you are satisfied with the map alignment, as shown in Figure 13.4, example 3. This image shows Dr. Quin with the hair made with the Shag Hair plug-in that is explained in a tutorial in Chapter 17, "Plug-Ins."
8. Save the file as GenManFace.max.

In the following tutorials, you will work through the process of creating a texture map for the face of a soldier using the Unwrap UVW Modifier and Adobe Photoshop.

USING UNWRAP UVW TO CREATE TEXTURE MAPS

Instead of using conventional mapping that uses planar or cylindrical mapping coordinates for the head, you can use the Unwrap UVW Modifier to break the surface into smaller segments with planar mapping coordinates on each piece. This is done by using *flatten mapping*. This method results in the least amount of distortion of the texture and is effective on complex surfaces. This is also the de facto standard mapping technique in the game industry and many high-end animation studios. This section describes how to use Photoshop to make a face texture using a picture of the mapping coordinates. The example used for this tutorial is the head of a soldier model in *Homing Instinct*. He is designed to look rugged and dirty, with scars on his face, as shown in Figure 13.5. By using Adobe Photoshop and the Unwrap UVW Modifier in 3ds max, you can create a good-looking texture map very quickly.

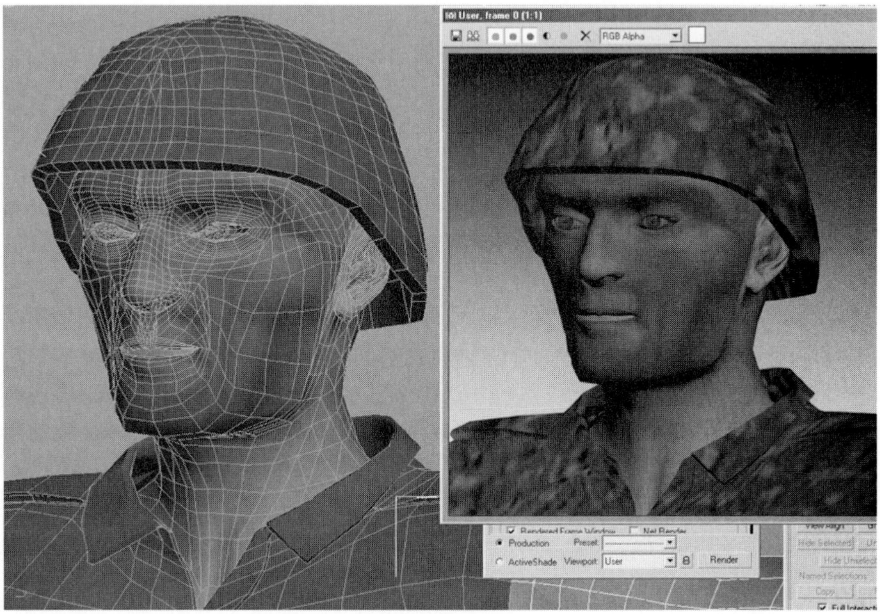

FIGURE 13.5 Facial texture created using Unwrap UVW and flatten mapping.

The usual workflow is to first apply Unwrap UVW to a mesh. Then, in the Unwrap UVW Editor, you select flatten mapping to break the texture coordinates into small, flat sections. Once the correct areas of the flattened face are associated together and mapped, the image from the UVW Map Editor is cloned using the Print Screen button, and that information is pasted into a new picture in Photoshop. There the painting is done to create the desired look. You can convert a copy of the image to a grayscale map to use for a bump or a displacement map. These secondary maps can provide character lines on the face, and will greatly enhance the realism if carefully done. Once the maps are done, they are brought back into 3ds max and placed in the diffuse mapping channel of a standard Max material. This material is then applied to the character head and test-rendered for alignment. If there is distortion, or if the features are not aligned correctly, go back to the Unwrap UVW Editor workspace and move specific vertices to move the affected portion of the map on the face. In this way, you can shift parts of the map on the model so that it will match the facial features perfectly.

TUTORIAL 13.2 USING UNWRAP UVW TO MAKE A MAP FOR A HEAD

To create a map for the head:

ON THE CD

1. Load the UVWMap.max file from the Chap13 folder on the companion CD-ROM.
2. Select the head in the front view and click Hide Unselected. Open the Modify Tab Panel and apply an Unwrap UVW Modifier to the head. Do not apply any other mapping.
3. In the Unwrap UVW > Parameters roll-out menu, click the Edit button. The Edit UVW's dialog and workspace will open and you will see a small wireframe head near the top of the window.
4. Click Mapping > Flatten Mapping in the editor's menu bar. In the Flatten Mapping window, enter 105.0 degrees in the Face Angle Threshold data window and click OK. After a short calculation, you will see the face mesh broken into separate sections, as shown in Figure 13.6.

The Face Angle threshold you choose determines how the face is divided into sections. By changing this number, you can create larger or smaller sections. 75 was chosen as the best setting for mapping the face area after trying a range of angles from 30 to 120. A higher numerical angle results in fewer larger sections, which are easier to paint in Photoshop.

5. After the editor flattens the face, you will see a left and a right side view of the face. These are the texture coordinates for the face. The next step is to take one of the wireframe face sides and put it on top of the other side.

   When you are using flatten mapping, you are essentially applying planar maps to each of the separate sections of the head. Because the left and right halves of the face are nearly identical, you can use the same part of the texture map to texture both halves of the face.
6. To put one side of the face on the other, draw a region selection box around the lower face coordinates group in the Unwrap Editor window. They will turn red. Then click the Flip Vertical icon in the Unwrap toolbar.

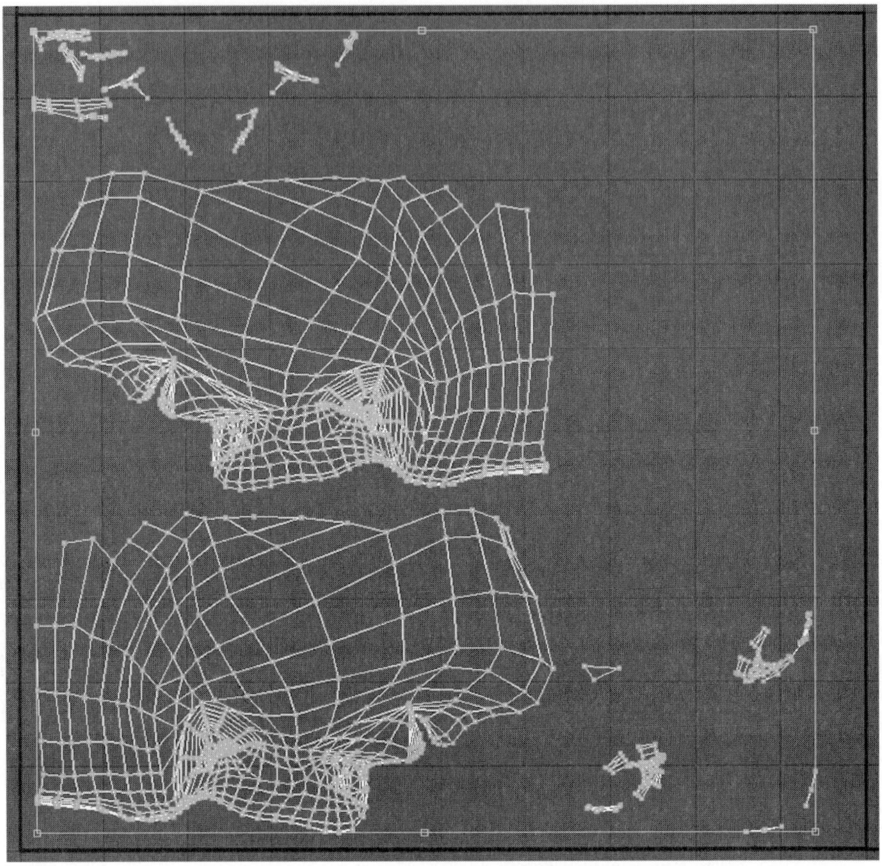

FIGURE 13.6 105-degree flatten mapping applied to the soldier's head.

The face will be inverted and should now be facing the same direction as the upper-face side view. Next, drag the selected face up and position it over the unselected face. Rotate it slightly to align it and then de-select (click in the gray area), as shown in Figure 13.7.

7. Now you are ready to snapshot the Editor window, but before you do, it is essential to change the editor workspace background color and turn off the blue grid lines. To do that, click Options > Advanced Options. In the Unwrap Options window, turn off Show Grid. Then select the background color swatch and change it to an RGB color value of Red = 186, Green = 161, Blue = 122. Then click OK and close the menu.

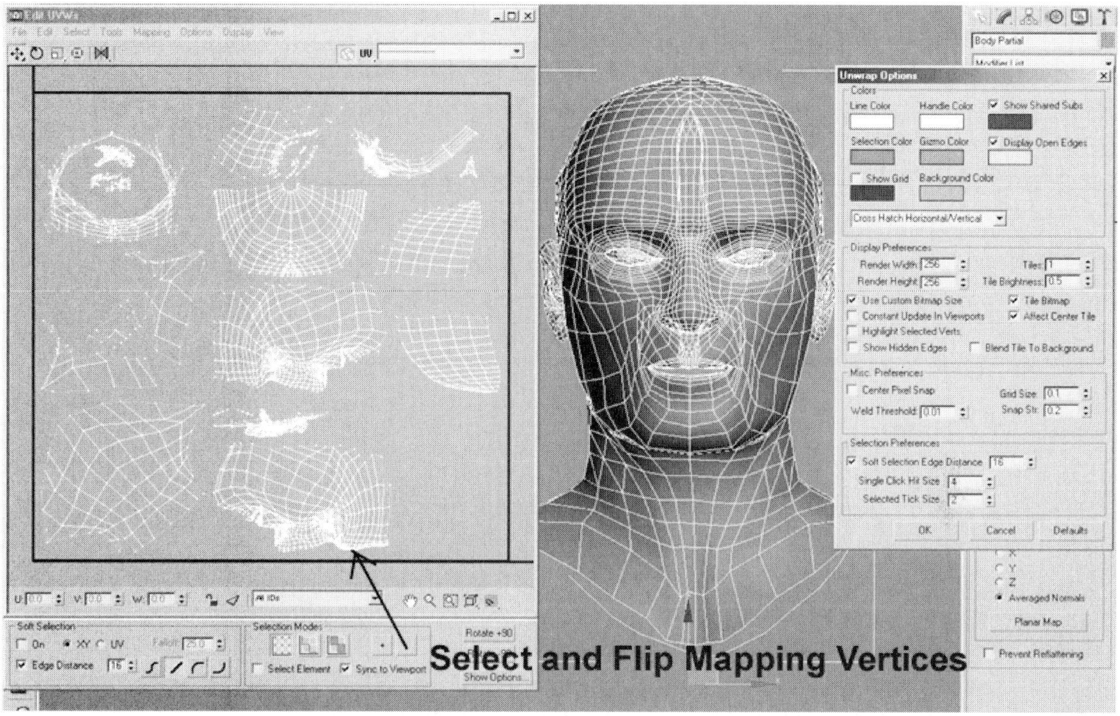

FIGURE 13.7 Flip and superimpose the two face maps.

8. Now you will do a screen capture by pressing the Print Screen button (next to Home). First, however, click the Maximize button in the upper right corner of the Unwrap UVW Edit window to enlarge the image. Then press the Print Screen button on your keyboard to capture the screen image to the Windows buffer memory. Minimize Max, and open Adobe Photoshop.
9. In Photoshop, Click File > New and change the resolution to 150 pixels/inch. Click OK, and then click Edit > Paste. The image of the Unwrap UVW Editor workspace should appear. Before going any farther, use a rectangular selection box to select only the center of the image inside the exact edges of the square around the mapping coordinates. Then click Image > Crop. You should now have a square image.

If you do not crop the image, your texture map will be the wrong size when you import it into 3ds max 6.

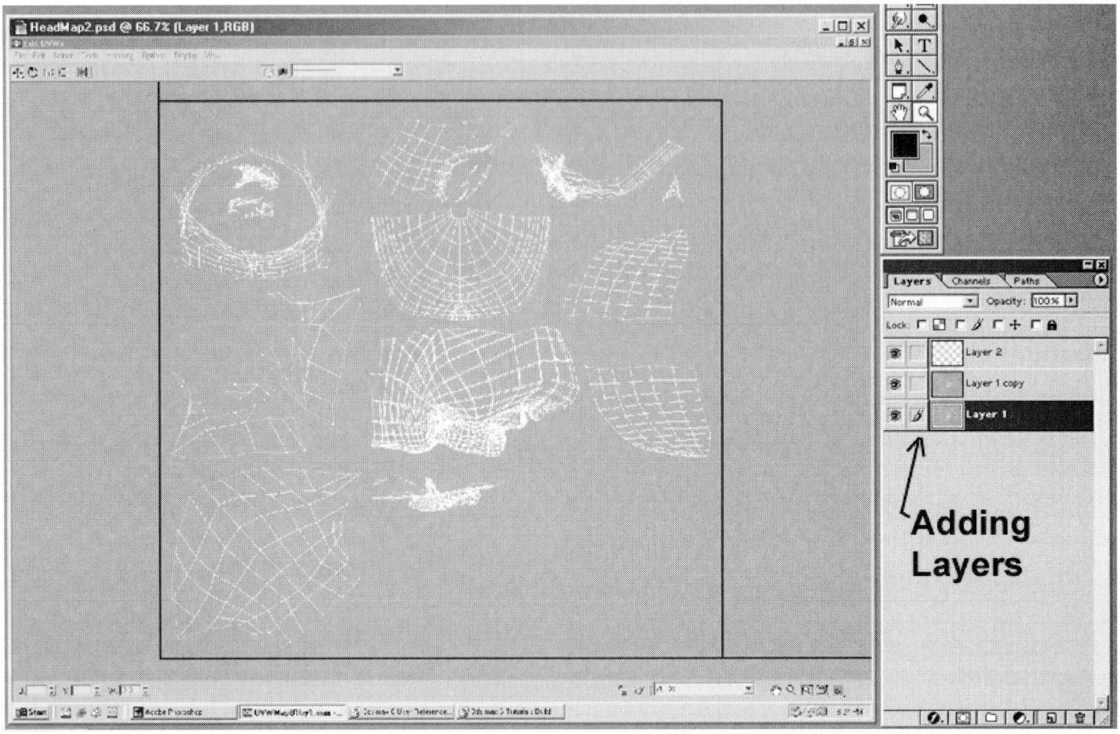

FIGURE 13.8 The screengrab of the Unwrap UVW Editing window, imported into Photoshop.

10. Next, rotate the image 90 degrees clockwise so that the side view of the face is vertical. Then, in the Photoshop Layers window, click the Options arrow. Click New Layer. Repeat that to create a second new layer. You should now have four layers: Layer 1 is a white background layer, Layer 2 is the screengrab of the Max6 Unwrap UVW Editor window, and Layer 3 is a transparent new layer, as shown in Figure 13.8. Layer 4 is the layer on which you will paint.
11. You are now ready to paint the face in Photoshop. Save the image file as HeadMap.psd. Continue on to the next tutorial without closing Photoshop.

In the next tutorial, you will paint the texture for the face. Then you will import it into 3d studio max 6 as a diffuse map and apply it to the head of the soldier.

TUTORIAL 13.3 PAINTING A FACE IN ADOBE PHOTOSHOP

To paint the texture map:

ON THE CD

1. Continue on in Photoshop with the previous tutorial. You should see the HeadMap.psd image in Photoshop. If not, you can load it from the Chapter13\Images folder on the companion CD-ROM. Next, load the FaceSample.tif image into Photoshop from the same folder. Use this image as a guide for painting your texture map.

It is helpful to move all of the images that you will be using for these tutorials into a folder in your 3ds max 6\Maps directory. The author recommends creating a Homing_Instinct folder in your Maps directory, and then creating individual folders for each chapter to hold the image files. For example, the images for this tutorial were put in a folder moved to the author's machine with the following path: C:\3dsmax6\Maps\Homing_Instinct\Chap13\Images. That way, you can remove the CD-ROM that comes with this book and put it away for safekeeping, and still have access to the necessary image files for the tutorials. The same recommendation holds true for all tutorial image files. Remember that all files on the CD-ROM are write-protected.

2. Before starting to paint the top layer, first use the Eyedropper to sample the skin background color of Layer 2. Use that color to fill Layer 3, and then set the opacity of Layer 3 to 65 percent, as shown in Figure 13.9.
3. Zoom in on the side view of the face. Select a small soft-edge brush and set opacity to about 20. Then, choose a darker hue of the skin-like color and paint a dark ring around the eye socket. Observe where the color has been applied to simulate dirt on the face and dark beard growth. This shading is done with a medium-gray, slightly orange color.
4. Paint the side of the face to your taste and then save the image as HeadMap2.psd. This will not be your map. To create the map, go to the Layers menu, select Layer 3, and increase opacity to 100 percent. You should no longer be able to see the original wireframe background image. Now, save the .PSD file with its layers, and then click the Options arrow in the Layer menu and select Flatten Image.
5. Before saving the texture map, be sure to rotate the image 90 degrees counterclockwise, or it will not fit the face of the soldier when you import it into Max. Remember to flatten all image layers and then save the image into your working directory as HeadMap2.tif. You should never try to use the .psd image for a texture map in 3ds max without flattening the image layers.

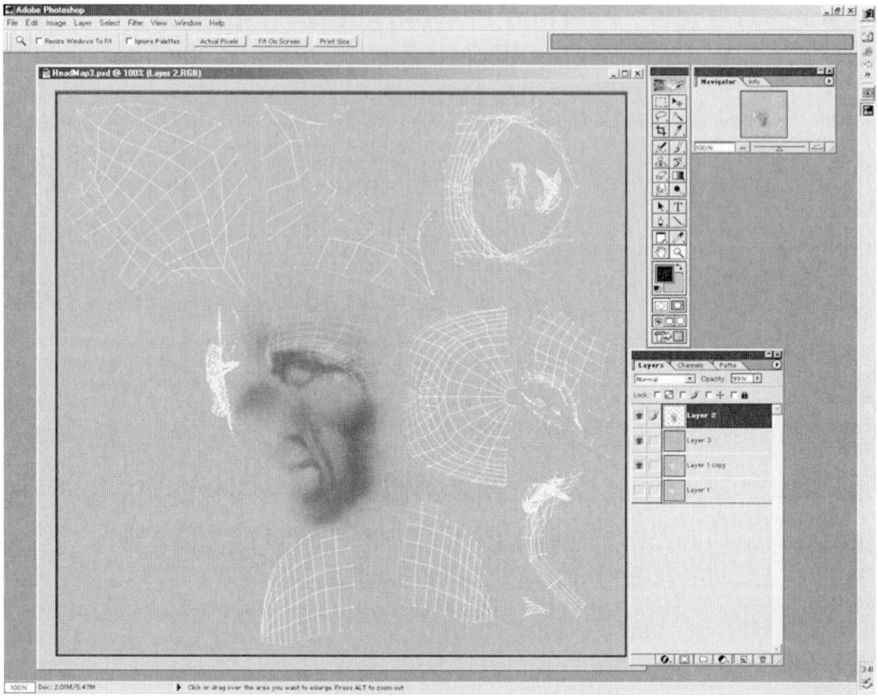

FIGURE 13.9 Setting up the layers in Photoshop.

6. Now return to 3ds max 6 and open the Materials Editor. Select a standard material and then click the Map Requester button beside the Diffuse color swatch. Load the map you just made in Photoshop and then apply that material to the head and click the Show Map In Viewport icon. You should now be able to see the results in the viewport. Render it to check how the texture aligns with the face.
7. You can add a bump map for additional surface texture. The author used the Sandshor.jpg map as a bump map from the 3ds max 6\Maps\Ground folder with the Bump Amount set to 5.
8. After rendering the face, you should view the results, shown in Figure 13.10. If any part of the map does not fit, you can adjust the vertices in the Unwrap UVW Edit window. You can also reposition the map by clicking the Diffuse Map button in the Materials Editor and then selecting Extended Parameters. There, you can adjust the map's Offset and Rotate settings to move the map up or down, or left or right.
9. Because this model was not used for close-up shots, no facial lines or displacement maps were needed. For more realism, you can prepare a

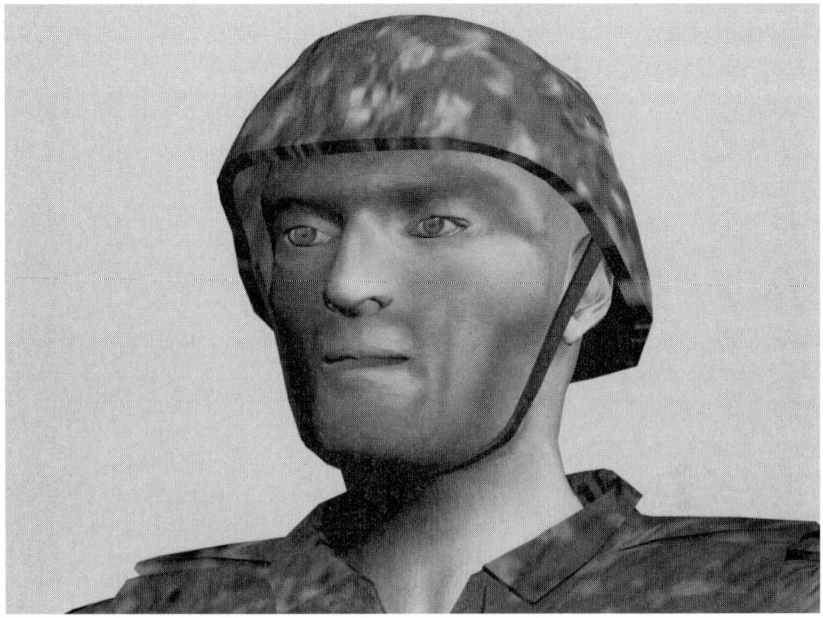

FIGURE 13.10 The finished texture map applied to the soldier's head.

grayscale displacement map of the scars and lines in the face. Be sure to start with a low displacement strength amount, between 1 and 5, when applying any displacement map. Save the file as UnwrapUVW133.max.

This completes the Unwrap UVW texture-mapping tutorial. This procedure was used for nearly all of the organic models in *Homing Instinct*. Only the buildings and environment had conventional texture coordinates and maps applied to them. This technique can yield very good results very quickly. It can also be used for photo-realism, but for *Homing Instinct* that was not necessary.

In the next section, you will explore the special materials that are new in 3ds max 6.

Architectural Materials and Textures

The new architectural materials in 3ds max 6 are meant primarily for architectural rendering and visualization where light transmittance and reflectance are important. These special materials greatly expand your capability to quickly apply believable, realistic textures and obtain a true-to-life depiction of what a building is going to look like. Architectural materials are meant to be physically accurate, and are best suited as realistic materials for high-end rendering with radiosity. If you are creating photo-realistic images of your models, these materials will yield beautiful interiors and realistic scenic environments.

Architectural materials cannot be used with the 3ds max scanline renderer or with standard lights. They will generally render correctly using Mental Ray and the Mental Ray lights with good results. The Architectural materials function very much like the Mental Ray shaders, and are based on a pre-made material template. They are meant to be used with photometric lights. A typical example is the Metal material template. There are four Metal material templates: Metal, which is shiny and reflective; Metal-Brushed, which is somewhat less shiny; Metal Flat, which is even less shiny; and Metal Polished, which is highly shiny.

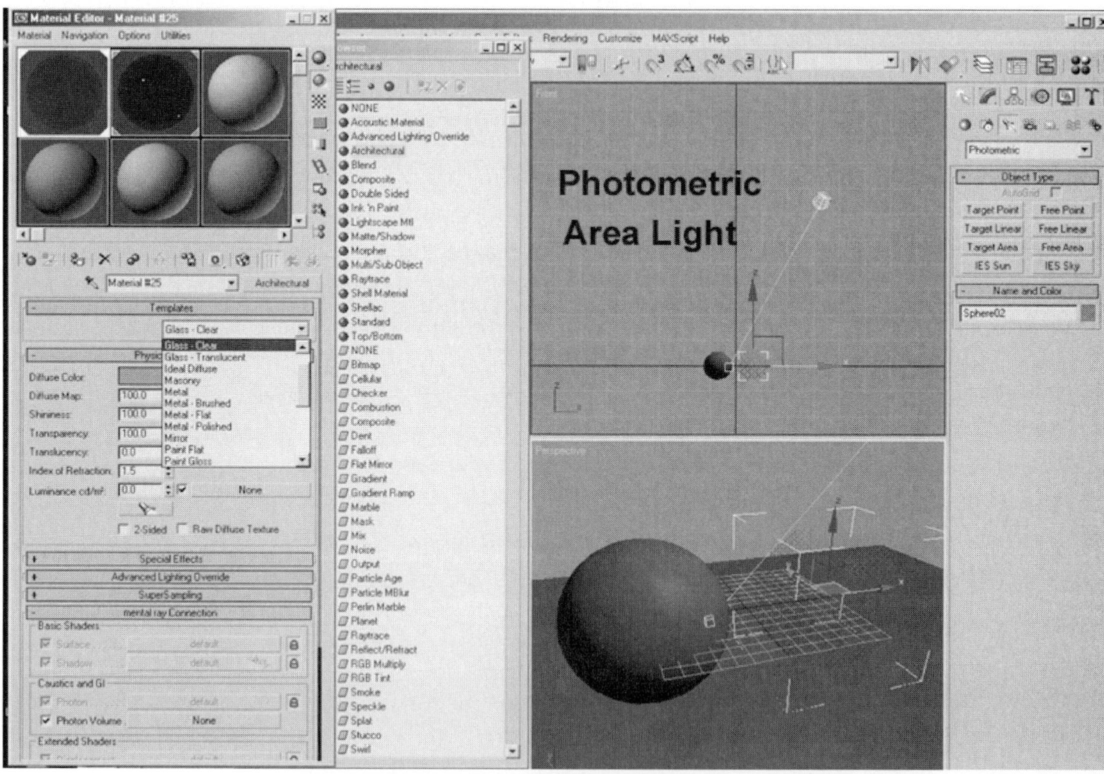

FIGURE 13.11 Three architectural materials applied to primitive objects with two photometric area lights.

To render a scene with these materials, you must set the architectural material parameters in the Adjust Radiosity roll-out menu, which is designed to control the way light is absorbed and reflected from wall and structural surfaces. You can also set reflectance and transmittance factors for glass to ensure that a room interior does not "burn out" from having too much light, and you can use exact luminance values for the lights in the room.

A sample rendering of two spheres and a plane was set up using three architectural materials: Metal-Glossy, Glass-Clear, and Masonry, as shown in Figure 13.11.

Advanced lighting was used and Radiosity was selected. The geometry was subdivided for the Radiosity solution, and then two photometric lights were added to the scene: a *target area light* and a point area light. Once the objects were re-meshed, the Radiosity solution was run. Then they turned black in the viewport and a Logarithmic Exposure control was applied in the Environment dialog so that a preview could be seen when the lighting was changed, as shown in Figure 13.12.

The spheres were then rendered, and it was determined that more adjustments were needed before the masonry material would show. It was also determined that this type of material was too rigorous to set up for use in *Homing Instinct*.

Mental Ray Materials and Shaders

The Mental Ray renderer is a major step forward in the direction of photo-realism in 3ds max 6. It comes with a large number of pre-built shaders that cover most of the types of materials you would want. It can also use most of the standard Max materials by using the Max to Mental Ray translator feature. Max materials that use discreet Radiosity or Max ray-tracing will not work with Mental Ray. Mental Ray has its own ray-tracing and indirect illumination technology. Those features are described in Chapter 14, "Lighting and Rendering."

Mental Ray shaders differ from Max standard materials, which are also shaders, in a few significant ways. The obvious difference between Mental Ray and Max shaders is the method used to calculate the surface and render the image. Mental Ray (MR) is based on ray-tracing and all of the MR shaders have settings for number of rays, regathering the rays, changing the number of photons, and a host of other processing settings.

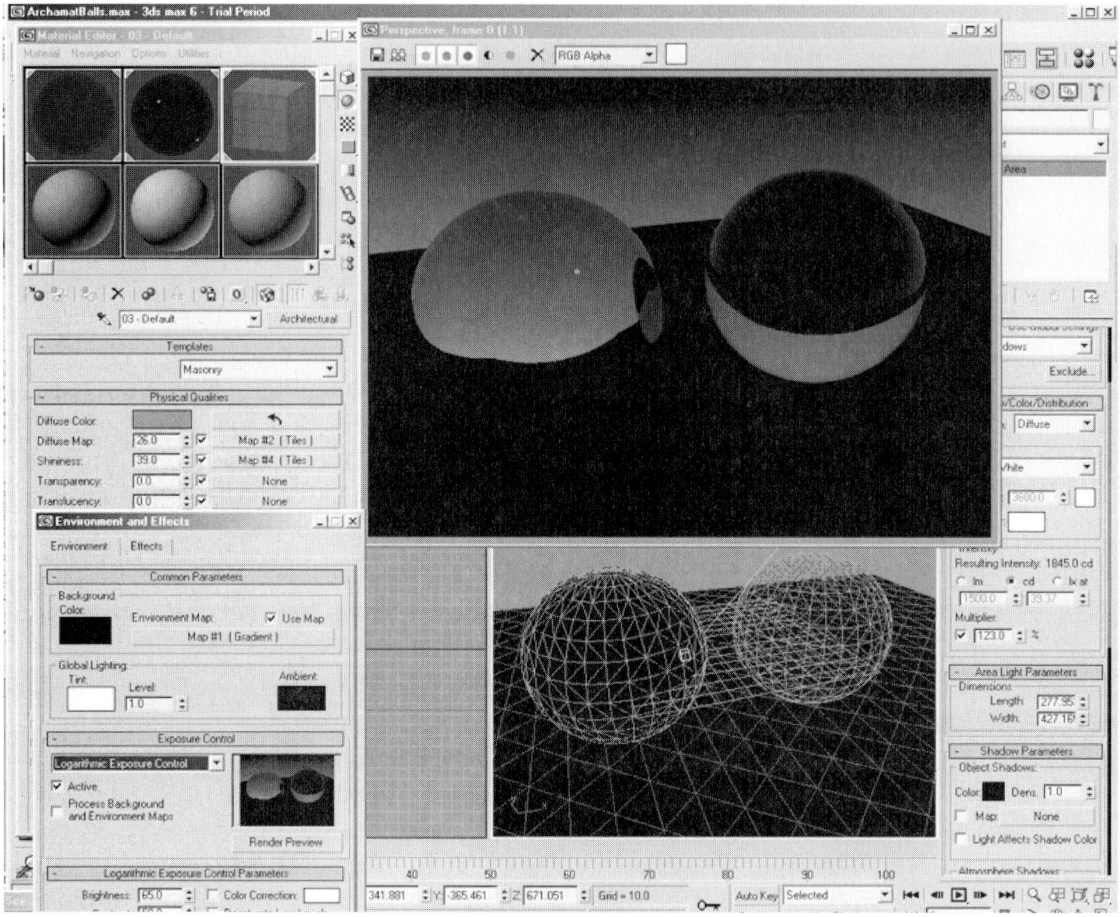

FIGURE 13.12 Two spheres rendered using the Radiosity lighting solution with architectural materials.

To fully describe all of the Mental Ray shaders and how to use them would take a separate book, and is far beyond the scope of this chapter.

The most straightforward way to get used to Mental Ray materials is to start with objects to which 3ds max 6 materials have been applied. Then switch to the Mental Ray renderer and render them with default settings. The author tested Mental Ray with a scene from *Homing Instinct* that was set in the sewers of Titan City. He found that all of the Max materials, except for the ray-trace material on the sewer water, which had to be changed, worked fine when rendered with Mental Ray, as shown in Figure 13.13.

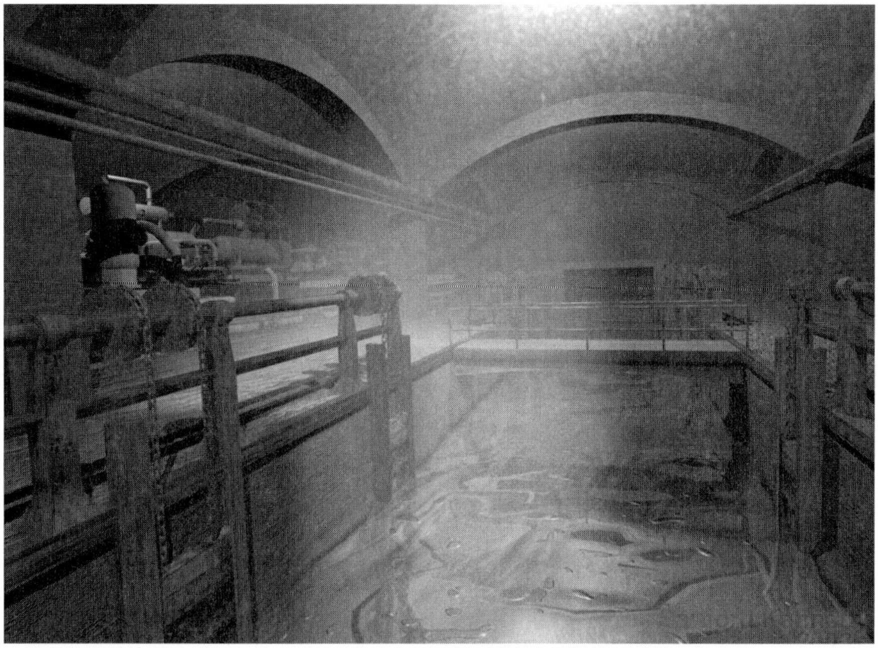

FIGURE 13.13 The Titan City sewer plant, with standard Max materials rendered using Mental Ray.

Concrete materials were used in most of the scenes in *Homing Instinct*. 3ds max 6 comes with four basic concrete bitmaps. The author used a Mix map type in the Diffuse map channel to combine different bitmaps and procedural maps, such as Noise, Mask, Gradient Ramp, and Cellular, to create a variety of different concrete surfaces for different aged buildings, structural members in bridges, and road surfaces. In reality, most of the fine details of the porous concrete surface were lost in the film. All of these materials were tested in Mental Ray and they worked very well.

After viewing rendered scenes, it was determined that audiences would never see the concrete material in a close-up shot. Scintillation, or "swimming," caused by the dots or lines of a repetitive texture in the rendering, forced the author to drastically blur many of the concrete and asphalt surfaces when the camera was moving. Much of the bump mapping detail was lost, except when the camera was still or in a close-up shot. Clearly, for an action film, you can use much less accurate materials, and simply "dirty up" a basic gray material to make it look good—for example, when a speeding vehicle is driving along a road and the surface is continuously moving, or when buildings are streaming by in the background.

Any material with repetitive parallel lines should be avoided, to prevent unwanted artifacts during rendering. An example of this type of material would be corrugated metal on building roofs and walls. At certain distances from the camera, the lines will begin to merge and create moiré patterns that move and undulate on the surface. Another example is the old-fashioned, narrow plank siding on buildings. A typical nineteenth-century wooden house could have hundreds of parallel lines all over its surface, plus the edges of the shingle roof and the rungs of a picket fence or iron gate. All of these repetitive line examples will cause rendering problems and should not be used in your sets or backgrounds. In film, these repetitive line surfaces pose no problem because horizontal scan lines do not exist. These are only bothersome in video and computer renderings.

To see the available Mental Ray shaders in the Materials Editor, you must select Mental Ray as your renderer. To select Mental Ray as the active renderer, open the Rendering dialog and click the Rendering tab. Now scroll down to the Common tab. Then, in the Common Parameters menu, open Assign Renderer and click the square chooser button beside Production Slot. Choose Mental Ray Renderer and click OK. Once you select Mental Ray as the active renderer, you will notice that the tab names have changed into Mental Ray menus in the Render dialog. You now have Processing, Indirect Illumination, and Caustics. The Rendering tab now contains three additional menus dedicated to Mental Ray: Sampling Quality, Rendering Algorithms, and Camera Effects.

Materials such as the Advanced Lighting Override material, the Lightscape material, the Morpher material, and the Shell material will not work with Mental Ray. However, Mental Ray usually has its own equivalents, so nothing is lost, and much more is gained.

An example of a very useful Mental Ray shader is the Edge (lume) shader, which can make a bump map look like a displacement map. Many of the available MR shaders in max 6 are lume shaders. These shaders are designed for production and are created especially to solve production problems. An example of this is the Edge (lume) shader that works with bump mapping. When you apply a bump map to an object, all of the surface will look bumpy except for the outer edge, which shows no bumps and therefore makes the object look fake. The Edge shader detects the edges of the object and makes part of the edge transparent, to make the bump visible on the edge of the object. This often eliminates the need to use a displacement map, and looks very good.

The environments and buildings in *Homing Instinct,* such as the temple and the buildings you worked on in Chapter 3, "Modeling Environments, Buildings, and Aliens," were all textured using standard 3ds max 6 materials. They were rendered using the scanline renderer. Mental Ray shaders were not used because of their rigorous setup procedures and the time penalty that Mental Ray photo-realistic imagery exacts. For the film, which needed to be rendered as quickly as possible while still maintaining a semi-realistic look, the Light Tracer and a Skylight with no more than one light ray bounce was adequate and quite fast. Max standard materials generally work very well, even if they always look like they are computer-generated. For those of you who want photo-realism, Mental Ray is a powerful and exacting rendering solution.

CONCLUSION

In this chapter, you explored the multilayer capabilities of 3ds max, and you applied a facial texture to a model using Unwrap UVW. Then you looked at the new architectural materials and Mental Ray shaders. In the next chapter, you will work with lighting and rendering to create scenes using Global Illumination.

CHAPTER

14 LIGHTING AND RENDERING

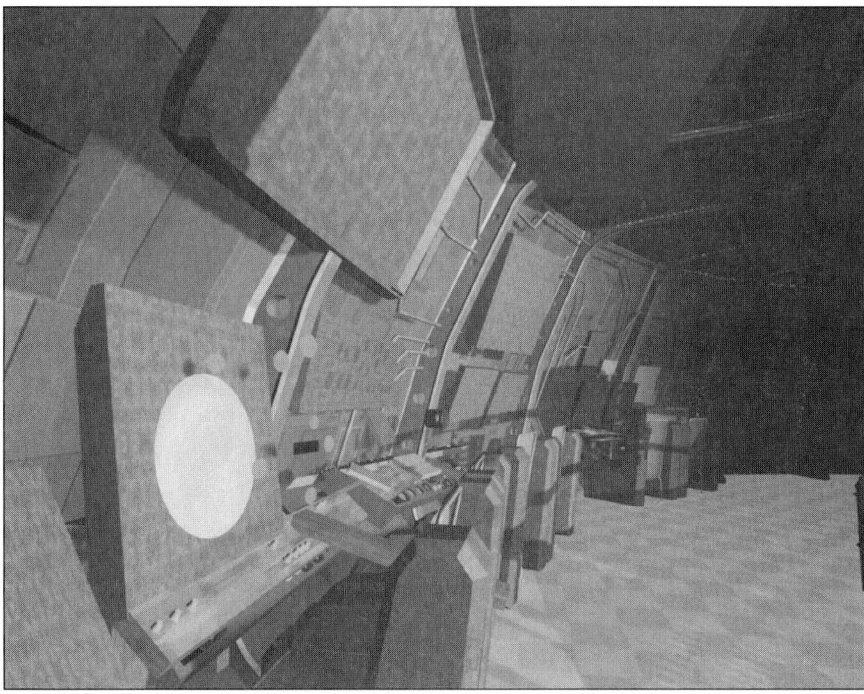

In this chapter, we discuss the standard and Radiosity lighting systems in 3ds max 6. You will explore some of the rendering issues that are important in finishing your animation and visual effects scenes

In 3D computer graphics, lighting is extremely important. You must take care to control the lighting to ensure the visual quality and dramatic impact of your animation, in much the same manner that lighting is used to control the look of a live-action motion picture scene. In this chapter, you will look at rendering features. Render Layers is a feature designed to break images into layers for compositing. It can help you modify the look of your images in high-end packages such as flame and combustion 3. Render to Texture is a very useful feature for burning the lighting in a scene into the texture applied to an object. Examples will demonstrate how the Mental Ray renderer works differently from the Max scanline renderer. You will explore the changes in lighting that must be made when you switch from one to the other. Then you will look at the requirements for using Backburner for network rendering.

Composition, Lighting, and Rendering

The principles of composition of a frame of animation are no different than the principles of composition for a still photograph or a painting, as shown in Figure 14.1. There are a number of problems that you must solve when you place cameras in a scene and prepare for the final rendering. Camera angles and camera movement are often difficult to plan to cover all the aspects of a fast-action or visual effects scene.

In addition to the technical considerations of rendering, there is the issue of render time. Lighting and rendering take up a major portion of your production time in any animated film project. For example, the first *Toy Story* by Pixar took over two years to render using a network of more than 250 Sun computers working every day. Even a small project can take many weeks to light and months to render. The style of lighting you choose directly affects the rendering speed, and the style of rendering you choose determines how quickly you can finish your film. A third factor that affects rendering speed is the number and resolution of the surfaces or mesh objects in your scenes.

3ds max lighting offers a variety of ways to light scenes. We will begin by looking at Radiosity and Global Illumination. Radiosity is best

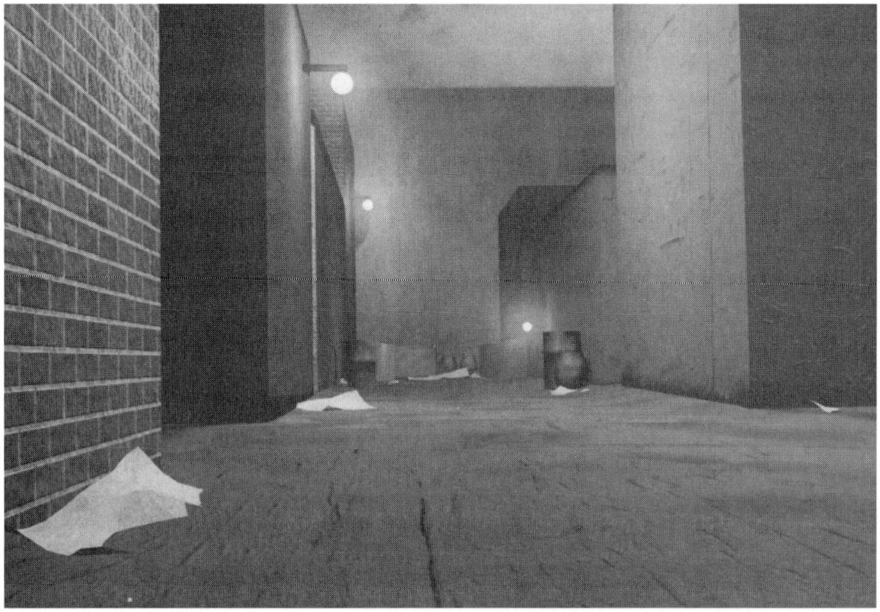

FIGURE 14.1 A scene rendered with multiple lights using global illumination.

used to light interior scenes, whereas Global Illumination is intended to light exterior scenes. Global illumination can be combined with conventional 3ds max lighting in the same scene, and special-purpose lights can be used for visual effects as well as for lighting the environment.

RADIOSITY AND GLOBAL ILLUMINATION

The Advanced Lighting capabilities for 3ds max include two different methods of creating Radiosity lighting: the Light Tracer, and Radiosity. Both of these methods will yield photo-realistic lighting solutions, but Radiosity is the most accurate because it is fully based on light physics. The Light Tracer is designed for quicker animation rendering and does not have the exhaustive accuracy of Radiosity. Radiosity is actually discreet Lightscape, which has been ported into 3ds max and can be used to build and analyze accurately the lighting of architectural or virtual movie set models, and to export Lightscape lights and data to the stand-alone version of Lightscape. A good solution for creating Global Illumination in a 3ds max scene is the Skylight, generally used for exterior scenes along with Light Tracer. The Photometric Light Creation menu gives you a choice of eight different types of lights, including Area, Point, and Linear lights used for Radiosity rendering. You can control light intensity measured in lumens or color temperature in degrees Kelvin, as well as create reflective colored shadows with edge softness.

The way Radiosity works is to first create a virtual mesh over every surface of the scene. Then, the system creates a virtual mesh of its own over those surfaces, as shown in Figure 14.2. It then analyzes the amount of light intensity and reflected light falling on each surface in the scene, and from that data it calculates the lighting solution that will be used for the rendering.

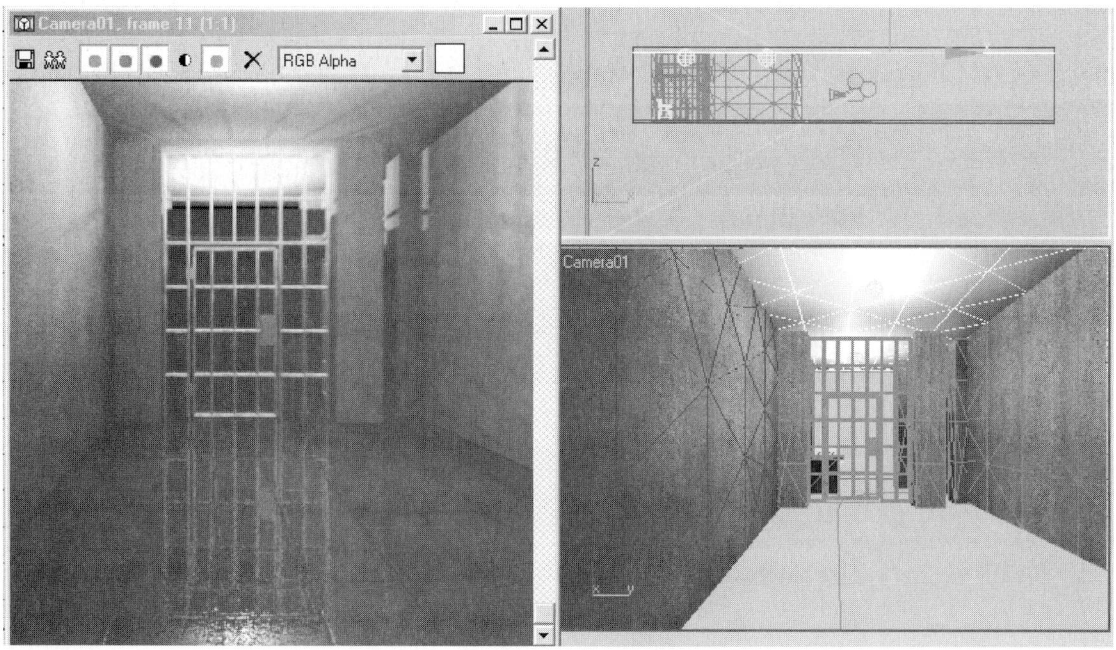

FIGURE 14.2 The re-meshed surfaces used to calculate the Radiosity solution.

Radiosity is quite fast with most scenes, but can be quite demanding if there are a large number of surfaces in a scene. However, even though it could take a long time to calculate and render, the photorealistic results are worth the wait. However, if you are pressed for time in a production situation, it might be better to use the less rigorous Light Tracer system to calculate a lighting solution and render the scene.

While working on both interior and exterior scenes in *Homing Instinct*, it was found that using one skylight, one shadow-casting target spot, and one Omni Light set to a low value to light the scenes, along with Automatic Exposure Control and the Light Tracer, gave a wonderful soft look to exteriors, interiors, and character's skin, and added nice reflected light in shadow areas. This was ultimately the combination that was used for almost all of the rendering throughout the film, as shown in Figure 14.3.

The tutorial that follows explains how to work with a Skylight and the Light Tracer to render a scene.

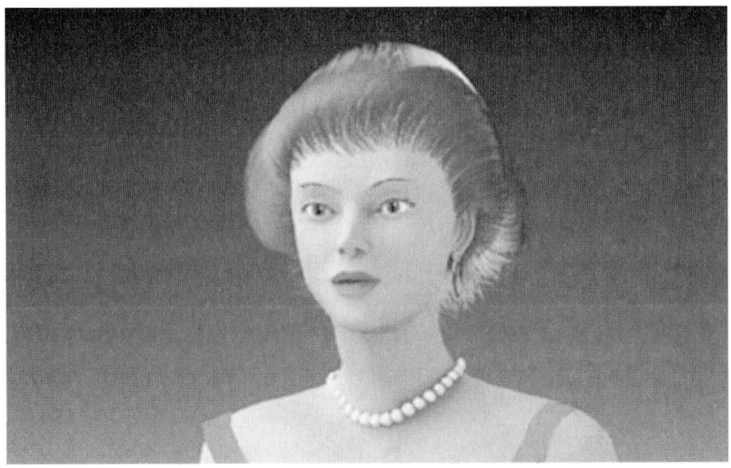

FIGURE 14.3 Rendering Xzulixia with a Skylight and the Light Tracer.

WORKING WITH THE SKYLIGHT AND LIGHT TRACER

The beauty of Global Illumination comes from the way it creates reflected diffused lighting and delicate shades. The shadow areas contain visual information that would not be seen in the dense shadows generated by conventional lighting. To understand how to use the Skylight, you will render a scene containing a military shuttle, as shown in Figure 14.4. When you load the scene, it will contain conventional lighting. Your task is to remove the conventional lighting and replace it with global illumination.

The Skylight can be used by itself as a single diffused light source for exterior lighting situations. In most cases, however, you will want to use one or two additional normal lights set to a low level to add highlights and shadows details to the scene.

The Light Tracer works with the Skylight to generate a realistic lighting solution for the Renderer. The primary effect of the Skylight is to

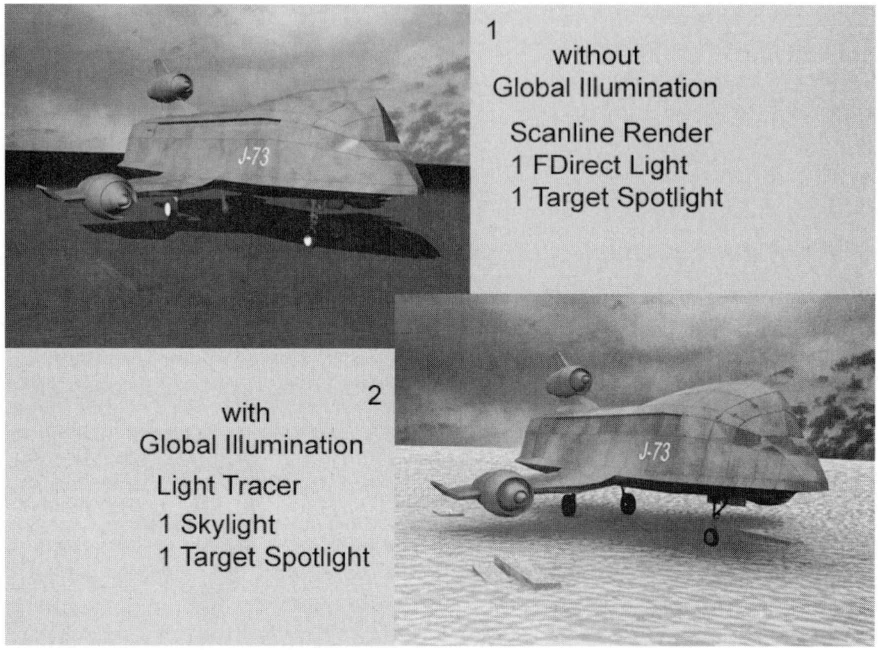

FIGURE 14.4 A normal scene compared to the same scene with Global Illumination.

create soft shadows and to reflect colors between objects and surfaces in the environment. For example, when using this lighting system, a girl in a red dress leaning on a white wall would reflect red light on to the wall from her dress.

In the next tutorial, you will place a Skylight and two auxiliary lights in the scene to render the shuttlecraft to see how Global Illumination increases the realism of the scene.

TUTORIAL 14.1

USING A SKYLIGHT FOR GLOBAL ILLUMINATION

To use the Skylight lighting system:

ON THE CD

1. Load the Shuttle1400.max scene file from the Chap14 folder on the companion CD-ROM. This scene is illuminated with a standard FDirect Spotlight (Free Direct) to simulate sunlight and cast shadows, and a Target Spotlight set to a low intensity to project light form a different angle.

2. Maximize the Camera03 view, press F10 to open Render, set Time Output to Single, and in Render Output, turn off Save. Then, click Render to see what the shuttle landing gear looks like before adding Global Illumination, as shown in Figure 14.5. Notice that there is no reflected light under the shuttle or on the landing gear.

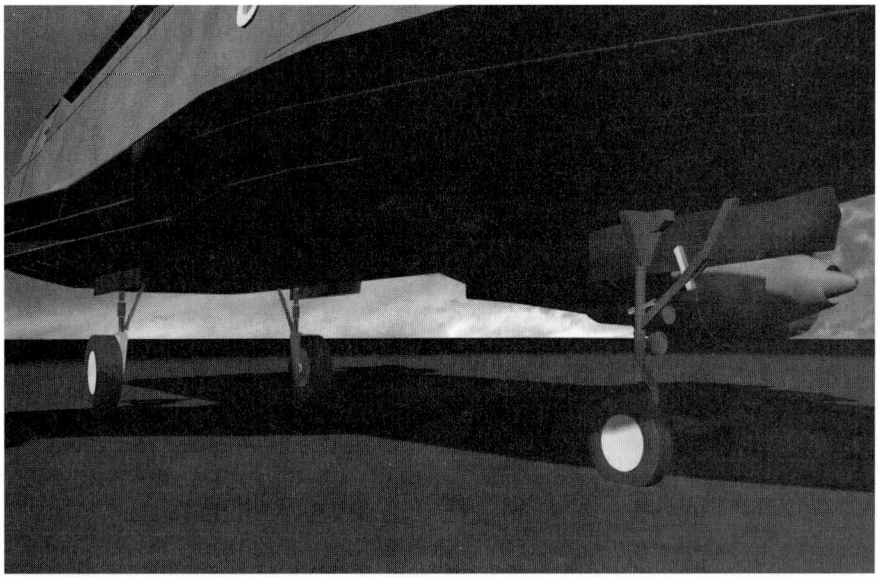

FIGURE 14.5 The shuttle landing gear illuminated without a Skylight or Light Tracer.

3. To add reflected light under the shuttle, create a Skylight. Maximize the front view. You should see two lights there already, an FDirect and a Target Spotlight. Select and delete both lights. Next, create a Skylight. In the Create > Lights Command Panel menu, select Skylight in the Object Type menu. Click in the front view in the sky area above the shuttle model to place the new Skylight, as shown in Figure 14.6, example 1. Then, right-click to turn off Skylight creation.
4. Rotate the hemispherical Skylight icon so the bottom is horizontal, and then click Modify. In the Skylight Parameters, use the default Multiplier value of 1.0. You must turn on the Automatic Exposure Control. In the Main menu bar, click Rendering > Environment. Then, in the Environment dialog, find Exposure Control and click the small arrow that says <no exposure control>. When it opens, select Automatic Exposure Control. The Automatic Exposure Control Parameters menu will open. Use the defaults. If you want the scene darker, Set Brightness to 45.0 and Contrast to 40.0.

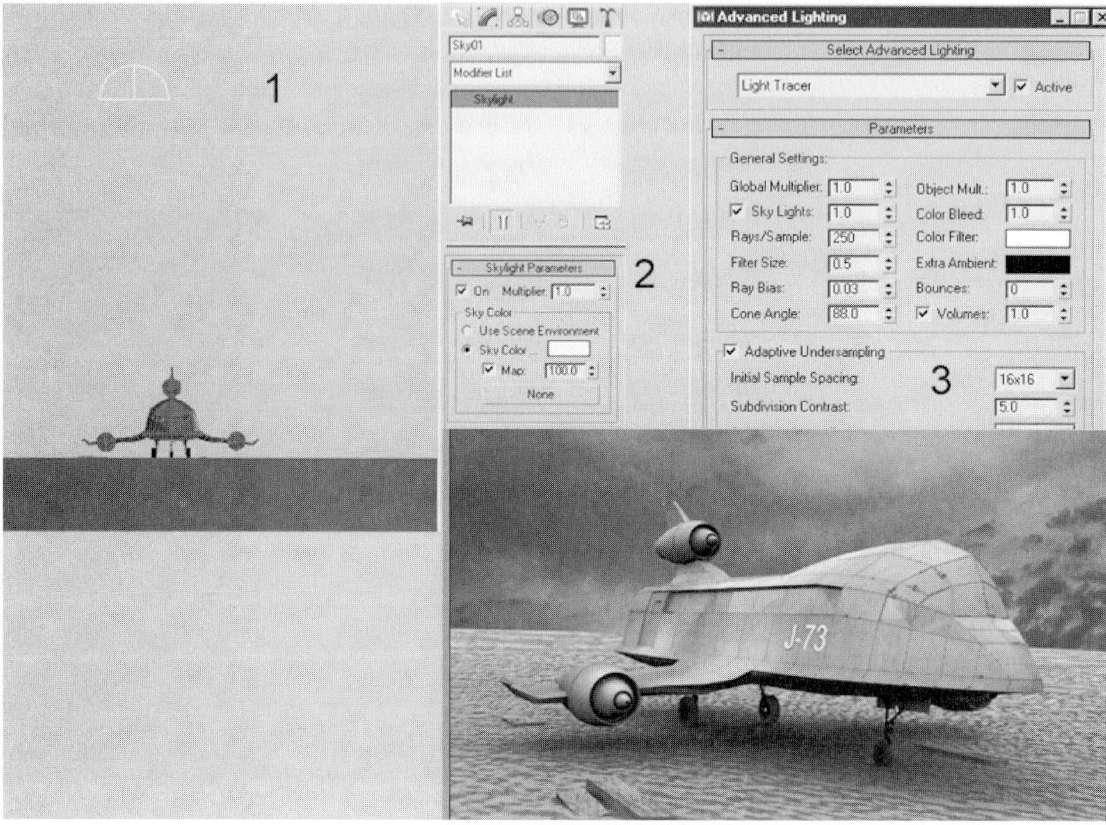

FIGURE 14.6 A Skylight in place of the FDirect light.

5. Click the small Render Preview radio button to see a mini-render view of what the light balance is with those settings. Next, activate the Camera03 viewport and press F9 to render a full-sized image to see what changes there are with the Skylight instead of the FDirect light. You should now see diffused illumination on the landing gear, under the shuttle, and on the ground. Switch to the Camera01 view and render it to see the exterior appearance of the shuttle. Notice that the textures on the shuttle are quite prominent and the ground is dull, as shown in Figure 14.6.
6. To obtain the best lighting effect with Global Illumination, turn on the Light Tracer. Click Rendering > Advanced Lighting, and in the dialog, click the white window and select Light Tracer. The Parameters menu will open. Set the Bounces value to 1 bounce, as shown in Figure 14.6, example 3. This gives you a Radiosity type lighting solution, and ensures that the

shadow areas will not be pure black, but will have some reflected light on them to enhance realism.

7. Render the Camera03 view again. Make sure that Use Advanced Lighting and Computer Advanced Lighting when Required are both turned on in the Render dialog.
8. With the Light Tracer working in combination with Global Illumination, the rendering takes longer. That's because the Light Tracer is calculating a shadow solution that will reflect natural diffused light and the reflected light on all surfaces.
9. Save the scene as Shuttle_Global.max.

The same lights can be used in an entirely different situation and setting to create a good Global Illumination solution to light the interior bridge of the satellite model. Skylight works as well on an interior as it does on an exterior, even though it is primarily intended to be an outdoor light.

In the next tutorial, you will use a Skylight and the Light Tracer to light an interior scene.

LIGHTING AN INTERIOR SPACE

Exterior lighting to simulate outer space is very harsh because objects are normally lit by only one source: the sun. Interior lighting is much softer and diffused with lots of reflected light on nearly every surface. We expect to see small details, familiar surfaces, plastic, and metals, as shown in Figure 14.7.

Reflected light from the colored instrument panel lights would paint the objects with different patterns of light. Shadows from the overhead lights would add shadows and richness to the composition. Lighting should be dramatic. Dramatic lighting generally has large dark areas to contrast with the highlighted center of interest. This draws the attention of the audience to the action.

In the next tutorial, you will explore the Global Illumination and the secondary system of conventional lights that has been set up to light the satellite interior, as shown in Figure 14.7. Your task is to investigate which lights to turn on or off, and at what level to set them at to obtain the best image.

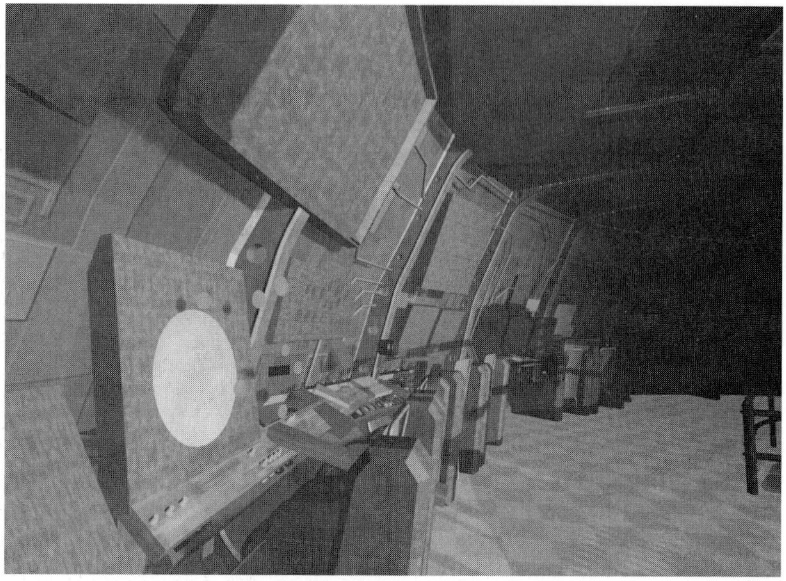

FIGURE 14.7 The satellite bridge without characters, lit by a Skylight and Light Tracer.

TUTORIAL 14.2

Adjust the Lighting of the Satellite Bridge Interior

To adjust the lighting of the interior:

ON THE CD

1. Load the Light_Interior.max scene file from the Chap14 folder on the companion CD-ROM. This is a complex scene that might be slow in loading and refreshing for people whose computers have less than 500MB RAM.
2. The scene is lit with a Skylight and six conventional lights. Select the Camera08 view and render a frame at 640 × 480. You should be able to render if your bitmap path points to C:\3Dstudio5\Maps\. All of the maps used in the scene at this point are standard 3ds max maps. The production design calls for floating-text holo-projections for imaging devices, as shown in Figure 14.8.
3. The crew member in the foreground is working with the floating text. In the script, the character can control the ship by moving the virtual text in 3D space. To simulate that, the character is first animated touching the text, and then the material on the individual text letters is animated to increase the self-illumination value as long as he touches a letter.

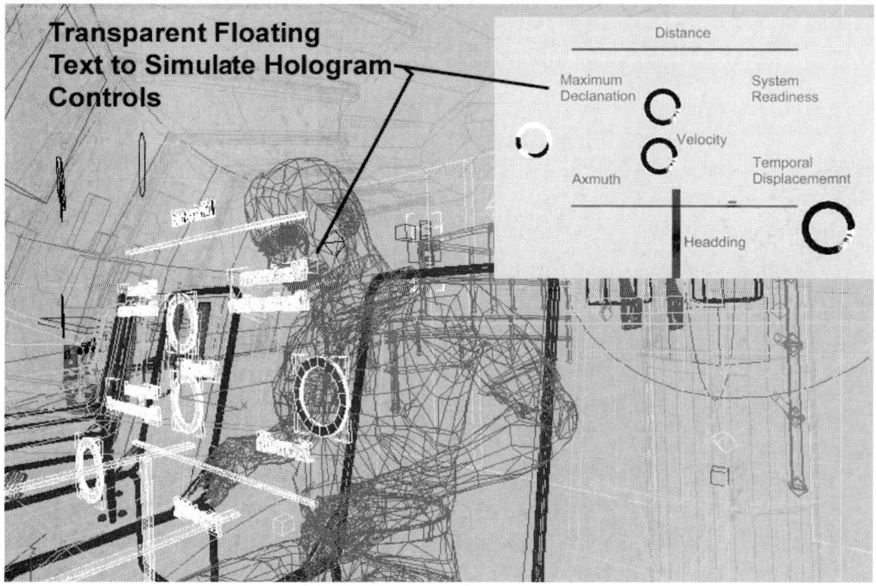

FIGURE 14.8 Adding floating text objects.

4. Open the Light Lister. Click Tools > Light Lister, as shown in Figure 14.9. The Light Lister shows the settings for all lights as well as the Skylight. Notice that about half of the lights are turned off, including the Skylight. Render the Camera08 view and save the image. Then, turn on all of the lights, except the Skylight, and render the Camera08 view again. You will see that the image has actually been flattened and has less depth when more lights are added.
5. Next, turn off Omni Lights 2 through 6. Then, turn on the Skylight. Your list should now look like Figure 14.9. Close the Light Lister. You will need to turn on two more settings to make the Skylight active. First, go to Rendering > Advanced Lighting and click <no lighting plug-in>. From the drop-down menu, select Light Tracer, and then close the window. Next, go to Rendering > Environment, and in the Exposure Control menu, click <no exposure control>. From the menu, select Automatic Exposure Control and close that window.
6. Render the Camera08 view again. Notice that this version is much more dramatic. The Skylight and the Light Tracer have added depth, shading, and reflected light. By turning off the extra Omni Lights you have created

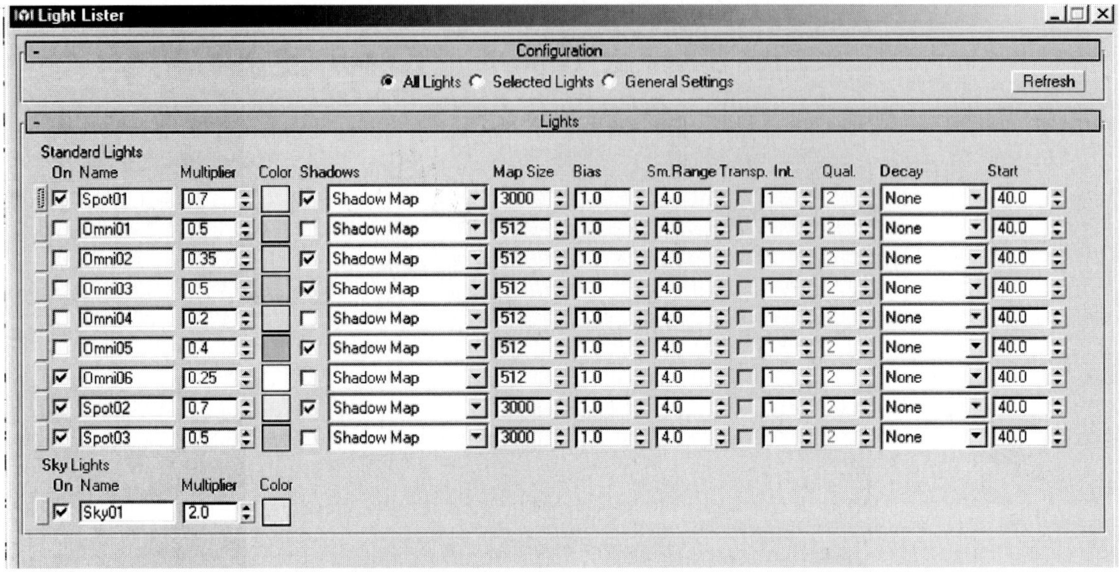

FIGURE 14.9 The Light Lister shows the settings of every light in the scene, including the Skylight.

a dark area behind the crew member, which adds greatly to the contrast and drama of the image, as shown in Figure 14.10.

7. Experiment with the different light values and different camera views available in the scene to see what the best light balance is.
8. In the Advanced Lighting > Light Tracer dialog, locate the Bounces setting and change it to Bounces = 1. You should see an increase in small shadow details and a general improvement of the image. Adding more than two bounces generally does not improve the image.
9. Render a final version in a large size to see how the finished film image would look, as shown in Figure 14.11. To make it more interesting, you can add a Lens Effect Glow to the lettering material, using the Rendering Effects menu. Bright colored reflected light on the crew member's face from the glowing letters can be simulated by placing a small Spotlight of that color pointing at his face. For more realism, you can set keyframes to turn on the light whenever the character touches a letter, making it glow. Exclude this light from all other objects.
10. Save the scene as Light_Interior02.max.

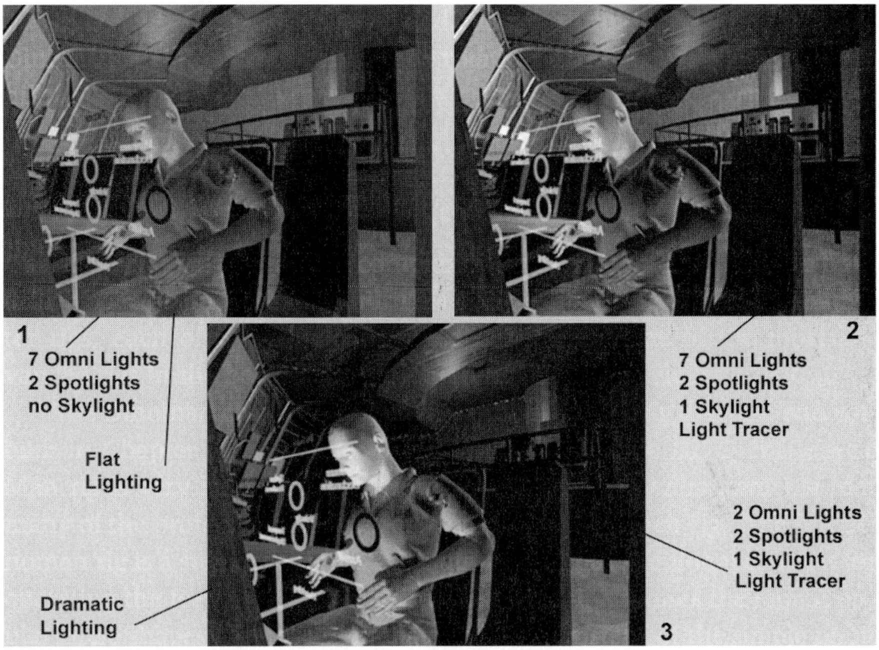

FIGURE 14.10 Effects of turning lights on and off.

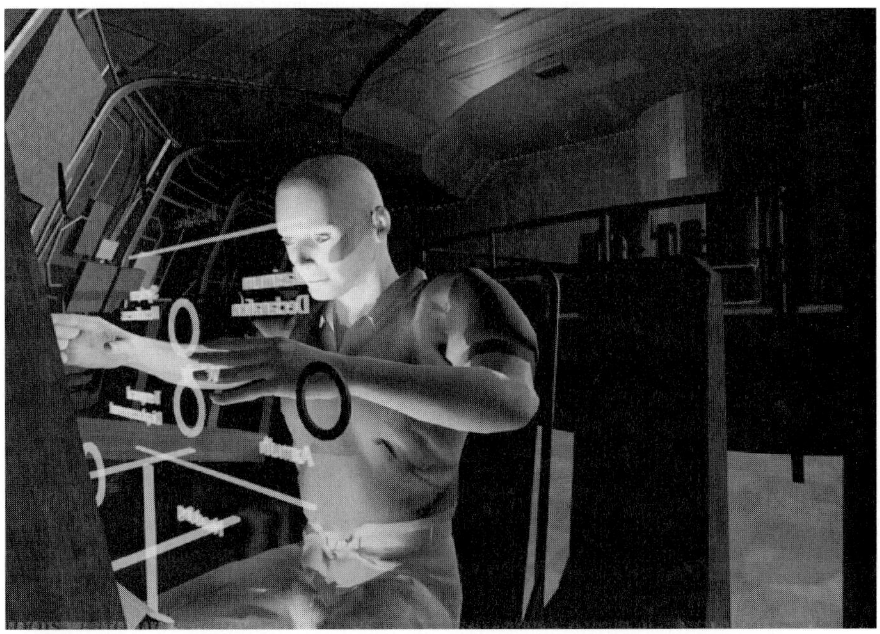

FIGURE 14.11 A Poser 4 Casual Man model is used to pre-visualize the scene with floating text, a Skylight, and Light Tracer.

Advanced Lighting Override Material with Radiosity

Using the advanced lighting Radiosity solution, you can light scenes by creating a special self-illuminated material in 3ds max called the Advanced Lighting Override Material. The ability to emit light from a material opens a whole range of lighting possibilities, such as neon tubes, instrument panels, flat florescent fixtures, translucent wall panels, and flush-mounted lights in settings like spaceships and modernistic buildings, as shown in Figure 14.12.

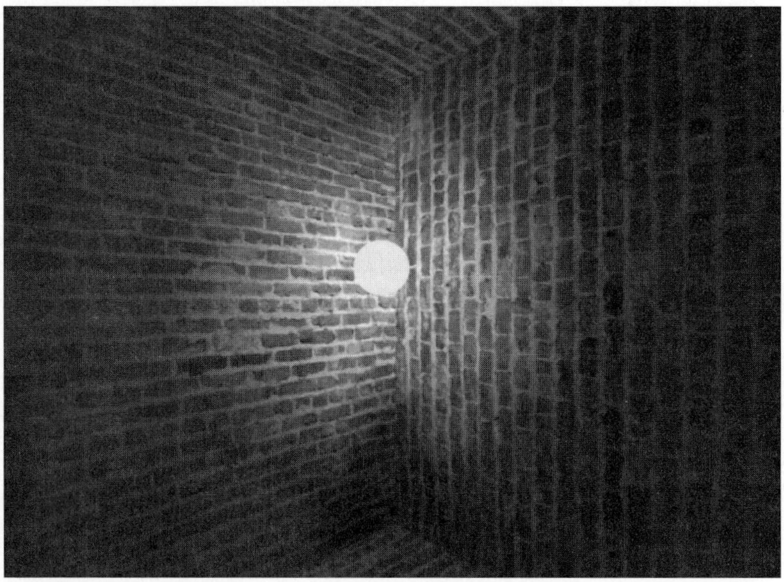

FIGURE 14.12 A room illuminated only by the Advanced Lighting Override Material.

The workflow for creating self-illuminating materials that contribute to the light in a scene is as follows: Create a room from a box primitive and apply mapping and a brick material. Flip the normals so they point in. Place a camera in the room and create a sphere that will become the light source, as shown in Figure 14.13, example 1. In the Materials Editor, click a material sample sphere and then click Get Material.

In the browser, select Advanced Lighting Override and drag it onto the sample sphere. In Material menu click the Base Material button. Set the Diffuse color to orange and set Self-illumination to 100. Click Go to Parent, and set Override Material Physical Properties > Reflectance Scale to 78.0, and set Special Effects > Luminance Scale to 1570.0, as shown in Figure 14.13, example 2. Select the sphere in your room and apply the Advanced Lighting Override Material to it. Open the Rendering > Environment menu and turn on Exposure Control > Linear Exposure Control. Next, open the Rendering > Advanced Lighting menu, and in the Select Advanced Lighting menu, select Radiosity.

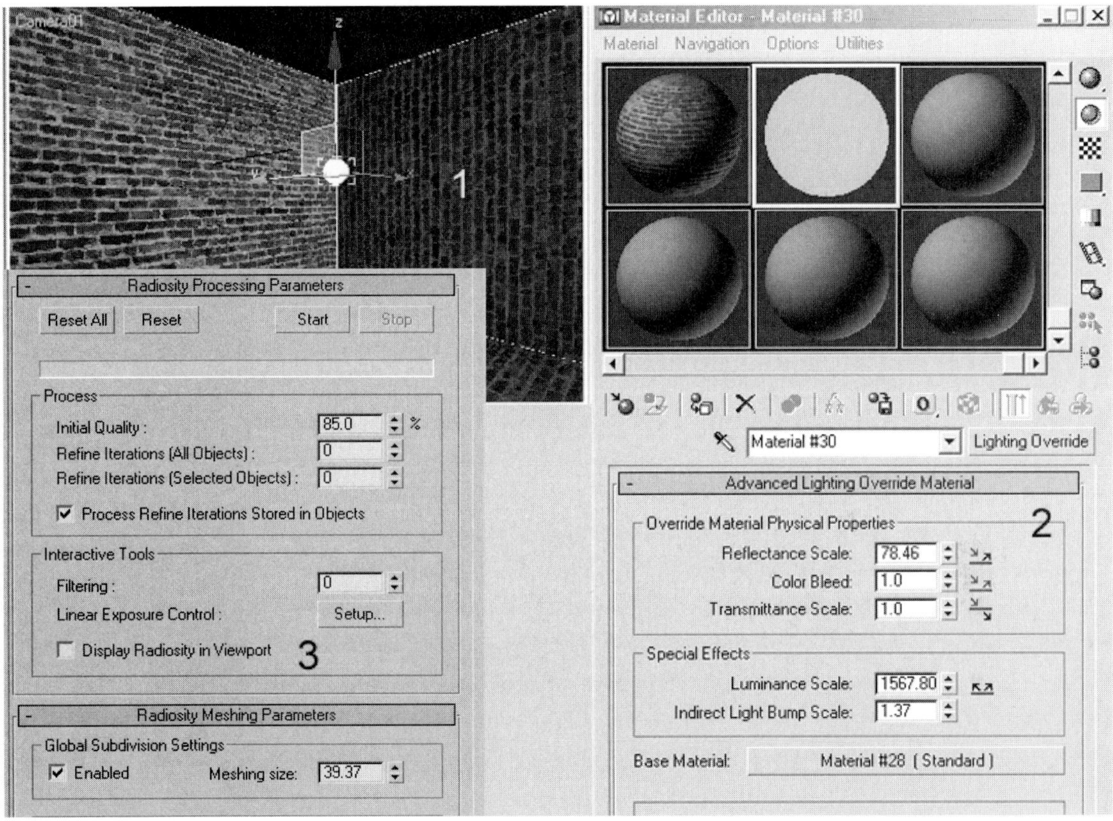

FIGURE 14.13 The Radiosity and Advanced Lighting Override Material menus.

Switch to the camera view, and position the camera to see the sphere at the other end of the room. In the Radiosity Meshing Parameters menu, click Global Subdivision Settings > Enable, as shown in Figure 14.13, example 3. In the Radiosity Processing Parameters menu, click Start. A Radiosity solution will be calculated. Select the Camera window and render the view. If you followed these somewhat complex directions correctly you should see the image, as shown in Figure 14.12.

USING 3DS MAX STANDARD LIGHTS FOR DRAMATIC LIGHTING

Standard lighting in 3ds max works very effectively to light complex scenes in a way that emphasizes certain areas where important events are taking place. For the purpose of this discussion we will call this style of lighting "focused" lighting, which means that the lights are focused only on the center of interest. This approach to lighting is different from a Radiosity lighting solution, which aims to create the illusion of realistic natural lighting. In *Homing Instinct,* as well as most motion pictures, the lighting is designed specifically to control the viewer's perception and draw attention to important actions, clues, or events. This type of lighting adds to the visual impact and drama of the scene; hence, it is often called "dramatic lighting."

In an animated scene you have the ability to animate the position, color, and intensity of the lights and to move them easily to follow a character through a complex environment. Lighting, when combined with well thought-out camera moves and angles, can become as fluid as the movements of the characters. You can also link the lights to the characters so that they never go dark and their facial expressions remain visible even when they enter shaded areas, or creep around during a battle scene. The constantly lit face technique is used in many science fiction movies where the main characters wear space suits with a ring of lights inside the helmet. Of course, this is totally unrealistic, but it is universally accepted as dramatic lighting.

There are many other styles of lighting in constant use in films. Some different lighting techniques you can use include:

- **Back light:** The light is trained on the back of the subject pointing toward the camera, and is used to separate an object or character from the background.
- **Hard light:** The contrast of light and shadow creates a hard edge that is used for dramatic lighting in mystery films, or scenes with intense conflict and fear.
- **High Key lighting:** The entire scene is brightly lit and the character's costumes are bright, similar to television comedy shows, animated cartoons, and nondramatic films such as *Toy Story*.
- **Low Key lighting:** The majority of the scene is barely lit, character costumes are dark colors, and shadows are deep, commonly used for

horror and mystery films, and popular for depicting suspense, war, and fantasy films where heroes fight dragons in their lair, such as *The Lord of the Rings*.

VISUAL EFFECTS LIGHTING

There are many cases where standard lights are used in 3ds max to simulate roving searchlights or the pulsing light thrown by an explosion or flames. These lights are not considered visual effects themselves, but are used to enhance the realism of many types of visual effects. An example of this is the Alien Ship Crash that is presented in the next tutorial. In that scene, an alien ship has been badly damaged and is headed for a crash landing in a coastal swamp area of low hills and islands.

In the next tutorial, you will explore how to add lighting to the visual effects in the Alien Spaceship Crash scene.

LIGHTING THE CRASH OF THE ALIEN SPACESHIP

The opening act of the film starts with a space battle and climaxes with the crash of an alien spaceship on Titan. The ship crashes on a small island in a swamp and comes to rest against a ruined temple hidden under vegetation. The heat of the ship catches the vegetation on fire and creates a cloud of smoke. The back part of the hull is immersed in the water, which throws up steam as it cools. The visual effects for the shot are a combination of 3D and 2D effects. The master shot of the crash uses a wide angle camera looking down over the coastal swamp, as shown in Figure 14.14. Additional cameras have been placed in the scene that you can use to cut to different viewpoints and close-ups during the crash sequence.

In the next tutorial, you will explore how the lighting was set up to enhance the visual effects for the crash scene. It is too time consuming to take you through building the entire scene from scratch, so a completed scene containing the models, the animation, and the lighting of the crash scene has been supplied on the companion CD-ROM.

ON THE CD

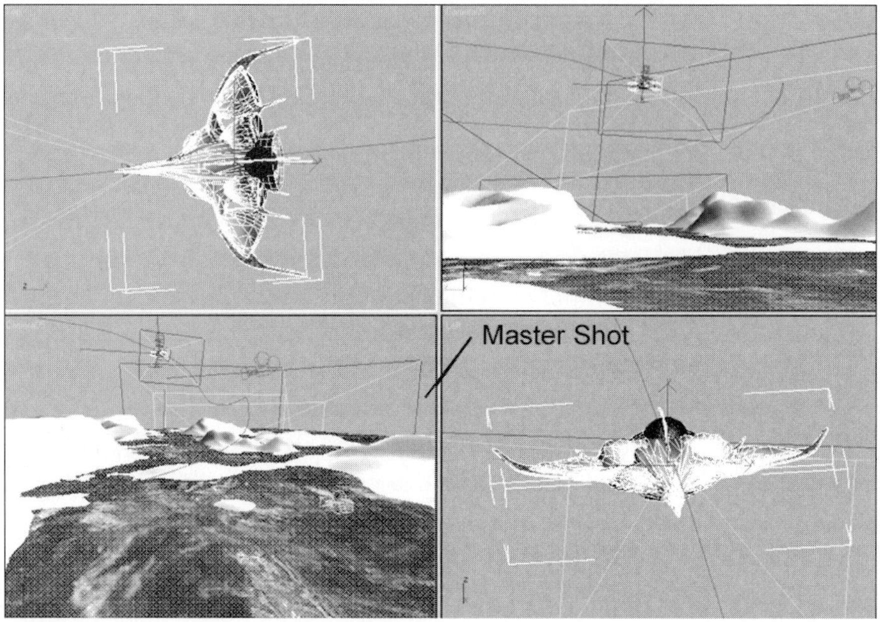

FIGURE 14.14 The master shot of the alien crash site and views of the alien ship.

TUTORIAL 14.3 LIGHTING THE ALIEN SHIP CRASH

ON THE CD

1. Load the AlienShip.max scene file from the Chap14 folder on the companion CD-ROM. Maximize the CamCrashMain view and then press Play to see the flight of the alien ship along the motion path. The alien ship model is linked to a dummy object that is already animated to follow a motion path, as shown in Figure 14.15.
2. The scene is 1,500 frames long, but the ship does not get close enough to see until around frame 900. For that reason, the playback range of the scene has been set from frame 900 to 1,350. The ship impacts the surface of the swamp around frame 1,180, and comes to a stop at frame 1,292.
3. The lights have been hidden. To see the lights, click the Display tab in the Control Panel. Then, in the Hide by Category list, turn off the Lights switch. The lights should now show in the scene. Select the alien ship. Notice that the ship already has lights and Fire Effects applied to it. Switch to the front view, and then Press the H key to see the Select Objects dialog. Click the Invert button on the right, and then click Lights. You will see a list of the six lights in the scene. The Fdirect01 light is the main shadow casting illumi-

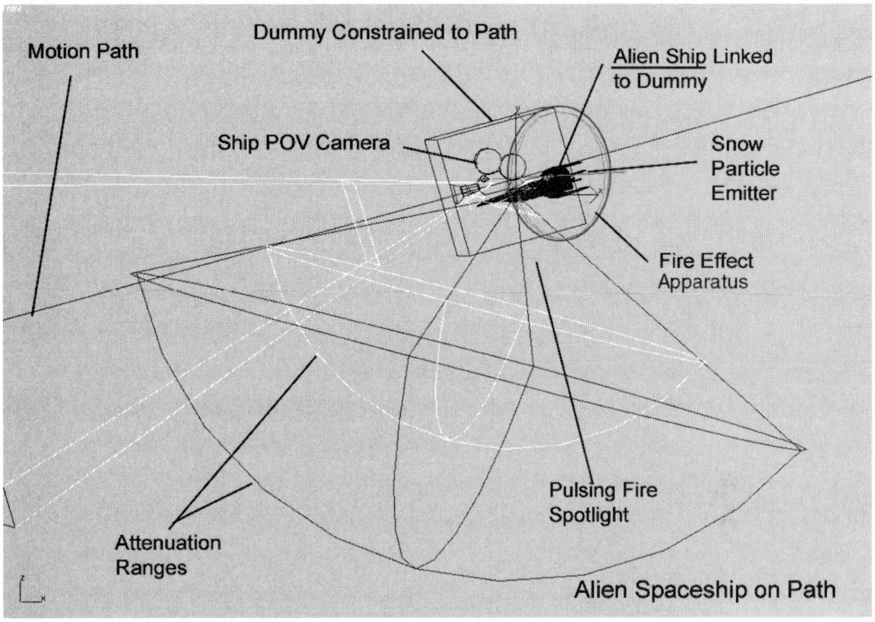

FIGURE 14.15 The alien ship is linked to a dummy with a path constraint.

nation for the entire scene that simulates the sun. Its Hotspot/Beam = 2000 units, and Falloff/Field = 3000 units.

4. There is a brown dummy object surrounding the ship, as shown in Figure 14.15. The ship is linked to this dummy along with its associated lights, which is constrained to the motion path. The ship itself is not constrained directly to the motion path. That is done so that it can be animated separately from the dummy in the vertical axis to shake it whenever onboard explosions occur.
5. Linked to the ship, and pointing down at the ground, is an animated FSpot light. It is designed to throw pulsating orange light on the ground to simulate reflected light from the flames. Select the Fspot01 light and then open the Track view – Curve Editor. In the hierarchy window, scroll down until you see the Multiplier track. Select Multiplier, right-click, and select Properties to see the noise controller that is applied to the light strength, as shown in Figure 14.16. Multiplier Strength should be set to 1.0.
6. Move the Time Slider to frame 1,265 and set the Rendering dialog to render a single image without saving. Turn off different lights to see what effect they have. Notice that there is a light illuminating the bottom of the

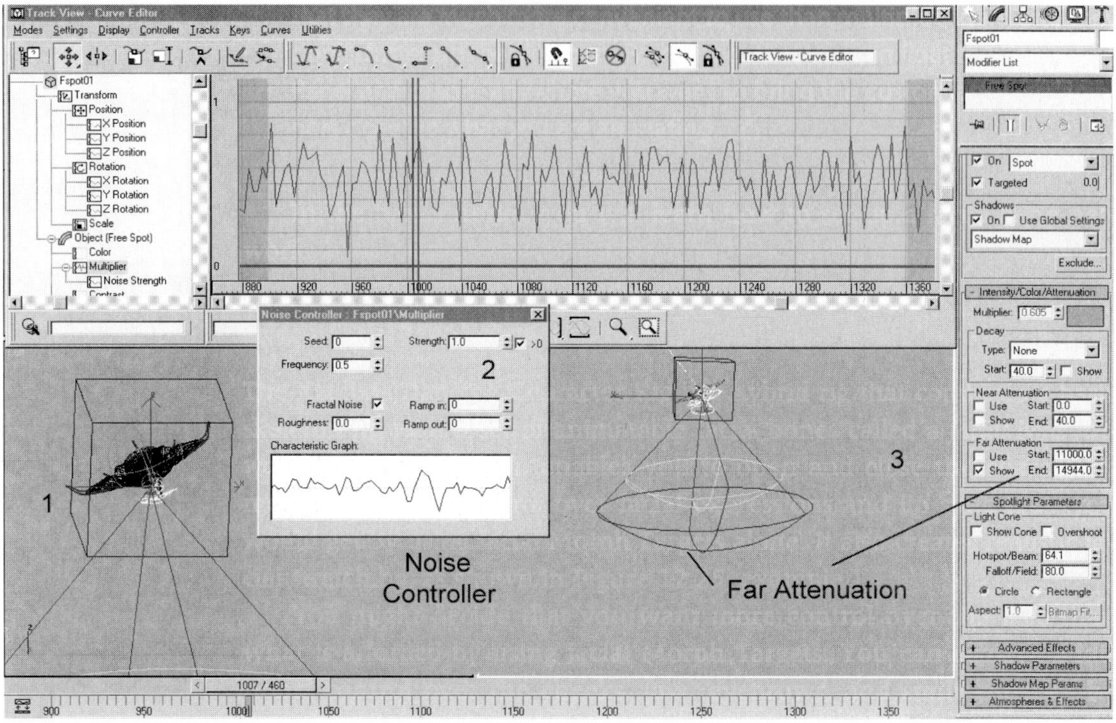

FIGURE 14.16 A noise controller used to pulse the light.

ship to give an orange glow. There is also an Omni Light behind the ship that casts blue light on the hull to improve its appearance. It is always a good idea to include some red and blue light on either side of the main subject to help separate it from the background and to improve the appearance of the surface textures and shadows.

7. The water is a raytrace material. It reflects the light, fire, and atmospheric effects, as well as the ship, as shown in Figure 14.17. The water includes diffuse and bump maps and has 20% transparency. No water splash or spray effects are created in 3D; they will be added later in Chapter 16, "combustion 3, Compositing and 2D Visual Effects," in post production using combustion 3.
8. In the alien ship exhaust port is a Snow particle emitter. Snow is used to create a trail of particles behind the ship. Facing type particles were used with a radial gradient material. This simulates a smoke trail quite nicely except when the ship moves up or down too rapidly. You can see this problem by rendering a 640 × 480 still image of the scene at frame 1260. The

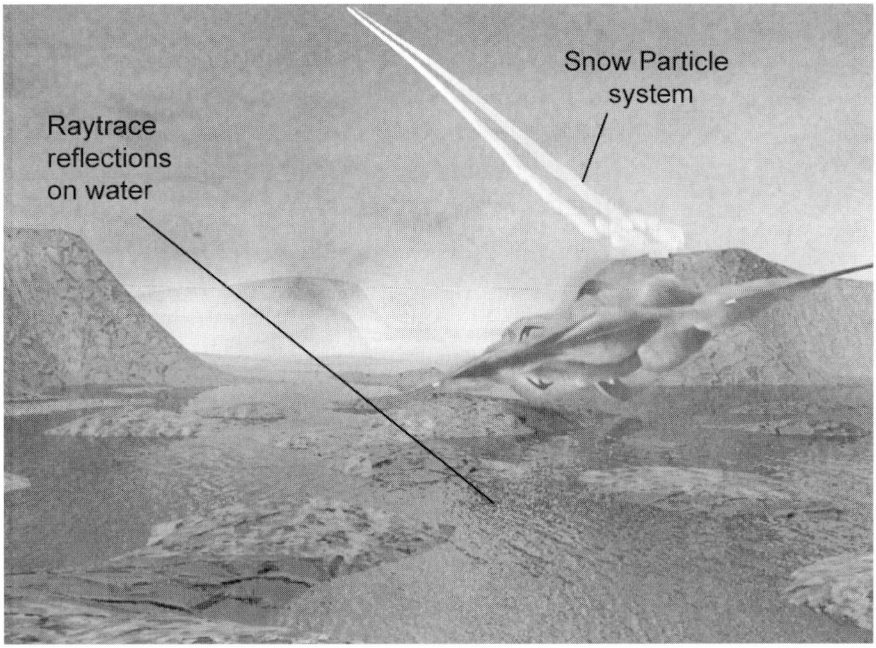

FIGURE 14.17 Basic visual effects for ship crash.

dual smoke trails look fine, but break up when the ship lurches up as it impacts the cliff at the edge of the swamp. For that reason, the 3D trailing smoke effect will be deleted in the next tutorial so it can be re-created as a 2D trailing smoke effect in combustion 3.

9. Since there are no changes, do not save the scene, but go on to the next tutorial where you will render the scene.

In the next tutorial, you will render a group of frames to use in Chapter 16 with combustion 3 to add 2D visual effects to the scene.

Rendering a Scene

Good rendering is one of the areas of 3D animation that can be considered an art, along with creating good materials. 3ds max actually has a number of built-in renderers. The basic render is the Scanline renderer that is used for normal production work. A second renderer is the Raytracer that operates within the Scanline renderer and is applied to specific objects as a raytraced material. Ink and Paint is another rendering system that is used as cell shader material. It simulates 2D cartoon-style rendering of 3D objects and is capable of showing reflections on surfaces, and works with fog. Mental Ray is a high-end renderer that is used by many production companies for motion picture quality output. It can be purchased with 3ds max from discreet. It is capable of very good glass, caustics, vibrant colors, and Global Illumination.

In the following tutorial, you will render multiple layer elements for export and compositing in combustion 3. *Element* is the standard term used for any full or partial image sequence that will become part of a visual effects composite. These elements become layers in the combustion 3D composite. They are rendered in three separate passes in 3ds max. In the background render pass, everything will be visible except the smoke trails from the exhaust and the Tracking Sphere. In the second render pass, only the alien ship will be visible. In the third render pass, everything will be hidden except the Tracking Sphere.

The elements will be rendered at a resolution of 320 × 240 pixels. High resolution is not necessary for learning how the particle effects work in combustion 3. You might prefer to render the images at D1 image resolution, which is 720 × 486 pixels, but this will generate a huge image sequence that will use up a large portion of hard drive space. Rendering at this size will also make it difficult, if not impossible, to load the animation into combustion 3 and play back the entire sequence in real time. The 320 × 240 image sequence can be thought of as a half-sized proxy version of the scene. If you want to render this or any other scene at high resolution, combustion 3 can create its own proxy using its Make Proxy command. The QuickTime movie format is not recommended for rendering elements. Advanced users are aware that you could render these layers as QuickTime+ movies (.mov) with Alpha, but QuickTime movies are not used as visual effects elements in animated film production. They are mainly used for previewing an animation, or for creating animated bitmaps that serve as animated textures. Animated textures are used in *Homing Instinct* to simulate instrument, computer, and video displays in a number of building and vehicle interior scenes.

In the next tutorial, you will render a scene three times to generate three image layers for compositing and 2D visual effects.

TUTORIAL 14.4

RENDER IMAGE LAYERS FOR COMPOSITING AND EFFECTS

ON THE CD

To render image layers:

1. Load the AlienShip.max scene file from the Chap14 folder on the companion CD-ROM, if it is not already loaded. Maximize the CamCrashMain view and then press Play to see the flight of the alien ship along the motion path. The alien ship model is linked to a dummy object that is already animated to follow a motion path, as shown in Figure 14.15.
2. The scene is 1500 frames long, but the ship does not get close enough to see until around frame 900. For that reason, the playback range of the scene has been set from: frame 900 to 1350. The ship impacts the surface of the swamp around frame 1180, and comes to a stop at frame 1292. You will render these 451 frames.
3. Press the H key, and in the Select by Name dialog, find Snow01. Click Select and then delete the snow particle system.

Combustion 3 has a wide variety of excellent particle smoke and explosion effects. When the footage in this tutorial is taken into combustion 3 in Chapter 16, you will need to track the exhaust port of the ship in order to attach a combustion particle emitter to it. Combustion will need a specific point to track. This point is provided in the scene by a small white sphere called a Tracking Sphere, which is positioned inside, and linked to, the ship's exhaust port. A separate element is rendered containing only the sphere moving along the path with an alpha channel. As an aid to visualizing the movements of the sphere, or any object in the scene for that matter, you can turn on Views > Ghosting, and set it to every third frame to view the motion path, as shown in Figure 14.18.

4. Before rendering the image sequences, create an image directory on your hard drive with at least 600MB of available space and name it Crash_Elements.
5. You are now ready to render the background element, which consists of the entire scene and all of the Fire Effects, as shown in Figure 14.19. To render the background element, open the Render menu, select a Frame Range of 900 to 1350, set 320 × 240 as the Output Size, and save the file as Crsh_Bak0900.tif, uncompressed. Render every frame of the background sequence to your Crash_Elements directory. Make sure to delete the Snow01 particle emitter before rendering.

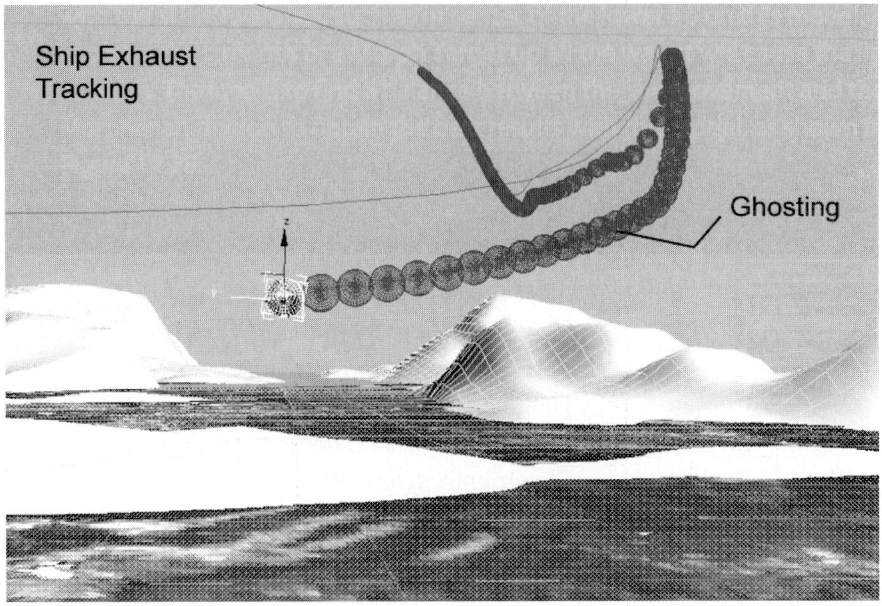

FIGURE 14.18 The Tracking Sphere represents the center of the alien ship's exhaust port.

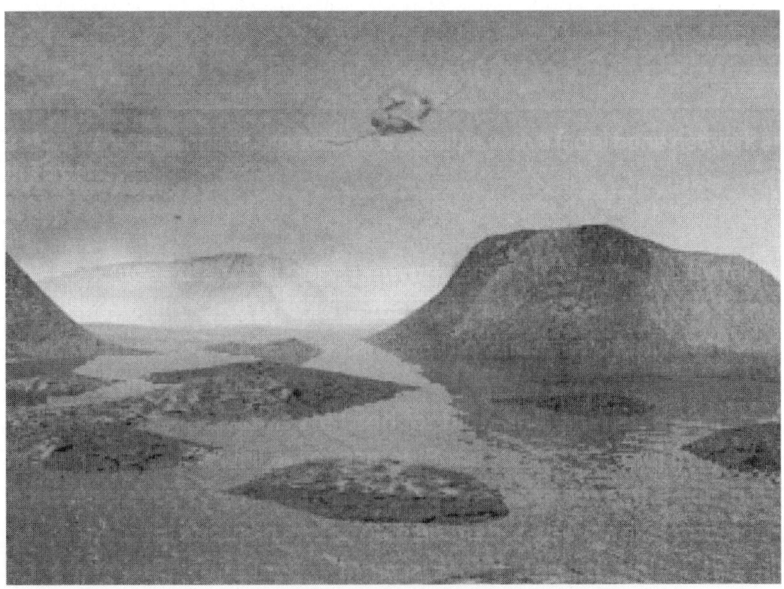

FIGURE 14.19 The rendered background element with water reflections and fog.

With a machine in the 800-MHz to 1-GHz speed range, it should take about three hours to render all 451 frames of the background element because raytracing and atmospheric effects are slow to render.

6. The second element is called Crsh_shp, which indicates that the entire image of the crash is hidden except for the ship itself. It should contain nothing but the alien ship with an empty black alpha channel background. To set up this render pass, hide everything except the alien ship, and then turn off the environment background bitmap display. To do so, click Render > Environment, and then in Common Parameters, turn off Use Map. Set Background Color and Ambient color to Black. This setup will generate the black alpha channel background.
7. To disable all atmospheric effects, go to the Environment > Effects window, select each effect, and turn off the Active switch. The sequence of frames should be named Crsh_Shp0900.tif and it should be rendered from frame 900 to frame 1350 at 320 × 240 resolution, uncompressed. This layer will render quickly with the raytraced water hidden and atmospheric effects turned off.

The purpose of the Ship Only element is to give you a clean ship layer with no visual effects overlapping the ship. This layer can function as a mask to either hide or reveal portions of the background ship.

8. The final effects element you will render is the Tracking Sphere element. It should show only the white sphere that is linked to the center of the alien ship exhaust, and will have an alpha channel background. To set up this shot, hide the alien ship and unhide the Tracking Sphere. Make sure that all atmospheric effects are still disabled.
9. Render the Tracking Sphere element. Name the file Crsh_trak0900.tif. You will compress this layer to save hard drive space. To do that, save the image. The Settings dialog should open. Turn on Compression Type > Packbits. This will reduce the frame size from about 280k to 5k. It should take no more than three minutes to render all 451 frames. You should see only the white sphere crossing the black background.
10. After you have rendered the all three layer elements, save the scene file as Crash_LayersFinal.max.

To view an image sequence, you can load it into the Ram Player. To do so, click Rendering > Ram Player. Then, in the Ram Player window, click either the Channel A or Channel B yellow File Open icon, and browse for the first image of the sequence. In the Ram Player Configuration dialog, turn on the Sequence switch. The file sequence will load. An .ifl (image file list) will be generated. When all 451 images are loaded, click the Play arrow to see the animation.

ON THE CD

These images will be used in Chapter 16. They can be found in the Chap16\Ch14_Render folder on the companion CD-ROM.

RENDER EFFECTS

Render effects play a major role in finishing animations and visual effects shots. There are many rendering effects that you can add to your scenes, ranging from lens effects and glow to motion blur. They can be found in the Rendering Effects menu, as shown in Figure 14.20.

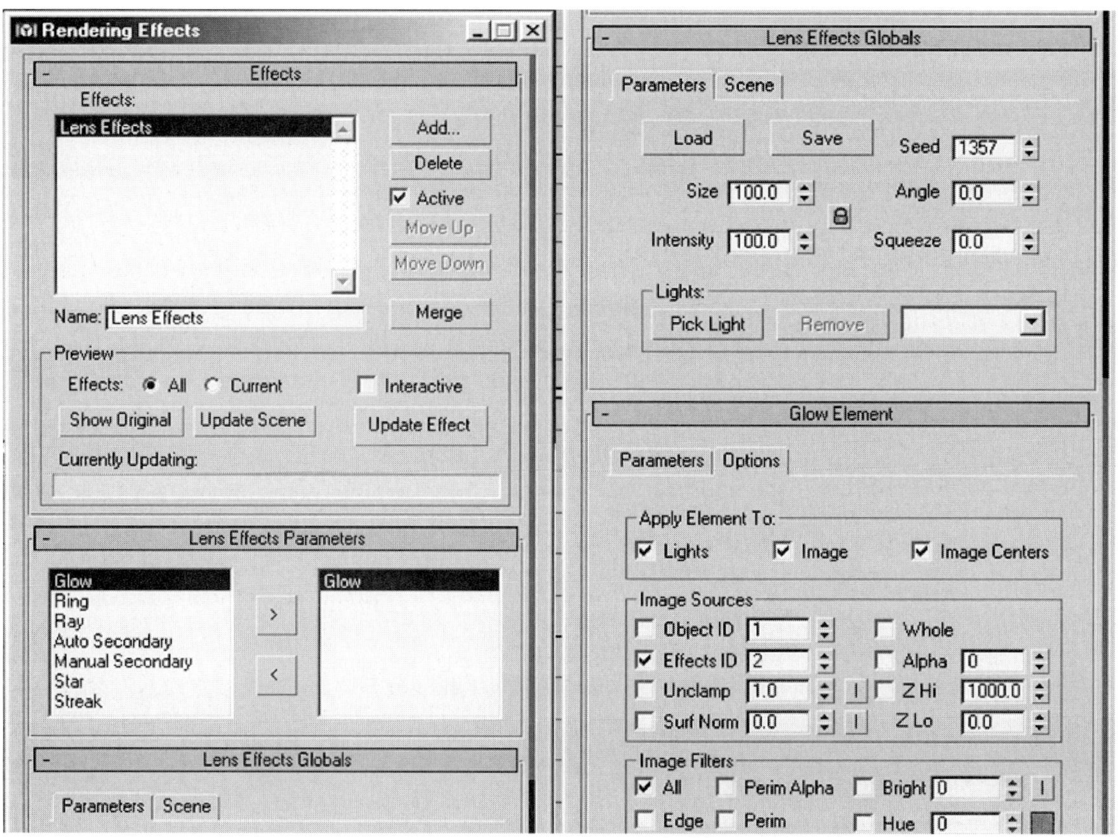

FIGURE 14.20 The Rendering Effects menu showing Lens Effects.

RENDERING IMAGE ELEMENTS

Image elements are an advanced approach to rendering in which each component of an image is rendered as a separate named element file. The Render elements dialog is found in the Render Scene menu. Use the Add button to open the list of elements and add them to the Render Elements queue, as shown in Figure 14.21.

These elements can be used by high-end compositing systems such as discreet flame or combustion 3 to manipulate any of 16 different aspects of an image, such as Specular, Diffuse, Shadow, and Z-Depth. Most of them can be used by Adobe Photoshop; however, it does not recognize Z-Depth elements.

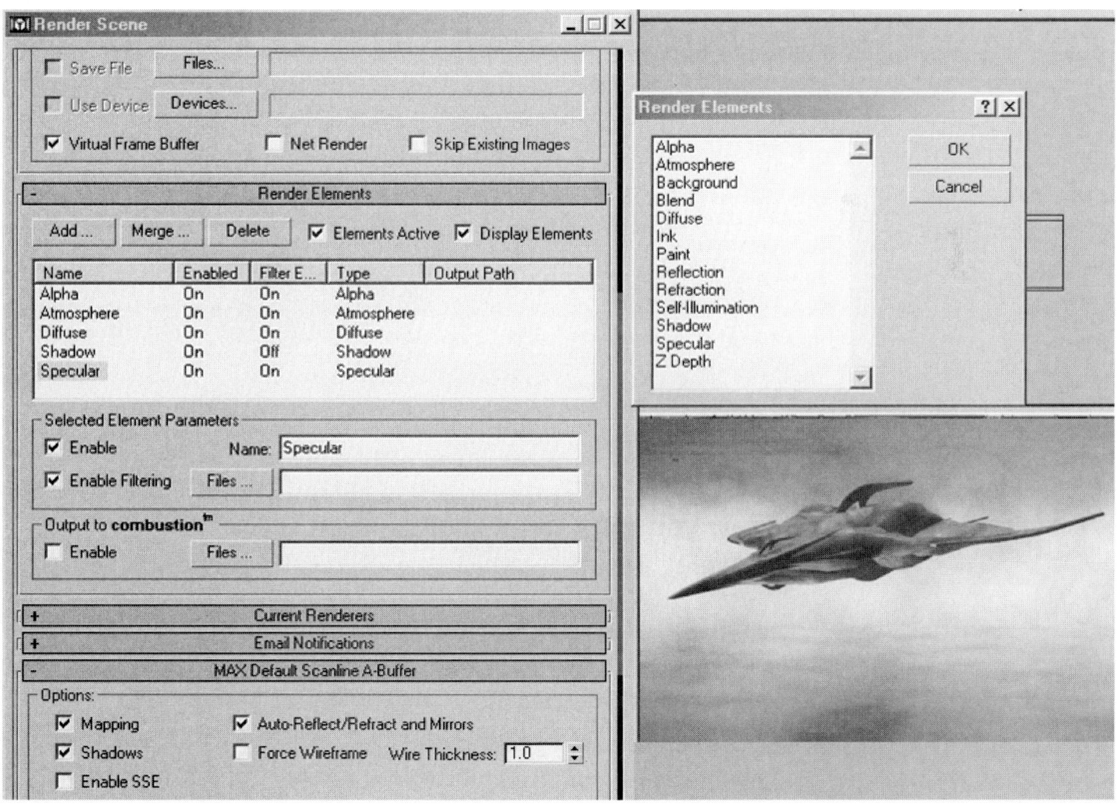

FIGURE 14.21 The Render Elements queue and selection menu.

RENDER TO TEXTURE

Render to Texture is a specialized rendering tool that lets you "bake" the scene lighting into a material. The main benefit of this technique is to eliminate the need for special lighting on a model. This is very valuable for game production, where the materials are not lit in the game engine. It also can be used to good effect by baking the shadows into the material on a character, and then turning on self-illumination. This makes the model "self-lit" and eliminates the need for individual lights to make every character stand out in a complex multiple-character scene.

Rendering to texture can now be done over a network and is useful for lighting interiors of rooms, landscapes, and mechanical structures where the perceived angle of the light does not change very much. Render to Texture is accessed by clicking Rendering > Render to Textures. It actually creates a surface texture map of the selected object by using Automatic Unwrap Mapping. The material texture and lighting are backed into a single map or into a group of map elements. The maps are square and typically range in size from 32 by 32 pixels to 1024 by 1024 pixels. This is the preferred method of texturing game figures and objects in the game environments.

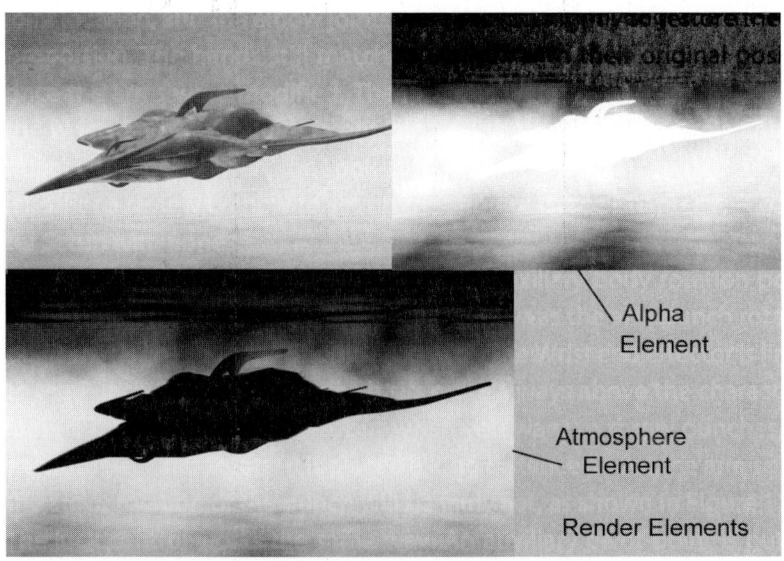

FIGURE 14.22 Some of the render elements generated by 3ds max.

LIGHTING AND RENDERING WITH MENTAL RAY

The Mental Ray production renderer has been incorporated into 3ds max 6, adding high-end motion picture-quality distributed rendering capabilities to the suite of renderers that ship with Max. It can do things that the Max scanline renderer cannot do, such as photo-realistic glass and caustics for water. It uses the "bucket brigade" rendering system whereby small squares of the image are rendered one at a time. This system can spread the rendering process over a number of computer processors and is designed for large rendering jobs using render farms. Mental Ray is used by the top animation studios, including Industrial Light and Magic, Digital Domain, Disney Studios, Sony Pictures Imageworks, and DreamWorks. It is also used by DaimlerChrysler AG, BMW, Honda, and Boeing for their design work.

Mental Ray materials are based on shaders, which are explained in Chapter 13, "Materials and Textures." The 3ds max 6 standard scanline renderer also uses shaders, but the Mental Ray (MR) shaders are quite different, and much more powerful. With Mental Ray, you can combine multiple shaders to achieve far more detailed control over the appearance of the final rendered surface, as shown in Figure 14.23. Up to 10 shaders can be combined at one time to create a material.

Mental Ray 3.2 for Max is designed to use MR shaders as well as most standard 3ds max 6 materials. It does this by translating Max materials into special Mental Ray shaders. MR shaders that were written for the stand-alone version of Mental Ray are not compatible with 3ds max 6; and, conversely, the Mental Ray shaders in 3ds max 6 will not work in the Maya or Softimage versions of Mental Ray. However, you can write your own custom shaders using the shader design facilities in the Max version of Mental Ray. Additional shaders are also available from third-party vendors, such as Lume, which wrote about half the MR shaders you will find in 3ds max 6. One of the unfortunate omissions in the Max collection of shaders is the MR Hair shader that is used in Softimage MR to create very good hair for motion pictures.

Using Existing Scenes with Mental Ray

Once you have activated Mental Ray, you can continue working on most of your files that originally have Max materials applied to objects. The exception is any file that uses Radiosity, the light tracer, or photometric

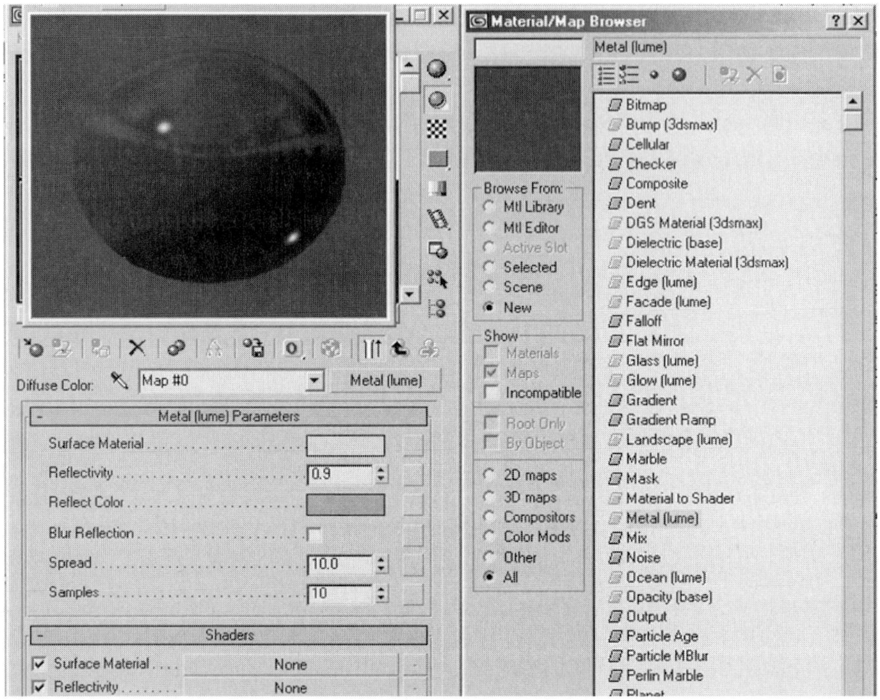

FIGURE 14.23 The Mental Ray Metal (lume) shader includes its own ray-traced reflections.

lights. These scenes cannot be rendered by Mental Ray. To render those scenes, you will have to delete all of the Radiosity lighting and material setup, turn off advanced lighting, and delete the Radiosity solution. Then you can re-assemble the scene using Mental Ray shaders, Mental Ray area lights, and Mental Ray's Indirect Illumination. The one light that will work correctly with Mental Ray is the Skylight. In fact, you *must* use this light is you want to use HDRI maps to light your scene. This is the only way Mental Ray can use HDRI maps.

Using HDRI Lighting Maps with Mental Ray

High Dynamic Range Image maps, commonly called HDR maps, are the newest method for simulating realistic lighting in 3D computer graphics. This process was pioneered by Lucas Film on the film *Star Wars, Attack of the Clones*. The process starts with taking a spherical photograph of the set or location that you want to use as a lighting source. You light the live action scene on a set, and then during the shoot you take a series of HDR images of the chrome sphere that capture the environment of the stage. Then, when you are ready to create the digital scenes and characters to match the live action scenes, you use the HDR images as lighting and reflection maps to supply the correct highlights and contrast ratios of the light in the environment, as shown in Figure 14.24. This map is used as the spherical environment map in the computer. This is infinitely more accurate than trying to manually create lighting to match the set. The resultant highlights on a digital object look very realistic and the colors are well saturated. This is a great help in getting a digital model to blend seamlessly into a scene.

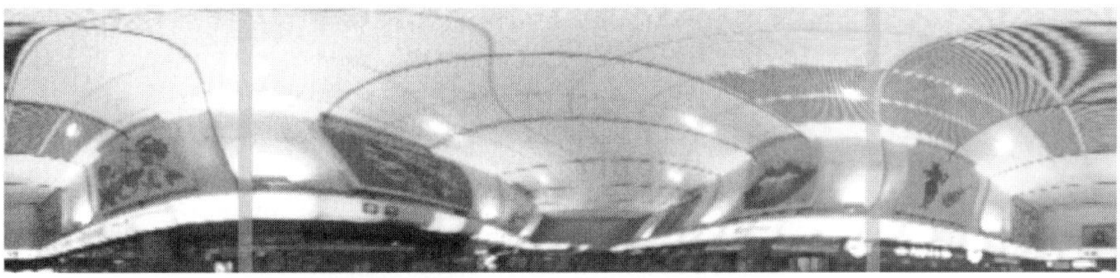

FIGURE 14.24 An HDRI map used with Mental Ray Indirect Illumination and a Skylight.

Mental Ray and other advanced renderers, such as Brazil® and Final Render®, can take advantage of this lighting scheme, and it has become the standard in high-end rendering. 3ds max 6 can now load most HDR images, including the HDRI ESX image files licensed from Lucas Film. Note that the ILM visual effects division uses Mental Ray for some of its rendering in addition to Renderman. An example of the use of Mental Ray is the film *The Hulk*. The ability to use this image format gives Max users access to the same high-end lighting tools as those used by ILM.

There are some rules that must be considered when using HDR maps and the Max Skylight with Mental Ray. First, when using a Skylight with Mental Ray, the scene will render incorrectly unless you turn on Final Gather in the Indirect Illumination roll-out menu, as shown in Figure 14.25. This will increase the rendering time substantially, but the results should be worth it. Second, you must put the HDR map into the map slot of the Skylight and turn on Use Scene Environment.

In most cases, no other lights will be needed except for one or two small detail lights. If you want to add lights to an Indirect Illumination scene, they must be MR area lights. You have two types to choose from:

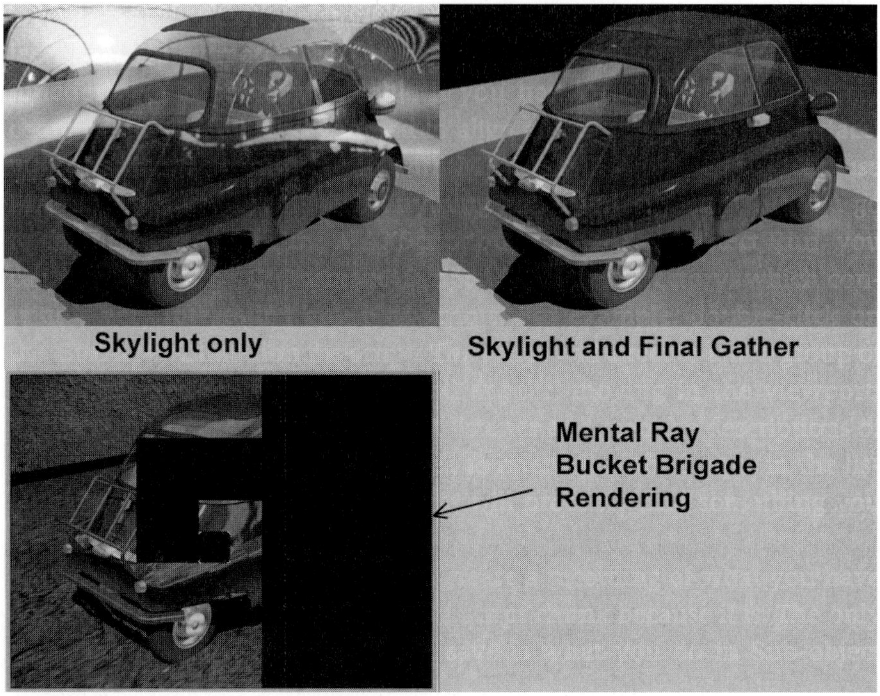

FIGURE 14.25 Rendering with Mental Ray, and a Skylight showing the effect of Final Gather on the right.

the MR Area Omni and the MR Area Spotlight. By default, they both use ray-traced shadows. The Skylight generates soft shadows, so you might want to use area shadow mapping with the area lights if you want to have sharper-edged shadows. Third, when using Mental Ray shaders, you must always put a shader in the surface slot of the Mental Ray Material or you will see nothing in the renderer. The fourth rule is: never try to use the standard 3ds max 6 Displacement Map channel with Mental Ray. You might crash Max. Always use the Mental Ray displacement map when doing a Mental Ray render.

CASE HISTORY OF A MENTAL RAY IMAGE

The Ferrari model that was used by the author to test Mental Ray rendering in 3ds max 6 is a model from Rem Infographica. Many of these models were free on the Word Creating Toolkit disks that were included with early versions of 3ds max. All of these models are excellent and will work well with Mental Ray. To see how the scene was constructed, load the Ferrari.max file from the Chap14 folder on the companion CD-ROM.

ON THE CD

The rendering was set up as follows. First, the model was positioned in the camera view and a Skylight was placed over the model, as shown in Figure 14.26.

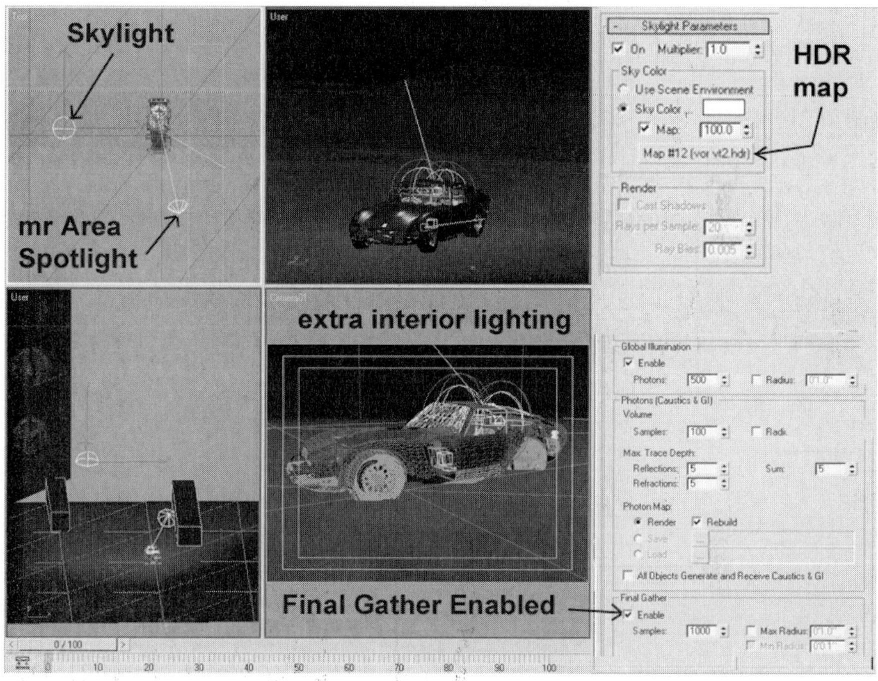

FIGURE 14.26 The setup for rendering the Ferrari in Mental Ray with HDRI lighting.

An HDRI map was put into the map channel of the Skylight and Use Environment Map was turned on. Then, a Mental Ray Metal (lume) shader was applied to the body panels of the car. Next, a black backdrop made of a box primitive was placed behind the car to hide the HDRI map image in the environment background. A number of test renderings were done and it was determined that the interior of the car needed additional illumination. Two MR Area Onmi Lights were placed in the car's interior. After more renders, a MR Area Spotlight was added to create more prominent shadows and increase the intensity of the highlights on the spoke wheels. More renderings showed that the fender line highlight was not as prominent as it should be, so two long, black boxes were placed above the car so that they would be reflected in the body panels. The final results are shown in Figure 14.27.

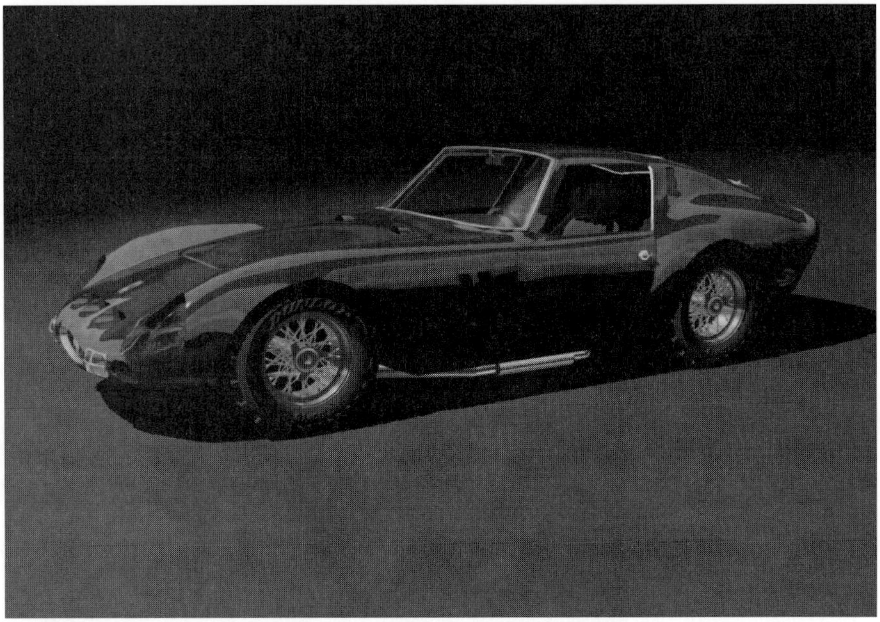

FIGURE 14.27 The final rendering of the Ferrari using a Skylight and an HDRI map.

The final image took 1 hour and 30 minutes to render at 800 by 600. Because photo-realistic image quality was not important to the author, and quick render times were very important, Mental Ray was not used in the production of the semi-realistic animated film *Homing Instinct*.

Rendering Glass and Liquids

Mental Ray is well known for rendering great glass and water caustics. It has the ability to render caustics that simulate the real behavior of light when it is transmitted through, or reflected from, glass, water, or other refractive materials. The 3ds max 6 Tutorial Help files cover this subject very well.

When rendering a sequence of images for an animation using indirect illumination, Mental Ray first calculates the photon emissions. Then it computes the final gather of the light ray points on the objects. This is done before it starts to render any images. Render times in the hours-per-frame range are not unusual for photo-realistic images of scenes with multiple reflections. For that reason, Mental Ray was not used on the film *Homing Instinct,* for which the production design stresses fast action and visual effects, not elegant realism. Mental Ray 3.2 for 3ds max 6 represents a great expansion in the ability of animators to generate great photo-realistic imagery.

USING BACKBURNER 2 FOR NETWORK RENDERING

Backburner is the built-in network rendering manager that works exclusively with the 3ds max 6 scanline renderer to let you use a large number of computers to render projects across a computer network. It includes a Rendering Server Manager and a Rendering Queue, in which all the jobs currently running are listed. You can set priorities on rendering jobs, and edit job settings. It functions equally well with 3ds max 6 and combustion 3. One of the new features for 3ds max 6 is the capability to Render to Texture over a network. Another feature is the capability to control network rendering with a MAXScript. The 3ds max 6 scanline renderer can render over a network containing up to 9,999 computers at no additional cost. The Mental Ray renderer comes with one local rendering license and does not work with Backburner. Mental Ray does not support network rendering unless you purchase additional render node licenses from Discreet. Network rendering only works with Windows 2000 or Windows XP Pro. It will open in other Windows versions, but it will not function.

To use Backburner 2, you must have Backburner 2 installed in the Backburner directory of the machine for which you have a 3ds max 6 commercial license. The 3ds max 6 installer will do this for you. This is the machine from which you will launch the network render sessions. On every machine that you want to use for rendering only, such as all the machines of a render farm, you must install the 3ds max 6 core. These machines do not need to be licensed. You do this by using the minimum install option in your 3ds max 6 disk installer. You must have a functional network connection to each machine on which you have set up a TCP\IP address protocol with distinct addresses.

Once everything is installed, and you are ready to render a job across the network, go to the Render dialog and turn on Net Render. That will bring up a Backburner dialog that will let you submit jobs and check to see which machines are connected to the network and which ones are ready to render. There is a stand-alone Queue Monitor called Manager.exe that you can run outside of Max to check the progress of your network render locally on machines in the render farm. If you have only one machine, you can use Backburner as a Batch Render service to load up a series of rendering jobs that will run overnight without supervision. Please see the Max Reference Help for information on how to set this up. The details of these procedures can be found in a series of documents in the 3ds max 6 Reference help file in the section entitled "Introduction to Network Rendering."

Command-Line Rendering

A command-line rendering system has been implemented for 3ds max 6. It allows rendering with Max on machines without actually starting 3ds max 6. This is a render-only implementation for a large render farm, and Max software cannot actually be started or used on these machines. The 3ds max 6 core must be installed on a machine for this to work.

This service can be accessed by opening an MS-DOS command window and entering the following command line:

```
C:\3dsmax6\3dsmaxcmd –7
```

This is a professional rendering service for local and network rendering, and it can overwrite files without telling you, so do not use it unless you have read the help files.

Brazil, Final Render, and V-Ray

Brazil is an excellent global illumination third-party rendering plug-in for 3ds max 6. It is has been gaining worldwide recognition and is currently in use at Industrial Light and Magic for rendering their digital mat paintings. This represents a breakthrough for 3ds max because ILM does not normally use 3ds max 6 except in their games division for creating backgrounds. Maya and Softimage are their normal softwares of choice, and Renderman from Pixar is their renderer of choice. This speaks well for the quality of Brazil from *www.splutterfish.com*. Brazil uses HDRI lighting maps and has a very advanced global illumination system.

Two other global illumination renderers of note are the Final Render plug-in from *www.cebas.com*, and V-Ray from the Chaos Group at *www.vrayrender.com*. Both of these renderers offer better quality than the standard 3ds max 6 global illumination scanline renderer. They also can handle larger scenes more efficiently than the standard Max renderer. There are more third-party renderers, such as Illustrate. Obviously, these third-party developers are convinced of the high quality that can be obtained by using 3ds max 6 as the platform for their products.

CONCLUSION

In this chapter, you explored scene lighting. You worked with Global Illumination, the Light Tracer, and standard lighting. You looked at Render Elements, and you rendered image layers for compositing. Then you explored the functionality of the new Mental Ray renderer. In the next chapter, you will be introduced to character studio 4 and learn to use some of its extensive character animation features.

CHAPTER

15

character studio 4

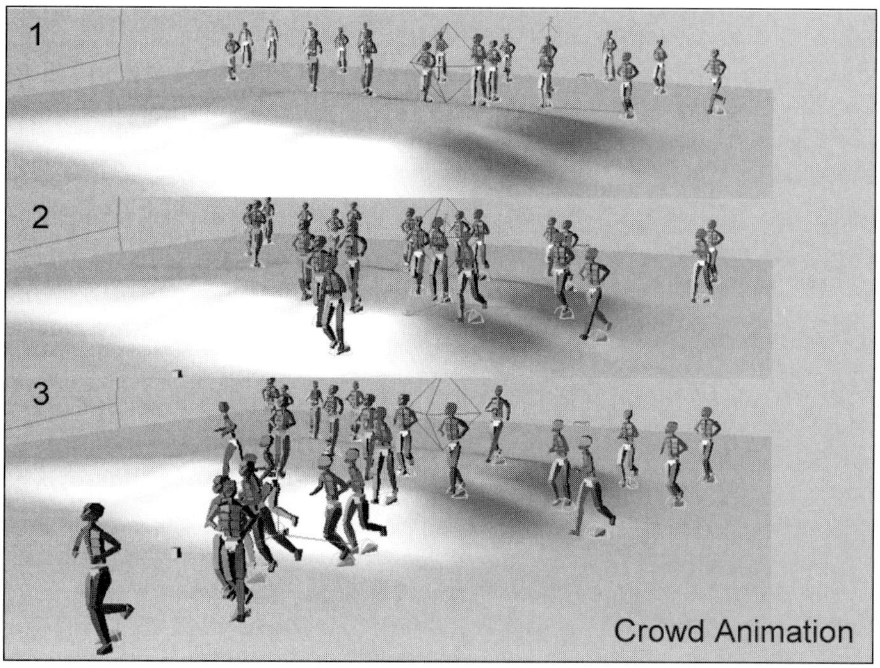

Character studio 4 is a sophisticated character animation plug-in program for 3ds max 6 from discreet. It adds a wide array of professional animation capabilities that go beyond the built-in Inverse Kinematics (IK) animation system that is part of 3ds max. The power of character studio 4 lies in its ability to take Motion Capture files and modify and mix them to suit your needs. When this capability is combined with the nonlinear character animation Motion Mixer, you have an extremely flexible system that can combine numerous different biped motion and Motion Capture files together at variable strengths just as you would mix different tracks of music, each with its own volume level.

At the most basic level, character studio 4 is a footstep-driven animation system. This means that you can paste a series of footstep icons on a ground plane in 3ds max, and then let the system calculate the animation of a biped skeleton so that it follows those footsteps over time. However, a walk generated this way is a rudimentary human walk cycle that has minimal upper body movement. This is because the Create Footstep Generator is only meant to be a basis upon which to build a specific walk motion using the Layer animation tool. It gives you a foundation on which to tailor your own motion to fit your needs. To better understand the capabilities of character studio 4, this chapter presents a crowd tutorial that explains how to create a charging army of Dinomen warriors using crowd animation techniques.

There are many specialized features and interfaces in character studio 4. The Animation Workbench is a Motion Curve Editor dedicated specifically to working with motion files and the biped. The Motion Mixer lets you load a number of different motions into a biped character and then use the Motion Mixer to blend and combine parts of different .bip motion files together to create new motions, as shown in Figure 15.1. For example, you can mix several different upper and lower body movements at the same time on the same biped, cross-fade between multiple motions, and move motions in time. You can vary the speed of a motion over time, and keep the feet planted on the ground during the transitions.

Motion Capture is used extensively in the games industry, and is becoming the most widely accepted method for animating characters in motion pictures. An example of this would be the "Gollum" character in the film *The Lord of the Rings, the Two Towers*. For a small studio, Motion Capture can save money and time, which is a great help when a deadline

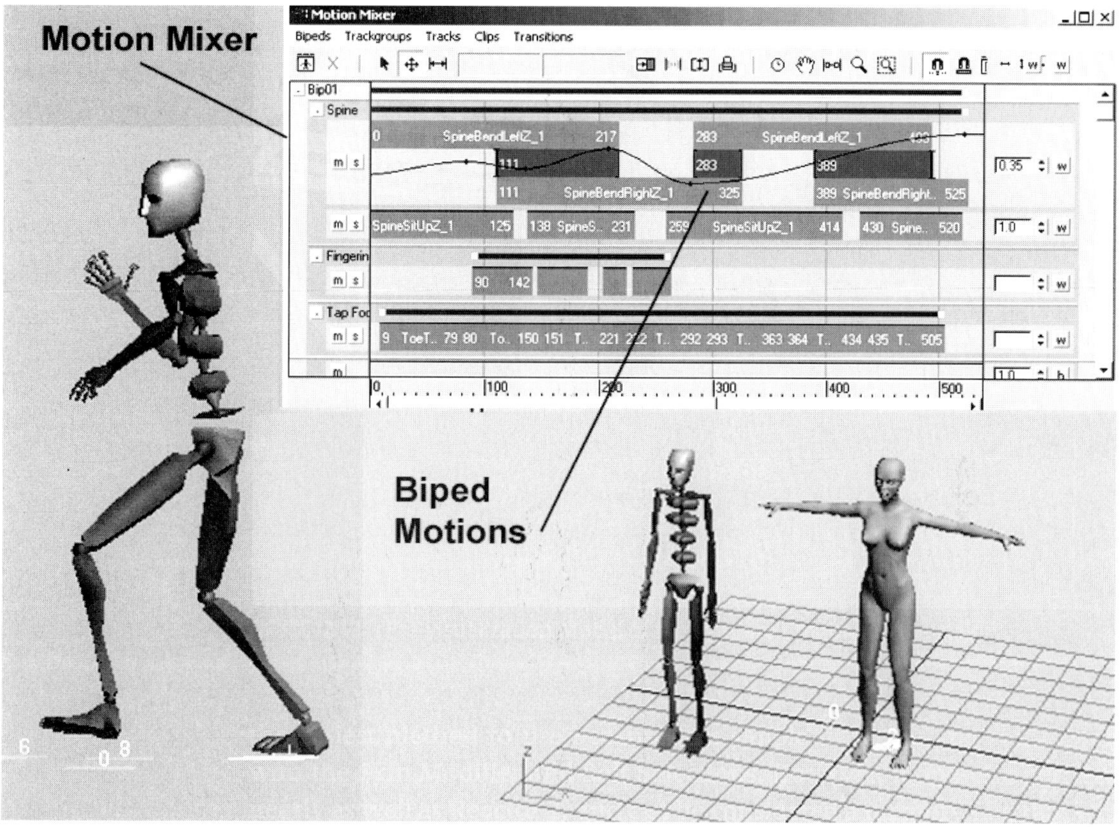

FIGURE 15.1 The new character studio 4 biped skeleton and the Motion Mixer.

is looming and you need to turn out a large volume of animation in a short time.

The 3ds max export to the .fbx (Filmbox) file format enables you to convert any biped motion to a bones animation. The procedure is to export the .max scene file as an .fbx file, and then import it back into 3ds max. This automatically creates one 3ds max bone for every biped bone and preserves the animation keys. In this way, you can use Motion Capture to animate a model with a 3ds max Bones skeleton, as shown in Figure 15.2.

To work with Motion Capture data in character studio, you can either use Motion Capture data directly, such as a .bvh (Biovision) or a .csm (character studio marker) file, or you can convert the data to biped (.bip) footstep files. The most practical approach is to convert all Motion

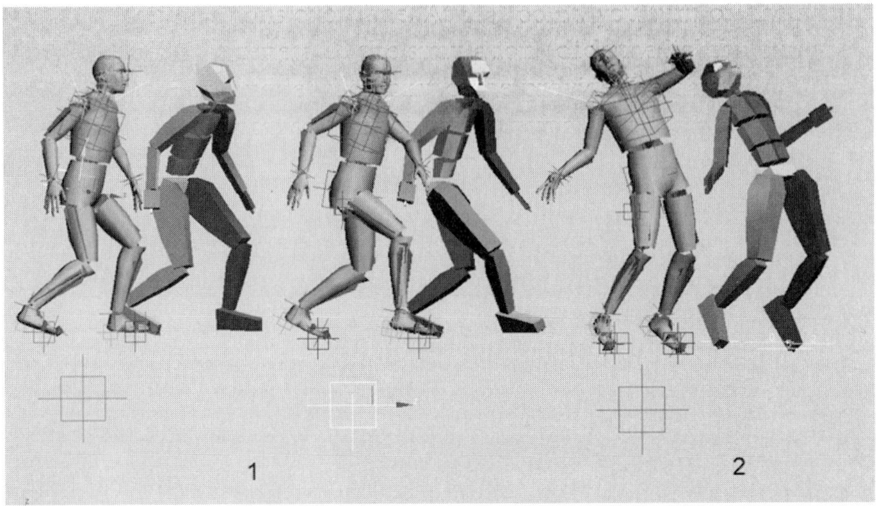

FIGURE 15.2 .fbx file conversion can be used to animate 3ds max bones with character studio 4 biped motions.

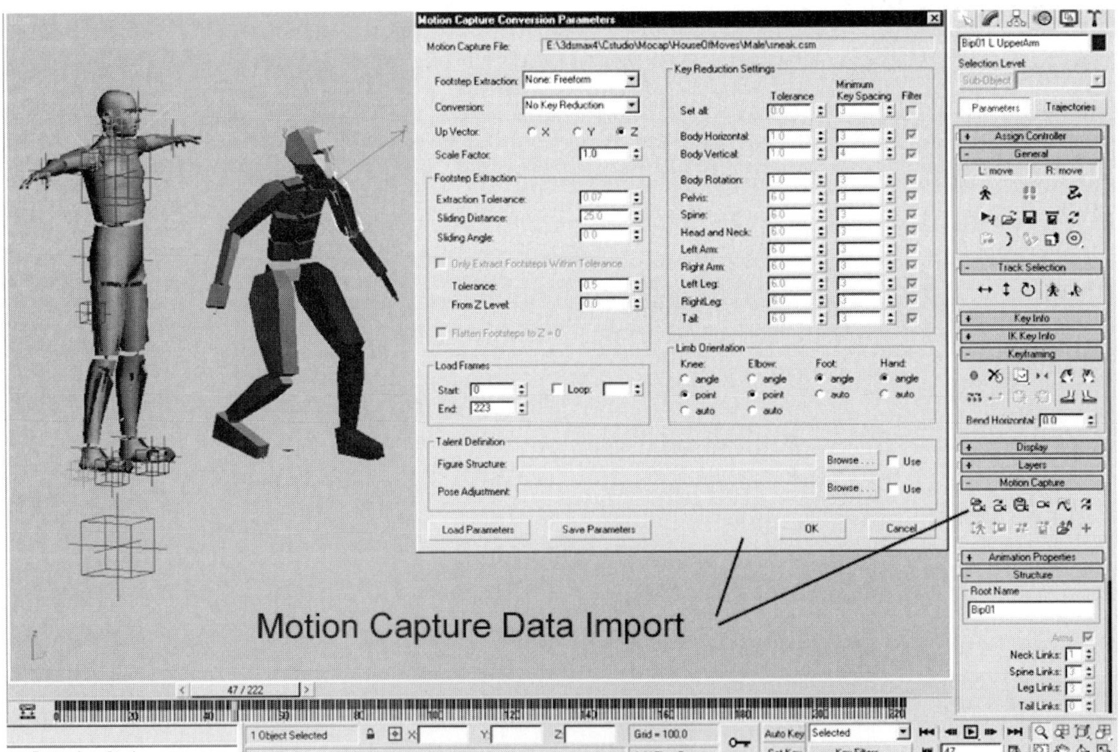

FIGURE 15.3 The character studio Motion Capture Data Import menu.

Capture files to .bip files with footsteps in the Motion Capture Import dialog. Once they are converted to .bip files, you can modify or combine the motion sequences using the Motion Flow Editor, the Layer Animation tool, or the Motion Mixer.

Most of the .bip (biped motion) footstep files that ship with character studio 4 are based on Motion Capture data that has undergone key reduction, so the movements are life-like. Character studio 4 also provides an extensive library of .cam and .bvh Motion Capture files. The Motion Capture Import dialog provides a file conversion utility where you can rename and map the correct joint data in the .bvh file to the same joint in a biped, generate biped footsteps, and perform keyframe reduction, as shown in Figure 15.3. If you want to use custom Motion Capture data, most Motion Capture studios can supply you with files in the .csm format that are compatible with character studio.

SLIDERS AND WIRED PARAMETERS

A slider is a manipulator helper object that looks and acts much like a traditional volume control on a stereo radio, but instead of changing volume, it can be assigned to change any parameter such as the rotation angle of a finger joint. A slider normally floats in the viewport at all times, but can be hidden or minimized. If you want to add slider manipulators to the viewport to animate the hands or fingers of a character studio 4 biped, you must first apply an Euler XYZ controller to the Rotation List Controller of each finger bone. This is done in the Motion Tab menu, in the Assign Controller dialog. It is not a difficult procedure, but it takes a little while to set up, depending on how many joints you want to animate. A benefit of this operation is that once you are finished, there will be a separate animation track for each finger bone of the biped in the Trackview – Curve Editor and the character studio 4 workbench.

In the next tutorial, you will add an Euler XYZ controller and a slider to animate the fingers of a biped's left hand.

This tutorial assumes that you have installed character studio 4 in 3ds max on your computer. For information on obtaining a demo version of character studio 4, go to the www.discreet.com Web site, click character studio 4 in the product list, then go to Downloads and follow the instructions.

For more in-depth information on using sliders and wired parameters, see Tutorial 8.5, "Create a Slider and Wire It to a Finger" in Chapter 8, "Preparing for Character Animation."

TUTORIAL 15.1 ANIMATING BIPED FINGERS WITH SLIDERS

To animate biped fingers with sliders:

1. Create a character studio 4 biped. This tutorial will not work with version 3 bipeds. In the Structure rollout, set Fingers = 5 and Finger Joints = 3. Then, zoom in on the left hand in the perspective view.
2. Select the first bone of the Index finger, open the Motion Tab menu, and then open the Assign Controller drop-down menu. In the menu, you should see a main heading called Transform: Finger1. Below that is a subheading called Biped SubAnim , and under that, you will find the BipRotationList: Rotation List, as shown in Figure 15.4, example 2.

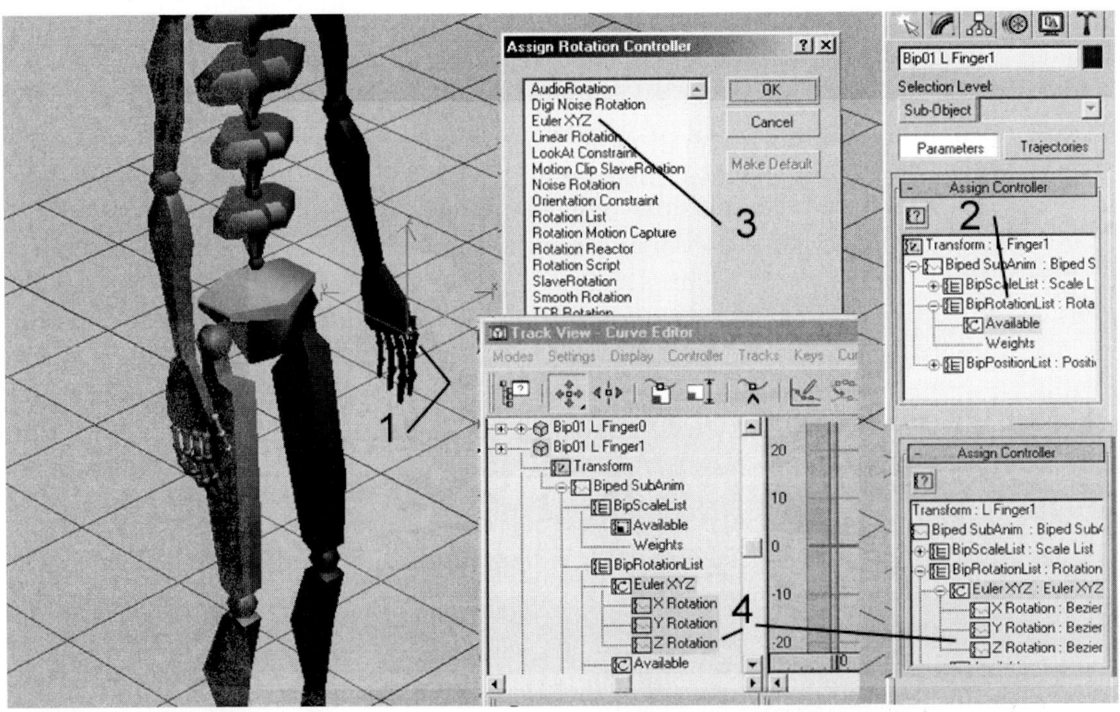

FIGURE 15.4 Applying a Euler XYZ Controller to the biped fingers to make them animatable with sliders.

3. Below BipRotationList: Rotation List you will see the word "Available." Click Available and then click the "?" button at the top of the Assign Controller window to open the Assign Rotation Controller menu. In the menu, select Euler XYZ and click OK, as shown in Figure 15.4, example 3.
4. Open the Trackview – Curve Editor. In the Hierarchy window, you should see Bip01 L Finger1 highlighted and below it, the BipRotationList with its three Euler XYZ tracks, as shown in Figure 15.4, example 4.
5. Repeat these steps to set up all of the biped finger bones to accept data from a slider.
6. Save the file as EulerSetup.max.

In the next tutorial, you will create slider manipulators and wire the finger bones to open and close by moving a slider.

WIRED PARAMETERS

When used with wired parameters, the slider can be set up to control any object you want to animate with an external control. 3ds max enables you to create a physical connection between one parameter and another by "wiring" them together in the Wired Parameters dialog.

A wired parameter can be either a driver or a driven parameter. A slider is considered a driver object that controls a parameter of the driven object such as a finger bone. In this skeleton rig, the movements of the hand and fingers are controlled by the Y-axis Rotate parameter. To animate the hand or finger closing, you move the slider, which then changes the angle of the Y-axis. One of the fingers can be wired to control all the other fingers in a Parent > Child relationship. For example, when the index finger bends or closes, the entire hand can be made to close with it. Alternatively, if you want to control the fingers individually, you would create one slider per finger.

In the next tutorial, you will set up a slider to control index finger movement.

TUTORIAL 15.2 CREATE A SLIDER AND WIRE IT TO A BIPED FINGER

To create a slider and wire it to control a biped finger:

1. Load the EulerSetup.max scene file if it is not already loaded.
2. To create a slider manipulator, click Create > Helpers > Manipulator, and in the menu, click the Slider button. In Parameters, put a label on the slider before you create it. Label it: Left Hand Close. In Slider Parameters, leave Value = 0, and then set Minimum = 0, and Maximum = 1.0. Click in the lower-right corner of the viewport. A new horizontal slider now floats on the viewport, as shown in Figure 15.5, example 1. Right-click in the viewport to turn off slider creation.

   The next operation will determine how the hand will work. The basic idea is to select the slider, right-click, and choose what parameter it will control. Then, select an object, such as a bone, right-click, and choose which

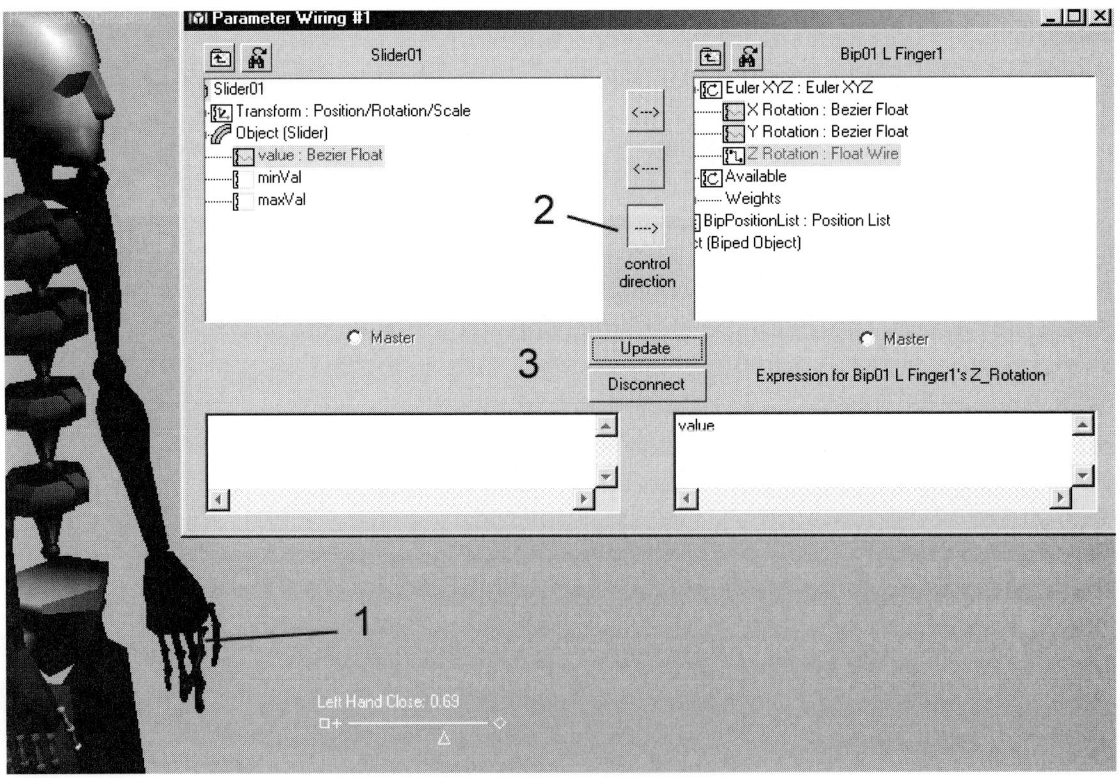

FIGURE 15.5 Connecting wired parameters from a slider to a finger bone.

bone parameter you will control with the slider. In this case, you want the slider to control bone rotation in the correct axis to close the finger.

3. During this operation, a floating window is going to cover part of the front view. Pan the biped in the view downward to leave room at the top. Select the slider, and then right-click. The Quad menu will pop up, as shown in Figure 15.5, example 2.
4. Click Wire Parameters. As soon as you click it, a small pop-up menu opens. The menu will probably be over the lower part of the interface. In that pop-up menu, click Object (which refers to the slider), and then click Value. Don't release the mouse button.
5. Drag the cursor over and select the root bone of the Index Finger (Bip01 Finger1). A dotted line will follow the cursor. A second Parameter pop-up menu will appear for the finger bone. Click Transform, then select Rotation List, then Rotation, and finally select Z Rotation, and release the mouse. The Parameter Wiring dialog window will open, as shown in Figure 15.5, example 3.
6. Notice that the slider is listed on the left with Value highlighted in yellow. The finger bone is listed on the right with Z Rotation: Float Wire highlighted. In the center of the Wiring dialog box is a column of arrows. Select the arrow pointing from the slider side toward the finger side of the dialog. The arrow will turn yellow to indicate the Control Direction, as shown in Figure 15.5, example 3.
7. Click the Connect button below the arrow to create a connection between the slider and the index finger's Z rotation axis.
8. To test the function of the new Left Hand Close Slider, click the Select and Manipulate icon in the Main toolbar (next to Move), and then click and drag the small triangle handle under the slider to the right and watch the finger move.
9. The finger bone should rotate downward in the Z-axis. To finish the hand, refer to Tutorial 8.5 in Chapter 8. That tutorial explains how to use the first joint to drive the second joint rotation, and then use the second joint to drive the third joint. Then, you use the rotation of the first finger to control the rotation of the second finger. The wiring of the fingers of the biped is the same, from this point on, as the wiring of the Generic Man 3ds max bone hands.
10. This completes the explanation of the process of wiring the hand of a biped to a slider. Close the Parameter Wiring window. Rather than go through the entire wiring process, you can move on to the next tutorial

and load a biped file that already has the fingers of the left hand wired to a slider.

11. Save the file as EulerSetup2.max.

Once you have wired and animated the hand of the biped, you can save that data as a 3ds max file, and then export the file to the .fbx (Kadara Filmbox) file format. This automatically converts the animation motion of the body and the fingers into data that will create an animated 3ds max skeleton when it is re-imported back into 3ds max.

The next tutorial explains how to apply Motion Capture data to animate a biped, export the biped animation to an .fbx (Filmbox) file, and then import it into 3ds max as a 3ds max bones skeletal animation.

The .fbx conversion procedure works with any version of biped compatible with 3ds max 6.

TUTORIAL 15.3

Convert Biped Animation to 3ds max Bones Animation

ON THE CD

1. Load the BiptoFBX.max scene file. There should be three sliders visible in the selected viewport.
2. There is a biped in the scene that uses the Dodge.bip motion file. If you do not have the commercial version of character studio installed, you will not be able to find the Dodge.bip file in the Cstudio directory in 3ds max 5 on your computer. However, you can load it from the Chap15\BipedMotion folder on the companion CD-ROM.
3. To use slider manipulators to operate the biped hand and close the thumb and fingers, first select any biped bone, and then go to the Motion tab in the control panel. Then, open the Keyframing Tools menu. Turn on the Enable Subanims (subobject animations) and Manipulate Subanims icons, as shown in Figure 15.6, example 1.
4. Next, click the Select and Manipulate icon in the Main toolbar. The sliders will turn green. Now you can move the sliders to animate the fingers on the left hand.
5. Let's assume that you have animated the fingers, and want to include the finger motion in the file that you converting to a 3ds max bones anima-

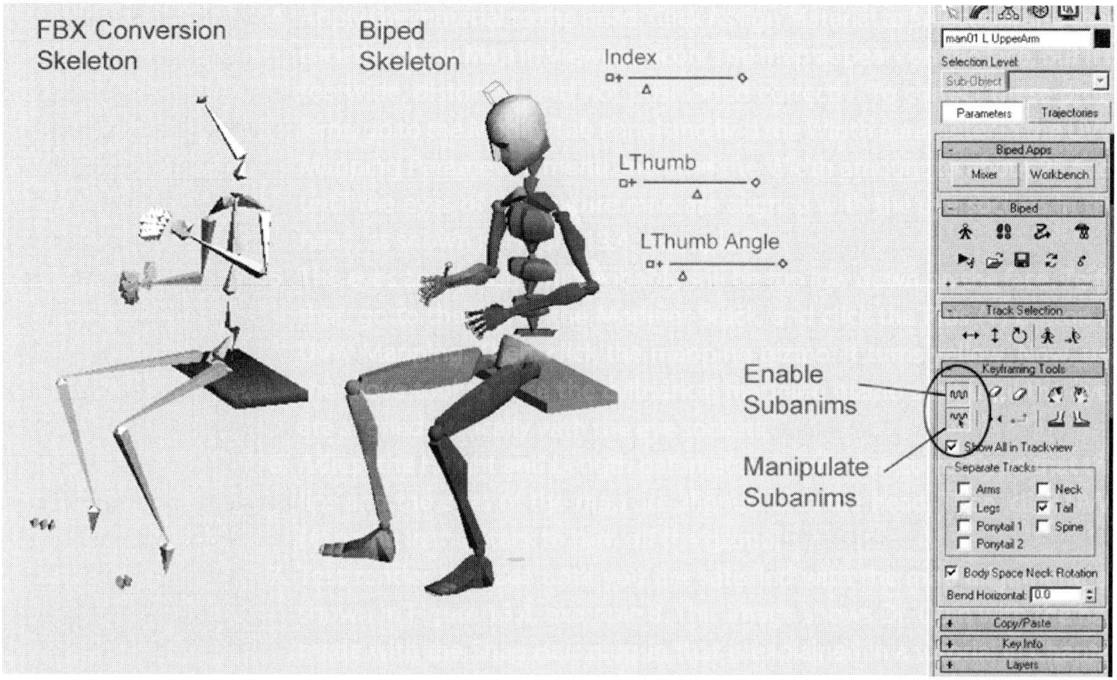

FIGURE 15.6 The Enable Subanims icon lets you animate the biped fingers with sliders.

tion. To do that, you must first save the .bip file with the finger animation keys before you export the file to .fbx format. This incorporates any new finger track keys into the .bip motion file.

6. To export the Biped animation to an .fbx file, click File > Export, select Import .fbx to .max., and resave. Biped is now converted into bones with finger tracks intact.
7. You can rig the bones skeleton with IK to modify the original Biped animation, but you will lose the original animation wherever you apply an IK Chain.
8. Save the file as Bip2Bones.max.

Motion Flow and Layer Animation

Because Motion Capture files have one key for every frame applied to every joint in the skeleton, you need to reduce the density of the keys by turning on Conversion > Use Key Reduction. This reduces the file to a point where it can easily be edited using the Layer Animation tool. You also need to turn on Footstep Extraction > On. All other settings should work in their default values. Click OK to convert the .csm file. The system calculates the conversion and creates a set of footsteps in the viewport. You can then save the animation as a .bip file and then use it in the Motion Flow Editor to create a sequence of motions, as shown in Figure 15.7.

The Motion Flow tool is designed to create Motion Flow Scripts by importing clips (biped motion files) and arranging them in the Motion Flow Graph window, as shown in Figure 15.7, example 1. The procedure is to open the Graph, load a number of clips, and create transitions between them (the arrows). Then, in the Motion Flow Script Editor, click the Define Script icon and give the script a name. Once it is named, click on each clip in the Graph to add it to the script. You can then play the script and watch the biped to see how the motions work together. If you are satisfied, save them as a .mfe file (Motion Flow Script). This file can

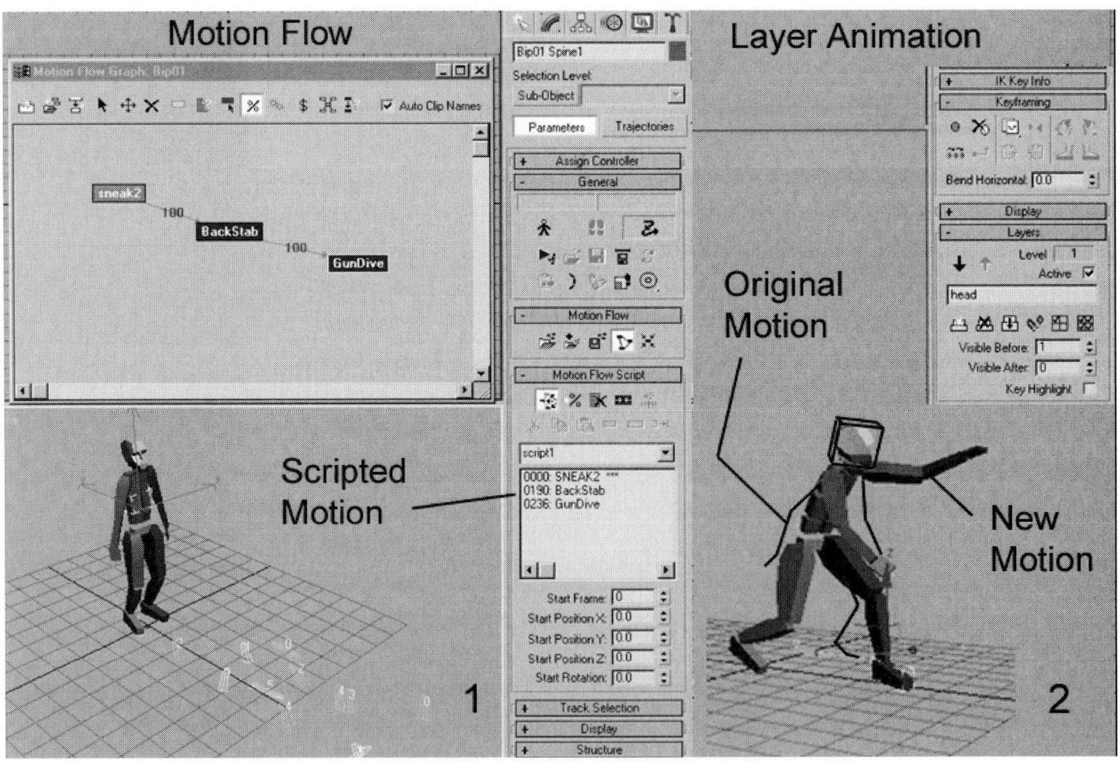

FIGURE 15.7 Motion Flow and Layer Animation menus.

then be used on any character or any number of characters and given random offsets. For example, if you wanted soldiers to be mowed down by a machine gun, you would create one Motion Flow Script for the action of the soldiers getting shot and falling. Then, you would create your biped soldiers, apply the motion script to each or to a group of them, and then offset in time and randomize the keys to have soldiers getting shot and falling at different times to create a realistic battle simulation.

One of the most important and commonly ignored tools in character studio is the Layer Animation tool, found in the Layers rollout menu. It lets you create many different versions of the same movement and then only save the one you want. The original movement keys are represented by a red stick figure. The new movement you add is represented by the current position of the biped, as shown in Figure 15.7, example 2.

This tool also functions as a Motion Capture Data editor because you can change movements in a Motion Capture file without having to convert it to a biped footstep file. When the new keys are collapsed, they are integrated into the original motion data. You then have an edited .csm Motion Capture file tailored to fit your needs. However, you can only save it as a .bip motion file for use within character studio, so you cannot export edited Motion Capture files unless you convert them into .fbx (Filmbox) files.

Filmbox motion files are compatible with Maya and Softimage provided you have the free Kadara Filmbox file loader plug-in installed. This plug-in allows you use character studio 4 to animate a character that can be used in Maya. The Filmbox file loader is available on the *www.kadara.com* Web site.

In *Homing Instinct*, bipeds were used for all of the secondary characters, creating the crowds of people, soldiers, background pedestrians in exterior scenes, customers in restaurants, and so on.

CROWD ANIMATION

Charging armies are impressive spectacles in films such as *Lord of the Rings, the Two Towers,* and most of the *Star Wars* films. Game Cinematic movies, which are used to promote the games, also incorporate charging armies, such as the excellent charging army animations from the *War Craft* game series, produced by Blizzard Entertainment (*www.blizzard.com*). Character studio was used on *War Craft* and is used regularly for this kind of game animation.

The character studio 4 Crowd system lets you create an environment where biped characters can move seemingly under their own volition, making decisions such as seeking or avoiding obstacles The system works by creating delegates, which are like children of the crowd object, who have specific behaviors and goals that they must fulfill. Delegates can hold or move biped skeletons. They can be scattered randomly across an area in which you want them to move, such as a battlefield or a shopping mall. To attach biped characters to these delegates, you associate a biped skeleton with each one, as shown in Figure 15.8.

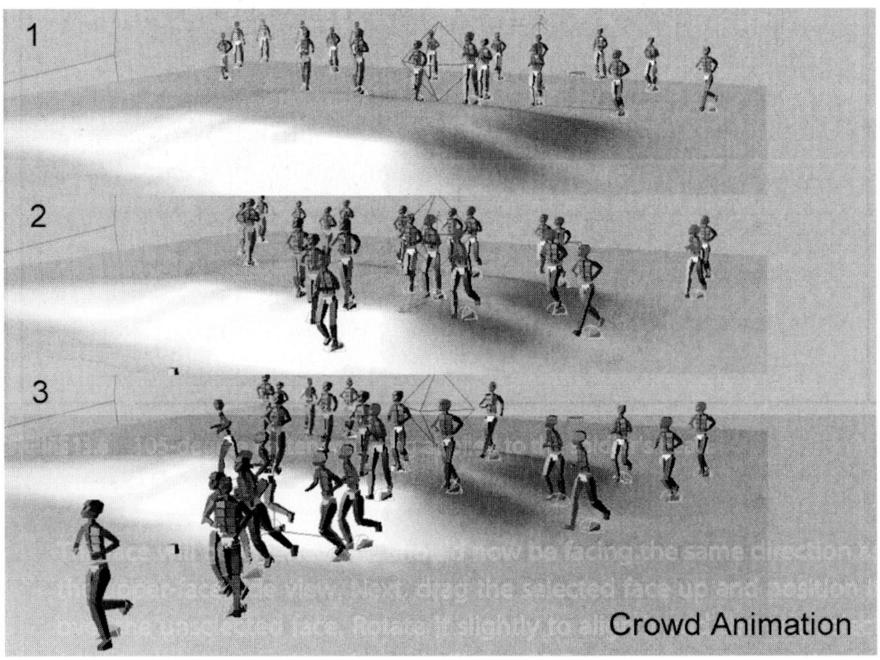

FIGURE 15.8 A crowd of running bipeds with avoid and seek behaviors moving toward a goal.

The bipeds can have a number of behaviors programmed into them. Delegates are assigned behaviors in the Delegate Behavior Assignments and Teams dialog. Any behavior, such as orientation, repel, seek, wander, and speed vary, can be triggered by outside events, such as impact with another delegate or obstacle. These behaviors happen automatically, so

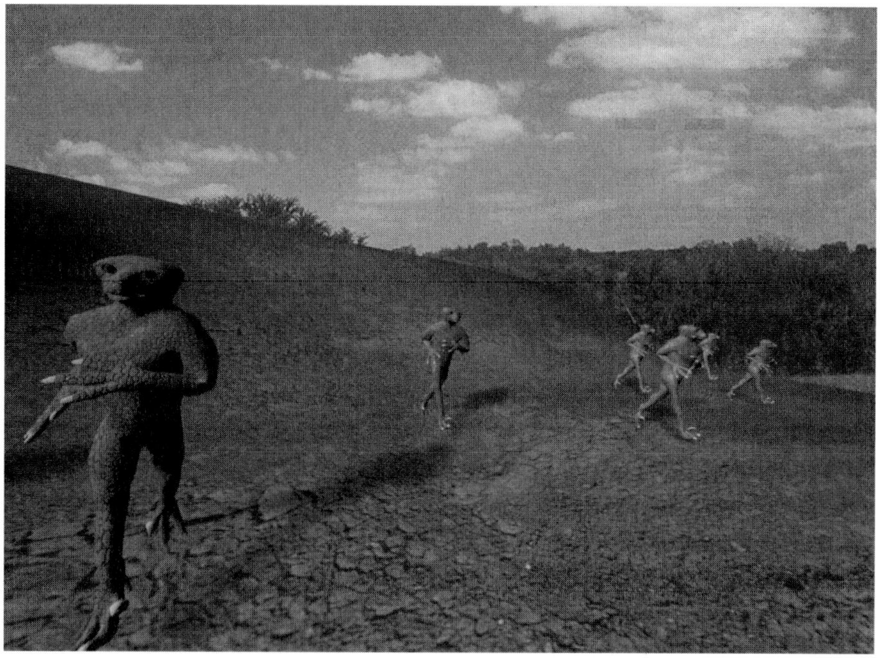

FIGURE 15.9 Crowd simulation of Dinomen Warriors charging down a hill.

once the delegates are set up and started, character studio 4 animates them for you. You can sit back and be entertained, watching them trying to accomplish the tasks you assigned to them, as shown in Figure 15.9.

Motion clips are assembled as a Motion Flow script. This script can be applied to many bipeds in a single scene. You can program the delegates with triggered *cognitive behaviors*. These behaviors can include events such as searching for a doorway or raising an arm when they get close to another biped. This means that you can simulate intelligent interactive behavior in any character, or team of characters, in a crowd. They can act autonomously within the boundary space of the crowd environment, and perform any action that you assign, including the typical actions of a soldier, a tourist, or a child at play, and all the motions can be created from biped motion files. The forward motion of the delegate must match exactly the speed of the character's feet as they stride along. When you use bipeds animated with a Motion Flow script, character studio 4 takes care of moving the feet at the correct speed, automatically matching it to the forward speed of the delegate.

ANIMATING A CHARGING ARMY

The first task in animating an army of warriors charging down a hill is to get a line of delegates positioned on the hill. The second task is to assign them all a behavior that will get them to move down the hill together. In the following tutorial, you will set up a crowd and cause delegates to move down a hill. This must be done before the biped warrior characters can be brought into the scene.

TUTORIAL 15.4

SETTING UP A CROWD ANIMATION

ON THE CD

To set up a crowd animation:

1. Load the Army_Start.max file from the Chap15 folder on the companion CD-ROM. You should see a hill terrain object with a Crowd icon and eight Delegate icons at the top. The delegates point in the direction they are going to travel and will eventually have eight biped warriors attached to them.

Avoid moving any of the delegates up or down. Each delegate center pivot is aligned with a vertex on the surface of the hill. If you raise or lower a delegate, it will flip up or down during the first few frames, trying to align itself when you run the simulation. If you have a warrior linked to the delegate, you will also see it flip up or down.

2. To animate the delegates, you will apply a behavior to them. To do that, select the Crowd icon in the top view (the large green diamond shape) and then open the Modifier Panel. In the Setup menu under Behaviors, click New. From the list of behaviors pop-up dialog, select Surface Follow Behavior, as shown in Figure 15.10, example 1, and then click OK. It will show in the Crowd Behaviors list. Then click Surface Follow and rename it Surface Follow01. This behavior will later be associated with Delegate01.

In an ideal world, you should be able to use one behavior for all of the delegates. The problem is that this strategy works only if you are willing to accept all of the delegates moving around the surface randomly. If you want them all to go in the same direction, as you would with a charging army, you must assign a separate behavior to each delegate so that their Z-axis direction projections will work. This feature does not work when you have multiple delegates being directed by one instance of the surface follow behavior.

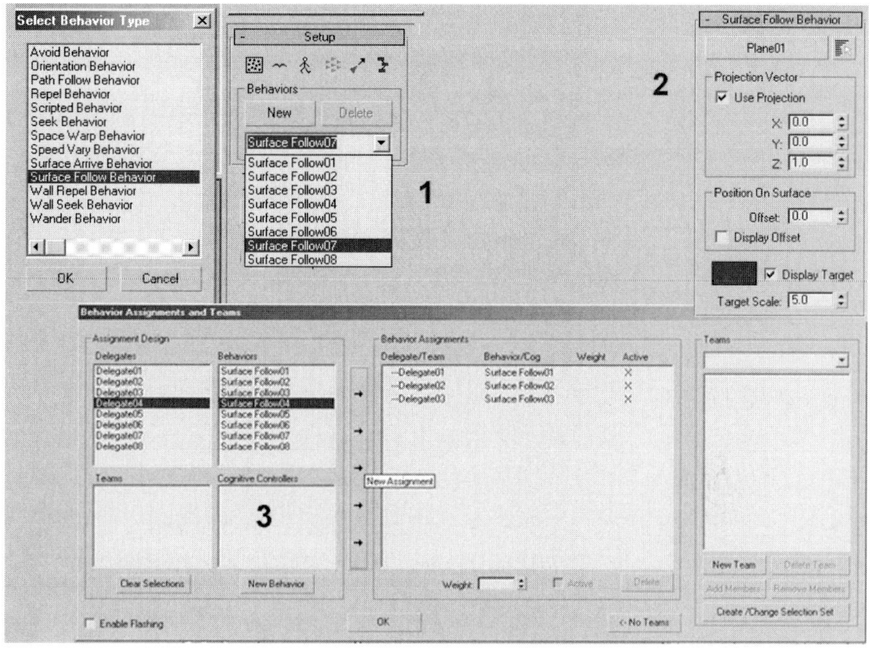

FIGURE 15.10 Assigning delegate behavior.

3. Create seven more Surface Follow behaviors and name them 02 through 08. They will be associated with Delegates 02 through 08. As you create and rename each instance of the behavior, also click the large button marked None in the Surface Follow Behavior drop-down menu, as shown in Figure 15.10, example 2. In the viewport, select the hill (plane01) as the surface follow object. Next, turn on Projection Vector > Use Projection with the Z-axis set to 1.0 (the default). Do this for each behavior. This vector will make the delegates proceed in a straight line down the hill, instead of wandering around at random.
4. Now that you have created eight behaviors, you will associate the delegates with their behaviors. To do that, click the Behavior Assignment icon (the arrow) in the Crowd Setup menu, and open the Behavior Assignments and Teams dialog. Eight delegates and eight behaviors should show in the lists, as shown in Figure 15.10, example 3. The process of creating the association is quite simple. In the Assignment Design window, select Delegate01, and then select the behavior, Surface Follow01. Next, click the large vertical button with five arrows to move then to the Behavior Assignments window. When you have done all of them, click OK.

5. You are now ready to test the crowd simulation. Before solving, you need to set the length of the simulation. In the Crowd > Solve menu, set End Solve = 145, and turn on Delete Keys Before Solve, as shown in Figure 15.11, example 1. Then, click Solve. If any of the delegates do not follow the surface of the hill, go back to the Setup menu, find the behavior associated with that delegate, and ensure that Plane 01 is selected as the follow surface object.
6. When you run the solution, you should see the delegates make their way slowly from the top of the hill to the bottom, as shown in Figure 15.11, example 2. You are now ready to merge in the biped Dinomen warriors to complete the second part of the scene setup. Save the scene as Army01.max in case you need to go back to this stage. The next part of the process is a bit more complex.

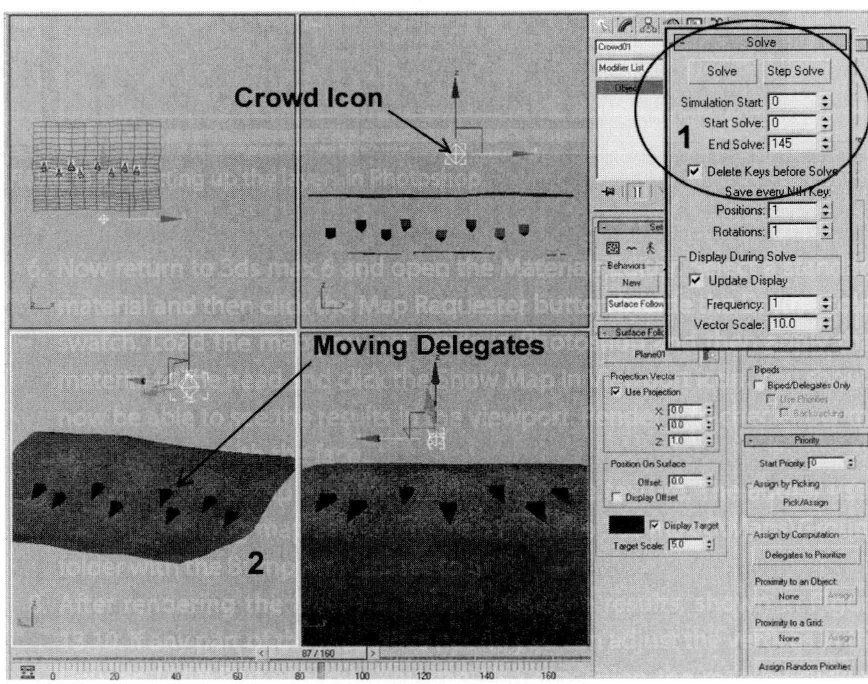

FIGURE 15.11 Solving the crowd simulation.

7. There are eight different Dinoman Warrior files, each with unique names for all of the components of the biped skeletons and the mesh skins of the models. The names range alphabetically from A through H. Crowd does

not accept duplicate names for different bipeds, so you cannot use the same biped repeatedly to make a crowd. Merge them into your scene one at a time by clicking File > Merge, and then in the file browser, go to the Chap15\8Warriors folder on the companion CD-ROM and click WarriorA.max. In the Merge dialog, click the All button and then click OK. The warrior will appear under the top of the hill on the ground plane. Later, it will be elevated up to the delegate when you go through the association process in the next tutorial. Do not move any of the warriors. Crowd will move them to their correct places.

ON THE CD

8. Merge in WarriorB.max, and so on, until they are all in the scene. All warriors will be on top of each other because they all have the same Walk.bip motion file on them, so it will appear is if there is only one warrior. This is the correct result after merging. Crowd will separate them later. During the merge operation, 3ds max will ask you if you want to use the Merged or the Scene Material. Click Scene.
9. When you are finished, to speed up the scene you should select and hide all of the skin meshes of each warrior. For example, in the WarriorA.max file, the skin mesh is named ADinoBodyLowRez02. For WarriorB, it would be BDinoBodyLowRez02, and so on. The quickest way to select all skin meshes at once is to press H to open the Select by Name dialog, and in the top window, type *Dino. That will highlight all the skin objects. Click Select and then Hide Selected. Do the same for the eyes (Type *eye) and hide them.

The Crowd simulation works much faster when only the biped skeletons are visible. Each of these Warrior files is about 2.5MB, so your scene will get somewhat large, but as long as only the bipeds are visible, it should not slow down your machine. It is not unusual in crowd simulations to have files of 500MB or more. The author worked with one file that took 20 minutes to load and contained 300 bipeds.

10. After you have finished merging all of the warriors into the scene, save the scene as Army02.max. Go on to the next tutorial to begin setting up the Biped Crowd animation.

In the next tutorial, you will use a Motion Flow Script to animate the bipeds for the Biped Crowd simulation.

The next tutorial assumes that you have a basic familiarity with character studio 4 biped commands and that you understand how to use the interface.

TUTORIAL 15.5

SETTING UP A BIPED CROWD SIMULATION

To set up a biped crowd:

ON THE CD

1. Transfer the Chap15\Crowd\MotionFlow folder from the companion CD-ROM to your hard drive. Put it in your 3dsmax6\Scenes directory. The next two tutorials assume that you have done this.
2. Load the Army02.max file. If it is not already loaded, load it from the 3dsmax6\Scenes\Tutorials folder that you have placed on your hard drive.

The next step is to create two motion clips that the crowd simulation will use for biped motion synthesis. The bipeds already have a Walk.bip motion applied to them, but that will be removed shortly. You will be creating a Motion Flow Graph. If you are not familiar with the interface, hold the cursor over each button to see a description.

3. Select the WarriorA biped root object. This is the COM (Center of Mass) object of biped A. To do that, press the H key, and in the Select by Name dialog that opens, select object Aip02. That will enable the Biped menu. In the Command Panel, click the Motion tab. The Biped menu will open. Then, in the Biped roll-out menu, click the Motion Flow Mode button. The Motion Flow menu will open, as shown in Figure 15.12, example 1.
4. In the Motion Flow menu, click the Show Graph button. The Motion Flow Graph will open. The Graph has a row of buttons along the top. To create the motion clips for the biped, click the Create Multiple Clips button, as shown in Figure 15.12, example 2. A browser will open. Navigate to your 3dsmax6\Scenes\Crowd\MotionFlow folder. Hold down the Ctrl key and click jogStraight.bip. Then click AlsoJog.bip. Next, click OK. Two blue clip boxes will appear in the window, one for each .bip file. Next, you will create transitions between the two clips so that they blend their motions together smoothly.
5. To create transitions between the clips, select both clip boxes, and then click the Synthesize Motion Flow Graph button, as shown in Figure 15.12,

example 3. A pop-up message will ask you if you want to create two sets of transitions. Click No. You should now see two arrows joining the clips. If you see four arrows, delete the ones that extend from each clip to itself. The transition function automatically uses the beginning and end of each clip to create transitions. Now reselect the clips, including the arrows, and click the Optimize Transitions button to remove any roughness in the transitions, as shown in Figure 15.12, example 4. Accept the default 10 frames and click OK.

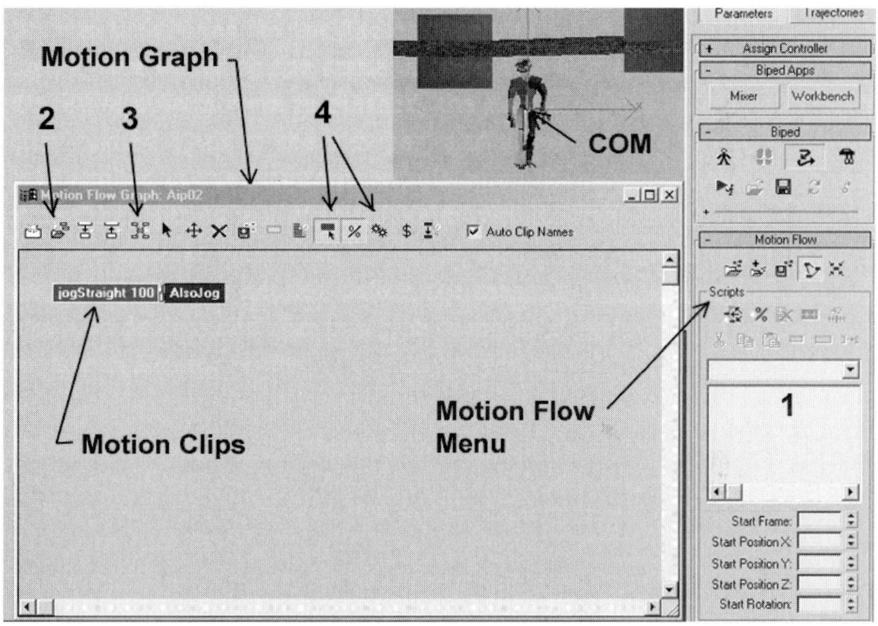

FIGURE 15.12 Creating a Motion Flow Graph.

6. These clips will become the shared Motion Flow Graph used by all eight bipeds in the Crowd simulation. The next step is to select the Random Start clip. If you do not do this, the simulation will fail. Click the Random Start Clips button, and then click the jogStraight clip. The number 100 will appear to the right of the selected clip, indicating a 100% chance that your animation will always start with this clip. If you have different clips in the Graph, you can change this percentage to create some randomness among the bipeds.

7. Now go to the Biped > Motion Flow menu and click the Save File button. Save the Graph in your 3dsmax6\Scenes\Crowd\MotionFlow folder as Warrior1.mfe. (motion flow format) You are now ready to use the Motion Flow Graph with the bipeds to create the Crowd simulation.
8. Save the Max scene as Army03.max in your 3dsmax6\Scenes\Crowd folder. Now Reset max to clear and reset all data, and then reload the Army03.max file. Be sure to drag the left edge of the Control Panel wider (to the left) so you can see all of the Crowd menus. Continue on to the next tutorial for the steps needed to attach the bipeds to the delegates for the Crowd simulation.

In the next tutorial, you will complete the Biped Crowd simulation.

TUTORIAL 15.6 COMPLETING THE BIPED CROWD SIMULATION

To complete the biped simulation:

1. Load the Army03.max scene file if it is not already loaded. You previously associated each delegate with a behavior. Now you will link each biped to a delegate.
2. To link all of the bipeds to the delegates at once, select the Crowd icon in the viewport. The Modifier Panel will automatically open. In the Setup menu, select the Biped Delegate Associations button to open the Associate Bipeds with Delegates dialog. On the left, click the Add button and select all of the bipeds. Only the COM or root object will be listed for each biped. Then, under Delegates, click the Add button and select all of the delegates, as shown in Figure 15.13, example 1. Make Specified Associations and Set Delegates to Use Biped should be checked by default. Next, click the Associate button.
3. The next step is to tell each biped to use a random Start clip. To do this, click the Multiple Delegates Editing button in the Crowd Setup menu, as shown in Figure 15.13, example 2. In the dialog that opens, go to the Delegates to Edit window in the upper left, and click the Add button. Select all of the delegates. Then move down to the Biped menu and click Use Biped, and Random Start Clip, as shown in Figure 15.13, example 3. Finally, click the Check all Sets button and then click Apply Edits. The window will close.

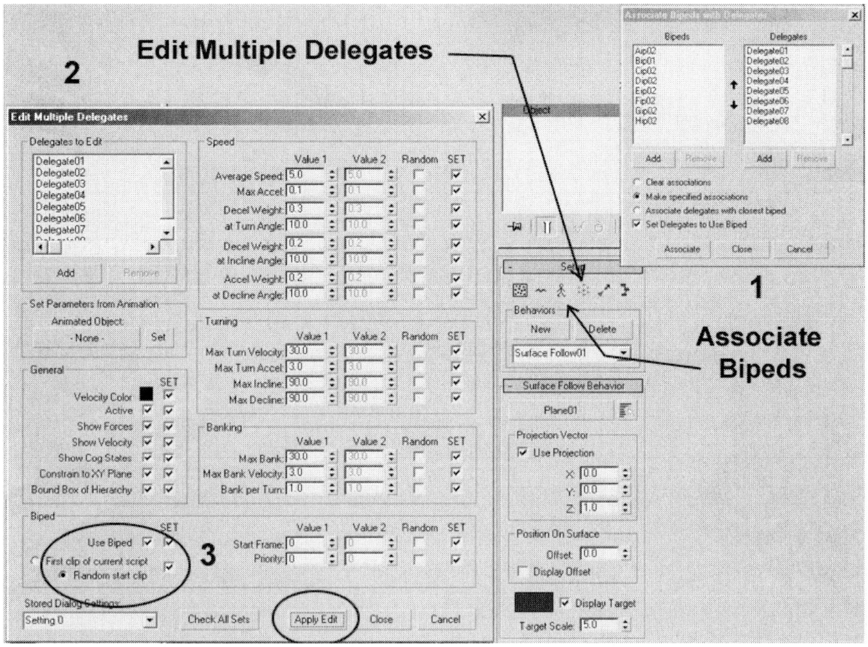

FIGURE 15.13 Associating the delegates with the bipeds.

Next, you will use Shared Motion Flow to apply the Motion Flow Graph file you created earlier.

4. To apply shared motion flow, select a bone in any biped, and then open the Biped menu in the Motion Panel. Click the Motion Flow Mode button. In the Motion Flow menu, click the Shared Motion flow button, as shown in Figure 15.14, example 1. When the dialog opens, click the New button to create a new shared motion flow with the name SharedMoflow1.
5. Now you will load the Motion Flow Graph file you created earlier. To load the file, click the Load.mfe button in the Parameters window, and then navigate to your 3dsmax6\Scenes\Crowd\MotionFlow folder and select Warrior1.mfe. Now, click the Add button and select all of the bipeds (only the names of their COM objects will show). You will get a warning. Go ahead and click OK. When they load, you will see that biped Aip02 has the wrong scale, as shown in Figure 15.14, example 2. This is not uncommon and has been done here purposely to show how to fix this problem.
6. To fix the scale problem of biped Aip02, click the Reset Wrong Scales: Just Legs button. Do not click OK yet. This step ensures that all the bipeds will

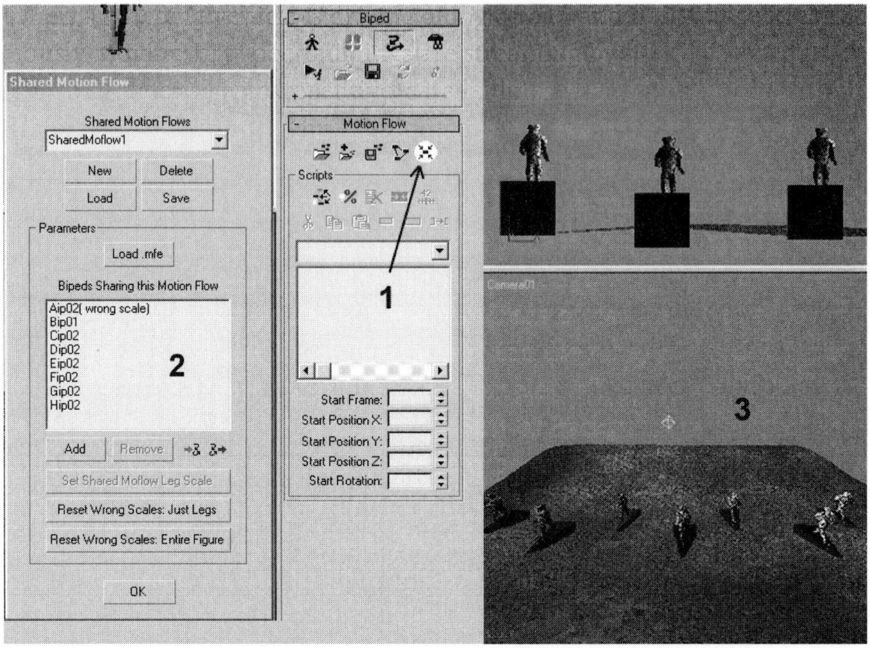

FIGURE 15.14 Creating a shared motion flow.

move at the same speed by scaling Aip02's legs to make them the same length as the other bipeds. The final step is to click the small green button called Put Multiple Bipeds in Motion Flow. Now click OK.

7. Next, select the Crowd icon and open the Modifier Panel. In the Solve menu, make sure that Start Solve is set to 0, and End Solve is set to 160. Click the Solve button. You will see all of the bipeds pop up and stand on their respective delegates. As it solves, it will look strange because the bipeds go straight into the air, while the delegates follow the surface of the hill. When the solver gets to the last frame, the bipeds will pop down to the surface and end up standing on their respective delegates. Rewind to frame 0 and play to see the final Crowd simulation with the bipeds correctly following the hill, as shown in Figure 15.14, example 3.
8. At the very end of the simulation, the bipeds might pop up again. Don't render that far. Before you render the scene, Unhide All to unhide the Dinoman Warrior skin meshes, along with their eyes. Then select and hide all the bipeds. The quickest way to hide the bipeds is to press the H key and, in the top window, type "ai," which are the first two letters of all of BipedA's bones. Click Select, and then Hide Selected. Repeat that for

BipedB by pressing H and typing in "bi," the first two letters of all of BipedB's bones. When they highlight, click Select and then Hide Selected. Repeat this operation for all bipeds and they will be hidden very quickly.

You will notice that part of the mesh of BipedA is being left behind its feet. This has happened because Crowd has scaled the legs down to make the simulation work. Making the skin envelopes larger to begin with does not seem to help. If you try to go into the Skin Modifier and adjust the skin on that biped after it has been simulated, max will crash. You can achieve better results by simply deleting that biped or hiding it. In a big army, you will not miss one warrior, especially if you create some dust as they run. You can go to Chapter 11, "Visual Effects," and set up a Particle Flow particle system to make dust rise up from each Dinoman's footsteps.

ON THE CD

9. This concludes the Biped Crowd simulation of the army of Dinomen warriors charging down a hill. Save the file as Army04.max. For a movie of this animation, open the Warriors.mov file in the Chap15\Images folder on the companion CD-ROM.

CONCLUSION

In this chapter, you were introduced to some of the specialized features of character studio 4 including the Motion Mixer. You worked with the wired parameters to enable hand animation with sliders. You explored how to export biped animation in the Filmbox format and then re-import it into 3ds max 6 as a 3ds max bones animation. Then, you looked at the Motion Flow tool and Layer animation, and used the Crowd feature to animate a charging army of warriors in a crowd simulation. In the next chapter, you will be introduced to combustion 3 and work with compositing and 2D visual effects.

CHAPTER

16

combustion 3, COMPOSITING AND 2D VISUAL EFFECTS

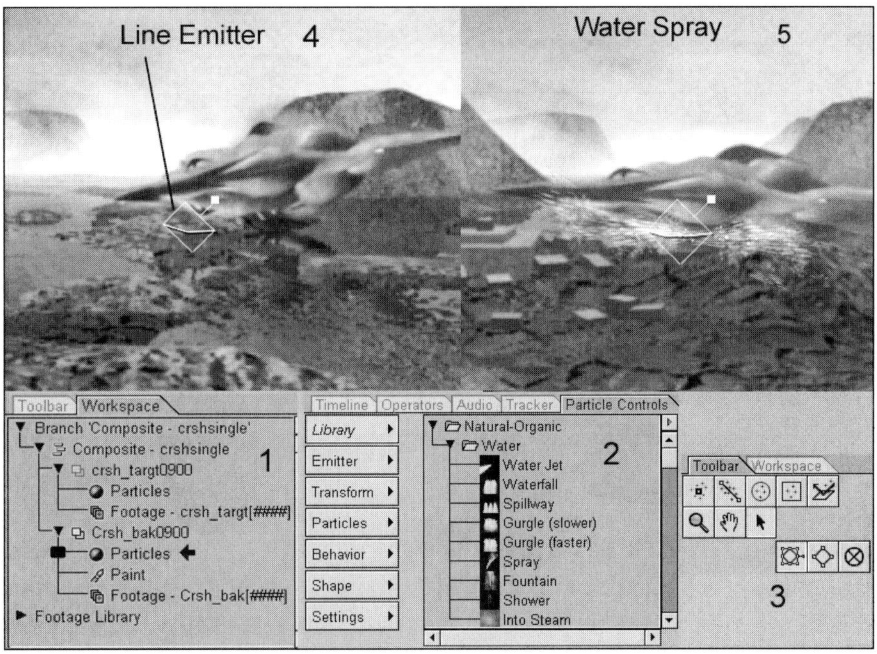

Whatever the length or size of your film, or the methods used to create it, you will need to apply a number of post-production processes to put all of the images, scenes, backgrounds, foregrounds, and visual effects together. This chapter explains how to use the keying, compositing, and visual effects tools. Then, we discuss the post-production process in combustion 3.

Combustion 3 from discreet is a 2D and 3D compositing and visual effects program that includes extensive tools for keying, tracking, color correction, creating mattes, generating a wide array of atmospheric and particle effects , and vector paint tools. New in version 3 is the Edit Operator, for editing clips and footage, and creating transitions, and the Macromedia Flash exporter, for making movies for the Web. Other improvements include a new system of Timeline markers, and a significant improvement in speed. A large number of plug-ins are now available, including RE:Flex®, which enables you to do animated morphing.

Combustion 3 offers a large number of image processing filters, a Z-depth buffer, depth of field, and motion blur capabilities; all of these can be applied to almost any type of image. The excellent tracker in combustion 3 uses the same technology as discreet flame™. It lets you lock particle effects or an image layer to any trackable point in an image sequence. The extensive particle preset library gives you hundreds of impressive ready-made effects, from wispy smoke and violent explosions, to raining numbers.

Combustion is often included in the 3ds max production bundle, along with character studio and a selection of Digimation plug-ins. Combustion and 3ds max can work with each other interactively through the special combustion material that has been integrated into the 3ds max Materials Editor. This material gives you the ability to paint combustion 3 textures directly on 3D objects in any 3ds max viewport. As you paint, you can watch the 2D paint image update in real time in the combustion 3 paint interface. This capability solves many of the mapping problems that make it difficult to map and apply textures to intricate organic 3D models.

The combustion 3 interface, as shown in Figure 16.1, has a number of different possible configurations, and is designed to be used with dual monitors. The timeline and the image display areas can be resized to speed the workflow.

The filmstrip display can run vertically or horizontally, and the Workspace can be changed to a schematic view that is structured as a workflow diagram showing all dependent operators as icons that are

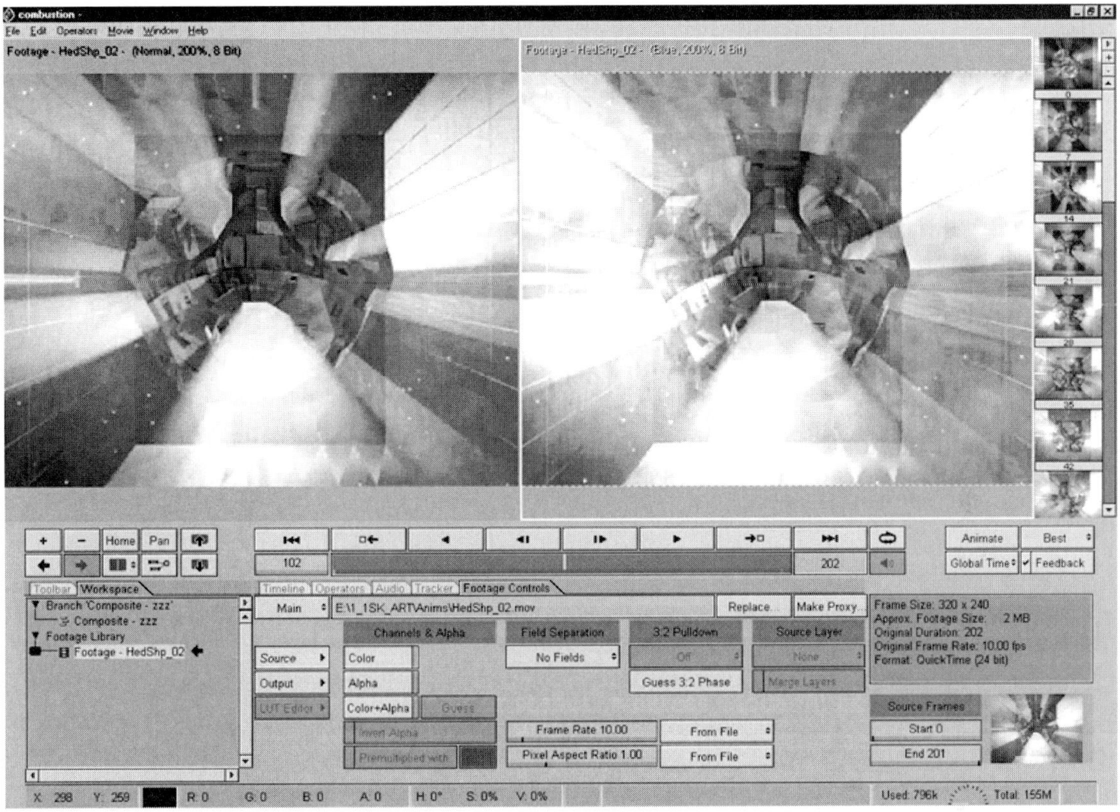

FIGURE 16.1 Visual effects footage displayed in the combustion 3 interface.

wired together. When a scene is rendered in the RLA or the RPF file format in 3ds max, you can save Z Depth data and GBuffer information from the 3D scene. The Z Depth data lets you add visual effects to an image in 3D space such as 3D fog, or lighting effects. The GBuffer information lets you select objects in an image, apply effects only to them, modify their materials, or delete them from an image.

Blue- and Green-Screen Compositing

Combustion is based on the use of operators that are applied to some aspect of an image to modify it. In a multilayer 3D composite, you can modify the characteristics of an individual image layer. The function of an operator in combustion 3 is analogous to the function of a Modifier in

3ds max. For example, a Keying Operator lets you key out any color in a layer to reveal the image layer behind it, as shown in Figure 16.2. Almost every function in combustion 3 starts by applying an operator. The most fundamental operator is the Footage operator. It is designed to load either an individual image or a clip containing a movie or a sequence of images into the combustion 3 Workspace to create an image layer. When you import footage into a composite, a new layer is automatically created in the Workspace.

Blue- and green-screen photography, when used with digital keying and compositing, is one of the most versatile tools a director has because it can stretch reality and create impossible illusions using digital compositing tricks. Blue-screen photography can put live actors into a computer-

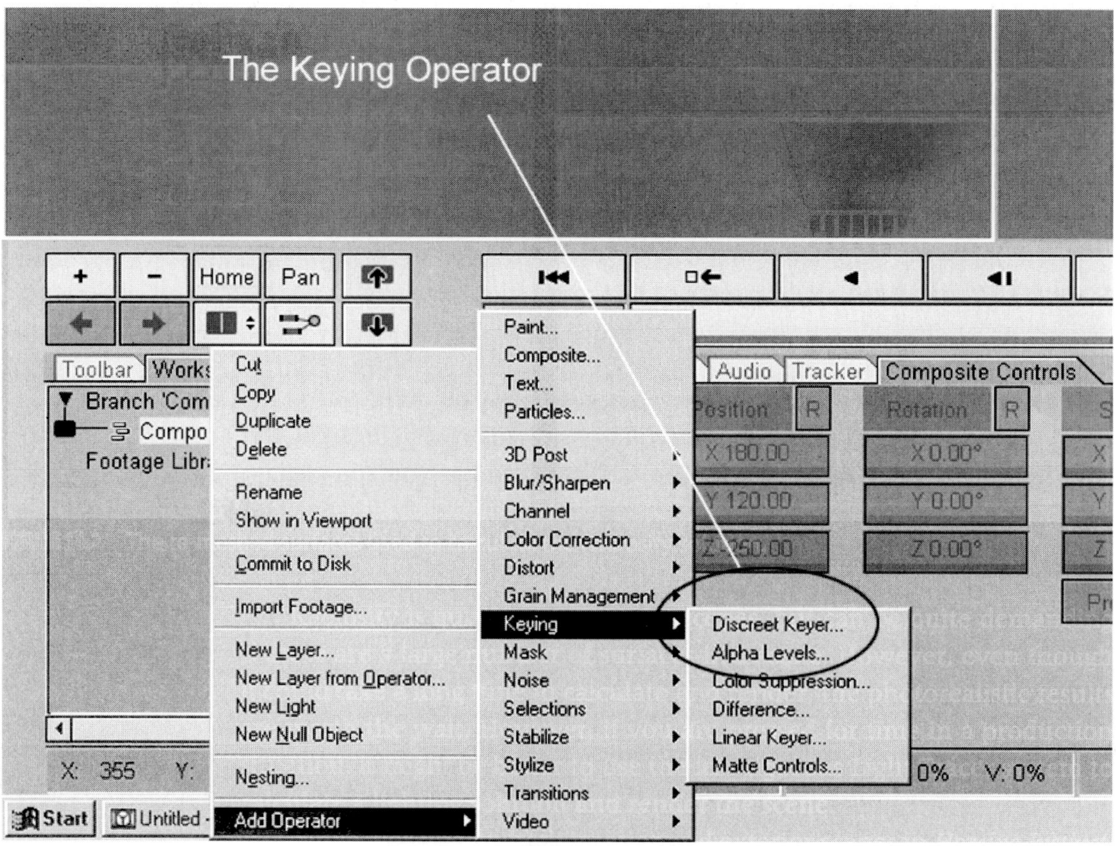

FIGURE 16.2 Adding a Keying Operator from the list of operators to the combustion 3 Workspace.

generated image or a digitally created fantastic background. There are many times in an action-adventure, science fiction, or fantasy film where the director needs to film an actor in a dangerous situation, or place the actor in an environment that does not exist except in the computer.

To create a blue- or green-screen shot, the actor is filmed giving his performance, standing in front of a blue or green screen on a bare stage. The issue that must always be carefully considered is how to light the blue or green background behind the actor. The success of your shot depends on how well you light the background, and how well you prevent any color spill or light reflected off the background from falling on the foreground subject. Any color on the foreground subject that is the same or close to the color of the background can cause a hole in your matte. When this happens, you must try a number of alternative ways to get rid of it. If it is too bad and you find that you cannot pull a smooth matte, you might be forced to re-shoot the shot. However, most productions cannot afford to re-shoot expensive scenes like blue-screen shots, so combustion 3 is equipped with a number of different keying methods designed to suppress color spill. There are also ways to either shrink or grow a matte and to feather the edge that become very useful when batting hair against a blue or green-screen.

Hair, smoke, and fire are probably the toughest images from which to pull good mattes. This is because of the subtle gradations of transparency in these shots such as the area around the edge of a person's hair where the background shows through. Fire can be especially difficult because it is so gaseous. The edge color of the flame is so transparent and subtle that it can take a lot of effort to get a matte that dissolves to nothing instead of having abrupt hard edges.

The traditional blue-screen shot is often replaced by the green-screen shot depending on the color of the actor's costume or props. Green-screen shots work well for skin, and you can pull good mattes in both the dark and light areas of the image. A blue-screen matte is a little harder to "pull" (create) than a green-screen matte because the blue color is of a narrower bandwidth, but it is still used when there is a prop like a vehicle or metallic object in the scene.

Background lighting for a blue- or green-screen shot can be done with tungsten light, which are normal stage lights. The only problem with them is that they have a large amount of reddish light in their output. To get a good matte with a blue screen, you need to add a blue gel filter to every light, known as Booster Blue. The blue subtractive filter blocks the red light frequency and generates a much better blue light on the blue screen. There is also a florescent lighting system used in the studios called Kino-Flo lights that only output blue light. This is the preferred type of light for blue-screen shots in the big movie studios. Outside light or sunlight has a different color temperature than indoor lights. Tungsten indoor lights are rated at 3200 degrees Kelvin, whereas outdoor light is rated at 5000 degrees Kelvin. Sunlight is commonly used when shooting high-speed or visual effects shots because more image information reaches the film, and it is white light that contains the full spectrum of all colors.

If you do not own combustion 3 and want to download a free 30-day trial demo of the latest version of the software, go to the www.discreet.com Web site and find combustion in the Product menu. On the left side of the interface, you will find a link to a Download page where you can enter your e-mail address and download the combustion 3 demo.

Inserting an actor into a photographic background in combustion 3 is done by importing the background and foreground footage, and then adding a Keying Operator, such as the Discreet Keyer, to the foreground footage.

This operator lets you sample the green color background and apply different tools and settings to pull a clean matte. In the next tutorial, you will use the Discreet Keyer to composite the green-screen image of an actor (the author) into a photographic background.

TUTORIAL 16.1 COLOR KEYING IN COMBUSTION 3

To composite an actor into a background:

1. Open combustion 3. Click File > New. In the New dialog, name the composite GreenScreen. In the Format Options field, accept NTSC 640 x 460 (the default). In the lower-left corner of the dialog window, click the Duration field and drag the mouse to set the Length to 302 frames. Make sure Mode is set to 3D, and then click OK. The Favorites pop-up window will appear. Close it without selecting anything.

ON THE CD

2. In the Workspace, right-click the Composite and from the pop-up menu select Import Footage. Browse to the Chap16\Images folder on the companion CD-ROM and load ChinaGate.jpg. Then, right-click again on Composite and select Import Footage. This time, browse to the same folder and load GrenScrn3.avi. Both image layers will load with the GrenScren3.avi image showing in the viewport, as shown in Figure 16.3.

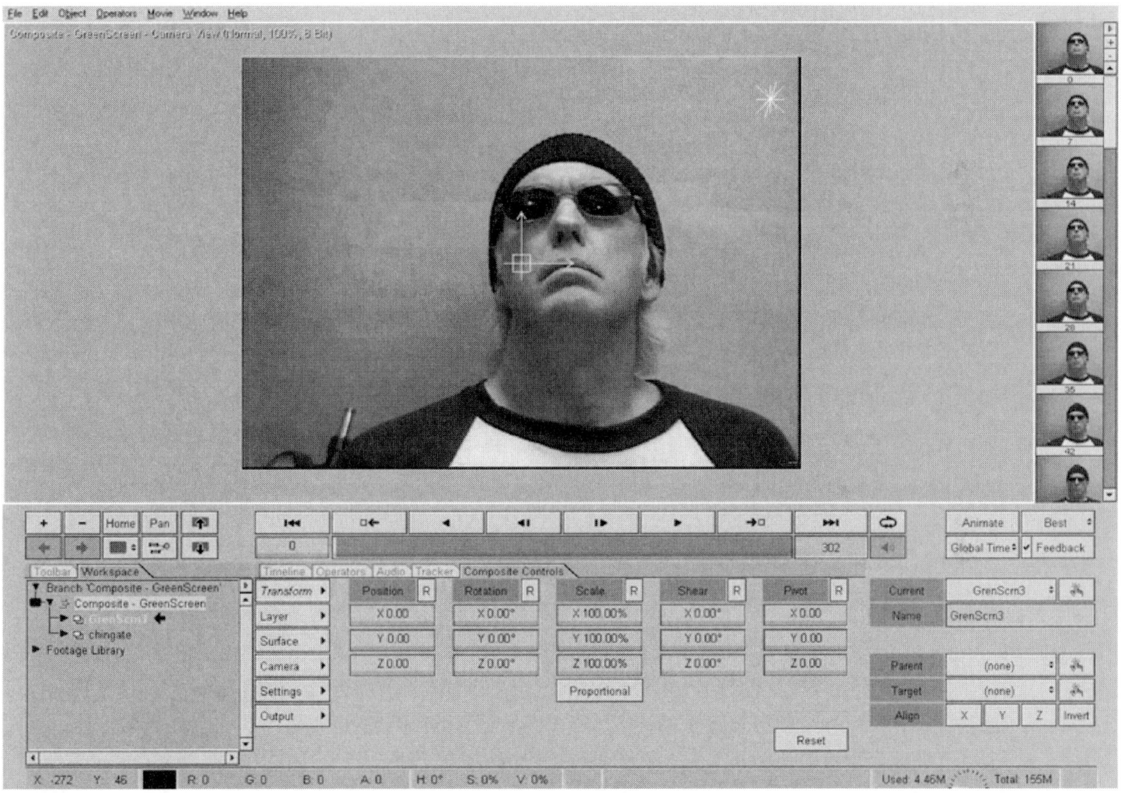

FIGURE 16.3 The combustion 3 interface with green-screen footage loaded.

3. In the Workspace, double-click ChinaGate. Notice that the ChinaGate background image now automatically spans 302 frames just as the GrenScrn3 footage does. Now you are ready to apply a Keying Operator to the GrenScrn3 footage.
4. Double-click GrenScrn3 footage in the Workspace to display it. Right-click on GrenScrn3, and then from the pop-up menu select Operator >

Keying > Discreet Keyer. The Keyer will load. The image will shift to a darker color, and the Keyer Controls menu will be displayed, as shown in Figure 16.4.

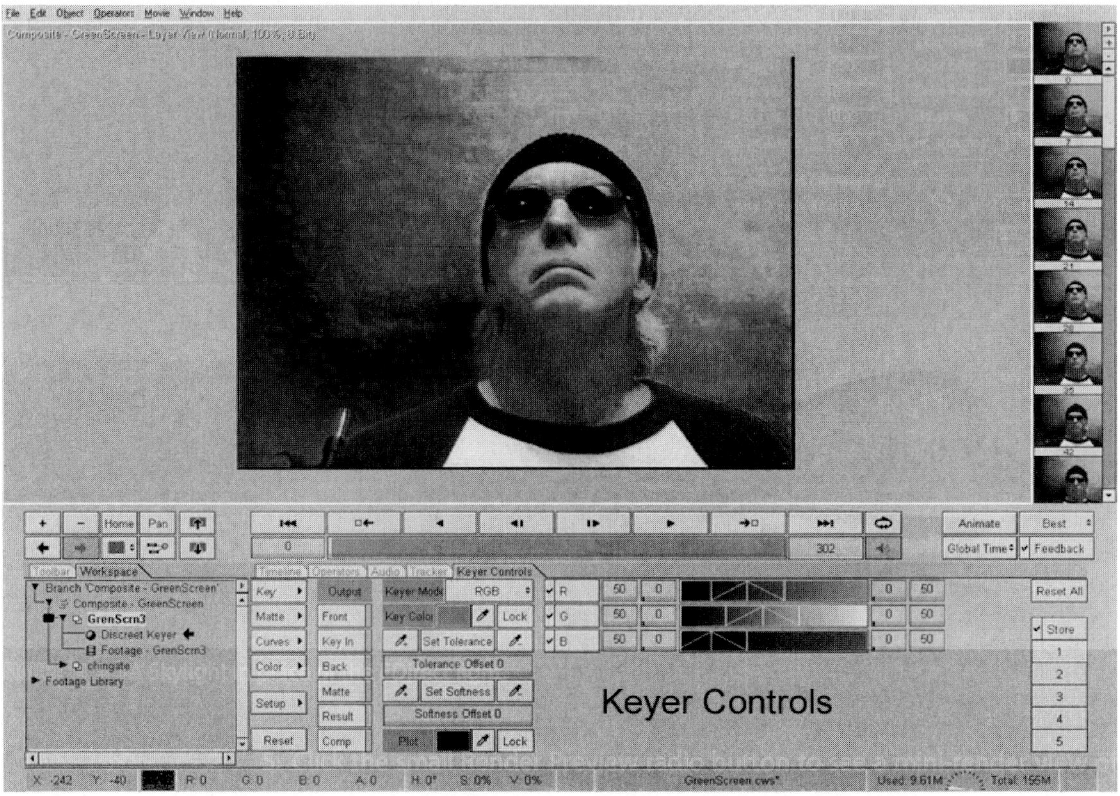

FIGURE 16.4 The Discreet Keyer applied to the GrenScrn3.avi footage, with the Keyer Controls.

5. To show two windows, go to the Tool Panel, and then below the Home button, click and slide the cursor down to the two side-by-side image icons. In order to create a matte, you must sample the color of the green background. In the Keyer Controls, click the Key Color eyedropper, hold down the Control key, and then click and drag in the green-screen area to sample the green tones. Then, under Output, click Result.
6. You will see a partial key created that shows the background image, which still leaves some large areas unkeyed, as shown in Figure 16.5. This points

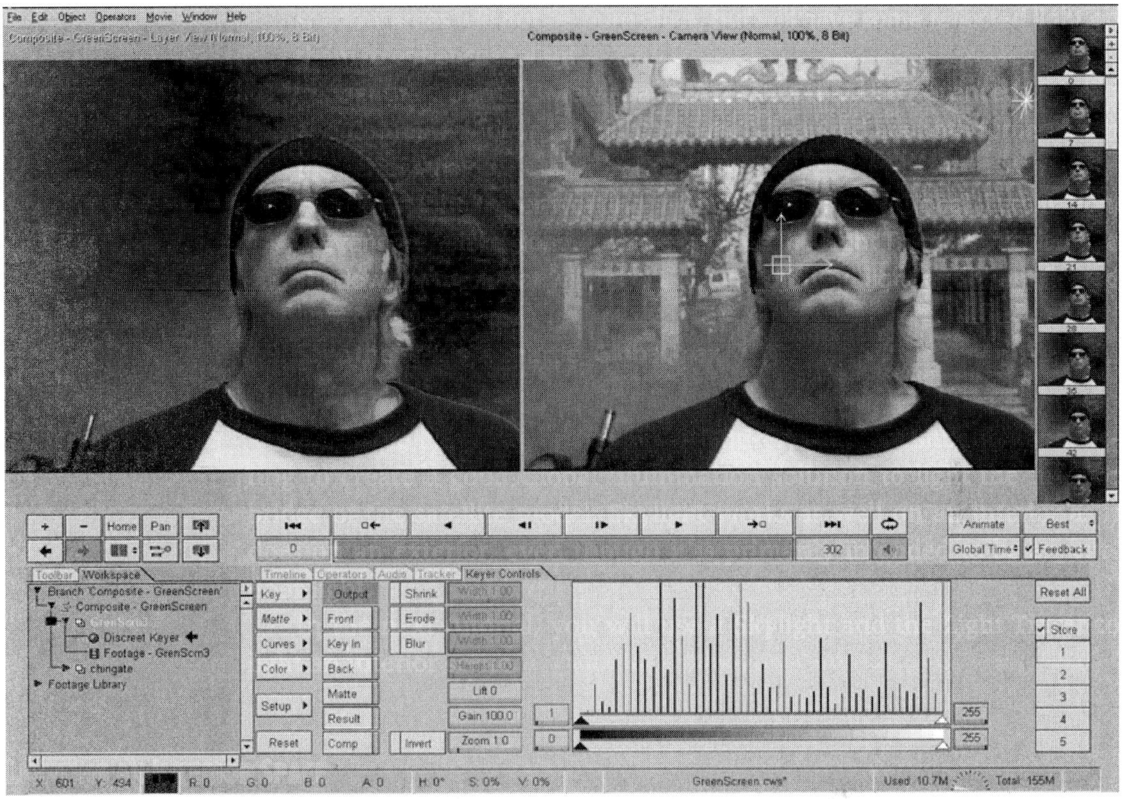

FIGURE 16.5 The Discreet Keyer applied to the GrenScrn3.avi footage, before adjustment.

out a major problem with the footage: it is much too dark and much too unevenly lit. This demonstrates the problems you face if the original lighting on the green backing was too weak or uneven.

7. By adjusting the RGB color ranges of the Key sample, as shown in Figure 16.6, you will be able to create a slightly better matte. However, it is nearly impossible to adjust enough to get rid of all the brownish-green shadow areas in the background without causing damage to the skin and other areas of the image.
8. A possible solution is to try color suppression. The problem with using color suppression on this footage is that the shaded area color on the face is modified when you suppress the brownish shade tones in the green background, damaging the mid-tones of the face.

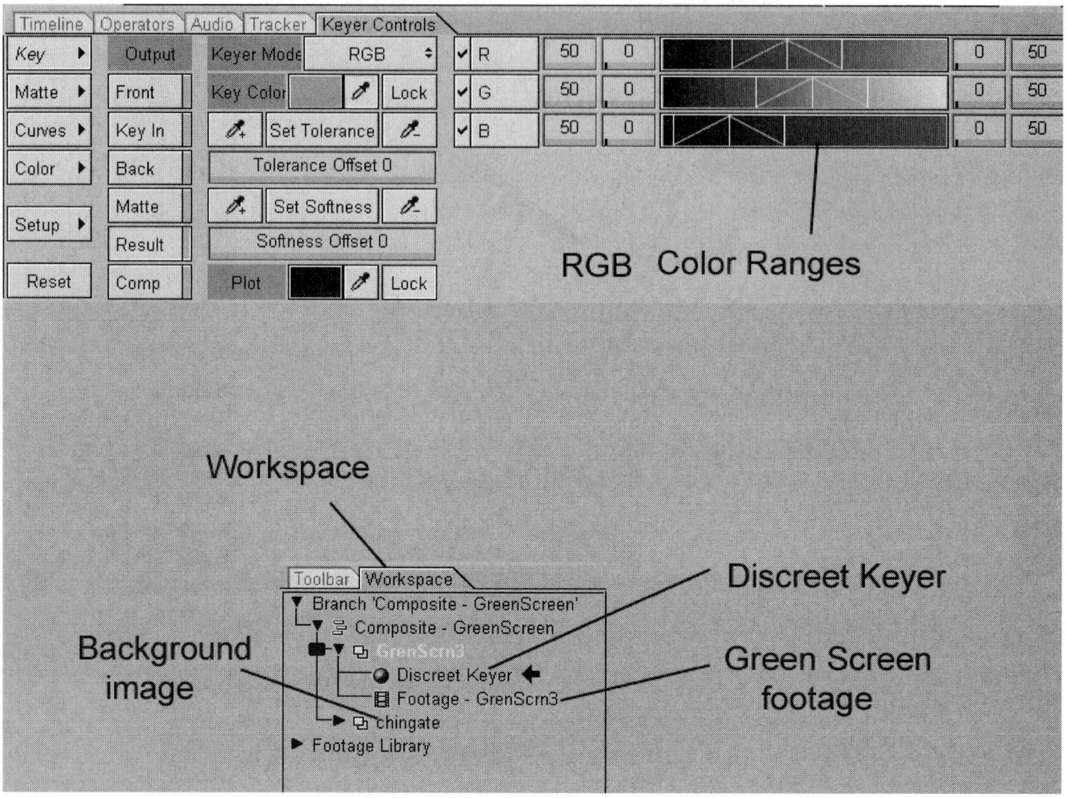

FIGURE 16.6 The Discreet Keyer Controls and the Workspace.

9. A realistic work-around for this sequence is to create an animated mask that tightly outlines the head, leaving only a small part of the green background as an edge around the figure to key out, as shown in Figure 16.7. To do that, go to the Workspace and place a Draw Mask operator on the GrenScrn3 footage below the Discreet Keyer. Then, use the Polygon/Bézier Mask Tool to click points around the actor and outer edges of the image. Complete the circle to generate the mask.
10. Turn on the Animate button and move the mask points every 15 to 20 frames to animate the mask following the edge of the head.
11. This tutorial demonstrates that it is sometimes better to use an animated mask to cut out the green, than to try to key out a bad green background.
12. Create an animated mask for the entire sequence, and then key out the thin green edge and suppress the green spill around the actor. Render the composite and save the Workspace file as GreenScreen2.cws.

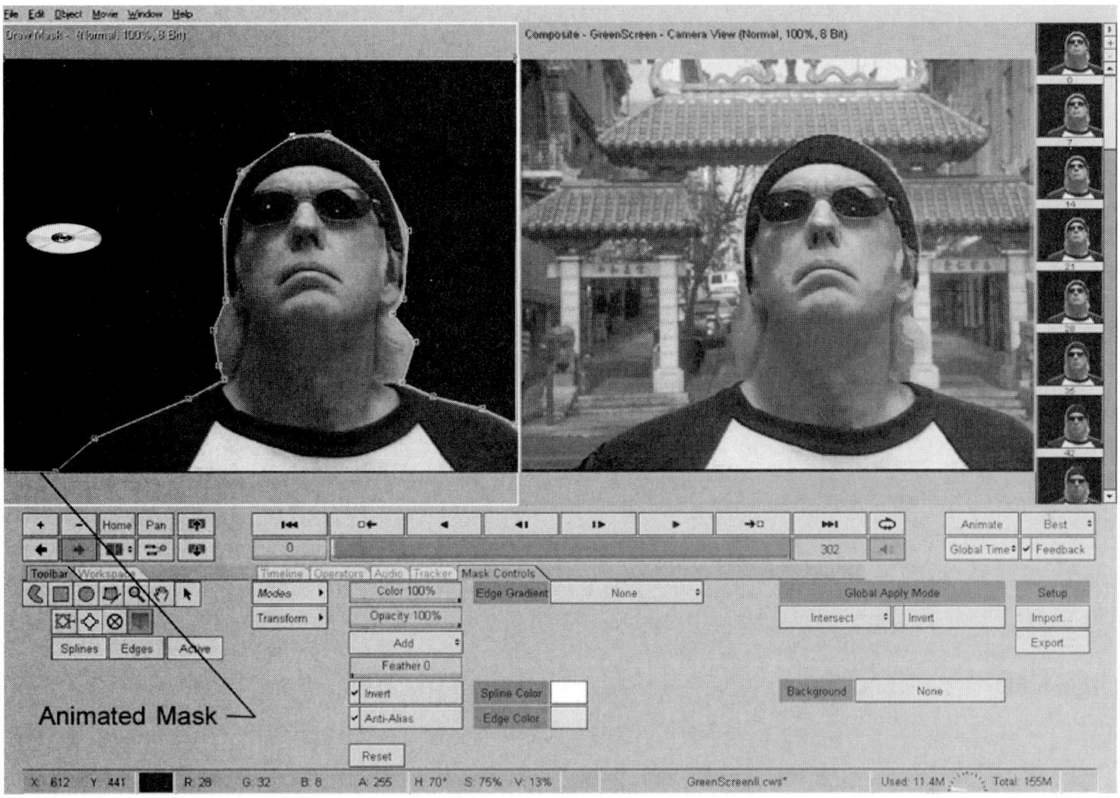

FIGURE 16.7 Using an animated mask to get rid of a bad green-screen background.

In the next tutorial, you will import the alien ship crash elements you rendered in the previous tutorial, create a 3D composite, and add a particle visual effect.

Adding 2D Visual Effects

Combustion 3 has a powerful 2D particle system generator that can be used to enhance footage and add 2D visual effects to footage rendered in 3ds max. The footage you will load and composite here was rendered in Chapter 14, "Lighting and Rendering," in the tutorial entitled "Rendering the Alien Ship Crash."

The object of this tutorial is to explore using the Particle Operator to add visual effects such as 2D water spray to an image sequence.

TUTORIAL 16.2 CREATE A COMPOSITE WITH PARTICLE EFFECTS

To create a composite:

1. Open combustion 3. Click File > New. In the New dialog, name the composite Ship_Crash. In the Format Options field, click NTSC (the default) and select Custom. Click and drag the mouse in the Width field to set Width to 320. Then, click and drag the Height field and set Height to 240. In the lower-left corner of the dialog window, click the Duration field and drag the mouse to set the Length to 451 frames. Make sure Mode is set to 3D, and then click OK, as shown in Figure 16.8, example 1. The Favorites pop-up window will appear. Close it without selecting anything.

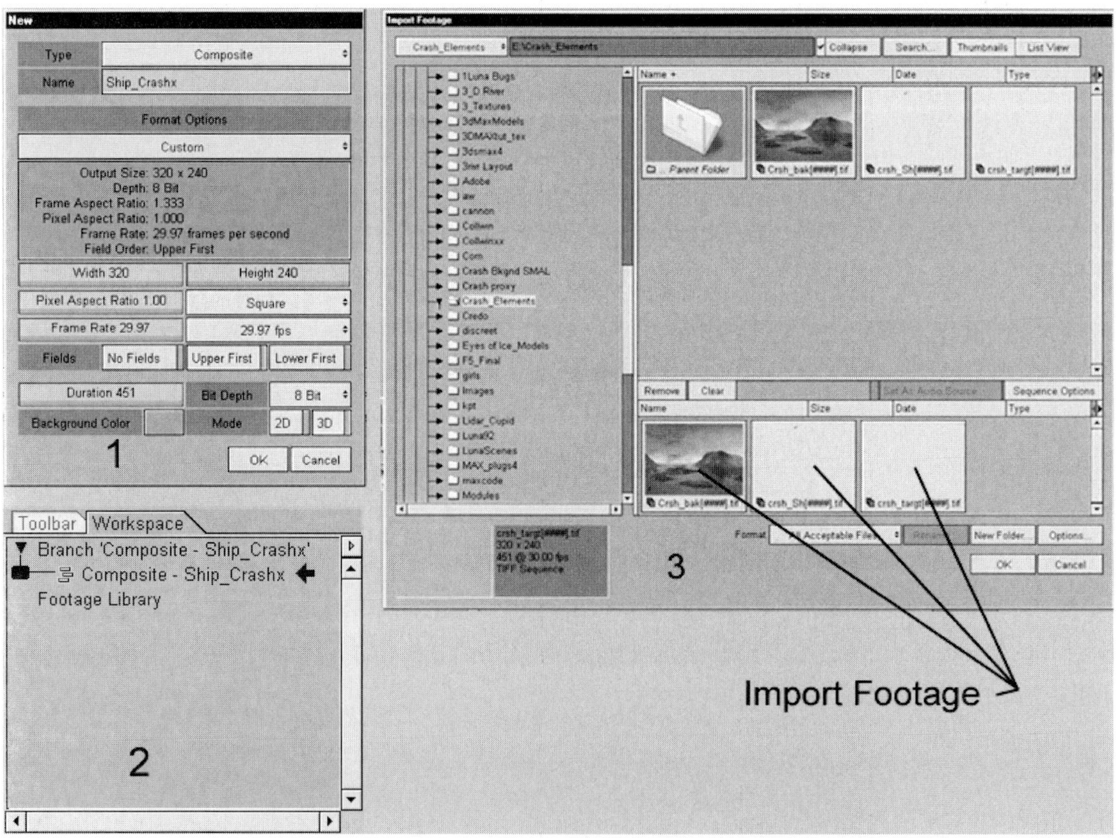

FIGURE 16.8 Menus for setting the size and length of the composite, and loading footage.

2. Notice that the Workspace already shows three entries: Branch Composite —Ship_Crash, Composite—Ship_Crash, and the Footage Library, as shown in Figure 16.8, example 2. Select Composite, and then click File > Import Footage (Ctrl-I). When the Import Footage file browser opens, locate the directory where you placed the image sequences.

ON THE CD

You can find these image sequences on the companion CD-ROM in the Chap16\Ch14_Render folder. Copy them to your hard drive. Do not try to work directly from the directories on the CD-ROM because playback performance in combustion 3 will be seriously degraded, and you will not be able to save any changes or additions.

3. In combustion 3, the image sequences are called "clips." For this tutorial, you will load only the background clip. To do that, click Crsh_Bak0900. A preview of the clip will appear in the queue of the Import Footage browser, as shown in Figure 16.8, example 3. Click OK to load the background into the composite.

You can scrub the mouse cursor across any of the previews in the browser to see the animation play or to review what is in the image sequence or clip.

4. After the clip is loaded, you will see it displayed in the interface. To enlarge it, click the + button above the Workspace. Next, go into the Workspace and click the arrow beside Composite to open it and see the Footage—Crsh_bak(###) layer, as shown in Figure 16.8, example 2.
5. Once the layer is loaded, right-click the footage. In the pop-up menu, select Add Operator. Then, from the Operator menu, select Paint. Paint along with a Paintbrush icon will appear in the Workspace. Next, click Paint, and right-click to again Add Operator. This time, add a Particle operator, as shown in Figure 16.9, example 1. The Paint operator will not interfere with the particles and will allow you to use the Paint tools to add details to the bottom of the ship over a large number of frames.
6. Double-click the Particle operator to make it active. You should see a black rectangle appear to the left of any active operator when you double-click it, which indicates that it is ready to be modified. Click the Particle Controls tab just below the timeline. The pre-set Particle Library menu will open. This library contains a wide variety of ready-made animated 2D particle effects that you can apply and modify to your needs, shown in Figure 16.9, example 2.

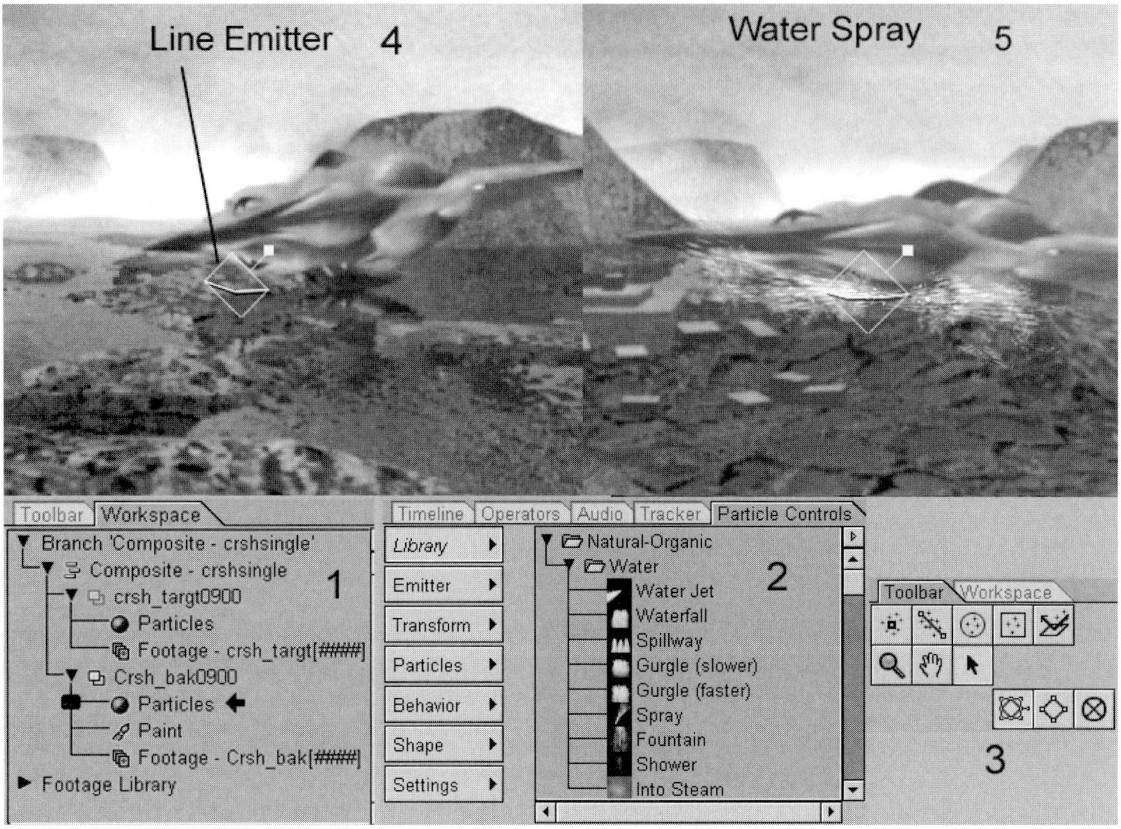

FIGURE 16.9 Adding a water spray particle emitter to the background layer.

7. In the Particle Library, click the upper-right arrow to select additional library pages. From that list, select Natural-Organic > Water. In the Water list, click Spray. Click the Enable button above the Preview window to the right of the Library window. It should begin to display an animated preview of the water Spray effect. You have now selected Spray as your particle type.
8. Move the Time Slider to frame 327 where the bottom of the alien ship is just contacting the water. At the top of the Workspace, click the Toolbar tab to open the particle system tools. Select the Line Emitter tool and then draw a line under the ship at frame 12,543 where it just touches the water, as shown in Figure 16.9, example 4.
9. The particles will begin to emit at the frame where you drew the emitter. To set the duration of the water spray, advance the Time Slider until you see the ship impact the island beside the ruined temple at frame 346. You should see a fairly uncontrolled spray of particles coming from the emitter.

To control its size, angle, and duration, click the Emitter button to the right of the Particle toolbar to open the Particle Controls. To taper off the spray and stop it gradually, you animate the Number value. Notice that there is a button labeled "Number" near the center of the Particle Controls.

10. Turn on the Animate button above the Preview window. Back up to frame 335, and then click and drag to the left to change the default Number 215% to 100%. Then, move to frame 346 and reduce the Number value to 0%. This will taper off the number of particles that the emitter outputs.
11. Turn off Animate, and then change the angle of the spray by clicking the Emission Angle button in the Particle Controls. Set the Emission Angle to 9 degrees, and play the animation from frame 310 to frame 360 to see the results, as shown in Figure 16.9, example 5.
12. Save the Workspace by clicking File > Save Workspace As, and name the file Ship_Crash01.cws.

To finish this shot and add all the particle effects, simply repeat the procedures you just performed with different particle emitters and particle effects from the library. You can use the same procedures as explained in the preceding tutorial to create a trailing smoke particle effect in the Tracking Sphere layer. Then, you can load the Ship Only layer as a mask over the top layer and render the scene to see the final effect.

ON THE CD

To see the finished scene and examine the finished project file, load the Ship_Crash_Final.cws file from the Chap16 folder on the companion CD-ROM. To see a rendered movie of this scene, load the Ship_Crash.cws movie file from the Chap16 folder on the companion CD-ROM.

MESH PAINT IN 3DS MAX

Combustion 3 is not a plug-in, but it can function like a plug-in to expand 3ds max's capabilities. Combustion 3 is a stand-alone program for compositing and visual effects, but it can function like a plug-in to add mesh painting to 3ds max. Combustion 3 gives you the ability to paint texture maps, bump maps, and specular maps directly on the surface of 3D models in the 3ds max viewport, as shown in Figure 16.10. To do this, both 3ds max and combustion 3 must be running, and the Max combustion material must be applied as active in the 3ds max Materials Editor.

The preceding tutorial only touched on one of the ways in which combustion 3 can be used. Combustion 3 is closely integrated with 3ds

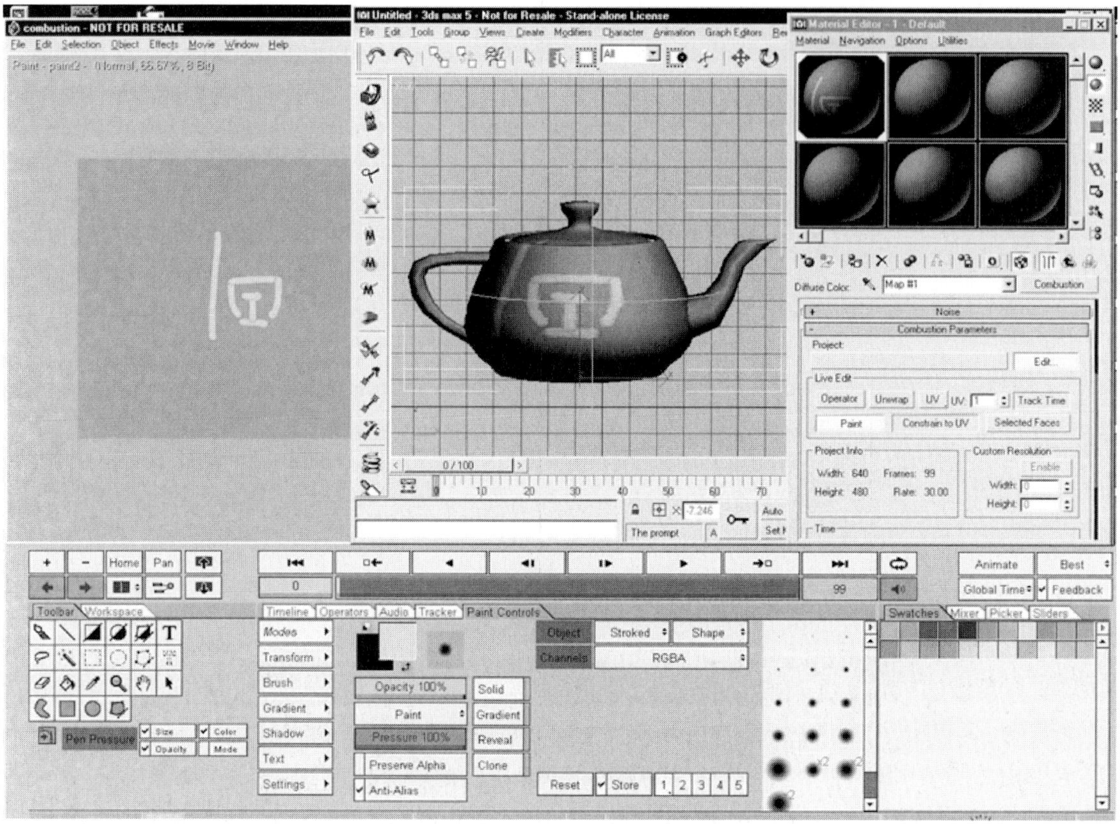

FIGURE 16.10 Using combustion 3 with 3ds max 6 for 3D mesh painting.

max. For example, there is a combustion material in 3ds max that creates a link between combustion and 3ds max when the combustion map type is chosen as the Diffuse Map. To examine this capability, first start combustion 3, create a new Paint Workspace, and name it Texture. Then, start 3ds max and open the 3ds max Materials Editor.

To test the paint capabilities in 3ds max, create a sphere in any viewport and apply mapping coordinates. Next, click the Get Map icon beside the Diffuse color swatch. The Material/Map Browser will open and you will see combustion as a material type. Select it and drag it onto the material sample sphere, which will then turn black. With both 3ds max and combustion open and running at the same time, you can then go to the combustion Parameters drop-down menu in the Materials Editor and click the Edit button.

Once combustion is recognized, click the Paint button to start using combustion to paint texture maps right inside the 3ds max viewport. You can use the mouse cursor or a Wacom pad to paint directly on the surface of a 3D object. This 3D mesh painting generates brushstrokes that are echoed in combustion 3, which can be saved as texture, bump, specular, or displacement maps.

Once everything is put together in combustion 3, it is ready to be output to film or video.

THE EDIT OPERATOR

Added to combustion 3 is a new Edit Operator that closes a major gap in the coverage of post-production functions. If you are working on a clip and need to add a cross dissolve or you need to ripple cut a few short clips together, the Edit Operator gives you the capability to do most standard editing operations, as shown in Figure 16.11.

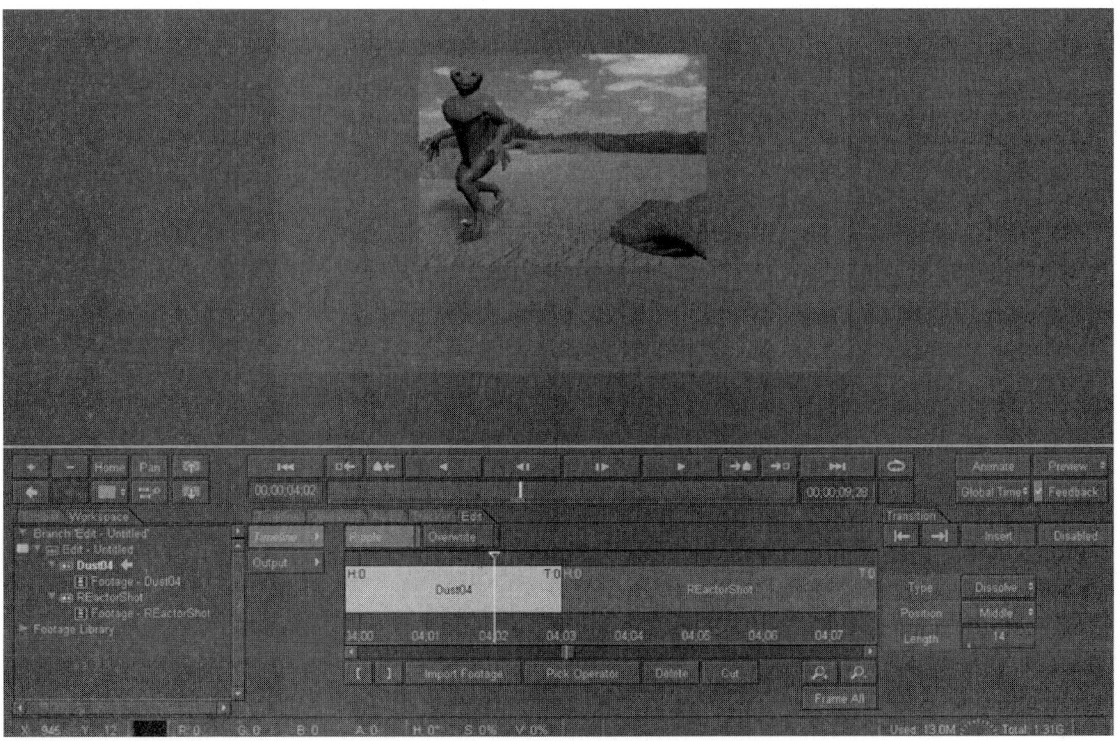

FIGURE 16.11 Creating a dissolve between two clips using the Edit Operator.

For multilayer editing, you can use the compositing tools along with the Edit Operator to do the same work that would have been previously done by a dedicated editing package. By using the combustion 3 Edit Operator, you keep everything in house and speed up production.

POST PRODUCTION

The final step in the animated filmmaking process is post production. This is where all of the animated footage and the visual effects elements come together. The post-production process includes editing, compositing, 3D and 2D visual effects integration, lighting and color correction, adding motion blur and atmosphere, dialog voice-over, sound effects, and music. The post-production team works with the editor and the director to smooth transitions from scene to scene, insert new footage, and correct errors in animation, lighting, and color. This ensures that the story flows cleanly from shot to shot and builds to an exciting conclusion.

OUTPUTTING ANIMATION AND VISUAL EFFECTS TO FILM

Imagica, an optical and digital visual effects company in Los Angeles, California, is one of the premiere facilities that offers film printing from digital files in the Hollywood area.

They can output digital files to a range of film formats, including 35mm, 65mm, and 70mm. Digital output from animation and visual effects studios comes to them on digital tape in many different formats. The oldest tape format still in use is the Exabite tape format. It has been around for at least 15 years and is a low-capacity slow tape that requires an extended time to transfer the digital data to the server that will control the printing of the images to film. The best and fastest tape formats in use are the DTL and the DTF digital tape formats from Sony.

The workflow is listed here:

1. The digital tape arrives.
2. It is put into the tape deck.
3. The data is loaded into the server computer into massive storage hard drives. (Companies like Imagica have many terabytes of storage space that allows them to work on many shows at the same time.)
4. A script is written to control the output to film recorders.

5. The script is run, which sends the data to one or more Solitare 3 CRT film recorders.
6. The film printers output film negative, which is then processed.
7. The negative then goes to a large film lab such as CFI in Hollywood where an answerprint is made.
8. The answerprint is then projected to check the image. They are usually viewed by the staff of the animation company, Imagica's client, at Imagica's projection facility. This film becomes the dailies that are viewed by the animators and the director at the animation company.

The work done at Imagica, and facilities like it, focuses on motion picture and television production, but they also do visual effects and short film projects. In most of the major cities in the United States, there are companies that can offer digital output to film on projects of any size. If your project is a short film, or perhaps a short animation or visual effect for a commercial, you might decide to take it directly to video tape rather than to film. In many cases, studios will rent a Beta-SP or a DigiBeta recorder and output the final computer imagery to tape themselves. Whatever the size of the project or the chosen output media, programs like combustion 3 make getting your project finished and ready for final output more efficient.

CONCLUSION

In this chapter, you worked in combustion 3 keying a green-screen shot. Then, you applied 2D particle effects to a scene that was animated and rendered in 3ds max. In the next chapter, you will work with some of the plug-in programs that are available for 3ds max 6.

CHAPTER

17

PLUG-INS

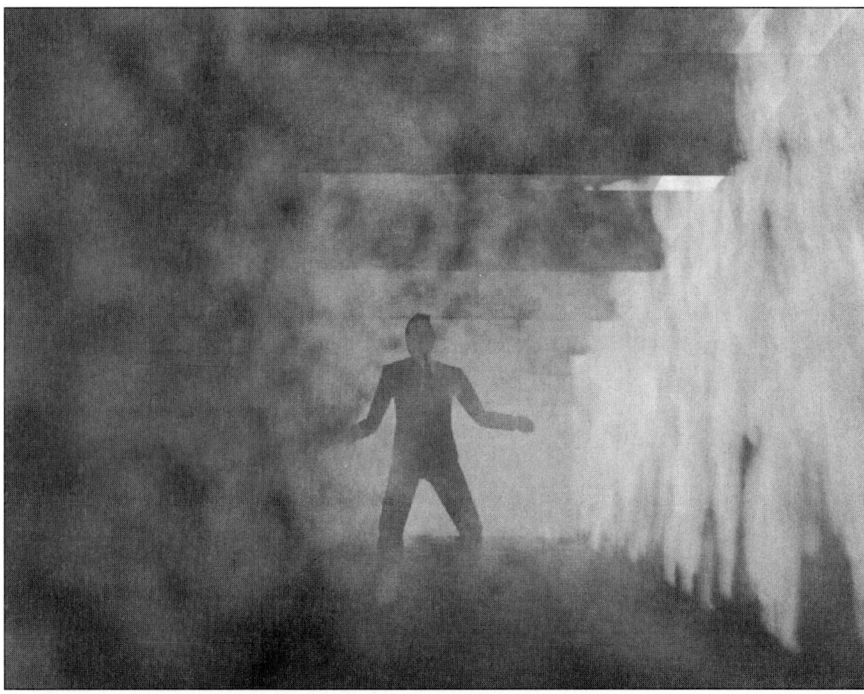

3ds studio max is designed with an open architecture that lets any developer write a plug-in that expands the capabilities of 3ds max. At the time of this writing, there are numerous third-party and freeware plug-ins available for 3ds max 6. Third-party vendors such as Digimation, Cebas, and others have extensive offerings that range from hair and fur plug-ins, to smoke generators and dynamic clothing packages. For a list of additional plug-ins and plug-in vendors, see Appendix B. Demo versions of all Digimation plug-ins are available for download from the www.digimation.com Web site.

CHARACTER STUDIO 4

Discreet character studio 4 is a nonlinear character animation plug-in that integrates seamlessly into 3ds max and gives you crowd animation with artificial intelligence, obstacle avoidance, flocking, and individual scriptable behaviors. This plug-in is covered in Chapter 15, "character studio 4."

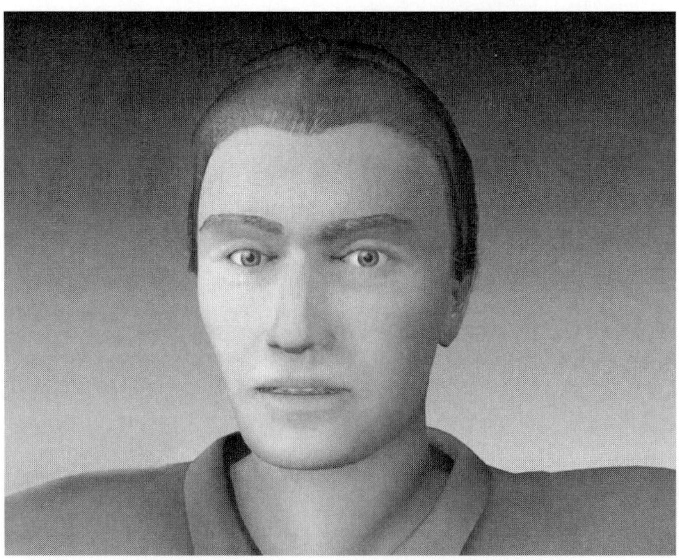

FIGURE 17.1 Shag Hair creates hair from a reference spline.

Shag Hair

Shag Hair, from Digimation, was used to create the hair and the fur, and the grass on the ground for the characters and the environments in the film *Homing Instinct*. This plug-in program is accessed through the Environment Effects menu in 3ds max 6 (Figure 17.1).

To put hair on the character models, a separate scalp mesh was created and positioned inside the head. It was then chosen as the hair emitter object. A Hair model was made from a spline that was linked to the scalp, and Shag Hair used it as a pattern to generate all of the hair on the head. An invisible Hair Cutter box was used to trim the unwanted hair by the neck, and create a hairstyle. Shag Hair is fully dynamic and reacts to gravity and wind. It has a special Hair Shader material that can create individual highlights on each hair and generate natural shadows for a life-like appearance. Shag Hair uses hair vectors to control the direction of the hair. In the next tutorial, you will create hair for Dr. Quin using the Shag Hair plug-in from Digimation.

The Shag Hair Plug-In

Shag Hair is a plug-in program that is designed to create long hair on characters. The hair can be shaped by creating a spline shape, which the hair uses to determine the shape of the hair and its length. Hair length and density can be controlled using grayscale maps loaded into a Multi-Subobject material. The hair can get its color either from the diffuse color swatches in the Shag Hair Modifier, or by applying the Shag Hair Shader type in the Materials Editor. Cutter objects, which are usually modified boxes or sculpted spheres, can be used to cut and style the hair. Attractors can be used to create clumping to simulate wet hair. Hair vectors can be used to control the angle of the hair or to cause the hair to lay against the head in a particular direction.

Shag Hair obeys the laws of physics and will react to forces such as wind and the Dynamics controls in the Dynamics menu in the Shag Hair rollout menu, such as Mass, Gravity, and Inertia. By running a dynamics simulation, you can cause the hair to fall naturally, and to lag behind the movement of the head, giving it a realistic appearance and behavior.

In the next tutorial, you will create a Scalp object to act as an Emitter object for the hair.

TUTORIAL 17.1 CREATE A NURBS SCALP TO USE WITH THE SHAG HAIR PLUG-IN

To create a scalp:

ON THE CD

1. Load the GenMan811.max scene file from the Chap17 folder on the companion CD-ROM. In the front view, zoom in on the character's head, and then select the head and Hide Unselected. Click Zoom Extents Selected.
2. To place the hair exactly where you want it, you will create a Scalp object. The hair will then be applied to the scalp, not to the original head. It is a good idea to turn off the Skin Modifier and the Relax Modifier during the following steps.

Shag Hair will not perform correctly when a scalp is made by cloning the original patch surface of the head. After experimentation, it was determined that Shag Hair works very well in the scene on a new Editable Mesh scalp. It was decided to create a NURBS (Non-Uniform Rational B-Spline) surface scalp and then convert it to an Editable Mesh. NURBS were selected because it is quick and easy to create a scalp by snapping NURBS splines on the patch head and then U-Lofting the scalp object from the curves. You start this process by first snapping a normal spline all the way around the head to draw the hairline. Once the hairline spline is on the head surface, you can turn the head at different angles to see if you are happy with the shape of the hairline. Then, you snap on the NURBS point curves and loft the scalp surface.

3. To snap a hairline to the head, click the 3D Snap icon in the Main toolbar, and then right-click it and set the Grid and Snap Settings to Vertex, Edge, Face, Midpoint, and Center Face. Make sure Grid Points is off. This setting lets you create an accurate line on the head.
4. Click the Create tab, click Shapes > Line, and in the Creation Type drop-down menu, select Initial Type = Smooth, and Drag Type = Smooth. Next, position the cursor about one "nose length" above the brow on the forehead. You should see a blue square wherever the cursor is. Click there to start the spline, and then click a row of points that go toward the ear, following a typical hairline. Continue around the sideburn area, and then up over the ear and down to the back of the neck. Right-click to end the spline creation, as shown in Figure 17.2, example 1.
5. In the front view, select the new spline and then Mirror Clone it and move the cloned spline to the opposite side of the head. You should now have a hairline spline that runs all the way around the head. Right-click the Scalp head, select Properties, and turn on See Through. Now, Arc Rotate the

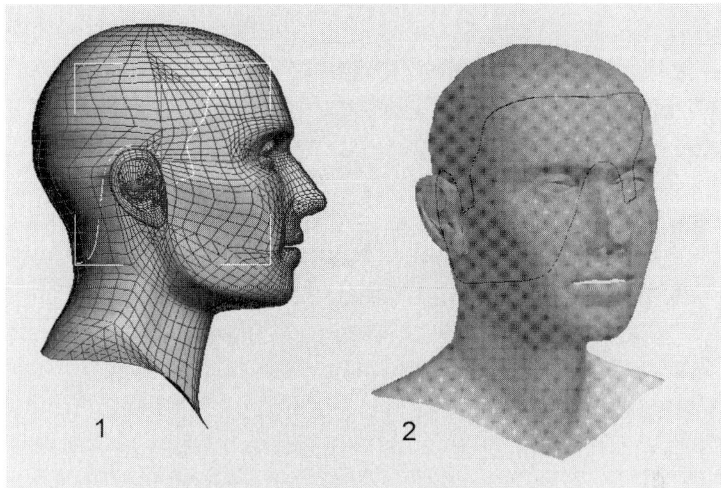

FIGURE 17.2 Creating a hairline and deleting everything but the scalp.

head around to see how the hairline looks, as shown in Figure 17.2, example 2. When you are satisfied with the hairline, you are ready to create the NURBS Scalp object.

6. To snap NURBS splines on the head, make sure that 3D Snap is turned on. Then, go to Create > Shapes and click the word Splines in the Object Type window. It will open and display the other choice: NURBS Curves. Select NURBS Curves, and then click the Point Curve button in the Object type drop-down menu.

NURBS surfaces behave best when all curves have about the same number of points. All curves must go in one direction. If any curves are reversed, the surface will twist into a knot.

7. You will snap a series of curves onto the head within the boundary formed by the hairline spline, starting at the front on the head and moving toward the back of the neck. Work in the left view, with the mesh shaded and Display Edges turned on. Start the first curve by clicking on the forehead just below the top of the head, right next to the hairline. Then, click repeatedly, about 10 times, along the edge of the head until you reach the back of the neck at the rear hairline, as shown in Figure 17.3, example 1.
8. Snap eight additional lines on the head starting at the front of the hairline, which cover the side of the head, as shown in Figure 17.3, example 2.

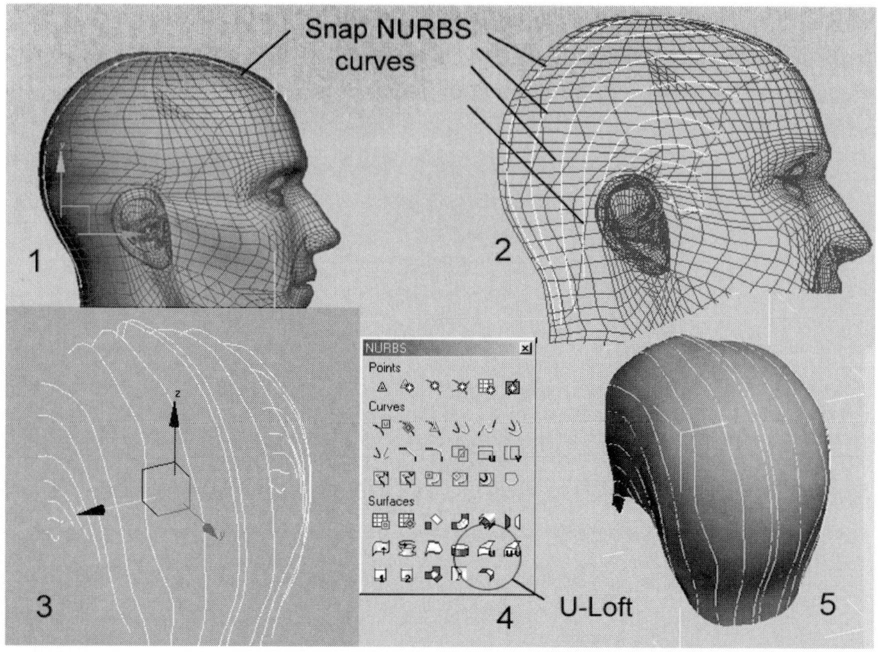

FIGURE 17.3 Creating the hairline.

Notice that the last small lines at the sideburns only have four points. The NURBS surface will still be created even though the number of points is reduced.

9. In the front view, select all of the new NURBS curves and Mirror Clone them. Click the Mirror Selected Objects icon, and then click Copy and OK. A new set of curves will appear. Use the Move tool to position them on the other side of the head surface. Next, in the left view, Arc Rotate the head up a little and snap a final curve down the center of the head to the back of the neck, as shown in Figure 17.3, example 3. You are ready now to attach the curves and loft them to create the NURBS scalp surface.
10. Hide the head and the hairline spline. Select one of the NURBS curves, and then click the Modify tab to open the NURBS Modifier. To attach them as one object, click the Attach Multiple button, select all the curves in the list, and click Attach. The object will take the name of the first curve you clicked.
11. To loft the NURBS surface, click the NURBS Creation Toolbox icon to open the NURBS menu. Arc Rotate the view so that you can see and select any curve easily. In the floating NURBS menu, locate the U-Loft icon, as shown

in Figure 17.3, example 4. Click the icon, and then click each curve sequentially starting with the small curve at the left sideburn. As you click each, the surface is generated between curves.

12. Continue clicking all the way over the head until you reach the right sideburn. This will create the lofted NURBS surface for the Scalp object, as shown in Figure 17.3, example 5. Now, convert the scalp to an Editable Mesh to automatically tessellate the surface, which will ensure even faces over the entire scalp. Right-click and select Convert to > Convert to Editable Mesh.
13. Re-name the Scalp object as Scalp Mesh. Save the scene file as GenManScalp.max.

In the next tutorial, you will create hair for Dr. Quin using Shag Hair. Shag Hair is a sophisticated hair generation program that creates hair with dynamic capabilities that can be styled to your taste. This tutorial assumes that you own Shag Hair and have installed it.

TUTORIAL 17.2 CREATE HAIR USING THE SHAG HAIR PLUG-IN

To create hair:

1. Load the GenManScalp.max scene, and maximize the front view. Unhide the Head object. Click Zoom Extents (Ctrl-Alt-Z). You should see the head, with the scalp sitting on it like a skull cap.
2. Select the Scalp object, and then Uniform Scale it down about 5% or until it just disappears inside the head. Next, turn off Edged Faces if it is on. Select the head, right-click, and select Properties. Turn on See Through and click OK. You should now be able to see the Scalp object inside the head. Right-click and select Freeze Selection.
3. Before applying Shag Hair, you need to create a spline that defines the shape of at least one hair. Switch to the left view. Create a spline by clicking on Create > Shape > Splines > Line, and then select Smooth as the Initial and Drag type. Click the cursor on the top of the scalp to start the spline, and then click three more times to draw a fairly short curved hair, as shown in Figure 17.4, example 1. Rename it Hair01.
4. Before the hair can be generated, you must apply the Model Hair Modifier to the spline. Select Hair01, and then click the Modifier List arrow and

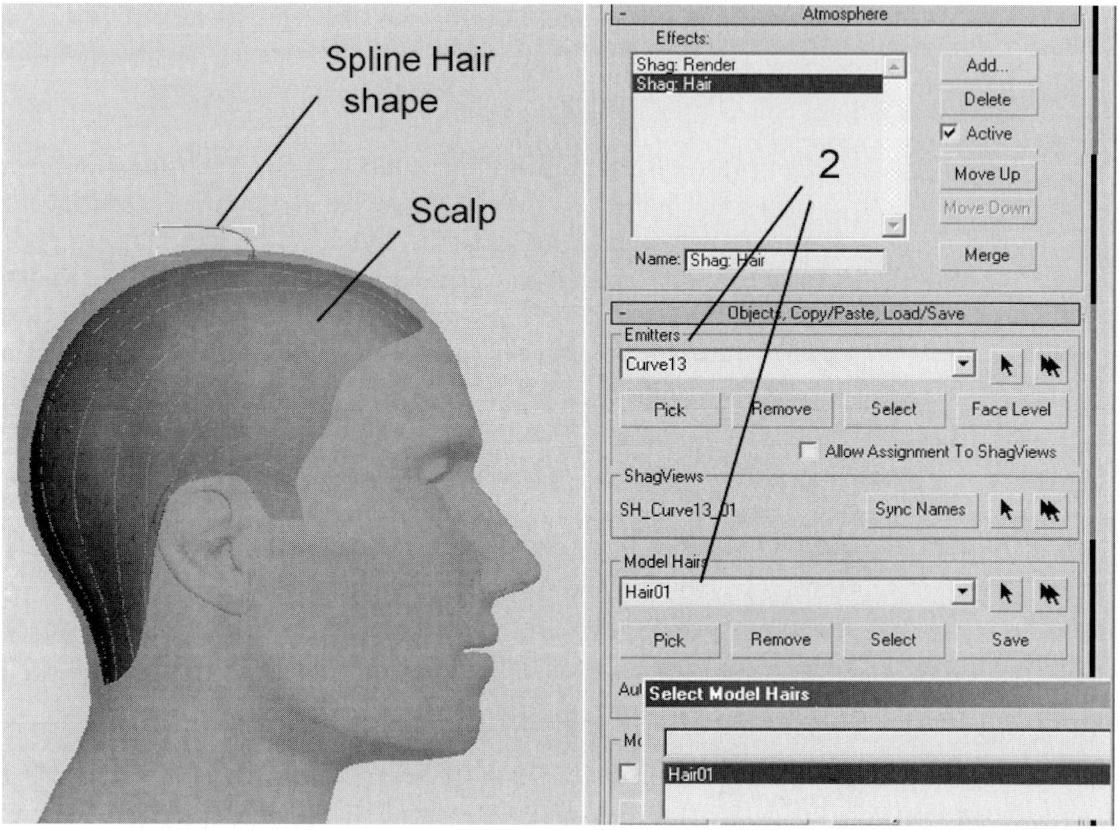

FIGURE 17.4 The head and scalp with the Shag Hair interface.

locate Model Hair. It is automatically applied. Apply Planar Mapping to the scalp, select the X-axis to project mapping coordinates from the side of the scalp, and unhide the eyes.

5. Shag Hair is an atmospheric effect and is located in the Rendering > Environment > Atmosphere > Effects menu. Click Render in the Main menu and select Environment. In the Environment > Atmosphere > Effects menu, click the Add button. In the Add Atmospheric Effect dialog, select the Shag Renderer, and click OK. It will appear in the Effects window. Click Add again, and then add Shag Hair.
6. Click Shag Hair to open the Shag Hair interface. There are a number of menus. The first menu is Objects, Copy/Paste, Load/Save. Below the first data entry field named Emitters, click the Pick button, and then select the

scalp in the left view. Then, in the second field called Model Hairs, click Pick, click Select, and in the pop-up list click on Hair01, and OK, as shown in Figure 17.4, example 2. Hair will immediately be generated that should cover the Scalp object.

7. Before rendering, you must reduce the number of hairs that will be generated by the Scalp object, and its thickness. In the Shag Hair interface, scroll to the Parameters roll-out menu, and in the Density menu box select Absolute and set it to 1.0. In Thickness, set Maximum to 0.03, and then in Curliness, click Enabled and set Turns to 1.5, as shown in Figure 17.5, example 1. Now render one of the views (F9).
8. It should render fairly quickly and you should see a full head of hair, as shown in Figure 17.5, example 2.
9. Save the scene file as GenManHair.max.

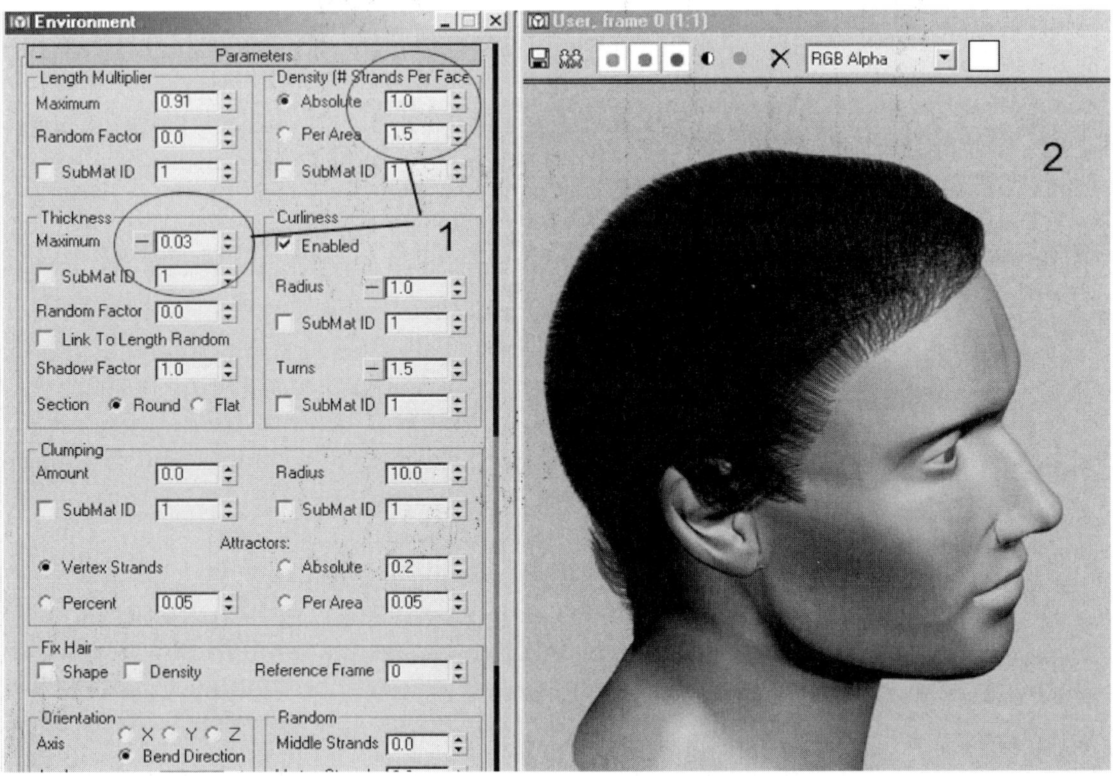

FIGURE 17.5 Setting the number of hairs per face and the hair thickness.

The hair style used for Dr. Quin is actually very conservative and does not complement his looks. This was done on purpose so that he would look a bit out-of-it compared to some of the other male characters, such as Chris Christianson, who has a big mop of blond hair. It was decided that because Xzulixia the vampire is capable of shape-shifting, she should have a number of different hair styles and colors. She wears many different styles in the film, ranging from a spikey Mohawk to a long ponytail. In the next tutorial, you will create a dynamic, full-bodied long hair style for her that moves as she turns her head.

Using Shag Hair for Dynamic, Long Hair

Animated hair makes a tremendous difference in how realistic a character looks. Stiff hair ends up resembling a hat more than hair. Long hair should move and fall on the shoulders like real hair when an animated character moves, and should obey the forces of gravity and wind. Shag hair can simulate the dynamics of long, soft hair as it reacts to gravity, inertia, and wind. You can add to the realism by using impact detection, clumping, hair vectors, and hair cutters to style the hair and keep it out of the face.

You can have a great deal more control over the shape and behavior of the hair if you use a number of splines to shape it. In the previous tutorial, you used only one spline to serve as the pattern for the hair shape. In this tutorial, you use four splines. Shag hair will fill in between the different shape splines and interpolate the length between multiple splines. This enables you to create many different hair styles by using different hair spline shapes and lengths on different areas of the head, as shown in Figure 17.6.

You can approach working with long hair in two different ways. You can try to put the hair on selected faces of the model you are working with by selecting some faces of the model's head. That will work, but the author has found that everything works quite slowly when you try to work on a scene that is already full of data and using up a chunk of RAM. The other alternative is to work out the hair style first on a simple sphere with selected faces that become the hair emitter. This works well if the sphere has been sculpted to fit the exact size of your model's head.

Note two benefits to the sphere hair emitter approach: first, there is no clutter in the scene and no sluggishness. Second, you can make a perfect hairline by cutting a line into the sphere in the shape you want the real model's hairline to be. Then you select the outlined scalp and scale

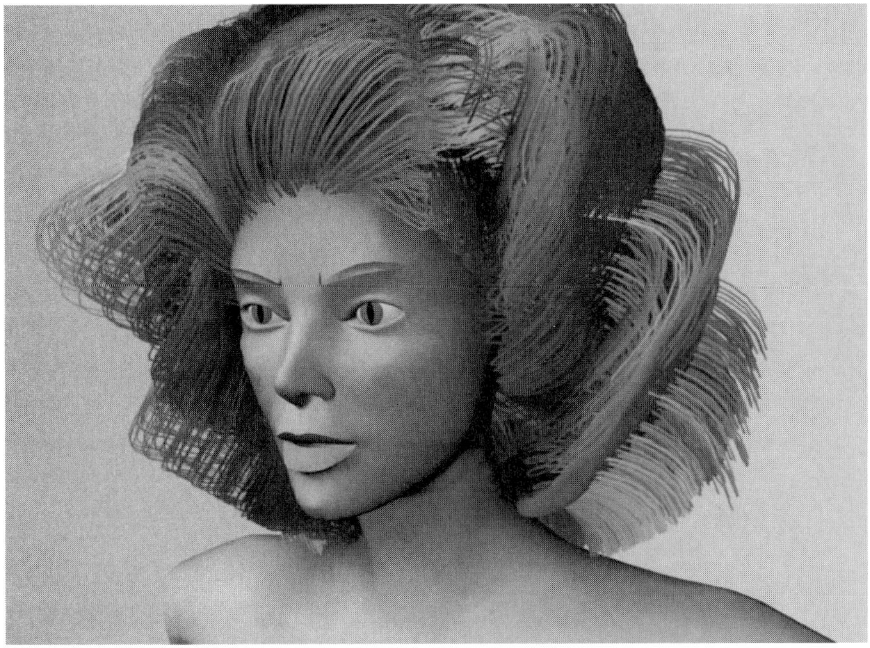

FIGURE 17.6 Many different hair styles are possible with shag hair.

the sphere down about 10% so it will fit inside your model's head. Once the hair is worked out on the sphere, and it behaves correctly in a dynamic simulation, the sphere and the Shag Hair splines are merged into the scene in which the original character model resides. The sphere is then placed inside the head of the character and linked to the skeleton's head bone, to be used as the Shag Hair emitter.

In the next tutorial, you will explore the process of setting up a dynamic long hair animation.

TUTORIAL 17.3 ANIMATING LONG HAIR

To create long hair:

ON THE CD

1. Load the Long_Hair.max file from the Chap17 folder on the companion CD-ROM. The file contains a polygonal head and splines on the scalp that are used as hair shape curves. If you get an "obsolete file" warning when you load the file, don't worry. Resave the file to your 3ds max 6\Scenes

working directory and it will work correctly as long as you have the max 6 version of Shag Hair installed in your plug-ins folder.

2. Four long splines are positioned on the head, as well as some simulated hair strands that are generated by Shag Hair. Notice also that there are a number of spheres around the face that can barely be seen. Three transparent spheres are used as "hair cutters" to keep the stray hair out of the face, as shown in Figure 17.7, example 1. Select the transparent spheres and hide them for now. The head is already animated and the basic hair shape and length has been determined by the hair splines. The splines have the Model Hair modifier applied to them to convert them to a form that Shag Hair can use in the hair dynamics solution. Their behavior is similar to a particle system. Model hairs can be affected by the same forces that affect particles such as gravity and wind.
3. All of the parameters for the shag hair can be found in the Rendering > Environment dialog. Shag Hair is an atmospheric effect, and both the Shag Render and the Shag Hair entries must show in the Atmospheric Effects window. Open the dialog and then click the Shag Hair option to open the roll-out menus. The first menu is the Objects Copy\Paste Load\Save menu,

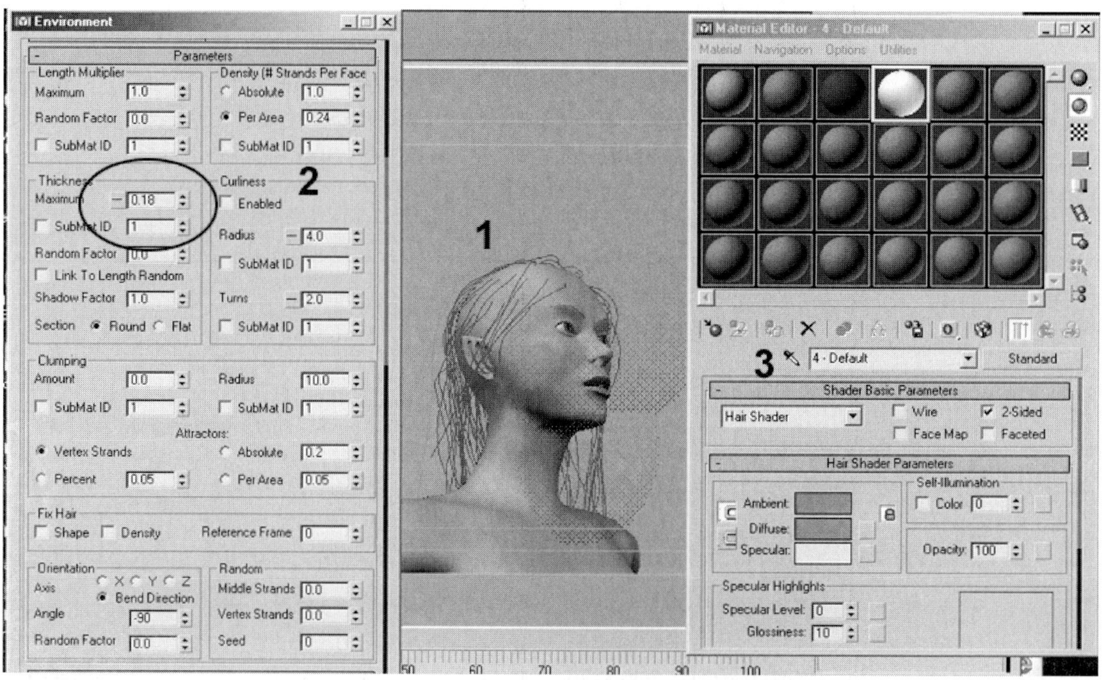

FIGURE 17.7 Hair splines positioned to create a long hair dynamic animation.

which is located above the Atmospheric Effects window, and might need to be opened manually. Here you select the hair emitter and the model hair splines that will be used in the hair simulation. Be sure that the Hair Cutter spheres are enabled in the Modeling Cutters section. The three Hair Cutter spheres should be selected and show in the Modeling Cutters list window.

The thickness of the hair is set in another menu called the Parameters menu, and has already been set to 0.18 units, as shown in Figure 17.7, example 2. A slight change in thickness will make a big difference in how good the hair looks. The length multiplier is set to 1.0, which means that the hair will be generated at the same length as the hair splines.

Your system Units Setup should be set to Max Generic International Units, as they are used in almost every tutorial in this book.

4. Included with Shag Hair is a special hair material called the Hair Shader. It enables you to set the hair color and modify the specular level. It can be found in the Shader Basic Parameters shader selection window of the Materials Editor, as shown in Figure 17.7, example 3. You cannot find it in the Maps Browser. It has nice highlights and gives the hair a very realistic look.
5. To create the animated hair simulation, you must enter the correct settings in the Dynamics menu. Start in the General section and turn on Pre-Calculated and Weighted (the defaults). Go down to the Collision Properties section and click the Select button. In the Select Collision Objects list, select XzuHead, and click Enabled. In addition, turn on Segment Collisions and Get Hair out of Colliders at Start, as shown in Figure 17.8, example 1.
6. In the Common Properties section of the Dynamics menu, click the Select button for Gravity, and in the dialog, select Gravity01. Then select Wind01 for the Winds entry, as shown in Figure 17.8, example 2. Be sure to enable them. The final setting is actually a graph in which you must modify the shape of a curve. To see the graph, go to the Weighted section of the Dynamics menu and click the Weights button, as shown in Figure 17.8, example 3.
7. The Weight Along Length graph will open. By default, the curve is backwards. It should be high on the left, not the right. Reverse the curve by selecting and moving the points on the graph line so that it matches the curve shown in Figure 17.8, example 4. Add points by clicking the curve. Now click the Inertia and Hardness buttons and reverse their curves the

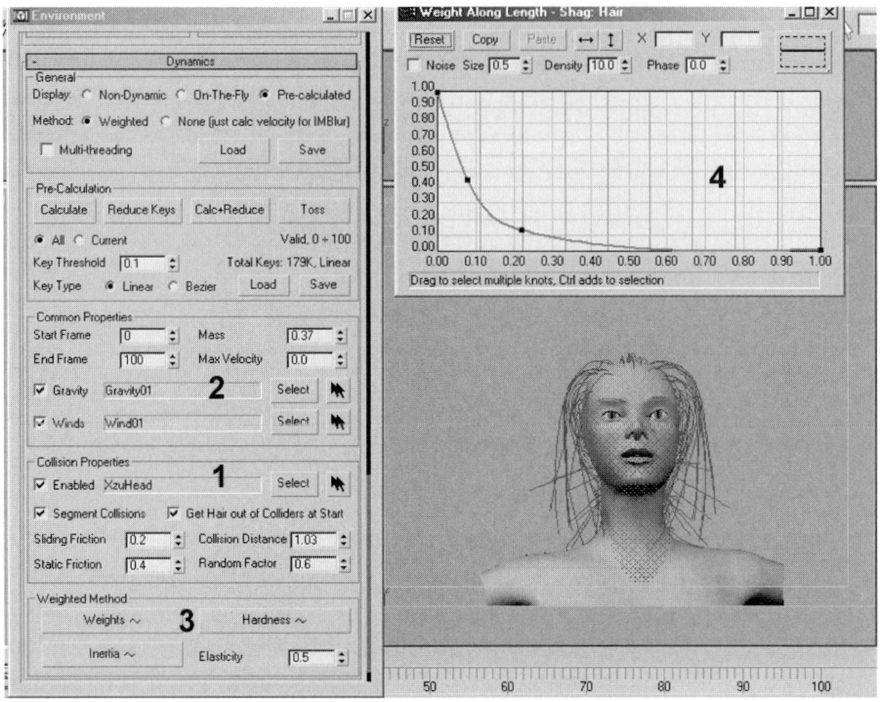

FIGURE 17.8 The Dynamic Hair Solver menu.

same way. All curves should be high on the left (Value = 1.00), and low on the right (Value = 0). If you do not do this, the hair will be stiff on the ends and flexible at the scalp.

8. Now you are ready to run the simulation. This is done by pressing the Calculate button in the Pre-Calculation section of the Dynamics menu. The calculation will run fairly fast and then you will be able to press Play and see how the hair behaves. Do that now. After it runs, you might find that the hair behavior is not as you want. You can change any of the variables. You can start by changing the Elasticity, or the two Friction values.
9. An important setting to look at is the Gravity setting, which should be set to a strength somewhere around 0.36. Changing this makes a big difference in the hair. It can be found by clicking Unhide by Name and then pressing the H key. Next select Gravity01 and open the Modifier Panel. The other important setting is the Wind strength, which is set to 0.95, and Turbulence, which is set to 1.44. Frequency is set to 0.22. By changing these settings, you can directly control the behavior of the long hair, as shown in Figure 17.9.

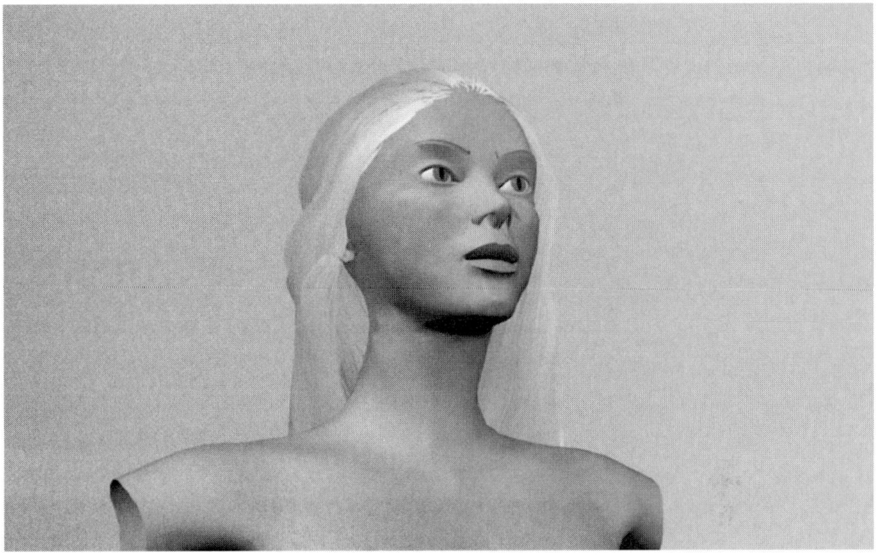

FIGURE 17.9 Xzulixia, with the finished dynamic, long hair.

10. Every time you want to re-run the simulation, you must click the Toss button in the Dynamics menu > Pre-Calculation section to clear out the old hair keyframes. Hair control is an art that is mastered by trial and error. Good luck. That concludes the Long Hair tutorial. Save your file as Long_Hair173.max.

    ON THE CD To see how the long hair behaves, load the LongHair.mov movie from the Chap17\Images folder on the companion CD-ROM.

In the next tutorial, you will work with the clothfx cloth simulation plug-in to discover how layers of cloth are animated.

CLOTHFX

The clothfx cloth simulation plug-in from Turbo Squid, *www.turbosquid.com,* has been used to create costumes for a number of excellent cinematic trailers for major game companies, including *Warcraft* from Blizzard Entertainment. A recent game cinematic using clothfx (formerly known as Stitch) was created with help of the author for the game *Grayhawk: The Temple of Elemental Evil,* from Troika Games. The cinematic movie can be seen at *http://grayhawkgame.com/movies*. Clothfx was also used to create numerous costumes for the main characters in the author's animated film *Homing Instinct*. Clothfx is a sophisticated cloth simulation software package that uses collision detection, springs, and dynamics to simulate the natural movement of cloth falling against a character's body.

Clothfx consists of two modifiers: GarmentMaker and clothfx. GarmentMaker is used to create cloth panels from splines and attach their seams together with Sewing Springs. Clothfx is then applied to pull the seams together using the Sewing Springs. Then, by running a local simulation, the garment is fitted to the figure, as shown in Figure 17.10. Clothfx lets you apply real physical properties to the cloth, such as gravity, friction, stretch, and stiffness.

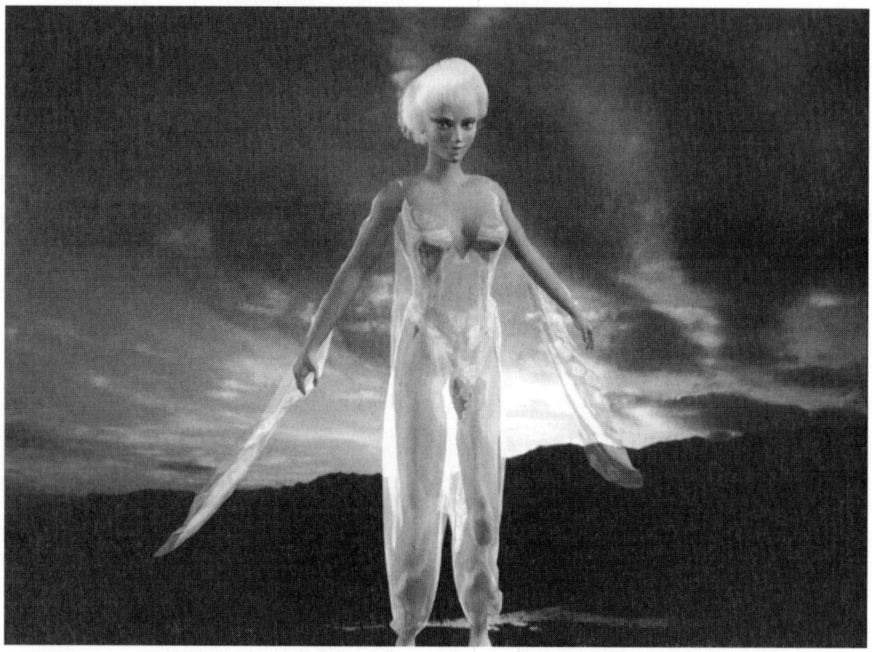

FIGURE 17.10 Xzulixia wearing a four-layer cloth costume.

You can choose from a range of pre-set cloth types, including silk, cotton, leather, wool, and rubber. Pockets and collars can be attached to the surface of the cloth to add details, and belts can be used to gather garments around a character's waist. Complicated costumes consisting of multiple layers of cloth can be created. You can create a costume consisting of pants or a skirt with an overlapping shirt or blouse, a coat that lies over that, and a scarf that lies over the head and drapes across the shoulders.

Clothfx was used to create fitted clothing for the Dancing Xzulixia character. Another example of a clothfx garment can be seen in the Color Plates section of this book. The dress Xzulixia wears in Color Plate 4 was made using GarmentMaker from spline shapes that were derived from a commercial dress pattern.

In the next tutorial, you will explore how clothfx is used to make a multilayered cloth costume. Xzulixia is animated doing a slow dance to demonstrate how the layers of cloth interact with each other. The costume design is similar to a "harem girl" costume, and is intended to simulate heavy silk.

Creating a Multiple-Layer Costume for Xzulixia

The dance costume for the Xzulixia character consists of a tight-fitting bodysuit, loose pants, a cape, and arm draperies. The bodysuit was made by trimming down and reshaping a clone of the polygonal Xzulixia body mesh. The Push Modifier was used to enlarge the mesh in the direction of the surface normals. The pants are a Patch model, which was made by creating a spline cage and then generating a surface with the Surface Modifier. They were then converted to an editable mesh. The cape and the arm drapes were made from splines using GarmentMaker, as shown in Figure 17.11.

Cloth simulation works by converting the mesh objects into soft objects that behave like particle systems. Therefore, the forces that work on particle systems can also affect the cloth. Multiple layers of cloth are a much greater challenge to manage than a single layer. With a single layer, you only need to pay attention to gravity and internal collision detection to prevent penetration of the cloth object into the underlying mesh. With multiple-layer cloth assemblies such as Xzulixia's costume, each layer of the costume functions as both cloth and collision object, and a certain separation distance must usually be maintained if the cloth simulation is to be successful. Penetration is the most common cause of cloth simulation failure.

You should understand a number of other concepts before you use clothfx. Many of them will affect how the cloth simulation performs in your scene. Local simulation is done to make the cloth settle into place

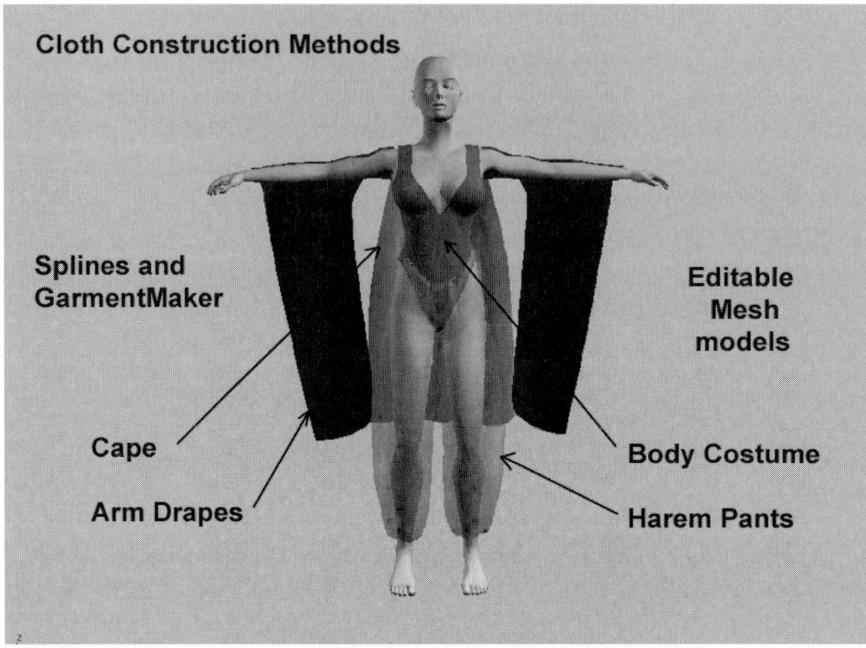

FIGURE 17.11 Different techniques were used to create different pieces of Xzulia's costume.

before you start the main simulation. Forces can include a Space Warp that affects a particle system, such as Wind and Gravity.

GarmentMaker

The GarmentMaker Modifier enables you to create garments from flat cloth panels, just as a tailor would do. Actual dress and shirt patterns can be used and the shapes derived from them will work very well to create clothing that fits well on a character and moves just like the real garment would, as shown in Figure 17.12.

GarmentMaker works by using splines to define the outside shape of each cloth piece. In the tutorial, the cape and the arm drapes were made by drawing their shapes with splines and then creating mesh with the irregular Dulanney tessellaton, which in a cloth simulation performs much better and creases less than a typical editable mesh object.

GarmentMaker is where you set up and select the seams to be pulled together by Sewing Springs during the simulation. For more information on using GarmentMaker, see the reference section of the clothfx help file.

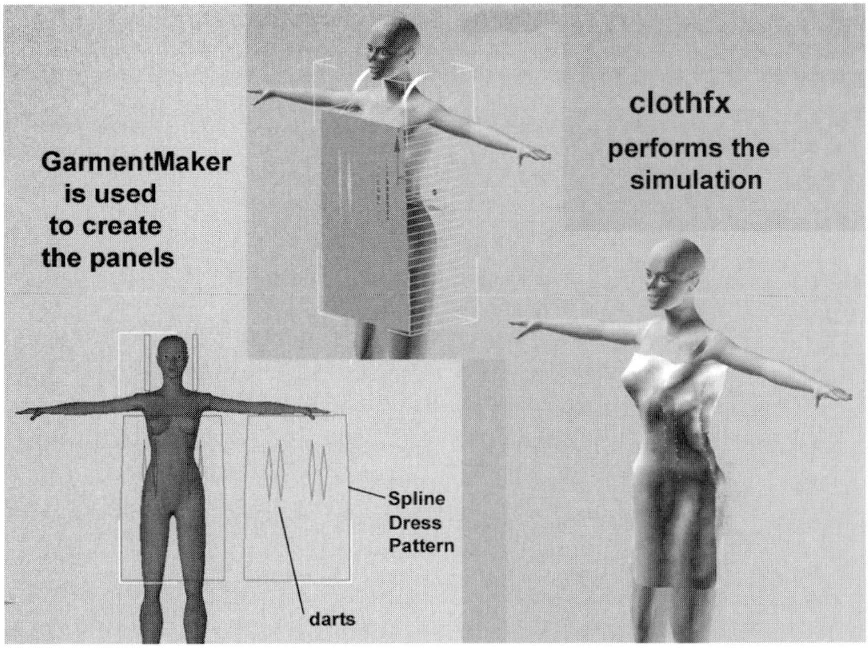

FIGURE 17.12 Using a dress pattern to create the cloth panels for a digital dress in GarmentMaker.

Using Groups to Attach Garments to a Character

One of the most important concepts to understand is *groups*. Without using groups, it is difficult, if not impossible, to work with garments of all shapes. The purpose of a group is to provide a way to attach a garment to a character. In clothfx, the term "group" refers to selected vertices in the mesh of the garment that are constrained to some area on the surface of the character mesh. Groups that are constrained to the model surface will stay put during the entire simulation. If you do not set up groups, the garments will be affected by gravity and end up sliding down to the character's ankles. Setting up groups is one of your most important tasks in doing a multilayer cloth simulation.

Standard 3d studio max 6 groups have nothing to do with clothfx. Max groups are completely different and have no function in clothfx. The clothfx plug-in was formerly called the Stitch plug-in, but during the preparation of this book, the name and the distributor of the plug-in was changed. The file you are about to use was created in Stitch, which is now called clothfx. In the file you will load from the

ON THE CD

CD-ROM, you will see the name Stitch on the modifier. Because only the name was changed, and not the functionality of the plug-in, you can be confident that the instructions apply equally to both versions of the plug-in. Any file made in Stitch will load into clothfx. We apologize for the confusion. All references to clothfx apply also to Stitch.

MATCHING THE MODEL SCALE TO REAL LIFE

Another very important problem that must be solved is getting the scale of the cloth objects correct so that physical forces in the simulation behave as they should. Clothfx is designed to work with real-world sizes and forces. If the scale of the cloth model is wrong, either too small or much too large, then the cloth will behave unpredictably. For example, the Xzulixia model is not scaled to life size. If the model were built in real life at the scale it is in 3ds max, it would be a giant 27½ feet tall. or 829 cm. She was built giant-sized because many visual effects in Max work much better on a larger-than-life-size model. This is not the case with clothfx.

Xzulixia was designed to be 5 ft. 9 in. or 1.752 m (175 cm) tall in real life. By dividing the actual height of the model in Max by the height that the character would actually be in real life, you get a multiplication factor of 4.731. In other words, Xzulixia is 4.731 times larger than life size in this file. Therefore, the cloth simulation multiplication factor must be set to instruct clothfx how to set the scale of the physical forces it applies.

To set the multiplication factor, you must enter the clothfx Modifier. Select any part of the costume that has clothfx applied and then click on the clothfx Modifier in the Stack. The Simulation Parameters drop-down menu will open and you will see the top entry, called cm/unit. By default, this value is set to 2.54. With the factor set to 2.54, the system assumes the model is the correct size and therefore will treat the cloth like huge tents of canvas that are 27 feet tall. To fix this, you must divide the 2.54 setting by the scale multiplication factor of 4.731 to tell the system how tall the character should actually be. The result is .536, so you should enter .5 instead of 2.54. That will make the system scale agree with real life. If you do not set this factor first, all of the physical calculations will be wrong and the behavior of the garment will be scaled for an object five times as big.

In the next tutorial, you will explore the way a four-layer cloth costume is attached to the figure of the model, and then you will work through the steps required to simulate the various cloth garments to create the animation. Because of the size and complexity of this project, most of the setup work has already been done for you.

TUTORIAL 17.6

MULTILAYER CLOTH SIMULATION USING CLOTHFX TO SIMULATE MULTILAYER CLOTH

ON THE CD

1. Load the Xzu_Cloth_Start.max file from the Chap17 directory on the companion CD-ROM. The file contains a pre-animated Dancing Xzulixia model and five mesh objects that form the costume. If you get an "obsolete file" warning when you load the file, don't worry. The file was originally created in max 5.1. Just resave the file to your 3ds max 6\Scenes working directory and it will work correctly in max 6 as long as you have the clothfx plug-in installed in your system.

This tutorial uses both the clothfx and the Shag Hair plug-ins. If you do not have the Shag Hair plug-in installed in your system, max will notify you with a pop-up message saying that there are missing plug-in files (usually .dlls) for an atmospheric plug-in. Shag Hair is an atmospheric effect. You can ignore the Shag Hair error message and continue on with the tutorial by clicking the Continue button. This will not affect the functionality of clothfx or the animation.

2. Set the Time Slider to frame zero. Then, in the Camera02 view, select the Body Costume by clicking on the character's stomach. Now open the Modifier Panel. You will see the clothfx (formerly Stitch) Modifier on the Stack above the Skin Modifier. When you click on the Modifier title bar, the Object Properties dialog will open. Here, you pick the object that will be the cloth, which would be the body costume. Then you pick the object that will be the collision object, which would be the XzuBody mesh. Next, you look at the groups used to attach the cloth to the surface of the model.
3. To see how the groups are set up, click the clothfx > Groups Sub-object. The vertices of the garment will turn blue. Select the vertices you want to attach to the model's surface and then click the Make Group button. In the dialog, give the group a name associated with that garment and click OK. The name will appear in the Groups list as "unassigned." Then click the Surface button, move the cursor over to the character model that you want the garment attached to, and click it. The entry will change "unassigned" to

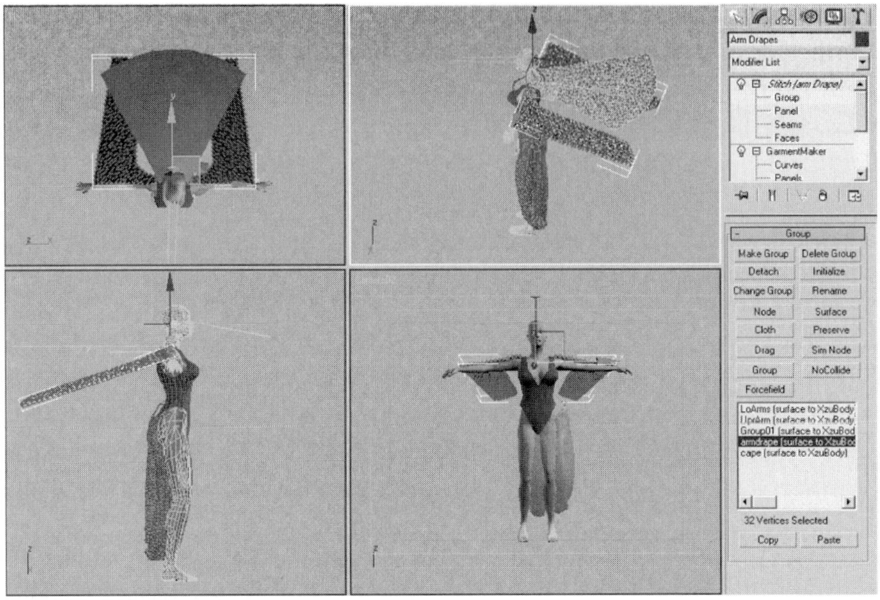

FIGURE 17.13 Garment pieces are attached to the model surface by selected vertex groups.

the name of the model, as shown in Figure 17.13. This must be done for all of the cloth pieces in order to hold them in place correctly. Groups can be soft selections to attach a larger area to the model.

All the groups have been created for you. Do not disturb or delete any of the groups.

4. The next step is to run the local simulations to make the cloth settle into place. To do that, first select the body costume. Then, in the clothfx > Object roll-out menu, in the Simulation section, click the Simulate Local button. The garment might jump away from the body and then slowly return and tighten up. When the body costume has settled onto the body and tightened up on the surface, press the Escape key. Now, go to the next garment, the harem pants. Again, select the garment, and then click the Simulate Local button and run it until the pants settle nicely onto the body.
5. Repeat this operation for each garment. When all of the cloth objects have been run through the local simulation and are nicely draped on the figure, you are ready to perform the simulation for the animation. Select one of

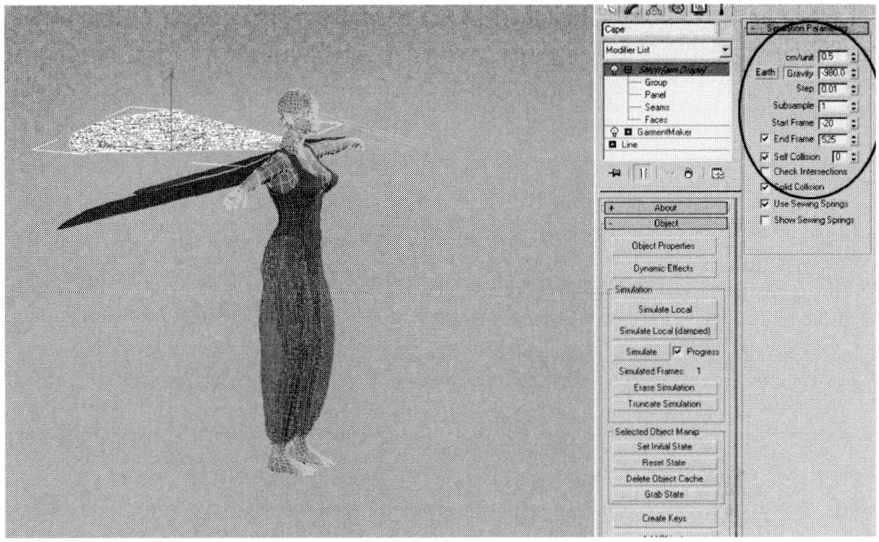

FIGURE 17.14 Running the Cloth simulations.

the garments. Now set the range of the simulation. In the Simulation Parameters menu, set the start time to –20 and the end frame to 250, as shown in Figure 17.14. Now click Simulate. It will take some time to calculate all 250 frames. It is a good time to go get a cup of coffee.

6. When the simulation finishes, you are ready to render the animation. You might find that some of the cloth pieces do not behave as expected. Numerous variables might need to be adjusted. Please consult the troubleshooting guide and the clothfx help reference guide for information on how to work out problems with the cloth. This tutorial is only an introduction to clothfx's functionality, and is not meant to teach you everything about clothfx. Save your finished file as Xzu_Cloth 176.max.

ON THE CD

To see the finished animation of the four-layer cloth costume, you can load the XzuDance.mov movie from the Chap17\Images folder on the companion CD-ROM.

WORKING WITH LARGE FILE SIZES

Cloth simulations use a great deal of memory. The finished animation generated by the file in this tutorial took 82MB. This is not uncommon for multiple-layer cloth animations in which every vertex of every piece of cloth is tracked for 500 frames. Clothfx is optimized to deal with large amounts of data, and has a built-in point cache system that stores the information for you.

It is recommended that you run clothfx on a fast machine with plenty of RAM. The author's PC runs at 2 MHz and has 1GB of RAM. It can be run on a less capable machine, but you will have to wait a long time for the simulation to calculate. Once the calculation is done, the Time Slider will move easily because the information resides in a large point cache. That is why multiple-layer cloth animations can run anywhere from 40MB to 200MB in size. A large file can take 15 to 20 minutes to load into 3ds max, depending on how many characters it contains. If you want to work with big scenes in a professional animation studio, you will have to get used to it. These large file sizes are common in professional 3D animation.

In the next section, you will be introduced to the Immersion Microscribe® and the Scrib-it® software, which enables you to digitize objects into 3ds max 6.

DIGITIZING A MODEL WITH THE IMMERSION MICROSCRIBE

It is generally not known that nearly all animated characters in motion pictures are first sculpted as clay models or maquettes before they are digitized and built in the computer. In films such as *Shrek, Ice Age, Lord of the Rings,* and *Jurassic Park,* all of the computer-animated creature and character models started out as clay sculptures first. The Immersion Microscribe was used in the production of the author's film *Homing Instinct* to create many of the costumes and some of the outlandish alien creatures from original clay models.

By working out the design in clay first, you can get a much better idea of the impression that will be created by the character than you can get from two-dimensional drawings. This is because even a nonartist (such as your accountant or your lawyer) can understand why the character should look as it does if he or she can see it and touch it as a three-dimensional physical model.

In many large studios, molds are make from the clay models and copies are painted and finished so that the digital department can get the director, the art director, and the producers to "sign off" on the final design before doing anything on the computer. Once approved, the model is given to the digitizing person, who will have a tool such as the Immersion Microscribe digitizing arm. He or she will proceed to draw contour lines and establish points on the surface of the model that will become points in 3D space in the computer. The skin and the clothing of a model can be input into the computer this way to create a spline cage for a surface patch model.

The Scrib-it and Surf-it® plug-ins from Ghost3D work together in 3ds max 6 to enable you to input the data from Immersion Microscribe directly into the Max viewport. Clothing is difficult to create and fit accurately over the surface of a model. The approach taken for many of the more complex costumes in *Homing Instinct* was to sculpt the clothing in clay, and then to digitize the clothing so that it could be built as a Spline Patch model for later use in clothfx, the cloth simulation plug-in.

USING SCRIB-IT

Scrib-it, from Ghost3D, is used to read the stylus positions as point data that is generated by the Immersion Microscribe, and then import the points into the 3ds max 6 viewport in a readable fashion, as shown in Figure 17.15.

The sculpted clay model is prepared by drawing lines around all of the seams, up the centerline and the sides of the torso, and then horizontally around the body. The lines on the arms run along the length parallel to the seam and then rings are drawn around the arm at the joints and the cuff. The collar, or other details, such as a pocket, can be digitized as separate pieces and joined to the garment later.

The next tutorial explains how to use the Scrib-it software and the Microscribe in the digitizing process to create spline curves in Max for the clothing. A subsequent section on Surf-it, which is bundled with Scrib-it, discusses the steps needed to turn the digitized splines into Patch Surface clothing that can be used in a cloth simulation.

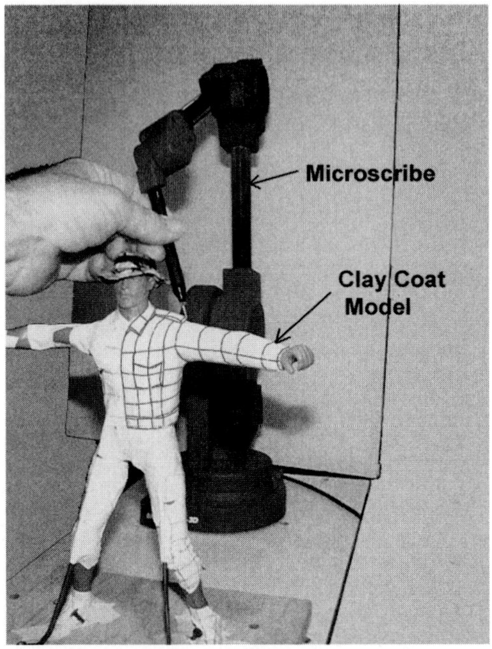

FIGURE 17.15 Digitizing a clay model of a coat with the Immersion Microscribe-3D.

TUTORIAL 17.7

DIGITIZING CLOTHING FROM A CLAY MODEL WITH SCRIB-IT

To digitize a clay model of clothing:

1. Connect the Immersion Microscribe to your serial port according to the directions that come with Scrib-it. It is assumed you have made all of the connections according to the instructions included with the Microscribe. This is tested by opening the Scrip-it[Scrib-it] menu in the Utility panel and clicking the Activate Device button.
2. You digitize the model by setting three reference points so that the Microscribe knows where the model is in 3D space. In the Scrib-it utility menu, click the Draw Spline button and then capture points on the model by moving the stylus along the surface, clicking on the Microscribe input pedal (or pressing 9) wherever you want the points to be, as shown in Figure 17.16. Only the left half of the coat was sculpted in clay. The curves and points you capture can be Mirror Cloned to create the other half of the coat when you are finished digitizing.

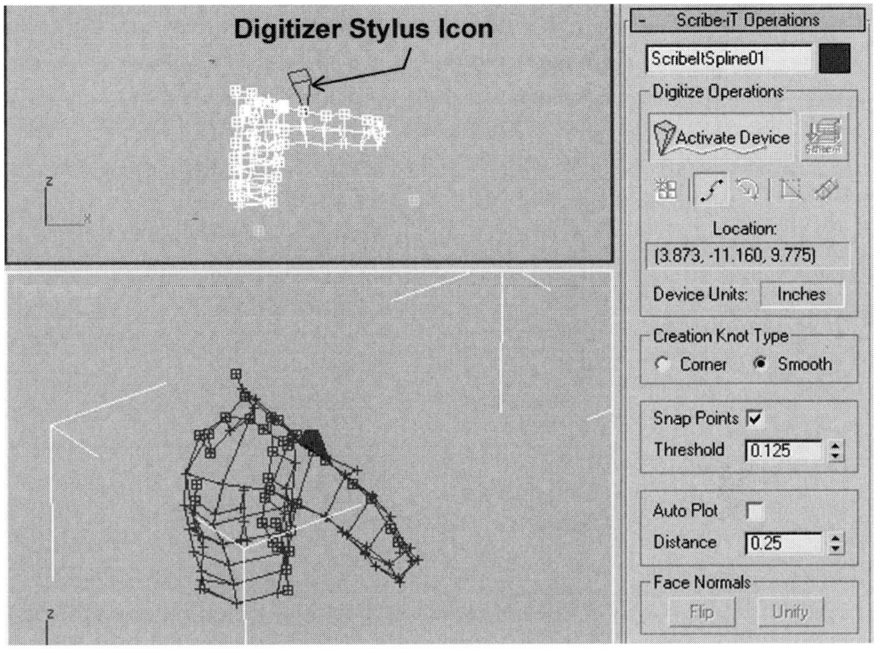

FIGURE 17.16 Inputting the spline points from the clay model into 3ds max 6.

For a Spline Patch model, you want to click only at the locations where the lines cross on the surface of the model. In some cases, you will want to use the Create Mesh Faces or the Create Mesh Strips capability of Scrib-it to generate a mesh object as you digitize the clay sculpture.

3. When the digitizing is done, you will have spline curves that are mostly linear and run straight from point to point. To correct this, you need to take the model into the Surf-it Spline Editor and change the shape of the spline segments. After you are done digitizing the model, disable the Microscribe and close Scrib-it.
4. Save the file as Digitize01.max. Go to the next section for a discussion of how to use Surf-it to finish the spline cage and apply a patch surface.

   The digitizing process yields a rough set of curves, but the points are accurate and reflect the original surface shape. Surf-it is designed to work rough curves into a smooth, finished spline cage suitable for skinning with a patch surface.

The next step, after saving the curves, is to open Surf-it. It was automatically installed into 3ds max when you installed Scrib-it.

USING SURF-IT

Once the data points from the clothing model are in 3ds max, the clothing is created as a Spline Patch surface using the tools in Surf-it. Then the surface can be collapsed to a quad mesh. Surf-it has excellent tools for creating a patch surface over a spline cage that has been digitized into 3ds max. It has the ability to output mesh as a quad polygonal mesh. It is important for cloth simulation to have the correct type of tessellation or subdivisions of the cloth mesh surface. Surf-it does this by generating quad polygonal surfaces from the original Spline Patch models. Quads are the recommended surface for clothfx cloth simulation.

To finish the model, open the Surf-it menu in the Max main menu and select Spline Editor. Fuse and weld all open pairs of points, and then convert to Bézier splines and adjust the handles to obtain the curvature

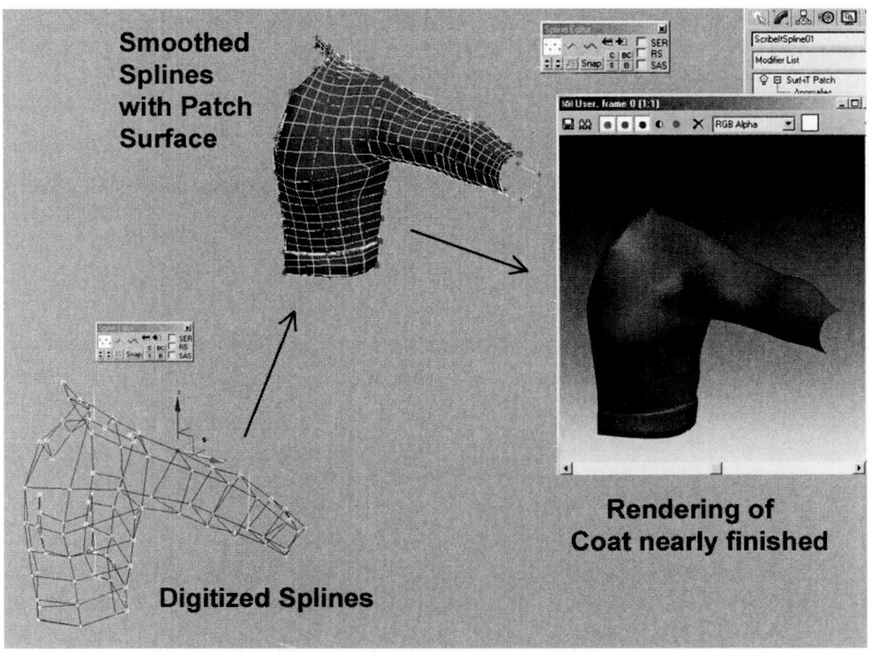

FIGURE 17.17 Adjust the spline curvature and apply the Patch Surface in Surf-it.

that you want. Next, use the Surf-it Patch to create the patch surface on the spline cage, as shown in Figure 17.17.

Next, re-adjust the Bézier handles to finalize the shape of the surface, and then convert the surface to a quad polygon mesh for use in the clothfx cloth simulator software. You now have a garment with the kind of surface tessellation that will behave well and act like real cloth in clothfx. Quad meshes are the preferred object type for creating clothing.

A Scrib-it and Surf-it demo can be obtained from the *www.ghost3d.com* Web site. The Microscribe digitizing arm is available from the Immersion Corporation on a trial basis at *www. immersion.com.*

In the next section, you will be introduced to a very powerful pair of programs that turn 3ds max 6 into a professional-quality multitrack sound effects studio.

FOLEY STUDIO AND SOUND TRAX FOR CREATING SOUND EFFECTS

The final impact of any animation in the theatre is 50% visual and 50% audio. Sound connects the emotions of the audience to the visual information and makes sense of it. Try turning the sound off when watching your favorite science fiction or animated movie. Boredom and confusion will set in rapidly without a sound track. The soundtrack is tremendously important to the overall production. Two plug-ins from *www.Boomerlabs.com* will enable you to do a great job of building a soundtrack inside 3ds max 6: Sound Trax® and Foley Studio®, which can be used together to turn 3ds max 6 into a sound effects creation studio.

Sound Trax was essential to all the scenes created for *Homing Instinct,* as shown in Figure 17.18, example 1. It allowed the author to construct multitrack sound backgrounds and position sound clips where they were needed, and mix in sound effects and ambient background noise. Sound Trax lets you keyframe the volume to get a final mix for the scene, and to slide sound clips to synchronize them perfectly with the action.

ON THE CD

Foley Studio was used for the visual effects and battle scenes in which numerous events were happening rapidly. Trying to lay in clips manually in Sound Trax becomes very difficult in a complex scene. Foley Studio uses the objects and events in the scene to trigger any number of sound effects at exactly the right moment, as shown in Figure 17.18, example 2. This gives a realism and validity to the soundtrack and elevates the production values of the film. Load the BattleSound.mov movie from

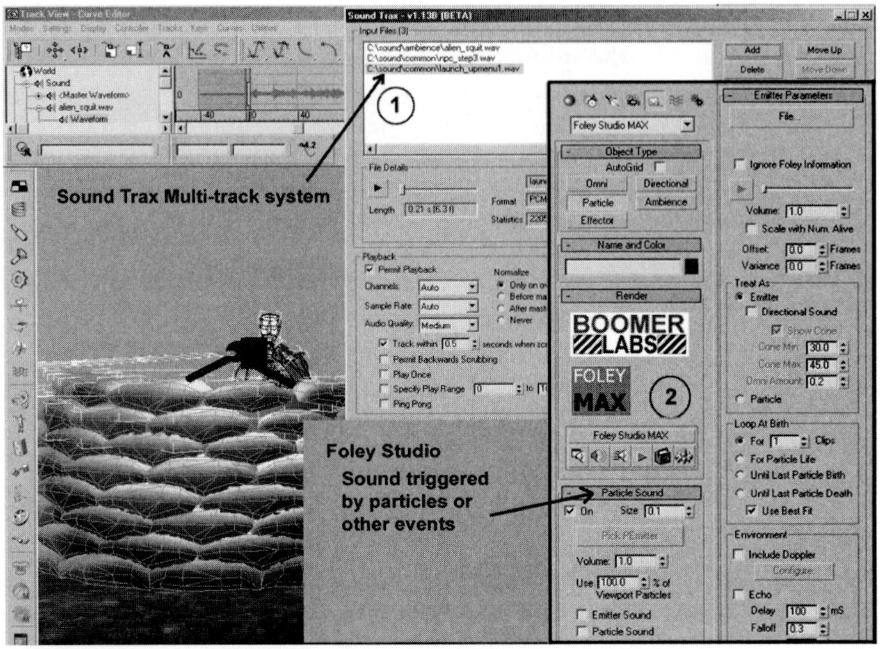

FIGURE 17.18 Sound Trax and Foley Studio provide multi-track background sound and sound effects.

the Chap17\Images folder on the companion CD-ROM to listen to a synchronized soundtrack created with Sound Trax and Foley Studio.

PHOENIX—FIRE THAT THROWS LIGHT

Phoenix® is a realistic light-emitting fire plug-in from Digimation. The sample scene contains a character studio character called Man(suit), who is animated with the Stagger.bip motion file. The flames are generated with default settings, as shown in Figure 17.19.

The volume fog atmospheric effect has been added with a density of 2.0 to create the appearance of smoke in the hall.

This tutorial assumes that you have the Phoenix plug-in or the demo version installed on your computer.

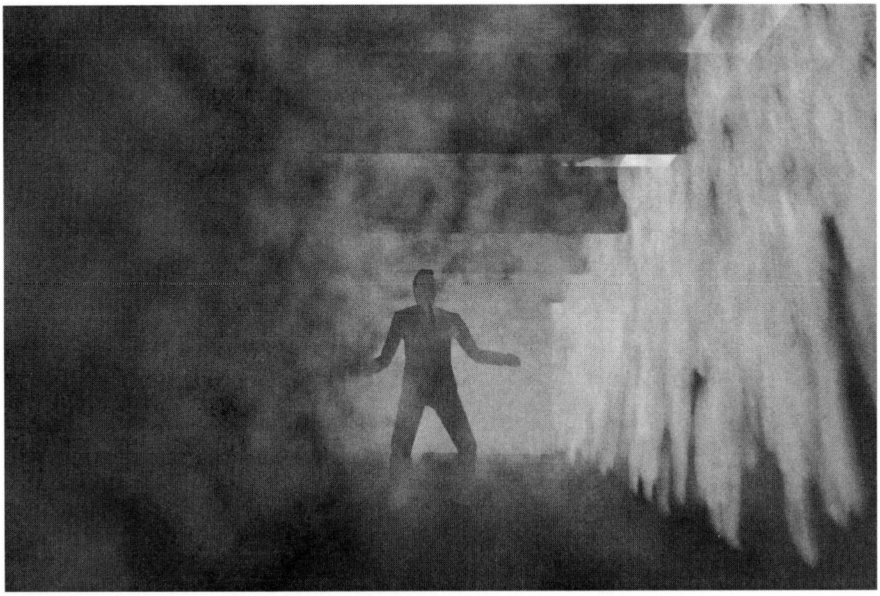

FIGURE 17.19 Burning Hall created with the Phoenix light-emitting fire plug-in.

TUTORIAL 17.11

USING PHOENIX TO CREATE FIRE THAT EMITS LIGHT

To create Phoenix fire:

ON THE CD

1. Load the Hallfire.max scene file from the Chap17 folder on the companion CD-ROM.
2. If you have the Phoenix Demo version installed, you will be able to render the camera view of the scene. To look at the settings, go to the Rendering > Environment > Effects > Phoenix menu, as shown in Figure 17.20.

The Phoenix interface lets you set the appearance of the flames and create special lights for the flames, as shown in Figure 17.20.

See the appendix for a list of other plug-in vendors and links to free plug-in and MAXScript sites.

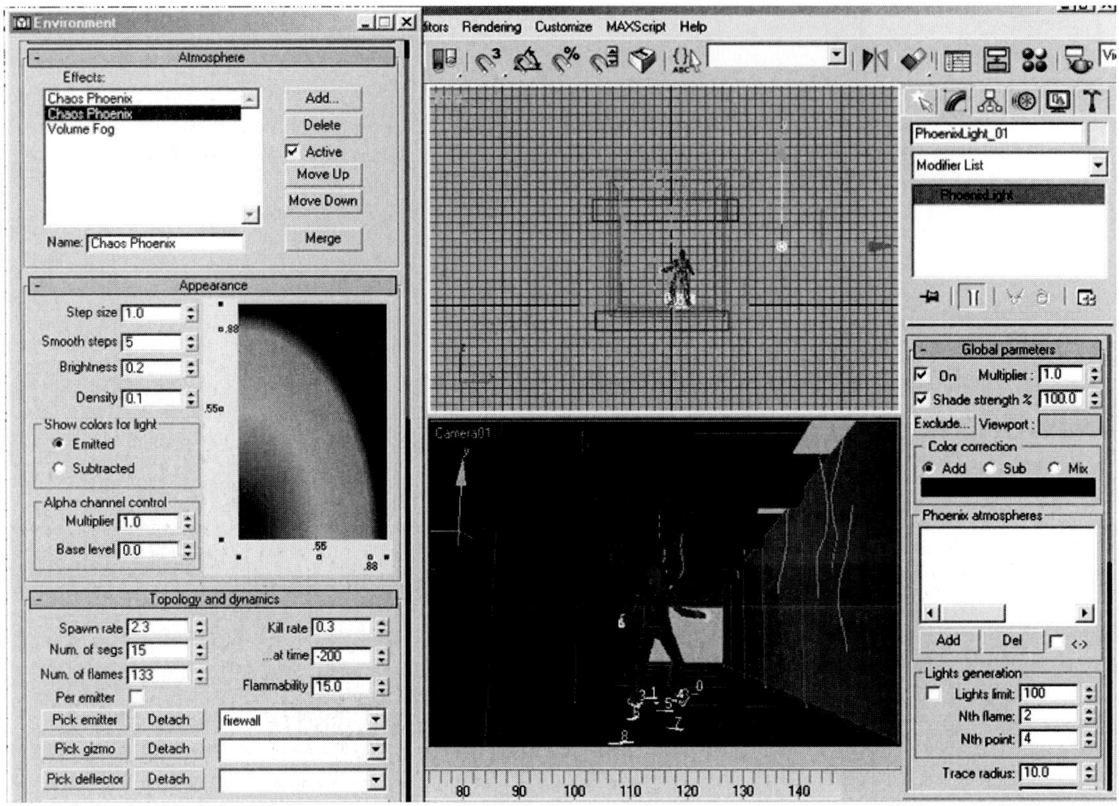

FIGURE 17.20 The Phoenix atmospheric effect and Phoenix Lights interface menus.

CONCLUSION

In this chapter, you were introduced to some of the plug-ins that are available for 3ds max 6. You worked with the Shag Hair plug-in to create hair for the Dr. Quin character, which was described and built in Chapters 6, 7, and 8. Then you created a multilayer cloth animation for the Xzulixia character using the clothfx plug-in. For more information on plug-ins, visit the Web sites listed in Appendix B under "Plug-In Vendors."

APPENDIX

A

ABOUT THE CD-ROM

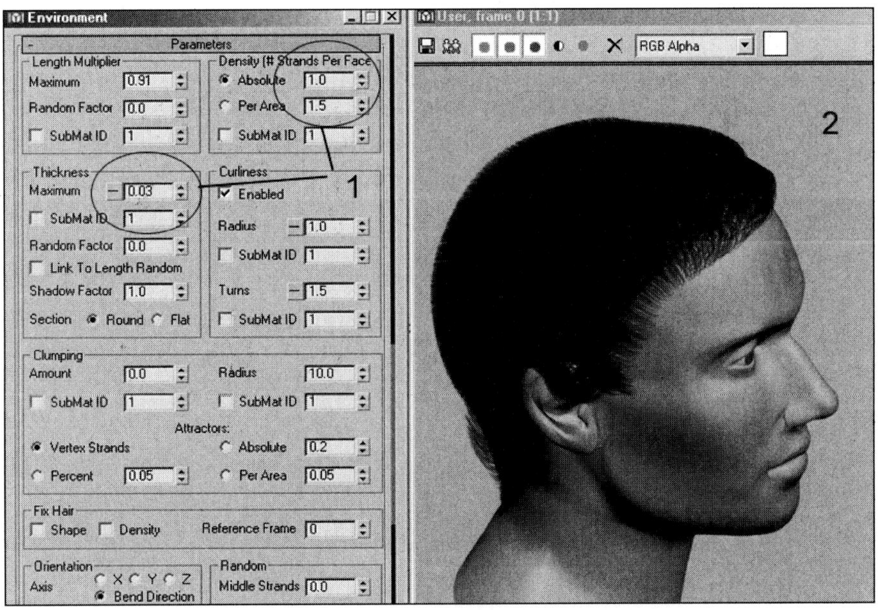

As you are working through the book you will find that many tutorials require you to load image files. The companion CD-ROM contains all of the tutorial files and the image files in separate subdirectories that are necessary for Chapters 3 through 17. Many of the chapters have extras folders that contain 3ds max materials libraries, and texture maps for your use.

The image folders contain both reference images and movies. Chapter 16 contains a directory with three image sequences zipped into an archive containing 1,353 frames that are to be used in the combustion 3 visual effects tutorial.

Demo versions of the plug-ins discussed in the tutorials in Chapter 17 "Plug-ins" have not been included on the CD-ROM. At the time this book went to press, the final release versions were not available yet for 3ds max 6. You can download the final demo versions of each plug-in by going to the Web sites mentioned in each tutorial in Chapter 17 "Plug-ins."

FINDING MAPS

To make the tutorials easier to work with, create a folder called "Homing Instinct" in your 3ds max6\Maps directory. Then create a folder for Chap03 through Chap17 inside the Homing Instinct folder. Finally, copy each of the chapter Images folders from the CD-ROM for Chapters 3 through 17, and place them in the corresponding folders you have created in your new 3ds max6\Maps\Homing Instinct directory. Then, click Customize > Configure Paths > External Files, and add Homing Instinct to your map paths. This is how the author set up all of the tutorials on his own machine. If you do this, you will have a much easier time locating all of the necessary maps and images for each tutorial.

SYSTEM REQUIREMENTS

The minimum system for doing these tutorials is as follows:

- 3ds max 6
- IBM compatible PC
- 800 MHz processor
- 256MB RAM memory

- Video display with 32MB RAM
- 600MB hard drive space
- Windows 2000 or Windows XP Pro

The recommended system for doing these tutorials is as follows:

- 3ds max 6
- IBM compatible PC
- 2.5 GHz or better single or dual processor
- 1GB or more RAM memory.
- Video display with 128 to 256MB RAM
- 4GB available hard drive space
- Windows 2000 pro or Windows XP Pro

APPENDIX

B

REFERENCES

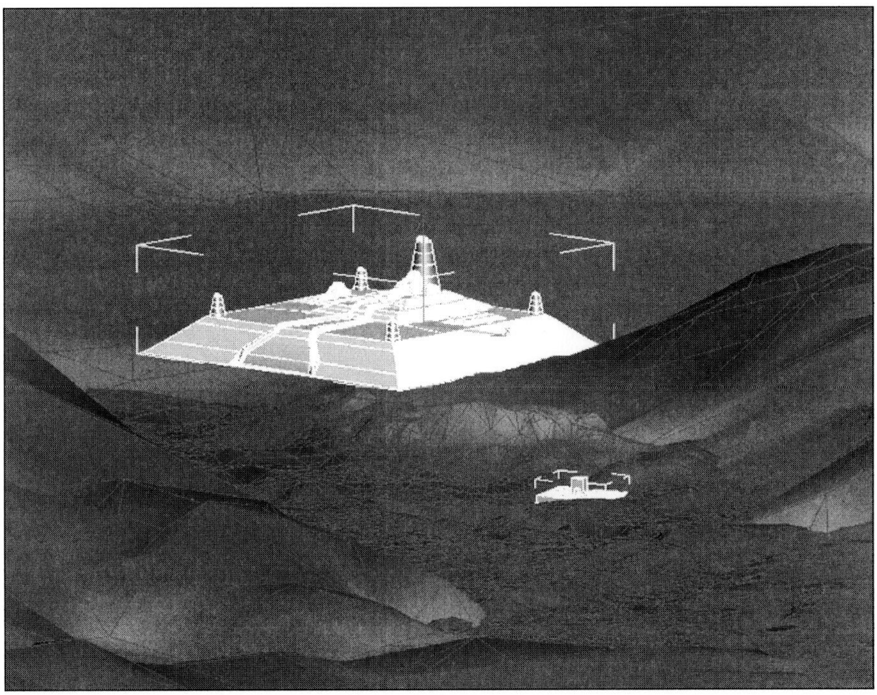

RESOURCES AND LINKS

www.discreet.com
www.sanfordkennedy.com
www.graphicresources.com
www.digimation.com
www.motionmedia.com
www.turbosquid.com

GOOD 3DS MAX SITES

www.splutterfish.com
www.neilblevins.com
www.scriptspot.com
max3d.3dluvr.com
maxunderground.com
www.blur.com
www.google.com just type "3ds max" or "3d studio max" into the search engine.

PLUG-INS

I was going to list the plug-ins for 3ds max, but there are over 200 available and space does not permit. Please go to the above links to discover for yourself the rich world of plug-ins for 3ds max.

3DS MAX FILMOGRAPHY

Some of the films made using 3ds max include *The Matrix, Xmen 2, Minority Report, Armageddon, The Majestic, Panic Room, Final Destination 2, The Core, Reign of Fire, X-Men, Blackhawk Down, Swordfish, Driven, The Mummy Returns, Inspector Gadget, Tomb Raider, South Park: Bigger, Longer & Uncut, Dr. Doolittle 2, Undisputed, Mighty Joe Young, Equilibrium, The Crow 2: City Of Angels, The Truman Show*, and many more.

INDEX

A

Active Shade renderer, 27
Adobe Photoshop
  Ghost Paint plug-in, 41
  visual effects and, 3–4
Advanced Lighting Override, 466
Afterburner plug-in, 41
AI behaviors
  character studio plug-in and, 37
  delegates for crowd animation, behavior assignment, 520–524
Animation
  acrobatic motion, 311–313
  armies, charging army animation, 522–531
  biped animation conversion to bones animation, 516–517
  .bip footstep files, 510–511
  body language, 219, 301, 337–338
  Character Assembly Node, 302
  of character studio bipeds, 353–354
  clinging motions, 299, 311
  collisions, dynamic, 398–403
  control points and natural motion, 207–208, 213–216, 280–281, 282
  crowd animation with character studio 4, 37–38
  curve graphs, 17–19
  custom attribute rigging, 417–424
  cutting and pasting animation keys, 19
  dusty footsteps, 383–390
  expression controllers and, 394–398
  facial animation, 12–15
  feature overview, 6–11
  fighting rigs, 429–434
  film design phase, 47–48
  film production overview, 46–47
  footstep driven animation systems (*See* character studio 4)
  Footstep Motion files, 411
  hair, dynamic long hair, 562–567
  of hands and fingers, 206–207, 251–257, 280–284, 346, 511–513, 514–516
  IK Solvers, 210, 218–221, 315
  IK Swivel Angle Targets, 315–316
  jumping motions, 311
  Kick Controls and, 312
  Layer Animation tool, 517–519
  leaning forward, 280–284
  of legs, 227–230 (*see also* Running and run cycles; Walking and walk cycles)
  Level of Detail utility and, 12

lifting objects, 288–290
lip synching, 12–15, 290–294
morphing and shape transformations, 23
Morph Targets for, 258–263
Motion Capture, 508–511
multiple objects (crowds and swarms), 37–38, 377–380, 519–531
picking up an object, 280–284
Point Cache Modifier, 445–446
pre-production phase, 48–52
rain or waterfall Particle effects, 362–365
Ram Player, playback, 41–42, 493–494
Reactor 2 and, 398–417
release and distribution issues, 64
resolution settings during, 204
rotations and, 280–281
running motion, 335, 337–346
secondary motion, 11, 444–445
sitting, 277–280
sliders and wired parameters, 511–513, 514–516
sliding feet, preventing, 310, 335, 337–340
smoke, steam, or exhaust effects, 380–381, 485–494
squash and stretch effects, 8
tools for character animation, 5
Tracking Sphere, 490, 491
upper body movement and gestures, 277
wired parameters and, 251–257
see also Bones and boning; character studio 4; Explosion effects; Inverse Kinematics (IK); Morphing; Running and run cycles; Walking and walk cycles

Animation key exports, 42
Animation supervisors, 62
Animation Workbench in character studio 4, 508
Animators and modelers, 62–63
Architectural elements
architectural detail tutorial, 80–85
doors, modeling, 80–85
new tools for design and visualization, 5–6
size and scale of models, 83
Temple of the Horns tutorial, 76–79
windows, modeling, 80–85

Architectural textures or materials, 79, 448, 461–463
Armies, charging army animation, 522–531
Armpits, adjusting skin envelopes at, 246–249
Arms
adjusting skin envelopes at joints, 246–249, 284–288
animating, 234–236, 280–284
modeling, 148–151
rigging for animation, 234–236
running cycle animation, 341–345
walk cycle animation, 309–311

Art Beats, 365–366
Art direction, 53, 54, 62
Artificial Intelligence, behaviors
character studio plug-in and, 37
delegates for crowd animation, behavior assignment, 520–524

Asset Browser, 30
Atmospheric effects, 23
explosions, 372–376

Attach command, 115
Attribute Holder Modifier Script, 419
Audience
character design and, 15, 55
explosion effects and appeal to, 365–366

Audio Controllers, 20
Audio Position, 25
Audio Rotate, 25
Author, contact information and bio, *xiii*
Automatic Exposure Control, 35

B

Backburner 2 for network rendering, 5, 503–504
Background lock toggle, 100–101, 146

Backgrounds
alignment with models, 146
visual effects and, 4
Back lights, 484
Bezier handles, 182, 201
Bezier Spline Patch modeling, 142
Bezier handles, revealing, 182, 201
see also Generic Man model
.bip files, 353–354, 510–511
Bitmaps, displacements and, 70
Blinking, animation, 316–323
Blob Mesh Compound Object, 391
Blue-screen compositing, 535–543
Bodies
polygon modeling tutorial, 87–89, 93–96
rigging for animation, 230–233
spine bones, 210–211, 219–220
see also Torsos
Body language, 219, 301, 337–338
Bones and boning
animation and, 206
biped animation conversion to bones, 516–517
bone stretch, 427–428
Bone Tools, 239
facial animation techniques with, 12
facial bone networks, 424–428
fins, adding, 239–241
of hands, 213–216
IK skeleton rig, 6–7
naming conventions and hierarchies, 216–218
splines used as, 12
Wired Parameters and bone rotation, 10–11
see also Skeletons
Bone Tools, 239
Brazil plug-in, 41, 504
Breasts, polygon modeling techniques, 93–96
Buildings. *see* Architectural elements
Bulge Angle Deformer, 10
Bump maps, Edge shader and, 466–467
Butterflies, instanced geometry particle effects, 378–380
Buttocks, modeling, 90–92

C

Camera angles and positions, 24–25, 50, 55
features overview, 42
location models and, 67–68
scene animation and, 345–346
tracking by linking to bones in models, 293
Video Post, 24–25, 42
Camera effects, 24–25
Caustics, Mental Ray and, 5
CD-ROM content, 586–587
Cell Block Zebra tutorial, 73–76
Character Assembly Node, 302
Character Control box, walk cycle animation and, 302
Character Node, 43
Character rigging. *See* Rigging
Characters
body language and expression, 219, 301, 337–338
character design, 55–56
personality and, 55–56, 301
character studio 4, 353
Animation Workbench, 408
crowd animation, 37–38, 519–531
features, 508–511
Layer Animation tool, 517–519
Motion Capture, 508–511, 517–519
Motion Flow, 517–519, 529–530
Motion Mixer, 508
"Circle rigs," 394–395
Cities, design and modeling, 68–69
Close-ups, landscape locations and, 73–76
clothfx plug-in, 15, 38–39, 567–572
groups, 571–572
multilayer clothing, 569–575
Clothing and costumes
bodysuits, modeling, 132–134

collars and cuffs, modeling, 268–270
costume design, 55
digitization of, 576–581
file sizes, 575–576
Garment Maker modifier, 568, 570–572
merging with skin and skeleton, 270–272
modeling techniques, 15
multilayer clothing, 569–575
pants and shirts, modeling, 263–270
Push Modifier to model, 15, 132–134, 263–268
Reactor 2 for clothes modeling, 15
scale, 572
Sewing Springs, 568
skin penetrated clothing, troubleshooting, 134
see also clothfx plug-in
Cloth (Reactor 2), hair simulated with, 436–442
Collisions
deformable meshes and, 398–399, 402
dynamic collisions with characters, 400–403
proxy collision objects, 398–399, 402
Color keying in combustion, 535–543
combustion 3, 30
blue- or green-screen compositing (color keying), 535–543
demo downloads, 538
Edit Operator, 534
Render Elements, 495
textures and, 547–549
2D visual effects, 543–547
Command-line rendering, 504
Command Panel, 20
Compatibility issues, 42–44, 519
Composite effects, 23–24
Composite materials, 32–33, 451
Compositing
blue- or green- screen compositing, 535–543
in post-production, 63–64
rendering layers, 491–494
visual effects, 23–24, 544–547
Composition, scene composition, 470
Concept art, for animated film projects, 47–48
Constraints, 21, 43, 311–312
Rag Doll constraints, 405–406
Controller effects, 25
Control Point Box Rigs, 207–208
Control Point Circle Rigs, 207–208
Costumes. *See* Clothing and costumes
Cross Section Modifier, 181
Crowds and swarms, 27
biped crowds, 526–531
character design issues, 56
character studio 4 for, 37–38, 519–531
file size and, 525
instanced geometry particle effects for animation, 378–380
setting up a biped crowd, 526–528
Cursor, slow movement, 199
Curve Editor, 17–19
Custom attribute rigging, 417–424
Cut tool, 101

D

Davis, Brandon, 360–361
Deformable meshes and collisions, 398–399, 402
Deform Along Surface, 25, 27
Delegates for crowd animation, 520–521, 522
Behavior Assignment and, 523–524
Demo downloads, combustion, 538
Dialog, recording, 295–297
Digimation, plug-ins from, 39–41
Digitization of clothing, 576–581
Directors, 54–55, 62
Disappearing, visibility keys and, 25
Display floater, 272
Doors, modeling, architectural details tutorial, 80–85
Dope Sheet, 17–18, 20

Dr. Quin Model
- basic skeletal rig for, 209–213
- faces, modeling, 192–197, 201–203
- feet, modeling, 190–192
- fingernails, modeling, 182–185
- hands, boning, 213–216
- hands, modeling, 179–182
- head, modeling, 192–195, 199–201
- Major Black, modifications to model, 429–434

Dusty footsteps animation, 383–390
Dynamic effects, 22, 60
Dynamic simulation, point caches and, 445

E

Ears, attaching to head, 115–118
Ears, modeling, 202–203
- patch ears, 172–175
- pointed ears, 112–115
- positioning of, 194

Edge shader in Mental Ray, 466–467
Editable Polygon modifier, tools in, 101
Editable Poly Meshes, *vs.* triangle meshes, 98
Editing, feature overview, 5
Edit Operator of combustion 3, 534
Elbows, adjusting skin envelopes at, 246–249
Engle, Volker, 360
Envelopes, skin envelopes, 8–9
- adjusting, 244–249, 284–288
- influence envelopes, 244–246, 284–288
- Mirror Skin Weights and, 249–251
- parts of described, 242–243

Environments
- design of, 57–58, 59
- landscape modeling overview, 66–68
- level of detail and, 68, 71
- Master Landscapes, 66–68
- Master Maps, 66–68
- materials and textures and, 448–451
- resources for creating, 57–58, 59
- scene animation and, 326–328
- *see also* Landscape locations

Exhaust, 380–381, 485–494
Explosion effects
- atmospheric explosions, 372–376
- audience appeal of, 365–366
- in battle scenes, 408–417
- creating with Reactor effects, 22
- dense explosions, 368–372
- fragmentation Particle effects, 367
- image sources, 60
- multiple effects used to create, 267–272
- Omni lights in, 373–374
- slow motion and, 366–377
- sources of stock explosion images, 365–366
- uses of, 365–368
- volume lights in, 376–377

Export
- animation key exports, 42
- file formats for, 42
- skeleton exports, 42

Expression, body language and, 219, 301, 337–338
Expression, facial
- Morph targets and, 258–259, 290–294
- *See also* Lip synching

Expression Controller, 395–398
Expressions, facial bone networks and, 424–428
Externally Referenced Objects, 357
Extrude Along Spline tool, 29
Eyeballs, modeling, 109–110
Eyelashes, animating, 320
Eyelids, modeling, 108–109
Eyes
- animation of, 316–323
- iris, animating, 316–319
- meniscus, wet-looking eyes, 138–140
- modeling, 102–103, 107–110, 160–161, 162–163, 203
- positioning and size of, 193–194
- realistic human and alien eyes, tutorial, 135–138

F

Faces
  animation, 12–15
  bones used in, 12
  facial bone networks and expressions, 424–428
  facial proportions, 192–193
  features, modeling, 108–110, 159–164, 192–197 (*see also Specific features i. e., Eyes*)
  features, positioning of, 192–193
  increasing resolution, 104–108
  maps for texturing, 459–460, 543–548
  modeling tutorials, 100–112
  Morph Targets, 197, 258–263
  painting texture maps for, 459–461
  photos as feature references, 203
  shaping the facial features, tutorial, 108–110
  subdivision tutorial, 104–108
  textures, applying to, 451–461, 543–546
  see also Expression, facial; *Specific facial features, i.e., eyes*
Facial bone networks, 424–428
Facial tracking plug-in, 41
Facing particle effects (Sprites), 22, 380–381
.fbx (Filmbox) file format, 42, 509, 516, 519
Feet
  animation, custom attribute rigging, 417–424
  dusty footsteps animation, 383–390
  footstep motion files and animation, 411
  modeling, with toes, 125–127
  modeling rudimentary feet, 190–192
  rigging for animation, 227–228
  sliding feet, preventing, 310, 335, 337–340
  walk cycle animation, 303–313
Female figures, modeling. *See* Xzulixia, alien vampire character
FFD (Free Form Deformation), 12
File compatibility, 42–44, 519
Film
  digital visual effects in, 2–4
  film design, 47–48
  filmography, 590
  outputting to, 550–551
Filmbox (.fbx) file format, 42, 509, 516, 519
Film design, 47–48
Filmography, 590
Final Render plug-in, 41, 504–505
Fingernails, modeling, 123–125, 182–185
Fingers
  animating, 206–207, 251–257
  animation with sliders, 511–513, 514–516
  modeling, 119–121, 179–182
Fin Tools, 239–241
Fire
  Phoenix plug-in for light throwing fire, 582–584
  see also Explosion effects
Flatten Mapping, 32, 453–454
Flex Modifier, 11, 444–445
Floating, Reactor 2 to create floating objects, 20
Folders, to organize projects, 459
Foley Studio plug-in, 41, 581–582
Footage Operator, 536
Footstep Motion files, 411
Forward Kinematics, walking cycle animation and, 304
Fracturing effects, 25
Fragmentation Particle effects, 367
Free Form Deformation (FFD), 12
Fuse command, 148
  vs. welding, 185

G

Garment Maker modifier, 568, 570–572
Generic Man Model
  adaptability of features, 203
  arms, modeling, 148–151
  ears, modeling, 172–175
  eyes, modeling, 160–161, 162–163
  facial features, modeling, 159–164

head, modeling, 157–159
legs, modeling, 151–154
modifications to create Major Black, 429–434
mouth, modeling, 158–162
neck, modeling, 155–156
nose, modeling, 159–161, 163, 165–168
nostrils, modeling, 157–158
patch ears, 172–175
pelvis, modeling, 144–145
shoulders, modeling, 146–148
torso, modeling, 143–146
see also Dr. Quin model
Ghost Painter plug-in, 41
Global Illumination (GI), 471–472, 504–505
Mental Ray and, 5
Gravity, using Space Warps, 363–364
Green-screen compositing, 535–543
Groups, clothfx *vs.* Max Groups, 571–572
Grow edge selection command, 29

H

Hair
dynamic long hair, 562–567
Reactor 2 Cloth to simulate, 436–442
Shag Hair plug-in, 37–38, 555, 559–567
Hands
animation of hands and fingers, 206–207, 213–216, 251–257, 280–284, 346, 511–513, 514–516
bone placement in, 213–216, 224–225
gestures during running, 346
modeling, 118–125, 179–182
picking up objects with, 280–284
skinning, 244–246
Wrist Control points, 213–216, 282
Hard lights, 484
HDRI lighting, 498–500, 505
Heads
attaching to bodies, 199–201
cloning for animation, 260–261
mapping with Unwrap UVW, 453–458
modeling, 99–100, 127–130, 157–159, 192–195
Morph Targets for, 258–263
rigging for animation, 230–233
scalps, modeling with NURBS, 556–559
smoothing surfaces, 197–201
see also Hair
Helicopter chase animation, 347–353
"Hero" models, 14–15
Hierarchies
bone naming conventions and, 216–218
Schematic view and, 272
High Key lighting, 484
Hinge From Edge tool, 29
Hips, bone placement in, 212–213
Hotkeys
background lock toggle, 100–101
Bezier handles, 182
Gizmo, 201
QWERTY hotkeys, 42–43
Snap Tool, 160–161

I

IK HI (History Independent) Solvers, 210, 219–221
IK manipulator handles, 231
IK Solvers, 218–221, 315
Illustrators, 47–48
Image elements, 495
Immersion Microscribe, 576–577
Impacts, dynamic collisions with characters, 400–403
Initial Velocity settings, 404
Ink and Paint, 30, 490
Interface, 16–20
Command Panel, 20
Curve Editor, 17–19
Dope Sheet, 17–18, 20
toolbars, access to, 16
Interiors
lighting for, 477–481, 538

modeling interior locations, Cell Block Zebra tutorial, 73–76
International Generic Units, 83
Inverse Kinematics (IK), 5, 206–207
chains, creating with HI Solver, 219–221
custom attribute rigging and, 417–424
defined, 218
IK HI Solvers, 210, 219–221
IK Solvers, 218–221, 315
manipulator handles, revealing, 231
Swivel Angle Targets, 315–316
walking cycle animations and, 304
Isolines, 30

J

Jail cells, Cell Lock Zebra tutorial, 73–76
Jiggles, secondary animations, 11, 444–445
Joining model parts together, 115–118, 130–131, 148
Joining vertices, Fuse tool for, 148
Joint Angle Deformer, 10
Joint manipulator handles, 418
Joints
IK Solvers to align, 218–221
Joint Angle Deformer, 10
skin control at, 10
skin envelopes, adjusting, 246–249, 284–288

K

Kadara Filmbox file loader plug-in, 519
Key Frames
Dope sheet and, 17–18, 20
Initial Velocity and collisions, 401
Keying Operator, 536
Kick Controls, 312
Knees, adjusting skin envelopes at, 246–249

L

Landscape locations
building, 69–72
cities, design and modeling, 68–69
close-ups and, 73–76
level of detail and, 68, 71, 73–76
multiple displace plane tutorial, 70–72
Quad Patch building technique, 69
Terrain Modifier option and, 69
Landscape modeling, multiple displaced planes technique, 70–72
Layer Animation tool, 517–519
Layers, 16–17
access to Toolbars, 16
Composite materials for texture layers, 32–33
Layer Animation tool, 517–519
model organization and, 84–85
moving objects between, 17
rendering, 491–494
Leaning during running cycles, 342
Legs
attaching to torso, 151–154
kick controls, 312
modeling, 90–92, 125–127
rigging for animation, 227–230
see also Running and run cycles; Walking and walk cycles
Level of Detail (LOD)
close-ups and, 68, 71, 73–76
Level of Detail utility, 14, 357
refresh rate and, 355–357
in visual effects, 2–3
Level of Detail utility, 14, 357
Lighting Override material, 482–483
Lights and lighting
Advanced Lighting Override Material, 473–477, 473–477, 482–483
architectural textures and, 462
Back lights, 484
for blue- or green-screen shots, 535–543
color temperature of, 538
composition of scenes and, 470
dramatic impact of, 451
in explosion effects, 373–374, 376–377
features overview, 5, 33–37
firelight, 582–584
Global Illumination, 471–472

global illumination (GI), 504–505
Hard lights, 484
HDRI lighting, 498–500, 505
High Key lighting, 484
indoor *vs.* outdoor light, 538
for interior spaces, 477–481, 538
Lighting Override material, 482–483
Light Multiplier, 374–375
Light Tracer, 33, 473–477
linking spotlights to moving objects, 347–348
Low Key lighting, 484
Materials Editor and, 30
Mental Ray renderer and, 497–500
Omni lights, 473
Phoenix plug-in, 582–584
Photometric Light Creation menu, 34
photometric lights, 34
Radiosity, 33–35, 470–473, 482–483
Render to Texture, 470, 496, 503
satellite bridge interior, lighting tutorial, 477–481
scene animation and, 347–348, 352
self-illuminated materials, 482–483
Skylight, 33, 471, 473–477
spaceship crash, lighting tutorial, 485–489
standard lighting, 484–485
for textures, 451–452
three-color lighting, 451
visual effects and, 485
Light Tracer, 33, 35, 473–477
Lip synching, 12–15
animation tutorial, 297–301
phonemes and Morph targets for, 258–259
set up for, 291–294
soundtracks, recording, 295–297
Liquids, 26, 27
Metaball Blob Mesh and, 391
rain or waterfall Particle effects, 362–365
Location lists for animation projects, 49–50
Location models, 67–68
scale for, 68
Loop edge selection command, 29
Low Key lighting, 484

M

Macro reader, 436
Major Black, Generic Man model modified to create, 429–434
Male figures, modeling. *See* Dr. Quin Model; Generic Man model
Maps, Master Maps for environment planning, 66–68
Maps and mapping (textures and material maps), 6, 30, 31
bitmaps, displacements and, 70
bump maps, 466–467
Cellular maps, 450–451
Flatten Mapping, 32
Flatten mapping, 453–454
HDRI lighting maps, 498–500
Mix maps, 449–451
organizing maps and images, 586
painting texture maps for faces, 459–461
with Unwrap UVW, 453–458
Materialization, visibility keys and, 25
Materials. *see* Textures and materials
Materials Editor
combustion materials, 30
feature overview, 30–32
Mattes for compositing, 537
Max Man plug-in (Animal Logic), 42
MAXScript, 41, 434–436
Maya, compatibility with, 42–44, 519
Meniscus, wet-looking eyes, 138–140
Mental Ray renderer, 5, 33, 36–37, 463–467, 490
existing scenes and, 497–498
Ferrari model, case history, 500–502
HDRI lighting maps and, 498–500
lighting and rendering with, 497–500
shader access, 466
Mesh painting, 547–549
MeshSmooth Modifier, 86–87, 104
MeshSmooth Subdivision Surface, 29

Metaballs, 391
Metaparticle systems, 391
Mirror Cloning, 106, 130–131, 188–190
Mirror Parameter menu, 250
Mirror reference copies of models, 87
Mirror Skin Weights, 8–9, 249–251
Mirror Skin Weights and, 249–251
Mix maps, 449–451
Modeling
  attaching model parts, 199–201
  Bezier spline patch modeling, 27
  feature overview, 27–30
  "Hero" models, 14–15
  joining model parts together, 185–188
  mesh modeling, 27
  mirror-cloning, 106, 130–131, 188–189
  NURBS modeling, 27, 556–559
  NURMS modeling, 104
  physical models used in production design, 54
  Polygon modeling, 29–30
  in production phase of animation projects, 63
  tools and features, 5
  see also Bones and boning; Skinning; specific parts (i.e., hands) or models (i.e., Generic Man Model)
Morph Along Path, 25
Morph Angle Deformer, 10
Morphing
  for faces, 12, 197, 258–263, 290–294
  full-body morphing, 442–446
  lip synching and, 297–301
  missing Targets, 294
  Morph Along Path, 25
  Morph Angle Deformer, 10
  Morph Modifier, 12–13
  Morph Targets, 23, 197, 258–263, 297–301
  nudging, 300
  Re-Flex plug-in, 534
  sculpting, 261–263
Morph Modifier, 12–13
Morph Targets, 23
  for faces, 12, 197, 258–263
  facial expression and, 258–259, 290–294
  on heads, 258–263
  lip synching and, 297–301
  missing Morph Targets, 294
  nudging, 300
  sculpting, 261–263
Motion Blurs, 35–36
Motion Capture
  in character studio 4, 508–511
  Layer Animation tool and, 519
Motion Curve Editor, 508
Motion Flow
  scripts, 521
  shared motion flow, 529–530
Motion Mixer in character studio 4, 38, 508
Mouths
  inner mouth spline cage, 196
  lips and inner mouth openings, 195–197
  modeling, 103, 107, 158–162, 168–172, 202
  see also Lip synching
Multiple displaced planes, landscape modeling technique, 70–72
Multiple moving objects, 25

N

Named Selection sets, 16
Naming conventions, bone hierarchies, 216–218
Necks, modeling, 155–156, 199–201
Network rendering
  Backburner 2 for, 503–504
  Render to Texture, 503
New Caledonia Landscape tutorial, 70–72
Noses, modeling, 102, 107, 110–112, 160–161, 163, 165–168
Nostrils, modeling, 111–112, 157–158
Nudging, 300
NURBS (Non-Uniform Rational B-Splines), scalp modeled with, 556–559

NURMS (Non-Uniform Rational MeshSmooth objects), described, 28, 104

O

Omni lights, 473
Organization of projects, 61, 84–85, 451, 459, 586
Output
  file format options, 42–44
  to film, 550–551

P

Paint Weights, 8–9, 241
PArray particle system, 362–365
Particle effects, 22
  combustion and, 544–547
  Facing effects (Sprites), 380–381
  instanced geometry, 377–380
  Max standard particles, 414–415
  Metaparticle systems, 391
  object fragmentation effects, 367
  PArray, 362–365
  steam, smoke, or exhaust, 485–494
  uses of, 360–362
Particle Flow system, 381–391
Patch modeling
  ears, 172–175
  fingernails, 182–185
  hands, 179–182
  Relax Modifier to eliminate irregularities, 198
Path layout for scene animation, 338–340
Pelvis, modeling, 154–155
Phoenix plug-in, 582–584
Phonemes and Morph targets for lip synching, 258–259
Photometric Light Creation menu, 34
Photorealistic rendering, plug-ins, 41
Physical models, 63, 577–580
Planning, animated film projects and, 47
Plug-ins
  Afterburner, 41
  availability of, 4
  Brazil, 41
  clothfx, 15, 38–39, 567–572
  Digimation plug-ins, 39–41
  for facial tracking, 41
  Final Render, 41
  Foley Studio, 581–582
  Ghost Painter, 41
  Kadara Filmbox file loader, 519
  Max Man (Animal Logic), 42
  Phoenix, 582–584
  Re-Flex, 534
  Scene Genie, 41
  Scrib-it, 577–580
  Shag Hair, 39–41, 555, 559–567
  Sound Trax, 41, 581–582
  Surf-it, 580–581
  value of, 41
  Vehicle Simulator, 41
  see also character studio 4; combustion 3
Point caches, 11
Poly counts, reducing, 355–357
Polygon modeling
  advantages of Editable Poly Meshes, 98
  feature overview, 86–87
  leg and buttock modeling tutorials, 90–92
  NURMS and, 104
  Polygon Selection tools, 29–30
  technique fundamentals, 87
  see also Specific objects to be modeled
Polygon Selection tools, 29–30
Polytrans, 42
Poser 4, 206
Post-production phase, 64, 550
Pre-production phase, 48–61
  art direction, 53
  character design, 55–56
  environment design, 57–58, 59
  production design, 53–55
  storyboards, 50–52
  visual effects design, 58

workflow chart, 49
Pre-visualization / physical models, 63, 577–580
Primitives
jail interior modeling tutorial, 73–76
temple modeling tutorial, 76–79
Production design, 53–55
Production managers, 61, 62
Production phase, 61–63
workflow chart, 62
Proxy collision objects, 398–399, 402
Proxy skins, 328–331
Push Modifier, clothing modeled with, 132–134, 263–268

Q

Quad Patches, 69
Quick Slice tool, 101
QWERTY hotkeys, 42–43

R

Radiosity, 5, 33–35, 470–475, 482–483
Radiosity Processing Parameter menu, 483
Rag Doll stunt doubles
battle scene with two Rag Dolls, 408–410
constraints and, 405–406
"convulsions," troubleshooting animation problems, 407
"shooting" animation, 404–408
Rain or waterfall Particle effects, 362–365
Ram Player, 41–42, 493–494
Raytracing
glass and water materials, 448–449
rendering, 493
see also Mental Ray renderer
Reactor 2 (Havok), 5, 20–26
Atmospheric effects, 23
battle scene with explosions, 408–417
Cloth to simulate hair, 436–442
constraining object motion, 21
described, 398–399
Dynamic effects, 22
floating objects, creating, 20
interface for, 399
particle effects in, 22
Rag Doll stunt skeleton, 403–410
soft body dynamics and secondary motion, 444
Realism
animation and, 53
dynamic effects and, 60
Re-Flex plug-in, 534
Refresh rates, 327–328, 355–357
Relationship viewer, 272–273
Relax Modifier to eliminate irregularities in patch models, 198
Relax UV tool, 5
Render Effects, 25, 494
Render Elements, 36, 495
Rendering
architectural textures and, 462–463
artifacts, avoiding, 466
Backburner 2, 503–504
Backburner network rendering manager, 5
Brazil, 504
command-line rendering, 504
composition of scenes and, 470
feature overview, 5
Final Render, 504–505
image elements, 495
Ink and Paint, 30, 490
layers, 491–494
Mental Ray renderer, 5, 33, 36–37, 463–467, 490, 497–500
on multiple machines, 42
network rendering, 496, 503–504
new features described, 5
output formats, 44
photorealistic rendering plug-in, 41
during post-production, 64
Render Effects, 25, 494
Render Elements, 36
Render to Texture, 470, 496, 503

Scanline, 489
speed, 493
Video Post for test renders, 349
V-Ray renderer, 504–505
Render Layers, 470
RenderMan Pro, 42–44, 504–505
Render to Texture, 470, 496
network rendering, 503
Resolution
faces, modeling and resolution, 104–108
facial animation and, 14–15
low-resolution proxy skins, 328–331
of Patch Models, 204
scene animation and, 327–331
Resources, Web addresses, 590
Rhino, 42
RIB files, 44
Rigging, 5
for arms, 234–236
Attribute Holder Modifier Script, 419
for bodies, 230–233
character rigging, 5
"circle rigs," 207–208, 394–395
Control Point Box Rigs, 207–208
Control Point Circle Rigs, 207–208
custom attribute rigging, 417–424
defined and described, 226
for feet, 227–228
fighting rigs, 429–434
for heads, 230–233
for legs, 227–230
for shoulders, 234–236
skeleton rigging, 217–227
walk cycles and, 304
Rigid Body (RB) Collections, 398–399
Ring edge selection command, 29
Running and run cycles, 335, 337–346
hand gesture animations, 346
leaning during, 342
sliding feet, preventing, 310, 335, 337–340

S

Satellite bridge interior, lighting tutorial, 477–481
Scale
for clothing, 572
International Generic Units and, 83
for location models, 68
Master Landscapes and, 86
Scalps, NURBS to model, 556–559
Scanline renderer, 489
Scene animation
adding characters to scenes, 353–354
camera setups, 345–347
demands on system, 327–328
lighting and light effects, 347–348
multiple scene files, efficiency of, 347
path layout for motion, 338–340
Proxy skins for, 328–331
setting up scenes, 334–336
Video Rotoscope techniques, 354, 357–358
Scene Genie plug-in, 41
Schematic View, 5, 272–273
Scrib-it plug-in, 577–580
Scripts, film scripts
analysis during pre-production phase, 48–49
dialog and soundtracks, 295–297
environment and location design, 66
film design and, 48
shooting scripts, 49–50
visual effects, assessing script requirements for, 331–334
Scripts and scripting languages
Attribute Holder Modifier Script, 419
macro reader, 436
MAXScript, 41, 434–436
Motion Flow scripts, 521
particle systems and, 22
Secondary animation, jiggles, 11, 444–445
Semi-realism of materials and textures, 448–451
Sewing Springs, 568

Shaders. *See* Mental Ray renderer
Shadow Matte, 24
Shadows. *See* Lights and lighting
Shag Hair (Digimation), 39–41
  long hair, dynamic, 562–567
  NURBS scalp for, 556–559
  previsualization and, 331
Shell Modifier, 434
Shoulders
  modeling, 146–148
  rigging for animation, 234–236
Shrink edge selection command, 29
Skeletons, 5
  arm bones, 210
  basic skeletal rigs, 207–213
  binding to skin, 241–244
  body language and, 210, 301–302
  bone fins, 7–8
  Control Point Box Rigs, 207–208
  Control Point Circle Rigs, 207–208
  creating, 206–207
  custom attribute rigging, 417–424
  for Dr. Quin Model, 209–213
  exporting, 42
  facial animation and, 12–13
  fitting to character models, 223–224
  hands, boning, 213–216
  IK and, 7
  leg bones, 211–212
  naming bones, 216–218
  proportions of, 206–207
  purposes and complexity of, 206, 207
  Rag Doll stunt skeletons, 403–410
  resizing, 301–302
  rigging for animation, 217–227
  spine bones, 210–211, 219–220
Skin, human, materials and textures for, 451–461
Skin Modifier, 7–9, 241–244, 434
Skinning, 6–7
  binding skin to skeleton, 241–244
  control at joints, over muscle bulges, etc., 10
  features overview, 6–7
  problem areas, identifying and correcting, 244–246
  Proxy skins, 328–331
  wrinkles and creases, eliminating unwanted, 133
  see also Envelopes, skin envelopes
Skin Weights Assignments Table, 8
Skin Weight Table, 8–9, 251
Skylight, 33, 35, 471, 473–477
  Mental Ray renderer and, 498–500
Slice Plane tool, 101
Slider controls, 251–254, 511–513, 514–516
Smoke, steam, or exhaust effects, 380–381, 485–494
Soft body dynamics, 444
Sound effects
  Foley Studio plug-in, 581–582
  Sound Trax plug-in, 41, 581–582
Soundtracks
  loading, 294
  recording, 295–297
  Sound Trax plug-in, 41, 581–582
Sound Trax (Boomerlabs), 41, 581–582
Spaceship crash, lighting effects for, 485–489
Space Warps, 363–364
Spine bones, 210–211, 219–220
Spline Patch modeling, 132
  see also Generic Man model
Spotlights, 347–348
Sprites (Facing particle effects), 22, 380–381
Squash Modifier, 8
Steam or smoke effects, 380–381, 485–494
Stitch plug-in. *See* clothfx plug-in
Storyboard artists, 47, 52, 54
Storyboards, 47, 50–52
Stride Markers, 305–306, 337, 338–340
Stunt doubles, Rag Dolls, 403–410
Subdivision
  faces, modeling tutorial, 104–108
  MeshSmooth *vs.* MeshSmooth Modifier for, 104

NURMS and, 104
Subdivision Displacement, 29
Surface Modifier, 170–172, 199
Surf-it plug-in, 580–581
Swivel Angle Targets, 315–316
System requirements, 586–587

T

Temple of the Horns tutorial, 76–79
Textures and materials
architectural materials, 79, 448, 461–463
baking textures, 5, 496
combustion for mesh painting, 547–549
composite materials, 32–33, 451
features overview, 29–32
file organization tips, 451
lighting for, 451–452
Mental Ray renderer and, 463–467
raytracing for glass and water materials, 448–449
self-illuminated materials, 482–483
semi-realism, 448–451
Unwrap UVW Modifier, 5, 31, 434, 453–458
see also Maps and mapping (textures and material maps); Materials Editor
Three-color lighting, 451
Thumbs, modeling, 121–123
Time, required for animation projects, 47
Toolbars, displaying, 16
Torsos
modeling, 130–131, 143–146
polygon modeling tutorial, 87–89, 93–96
see also Bodies
Tracking Sphere, 490, 491
Track View, 17, 20
Transform effects, 23
Translucent Shader, 30
Triangle meshes *vs.* Editable Poly Meshes, 98
Troubleshooting
artifacts during rendering, 465–467
cloth modeling, file sizes, 575–576
crowd animation anomolies, 522
cursor, slow movement, 199
distortion of spline cage, 148
patch models, irregularities in, 198
"Rag Doll" convulsions, 407
scintillating materials, level of detail and, 465–467
skinning problem areas, 170–172, 244–246
sliding feet, preventing, 310, 335, 337–340

U

Unwrap UVW Modifier, 5, 31, 434, 453–458
Face Angle threshold, 455

V

Vehicle Simulator plug-in, 41
Vertices
Cross Section Modifier and joining, 181
joining, 116, 130–131
Video Post, 24–25, 42
for test renders, 349
Video Rotoscope techniques, 354, 357–358
Viewport Layer manager, 16
Virtual actors, 3
Visual effects
Adobe Photoshop and, 3–4
combustion and, 543–547
compositing and, 23–24, 544–547
defined, 60
design of, 58
disabling, 493
feature overview, 20–27
lighting and, 485
Particle effects, 360–362
pre-production phase and design of, 58
Reactor and, 20–26
scripts and assessing need for, 331–334
state of the art, 2–4
see also Explosion effects; *Specific* effects
Visual effects supervisor, 62

Volumetric clouds, plug-in, 41
V-Ray renderer, 504–505

W

Walking and walk cycles, 227–228, 301
  arm motions, 309–311
  described, 303–304
  expression controllers applied to, 394–398
  foot movement, 303–313
  Forward Kinematics and, 304
  hip and shoulder counter-rotation, 308–309
  reference films on CD-ROM, 309
  skeletal structure and linking, 303–304
  sliding feet, 310, 335, 337–340
  stride length and Stride Markers, 305–306
Waterfall Particle effects, 362–365
Weapons fire, "shooting" a Rag Doll, 404–408
Web resources and links, 590
Weigert, Marc, 360
Weighting
  Mirror Skin Weights, 8–9, 249–251
  NURMS and, 104
  skinning and, 8–9
  Skin Weight Table, 8–9, 251
  welding vertices and, 148
Welding, 130–131
  weighting affected by, 148
Windows, modeling, architectural details tutorial, 80–85
Wired Parameters, 5, 10, 251–257
  bone rotation and, 10–11
  character studio 4, 513–516
  slider creation and, 251–254
Workflow chart, 49
World Creating Tool Kit, 68, 500–502
Wrinkles and creases, eliminating unwanted, 133
Wrist Controls, hand animation and, 213–216, 282
Wrists
  adjusting skin envelopes at, 284–288
  joining hands to arms, 185–188
  Wrist Control points, 213–216, 282

X

X-refs, 357
Xzulixia, alien vampire character
  breasts, modeling, 93–96
  clothing, modeling, 569–575
  ears, modeling pointed ears, 112–115
  eye and eyelash animations, 316–323
  eyeballs, modeling, 109–110
  eyelids, modeling, 108–109
  eyes, modeling, 102–103, 107–110
  eyes and eyelash animations, 316–323
  face, modeling, 100–112
  face, shaping the facial features, 108–112
  feet, modeling, 125–127
  fingernails, modeling, 123–125
  fingers, modeling, 119–121
  full-body morphing animation, 442–444
  hands, modeling, 118–125
  head, modeling, 99–100
  legs and buttocks, modeling, 90–92, 125–127
  morphing animation, 442–444
  mouth, modeling, 103, 107
  nose, modeling, 102, 107, 110–112
  nostrils, modeling, 111–112
  overview modeling techniques, 86–87
  thumbs, modeling, 121–123
  torso, modeling, 87–89, 93–96